THE ROTISSERIE BASEBALL ANALYST 1991

BY JOHN BENSON

EXECUTIVE EDITOR: PETE DeCOURSEY
ASSOCIATE EDITOR: RANDALL BARON
SCOUTING DIRECTOR: LARY BUMP

Published by
Devyn Press, Inc
Louisville, Kentucky

1990 stats compiled by J. P. Martin, Mike Dalecki, and contributing writers; information provided by team media offices. Second half stats are available on Compuserve Sports Forum.

1988 and 1989 stats provided by Project Scoresheet
6 Penncross Circle, Newark, DE 19702

Cover design by Rob Pawlak

Rotisserie League Baseball (R) is a federally registered trademark of the Rotisserie League Baseball Association, Inc. For more information contact: R. L. B. A., 41 Union Square West, Suite 936, New York, NY 10003.

Copyright © 1991 by John Chapman Benson

All rights reserved. No part of this book may be reproduced in any form without the permission of Devyn Press and John Chapman Benson.

Printed in the U. S. A.

Devyn Press, Inc.
3600 Chamberlain Lane, Suite 230
Louisville, KY 40241

ISBN 0-910791-91-0

TABLE OF CONTENTS

Foreword by Bill Gray 5
Introduction: Consumer Safety Information 6
Acknowledgements and Credits 9

I. THE GAME

The Game 13
Winning the Game — The 4 Essentials 14

IA — FORECASTING PLAYER PERFORMANCE

Scouting and Forecasting 16
Last Year's Numbers 19
Second Half Signals 21
Winds of Winter 25
Strikeout/Walk Ratios by Rob Wood 27
The Problem with Pitchers and What to Do About Them 29
Pitchers: Quality Measures 32
Top American League Pitchers — 1990 Quality Rankings 34
Top National League Pitchers — 1990 Quality Rankings 35
The Quality Start 36
Age 26: Most Bang for the Buck, 1991 38
Ballpark Effects by Fred Percival 40

IB — PLAYER VALUATION

Player Valuation 101 — Basic Scarcity 41
The Concept of Value in Position 45

IC — CONDUCT OF THE DRAFT OR AUCTION

Optimal Bids, Revisited 1991 47
Optimal Bids at Work 50
Draft Price Inflation and What to Do About It 55

ID — MANAGING YOUR ROSTER

Midcourse Corrections 58
Yes, You Can Manipulate the Standings, Legally 63

II. THE PLAYERS

Introduction to the Player Essays ...71
American League Catchers ...72
National League Catchers ...84
American League First Basemen ...92
National League First Basemen ...104
American League Second Basemen ...112
National League Second Basemen ...129
American League Third Basemen ...140
National League Third Basemen ...148
American League Shortstops ...157
National League Shortstops ...165
American League Outfielders ...181
National League Outfielders ...199
American League Designated Hitters ...199
American League Starting Pitchers ...203
National League Starting Pitchers ...217
American League Relief Pitchers ...234
National League Relief Pitchers ...247

III. THE NUMBERS

Hitters 1991 Forecast Stats ...258
Introduction to Pitchers 1991 Forecast Stats ...272
Pitchers 1991 Forecast Stats ...273
Hitters $ Values ...285
Pitchers $ Values ...300
Introduction to Second Half Stats ...306
Hitters 1990 Second Half Stats ...307
Pitchers 1990 Second Half Stats ...313

IV. GRADUATE STUDIES

Leaguesmanship ...320
Their Batting Stats Will Deceive You ...325
Better Models of Baseball by Pete DeCoursey ...326
Extra Innings ...330

FOREWORD

By opening this book, you have taken a giant step toward winning your Rotisserie league in 1991. From the first moment you begin reading, you will improve your skills. Trust me. I did it. This book is a powerful tool.

John Benson says that his book is not for beginners, but I think it is for everyone. The more you study it, the more you learn. It is THE definitive textbook on the subject of winning Rotisserie baseball.

Four years ago, I was a novice, possessing plenty of knowledge about baseball but little understanding of Rotisserie. Three years ago, I was lucky to finish sixth. In 1990, I won my league. In fact, I beat John Benson, using his own methods against him. I literally owe all my success to John and his work. He has spent years researching, testing and detailing the strategies and tactics that he gives to the public in his book and monthly newsletter. It was no coincidence that I moved into second place in 1989, when I first got hold of this book.

While ending the Benson Dynasty in one league (I hear he finished first in three other leagues in 1990), I didn't exactly run away with the title. The points were tied exactly, and I won the tie-breaker. The interesting fact is that, one year ago, I would have given up in late August; I mean I would have tried and hoped to win, but I wouldn't have had the foggiest idea that victory was possible. But in August 1990, the Benson newsletter had just published an essay about something called Unsettled Points (a chapter in this year's book, I believe).

Following the Benson method of roster management, I sifted through the numbers behind the numbers, and found the only possible series of events that would give me a chance to win. The Unsettled Points method showed me that, if I loaded up on starting pitchers, and accumulated a huge number of good innings in September, I had a remote chance (maybe 10%) to finish first. One in ten isn't much, but it's better than zero. Bingo! The events all happened. John's team didn't collapse, but everything else worked perfectly. David Cone and Jose Rijo led my beefed-up starting rotation. The other teams in the league all cooperated perfectly by sniping points from Benson in every close category, including a three-way tie in Wins. Talk about close. For me, the last day of the 1990 season had the Bill Mazeroski and Bobby Thompson homers, and Mookie Wilson's grounder to Buckner, all rolled into one. And if I hadn't studied the Rotisserie Baseball Analyst, it would have been just another Wednesday.

Now, I'm not writing this to let you know that the GRAY MATTER beat BENSON BURNERS for the first time. I'm using myself as a case study to demonstrate that anybody who uses this book properly can improve to the extent that VICTORY is possible, and you can beat the best players, with some hard work and a little good luck.

Rotisserie books and magazines abound. A FEW of them can help you. But in any field, there can be only one person or one product that is clearly THE BEST. John Benson is the best writer and teacher about Rotisserie baseball, and the book that you are holding is the best on the subject. I've read them all, and I know. In fact, I don't even know one person who thinks there is a better book than this one, and I know a lot of people. Honest. Read 'em all! Decide for yourself. Trust me.

— Bill Gray
Columbus, Ohio
October 1990

INTRODUCTION:
CONSUMER SAFETY INFORMATION

Like art, music, great literature and the World Series, Rotisserie baseball has the power to make men happy. Like all sports and games, Rotisserie is most satisfying when played well. For those who do poorly, the game can be a prolonged source of frustration and profanity.

The purpose of this book is to move more people from a level of vexation, up to the class of satisfied winners. "Satisfaction" may imply different goals for different people. Many (like me) simply want to finish first: number one, the champ. Others are happy if they can perform at an average level among their peers, and are thrilled if they finish near the top. Finally, there are some with only the most modest ambition: "please don't let me come in last!" This book will help them all.

Rotisserie is a very new game, compared to pursuits like golf, poker, chess and bridge; Rotisserie publications reflect this young age. Most material is written for beginners: how to organize a league, and how to sift through major league rosters to find names that have more value in Rotisserie than in "real" baseball. The quality of books and magazines is improving, but compared to other sports and games, there is little writing for the more serious students of the game.

In previous editions, this introduction has made allusions to various Rotisserie books that fell short of expectation. In late 1990, I have a more charitable attitude, and a more optimistic outlook. Some of the worst books have disappeared. Some authors who stretched their credentials to appear as experts have now vanished from the Rotisserie scene. They didn't fool anyone but the gullible publishing executives who paid them for work that was, at best, irrelevant to the study of this complex and esoteric subject. Some weak material remains, and new books without much value will continue to appear, but I see a genuine movement toward honest quality. The buying public [always a smart group] has begun to educate the people who decide what gets published.

It is obvious to me that within five or ten years, Rotisserie will have a body of literature aimed at advanced players, just like chess and bridge (for example), with numerous serious authors producing treatise works. Some of the existing books and publishers are improving. The official Rotisserie League Baseball book is enlarged and strengthened this year. Peter Golenbock's "How to Win" has likewise expanded its intentions and accomplishments. The Sporting News has a wholly new annual which is aimed at beginners but which contains player profiles that will be useful for everyone. Fantasy Baseball Magazine is constantly adding new and better writers.

For my own book, however, I still claim the most disciplined approach, the most comprehensive delivery of information, and the most sophisticated readership. Two simple concepts make The Analyst different from other books:

(1) We approach Rotisserie as a serious game, susceptible to careful analysis just like poker, chess, or bridge, and we treat the game with this single-minded perspective. Certain strategies and tactics are known to give better chances for victory. The best players have understood them, intuitively, for years. There is no reason why these methods should remain a secret. We attempt to gather the best available wisdom and write it down (that simple). And we are always trying to learn more.

(2) We had 49 writers last year, and a similar number this year. With this depth of writing talent, we can examine every position on every major league team, down to the Double-A level, and make informed predictions about who is going to play, and how well they are going to do. We often predict changes in lineups before the major league teams themselves see the necessity of making those moves. This isn't "Benson brilliance" — it is the simple, hard work of 49 people, collected and presented for your consideration.

Concerning the technical aspects of Rotisserie baseball — those winning methods that pay dividends year after year — there are some myths that have grown up in the absence of codified guidelines. Lacking written materials that fully explain the winning methods and why they work, most of the chronic non-winners in Rotisserie baseball have passively accepted the notion that there is some kind of inborn, elusive skill or insight that separates the winners from the rest of the pack, something in the mystic realm of "card sense" that makes some people good at bridge or poker. The winners are happy to perpetuate this myth, because it discourages the mediocre players from advancing.

The truth is that winning methods can be learned by anyone. Having a good memory helps, but the keys to victory are experience, enthusiasm, concentration and hard work. If you ever doubt this statement, consider the progress made by every player after one year of experience. Does the second annual draft/auction in any league resemble what happened in the first year? And consider the success of those who follow the news religiously (year-round), compared to those who scan their stats only once every week or two (and ignore baseball during the winter). It doesn't take too many cases of missed DL listings or overlooked call-ups to separate first place from sixth place.

The learning curve doesn't stop after one year. With the game only ten years old, I feel safe in saying that nobody can even define the learning curve at this point. Every day, somebody calls or writes to me: "I wish you hadn't printed THAT in your book/newsletter; in my league I WAS the only person who knew it. Now . . ." Truly, there are no born winners in this game. Anyone who wants a practical example of clear thinking and paying attention should hope to meet and chat with Harry Stein, the winningest member of the original Rotisserie League. He would quickly put an end to any notions you may have about victory coming easily to those who are blessed with some innate form of good luck. Plain hard work and application of sound principles are the stuff that wins pennants.

The issues of scouting every position on every team, and forecasting player performance, are both subject to common misconceptions as well. The watchword in winning Rotisserie baseball is "CONTEXT." Some readers of this book will unwittingly reveal their narrow-minded approach by taking things out of context, and saying thing's like, "Benson uses second half stats to forecast performance; Joe Bimbleman had a great second half, so Benson must like him," or "Benson uses age to forecast performance; Mario Mendoza is 27 this year, so he must be due for a great year." If you hear anybody make such comments, get them into your league, because they are genuine, cash-paying fish.

Always think "context." If you see some fact or number that catches your eye — take a superstar performance in Winter Ball for example — put that piece of information into context. Is the player on a major league roster? Has he ever before done anything similar in baseball? Is he somewhere between the ages of 19 and 39? Does he have a chance to play, or is he waiting in line behind Will Clark, with no chance of being traded? If he does get to play, will he bat leadoff or clean-up like he did in Puerto Rico this winter, or will he bat ninth and be used only against occasional lefty pitchers? To reiterate: think CONTEXT.

The most important context is one that you must gauge yourself: the strength of your own Rotisserie league. People call me all the time and ask the question, "Who's a good sleeper?" I need just a little more information to answer that question. Answers with no context might make you think, "All your sleepers were busts; EVERYBODY knew about them," or "Those sleepers you gave me never even came up for bids; they're ALL still available!" And the same names generated both comments. In 1989, Joe Boever sold for $1 to $3 in about one third of all auctions, and he went for more than $20 in about one third of all auctions. Obviously, some leagues had two or more people who saw Boever coming, and some leagues had only one person (or nobody) who expected him to get 20 saves. It takes a league context to create a sleeper.

If you opened the bidding for Cecil Fielder at $20 last year, and everyone snickered and let you have him, you made a good buy, but not a wise buy. He was available for $10 to $12 in most auctions, and $2 to $4 in many. From reading this book, you cannot possibly find out how well the other players in your league have done their scouting, but you can find this advice: study your competition, and think context.

The Rotisserie Baseball Analyst will be what you make of it. People who win their leagues always love this book (and my newsletter), and people who love this book consistently win their leagues. Do they win because they read my stuff, or do they read my stuff because they are doing what winners do (studying all informed opinions)? The cause and effect doesn't really matter. The high correlation tells you a great deal, however.

Finally, I hope you find that this book contains a minimum of dogmatism suggesting, "This is the only way." My readers implore me to be opinionated, to take strong stands, and to avoid words like "but" and "however" when telling how the game should be played and how individual athletes are likely to perform. I try to fulfill this service as requested, while hoping for individual experimentation and enjoyment. The game is young. We need more discoveries. And if everyone thought the same thing, the game would be much less exciting. Tell me what you think, especially if you have an insight.
— John Benson, PO Box 7302, Wilton, CT 06897

ACKNOWLEDGEMENTS AND CREDITS

One year ago, at the last minute before going to press, I threw together some acknowledgements and rushed the disk to Federal Express, just barely making the departure cutoff. This year, I spent more time on the acknowledgements, leaving the players stats and $ values to be thrown together while the last Fedex plane was fueling up. This new method has two advantages: (1) Carney Lansford is not valued at $30, and (2) some of the people who worked very, very hard (or did other good deeds) to make this book possible, get a small measure of the recognition they deserve. Undoubtedly, I have omitted or faint-praised somebody somewhere; please be assured that it wasn't intentional.

In the beginning, there was "Our League," which begat the Armchair League, which begat the GS&FP League, which begat the MLBE League, for which I thank Bill Cunningham, Mark Giannini, Bill Smith, Ernie DiBello and Steve Walsh, in particular.

Bill Gray, the MLBE's current secretary-for-life, has been a major source of inspiration, knowledge, and creative hard work. Bill has performed innumerable services to make this book possible, ranging from flash updates on the life and times of Albert Joey Belle, to helping me fix a blown-out hard drive in my computer. There is a link in there somewhere. Keep up the good work, Bill.

For Rotisserie League Baseball (the game, the book, and now the movie), the world is indebted to Glen Waggoner and Dan Okrent, among others. I am personally grateful to Glen for encouraging my work, for introducing me to giants in the field like Harry Stein, for listening to my far-ranging ideas with Iron Horse patience, for giving me a valid business reason to visit Mickey Mantle's, and for not putting Mantle out of business by naming a league after his restaurant.

Peter Golenbock has been a friend and supporter since the earliest days of my work for the Rotisserie audience. His book **Dynasty** got me in trouble in 1976, because I couldn't put it down even when my boss said I ought to; one of his other books, How to Win at Rotisserie Baseball, long ago lifted my own level of play at this game that we all love. And I am eternally indebted to Peter for giving me the inside information (Joe Sambito, Steve Henderson, and that "kid" who came up in midseason . . .) which carried me to a stunning victory in the first Senior League Rotisserie of 1989-1990.

During the bleak winter of 1988-89, when there was no Senior League, and when it appeared that neither the GAB Statbook nor the Bill James Baseball Abstract would be in print by summer, Fred Percival helped me realize that many writers and analysts had timely work that just needed an entrepreneur to provide an outlet, and this book was born. Fred is a visionary thinker and a cutting-edge sabermetrician whose help has continued right up to the present moment, extending in uncountable directions. I know I don't say "Thank you" every time you do something, Fred, but I always appreciate every single contribution. The Ballpark Effect research is one of the recent products flowing from Fred's prolific computer.

Don Zminda encouraged my early efforts with his positive attitude. If he had simply given a lukewarm reaction to my first writings on Doug DeCinces and Mike Davis, you wouldn't be reading this now. Don has been a friend and counselor, and like all the people at STATS, he brings pleasure and professionalism into the world of baseball research and writing. In late 1989, he gave me the once-in-a-lifetime opportunity to show the world how many 400 word player essays a person can write in one week, adding a page to Guinness. Don is one of several people who shared their insights with me, but didn't want any by-lines. I have no doubt all his predictions are perfect, and next year he will want credit.

Pete DeCoursey, a mild-mannered reporter for a great metropolitan newspaper, brings a wealth of talent to the job of Executive Editor for this project. He is the world's foremost researcher on the subject of defensive performance measurement, the creator of Defensive Average, and a Daniel Boone on the frontier that makes up the other half of baseball: stopping the other team from scoring runs. Pete's annual research presentations are a highlight of SABR conventions. While maintaining his knowledge of defense, Pete accumulates an encyclopedic knowledge of teams and players. At any time during any summer, he can tell you who is the backup third baseman in San Diego, Seattle or Houston. [Can you do it?] Pete works for the daily Reading Times, and writes the world's only column on baseball statistics. In his spare time he covers the Phillies for the Harper & Row Scouting Report, helps Jayson Stark and the Philadelphia Inquirer with their baseball work, and publishes the Philadelphia Baseball File (215-926-8170).

You will find Lary Bump's name everywhere in the player essays. Lary devotes himself to following minor league baseball. He has covered the International League for a major daily newspaper, and served as an IL official scorer. Lary could match his knowledge of the minors against any "real" GM and hold his own. For the huge effort that Lary contributed to this year's book, I am deeply appreciative. In fact, I am a little embarrassed that Lary's name doesn't appear on the cover; sorry Lary — they designed the cover back in September.

Mike Dalecki is a stalwart of fundamental and applied research in the world of Rotisserie baseball. He's an assistant professor at East Carolina University where he teaches statistics and research methods among other subjects. Professor Dalecki got his Ph.D. at Penn State. What I like best is that every time he calls me, he has at least three good rumors about baseball.

Harry Conover of Compuserve Sports Forum, while running a high quality service (see Graduate Studies at the back of this book) has made available a huge volume of statistical baseball data, including average prices paid in 1990 auctions (with standard deviations, even). Two of the Forum Sysops, Adam Stein and Owen Mock, did yeoman service. Owen developed the pitcher quality rankings that appear in this year's edition. Owen and Adam both helped with quick and meaningful correlations and regression analyses. Adam wrote on many players, as you will see; he is an emerging authority on the subject of player valuation and Rotisserie science. Others among many, many Forum adherents who helped this book along include Bob Aube, Paul Clements, J.L. Feinstein, Steve Hammond, Bob Hazlewood, Andrew Ingal, Michael Lesher, Walt Marchinko, Michael Purius, Thom Rogers, Steven Rubio, Ben Schilling, and Chuck Wright.

John Wallwork of Roti-Stats (the MLBE league's own Price Waterhouse) has shaped my thinking, entertained me, helped me reach a wider audience, and shared his vision of the future. John has made numerous suggestions that improved this book since it first appeared in 1989.

My publisher and associate editor Randy Baron has been himself: enthusiastic and supportive, while keeping our attention focused on the business implications of everything we do. Randy allows me a unique range of freedom in the production and promotion of this work. Our proceeding without many formal guidelines is only made possible by Randy's dovetail personality, powerful memory, and positive approach to life. Before ascending to the captain of industry position that he now occupies, Randy became a world class writer and teacher on the subject of bridge. He knows how to make a book about a game, if anyone does.

Betty Mattison did the typesetting and arrangement again this year, with obvious professional talent and amazing grace under pressure. Thanks for the quality work, Betty. The book obviously wouldn't be anything without you.

Rob Wood has graced our pages with some of the finest work on the cutting edge of baseball analysis. The annual "washed up" list is a classic example of the type of contribution upon which the world has come to depend. Thanks for thinking of me, Rob.

Alan Boodman was a major contributor and a great pinch-hitter for me as 1990 drew to a close. He researched the Age 26 essay among his numerous other contributions.

Dave Smith continues to personify the original purpose of Project Scoresheet: unselfish, enthusiastic sharing of information and attention to detail. Dave contributed numerous items including the Quality Start research. He has a unique ability to present numbers in a manner that communicates in a smooth flow, without requiring words to explain. Quite a talent.

Gary Levy of The Sporting News has given the Rotisserie world an outstanding new publication, the TSN FBB Owners Manual. He helped my RBA book along by getting me to focus on key issues on a timely basis. Gary is a fine example of the publishing executive who will shape our thinking in the year 2000: fast-moving, flexible, multi-talented. I will follow his career with great interest.

Kit Kiefer, the backbone of Fantasy Baseball Magazine, has been a friend and confidant. He has focused my attention on the seasonality of the Rotisserie cycle, made numerous helpful suggestions, and always gives me a wonderful, color spread in his pages. I am proud of my association with Krause publications, and get considerable enjoyment and insight from Kit and his colleagues. The improvements in this year's book, dealing with roster management during the baseball season, are largely attributable to Kit Kiefer's prompting.

Jerry Heath of Heath Research continues to be a pillar of the Rotisserie community, once again providing a complete almanac of auction prices and team standings from the many leagues that he oversees. Jerry is always a big contributor to the work that ends up in these pages, and he is a pleasure to work with.

Lynn Busby and his colleagues at Baseball America have been friendly and helpful at every opportunity.

A large number of real baseball people added to my knowledge during 1990. Several hours of tapes that I recorded for the Scouting Report book (for example) provide a good library of insight into the game between the white lines, and the thinking that shapes it. I enjoy this work without reference to the subject of paper leagues; dealing with the real people helps me maintain a sense of perspective and remember why we like to watch pitchers pitch, hitters hit, and fielders field. It's great fun. I acknowledge and thank Major League Baseball for making this book necessary.

The writers all have by-lines on their work (I hope!) so I won't list them here. Obviously, the main strength of this book is the large network of writers nationwide, scouting and analyzing. They include not only sportswriters, but also player agents, lawyers, high school and college coaches and teachers, physicians, data processing consultants, all types of professionals and executives, and students aspiring to these careers.

For that person who got left out (some electromagnetic glitch removed your name from your work) I offer Thanks to the Unknown Writer: You researched thoroughly in August; you did an excellent analysis in September, you wrote a brilliant essay and sent in your material on time in October; you got no acknowledgement or thanks in November; I didn't even return your phone call in December; and then I sent this book to the printer without your name in January. Hope you'll be back next year, because I need you.

John Benson Wilton, CT January, 1991

I
THE GAME

THE GAME

"Rotisserie baseball is a way to compete with other fans, using real major league statistics. At the beginning of the season, you get together with a group of friends, and you have a draft or auction to select players. If there is an auction, there is a spending limit or salary cap for each roster, for example $50 or $200 or whatever you want to invest. Each team has to fill out a whole roster with a specified number of players at each position, for example two catchers, two first basemen, two third basemen, two or three middle infielders, etc. If the players are selected by draft, I might pick Eric Davis first, you pick Dwight Gooden second, and so forth. You keep going until everyone has filled out a team. Everybody gets a few superstars.

"After the draft or auction, you compile stats, and do standings. Most rotisserie leagues use eight categories, four hitting categories (batting average, homers, RBI's and stolen bases) and four pitching categories (Wins, Saves, ERA and a fourth category, either strikeouts or opponents on-base average). You give points according to rank in each category. If you have ten teams in your league, the team with the most home runs gets ten points, second best gets nine points, etc.

"The rotisserie league gives you an incentive to check box scores, and gives you a reason to follow players in other cities. If people in New York didn't play rotisserie, they wouldn't know about Harold Reynolds or care about his performance. Rotisserie gives you an interest, a good way to bandy back and forth with friends, and a fun way to compete."
— Jody McDonald on WFAN radio

Jody has a broad definition of The Game. I think he would include all types of contests where people select players at the beginning of the year, and then check stats in predetermined categories at the end of the year, to see who picked the best team. Jody's comments indicate that he probably plays in a "mixed" (AL and NL) league, where most players selected are stars or regulars.

If you ask Ferguson Jenkins, he will tell you that "rotisserie" is so named, because the draft "rotates" the selection of players.

There is another, narrower definition of The Game, a definition that carries some weight of authority, because it comes from the people who first used the word "rotisserie" to describe their activity. I am speaking, of course, about Rotisserie League Baseball, a trademark of the Rotisserie League Baseball Association, Inc., as described in the book, "Rotisserie League Baseball." Glen Waggoner, Dan Okrent, Robert Sklar, and their colleagues named their league after a New York restaurant, La Rotisserie Francais. Their book, magazine articles, publicity and hard work all contributed immensely to the spread of rotisserie baseball to the far corners of the world.

I could go on at length about other factors that have led to the increased popularity of rotisserie baseball, such as the proliferation of personal computers and modems, and the explosion of timely information that grew out of America's natural fascination with the numbers of baseball. But I want to give credit to the Rotisserie League Baseball people. I recommend their book; it is entertaining and informative, and it contains the set of rules that has been most widely adopted. I also recommend Peter Golenbock's book, "How to Win at Rotisserie Baseball" which, I understand, will also contain the official rules in this year's edition.

My book (the one you have in your hands now) should be useful to people who play all kinds of rotisserie baseball, but it is specifically intended to aid people who play according to RLBA rules.

Player valuations are based on separate AL and NL rosters, with 23 players and $260 per team. The rankings remain valid for rules that are slightly different, but if you play by radically different rules (e.g., a "mixed" league) you will want to make adjustments. Suggestions are included in the text.

WINNING THE GAME
THE FOUR ESSENTIALS

Winning Rotisserie baseball is a lot like winning the horse race game, just more complex. There are a thousand horses in the field. It takes over six months to run the race, and many horses enter or leave the field while the race is in progress. You bet on 23 to 40 horses, not just one. You must bet on specified numbers of certain types of horses. You can move your bets from one horse to another while the race is in progress. If your horse breaks a leg, you can pick another horse, but only after he is officially scratched. And at the end of the race, you must parlay some of the bets. And one more minor detail: your horses are running in four different races, simultaneously.

These complexities make it difficult to see the big picture. Most writers have adopted a worm's eye view, not a bird's eye view. They have gone down one of two paths:

(1) Some see the complexity, and turn away from it. They choose to write about the fun of the game, how to get started, the fascinating twists and turns, and the joy of winning. If they give any advice, it is anecdotal, always entertaining, and seldom rigorous.

(2) Other authors seize on one small aspect of the game. Like the blind men touching parts of an elephant, they make valid observations but fail to see the whole beast. They draw false conclusions. Feeling a leg, they say the elephant is like a tree. Touching his trunk, they think they have found a type of snake. One grabs the tusk, and says the elephant is a sort of spear. They are all right, and all wrong.

The favorite elephant-part for Rotisserie analysis is player valuation. Given a set of player stats, what is the dollar value that should be assigned to them? This is a vital question, but it is hardly the most important question. For 1991, which would you rather know . . .

a. who is going to play and how well they are going to do? or:

b. the precise value of a home run (versus a stolen base) using 1990 scarcity and impact on league standings?

I hope you said (a). If I had told you, in April 1990, that Cecil Fielder was going to hit 51 home runs, you wouldn't need to know much about the relative scarcity of homers or their impact on standings points. If you had known that Bobby Thigpen was going to get 57 saves, you wouldn't have cared much about the comparative value of saves and wins. You would have done just fine in the auction, with little knowledge of player valuation.

No, I didn't tell you about Fielder or Thigpen last year, but I did tell you (last February) that Ron Gant was one of the best picks for 1990, that "Doug Drabek is a gem," that Hal Morris was the best 1B prospect, that Edgar Martinez would play 3B for Seattle, that Pete O'Brien was "fading rapidly," that Gerald Young had lost his base-stealing ability, that Mitch Williams would lose the Cubs saver role "any day," that Rickey Jordan was the Phillies fourth best first baseman, that Bobby Bonilla was the player most likely to break out with a big season, etc., etc. I am not trying to make the point that I can always see the future (I made a lot of wrong predictions, too). The point is that other "analysts" didn't even face these questions.

Let's get back to the question of perspective. There are FOUR essentials to winning Rotisserie baseball, and you better be good at all of them, if you want to finish first:

1. Forecasting player performance.

2. Player valuation

3. Conducting the draft or auction.

4. Managing your roster after the draft.

It is intuitively obvious that number 1 (forecasting) is the most important, yet number 2 (valuation) gets many more pages in most books.

If you mess up number 3 (conducting the draft), your work on (1) and (2) will be wasted. Three bad minutes in a draft or auction can undo three months of preparation. But no one ever applied the basic rules of auction economics to the game of Rotisserie baseball, until we did.

In this section, we will review each of the four essentials. They will be given attention appropriate to their relative importance, which is (roughly):

Forecasting player performance — 50%

Valuation based on expected stats — 20%

Conducting the draft or auction — 20%

Managing the roster (trades, injuries, etc.) — 10%

You may quibble with my percentages, but you cannot deny the necessity for competence in all four areas. Without good forecasts, your valuations will be worthless. Without a rational valuation method, your forecasts will only occasionally lead to wise draft decisions. If you go to an auction and bid up to full, calculated value, without recognizing the independent dynamics of a competitive auction, you will never finish higher than third, even if your forecasts and valuations are perfect. Finally, if you traded Cecil Fielder for Sam Horn on May 15, you wasted your scouting, your valuation, and your successful draft.

Much of what follows is common knowledge. Much of it, I like to think, is fairly innovative, at least in the world of Rotisserie baseball. If it bores you, consider it a checklist, and move quickly to the player essays and 1991 forecasts stats and values. If you find some of this stuff new, however, you will do well to take time and understand it. Winning isn't everything, but losing is nothing.

SCOUTING AND FORECASTING

Some of the promotional and marketing people working on this book last year asked me for some biographical stuff. They were especially interested in knowing what a professional forecaster does, and what I had done. "Forecasted what?" Randy, my publisher, asked me. When pressed to recall some of the numbers that I had predicted, I produced a list so long that it impressed even me. I had forgotten: gold, silver, and copper prices, factory output, GNP, inventory levels, company revenues, expenses, cash flow, market size, market share, product performance, competitors' earnings and strategies, etc. My suggestion to the promoters was to highlight some of the baseball predictions that I had made. That's what you're interested in, anyway. Isn't it?

Anyway, I made this long list of planning tools and disciplines. From my point of view, much of it was true but irrelevant techno-BS. It is hard to describe the nuts and bolts of planning and forecasting to someone who has never worked in the profession. Technically, I became a manager of planning and forecasting, and generally stopped doing the numbers myself, around 1983. When you have math PhD types and MBA computer jockeys working for you, it is pointless to get too deeply involved in doing calculations.

The most important aspect of forecasting, in my opinion, is to think comprehensively. Look at everything. Hold no preconceptions about what is meaningful. Consider the possible reasons behind every event, especially events that can be characterized as changes. Always ask: "Why?"

My two best business/economic forecasts had nothing to do with arithmetic. During the first week of January, 1980, I saw people lined up outside a coin shop in Westport, selling tons of silver and silverware. With all those sellers, I reasoned, it was time for the price to go down. Remember when silver was $50 per ounce? The market collapsed two weeks after that line of people caught my attention. I did fine, thank you.

About three years later, in December 1982, I was driving to work on I-84 east of Danbury, the same road at the same hour as I had taken for years. You get used to routines. I was accustomed to seeing a flat-bed trailer full of two-by-fours on the road with me, the same truck every day. During the recession of 1982, this truck had grown increasingly empty. Some days, it hadn't even appeared. Then, on this one occasion in December, I passed TWO huge truckloads, and hypothesized that the recession was over. Phone calls to a couple of my friends in other companies' purchasing and sales functions generally supported my belief. My boss was very skeptical. He accepted my suggestion to enlarge our capacity slightly, but he took the unprecedented step of requiring me to write down my economic "assumption," to cover his ass. I welcomed the challenge, and put a copy of my forecast memo on the bulletin board. Two months later, the government announced that the recession had ended in December.

To see the future in baseball, all you have to do is keep your eyes open. Read a lot. Talk to people. Ask yourself questions that begin with "what if" and "why." Make a depth chart of every major league team, and write down who you think is going to play at each position. That's how this whole book is organized; somebody has to play at every position, every day. If you make a list of who you think will play, some glaring duplications and vacancies will jump out at you. You will see changes for 1991, before some of the major league teams themselves see what is needed. You can predict trades, emerging rookies, and fading veterans, before they even become rumors.

True, forecasting is partly arithmetic. You need a method to come up with "base case" numbers. You can't just sit down and guess all the stats for all the players (if you can do that accurately, you should become a bond trader for six months, and then retire). But the main question for every hitter is: how many at bats will he get in 1991?

My recommendation is that you should simply collect information: news, stats, observations, whatever you find helpful. And keep asking yourself: who is going to play at every position, every day? (If you can't maintain such a large and detailed inventory, subscribe to my newsletter.)

To win Rotisserie baseball, you need a nationwide network. I have the benefit of a decent national network: people who know what they're talking about, in every city. If you join, your Rotisserie performance will benefit. I also have the benefit of working nine years for a company with an office in every city, providing instant access to people who follow every team and read every newspaper.

Speaking of newspapers, you should be receiving AT LEAST 500 pounds per year. That's only about two or three per day, depending on their size. I assume you know about Baseball America and USA Today. You should intensify your reading during spring training. Here are some names and phone numbers that you will want to use. Where two numbers are given, the second is the sports department.

Arizona Republic 602-271-8503
Atlanta Journal .414-522-4141 — 414-526-5331
Baltimore Sun (esp. Sunday) 301-539-1280
                                  301-332-6200
Baseball America. 800-845-2726
Boston Globe 617-929-2000
Camden Courier Post 609-662-4700
                                  609-486-2424
Chicago Tribune .800-874-2863 — 312-222-3232
Cincinnati Inquirer .513-651-4500 — 513-369-1917

Cleveland Plain Dealer 216-344-4080
                                  216-344-4580
Dallas Morning News 214-745-8383
                                  214-977-8444
Houston Post. . .713-840-5000 — 713-840-5184
K.C. Times . . . .816-234-4545 — 816-234-4355
L.A. Daily News .818-713-3131 — 818-713-3600
L.A. Herald Examiner 213-744-1122
                                  213-744-8000
L.A. Times 213-626-2323
Miami Herald . .305-350-2000 — 305-376-3500
Milwaukee Journal 414-224-2020
                                  414-224-2310
Minneapolis Star Tribune 612-372-4343
                                  612-372-4447
New York Daily News 800-692-6397
New York Post 800-552-7678
Oakland Tribune 415-839-3939 — 415-645-2000
Philadelphia Inquirer 215-665-1234
                                  215-854-4550
San Francisco Examiner 415-778-7800
                                  415-777-2424
Seattle Post Intelligencer 206-464-2121
                                  206-448-8370
St. Petersburg Times 813-893-8166
Towson Times 301-337-2400
Orlando Sentinel 407-420-5305
                                  407-420-5474
Philadelphia Daily News 215-665-1234
                                  215-854-5700
Pittsburgh Press 412-263-1121 — 412-263-1100
San Diego Union 619-299-3131 — 619-293-1341
Sporting News 800-669-5700
St. Louis Post Dispatch 314-622-7111
                                  314-622-7597
Toronto Star . . .416-361-2138 — 416-869-4300
The National Sports Daily 800-677-0707

There are probably some very good dailies missing from the above list, but that should keep you busy. Peter Golenbock has some excellent suggestions on how to get information from sports desks. See his book, "How to Win at Rotisserie Baseball." He also discusses calling major league teams' P.R. departments, but my personal opinion is that, unless you know someone pretty well, calling the teams is a waste of time. They don't want to be bothered, and have no reason to help you.

What P.R. department is ever going to say, "That pitcher's arm is all screwed up; he can't throw his slider," or "Bimbleman's leg is broken, but we're not going to tell the newspeople until tomorrow." Be realistic. They always tell you that Bimbleman is "being examined by a doctor today." Didn't he see a doctor yesterday, after his teammates carried him off the field? Or did the trainer just give him a beer, and tell him to keep his stay off his feet?

If you do call the teams and succeed in getting someone to tell you their status reports, or if you just wait to read about them in the papers, you will need to translate what they tell you. The general theme is that P.R. people are extremely optimistic. They are propagandists, not informants. For example:

"He is being examined by a doctor today," means he is going on the DL today, unless a miracle occurred during the night.

"He has a sore knee and will miss a few days," means he has torn ligaments and may never play again.

"The rookie has an excellent shot at winning the first base job . . . it's wide open," means they wish the regular 1B would practice his fielding more.

"We haven't made any decision," means the rookie is being sent down, but they haven't told him yet.

You get the idea.

SPRING TRAINING

Definitely, go to spring training. If you are serious about scouting, however, do not fall into the trap of a whirlwind tour. You cannot see all the players no matter how much you move around, and you are much more likely to gain some real insight if you watch one team for several days. Pick a team and a week. Every player in spring training is capable of going 5 for 5 one day, or he wouldn't be there. It is harder to be outstanding for a whole week, against 20 different pitchers.

Get your variety by perusing the visiting teams. Your "home team" players, coaches and other visitors (who can be an excellent source of insight) will get to know you after a few days, and become increasingly relaxed about what they will discuss with you, or within your listening range. If you have two weeks, pick two teams, and visit two camps extensively.

The exception to the "one team" rule is Phoenix. If you set up base a few miles northeast of the airport, you can watch the Giants take BP in the morning, see an A's game in the afternoon, and catch a Mariners game at night, all within ten minutes drive of each other. That's five teams in one day, with no rushing around.

Do not neglect your local media, especially the radio. Television stations are not likely to spend much time with baseball insiders, but your local radio sports producer (if he's any good) should get a couple of major league GM's, a scouting director, a field manager, and several out-of-town columnists on the phone to answer questions. I have been spoiled by WFAN all sports radio in New York, but you can get your local station to do some quality broadcasting, just by asking for it.

Finally, when you pull together all your scouting and analysis, search for combinations of clues. Do not take anything out of context. If you saw a hot rookie in spring training, but the Baseball Register says he is 29 years old and has never hit over .260 in seven minor league seasons, assume he had one terrific week, and forget him. If you see that 25 year-old Jose Cabalero hit .400 in winter ball, and .340 at Triple A last year, and that his team's regular first baseman can't run, while Cabalero has been looking like a gold glove at 1B in spring training, well, then you have something.

Before draft day, make lists, lots of lists. Then about a week before the draft, go through all these lists and see who appears near the top of several lists. For your draft, you will want just one list, a digest of all the others. Put a little time and effort in, and that one list will be a winner.

LAST YEAR'S NUMBERS

Spend less time looking at last year's numbers, and you will do better. True, you have to start somewhere, and last year's numbers are convenient, because:

— The calendar year is the official "accounting period" for major league baseball stats.

— Last year covers the same length of time that you are now trying to forecast, i.e., one season.

— Almost all existing data is sorted and analyzed by year.

— Almost all publications are focused on last year.

The main problem with last year's numbers is that there is TOO MUCH material focused on last year. It is so easy to get your hands on last year's stats, all exquisitely computerized and scrutinized and summarized, that there is an overwhelming temptation to stop after you have seen enough of last year's numbers, because you are fed up with them. After spending 600 hours during the winter, reviewing 1990 stats and having them almost memorized, you feel justified in calling it quits. You know that you have studied just as hard as anyone else in your league. Isn't that enough?

The problem is not that you must study MORE, but that you must study DIFFERENT. I am advising you to spend LESS time studying last year's numbers. They make you blind, after a while.

Another problem is that everyone else in your league will also know last year's numbers, backwards and forwards, because they have been deluged with the same "information" that you have. To win Rotisserie baseball, you must have some new ideas, some insight, some different way of looking at the past. When everybody uses the same information exclusively, the game becomes a contest to see who can perform the most rigorous manipulations of last year's numbers. That is no fun, and (even worse) it will make you a mediocre player.

My advice is to get last year's numbers into a new context, as fast as possible after you receive them. Keep a historical file on a computer. Dump the most recent year's numbers in, as soon as you get them, and produce a new "model" of long term performance. A quick and dirty method to put career hitter stats into context, is to weight them 50%/25%/15%/10% for the past four years, and create a "weighted average" annual performance.

Another step you can take is to break down last year's numbers into first and second half. For three years, this book has devoted a major essay to the subject of second half numbers. Other publications are just beginning to include second half numbers. I started the practice in this book, and I am confident that within three years, second half stats will be a standard report in every baseball annual, right up there with left/right breakdowns. They are just too important to ignore, and too easy to compute.

You do not need to wait for my book to start analyzing second half numbers. Save a file of stats at the All Star break, and when you get the full year numbers, just subtract the first half to get the second half. You can begin scrutinizing the second half before the LCS is finished, and it will do you more good than scrutinizing those full year numbers that have always caught your attention in October.

Need another idea? Start looking at players' careers in terms of playing time, not calendar time, especially where younger players are involved. A rookie season of 150 at bats is not the same as a rookie season with 500 at bats. Three or four "years" as a utility player may produce only as much development as one year as a regular. Robert O. Wood has made a science of splitting players' careers into 10 equal parts, so that every player has a "first decile" equal in significance to every other player's first decile. You can do the same thing yourself. If the activity does nothing more than focus your attention away from last year's numbers, it is a worthwhile activity.

You can also transform last year's numbers into per-at-bat statistics and then make comparisons. You can match last year against two years ago, and do a "fluctuation analysis" to see who is most improved and who is fading fastest. You can combine the two methods and compare per-at-bat numbers for current year versus per-at-bat for the previous year.

The point is, anything you can do to move your attention away from last year's numbers, will offer you the possibility of a competitive edge. You will be inundated with last year's numbers anyway, from everywhere you look, everything you read, everyone you listen to. Don't waste your time seeking out last year's numbers. Let them find you. They will, too. I guarantee it.

SECOND HALF SIGNALS

This is a quiz. No notes, please. We are testing your memory. If you do well, you can skip this chapter. Just a few questions. Any close answer will be acceptable:

1. What was Lenny Dykstra's batting average in mid June 1990?

2. What was Jack Armstrong's won/lost record at the All Star break last year? Do you remember his ERA?

3. How many home runs did Cecil Fielder have, half way through 1990?

Now, those aren't too hard; are they? The answers were printed repeatedly in newspapers everywhere last year. The average baseball fan should be able to make some close guesses on one or two of them, anyway.

The answers: Dykstra was hitting around .393, plus or minus ten points, depending on which day you pick from "mid June." If you guessed, "about .400," you got 1 correct.

Jack Armstrong? If you watched the All Star game, you might remember that he was 11-3 at that point; they put the graphic on TV enough times to educate people who don't read newspapers. His ERA was 2.28. If you just remembered "around 2.00," or "in the low 2's," that's a good answer.

And Cecil: 28 homers at the All Star break; again the TV graphics helped. By early July, most fans saw the clear possibility that Fielder might hit 50 HR in 1990.

Now, three more questions:

4. What was Dykstra's batting average in the second half of 1990?

5. What was Armstrong's won/lost record and ERA after the All Star break?

6. How many homers did Fielder hit in the second half?

These are a little harder, aren't they? The Dykstra BA and Armstrong ERA are very tough, because you can't do the arithmetic in your head (I can't, anyway) even if you have a perfect memory of their final 1990 stats. Fielder you might get without too much trouble: since he had 51 HR in total (a very memorable number) and 28 at the break, he must have had 23 in the second half. Dykstra hit .292 in the second half, and Armstrong was 1-6 with a 5.96 ERA and a 1.64 ratio.

In case you haven't gotten the point yet, it is this: every year, we get inundated with first half numbers, and they stick in our memory. April numbers: I still remember that Graig Nettles once hit 9 HR in April. Ron Cey hit 11 in April one year. It was big news at the time. Did you ever hear about how many homers anybody hit in July? It would have to be a huge number to get national attention. Maybe Kevin Maas might be a case of July attention, but nobody said, "See what he's doing in the month of July." People simply focused on his full year and career numbers, because they were rare.

We get early-season and full-year numbers continuously. First they are focused on April and May, then April through June, then April through July, and (finally) April through October. We see these numbers, we read them, and we remember many of them. But when do we get lists of the best players from August 15 to the end of the season? Isn't that just as important as April 1 through May 15? For predicting next year, the August-September numbers are MORE IMPORTANT than the April-May numbers, because they are newer. But we never see them!

If you want to win Rotisserie baseball, you better get used to the idea of studying second half numbers. Many magazines and annuals have started focusing on second half numbers within the past twelve months, just as I predicted they would. They are just as important as right/left breakdowns.

For example, last year at this time, you could have noticed:

George Brett hit .316 with 53 RBI in the second half of 1989. If you concluded that Brett was NOT washed up, you got him cheap in your 1990 auction and did very nicely. Last year, The Analyst had Brett rated as the 2nd best first basemen in the AL when we went to press in February.

Barry Bonds stole 20 of his 32 bases in the second half of 1989. We said he could steal 40 bases in 1990, and he stole 50.

Gerald Young stole only three bases in the second half of 1989, while getting caught nine times. We concluded that there was something wrong, and warned you off. People who went into 1990 expecting him to steal 65 bases, like he did in 1988, are now scrutinizing second half stats.

Neal Heaton began throwing a forkball in the July 1989. In the second half of '89, his ERA was 1.66 and his Ratio was 1.03. No one noticed Heaton's new form, because his full year numbers kept reflecting the bad first half that had motivated him to experiment. The conventional media didn't start asking what had happened until early 1990, when the glamorous numbers finally caught people's attention. It pays to look. Going into 1990, we had Heaton valued higher than Todd Worrell, Rick Reuschel, John Smoltz, and Tom Glavine (for example).

Which told you more about Todd Worrell's outlook for 1990, the fact that he had a 2.96 ERA in 1989, or the fact that he had a 5.09 ERA in the second half of 1989? Worrell developed arm trouble, and the second half highlighted that fact, while his full-year stats didn't.

The anecdotal evidence goes on and on. The 1990 Analyst gives many more cases of second half stats foretelling the downfall or emergence of specific players. If you like to learn from examples, by all means go back and look at the 1990 book again. But the point is already clear: second half stats are surely worth a long, hard look, as PART of your effort to forecast player performance for the coming year.

Why is the Second Half such a good indicator? Several reasons:

(1) The second half of the preceding year is chronologically close to the period that we are trying to predict. Events that occurred early in the preceding year (like Todd Worrell's 1.21 ERA in the first half of 1989) are less relevant than events that occurred late in the preceding year, because the older events are chronologically more remote.

In a baseball forecast context, events that happened ten years ago are meaningless. A two year old event is possibly meaningful, but is still suspect because of its age. Events just one year old are more relevant than two year old events, and things that happened late last year are even more meaningful. Second Half stats give us a picture, a valuable little snapshot, in which the more remote events of the previous year (i.e. April, May and June) have been eliminated. You could think of second half stats as a photographic blow-up of an important detail that is usually overlooked: not the whole picture, but certainly worth a look.

(2) IF SOMETHING HAPPENED during the preceding year that changed a player's abilities and output, that "something" will be more heavily reflected in the second half numbers than in the full year numbers. If whatever it was that happened, happened on July 4th, that event will be fully

reflected in second half statistics, 50% reflected in full year statistics, and not-at-all reflected in first half statistics of the preceding year.

Some events get into the news, and some don't. You could have researched Worrell's injury in 1989. If you lived in Pittsburgh you might have had a clue that Neal Heaton developed a new pitch in July 1989. But many changes are not publicized, and many are difficult to investigate.

As we all know, many things can happen during the long baseball season. A hitter may be moved in the batting order. The players batting in front of him or behind him in the batting order may change, or be changed. The player's whole team may be changed. Opposing defense may be relocated to a hitter's disadvantage, or his own fielding position may be shifted and have an adverse, or favorable, effect on his hitting. All these factors affect statistics even when a player's innate skills, attitude, concentration, and total playing time remain exactly the same.

(3) Skills can change, too. A young hitter may learn (finally!) to lay off the high fastball, or to go the other way with an outside pitch. He may learn such things gradually over the course of several years, he may learn them during one season, or he may learn them suddenly on July 4th. An older hitter may lose some speed and get to first base on time less often, or he may lose his ability to get around on a fastball. Or pitchers may simply LEARN that the old man can no longer jerk their fastball into the seats. Word spreads fast among pitchers around a league.

(4) Rookies, not veterans, are most susceptible to opposing pitchers and managers learning something that is going to impair their hitting performance. In fact, the cornerstone of the "second half theory" is the old baseball axiom that a rookie's true ability can be seen in his second tour around the league, i.e. in the second half of the season.

In January 1989 I began publishing detailed analyses of second half numbers, even $ values based on second half, and the response has been overwhelming. No, I don't claim that I invented second half analysis; that baseball axiom about rookies is at least ninety years old. I am proud to be the first person who pursued this idea extensively, in print, for Rotisserie and forecasting purposes, however.

My enthusiasm for second half numbers has been such that many people (who should know better) have suggested that second half stats are the sole basis for my forecasts and predictions. It is flattering to have people think "Benson's idea" whenever they hear about second half scrutiny, but it is obviously silly to see that association backwards, and say "second half stats method" whenever they hear the name, "Benson." Anyone who makes that mistake shows that they didn't read my book; they just scanned the chapter titles and looked at the tables in the back. They are also showing that they don't know beans about forecasting, either. Quoting from the first two editions of The Analyst: "Second half annualization is definitely useful, but it is just one tool available to the analyst. When you finally make a determination and put your money where your mouth is, you should have considered numerous factors and various points of view, not just second half performance." Sounds pretty clear, I think.

Forecasting is not a mathematical exercise. It does not begin or end with formulas. My method is to make an individual scrutiny of every single player, using original information directly from players and coaches, and second-hand (unpublished) information from "baseball people" wherever possible. Within the part that is purely analytical, second half stats are just one more place where people should look for clues. I stress the importance of looking, because so many people don't look, and they don't see.

Drafting players for Rotisserie purposes is a lot like hiring people for professional positions. In hiring, there are several steps that should be followed. You should look at credentials. You should consider experience. You should interview. You should check references. You should give a preemployment physical exam. But when somebody says, "That manager hires his people on the basis of physical exams," they are showing their ignorance of the total process.

Last summer, writer/analyst Adam Stein ran a regression analysis looking at second half 1988 and full year 1988 as predictors of 1989 stats. He found that, when the whole population of major leaguers is examined (not just rookies, geriatrics, and injury cases), the second half was a weaker basis for prediction than the full year (and even a shade weaker than the first half in this one year). I wasn't surprised. A large base period is always desirable; that's why I consider data from four years for a base case. No doubt, two year base periods give better indications than one year base periods. If you limit your thinking to the second half of the previous year, you will give up some valuable perspective. Many second half performances must be dismissed as anomalies.

So keep things in perspective, and you will find all kinds of nuggets that give you an edge in Rotisserie competition. When you like players for numerous reasons (the right age, the right ballpark, an enthusiastic manager, an established role, and a good second half in the previous season) then you are on the right track. The forecast stats in the back of this book are the complete and "official" forecast for 1991. Tables of second half stats from 1990 are presented for your reference and enjoyment. They are worth studying.

Continuing an annual tradition, I will highlight some of the second half performances that impress me as noteworthy:

NATIONAL LEAGUE:

Strong Second Half —

Tim Raines: 25 SB.
Eric Davis: .280-13-51-13.
Mark Grace: .351, 50 RBI.
Darren Daulton: .303 BA.
Alejandro Pena: 2.01 ERA, 1.14 ratio.
Joe Magrane: 6-5, 2.90 ERA, 1.21 ratio.
Joe Boever: 2.30 ERA, 6 saves.
Roger McDowell: 2.23 ERA, 9 saves.

Tim Burke: 1.73 ERA, 1.06 ratio.
Jay Howell: 1.45 ERA, 0.96 ratio, 12 saves.
Bruce Hurst: 6-2, 1.94 ERA, 1.01 ratio.
Terry Mulholland: 6-7, 2.86 ERA, 1.05 ratio.

Weak Second Half —

Kevin Gross: 1-7, 6.25 ERA
Tom Browning: 5.05 ERA and 1.39 ratio, despite the 7-4 record.
Alfredo Griffin: .179 BA.
Jose Uribe: .174-0-6-2.
Todd Benzinger: .190-1-7-0.
Terry Pendleton: .198-1-13-6.

AMERICAN LEAGUE

Strong Second Half —

Roberto Kelly: .285-11-36-24 (compare to Rickey Henderson .315-11-25-26).
Steve Sax: 24 SB
Shane Mack: .343-5-31-10
Carlos Baerga: .309-4-28-0
Jeff D Robinson: 2.49 ERA, 1.21 ratio.
Chuck Crim: 2.29 ERA, 1.08 ratio.
Eric Plunk: 2.40 ERA, 1.04 ratio.
Bobby Witt: 12-2, 2.64 ERA.
Eric Hanson: 9-3, 2.59 ERA, 1.00 ratio.
Ben McDonald: 8-5, 2.50 ERA, 1.05 ratio.
Billy Swift: 2.47 ERA, 1.14 ratio, 5 saves.
Steve Farr: 7-4, 1.80 ERA, 1.16 ratio.

Weak Second Half —

Jim Abbott: 1.50 ratio.
Kevin Brown: 4.06 ERA, 1.46 ratio.
Teddy Higuera: 5-8, 4.75 ERA, 1.40 ratio.
Mike Schooler: 1.53 ratio, 8 saves.
Ron Kittle: .118-2-6-0.
Kurt Stillwell: .208-2-18-0.
Chili Davis: .250-2-18-0.
Bob Geren: .188-2-15-0.

WINDS OF WINTER

Like any "short" record of baseball statistics, 170 at bats in winter ball can be misleading. You do not pick up the USA Today on May 25 and draw final conclusions about full season numbers (if you do, Bill Cunningham would like to make some trades with you). But on May 25 every year, you do have some good CLUES about who is going to do better or worse than the year before, who is going to be successful among the rookie crop, which veterans are in danger of losing their jobs, and which pitchers are getting powerful results out of those new pitches they have been developing. So it is with winter ball. You get clues, indications, and hints which, in combination with other information that you have available, may lead you to make accurate assessments about full year numbers, including some surprises.

To give you a feeling for the kind of insights that you can get from winter ball numbers, here are some of the cases that emerged in recent years.

In 1989, my "first best" selection from winter ball was Lonnie Smith. For San Juan of the Puerto Rican League, he produced a .366 average, 7 homers, 42 RBI, and 28 stolen bases in just 191 at bats. Combined with the knowledge that Atlanta was short of righty-hitting outfielders, I felt confident that he would get plenty of playing time.

Caracas pitcher Mike Schooler, the Seattle bull pen prospect, led the league in ERA with 0.59, and produced a Ratio of 0.81. The 1988 Sporting News Baseball Register contained no major league record for this guy, and showed his 3.96 ERA at Chattanooga in 1987. Think he went cheap in the 1988 spring drafts? For 1988 numbers including 15 Saves and a low ERA, many people paid very little.

Greg Maddux, who struggled through a 6-14 season with a 5.61 ERA for the Cubs in 1987, went to Venezuela and produced a 7-4 record for last place Zulia, with an ERA of 1.49 and a Ratio of 1.07 in 96 innings. Give you any ideas about who your $1 to $2 starter should have been in 1988? Maddux, of course, went 18-8 with a 3.18 ERA for the Cubbies in '88, and looked like a Cy Young candidate until he faded in the second half. NOTE! I will repeat this later, because it is important. Winter league pitchers often fade around July 31.

In pre-1988 winter ball, Roberto Alomar, a 19 year old middle infield prospect who had never appeared in the major leagues, hit .302 with 31 runs scored in 199 AB's. He went on to have a very successful rookie season in 1988, holding his own with a .266 average and showed he can steal bases and score runs (84 in 545 at bats) just as well as he did for Caguas.

The most exciting case for 1988 drafts in my opinion — I stared at these numbers for weeks in advance of the spring draft — soft-throwing Doug Jones of Ponce, led the Puerto Rican League in ERA with 0.51 and a Ratio under 0.91, with a strikeouts to walks ratio of better than 3 to 1. When the Indians removed Jones from their 40 man roster during spring training, for technical reasons totally unrelated to their plans and expectations, his value went down in the eyes of everyone else who had noticed him. He was my LAST pitcher taken in my AL 1988 draft; no one else wanted him. All Jones did in 1988 was get 37 saves for CLEVELAND with an ERA of 2.18 and a Ratio of 1.02. And of course he continued in 1989.

Jose Rijo produced an ERA of 1.81 and a Ratio of 0.88 in the pre-1988 D.R. league. He walked only 11 in 55 innings, while striking out 38, not the same "Wild Man" Jose who had given up over 100 walks for Oakland in 1986, before being demoted to Tacoma in 1987. Do you think he might have been ready to have a great season in 1988? Ask Pete Rose, who watched Jose go 13-8 with a 2.39 ERA and a 1.12 Ratio. Rijo, by the way, got 160 strikeouts and gave up 63 walks in 162 innings in 1988, not quite as good as the pro-rata numbers he had produced for the Licey team, but showing definite improvement.

Luis Salazar, after being demoted to Appleton [wow, does that sound like a demotion!] spent part of 1987 with Las Vegas and was real CHEAP in 1988 auctions. In many drafts, he went unmentioned. His 1987 major league totals of 3 homers and 17 RBI are not the kind of numbers that are going to inspire fierce bidding. But wait! Look here in Baseball America issue of March 10 . . . it says that Luis Salazar of La Guaira finished the season with a .371 batting average, with 10 HR and 39 RBI in 197 at bats. How good is this league, anyway, you wonder? Well, right below this Luis Salazar fellow you see a certain Andres Galarraga who hit .343 with 4 HR and 21 RBI — if this is the same Galarraga we all know and love, then that chap Salazar might well be worth a $1 speculative bid, or even $2, at the draft next month. Of course he turned out to be worth much more!

Ramon Martinez (7-1, 1.63 ERA, 0.88 Ratio in 1988-89 winter ball) looked like he would be the Dodgers annual pitching "surprise." He is still hot property for 1990, and more assured of making the rotation.

By now everyone knows that Tim Leary, nearing retirement after a horrendous 3-11 record with 4.76 ERA in 1987, went down to Tijuana for winter ball, developed a devastating split finger fastball, and came back to be 17-11 with a 2.91 ERA for the world champion 1988 Dodgers. Leary looked as good as, or better than, Orel Hershiser during the first half of the season. (Again, note the late-season fade.)

It is no coincidence that Leary, Rijo, and Greg Maddux, all mentioned above, weakened in the second half of their highly successful 1988 campaigns. Winter ball can lead to a syndrome of overwork usually setting in by late July or early August. If you are fortunate enough to identify one of these Big Surprise pitchers, and acquire them at a cheap price, you may want to capitalize on the envy that your insight has created, by trading in July for an even better player at an even cheaper price, and watch with pleasure as the guy you traded away comes unglued in August and September. It is sometimes difficult to shift your loyalties from rooting avidly for one of these phenoms, to hoping that their arm falls off, but there is great pleasure in seeing everything unfold on schedule, as you knew it would.

1991 PROGNOSTICATIONS:

Steve Decker, Pedro Munoz, Julio Valera, and Hensley Meulens were among those who helped their careers with their performance in winter 1990-91. The WINNING ROTISSERIE BASEBALL monthly will have a complete wrap-up.

STRIKEOUT / WALK RATIOS
— WHICH CURRENT STARS ARE WASHED UP? —

by Rob Wood

I have previously undertaken an extensive study on the evolution of a hitters's strikeout and walk performances over the course of his career. The results were originally published in the 1989 Baseball Abstract.

To summarize, I found that a player's strikeout ratio and his walk ratio (walks/AB's) both improve during early part of his career. As the player's prime passes, these two ratios level off. Then as he enters the twilight of his career, both ratios become precipitously worse, until the player is forced into part-time duty and eventually into retirement.

As a single measure, the hitter's strikeout to walk ratio is a valuable tool for tracing the progress of his career. This measure is useful for all types of hitters. Good hitters and bad hitters all show the same cycle: the K/BB ratio improves steadily in the early part of a player's career, levels off in his prime, and worsens dramatically in his twilight.

The hitter's predilection to strike out, or draw a base on balls, does not affect the relevance of this ratio during his career. Virtually all hitters' strikeout to walk ratio improves in the first part of his career (constituting roughly 70% of his career), levels off for a while (for about 20% of his career) and then deteriorates sharply at the end of his career (roughly the last 10% of his career).

To form a simple statistic to identify in which of the three career stages a hitter currently resides, I calculate each hitter's strikeout/walk ratio in the previous season, and compare it to the strikeout/walk ratio for his entire career. From these two ratios, I calculate a "meta-ratio" (season ratio / career ratio) for each hitter. I have found these meta-ratios to be quite useful. As a rough guide, once a player's metaratio exceeds 1.25, he is typically in decline. A meta-ratio of exceeding 1.4 is almost always s a sure sign that the player's abilities have permanently vacated.

There are a myriad of criteria we can use in deciding whether a player is "washed up." Batting average, slugging percentage, and range afield are useful measures in their own right. You may have some other particular favorite. A hitter's strikeout to walk ratio is another in this list, one that can be of value not only as a monitor of current decline, but also as a predictor of imminent decline.

It is hardly uncommon for a player past his prime to have a poor season. But sometimes by looking at his traditional statistics we cannot be sure of he had an "off year" (and is likely to rebound) or if it is a signal of trouble immediately ahead. Especially for this type of player, I have found that looking at his strikeout / walk ratio can help discern the difference.

I have crudely classified every player who batted at least 250 times in the 1990 season, and who has at least 2500 career at bats, into four categories: (1) washed up, (2) on a banana peel, (3) in transition; and (4) safe and sound.

This classification has helped me stay clear of a few players, while sometimes encouraging me to acquire a player coming off a poor season.

Following the 1988 season, the strikeout / walk ratio put up a red flag on Fred Lynn, Gary Carter,

Keith Hernandez, and Willie Wilson. Each had a poor 1989 season (and they generally followed up with poor 1990 seasons).

Following the 1989 season, this classification told me that Eddie Murray and Candy Maldonado, coming off poor seasons, were poised for good years in 1990. I also found Andre Dawson comfortably in the "safe and sound" category. All three did indeed have stellar 1990 campaigns.

However, the strikeout / walk ratio must not be used indiscriminately. For example, Brian Downing fell into the "washed up" classification after the 1989 season, but I thought Downing was still a solid major leaguer, even at his advanced age. The red flag did not make me dismiss Downing entirely. In fact, I ranked him as the third best DH behind Baines and Parker.

I was not the only analyst to make the right conclusion. After examining Downing's "washed up" classification, John Benson predicted a .251-14-51 season. Brian actually produced .275-14-51 in 1990. John, you better work on your batting average predictions!

The following players are the most interesting of the roughly 100 veterans who meet my two requirements for evaluation (minimum 250 at bats in 1990, and 2500 career at bats). I list only those hitters whose evaluation was altered (at least in my mind) by looking at their strikeout to walk ratio vis a vis other more traditional statistics.

WASHED UP:

Johnny Ray
Mel Hall
Mike Heath
Willie Randolph
Mike Marshall

ON A BANANA PEEL:

Dale Murphy
Dan Gladden
Hubie Brooks
Frank White
Tommy Herr
Scott Fletcher
Vince Coleman
Dickie Thon

IN TRANSITION:

Paul Molitor
Alfredo Griffin
Gary Gaetti
Terry Pendleton
Dave Henderson
George Bell
Tom Brunansky
Pedro Guerrero

SAFE AND SOUND:

Joe Carter
Robin Yount
Kevin McReynolds
Tony Fernandez
Carlton Fisk
Andre Dawson
Brook Jacoby
Juan Samuel

As a general rule, stay clear of the "washed up" bunch, since the down side risk is far too much compared to upside return. The "banana peel" bunch should only be acquired if you have an overwhelming reason (e.g. a slugger just traded to the friendly confines of Wrigley Field). The "in transition" group is roughly in the middle of the road. Most will be mediocre to good in the coming year. The "safe and sound" group can be acquired with impunity, provided, of course, that they have playing time reserved for them.

THE PROBLEM WITH PITCHERS AND WHAT TO DO ABOUT THEM

Starting pitchers are the most unreliable, unpleasant group of people in the world, statistically speaking that is. There is something about the art of pitching that causes a tiny shift in ability to become a tremendous difference in measured performance statistics. Think about the difference between a good pitcher and a bad pitcher. An ERA of 2.70 is good; an ERA of 4.70 is bad.

The same pitcher can have an ERA of 2.70 one year, and then 4.70 the next. That's a 74% deterioration. Hitters do not produce such erratic numbers. An extreme case of a hitter going bad might be a .300 BA one year, and .239 the next. That's a 20% deterioration. Nobody goes from .330 to .180 in one year.

I will let somebody else do the arithmetic showing the standard deviations, standard errors, etc. describing pitcher performance from year to year. [If you want to do it, I will be happy to put your work in the Winning Rotisserie Baseball newsletter, and in next year's book.] One reason that I have not done this work is that I already know the answer: pitchers are dangerously unpredictable. It amazes me that some major league owners/GM's have not yet discovered this fact; they keep paying millions for Andy Messersmith and Dave LaPoint.

There is a high degree of risk in pitcher performance. When you pay $20 for a good, solid pitcher (value based on prior years' numbers) you might get $1 or $40 value this year. Intuitively, I can estimate the ranges and probabilities:

THE PROBABILITY THAT A $20 PLAYER (LAST YEAR) WILL BE WORTH $ X THIS YEAR

	PITCHERS	HITTERS
$18 to $22	10%	40%
$15 to $25	30%	75%
$12 to $28	50%	90%
$10 to $30	60%	95%
$5 to $35	75%	98%
$0 to $40	90%	99%

Yes, there is about a 10% chance that a pitcher worth $20 last year would be worth zero this year. You get the same level of confidence that a hitter worth $20 last year will be worth $12 to $28 this year. If you see that you would rather spend $20 on the hitter, you have a good feel for the risk involved. The reliability of the hitter is worth money. Conversely, the unpredictability of the pitcher is a cost factor. If you could buy insurance, to keep the value of the pitcher above $12, you would pay money for that safety. Since you can't buy insurance, you must take something off the $20 price tag (whatever you would have been willing to pay for that insurance).

Good hitters and bad hitters are not all that different from each other, not in baseball, and not in Rotisserie. A bad hitter (Mario Mendoza for example, a .215 average) makes an out 78.5% of the time. A good hitter (.300 average) makes an out 70.0% of the time. Only 8.5% of the time does a good hitter (Robin Yount, Jose Canseco, Andre Dawson, Ruben Sierra) get a hit when a bad hitter

(Mario Mendoza, Jay Bell, Jim Walewander, Bobby Meacham, Jim Pankovitz, or Rafael Belliard) would make an out. They do the "same thing" statistically (either both make an out or both get a hit) 91.5% of the time. Therefore you could argue that a bad hitter, based on Batting Average, is 91% as good as a good hitter; while a bad pitcher is only half as good as a good pitcher, based on earned run average.

For Rotisserie purposes, a bad pitcher hurts you even worse than it first appears, because there are TWO percentage measurements for a pitcher (ERA and Ratio) and only one percentage measurement for a hitter (BA). In all the other categories, the worst a player can do is zero. The pitcher has twice as much opportunity to take value away from your roster. That point is presented clearly by Alex Patton. I would add another point, that a pitcher can hurt you much worse in each category where he hurts you. Hitters with a BA of .110 and 400 at bats are non-existent; pitchers with extremely painful ERA's are common.

The above numbers are not intended to be rigorous mathematics. They are only intended to make a point: there is a big, big difference in stats between the best and worst pitchers in baseball. Can the difference in skill really be that widely spread? Heck, no. If there are 260 pitchers in major league ball at any given moment, that is 260 people out of about 100 million males between the ages of 18 and 39 in the U.S., Canada, and the Central America / Caribbean area. How good are those 260? All of them are very, very, very good! How big is the real skill difference between the best and the worst among those 260? Pretty darn small.

Conclusion? The stats we use to measure pitchers, especially ERA and Ratio, tend to grossly (!) magnify and distort the real differences in quality of performance. On any given day, a tiny factor like a skinned knuckle, a hangnail, a sore toe, or a distraction like bank account or romantic worries, can have a huge impact on a pitcher's observable performance, while the same factors in a hitter's life could be completely invisible for a week or longer. Did the pitcher really throw much different when he had a bad day? Not possible. If his throwing really looked that bad, the pitching coach and manager would notice right away, and make a change. Very seldom can the best observers in the universe detect ANYTHING visible, until it is too late, and the stats are cast.

What do you do about it? Spend less time and less money on pitchers, especially starting pitchers. Follow a few simple rules. Put your money on proven relievers whose teams will not change their stopper role, and your saves are safe. Pick tall, healthy, hard-throwing left-handed starters with teams that win a lot, and your W's will be more predictable than if you pick small righties who just won 18 games in a small stadium with a bad team behind them.

Generally avoid pitchers from the Mariners, Red Sox, Cubs, and Braves. Study park effects, not just pitchers' performances. Look for (believable) announcements about who will get the stopper role, rather than spending your time scrutinizing spring training box scores. (In each of the past three years, I have made lists of pitchers who had good spring training box scores, and pitchers who had bad spring training box scores. By mid May, it is always obvious that both lists are totally worthless.)

From an editorial perspective, I have followed my own advice. Pitching does not get as much attention as hitting. Struggling to identify the fifth starter on each team is NOT a worthwhile use of time. The person you end up identifying is probably going to have negative value anyway — one of the worst among those 260 that make it to the big leagues. Where information looked valuable (and in some cases where it did not) we have speculated, we have made observations, and we have shared opinions. But we know that finding the third and fourth outfielders and identifying the DH against righty pitching on every team, is an activity that has positive value in Rotisserie, while finding the fifth starter on every team will usually have little, if any, value, and we have acted accordingly.

Some of the high price talents, like Dwight Gooden and Roger Clemens, have been subjected to intense scrutiny, and we have tried to identify all the probable effects due to changing teams, changing ball parks, new pitches, new bullpens, etc.

There are some valid strategies that emphasize starting pitchers over star hitters. One is the case of a new (expansion) team in a league where all of the great hitters are taken before the draft begins. Chasing points in HR and RBI would be unproductive in such a situation. Hoping to build a great corps of starting pitchers is about the only chance to be a winner your first year in such a league. As noted above, pitchers that cost $20 will often turn out to be worth $5 or $35. A new team, or a weak team, is well advised to roll the dice and hope for the best. What have you got to lose?

Another strategy is to be contrarian. If you compete in a league that loves hitters with a passion, you may be unable to buy any hitters at fair value. In such a case, you could do very well by bringing up the names of star hitters early in the auction, and watching people overbid for them. Save your own purchases for the end, when the names of the more consistent moundsmen can be brought up with confidence that they will be bargains. You can cheaply pick up a few points in hitting by going for batting average and SB, and hoping that your pitchers all have great years. Remember: pitchers are not bad; they are just unpredictable.

Finally, if you play in a "mixed" league, you should obviously get your pitchers from the NL and your hitters from the AL.

PITCHING: QUALITY MEASURES

As a business forecaster, I have often come across numbers that were clearly dependent on external factors, but which could not be linked to these causative factors using standard methods. What we wanted was a nice set of regression equations that could be used for long-term or short-term forecasting, but sometimes that just proved impossible. For example, we always wanted to forecast company revenue: next month, next year, and the next five years. At one company, we threw the kitchen sink into regression analyses, and came up with nothing meaningful. (We got high R squareds, but only because of the huge number of variables.) Anyway, we were able to see that revenue (obviously) varied with total business volume; in this case, pounds of product. And we knew, without any arithmetic, that pounds of product was a direct result of orders received. And we were able to see that orders received was a function of the Industrial Production Index for durable goods factory output (IPID). The nice thing about IPID is that it is an official government index; all sorts of professional economists were issuing long-term and short-term forecasts of IPID. We ended up with a group that employed Alan Greenspan to help do IPID forecasts (that was before Greenspan became really famous).

Strangely enough, even though we knew the answer, when we tried to correlate our revenue with IPID, we always came up empty. We tried lagging, ridge regression, and everything else you could think of. No dice. That was OK, of course, because we were able to do our forecasts in separate steps, as mentioned. We didn't have to jump from Alan Greenspan's IPID outlook directly to a forecast of our company revenue. The outlook for IPID told us the outlook for our orders. We looked at the recent trends and seasonality of pounds per order, and got a reasonable forecast of business volume. We then looked at recent trends and seasonality of our prices, and came up with a reasonable forecast of our revenue.

The point of this little digression is that you do not have to "forecast" a pitcher's ERA and wins, directly. We "know" that ERA and wins, on average, will get better when the pitcher yields fewer walks, fewer hits, and fewer homers. We also know that, on average, strikeouts have a tendency to reduce earned runs and increase wins. We therefore focus significant attention on the question of forecasting "intermediate" measures.

The solution is, simply, that we forecast those things that can be forecast: hits per inning, walks per inning, homers per inning, and strikeouts per inning, assigning weights as emphasis in a never-ending trial and error process, to make these components into predictors of ERA and wins.

Thus we deal with one of the most frustrating aspects of Rotisserie baseball: the unpredictability of pitching performance. Wins, Saves, ERA, and Ratio all depend on factors other than the pitcher's own performance. Wins depend on a team that is able to field and hit, and to do so at the right moments, and to hold a lead once attained. The pitchers holding the lead could obviously be different from the pitcher who is going to get the "W" — no connection but team spirit (if any). Saves depend on a save situation being available, and again depend on the pitcher's own team winning; a loss means that no save is possible. ERA depends on good fielding, timely fielding, and quality of the relief pitchers who enter a game with men on base. Ratio is the most "independent" number, although the pitcher must rely on his catcher and manager to be well-prepared and know what they are doing, and rely on fielders to change hits into outs as often as possible, and even walks can be largely attributed to the catcher's glove-work.

Pitchers' actual skills seem to rise and fall from year to year, more than hitters' skills. The importance of numerous factors beyond the pitcher's control tend to aggravate the natural fluctuations, meaning that accurate forecasts require luck. That is the main reason why you should spend only 35% of your money on pitching: unpredictability and risk.

Some aspects of pitching performance are more predictable than others. Most of these predictable factors are statistics that are mainly within the control of the man on the mound: strikeouts, walks, hits, and homers. Looking at numbers such as strikeouts per inning, we see reasonable consistency from year to year. Unfortunately, such numbers are not part of standard Rotisserie. Some day they will be. In the meantime, we can use the more predictable numbers as measures of past performance, measures that are more accurate than the Rotisserie categories, of wins, saves, and ERA. Ratio really seems to be a "fair" measure of pitcher performance and is the most predictable, consistent number among the Rotisserie pitching categories.

Back in 1989, I had many lists of pitchers ranked according to various stats. This year, I am going to spare you the many pages of lists, and simply tell you the top "quality" pitchers in each league in 1990.

TOP AL PITCHERS — 1990 QUALITY RANKINGS

Prepared by Owen Mock using Compuserve Sports Forum as a source.

Notes: (1) Rank is counted from top to bottom, where 1 = worst in league.
       (2) Total is a scale where 10 = perfect/highest.

Name	Team	IP	SO/IP	RANK	HIT/IP	RANK	BB/IP	RANK	HR/IP	RANK	TOTAL
Eckersley,D	OAK	73.3	0.995	166	0.559	174	0.055	174	0.027	165	9.8
Clemens,Roger	BOS	228.3	0.915	160	0.845	143	0.236	163	0.031	164	9.1
Hanson,Erik	SEA	236.0	0.894	158	0.869	133	0.288	138	0.064	130	8.0
Jones,Doug	CLE	84.3	0.652	112	0.783	158	0.261	152	0.059	137	8.0
Olson,Gregg	BAL	74.3	0.996	168	0.767	61	0.417	63	0.040	158	7.9
Thigpen,Bob	CHW	88.7	0.789	140	0.677	171	0.361	97	0.056	142	7.9
Aguilera,Rick	MIN	65.3	0.934	162	0.842	144	0.291	137	0.077	98	7.8
Gleaton,Jerry	DET	82.7	0.677	118	0.750	164	0.302	129	0.060	135	7.8
Montgomery,Jeff	KC	94.3	0.996	169	0.859	137	0.360	98	0.064	129	7.7
Henke,Tom	TOR	74.7	1.004	170	0.777	160	0.254	155	0.107	51	7.7
Ward,Duane	TOR	127.7	0.877	153	0.791	157	0.329	113	0.070	111	7.7
Farr,Steve	KC	127.0	0.740	130	0.780	159	0.378	83	0.047	153	7.5
Delucia,Rich	SEA	36.0	0.556	71	0.833	147	0.250	158	0.056	143	7.5
Honeycutt,Rick	OAK	63.3	0.600	86	0.726	167	0.347	105	0.032	162	7.5
Ryan,Nolan	TEX	204.0	1.137	173	0.672	172	0.363	94	0.088	81	7.5
Schooler,Mike	SEA	56.0	0.804	142	0.839	145	0.286	141	0.089	79	7.3
Schilling,Curt	BAL	46.0	0.696	122	0.826	150	0.413	64	0.022	171	7.3
Harvey,Bryan	CAL	64.3	1.275	174	0.699	170	0.544	22	0.062	132	7.2
Nelson,Gene	OAK	74.7	0.509	49	0.737	166	0.228	165	0.067	118	7.2
Stewart,Dave	OAK	266.7	0.622	94	0.847	141	0.311	124	0.060	136	7.1
Gray,Jeff	BOS	50.7	0.987	165	1.046	59	0.296	130	0.059	138	7.1
Stieb,Dave	TOR	208.7	0.599	85	0.858	138	0.307	125	0.053	147	7.1
Nunez,Edwin	DET	80.3	0.822	147	0.809	153	0.461	40	0.050	152	7.1
Olin,Steve	CLE	92.3	0.693	120	1.040	60	0.282	143	0.032	161	7.0
Eichhorn,Mark	CAL	84.7	0.815	145	1.157	22	0.272	148	0.024	170	7.0
Wells,David	TOR	189.0	0.608	89	0.873	131	0.238	161	0.074	103	7.0
Witt,Bobby	TEX	222.0	0.995	167	0.887	126	0.495	35	0.054	145	6.8
Comstock,Keith	SEA	56.0	0.893	157	0.714	169	0.464	39	0.071	108	6.8
Guthrie,Mark	MIN	144.7	0.698	124	1.065	53	0.270	149	0.055	144	6.8
McDonald,Ben	BAL	118.7	0.548	67	0.742	165	0.295	133	0.076	100	6.7
Appier,Kevin	KC	185.7	0.684	119	0.964	98	0.291	136	0.070	114	6.7
Williamson,Mark	BAL	85.3	0.703	126	0.762	162	0.328	114	0.094	67	6.7
Finley,Chuck	CAL	236.0	0.750	131	0.890	125	0.343	106	0.072	107	6.7
Guetterman,Lee	NYY	93.0	0.516	55	0.860	136	0.280	144	0.065	125	6.6
Leach,Terry	MIN	81.7	0.563	72	1.029	64	0.257	154	0.024	169	6.6
Radinsky,Scott	CHW	52.3	0.879	154	0.898	120	0.688	6	0.019	172	6.5
Jones,Barry	CHW	74.0	0.608	88	0.838	146	0.446	52	0.027	166	6.5
Kiecker,Dana	BOS	152.0	0.612	90	0.954	104	0.355	100	0.046	154	6.4

TOP NL PITCHERS — 1990 QUALITY RANKINGS

		IP	SO/IP	RANK	HIT/IP	RANK	BB/IP	RANK	HR/IP	RANK	TOTAL
Dibble, Rob	CIN	98.0	1.388	150	0.633	149	0.347	85	0.031	146	8.8
Smith, Lee	STL	68.7	1.019	147	0.845	126	0.291	117	0.044	137	8.8
Andersen, Larry	HOU	73.7	0.923	140	0.828	130	0.326	99	0.027	148	8.6
Pena, Alejandro	NYM	76.0	1.000	145	0.934	90	0.289	120	0.053	129	8.1
Darwin, Danny	HOU	162.7	0.670	90	0.836	129	0.191	147	0.068	106	7.9
Smith, Dave	HOU	60.3	0.829	129	0.746	143	0.331	95	0.066	107	7.9
Gooden, Dwight	NYM	232.7	0.958	144	0.984	70	0.301	113	0.043	139	7.8
Martinez, Ramon	LA	234.3	0.952	142	0.815	135	0.286	121	0.094	59	7.6
Martinez, Dennis	MON	226.0	0.690	94	0.845	124	0.217	141	0.071	98	7.6
Viola, Frank	NYM	249.7	0.729	107	0.909	100	0.240	134	0.060	118	7.6
Neidlinger, Jim	LA	74.0	0.622	76	0.905	102	0.203	146	0.054	126	7.5
Rijo, Jose	CIN	197.0	0.772	119	0.766	141	0.396	58	0.051	132	7.5
Howell, Jay	LA	66.0	0.894	136	0.894	104	0.303	112	0.076	94	7.4
Harris, Greg W.	SD	117.3	0.827	127	0.784	140	0.418	45	0.051	131	7.4
Tomlin, Randy	PIT	77.7	0.541	43	0.798	136	0.155	148	0.064	113	7.3
Cone, David	NYM	211.7	1.101	148	0.836	128	0.307	111	0.099	49	7.3
Myers, Randy	CIN	86.7	1.131	149	0.681	148	0.438	39	0.069	101	7.3
Drabek, Doug	PIT	231.3	0.566	57	0.821	132	0.242	132	0.065	110	7.2
Franco, John	NYM	67.7	0.828	128	0.975	74	0.310	108	0.059	119	7.1
Hartley, Mike	LA	79.3	0.958	143	0.731	144	0.378	70	0.088	71	7.1
Brantley, Jeff	SF	86.7	0.704	98	0.888	111	0.381	68	0.035	143	7.0
Whitehurst, Wall	NYM	65.7	0.701	97	0.959	80	0.137	149	0.076	92	7.0
Searage, Ray	LA	32.3	0.588	65	0.928	93	0.309	110	0.031	145	6.9
Crews, Tim	LA	107.3	0.708	100	0.913	96	0.224	138	0.084	79	6.9
Hurst, Bruce	SD	223.7	0.724	104	0.841	127	0.282	123	0.094	58	6.9
Fernandez, Sid	NYM	179.3	1.009	146	0.725	145	0.374	74	0.100	45	6.8
Smith, Zane	PIT	215.3	0.604	72	0.910	98	0.232	136	0.070	100	6.8
Whitson, Ed	SD	228.7	0.555	51	0.940	88	0.206	144	0.057	121	6.7
Belinda, Stan	PIT	58.3	0.943	141	0.823	131	0.497	23	0.069	102	6.6
Tudor, John	STL	146.3	0.431	14	0.820	133	0.205	145	0.068	103	6.6
Patterson, Bob	PIT	94.7	0.739	110	0.930	92	0.222	140	0.095	55	6.6
Grimsley, Jason	PHI	57.3	0.715	103	0.820	134	0.750	3	0.017	150	6.5
Armstrong, Jack	CIN	166.0	0.663	86	0.910	99	0.355	81	0.054	125	6.5
Gardner, Mark	MON	152.7	0.884	134	0.845	125	0.400	55	0.085	76	6.5
Assenmacher, P	CHC	103.0	0.922	139	0.874	114	0.350	83	0.097	53	6.5
Charlton, Norm	CIN	154.3	0.758	116	0.849	123	0.454	35	0.065	111	6.4
Downs, Kelly	SF	63.0	0.492	29	0.889	109	0.317	102	0.032	144	6.4
Lefferts, Craig	SD	78.7	0.763	117	0.864	117	0.280	125	0.127	21	6.3
Castillo, Tony	ATL	76.7	0.835	131	1.213	12	0.261	129	0.065	109	6.3
Schatzeder, Dan	NYM	69.7	0.560	53	0.947	84	0.330	97	0.029	147	6.3
Maddux, Greg	CHC	237.0	0.608	74	1.021	52	0.300	114	0.046	135	6.3
Burke, Tim	MON	75.0	0.627	77	0.947	85	0.280	124	0.080	86	6.2
Nabholz, Chris	MON	70.0	0.757	114	0.614	150	0.457	32	0.086	75	6.2
Landrum, Bill	PIT	71.7	0.544	48	0.963	78	0.293	116	0.056	122	6.1

THE QUALITY START

The Quality Start is not a new statistic, but it isn't a nineteenth century relic, either. In the 1987 Baseball Abstract, Bill James rated the quality start as being more meaningful than the pitcher's won/lost record; defining "meaningful" on the basis of importance, reliability, and intelligibility. The quality start attempts to measure how often a starting pitcher pitches well. The definition, simply, is a start in which the pitcher completes at least six innings, and gives up three runs or less.

One complaint against the quality start (Moss Klein, quoted in The Abstract) was the argument that with 6 IP and 3 ER, the marginal quality start, there is implication that the pitcher could have a 4.50 ERA. James dismissed this silly complaint with the assertion that no pitcher had an ERA higher than 3.20 in his quality starts. James was being conservative.

Dave Smith of Project Scoresheet sent me a summary of quality starts from 1986 through 1990 (a total of 10,519 games). The argument was over long ago, I think, but the numbers were eye-opening just the same. Consider the findings . . .

Quality Start summary for 1986-1990. Prepared by David Smith, December 1990:

1. Quality starts represent just about half of all starts. They are neither scarce nor common. The "quality" criteria separate all starts into two groups of equal incidence.

2. The combined ERA in all quality starts was 1.93.

3. Pitchers' won/lost percentage in quality starts was .694.

4. Quality starts lasted 7.53 innings, on average.

5. Non-quality starts produced a composite ERA of 7.64, lasted an average of 4.85 innings, and yielded a winning percentage of .309.

If those numbers aren't meaningful enough to keep you reading further, then you wasted the money that you spent on this book. Let's take a look at the Dave Smith "20 QS" list for the past two years:

Pitchers with 20 quality starts in 1990

Roger Clemens	27
Dave Stewart	27
Ed Whitson	27
Frank Viola	25
Doug Drabek	24
Chuck Finley	24
Zane Smith	24
Dave Stieb	24
Bob Welch	24
Mike Boddicker	23
Erik Hanson	23
Dennis Martinez	23
Ramon Martinez	23
Mark Portugal	23
Oil Can Boyd	22
Randy Johnson	22
Greg Maddux	22
Andy Benes	21
Mike Morgan	21
Tom Browning	20
Dwight Gooden	20
Bruce Hurst	20
Joe Magrane	20
Jose Rijo	20
Bobby Witt	20

Pitchers with 20 quality starts in 1989

Bret Saberhagen 30
Joe Magrane 28
Orel Hershiser 27
Bruce Hurst 26
Bert Blyleven 25
Bryn Smith 25
Roger Clemens 24
Ron Darling 24
Doug Drabek 24
Mark Langston 24
Dave Stewart 24
Ed Whitson 24
Mike Scott 23
Scott Bankhead 22
Bud Black 22
Chris Bosio 22
Tom Browning 22
Sid Fernandez 22
Mark Gubicza 22
Mike Moore 22
Pascual Perez 22
John Smiley 22
Rick Sutcliffe 22
Jeff Ballard 21
Jose DeLeon 21
Jim DeShaies 21
Chuck Finley 21
Scott Garrelts 21
Greg Maddux 21
Kirk McCaskill 21
Rick Reuschel 21
John Smoltz 21
Frank Tanana 21
Fernando Valenzuela 21
Frank Viola 21
Doyle Alexander 20
Tom Candiotti 20
David Cone 20
Dennis Martinez 20
Nolan Ryan 20

There is remarkable consistency from year to year, among those at the top, as you would expect from a list using consistency as a criterion. From the list of 1990 pitchers with 20 QS, the top six ALL appeared on the 20 QS list for 1989, as well.

Among the other 19 pitchers who made the list in 1990, only 6 were also there in 1989.

Finally, consider the "top ten" who made the list both years, and their totals for two years:

Roger Clemens 51
Dave Stewart 51
Ed Whitson 51
Doug Drabek 48
Joe Magrane 48
Frank Viola 46
Bruce Hurst 46
Chuck Finley 45
Dennis Martinez 43
Greg Maddux 43

If Whitson, Hurst, and Magrane catch your attention, you have an eye for Rotisserie scouting.

AGE 26:
MOST BANG FOR THE BUCK, 1991

by John Benson

Last year we told you all about the "Age 26" phenomenon. Hitters who have two or more years of major league experience at age 26 tend to emerge as stars, and they tend to be undervalued in drafts and auctions. The key points are as follows:

(1) After a couple of years of major league play, the general perception is that a player's full ability has been displayed. In the case of younger players, that perception is usually wrong. Almost all players keep improving until they reach a plateau at about age 27.

(2) Players who are good enough to get regular jobs in the major leagues at age 23 or 24 are above average. Most major leaguers are just beginning their careers around age 26. The young veterans of 1991 are the stars and superstars of 1992-1993.

These two factors combine to create the best buys in Rotisserie auctions, and the best late-round picks in fantasy drafts. This year, we are giving you a complete list of all the players who fit the "Age 26" description, a birth date between 7/1/64 and 7/1/66, and a career that includes 200 major league games with 500+ career at bats with 300 at bats in one season.

The rankings tell my expectation of who will be most undervalued in 1991 drafts and auctions. Obviously, if everyone in your league reads this list and believes it, they won't be undervalued for long.

Note that this ranking is NOT intended to list the "best players." It is my prediction of players who are likely to be undervalued for reasons of age and experience. Mike MacFarlane is not going to hit better than Jose Canseco, but MacFarlane could easily be worth double what you have to pay for him. No way Canseco will give you a 200% return.

Finally, note that there are many players age 23 or 24, or 28. or 29, who will soar in value in 1991. This essay is a test of one age/experience theory, not a comprehensive list of all players likely to be undervalued in 1991 auctions.

Within this age/experience group, this method of evaluation. considers:

1. The player's "safety" based on an established role.
2. Opportunity for increased playing time.
3. Probability of enhanced performance.
4. Probability of being underappreciated in 1991 drafts.

My notion of underappreciation is based on the belief that most people play far too much attention to "last year" stats I think. Will Clark will be underappreciated in the average leauge; in many leagues that just won't be true. The players at the bottom of this list match the age and experience criteria, but. are NOT good candidates to be bargains in 1991.

The Top Twenty:

1. Jay Bell
2. Manny Lee
3. Jerome Walton
4. Eric Yelding
5. BJ Surhoff
6. Gerald Young

7. Matt Nokes
8. Ruben Sierra
9. Jerry Browne
10. Jose Oquendo
11. Roberto Kelly
12. Rafael Palmeiro
13. Brady Anderson
14. Greg Briley
15. Steve Finley
16. Bill Spiers
17. Ellis Burks
18. Kurt Stillwell
19. Nelson Liriano
20. Jeff King

Also likely to be bargains:

Luis Polonia
Billy Ripken
Jeff Blauser
Mike Greenwell
Mike MacFarlane
Shane Mack
Dwight Smith
Charlie Hayes
Will Clark
Benito Santiago
Walt Weiss
Jose Lind
Craig Biggio
Pete Incaviglia
Stan Javier
Lance Johnson
Dave Martinez
Fred McGriff
Bip Roberts
Barry Larkin
Lenny Harris
Ozzie Guillen
Felix Fermin
Mark McGwire
Mark Grace

Unclear future:

Damon Berryhill
Craig Worthington
Andres Thomas
Carlos Martinez
Mark McLemore
Ken Williams
Dale Sveum
Ricky Jordan
Jeff Hamilton
Luis Rivera
Kevin Elster

Already at their peak:

Kal Daniels
Barry Bonds
Jose Canseco
Cecil Fielder
Ron Gant

BALLPARK EFFECTS

By Fred Percival

When a player changes teams, he also changes ballparks. This can have an important impact on performance, depending on how the man's skills match the shape of his new home. Home runs are the offensive Rotisserie statistic most affected by park variations. It's something to keep in mind when trying to project the next season's output for hitters. For pitchers, ERA is the category that concerns you most when they change teams.

We have two tables of park effects, one for HR and one for Runs. The data are totals for both teams in all games played at home and away during the last three years. The index represents the impact of the stadium of the offensive output. For example, the Braves and their opponents (combined) scored 2200 runs in Atlanta and 1936 runs in the other stadiums where they played. Since the same teams and the same players produced both totals, the difference can be attributed to the stadium in which they played. The index is computed as 2200 divided by 1936, or 113.6.

To estimate the impact of a player changing teams, you divide his normal expected output by the factor of his old ballpark, and then multiply by the factor for his new ballpark. If, for example, you expected George Bell to hit 15 HR in his home games at Toronto, you would estimate his output in Wrigley Field would be 15, divided by 89.8, multiplied 144.5, or 24 homers. (Bell's homer output on the road is not included in this calculation.)

Just to recognize the limits of this quick method, consider that (1) there is no adjustment for the difference between AL and NL "away" parks, (2) there is no adjustment for the change in opposition pitchers between leagues, and (3) there is no adjustment for Bell's individual propensities such as left/right or line drive vs. flyball power. For a player changing teams within the same league, the first two of these three considerations would not be any cause for concern.

The numbers:

EFFECT ON HR:		EFFECT ON RUNS:	
1. CHN	144.5	1. ATL	113.6
2. SEA	135.3	2. SEA	110.9
3. SD	126.2	3. CHN	110.4
4. ATL	117.7	4. MON	108.7
5. CIN	116.2	5. CIN	108.5
6. CAL	115.0	6. BOS	107.9
7. DET	114.4	7. CLE	107.4
8. TEX	107.2	8. PHI	107.0
9. MIN	106.7	9. TEX	106.8
10. BAL	105.0	10. MIN	105.0
11. PHI	100.2	11. STL	101.4
12. SF	100.0	12. MIL	100.6
13. NYA	99.2	13. KC	99.5
14. PIT	98.1	14. NYA	98.6
15. BOS	95.5	15. PIT	97.5
16. MIL	94.6	16. BAL	96.4
17. CLE	94.5	17. SD	96.2
18. NYN	93.7	18. CAL	93.9
19. MON	90.7	19. DET	92.0
20. TOR	89.8	20. HOU	91.7
21. OAK	82.6	21. LA	90.4
22. LA	81.0	22. SF	89.3
23. STL	75.6	23. OAK	88.8
24. KC	70.4	24. NYN	87.4
25. HOU	63.4	25. TOR	85.8
X. CHA	NA	X. CHA	NA

PLAYER VALUATION 101
BASIC SCARCITY

(Same essay as last year;
the method doesn't change)

Last summer, I got three or four letters with the same message: "It's all very nice," they said, "that you wrote a book for advanced Rotisserie players, but some of the books aimed at beginners are hard to understand. For example, writers keep referring to SCARCITY as a method of player valuation. I grasp the concept just fine — so much value per SB and per HR, etc., but I have no idea how to do the calculations and get player $ values. It's easy to say, just do it, but hard if you haven't done it before. Can you show me?"

Yes, good question.

First, let's think about the purpose and the big picture. What is the question that we are trying to answer? In this case, I am going to answer the following question: Based solely on 1989 stats, what was the value of each AL hitter?

Note that we were NOT doing forecasts of 1990 values. HOWEVER, that was our ultimate goal. In some places, we will tinker with a pure, retrospective valuation of 1989 performance, because we want to move toward 1990 values, not away from them. You will see what I mean, shortly.

The hitters question is part of the larger question: what is the value for all players? Assuming a 12 team league with $260 per team and 14 hitters and 9 pitchers, there is $3,120 in total to be accounted for, and we want to spend 65% of that money on hitters, i.e., $2,028. (See the 1990 book.)

Anyway, the first thing you need is stats on a computer. For 1989, I found the following AL totals:

HR 1718
RBI 9103
SB 1587

We'll get to batting average in a minute; it's not any harder, just different.

With four hitting categories, we want to assign one fourth of our hitting money to each category. That would be $507 per category. We could take homers, then, and say $507 for 1718 HR means they are worth 29.5 cents per homer. We are not going to do that exactly, however. Some of the players who contributed to the 1718 HR total will not end up on Rotisserie rosters. But:

Remember what I said about moving TOWARD 1990 forecasts. If we reject all the numbers from September call-ups, we are throwing away valuable clues about 1990 scarcity. If 75 prospects came up in September and each hit one HR in 4 at bats, that is a good indication that the league is going to have more HR's in 1990. True, none of those 75 people would ever make it to a Rotisserie roster for 1989, but their performance is important for 1990 values.

Focusing just on players actually purchased in April 1989 is an idea with good intellectual appeal (considering our stated question), but, again, we must keep in mind the ultimate purpose of moving toward 1990 values. Discarding all the players who emerged during 1989 would be counter-productive. So, we take the whole population to see what is scarce and what isn't.

Since many of our hitters are going to end up with no value, or negative value, we need a dollar amount larger than $507 to allocate to each category. If we spread the $507 over all 300 hitters, and then took only 168 into the Rotisserie population, there would be less than $507 value in the Rotisserie HR totals, and less than $2028 in the hitters' population in total. We don't want that.

Rather than spend an hour finding the correct number above $507, I am going to take $1000 (obviously, more than enough) for each category, and calibrate the values again later. $1000 is a nice number, because it's easy to remember, it lends itself to simple arithmetic, and it keeps you focused on the quantity of HR (and SB's, etc.) in existence.

For example, to make the 1718 homers worth $1000 of "play money" we simply divide each player's HR total by 1.718 and add up the sum of all players' HR values. Voila: $1000. Looking at that 1.718 while you're doing calculations again and again all winter, will help you get used to the idea that there were about 1700 homers in the AL last year. If your scarcity divisor is 1.500 or 1.850 next year, you will note the increase or decrease in scarcity by second nature. I do, anyway — but I spend a lot of time at this stuff.

Anyway, the "formulas" for 1989 were simply: HR / 1.718, RBI / 9.103, and SB / 1.587.

If your league uses other categories, e.g. runs, just go ahead and add them in using the $1000 method (another advantage of saving the calibration for later, is that we can throw in all the categories we want now, and adjust values later). [Runs would be R / 9.732 but we are NOT counting them in this exercise.]

That gives every hitter a "play money" value for HR, RBI and SB's. The total value in each category now stands at $1000. If you want to check your work, sort the hitters in alpha order. Aguayo, at the top, should have $1 (rounded) for HR, $1 for RBI, $0 for SB's. Allanson should round off to $2 for HR, $2 for RBI, and $3 for SB's.

Now, batting average . . .

I really do not understand the great mystery about batting average, and all the trouble it causes. True, I did go wrong myself, once, but it took only one year to see the answer (May of the first year, actually). Batting average does have scarcity, it is cumulative, it can be added and subtracted for Rotisserie value purposes. The unit is obviously HITS. The only question is, which hits count, and how much are they worth?

You should have a gut feel for Hits value just from experience. Think about box scores. If you are in a tight race for Batting Average, would you rather see your guy go 3 for 4, or 1 for 1 ? Hope you said 3 for 4. But that's only .750, and the 1 for 1 is a 1.000 BA. You know, however, that there's MORE batting average in a 3/4 performance than in a 1/1.

This theoretical discussion could go on forever, but I just want to give you the answer now, and we can argue theory later. My method (one of my methods, that is . . . the simplest, so I will put it in here) is to focus on the LOWEST team batting average in your league. In all the leagues where I get stats, the lowest team average was pretty consistent: .249 in 1989.

For purposes of valuation, I suggest that any hitter who hits over .249 has some value in batting average (market value, not theoretical value). A guy who hits .290 will have twice as much value as guy who hits .270. We could do valuations using league "average average," (.263 to .264) but the answers we got would be out of this world. The market seems to look at a .250 as about zero value in BA, not a negative, and to value a .310 hitter about twice as much as a .280 hitter, etc.

Looking at the AL for 1989, I see 148 hitters who hit .249 or higher. Conveniently, one hit .249, Finley. I sorted them on my worksheet, and added up all the at bats and all the hits for THOSE 148 hitters who hit over .249. There were 51,352 at bats and 14,304 hits. Now, if all those hitters had hit exactly .249, their hit totals would have added up to 12,786, not 14,304. The difference is 1,517 hits — and I propose that those 1,517 hits ("HITS IN EXCESS OF .249 PERFORMANCE") are the items about whose scarcity we should be concerned. When you see a box score of 3 for 4, you should see "2 hits in excess of .249." Oh for four is a minus one, etc. Using the .249 number fits well with the fact that 4 AB's is the most common total in a game: poetic.

Anyway, I write the formula: (Hits minus (at bats times .249)) / 1.517 and give each hitter a $ value for Batting average. Some will be negative. The people who hit over .249 have a total value of $1000 of Play Money.

Put in a total for each player. Total value equals HR values, plus RBI value plus SB value plus BAvg value. If we add up all the Play Money in all the categories, we get $3,580. It would be $4,000, but the "negative" batting averages removed $420. Anyway, the total value for Puckett is not $59, Lansford is $62, etc. — obviously too high, so . . .

First Adjustment: get the total back to $2,028. Make another column as Total Value of Play Money, times 2028, divided by 3580. Now we're getting close to true $ values, but we're not done yet!

Sort the players by position. (For convenience, I assign one primary position to each player.) Take a look at catchers. If your league has 12 teams with 2 catchers each, you need 24 catchers. The 24th catcher on my list is now Ron Hassey, and his value is $1. That's just as it should be. The 25th thru 27th catchers are also worth $1, which is just fine. You have your choice of four $1 catchers if it comes down to that at the end of the auction.

Now look at the other positions:

3B: 21 players worth $1 or more. The 18th 3B is worth $1, so are 19 thru 21. 2B: 20 players worth $1 or more. The 18th is worth $1, as are 19 and 20. 1B: 22 players worth $1 or more. The 18th is worth $1, as are 19 thru 22. SS: 22 players worth $1 or more. The 18th is worth $3, 21 and 22 are worth $1. OF: 90 players worth $1 or more. The 60th is worth $5, 84 to 90 are worth $1. DH: 2 players worth $1 or more, none worth exactly $1.

Now, we need certain rules to apply to the above numbers. I cannot quite write a computer program to cover all those rules and make the necessary adjustments, but I can tell what I considered, and what I did, for 1989.

1. The 24th catcher shall be worth $1. We're OK there.

2. There must be 36 corner men worth $1 or more, and 12 each of 1B and 3B. We came out fine on those rules. The 18th 3B and 18th 1B being worth $1 each is nice, but not necessary. It could be the 16th of one, and the 20th of another, and is actually like that is most years. In 1989 the symmetry is beautiful. No adjustments necessary.

3. Middle infielders, same test as corner men, and again, we came out fairly good in total. But, looking at the SS by themselves, $3 for the 18th guy is too much money. Subtract $2 from the value of every SS. Now the 18th is worth $1, as he should be, nice and symmetrical with 2B's. Symmetry is NOT necessary, but it's convenient.

4. Outfielders: the 60th guy must be worth at least $1, and the number of players necessary to cover all the OF positions and remaining DH slots must also have values of $1 or more. But beyond those requirements, we do not want any more players valued above zero, except for those who "tie" at the $1 level when we make our minimum number. In 1989, we have far too many outfielders, valued too highly. The 66th is now worth $5. We are able to count several DH candidates without using any of the OF pool: 2 pure DH's, up to 3 from the 3B slot (those in excess of 18 worth $1 or more), 2 from the 2B slot, 4 from 1B, none from SS after we took away $2 from every SS. It is not necessary to have exactly 12 DH's worth $1 or more. It's good to have a larger number, say five extras or so. Since we can see 11 DH's at positions other than OF, we don't need to enlarge the pool of OF worth $1 or more, much beyond the 60 required in OF slots. If we had only 2 or 3 total DH's coming from all other positions, we would want to make about 10 more extra outfielders (about 70 in total) worth $1 or more. In 1989, we do not need

anywhere near 90 OF's. The solution is to subtract $4 from every OF. Now, the 66th OF is worth $1, just about right. Just make a mental note, that when you're bidding on an OF valued using this table, he could be worth $4 more if you can put him at another position. You could even go back and reposition all eligible OF's, but that would make this paragraph even longer!

So: now check the total value of all your hitters. It's only $1724 because of the subtractions we made. Other years, there might be a surplus at this point, if we had to add money to make the 24th catcher or the 36th middle infielder worth at least $1. In some years, the pluses and the minuses at different positions might offset each other. For 1989 values, we need to divide all values by 1724, and multiply by 2028, to make the total fit. When we get done, we now have 180 hitters worth $1 or more, and $2028 total. Purists may note that we want $2028 assigned to 168 hitters, and remove $12 or twelve $1 players, but the amount of money involved is only six tenths of one per cent now, so I would recommend, leave it alone at this point.

We're done!

In this book we calculate values using 1991 forecast stats. The same method can be used to value any group of players for any time period; the valuation method is exactly as described above.

THE CONCEPT OF VALUE IN POSITION: WHAT IT IS HOW TO USE IT

Sophisticated player valuation systems all share one method in common: they break down player value into its smallest components (one HR, one SB, etc.) and then rebuild player value using these components for each individual player, summing up all the values that have been assigned. One player's performance of .265 with 16 HR, 54 RBI, and 3 SB is worth exactly the same as any other player's performance of .265 / 16 / 54 / 3. Right? Wrong!

This method of building up player value, and then stopping the valuation process, would work fine if we could pick ANY 14 hitters for our roster. Hitters would be fungible: take out one hitter, replace him with another who has exactly the same stats, and everything would remain the same. Unfortunately for those who like things simple, the rules of Rotisserie baseball include roster requirements, and do not allow such unrestricted substitutions. You cannot delete a catcher, and put in an outfielder; if you did, things would be out of balance, and the game would not work (or as Casey Stengel would have put it, you would have a lot of passed balls). Rotisserie says you must have two catchers, always, no exceptions, period.

How many times have you come to the end of your auction or draft, having just $1 left and needing just one catcher to fill out your roster? You look over who is available: Joel Skinner, Mike Stanley, Mark Salas, etc. — the Usual Suspects. So you bid $1 for somebody who is going to contribute 4 HR, 23 RBI, no steals, and a batting average so low that it will hurt your team. One of your competitors might even shock you by raising your bid to $2, because he likes the sound of this player's name, or once met him at spring training, or some other hair-brain reason. It happens. You may end up getting only 2 HR and 19 RBI with no steals and the same Mendoza-like batting average for your $1.

At such times, you may have been surprised, or even dismayed, to look over the pool of unselected players and see that, with every team's Outfield and 3B and 1B and 1st/3rd and DH positions all filled, there is an available backup 1B/DH from Texas or Chicago or California, who could be counted upon to hit 10 HR with 40 RBI and a (harmless) .260 average, just sitting there, unwanted, unvalued. "Why can't he be a catcher?" you wonder. You check your position eligibility listing one more time. No dice. He's a first baseman, and so are two other available players who are clearly worth more than this "last catcher" that you are going to end up buying. How can this happen? You look at the drafted players and check the last several names selected at first base and Outfield and DH, grabbed up at $1 apiece. Were they mistakes? Did everybody overlook this 10 HR wonder? No, indeed. The last half dozen 1B/DH's taken are all of similar value — maybe 10 SB instead of 10 HR, but similar value to be sure.

The question is: how can the 5 HR catcher be worth as much as, or more than, a 10 HR first baseman? The answer is the simple law of supply and demand. The rules of Rotisserie require 24 catchers and "only" 12 first baseman (or say 18 or 20 or even 23 first basemen to allow for the 1st/3rd position and the DH's). The 24th catcher is invariably worse than the 23rd first baseman. Hence, the value of a catcher's home run is more than the value of a first basemen's home run (or an outfielder's home run, for that matter).

The positions producing "surplus" talent will vary from year to year. One season there may be more than enough good outfielders; the next year there may be just enough outfielders but a surplus of valuable third basemen. But there has never been (within our collective memories) a surplus of catchers who produce good hitting stats.

The design of Rotisserie baseball is just right. One must be impressed by the amazing balance and symmetry of Rotisserie rules, the way in which the last few available outfielders and corner men are worth about the same. Often the middle infielders come into balance nicely after the DH's and utility men have all been selected. Only the catchers come up two or three men short every year.

Many of you know these ideas already. Some of you have quantitative methods and models to measure and adjust for this imbalance. Bill Cunningham has a separate valuation approach for each individual fielder's position on the roster: a .240 batting average is perfectly acceptable for a catcher, equivalent to a .270 average for an outfielder or first baseman. My method is not that complex, but I believe it is just as effective, if not more effective, than the building of valuation models for each individual position. (Note, for example, that a .240 average from ANY player is going to lower your team batting average, no matter if it comes from a catcher or a DH).

The basic concept to grasp is that the LAST PLAYER taken at every position is worth exactly $1. The last player taken in every rotisserie auction is obviously worth only $1, because there is only one bidder. The same rule holds within the bidding for each fielder position, because an owner who has filled out his roster at a given position cannot bid for players of that position any longer. There are, therefore, several separate auctions going on simultaneously, with the last winning bid in each of these subauctions always being (by definition) one dollar. We are assuming, that the bidders know what they are doing, although it is always possible that some fool may bid a preemptive $5 for the 108th (and final) pitcher.

THE CONCEPT IN ACTION

The implication is that $ values for each position need to be adjusted, up or down, to "force" the last person taken at each position to be worth $1. The adjustment factors will change slightly from year to year. Normally, first basemen and outfielders need a downward adjustment of $2 to $5.

CONCLUSION

The concept of Value In Position is a necessary part of every player valuation model. Differences in values may be small in some years, but every year in every auction, AL or NL or mixed, there is comparative surplus of talent at one or more positions other than catcher. Sometimes the appropriate adjustments may be as large as $5 in some years for some positions. If you fail to adjust values to reflect these little surpluses, you will end up paying more than you have to for some player(s).

The concept of Value in Position is not revolutionary; for many people it is not even new. But the players who use the concept consistently do better than those who do not, and the object of the game is to win.

OPTIMAL BIDS, REVISITED, 1991

The 1990 Analyst had a long and exhaustive discussion of auction economics, and mathematical proofs of "optimal" bidding methods, using 200 auctions nationwide as a statistical database showing actual prices paid for actual players and types of players. I will not repeat that complete presentation in this year's book. Editor Randy Baron thought it was too long, anyway, and it gives the mathematical segment of our audience a good reason to save the 1990 book for reference (or to buy the 1990 book if they don't have it already).

This year, we are just going to recap the concepts and comment on some of the most frequently-heard public reactions.

The first concept is that auction economics are not a new subject. There is no "Benson breakthrough" in any academic sense. It amazes me, however, that people could play an auction-based game for years, and no one previously has circulated and explained the long-trusted concepts used in big business to calculate the best competitive bids. True, in the real world, most bidding calculations are made by contractors in a sealed-bid environment, and in these circumstances the lowest bid wins, but the arithmetic is the same for all auctions. To apply the math to Rotisserie bids, you just have to change a few pluses into minuses, and it's all quite simple. Maybe it helped me to study at Columbia Business School, under David W. Miller, the guy who wrote our textbook (**Executive Decisions and Operations Research**). If you want more math and less Rotisserie, you can get your auction economics by buying his old book instead of my old book (but his costs more).

So there is no breakthrough on the frontiers of math, but there are many people whose eyes have been opened. And they are all delighted with what they see.

The second key concept is that lots of money gets wasted in every auction. Just glancing at last year's actual prices paid in Heath Research and Roti-Stats leagues, I see Brady Anderson at $17, Steve Balboni $17, Phil Bradley $38, Mickey Brantley $24, Ellis Burks $39, etc. That's just a few AL hitters whose names begin with letter "A" or "B". The foolish spending occurs on almost every player. [Burks, by the way, might actually earn $39 this year, but you shouldn't pay that much for him.]

All that wasted money means there are fewer dollars left to chase the remaining talent, so prices must come down. Other people got Anderson at $1, Balboni at $1, Bradley at $9, Brantley at $1, and Burks at $7, because the wasted money in their auctions was thrown away on different players. These price quotes are the extremes, but even if you look at the middle-of-the-pack price ranges, there is much variation. I did extensive bell curve distributions on many players and types of players. On average, the MEDIAN price paid is equal to true value . . . but that means, half the time people are paying too much, and half the time they are paying too little. The quantity of money that gets wasted is very large, and can be measured accurately.

Easier than counting "wasted" dollars and recalculating values, I can tell you the probability (using nationwide averages) that you can succeed buying a player at 90% of value, 80% of value, 50% of value, etc. For example, a star hitter can be bought for only 70% of value, about one fifth of the time. That may not sound like much, but it means (roughly) that if you bid 70% of value on five star hitters, you will get one of them. It happens, as history proves. You also know your "profit" when you buy a player. If you get a $20 (calculated) value for $14, that's a $6 profit.

Optimal Bid calculations simply take each incremental price ($1, $2, $3, etc.) and for each price, list the possible profit ($), and the probability of getting that player at that price. Example: When you bid $14 for a $20 star hitter, with 20% probability of getting him, that means you have an Expected Value of $1.20 (0.20 probability X $6.00 potential profit). If you bid higher, you increase the probability, but you decrease the profit. If you bid lower, you decrease the probability but increase the possible profit. Optimal Bid is simply the point at which your multiplication (probability times profit) yields the highest answer.

The "best" bids are in the 70% to 85% of value for the best players. Established star hitters and ace relievers are the best players, because their value is most predictable. Bidding history proves that bidders like these types of players. There is less variation in the range of bids.

Players like rookies, injury rehab projects, aging veterans, and other players who are more difficult to value, will lead to more widespread differences of opinion about value. The more widespread these differences, the more variation you get in bids, and the easier it is to get bargains. For rookies and comeback types, the best policy is to bid only 35% to 40% of what YOU think they are worth. You can buy your share in this price range, no problem. You will only be getting about one fourth of the players you bid on, but with a long list and many opportunities, one fourth will be plenty. Rookie starting pitchers are the most price-volatile group. You can bid 25% to 35% and buy plenty of them. You will never get Ben McDonald or Gregg Olson, but you will NEVER get stuck with Steve Searcy, Al Leiter, or any of the dozens who don't pan out every year, either; not for more than $1, anyway.

Two reactive comments came to my attention repeatedly during 1990, when my readers first applied Optimal Bids in real auctions. [Everybody loved the idea, but . . .] the two main objections were (1) "All players in my auction sold for higher than your optimal bids," and (2) "You can't get any good power hitters using optimal bids."

The first question is easy. It's really impossible that "all" players could sell for higher than optimal bid. There is always a difference of opinion about what a player is worth (if there wasn't, there wouldn't be any Rotisserie). And there is always a bell curve distribution for every player. Your league might have a unique, high opinion of Steve Balboni's value. It might be impossible to get Balboni in your league for less than $15. But "all" players? The tipoff came from one reader who told me, "All players in our league sold for higher than 100% of your fair values. Forget optimal bids; I had to pay over 100% of value for every player. No way 85% would work!" Hmmm.

Since your league has only $2600 (NL) to spend, and my values add up to $2600, it isn't possible for "all" players to sell above fair value. How could you spend more than $2600 as a group? The answer is that the complaining bidders forgot about draft inflation that results from freeze lists. We had a short discussion of this subject last year (see page 62, "Supply and Demand"). This year, we have a big essay on the subject, from Mike Dalecki, to make sure everyone understands. I won't steal Mike's thunder by recapping his work here; he did a marvelous job explaining the problem and how to deal with it. Just the arithmetic: if you should increase all your dollar values by 20% for your auction, optimal bids are not 85% of fair value; they are 85% of 120%, or 102% of fair value. Let Mike explain the rest. He's a PhD in statistics. Trust him.

The other complaint we get is more valid, but has nothing to do with optimal bids. You can, if you like, accuse me of undervaluing home runs. My method of "fair value" calculation is very simple. For precision, it's too simple. Alex Patton is far ahead of me on standings gain points and other valuation factors. I just want a rational, comprehensive method to get the $2600 (NL) applied to a suitable population of players.

Personally, I make mental adjustments during an auction. When you see that the whole league is overvaluing home runs (compared to what I think they "should" be worth), you MAY choose to go up to, or over, 100% of fair value on a player or two. More likely, I will avoid home runs in that auction, and trade for them later. People love home runs. They get emotional about Mickey Mantle; they don't get emotional about Maury Wills and Lou Brock. It's all rooted in their childhood, and it's their problem, anyway, not mine.

If you have trouble getting any particular type of player (e.g. sluggers) my advice is to buy other players, e,g. Coleman types and ace relievers, at the bargain prices that must emerge after all that money gets "wasted" on power. You can even help the process by bringing up names of sluggers and watching the money fly, but I think it's wiser to bring up a starting pitcher every time for the first 15 rounds or so. Anyway, get these other types of players at bargain prices, and trade for what you need. By July, it will be easy to show someone that if they had Vince Coleman instead of Glenn Davis, they would be higher in the standings. Don't try to convince them before the auction.

[Harry Conover owns the copyright to above comments, which were made by John Benson at a Compuserve Sports Forum live conference on March 12, 1990.]

OPTIMAL BIDS AT WORK

By Mike Dalecki

[Editor's note: you may not care much about optimal bids, but this essay contains an actual 1991 auction that gives you a sneak preview of perceived values in November 1990 (before the winter meetings). It's just one point of reference, but surely worth a perusal before you go to your own 1991 auction.]

I had the chance to test optimal bids in a new NL Rotisserie League, with no freeze lists. All players were available, and there was no draft inflation to complicate the picture. I recorded information on players bought and prices paid. I still don't believe how well optimal bids worked.

SOME BACKGROUND

This was a new league and we all liked the idea of starting early. So on November 10th, 1990, we held a draft to fill out the league, using the normal rules for filling out teams, including position eligibilities, etc. Players who had crossed over to the AL, and hadn't yet returned, were not eligible for drafting. Anyone else who played in the NL during 1990 was eligible. Unsigned NL free agents like Vince Coleman were eligible; players like Willie McGee were not.

I decided I'd conform to optimal bids as much as possible during the draft, to have a little test of the theory of optimal bidding. I used an early version of John's 1991 prices (those that he did for The Sporting News Owners Manual) as my reference point in deciding what to pay for players. If you don't agree with some of the prices, remember than John did them in mid-September; he probably doesn't agree with some of them anymore, either. But as you'll see, (and as Benson keeps saying) pricing/valuation precision is much less important than astute bidding.

As John has indicated, optimal bidding involves bidding up to, but not over, the optimal price (the one with highest reward probability) for players in an auction. Generally, you should bid up to 70 to 85 percent of fair value for established players, and no more than 35 percent of your calculated fair value for hotshot rookies and other hard-to-value situations like older players and injury rehab cases. "Fair value" means an allocation of all money ($3120 AL or $2600 NL) to all available players, considering how many players are needed at each position. See his essays on player valuation and optimal bidding for more details.

I didn't have time to compute exact percentage optimal bids for all types of players, so I used 85 percent as the nominal optimal bid ceiling for all players. With rookies or people with a story, I just tried to restrain myself.

What follows this essay is a list of the players bought in order of nomination.

SWEET SUCCESS

At an intellectual level, I knew that optimal bids should work. But Geez! I didn't think they'd work THIS well!

Besides my two catchers, I paid over JB's value for only ONE player, Ron Gant, (and like I said, John's $ values were still being re-worked during the winter, so I wasn't worried about going up on one player who is going up in the world of real baseball.) For 3 other players I went over optimal bid, but not over JB's price. For the rest, I NEVER PAID MORE than 85 percent of JB's allocated "fair value."

I added it all up; even with the $8 I lost on Gant, I came out with $97 in profits. I had $13 left at the end of the draft, so I bought a team presumably worth $344. And THAT puts me in the running for the title.

The guy who organized this league took the drafted players and figured out who would have won using last year's stats. I would have won, with 60 points; the second place team had only 46! I know last year's stats can be misleading, but the gap between my team, Da Lucky Streaks, and the second place team is most encouraging and instructive. Six of my fellow owners are veterans of our AL Rotisserie league, so they aren't babes in the woods. It's clear that I won the draft going away. They can all see that, and I did it with optimal bidding. At this point, I own most of the decent undervalued players in the league, so I am well positioned for winter trading.

THE DYNAMICS OF BIDDING

What optimal bids do, as much as keep you from overpaying, is force you to husband your money for the later rounds. That's where it starts to work! I went through FOUR full rounds before I bought a player. I had to endure the taunts of my fellow owners as I sat there with my $260 untouched. Player after player went down. Strawberry. Bonds. Myers. Dibble. Franco. Gwynn. It was hard! It was excruciating! The beer didn't even taste good! Would there be anyone left WORTH anything?

In retrospect, I needn't have worried. Look at the left-most column in the list of players bought. That's the cumulative LOSSES as players are bought over their fair (JB) value, or the amount of money being wasted. It peaks from the 10th to 11th rounds. Notice also the asterisks denoting players worth at least $10 who were bought for an optimal bid. Those asterisks don't start showing up in earnest UNTIL after the peak "cumulative loss point" was reached.

Dave Smith, $15? Glad to have you on my team. The Bipper for $16? Pleased to meet you. Hal Morris for $9? Love those Reds. Zane Smith for $4? How DO you do? And what about the guys I bought before the peak in losses? You can see on the list of players all those I picked up, and when. That team is listed below.

And what about John's prices? I think this exercise goes a long way toward validating the prices John produces. I used those prices almost religiously, except in a few cases where I knew some good or bad news about the player. In the case of bad things, I just wouldn't bid on the player. And you can see that the good things didn't matter. I bought Gant simply because I needed SOMEONE with bang for the buck. And he's 26 years old. Alomar I got "stuck" with because there were still 5 people bidding when I said "21." (I wish I had known about "The Trade" but nobody else knew, either. Since there was not even a hint of a rumor about the Alomar deal, it couldn't possibly have been reflected in our auction prices.)

I imagine most veteran NL rotisserie players would be pleased with the prices I paid. Optimal bidding works. And so do John's prices.

NOTES

Optimal bids are great, but they don't work unless you are organized. It was easier to remain calm than it would have otherwise been. I KNEW that guys like Dave Smith, Sid Fernandez, Bip Roberts, Bruce Hurst, Norm Charlton, Zane Smith, etc., etc., were STILL available, even in round 13. As you can see, I ended up with a lot of star pitchers. That where many of the big bargains were in this auction.

Optimal bids must be adjusted upward in drafts where people are freezing players. See the essay on the subject of Draft Price Inflation.

John has noted that people tend to overpay for power hitters, compared to "fair value." The old TV graphics and baseball card backs that show just "Average, HR, RBI" tend to make people forget speed and undervalue SB's. The list of prices paid for players would seem to bear that out. Benson values are likely to steer you toward a roster that is long on speed and pitching, and short on power. (I hear he often calls his own teams "Benson Burners" because they're so fast.) Anyway, that's where trades come in. After your auction, you can begin to educate other owners about the fact that stolen bases are almost as scarce as home runs (scarcer in the AL). Show them last year's actual stats to prove it. The guys who have "too many" homers will eventually see the light. If you show people a trade that will make them go UP in the standings, they will give up their romantic fascination with power.

In the following tables, the "n" next to the player number shows those I nominated in the draft. The first 7 players nominated were those whom I felt reasonably certain would create losses. I ended up with Lee Smith and Roberto Alomar, but they were at or under fair value. As the draft progressed, I continued to throw out players I felt would drain money, but NOT those whom I was interested in. I didn't want to throw out anyone I wanted until it was late enough that I had no serious bidding opposition.

Toward the end, all players I nominated were those I was interested in. By the 190th player, I had more than a third of all the money left of the active bidders (3 owners were done). I didn't want to nominate a player I didn't really want, only to find no one else had the money or desire to top me. So my last 7 nominations were players I wanted. Of course, I had the money to make sure I got them.

There were plenty of undervalued opportunities late in the auction, but I can only take 23 home. I was being choosy.

THE DATA

The headings of the columns:

N#   The order of the nominated players. Barry Bonds was first. It only goes up to 211 because by that time it was clear how optimal bids had worked, I'd filled out my team, it was 1:30am and I was tired, anyone left was going for a buck, and 211 is enough!

JB$ John's preliminary "morning line" full dollar value for a player.

A$ The actual price paid in the draft.

$D   The dollar difference between JB's prices and actual prices.

CUMD The running (CUMulative) total of the Differences between JB's prices and actual prices.

n   An "n" next to the nomination number indicates that it was a player I nominated (we drew lots and I got to go first).

-    A "-" to the left of the player's name indicates one I bought.

*   A "*" to the right of the $D indicates that the player's worth according to JB was at least $10, AND the price paid was at or under the optimal bid. There are always lots of optimal bids on CHEAP players; I wanted to see if it worked for the more expensive ones, too. Optimal bids were judged as being 85 percent of John's predicted 1991 value, or less.

CUMD	N	Name	Tm	JB$	A$	$D
-6	1n	Bonds	PIT	39	45	-6
-5	2	Gwynn	SD	31	30	1
-11	3	Grace	CHI	21	27	-6
-12	4	Dykstra	PHI	26	27	-1
-20	5	Sabo	CIN	22	30	-8
-20	6	Gibson	LA	9	9	0
-24	7	Myers	CIN	30	34	-4

CUM	DN	Name	Tm	JB$	A$	$D
-35	8	Justice	ATL	20	31	-11
-49	9	Gooden	NY	16	30	-14
-50	10	Scioscia	LA	11	12	-1
-53	11n	Franco	NY	31	34	-3
-61	12	Magadan	NY	12	20	-8
-60	13	Treadway	ATL	11	10	1
-71	14	Zeile	STL	11	22	-11
-66	15	Thon	PHI	12	7	5*
-65	16	Sasser	NY	10	9	1
-72	17	Berryhill	CHI	2	9	-7
-87	18	Martinez.R	LA	22	37	-15
-93	19	Drabek	PIT	24	30	-6
-93	20	Santiago	SD	15	15	0
-94	21n	Strawberry	LA	35	36	-1
-97	22	Larkin	CIN	24	27	-3
-102	23	Dibble	CIN	21	26	-5
-103	24	Murphy	PHI	19	20	-1
-110	25	Sutcliffe	CHI	2	9	-7
-111	26	Crews	LA	7	8	-1
-120	27	Viola	NY	23	32	-9
-125	28	Van Slyke	PIT	22	27	-5
-139	29	Rijo	CIN	13	27	-14
-144	30	Coleman	STL	35	40	-5
-150	31n	Raines	MTL	28	34	-6
-158	32	Smoltz	ATL	9	17	-8
-170	33	Stubbs	HOU	11	23	-12
-166	34	Ramirez	HOU	9	5	4
-171	35	Walk	PIT	0	5	-5
-178	36	Valenzuela	LA	1	8	-7
-188	37	Clark	SF	25	35	-10
-196	38	Mitchell	SF	31	39	-8
-196	39	Sandberg	CHI	37	37	0
-197	40	McReynolds	NY	24	25	-1
-194	41n	-Smith.L	STL	31	28	3
-195	42	Butler	SF	26	27	-1
-199	43	O'Neill	CIN	18	22	-4
-202	44	Carter.J	SD	28	31	-3
-203	45	Herr	NY	11	12	-1
-201	46	Braggs	CIN	11	9	2*
-212	47	Williams.M	SF	25	36	-11
-217	48	Davis.E	CIN	30	35	-5
-229	49	Armstrong	CIN	3	15	-12
-233	50	Burke	MTL	22	26	-4
-239	51n	Murray	LA	27	33	-6
-246	52	Hayes.C	PHI	7	14	-7
-246	53	Dunston	CHI	22	22	0
-251	54	Johnson.H	NY	27	32	-5
-256	55	McDowell	PHI	18	23	-5
-260	56	Salazar	CHI	5	9	-4
-260	57	Assenmacher	CHI	11	11	0
-268	58	-Gant	ATL	26	34	-8
-273	59	Daniels	LA	19	24	-5
-275	60	Walton	CHI	8	10	-2
-275	61n	-Alomar	SD	21	21	0
-281	62	Dawson	CHI	27	33	-6
-279	63	Hatcher	CIN	18	16	2
-283	64	Clark.Ja	SD	16	20	-4
-287	65	Schmidt	MTL	3	7	-4
-290	66	Boston	NY	9	12	-3
-291	67	Lefferts	SD	25	26	-1
-297	68	Deshields	MTL	24	30	-6
-307	69	Williams.M	CHI	10	20	-10
-305	70	Lavalliere	PIT	5	3	2
-306	71n	Hayes.V	PHI	22	23	-1
-307	72	Uribe	SF	4	5	-1
-314	73	Maddux	CHI	9	16	-7
-326	74	Bonilla	PIT	27	39	-12
-324	75	Thompson	SF	14	12	2
-322	76	Daulton	PHI	9	7	2
-317	77	-Martinez.D	MTL	22	17	5*
-325	78	Scott	HOU	7	15	-8
-329	79	Galarraga	MTL	19	23	-4
-331	80	Jefferies	NY	21	23	-2
-331	81n	Samuel	LA	17	17	0
-330	82	Heaton	PIT	10	9	1
-323	83	-Kruk	PHI	13	6	7*
-330	84	Magrane	STL	7	14	-7
-334	85	Tudor	STL	0	4	-4
-327	86	-Whitson	SD	22	15	7*
-331	87	Bedrosian	SF	10	14	-4
-336	88	Guerrero	STL	15	20	-5
-346	89	Hershiser	LA	9	19	-10
-343	90	Lind	PIT	9	6	3
-342	91n	Brooks	LA	19	18	1
-344	92	Oquendo	STL	6	8	-2
-343	93	Miller	NY	5	4	1
-344	94	Darwin	HOU	15	16	-1
-352	95	Avery	ATL	1	9	-8
-351	96	-Grissom	MTL	9	8	1
-357	97	Cone	NY	16	22	-6
-362	98	Presley	ATL	10	15	-5
-354	99	-Martinez.D	MTL	15	7	8*
-360	100	Yelding	HOU	20	26	-6
-362	101n	Davis.G	HOU	18	20	-2
-360	102	Smiley	PIT	7	5	2
-366	103	Glavine	ATL	0	6	-6
-363	104	Boyd	MTL	13	10	3*
-367	105	Howell.J	LA	19	23	-4
-372	106	Brantley	SF	16	21	-5
-372	107	Smith.D	CHI	8	8	0

Note: this was the peak of "wasted money." From this point, bidders had so little money that they had to start bidding smarter.

CUM	DN	Name	Tm	JB$	A$	$D
-368	108	Mercker	ATL	13	9	4*
-369	109	Dascenzo	CHI	2	3	-1
-369	110	Nixon	MTL	16	16	0
-364	111n	-Smith.O	STL	17	12	5*
-367	112	Harkey	CHI	8	11	-3
-362	113	Esasky	ATL	7	2	5
-364	114	Bream	PIT	11	13	-2
-369	115	Leibrandt	ATL	2	7	-5
-368	116	Oliver	CIN	5	4	1
-373	117	Bielecki	CHI	0	5	-5
-374	118	Sharperson	LA	6	7	-1
-377	119	King	PIT	5	8	-3
-377	120	Biggio	HOU	17	17	0

CUM	DN	Name	Tm	JB$	A$	$D
-376	121n	Walker	MTL	16	15	1
-377	122	Darling	NY	5	6	-1
-373	123	Smith.L	ATL	12	8	4*
-371	124	Wallach	MTL	24	22	2
-367	125	Browning	CIN	13	9	4*
-368	126	Boever	PHI	7	8	-1
-368	127	Boskie	CHI	1	1	0
-367	128	Pagnozzi	STL	2	1	1
-362	129	Fitzgerald	MTL	7	2	5
-362	130	Wilson.T	SF	3	3	0
-356	131n	Girardi	CHI	10	4	6*
-353	132	Carreon	NY	4	1	3
-354	133	Blauser	ATL	4	5	-1
-344	134	-Smith.D	HOU	25	15	10*
-346	135	Parrett	ATL	2	4	-2
-346	136	Stanton	ATL	5	5	0
-351	137	Nabholz	MTL	0	5	-5
-351	138	Griffin	LA	2	2	0
-342	139	-Roberts	SD	25	16	9*
-342	140	Caminiti	HOU	4	4	0
-331	141n	Harris.G	SD	15	4	11*
-334	142	Gardner	MTL	3	6	-3
-329	143	-Morris	CIN	14	9	5*
-327	144	Jordan	PHI	5	3	2
-325	145	Agosto	HOU	3	1	2
-325	146	Akerfelds	PHI	1	1	0
-324	147	Frey	MTL	4	3	1
-319	148	Reynolds	PIT	7	2	5
-312	149	Hudler	STL	10	3	7*
-309	150	Pendleton	STL	9	6	3
-305	151n	-Fernandez	NY	18	14	4*
-310	152	Anthony	HOU	1	6	-5
-307	153	Morgan	LA	8	5	3
-304	154	Gott	LA	5	2	3
-303	155	Backman	PIT	5	4	1
-297	156	Redus	PIT	7	1	6
-298	157	Manwaring	SF	0	1	-1
-301	158	Bell	PIT	0	3	-3
-303	159	Pagliarulo	SD	1	3	-2
-298	160n	-Hurst	SD	15	10	5*
-302	161	Mulholland	PHI	0	4	-4
-302	162	Elster	NY	3	3	0
-296	163	-Charlton	CIN	13	7	6*
-296	164	Oberkfell	HOU	1	1	0
-300	165	Jackson	CIN	1	5	-4
-291	166	Jose	STL	12	3	9*
-294	167	Doran	PIT	0	3	-3
-290	168	Harris.L	LA	7	3	4
-279	169n	-Smith.Z	PIT	15	4	11*
-280	170	Searage	LA	0	1	-1
-278	171	Teufel	NY	3	1	2
-272	172	Smith.B	STL	8	2	6
-269	173	Clark	CHI	4	1	3
-267	174	Whitehurst	NY	3	1	2
-263	175	-Duncan	CIN	10	6	4*
-262	176n	-Martinez.C	PIT	4	3	1
-256	177	Landrum	PIT	11	5	6*
-256	178	Gullickson	HOU	1	1	0
-247	179	Tewksbury	STL	10	1	9*
-244	180	Benzinger	CIN	5	2	3
-245	181	Schiraldi	SD	0	1	-1
-239	182	Slaught	PIT	7	1	6
-240	183	Riles	SF	0	1	-1
-243	184n	-Decker	SF	0	3	-3
-243	185	Ruskin	MTL	1	1	0
-238	186	Templeton	SD	6	1	5
-233	187	Pena	NY	7	2	5
-234	188	Ruffin	PHI	0	1	-1
-232	189	Olson	ATL	4	2	2
-231	190	Villanueva	CHI	2	1	1
-232	191n	-Fletcher	PHI	0	1	-1
-229	192	Winningham	CIN	4	1	3
-224	193	Deshaies	HOU	6	1	5
-221	194	Owen	MTL	4	1	3
-218	195	Thomas	ATL	4	1	3
-214	196	Kennedy	SF	5	1	4
-207	197n	-Bass	SF	10	3	7*
-207	198	Whitt	ATL	1	1	0
-208	199	Offerman	LA	2	3	-1
-208	200	Innis	NY	1	1	0
-201	201	Portugal	HOU	8	1	7
-200	202	Sampen	MTL	3	2	1
-194	203n	-Lankford	STL	11	5	6*
-187	204	McDowell.O	ATL	8	1	7
-194	205	Chamberlain	PHI	0	1	-1
-193	206	Wynne	CHI	2	1	1
-187	207	Belcher	LA	8	2	6
-187	208	Abner	SD	1	1	0
-182	209n	-Benes	SD	8	3	5
-175	210	Hartley	LA	8	1	7
-176	211	Palacios	PIT	0	1	-1

DA LUCKY STREAKS WINTER ROSTER, NOVEMBER 1990

JB$	A$	Pos	Name	TM	BAVG	AB	H	HR	RBI	SB
13	6	1B	Kruk	PHI	0.291	443	129	7	67	10
25	16	3B	Roberts	SD	0.309	556	172	9	44	46
14	9	13	Morris	CIN	0.340	309	105	7	36	9
21	21	2B	Alomar	SD	0.287	586	168	6	60	24
17	12	SS	Smith,O	STL	0.254	512	130	1	50	32
10	6	2S	Duncan	CIN	0.306	435	133	10	55	13
0	3	C	Decker	SF	0.296	54	16	3	8	0
0	1	C	Fletcher	PHI	0.130	23	3	0	1	0
4	3	UT	Martinez,C	PIT	0.240	217	52	10	35	2
26	34	OF	Gant	ATL	0.303	575	174	32	84	33
9	8	OF	Grissom	MT	0.257	288	74	3	29	22
15	7	OF	Martinez,D	MT	0.279	391	109	11	39	13
10	3	OF	Bass	SF	0.252	214	54	7	32	2
11	5	OF	Lankford	STL	0.286	126	36	3	12	8

JB	A$	Pos	Name	TM	W	S	IP	ERA	RATIO
31	28	P	Smith,L	STL	3	27	68.67	2.10	1.1359
22	17	P	Martinez,D	MT	10		226.00	2.95	1.0619
22	15	P	Whitson	SD	14		228.67	2.60	1.1458
25	15	P	Smith,D	HO	6	23	60.33	2.39	1.0774
18	14	P	Fernandez	NY	9		179.33	3.46	1.0985
15	10	P	Hurst	SD	11		223.67	3.14	1.1222
13	7	P	Charlton	CIN	12	2	154.33	2.74	1.3024
15	4	P	Smith,Z	PIT	12		215.33	2.55	1.1424
8	3	P	Benes	SD	10		192.33	3.60	1.2791

DRAFT PRICE INFLATION AND WHAT TO DO ABOUT IT

By Mike Dalecki

It's time to get ready for the spring draft. You have your freeze list ready, you know what you need, you know how to use optimal bids, and you know what it will cost to get players in the draft. Or do you? Unless you can correct for Draft Price Inflation (DPI), you will find it more difficult to fill out your roster effectively come draft day.

[NOTES: (1) This problem DOESN'T apply to leagues just starting up, or to leagues that start over with clean rosters every year. Just plain $ values are all you need in a start-up situation. (2) In this essay the term "fair-value" is used to describe a players calculated value using a rational method to take all available money (i.e., $3120 for a 12-team AL or $2600 for a ten-team NL) and allocate this money to all available players.]

WHAT IS DRAFT PRICE INFLATION?

DPI occurs when there is too much money available to buy too little talent. When freezing players prior to the draft, owners typically freeze the best values, i.e. players that are undervalued. Less talent is then available in the draft, relative to the money available to buy it. This causes the actual auction prices to rise above fair-value. Even when some owners keep players at salaries higher than their fair-value, the average salaries for all retained players are almost lower.

Consider the case of Dave Justice ($10) and Ramon Martinez ($5). Suppose they are frozen and thus not available in the draft. The two players together are probably worth somewhere around $42; their contracts, though, total only $15. The effect of freezing them is that $42 worth of TALENT has been removed from the pool of available players, but only $15 has been used up. In this case there will be 27 extra dollars available to bid on players in the draft.

When owners freeze many players like this, you have a problem. There will be TOO MUCH MONEY chasing TOO LITTLE TALENT, which is the classic inflation scenario. Under these conditions, PRICES MUST RISE; uncorrected bids will not work very well.

WHAT CAN YOU DO ABOUT DPI?

Three things. FIRST, you can correct your fair-value prices and optimal bids to reflect the inflationary conditions that exist in the draft. SECOND, you can consider the freeze-draft dynamics that result from too much unspent money, and make up your freeze list accordingly. And THIRD, you can determine which players are likely to be available, focusing your draft strategy on those expectations.

CORRECTING FAIR VALUE (AND OPTIMAL BIDS) TO REFLECT DPI

To correct prices to reflect DPI, start out by estimating the VALUE of the players who are frozen. John Benson's predicted prices are the easiest thing to use. While you might quibble with some of his predictions, in the aggregate they will give you an excellent estimate of how much VALUE has been frozen. (I'll use National League examples below, so if you are in an AL league, use $3120 rather than $2600 as the money available to owners.)

1. Add up the predicted prices (value) for all the

frozen players. Subtract from $2600. (AL: $3120). This is the VALUE AVAILABLE TO BE BOUGHT in the draft.

2. Add up the contracts for all frozen players. Subtract from $2600. (AL: $3120). This is the MONEY AVAILABLE TO BE SPENT in the draft.

3. To create the correction factor to multiply by each player's fair value, divide (2) by (1).

An example:

My NL Rotisserie League has frozen 120 players worth, according to John Benson's price predictions, $1500. Their contracts are worth a collective $1200. There is $300 in retained value that hasn't been "paid for." The money saved has to go somewhere!

To create the correction factor:

1. $2600 - $1500 = $1100 total value of available players.

2. $2600 - $1200 = $1400 total money available in auction.

3. The correction factor is $1400 available, divided by $1100 value, or 1.273.

The correction factor is then multiplied by each player's price prediction. This corrects upward the median likely price that will be paid in the draft. Optimal bids are then based on this NEW price, which in this example is 27.3 percent more than the usual "fair value."

Suppose Fred McGriff's predicted price for 1991 is $31. His DPI price will be $31 times 1.273, or about $39.46. The optimal bid is then 70 to 85 percent of $39.46, or about $28 to $34.

You can also multiply the correction factor directly by the optimal bids John lists in the player-data section of this book, without first multiplying by the predicted fair value.

The correction factors will be different each year in each league. In general, the better the players were in the previous year, the better the retentions will be, and the more draft inflation will occur. You can't reliably use any standard correction factor, certainly not the factor reported here, because they assume a particular league context. You need to create your own. It takes about 10 minutes with a calculator.

The DPI correction will not allow you to get bargains in the traditional sense. It will let you get bargains RELATIVE TO THE AVERAGE INFLATED PRICE. You can't expect to get a lot of "good deals" when extreme DPI conditions exist. What DPI correction does is make sure you spend less than you might have otherwise (using corrected optimal bids), and to sensitize you to the price changes which occur under these conditions.

MORE SPECIFIC: DPI CORRECTIONS WITHIN HITTING AND PITCHING

The same corrections can be calculated separately for hitters and pitchers. Just use the 65-35 percent splits for money to be spent on hitting and pitching, rather than the grand ($2600 or $3120) total. In an NL league, $1690 should be spent on hitting; $910 should be spent on pitching. (AL: $2028 and $1092)

Rarely will you find the two correction factors to be the same, although sometimes they're close. If they are very different, however, you are on to something.

Computing separate correction factors for hitters and pitchers allows you to see which category of player will be more overvalued in the draft. If pitchers will be more overvalued than hitters, then hitters are more likely to be relative bargains in the draft. In one of my recent drafts, the DPI correction factor for hitters was 1.34; for pitchers, 1.46. It was somewhat harder to get reasonably-priced pitchers than hitters in that draft, because a larger proportion of pitching talent was already frozen.

I try to predict which players will be retained before the draft (I ask; sometimes they tell). I can then produce approximate correction factors BEFORE ROSTER FREEZE TIME. If the two correction factors are wildly out of balance, it tells me that one type of player will be much more expensive than the other in the draft.

For example, suppose that the pre-freeze estimated correction factors are: Pitchers 1.62, Hitters 1.21. Under these conditions, pitching would be much more expensive in the draft than hitting. If I had several borderline freeze possibilities, I'd think about freezing borderline pitchers before borderline hitters, since it would be easier to get back the hitting than the pitching in the draft. I'd try to insulate myself from being burned by high prices for a particular category of player. Better to not need too many of that type of player.

DRAFT DYNAMICS — BEAT THE OTHER OWNERS TO THE PUNCH

It's very hard to get high-value players for fair-value in a draft where DPI exists. Joe Carter will probably go for $35-40 in our draft this spring, just because there won't be much available. Each time you buy a player like this, you throw away the profits that are necessary to win. Do this enough times in the draft, and you get a 5th-place team. I don't like spending $130 to get $90 in value.

When DPI is prevalent, I focus more on having the greatest amount of VALUE frozen, which is a combination of PROFITS and high value players who are not necessarily profitable. During a draft with DPI, the owners as a group MUST give back their profits when they buy players. The trick is to give back as little as possible, and this can be done by "pre-spending" some of your money.

I did exactly that last spring when I froze two players at a combined price of $66, even though I expected "only" $50 to $55 of fair-value. It was just obvious to me that these two star hitters would not be available in the auction for $55, or even $65. So I "bought" them early with my freeze list.

Under extreme DPI conditions, I don't want to take a lot of money into the draft, because it's almost certain that I can't get fair value for it. Which means I'll give back profits. I look to find BARGAINS in such a draft, not high value. Where are these bargains, you ask? They almost never appear among high-value players. Instead, they appear in the crapshoot, among the $1 to $5 players that are picked up at the end.

I'd rather take $50 into one of these drafts than $150. With $50 I can get a couple of decent role-players, or one expensive player that I really need, and spend the rest of the money on cheap players. That's where most of the profits are. The book you are reading is great at pointing out sleeper picks. Some of them are always unclaimed toward the end of the draft, and I collect them as $1 wonders. I specialize in $1 catchers, for instance. Some of these guys don't pan out, but the upside is good, there's rarely much downside, and as a group they're usually profitable.

Many owners simply try to freeze maximum total profits. I'm just suggesting that this isn't always the best idea.

PLAYER AVAILABILITY EXPECTATIONS CAN DICTATE WHO TO FREEZE

What's written above is a general set of rules I follow when setting up my freeze list and draft strategy. But there are other considerations as well. I won't freeze a shortstop if there are going to be a lot of shortstops available in the draft, unless he's very undervalued.

I try to make sure I need players at positions where there's a lot of talent available, which is where optimal bids have the best chance of working. Let others fight over players at the positions where talent is really scarce!

MIDCOURSE CORRECTIONS

[Krause Publications owns the copyright to this essay, which appears here with their permission.]

Several weeks after your draft or auction, you have a good idea how your team is going to do. If you have a good roster, you want to put your feet up, and watch the juggernaut roll. If your team came away from Draft Day with many weaknesses, you may find that weekly stats are unpleasant, and want to avoid studying them. Both reactions are premature.

True: the draft is important. But many Rotisserie pennants are won with clever transactions in May and June. The first half of the season is the most important time to be alert and pro-active, for several reasons:

1. Statistical variations are most extreme early in the season,

2. Trade opportunities are most plentiful when everyone is still in the hunt,

3. Most emerging rookies (and fading veterans) can be identified early, and

4. Most leagues have a deadline, after which you cannot "fix" your roster.

So, the first half is not the time to be a spectator. May and June are critical months to be actively involved in watching baseball, studying numbers, looking for opportunities, and taking advantage of those who don't work as hard as you do. There are proven methods to make this period most productive.

MAINTAIN YOUR SENSE OF PERSPECTIVE: DON'T OVERREACT

During the early part of each season, you will see many extremes of player performance, some good and some bad. The biggest danger (other than ignoring stats altogether) is that you might overreact. Lopsided trades result more from misunderstanding of early-season stats than from any other cause, with the possible exception of deliberate player-dumping.

With hindsight, the possibilities for poor trades are obvious. Take a look back at your late May, 1989, USA Today:

FAST STARTS, SLOW STARTS, 1989:

Hitters:	BA	HR	RBI	SB
Rick Cerone	.325	1	11	0
Carlton Fisk	.240	2	4	0
Rafael Palmeiro	.328	4	23	2
Wally Joyner	.218	1	11	1
Paul O'Neill	.312	5	30	7
Eric Davis	.238	6	18	3
Wade Boggs	.299	1	15	0
Kevin Seitzer	.303	2	17	3
Gregg Jefferies	.198	0	13	3
Ken Caminiti	.262	2	16	0

Which catcher would you rather have, Cerone or Fisk?

If somebody offered you Joyner for Palmeiro, you would laugh in their face, right?

Looks like Eric Davis is not the outfielder he used to be . . . want to trade him for a fine, young rising superstar named O'Neill?

Boggs is also past his prime, but I'm a Red Sox fan; so I will give you a great young star 3B who leads him in every category. That's fair, isn't it?

And that kid Jefferies: probably returning to the minors. But I might be able to use him next year, so I'll give you an established player for him. OK?

Checking in again at year-end:

Hitters:	BA	HR	RBI	SB	
You gave:					
Eric Davis	.281	34	101	21	(130/462)
Wally Joyner	.282	16	79	3	(167/593)
Wade Boggs	.330	3	54	2	(205/621)
Carlton Fisk	.293	13	68	1	(110/375)
Gregg Jefferies	.258	12	56	21	(131/508)
	.290	78	358	48	(743/2559)
You got:					
Paul O'Neill	.276	15	74	20	(118/428)
Rafael Palmeiro	.275	8	64	4	(154/559)
Kevin Seitzer	.281	4	48	17	(168/597)
Rick Cerone	.243	4	48	1	(72/296)
Ken Caminiti	.255	10	72	4	(149/585)
	.268	41	306	46	(661/2465)

In summary, if you made these trades, you blew the season, losing 37 HR, 52 RBI, 22 points on your batting average, and a couple of SB. But no one would ever trade those top five names, would they? Well, maybe not all at once, but all of them got traded last year, by hundreds of Rotisserie owners, in deals just like the ones you see in the table above.

The point is: Don't panic! Tony Gwynn was hitting .237 in June 1988. Would you unload him, or wait for the second half when he hit .400 and won the NL batting crown? I know somebody (a fairly good Rotisserie player) who WAIVED a slumping Eric Davis in May 1986. Likewise, don't get all goosepimpley about dazzling first-half numbers, especially when they come from rookies. Matt Nokes hit .313 (with almost 20 HR) in his first half year as a rookie. That would have been the ideal time to trade him; he has been a consistent .250 hitter ever since. Many rookies flash huge numbers in their first tour around the league, and then fade into obscurity. Remember Mitchell Page?

CREATE A CONTEXT FOR ALL STATISTICS

I could tell you: know the difference between statistical anomaly and true player performance. That is easier said than done, but your duties as a Rotisserie manager are easy to define. Do your homework. Look at numbers other than current stats. NEVER make a decision based solely on what you see in the newspaper on any given day. Create a context.

Context is THE watchword in Rotisserie baseball. The vital statistics about any player are NOT the numbers you see in the papers in June. Think about the player's role: Is he a regular or a platooner, and how long has he had that job? Is he in prime physical condition, or recovering from injury? Is he filling in for a disabled star who will be coming off the DL next week? Is he threatened by a rookie phenom or a contemplated trade?

And statistically, what is the player's background? How old is he? Does he have a firmly established major league performance level? Are his current numbers similar to stats he has produced in previous whole seasons? Has he shown POTENTIAL to produce similar stats? Is he a known, streaky player? Does his career show any trends, up or down?

When you do your homework, wild numbers have a way of becoming sensible again. Yes, you can see the future! Sometimes it's difficult, but sometimes it's downright easy. Tony Gwynn is not a .237 hitter. At that point in his 1988 season, he was playing with a sore thumb, and taking a lot of walks. Tony Gwynn is such a smart hitter, that he could swing with one hand and bat .280 if he had to.

Let's take another look at some fast (and slow) starts from 1989, this time with a little perspective added in the two right-hand columns:

Hitters:	Late May, 1989				Lifetime	
	BA	HR	RBI	SB	BA	Age
Harold Baines	.367	2	18	0	.286	30
Will Clark	.358	6	27	1	.292	25
Vince Coleman	.336	0	9	14	.262	28
Alvin Davis	.328	4	27	0	.287	29
Keith Moreland	.319	1	7	0	.279	35
Paul O'Neill	.312	5	30	7	.253	26
Kevin Mitchell	.296	12	37	1	.268	27
Eric Davis	.238	6	18	3	.273	26
Tony Armas	.222	1	2	0	.252	36
Darrell Evans	.205	3	5	0	.249	42
Craig Worthington	.205	2	17	3	(NA)	24
Craig Biggio	.204	1	6	1	(NA)	23
Fred Lynn	.202	1	7	0	.287	37
Gary Carter	.114	1	5	0	.267	35

(NA) = under 150 MLB at bats.

You need more information than ages and lifetime BA's to make sense out of early-season stats, but combined with a little knowledge of each player's skills and history, you can make some amazingly accurate predictions. Taking the above cases, you could reason as follows:

Harold Baines is a fine, professional hitter, young enough to be playing near his peak ability. No one suddenly becomes a .367 hitter at age 30, however, so you know that Baines is playing a little over his head. He is a possible candidate to be traded for some other high-value player.

Could Will Clark hit .358 in a season? Darn right, he could. At age 25, no player has yet shown his peak ability. Do you trade Will Clark, figuring he will fall back to earth? If you do, you miss a great season from a top player.

Is Vince Coleman a .336 hitter? No way. He was having a nice season at this point last year, but if you could have traded him for another true star, that wouldn't have been such a bad idea in June 1989. He ended up as the Cards' fourth outfielder by September.

Could Alvin Davis really improve from .287 to .328 at age 29? Sure he could! Lot's of players improve a little at that age, and he isn't playing that far above his established level, anyway. Classification: no hurry to trade.

Is Keith Moreland due for a big, upward movement at age 35? Very doubtful. Be thankful for the decent numbers he has produced thus far, and keep him on the table as trade bait, for anything of real, lasting value. (He retired at the end of '89).

Could Paul O'Neill be an emerging star at age 26? Yes he could. But is he in the same class with Eric Davis? Nope.

Is Kevin Mitchell for real? At age 27, players often reach a new peak level. And if you knew that Kevin had corrected his vision problem for the 1989 season, you wouldn't have considered trading him in June, no way.

Eric Davis hitting .238? Who cares? He is a notorious, streaky player. If he was hitting .138, you wouldn't trade him. As soon as you did, he would hit nine homers in one week.

Was Tony Armas washed up in early 1989? Checking his age, and looking at the crowded California outfield, one would have to be worried. Classify: candidate for quick trade or waivers.

Darrell Evans: with a .205 BA and 42 candles on the birthday cake, the best you can hope is that somebody will be attracted by the marquee name, and give you something of value. Classify: possible throw-in, maybe just waivers.

Craig Worthington: you probably got him for $1 or $2 in 1989 anyway. At this young age, you do not give up on a recent International League MVP, and in 1989, you got rewarded for your patience with 15 HR, 70 RBI, and a player well worth keeping for 1990.

To wrap up quickly, Craig Biggio in June 1989 should get the benefit of the doubt, because of his youth and glittering minor league accomplishments. If you stuck by him in 1989, you got the best catcher in the NL. Fred Lynn and Gary Carter were not just old in 1989, they were also prominent on Robert O. Wood's "Washed Up" list for deterioration of their strikeout/walk ratios in 1988.

(See Bob's 1990 "Woodview" book, a great work, tel. 415-961-6574.) Your correct decision last year would have been dumping Carter and Lynn early.

We haven't mentioned any pitchers; they tend to be volatile. There is some conventional wisdom to be followed, however. Veteran hard-throwers often have slow starts. For many years, it was a sucker punch to grab Jack Morris in June or July, just before he began his annual string of shutouts. That ancient trick even worked again in 1990.

Pitchers who start the year at marvelous new performance levels are great assets for lopsided trades. The Cardinals usually have a rookie hurler who gets off to a great start (Cris Carpenter, Greg Mathews, etc.) In 1989, the guy was Ken Hill: going into June, his ERA was around 2.00, with a splendid ratio and a great W/L outlook. My point about conext now comes into play. Hill's last five lines in the Baseball Register read: 5.14, 4.50, 5.20, 5.14, and 4.92 in the ERA column. It is POSSIBLE that someone with such minor league numbers could suddenly become a major league star, but it is highly unlikely. You have to look at SOMETHING other than the June 7 USA Today to know what a rookie pitcher is worth. When Hill produced a 4.65 ERA and a sickening ratio in the second half, and proceeded to lose 15 games, nobody with any baseball sense should have been surprised. My friend Bill, who traded Hill to a novice owner in June, in exchange for a star reliever, was pushing "clever" into the realm of "unscrupulous." Please: think "context."

Like many skills, Rotisserie judgment requires hard-knocks experience, not just cook-book recipes. But you can learn from the past as well as the present. The above examples should equip you to know the issues for your midseason 1991 roster moves.

Another "duty" for the diligent Rotisserie owner:

STUDY YOUR OPPONENTS' ROSTERS, NOT JUST YOUR OWN.

It is amazing how many smart owners plod through their Rotisserie seasons with only brief looks at the opposition. You can create amazing benefits by knowing your opponent's point of view.

All of the above advice ("don't panic, don't overreact," etc.) has a flipside: try to create panic in the minds of your rivals. Call them and chat about their worst performers in June: "Is it true that Joe Bimbleman's wife left him, and he cannot concentrate on hitting?" With a little deeper research, you can develop your own rumors: "I see that Wally Whizzer is hitting .440 for Edmonton, and playing flawless shortstop! Aren't you worried about Schofield?" Let's be clear: I never advocate lies or deception, but when you're buying a used car, it is only prudent to point out the flaws. The same thing is true in Rotisserie trading.

In addition to finding underperformers on your opponents' rosters, there are two other benefits to be obtained through "competitive intelligence" . . .

(1) You can find the needs and weaknesses (and/or surplus numbers) in the other rosters, and

(2) You can find prejudices in your opponents' player selections, and take advantage of them.

Knowing your opponents' needs and weaknesses is vital if you hope to make beneficial trades. Other owners don't want to trade for YOUR most obvious surplus; they want to trade for THEIR most obvious need. When you see a player you want on someone else's roster, you better know what they need before you begin talking. Dangling a marvelous reliever isn't likely to help, if they already lead the league in Saves.

Not all players are perfectly rational, however, and that's where prejudices come in. You all know the owners who covet home town favorites, and you know how to take advantage of them. Other owners just love certain statistics, and certain types of players. It isn't rational, but one owner I know just loves high batting averages. He will always trade a slugger for a spray-hitting .300 type, even when he already leads the league in BA and needs HR and RBI. Knowing these irrationalities can make you rich.

Some prejudices are fairly obscure, but still quite powerful. In early 1987 while checking my arch-rival's roster with the Sporting News Register, I stumbled across a gold mine: his roster was a virtual alumni club of Arizona State University! He had Alvin Davis, Oddibe McDowell, Reggie Jackson etc., and all at high prices. Within 24 hours, I had traded ASU grad Floyd Bannister and spare change for a $10 kid named Ruben Sierra. And the other guy was thrilled!

TRADING TACTICS

You could write a whole book about trading. Indeed, business skills books about selling, buying, and negotiating are all useful for Rotisserie. I am going to cover just a couple of ploys that will help you in 1991.

1. Early in the year, make a bad trade.

I am NOT suggesting that you should give up a star for garbage. My favorite method is to trade a player of small (but obvious) value, for someone who is overwhelmingly worthless. For example, trade a healthy, established utility player for a crippled veteran or a failed prospect. Call up and ASK for Doug Strange or Skeeter Barnes. The weirder the name, the better. You will always be remembered for that flaky move. Everyone else in the league will become relaxed about dealing with you.

This method is similar to the old poker maxim: make sure you get caught bluffing (once) early in the game. A little visible stupidity, when you first start playing, can lead to riches later.

2. Never ask directly for the player that you really want.

Call and show that you know the other owner's needs: "I see that you are short of stolen bases." (Say s-t-o-l-e-n b-a-s-e-s real slow; let it sink in.) Dangle a good name: "Well, I have Speedy Gonzalez. Would you be intersted?" (If he says no, he's a dope, and you can proceed to pick his pocket without further advice from me.)

Then you ask for Barry Bonds or Ruben Sierra, clearly stating that you know you must give more to make it fair: "Are there any stars on my roster that might interest you?" If he says yes, you may end up with Barry Bonds AND the guy you wanted. Assume he says no. You chat about his strengths: nice homers, nice RBI, solid pitching. Then you come back to his weakness: "But you still need SB's, and I have Gonzales. Too bad you can't part with anybody I like. Well, good bye — oh — how about your shortstop, Mickey Strong; I see you've got two shortstops on your reserve list, and might be able to get along without him. Yeah? Deal? Great!"

And that's all there is to it. If you had called up and said, "I want Mickey Strong," how high do you think the price would have been?

The following chapter on "Manipulating the Standings" is useful at any time of year, and should be read and understood before implementing any mid-course corrections. The standings are still very flexible in May and June, however, and you should be open-minded about the fact you can win (or lose) any category by changing your roster during the first half of the year.

YES, YOU CAN MANIPULATE THE STANDINGS, LEGALLY

[Note: Krause Publications owns the copyright to this essay, which appears here with their permission.]

One of the prime attractions of Rotisserie baseball is that you always get a pennant race. There is no such thing as mathematical elimination, and no "magic numbers." No one ever says, "I clinched the pennant today," and nobody pours champagne (or Yoo Hoo) before October.

Like the game of baseball itself, Rotisserie offers myriad possibilities and surprise endings. Standings can tell you the probabilities of winning, but they can never tell you that the game is over — not until the last pitch has been thrown.

Rotisserie standings can change faster than "real" baseball standings, because there is more at risk every day. When the Mets and Dodgers take the field, there is only one game at stake, even if the score becomes 27-0. But whenever a pitcher takes the mound, his fantasy owner is at risk for unlimited damage. Ask anybody who owned Jim Clancy and Bob Forsch last year.

Strategy 1: LOOK FOR THE NUMBERS BEHIND THE NUMBERS

The first step in managing your roster toward September is to find the true meaning of your league standings. Too many people take their standings as gospel; it pays to be skeptical. Don't relax just because you look "safe" in the standings, and don't throw in the towel just because the standings say your team is lousy. The standings are not some external force that determines whether your team is good or bad; the standings are a passive set of numbers that can be manipulated.

Some standings can be downright misleading. We have a real league case study to illustrate "Standings Theory and Practice." We chose a time frame of August, because probabilities become clearer when you get closer to the end of the year; but these ideas are useful any time from July 1 to September. Names have been changed to protect the innocent.

GOODFELLOWS LEAGUE —
AUGUST 25, 1990

Burners 69
Aces 68
Firemen 60
Bushers 56
Veterans 45
Sliders 36
Bombers 30
Hangers 29
Gappers 28
Bums 19

In this league, it looks like the Burners and Aces have a tight pennant race going, just one point apart with a month to go! But these standings are deceptive. With more information (the numbers behind the numbers), you will see that the Aces have almost no chance of winning.

These standings also show the fifth place Veterans pretty far away from fourth place (eleven points). When you see the numbers behind the numbers, however, you will realize that the Veterans have almost a 50/50 chance to finish fourth.

The complete stats and standings for our sample league appear on page 69.

Let's examine the "tight" Burners/Aces pennant

race by looking behind the numbers. The Aces are just one point out of first place. The simple question is: where are they likely to gain one point? Or where might the Burners lose a point?

To answer such questions, my method is to count "Unsettled Points," any standings points where luck or random variation will be a major factor in determining the final outcome. (I like the acronym U.P.'s, or "ups" when I do this analysis myself, because these numbers truly represent the ups and downs likely to be seen. But there is enough new thinking here that I will spare you.) Unsettled Points are those that can be grabbed by a team that makes a strategic shift to emphasize the category in question. During April, May, June and July, almost all points are unsettled. By the end of August, however, 80% of all games have been played, and points do not fluctuate much from week to week. Some categories may be "clinched" by teams with big leads.

In most categories, there will be tight groupings, in or around the middle. The 1 HR that separates the Bushers from the Firemen in our case study, is worth one point in the standings. The 31 Homers by which the Veterans lead the Aces are also worth one point. With a 31 HR lead, that point apparently has been settled. When a standings point is based on a tiny REAL difference (like 1 HR), that is what I call Unsettled.

Unsettled points represent upward potential for one team, and downward risk for another. The strategic implication is that each team should set their roster to capture (or retain) the most Unsettled Points going into September. The first step is to list all the opportunities and threats for the team in question.

Take the Aces for example. Their 10-9-10-10 in hitting is an immediate tip-off that they have almost no upward potential. Topping a category often means that you have "Wasted Value" (see below); it ALWAYS means that your Unsettled Points represent only downward risk. There is no upward movement possible when you lead a category.

The Aces have no reasonable hope to pick up even one point in hitting. They have a remote possibility to improve from second place in HR, but they trail by a big margin. What about downward risk from Unsettled Points in hitting? Batting average looks safe (.271 to .264). Three teams are within 9 HR of catching the Aces; that situation bears watching, but I wouldn't quite call those Unsettled Points. In RBI, I see one Unsettled Point between the Aces and the Burners. The difference of 11 RBI is only 1.8%, and we have 20% of the season yet to go. That's within the range that I call risky; one player in one week could make up the difference. In Stolen Bases, the Aces' lead over the Burners is only one SB, clearly an Unsettled Point.

You can study the standings table yourself, and you can argue about what constitutes "Unsettled" [if you want all the definitions and formulas, write to me] but when you get done, you will have a list that looks something like this:

UNSETTLED POINTS

	Burners		Aces	
	Up	Down	Up	Down
Batting Average	2	0	0	0
Home Runs	2	0	0	0
RBI	1	0	0	1
SB	1	0	0	1
Wins	1	0	0	4
Saves	0	0	0	1
ERA	1	0	0	2
Ratio	0	1	0	2
Totals	8	1	0	11

Considering the Unsettled Points behind the standings, it becomes obvious that the Aces are in danger of losing 5 or 6 points with just a few unlucky bounces. The owner of the Aces should forget about chasing the Burners, and try to minimize his downside risks and hang on to second place. Considering which categories are most sensitive at this point, he should be looking to trade a star hitter for an ace starter, to prepare his roster for September.

Strategy 2: SHRINK YOUR PITCHING STAFF WHEN YOU HAVE A BIG LEAD

The Burners look pretty safe in the above analysis, but when you have a 95% chance of winning, you should take steps to make it 99%. Based on Unsettled Points, there is only ONE scenario that could knock the Burners out of first: their hitters fail to pick up any points, while their pitchers wreck their ratio, the Aces hold strong in every category, and the other eight teams all go sour (leaving the Aces unimpaired in any category). Likely? No. Possible? Yes! So why take a chance?

The best way to preserve an excellent ratio is to stop pitching. Assuming that the Burners will satisfy their league IP requirement, they would be wise to remove any starters who look shaky, before September. If they have no shaky starters, the Burners' owner should be looking for any flyball pitchers due to start at Wrigley or Atlanta (in the A.L., avoid Fenway and the Metrodome).

League rules vary widely about what is permitted in roster changes. In one league in 1988 (that allowed extensive access to free agents), I loaded my September roster with pitchers from the U.S. Olympic Team, (plus David Wainhouse, a token Canadian). [I also drafted a high school kid named Alex Fernandez who was recently the subject of tampering charges against the Yankees and later surfaced with the White Sox.] My ace relievers stayed active to keep my Save total high, while my ERA and ratio stayed nice and low.

You may be unable to draft free agents in August, and your trades may be limited to contiguous teams, but you can still pursue your goal of reducing IP. Somebody who needs to take chances will always be looking for an interesting starter, right up to the trading deadline. Short, situational relievers — you know, those guys who face only one or two hitters and then leave — are the safest selections for risk limitation.

If you feel confident that a minor leaguer or injured pitcher will NOT appear during September, go ahead and use them as "ghosts" on your roster. But be careful. September produces many experiments, just like spring training. Remember Jim Bouton's comeback?

One final caution: don't assume that freezing your ERA and Ratio will freeze your place in the standings. Most good pitchers improve their ERA's and Ratios in September, when they get to face many minor-leaguers. So make sure you have a big lead before cutting your IP.

Strategy 3: DON'T FOLD A WINNING HAND.

It is surprisingly common to find people who give up too early. In our case study league, the fifth place Veterans look like a longshot, 11 points out of fourth place, with a only month to go. But if you counted the Unsettled Points, you would find the following:

UNSETTLED POINTS

	Veterans		Bushers	
	Up	Down	Up	Down
Batting Average	0	3	1	1
Home Runs	0	0	0	2
RBI	2	0	0	1
SB	2	0	2	0
Wins	4	0	2	2
Saves	1	1	1	1
ERA	2	0	1	1
Ratio	2	0	1	1
Totals	13	4	8	9

Between the Veterans' upward potential and the Bushers' downward risks, there are 22 points blowing in the wind. And the Veterans are generally low in their tight-pack categories; they could easily gain four or five points without making any changes.

By making some strategic adjustments, the Veterans could gain about ten points, without losing any. Meanwhile, they can make life difficult for the Bushers, who could drop five or six points if their competitors do well in critical categories. The following strategies will increase the Veterans' chances of catching the Bushers. All of these moves are standard, prudent actions going into September.

Strategy 4: TRADE AWAY "WASTED VALUE"

With a 31 HR lead over their closest opponent, the Veterans could lose 30 HR without losing a point in the standings. One month from one very hot slugger would be 10 HR (that's a pace of 60 per year). So the Veterans can trade away one slugger, or even two, without risking much in the HR category. Considering their Unsettled Points at risk in Batting Average, they would be wise to move a slugger who hits for low average. Removing a .225 hitter from your lineup will always make your team BA go up nicely.

Almost every team has wasted value somewhere. If you cannot find any category where you lead your closest opponent by a wide margin, you have done a fine job of mid-season roster management AND you have been lucky.

Note that "victory" in any category usually creates wasted value. In this league, the Aces have wasted value in their high Batting Average. The Veterans have excess homers. The Burners and Bums have only one point at risk with 10 or 15 Wins to throw away. And the Burners have 9 or 10 extra Saves.

Strategy 5: USE YOUR KNOWLEDGE OF STANDINGS TO FIND TRADING PARTNERS

The same way you look at Unsettled Points to plan your own strategy, you can look for teams that have Unsettled Points in the categories that you want to trade away. For example, the Veterans want to trade away Home Runs. The teams that should be most interested are the Burners, Firemen, and Bushers, who are in a virtual three-way tie in Homers.

Obviously, if your objective is to catch the Bushers, you are not going to give them the critical HR's that they need. The Burners and Firemen are safer places to put those extra HR, and both should be eager to get them.

Strategy 6: HELP TEAMS THAT WILL HURT YOUR RIVALS.

When you look for trading partners, you should give special consideration to teams that can take points away from your arch rivals. If you own the Veterans roster, and your objective is to catch the Bushers, you should be delighted to place a good HR hitter with the Burners or the Firemen. Both teams are likely to take a point away from the Bushers by passing them in HR. In fact, you should consider helping both the Burners and the Firemen, and taking two points away from the Bushers.

Your main purpose in trading is to improve in the categories that you need most. The Veterans need help in Wins, SB, ERA and ratio, to get a big lift in September. Sometimes, however, you cannot find anyone who is willing and able to give you what you need. What do you do then?

As the trading deadline approaches, there is no reason to be stubborn. If you tried and failed to swap for the players you need, consider just "giving" a player to a team that can take points away from your closest rival. The Veterans, in this example, would benefit from "giving" some HR to the Burners or Firemen, if they cannot trade them for fair value. Trading a good, full time player for a mediocre parttimer would be an example of giving something away. [As a personal note, I favor good sportsmanship over cut-throat tactics, and I hate collusion. As long as both teams benefit immediately, I don't think any trade should be considered collusive.]

Finally, some people just won't trade, even when you're willing to give more than you get. In such cases, you can still give free advice and insight. So, in our case study, if you are trying to help the Burners and Fireman get more HR (to hurt the Bushers), you can simply make sure the Burners and Firemen understand that HR is a critical category for both of them, with points readily attainable. You may be able to steer them toward a trade with some other team, or point out a free agent who could help them.

Strategy 7: KNOW WHEN TO FOLD.

The commonest mistake in September strategy is the dogged pursuit of sixth place. Long after a money-winning finish is impossible, many owners keep fighting to get the best possible standing. If you have a fierce rivalry, and want to finish as high as possible at any cost, that's your business. But you must be aware that playing for the current year will necessarily hurt your chances for next year. You simply do better when you concentrate on one or the other.

The ideal time to shift your attention from this year to next year can depend on factors other than standings. You need to look at the quality of opportunity available in pursuing each alternative. If you want to play for this year, but no one will trade you the established players you need to be competitive, it may be time to shift your strategy toward the youngsters.

If you want to build for next year, but find that all the low-salary, emerging stars are being pursued by every team in the league, you might seize an opportunity by trading away all your low-priced talent for high-salaried stars who can help you this year. Losing rosters can be miraculously transformed in rare cases when the league attitude is too lopsided toward next year.

In the final results, only four teams finish in the money. That means that six (NL) or eight (AL) teams should give up at some point. If you have one of those six or eight teams, it pays to realize that fact as early as possible. There is no magic formula, but here are some basic guidelines to determine when you should fold up your tent:

1. No one should ever give up before July 1. If you're that badly outclassed, you should get out of your league, and find weaker opponents.

2. Periodically after the All Star break, you should make a serious assessment using the same approach as the Unsettled Points method. Almost everything is unsettled in July, but you want to ask the same questions: How many points separate you from where you want to be in the standings? What would it take to close that gap? Remember that gaps are smaller in July than in September. Gaining 25 HR in three months requires only 2 dingers per week with three months to go, or two HR from each of your hitters, over half a season. Gaining 25 HR in one month is darn near impossible.

3. Consider the physical condition of your players. Did you just get Canseco back after he missed half a season? Or did you just lose Canseco after he gave you a tremendous first half? Make estimates of the impact from such changes, and re-cast the standings to see what injuries and recoveries will really mean.

4. If you feel the inclination to call it a season, DON'T tell anyone. Check out available low-priced talent first. The price is going to skyrocket after you tell people, "My whole strategy is to build for next year; please give me some rookies and $1 bargains." Make your trades first, and then keep your mouth shut until October, anyway.

Strategy 8 DO YOUR PLAYER-DUMPING BEFORE IT'S TOO LATE.

Don't wait until the night before your trading deadline to begin moving your high-salary players. The top teams in your league may all look lucky, but there is a good chance that their owners simply know more about this game than you do. Hasty negotiations give a big advantage to the more knowledgeable party. Take the time to do your homework.

Talk to other owners all summer, and LISTEN extensively. When you start hearing, "You can't keep that guy at $40, and you're out of the money this year anyway," you waited too long. So listen carefully for subtler suggestions along those lines, and start making your moves before the situation deteriorates.

Strategy 9 KNOW YOUR ROOKIES AND MINOR LEAGUERS

Whether you're playing for this year or next, fine young talent will always help you. Checking for league-leaders in Double A and Triple A is important all year, but specially critical when you approach September. We could write a whole book about how to select your prospects, but here a few basics:

1. Forget pitchers. For every Greg Olson who bursts into the major leagues, there are ten or twenty Jack McDowells and Al Leiters. Only about 30% of the pitchers who get listed among the Top Ten in their league by Baseball America become major league regulars, and less than 10% become stars. Hitters on BBAs Top Ten lists have a 75% success ratio becoming strong regulars in the majors, and fully half of them could be called star material. The clincher: even the greatest pitchers can suffer as rookies. Sandy Koufax struggled for six years.

2. You must be able to visualize a starting role for the player, very soon. Cecil Fielder was a credible impact player for 1990, because the Tigers 1B situation was obviously undecided. (remember Torey Lovullo?) Backups for Eddie Murray and Cal Ripken have made bad picks in most years.

3. Know park effects and league averages. PCL and Texas League hitters produce notoriously inflated numbers; batting averages tend to move UPWARD when players advance from Pawtucket to Boston. Bill James' Major League Equivalents are goldmine material.

4. Don't bet on career minor leaguers. That 29 year-old outfielder hitting .344 in AAA knows why he isn't in the Bigs. You don't need to know; just avoid him. Pick a nice 24 or 25 year-old.

SUMMARY

Setting your strategy for September is a critical step in every season, whether you're playing for this year or next. The worst thing you can do is to have NO September strategy and make no late-season adjustments. So, formulate a vision of the future. Define where you want to be when the season ends. Make a list of the steps necessary to get there. And Execute!

CASE STUDY FOR STANDINGS ANALYSIS
GOODFELLOWS LEAGUE —
AUGUST 25, 1990

	TOT	WINS		SAVES		ERA		RATIO		PITCHING
BURNERS	69	74	9	54	10	3.02	9	1.08	10	38
ACES	68	66	8	25	5	3.38	8	1.20	8	29
FIREMEN	60	33	1	44	9	2.99	10	1.12	9	29
BUSHERS	56	64	6	38	7	3.41	7	1.21	7	27
VETERANS	45	63	4	38	7	3.42	6	1.22	6	23
SLIDERS	36	46	2	24	4	3.59	4	1.27	4	14
BOMBERS	30	57	3	38	7	3.55	5	1.28	3	18
HANGERS	29	64	6	22	3	3.61	3	1.26	5	17
GAPPERS	28	64	6	21	2	3.99	1	1.39	1	10
BUMS	19	75	10	11	1	3.63	2	1.33	2	15
	606	55	315	55	34.5	55	12.3	55	220	

	AVE		HR		RBI		SB		HITTING
BURNERS	0.262	7	91	6	590	9	130	9	31
ACES	0.271	10	100	9	607	10	131	10	39
FIREMEN	0.264	9	92	7	539	7	111	8	31
BUSHERS	0.263	8	93	8	540	8	103	5	29
VETERANS	0.253	6	131	10	461	4	79	2	22
SLIDERS	0.252	5	80	5	462	5	105	7	22
BOMBERS	0.250	3	74	3	336	2	81	4	12
HANGERS	0.251	4	69	2	390	3	80	3	12
GAPPERS	0.242	2	76	4	463	6	104	6	18
BUMS	0.241	1	60	1	309	1	62	1	4

II
THE PLAYERS

INTRODUCTION TO THE PLAYER ESSAYS

Long-time readers of this book know exactly what we're trying to do in the player essays. Some new readers may find the format and content a bit unusual. A brief orientation:

(1) The players are grouped by league, by position, and then by team. The position, not the team, is the first cut. For Rotisserie purposes, you may be looking a National League catcher, or an American League 2B. You don't play the game by saying, "I want to find a Yankee I can draft." You don't win with such thinking, anyway."

(2) Within the position section, each player is discussed along with his major league teammates and prospects who are competing for playing time at the same position. The discussion of Don Mattingly is part of the Kevin Maas story, and vice versa. If we gave you separate essays on Maas and Mattingly, they would be redundant about the interrelatedness. Also, if you are putting Mattingly on your Rotisserie roster, you need to know about Maas too, either as a backup or as a threat.

(3) We have tried to identify every player who might be a factor in the major leagues in 1991. "Be a factor" means to play frequently and well enough that you would want the player on your roster at some time, either as an original draft pick or as a mid-season replacement. We have not tried to identify every player who might be a September call-up; the 40-man September rosters are generally experimental, like spring training.

(4) Minor leaguers are included if they pass the test, "might be a factor." Other minor leaguers may be mentioned, if there is a reason to warn you off, or if there is a reason to feel certain about a major league impact in 1992 or later. Our treatment of minor leaguers is quite different from what you get in Baseball America (for example), because we are focused almost exclusively on the current year impact, not the five-year outlook.

(5) Starting pitchers are generally under-emphasized. The fifth starter on a major league team is important in "real" baseball, but fifth starters make lousy Rotisserie picks. Some exceptions are noted. The point is, we haven't made an exhaustive presentation of the major league pitching profession, because you shouldn't spend too much time looking for fifth starters. Even Cy Young winners have trouble producing good stats.

(6) In many cases we have a player or position covered by more than one writer. Essays have been selected and edited to eliminate duplication, but when differences of opinion are worth noting, we don't like to take them out of context. In all cases, the editor rationalizes or summarizes each section.

(7) The forecast stats and $ values in the back of the book are the latest thinking before we went to press, and are the single "official" source in this book. The essays point out likely variables and possible contingencies. If you want one opinion with no "buts" or "howevers," just check the forecast tables.

(8) On December 18, 1990 there were more than 30 free agents who had occupied positions on major league 25-man rosters during the 1990 season. Another dozen major leaguers had been released and remained unsigned. When these 30 or 40 players join new teams, changes will occur. In a few cases we have noted the probability of a free agent signing (such as Jack Clark going to the Red Sox), but we have generally avoided useless predictions about events that will be fully settled by draft day, anyway. Read your newspapers to see what happens, and read WINNING ROTISSERIE BASEBALL monthly for analyses of which players will be impacted, and how, whenever something changes. (See page 330.)

AMERICAN LEAGUE CATCHERS

IN GENERAL:

Same as last year, we do not see great buying opportunities in the top ranks of A.L. catchers for 1991. The best candidates like Fisk and Parrish are all aging and injury-prone, likely to attract high bids from people who expect peak performances, but offering little upward potential. Why take the risk? Look for your offensive guns at other positions, and consider taking TWO cheap catchers this year, instead of the traditional $1 on one and $8 or $10 on the other. The best opportunities among catchers are all in the $1 to $2 range anyway.

BALTIMORE

The free agency of Mickey Tettleton was one of the few fascinating questions in the catching picture when the winter meetings drew to a close. By the time you read this analysis, you will know Tettleton's affiliation, so we won't waste your time by stating the reasons why he would return to Baltimore, and why he might leave. Simply stated, The Orioles really wanted to re-sign Mickey Tettleton.

To roll out the first of many "I told you so" items, we may as well begin with the first team and the first position. From the 1990 book:

"Tettleton is NOT the hitter that he looked like in early 1989. He has shown double-digit homer output twice before, but we do not believe that he was suddenly transformed (at age 29) into a force at the plate. Fruit Loops' performance in early '89 was a fluke. After the All Star break, he produced only 6 HR and 14 RBI in 129 at bats. Even if you allow for improvement assuming his injuries are behind him, and if you believe that a guy who hits only .240 in the minors can become a .260 hitter in the majors (yes, it's possible), you still cannot expect much more from Tettleton than about .250, 15 HR and 55 RBI in 1990." Tettleton turned in .223-15-51. Once again this year, somebody in your league is going to have higher expectations, and you should let them have Tettleton.

Frank Robinson took a lot of heat for not utilizing Chris Hoiles in the majors last year, and Robinson deserved every bit of criticism. The O's did not field a lineup saturated with talent.

Hoiles is about the last residual asset from the Fred Lynn trade. After supplanting Carl Nichols (.228 in 1988) at Rochester, Hoiles produced .245 with 10 HR and 51 RBI in 1989. He led the Eastern League in HR in 1988, and at age 26 he is a very good bet for major league hitting success. Even if he gets only 300 AB, he should produce double digit homers.

Hoiles may need just a little more strike zone discipline, which is generally learned, not inherited. Do not let his .111 average from last September 1989 or his .190 average last year worry you. Overlooked by Baseball America in their ratings (partly because the International League had catchers like Francisco Cabrera and Brian Dorsett in 1989) Hoiles could still be a a sleeper and deserves watching in March.

Bob Melvin is nice little sleeper waiting to blossom, especially if Tettleton flies the coop, and/or if you don't care about batting average. Melvin has produced 11 HR before (the same career high that Tettleton had before his explosive 1989 season), and Melvin is a year younger than Tettleton. Melvin was a $1 catcher (or received no bids) in most auctions last year. He is better than a lot of the other $1 possibilities.

Hoiles' understudy at Rochester, Jeff Tackett, was absolutely nothing to write home about (.239-4-33-4 in 306 AB) and Hagerstown backstops Doug Robbins, Craig Faulkner, Mike Eberle, and Dan Simonds were likewise unimpressive.

Lary Bump:

Hoiles was simply too good for International League pitching last year — .348, 18 HR, 56 RBI in 74 games. If his season hadn't been interrupted by call-ups to Baltimore, we might be talking about Chris Hoiles, Triple Crown winner. He batted only .190 in 63 ABs for the Birds, but he also started slowly in the Eastern and International leagues. The real question isn't his bat, but his throwing arm. It's probably good enough to get by in the AL, unless Rickey Henderson or the Yankees come to town. The 26-year-old is a converted 1B, but Randy Milligan is blocking his way there. Hoiles' immediate future rests on whether the Orioles resign free agent Mickey Tettleton. They may need Hoiles' powerful bat in their lineup as a catcher or a right-handed DH. [Darren Daulton's new contract helps Hoiles indirectly, because the price of catchers just went up, somewhat diminishing the chance that Baltimore will end up signing Tettleton.]

BOSTON

Tony Pena got off to a great start within the Fenway Confines, and then leveled off in 1990. A little-noticed attribute is that Pena stole 8 bases last year, all in the second half. Can you imagine 16 SB in 1991? Not likely, but tantalizing. If there is a Red Sox fan in your league, Pena will probably be overbid; he is a clubhouse leader. If there are no Sox-ophiles bidding against you, groan something like, "Oh gosh, isn't he 40 years old?" when his name comes up, and you might get a bargain. His true age is 34, young enough to hit at Fenway. And young enough to run!

Fred Percival:

If not for Pena's arrival, the first string catcher at the Fens in 1991 might have been John Marzano. He failed to hit during his first trip to the show in 1988, but had a good effect on the pitchers. He sulked through the season after being sent down, failed to hit at Pawtucket in both '88 and '89, and caused a lot of people to write him off. But he adjusted his attitude in late 1989, and worked harder. John got to see a bit of action with the big club in September 1989, and more last year, and he made a good impression. Marzano's teammates from the 1984 Olympics have generally done well by now.

CALIFORNIA

The revival of Lance Parrish in 1990 didn't surprise us. Last year's comment is worth recalling, still valid: Contrary to popular belief, Lance Parrish did not suffer a terrible collapse during his two years with the Phillies. After 10 years in the AL, he had per year averages of 21 HR and 70 RBI per year. In Philadelphia, Parrish produced 17 HR and 67 RBI in 1987, then 15 HR and 60 RBI in 1988. There was a slight decline, but nothing dramatic. The stigma of "collapse" was assigned to Lance within his first few weeks in Philadelphia, when he was off to a slow start. Early-season numbers always get blown out of proportion and linger in memory.

If there is any real statistical evidence that Lance did not like hitting in Philadelphia, it was his lifetime low .215 batting average in 1988. But this came after a .245 year in 1987, and .245 is not much worse than what he had been doing in the AL. If you believe that Parrish hit .215 while trying his best, you may as well attribute the low average to old age as to dislike of Philadelphia, and devalue him accordingly. If, on the other hand, you believe that Parrish simply stopped trying during 1988, as some fans accuse, then you expected a return to about .240 in 1989, as we did, and the good numbers of 1990 followed naturally.

John Orton is interesting for 1991. His main problem in the past has been that he strikes out too much, lacking discipline and strike zone knowledge. If he shows a good Walk/SO ratio at Palm Springs in March, take a closer look.

We warned you off Bill Schroeder last year, and he's now gone.

Other than Orton and Tingley, the farm system holds nothing of interest for the next couple of years. At the Triple A level, Doug Davis and Mike Knapp are apparently continuing to get more enjoyment from Moosehead beer than they get from PCL pitching at Edmonton. Davis had the top power numbers among this pair, with only 2 HR and 23 RBI last year; in 1989 he had 3 HR and 22 RBI. At least he's consistent. In 1990 Davis also collected 18 RBI at AA Midland, where teammates Knapp and Dave Sturdivant were also unimpressive.

Lary Bump:

The Angels aren't going to re-sign Bill Schroeder, which gives John Orton, regarded as a top defensive catcher, a clear path to work his way into the lineup to replace Lance Parrish. Lance had his busiest, most productive season in five years, and isn't simply going to go away. But he is 34, so the 25-year-old Orton, who batted .241 in 50 games at Edmonton last season, should get significant playing time.

Ron Tingley, like Parrish and Orton, bats right-handed, so he has no platoon advantage. Also he is 32 years old. He batted .267 in almost the same number of ABs as Orton at Edmonton. Not much future for Tingley.

Mark Dennis Cladis:

Former 1 pick John Orton reminds people of Bob Boone in his conduct of the game, and may be ready in 1991. Fading prospect Ron Tingley has been cut loose by the Mariners and Braves, and stood in line behind Allanson and Skinner at Cleveland, so he cannot be too highly regarded. Tingley will be 32 years old this year; his place in history as a career minor leaguer seems assured. He bats right, like Parrish, so is not even a serious candidate to platoon. His 9 HR and 58 RBI in TWO YEARS at Colorado Springs are not the kind of numbers that push aside younger players with solid big league experience.

CHICAGO WHITE SOX

The White Sox catching picture is pretty clear: Fisk, Karkovice, and Matt Stark, in that order. Stark is a very good hitter, but will likely spend most of 1991 at Vancouver, unless something unusual happens (a great spring training wouldn't hurt). The Sox didn't really have a 3 catcher in 1990; Jerry Willard appeared in one game, and that was it. Stark appeared in eight games last year, as a DH/PH.

Carlton Fisk is way too old to be a regular catcher, but that hasn't stopped him during the past five years or so, so it shouldn't stop him in 1991, either. Note that we have been predicting Fisk's downfall every year for four consecutive years. Changing our tune may change Carlton's luck.

Ron Karkovice is waiting in the wings to take on more of the catching duties whenever called upon, and he is definitely ready. Karko has improved his game markedly, especially in offense. He has become a more disciplined hitter, and with his outstanding defensive skills he could be a 1 catcher for any team.

Fisk has overcome injury, age, being relegated to the outfield, and a number of other problems to become one of the best catchers ever. Reminiscent of Nolan Ryan's ageless quality, Fisk was still ranked the top catcher in the American League by the free agent rankings in 1990, and was similarly regarded by Rotisserians. Last year we said, "Look for one more productive year out of Fisk," and we'll put ditto marks under that line again this year.

Karkovice has the dubious distinction of once having a season batting average (.071) lower than his counterpart catcher's uniform number (72). But Ron Karkovice is the White Sox catcher of the future. He was handed the Chisox starting catcher role in the spring of 1987. Ron had just finished a highly successful 1986 campaign, jumping from Birmingham to the majors. At Birmingham he hit .282 with 20 HR in 319 at bats. You may think everyone hits 20 HR at Birmingham. Not true. Ron Karkovice has some latent offensive potential, that shined through at times during 1990. He is not a great hitter, and never will be, but he can put the bat on the ball in a good, workmanlike manner. As we told you last year, his .264 average in 1989 was a more accurate measure than his .071 or .174 of the previous two seasons. Even before the disastrous 1987 season started, the White Sox announced that 23 year-old Ron was their starting catcher. So Ron relaxed. He got a good tan. He signed autographs and chatted with fans, even during ''work time'' on the field. He was, stated briefly, the embodiment of all the reasons why fans come to spring training. And he played well, too: no big numbers at the plate, but he was making contact and hitting line drives.

Karkovice' great strength is defense. His arm is a gun: a powerful, hairtrigger, sharp-shooting cannon, in fact. Way back in that spring of 1987, Karkovice threw out Vince Coleman stealing second, by three feet! Then he threw out Tom Lawless by six feet, and at next opportunity he threw out Coleman again, making twice in one day. Granted, Coleman may have been experimenting with his jump and slide techniques, but the fact is: Karkovice did twice, in 45 minutes, what the entire Mets organization couldn't do until 1990: And Karko did not even use a pitchout to do it. The Mets, by the way, are not likely to catch Coleman again until 1995 at the earliest; they finally found a way to prevent him from stealing against them: give him money!

Karkovice is definitely learning to hit, at least well enough to play 130 games per year behind the plate. He is too valuable a commodity to keep off the field. The American League (especially) is beginning to think of Catcher as a DEFENSIVE position, sort of like a pitcher used to be, in the batting order. Managers in the AL have some room for such thinking, because they do not have to put their pitcher in the lineup, another spin-off effect from the disgusting DH rule. Gradually, AL managers are coming to think that a great defensive catcher who can hit .190 is a good man to have on the field. (Forty years from now, will we see the AL experiment with a ''second DH'' to hit for the catcher?)

What does all this mean for rotisserie players?

(1) Expect Fisk to play fewer games, even if he is healthy and productive.

(2) Expect Karkovice to play more games, maybe as many as 100, even if he hits poorly. If you think he can hit around .250 (like he did with the Chisox in 1986 and again in 1989 and 1990 — and I think he can do it in 1991) that makes Karkovice an asset. If you think his .216 lifetime BA is a true indicator, then you have to expect that 350 at bats could hurt you, bad, and you should keep him off your roster. We say buy him. He was very popular among owners who went on to win their leagues last year, and rarely cost more than $1 or $2.

Jon Dunkle:

Karkovice spent much of the 1989 season working with the White Sox hitting guru, Walt Hrniak, and Ron's natural abilities began to overcome his historic difficulties with major league pitching. He played in 71 games in '89 and hit .264, and the Sox used him once as their DH in 1990. Defensively, Karkovice is spectacular and with his improved hitting, the White Sox should have no qualms about increasing his playing time.

CLEVELAND

Sandy Alomar, Jr. finally got his chance in the big leagues in 1990. Unfortunately, after 2 years of hype and rumors and high expectations, he cost an average of $14 in last year's auctions, and that's about as much as he could have been expected to earn. If you were smart enough (and able by your league rules) to pick him as a speculation when he was still San Diego property (as I recommended) you are set for several years with a prime bargain. If he came into your league via the 1990 draft, he will probably be returned to the available pool every year or two for the rest of his career.

Farmhands Tom Magrann and Marc Sullivan (Colorado) and Ed Hearn (yes, he's still alive), Robby Wine, Carlos Matos, Barry Blackwell (Canton) were all utterly unattractive for our purposes. Lefty-hitting Allen Liebert at Canton produced 9 HR and 45 RBI with a harmless BA.

Steve Goldman:

No competition here: Sandy Alomar, Jr. is the man. He was the American League's top rookie last year, exhibiting the ability to catch, handle pitchers, throw out runners and hit for average with some power. I have only one message for him: For goodness sake, Sandy, learn to take a few more pitches! Even if he doesn't, though, he's still a fine player with a very promising career in front of him.

Joel Skinner is the backup, and he's good at that role. The Indians feel comfortable with him there, and will use him occasionally to give Alomar a breather.

Bill Gray:

Sandy Alomar, Jr.? It is rare that a "franchise" rookie lives up to the expectations of his team, fans and media. Much was expected of Alomar, and he actually delivered more. The most compelling component of Alomar's rookie year was consistency. Breaking down first and second half stats show Alomar taking a .291 BA to the All-Star game ("break" doesn't apply because he was the starter for the AL). He finished the season at .290. The nine homers were split 4 and 5. In short there were no spikes on the graph. Unfortunately, all the pre-season hype made him expensive before he even landed in Cleveland. Do you WANT to allocate 10% of your hitting budget for a catcher?

Joel Skinner backs up Alomar. Watch for a trade because some teams would love to have Skinner as their EVERY DAY catcher because of the way he handles the pitchers and throws out runners. As you know, calling a game and catching baserunners isn't a priority in Rotisserie.

Summary: If Alomar is available in your draft or auction, you can cause some other owner to waste some money. Keep in mind that Alomar is likely to be the most expensive catcher in AL auctions. He isn't as valuable as Fisk was last year, but should catch up by the time Carlton is 50. Anyway, if you look at John's valuation of catchers you'll see several who are likely to produce upwards of 80% of Alomar's offense and can be acquired for 50-60% of his price. Don't get suckered into a spending frenzy.

DETROIT

UPDATE — Mickey Tettleton's arrival hurts Mark Salas.

Last year we steered a number of people in the right direction: "Mike Heath is a relatively risk-free component. He should cost next to nothing and will be unlikely to hurt your roster badly. If he goes into a serious slump, you can expect to see his playing time and at bats diminish rapidly, so you can figure him as a .230 hitter with 180 or fewer AB's, or a .260 hitter with up to 300 AB. Both of the preceding scenarios are better than a catcher who gets 440 AB and hits an albatross number like .205." Heath hit .270 last year.

The tough comment on Heath is that he hit .323 in the first half of the season, and .209 in the second half, numbers tending to support a theory that Heath will get worn out if he has to carry the #1 catcher role all year.

Lary Bump:

Phil Clark, 22, once considered the Tigers' catcher of the future, had a lost year in 1990 and was last seen puttering around the Toledo outfield and around the Mud Hens' bat rack as a DH. If he can put his career back on course, he might be considered for 1992.

In the meantime, Rich Rowland, 24, also a right-handed batter, has climbed steadily through the Detroit system, a step at a time. Rookie Class Bristol in '88; Class A Fayetteville in '89; Double-A London, Triple-A Toledo and even Detroit, all last year. He batted .286 at London and .260 at Toledo, and totaled 15 HR and 52 RBI with the Tigers' top two farms. Detroit may give him a longer look this year and let Mike Heath develop his versatility at other positions.

KANSAS CITY

If you followed our advice last year, you let somebody else have Bob Boone, and made a small, speculative investment in Mike MacFarlane. Both ideas worked just fine.

Mike Macfarlane, at the age of 24, had earned the Royals starting catcher job in 1988. (In fact, he was only 23 on opening day.) The basic situation SEEMED to be great confidence in Mike's defensive skills and capabilities, with some slight doubt about his ability to hit major league pitching. At Omaha in 1987, he had shown a little power (13 HR and 50 RBI), but after three years in pro ball, he had never hit over .269. Offense remained a possible question.

Mike had apparently silenced his critics and skeptics by mid-July of his rookie year when he was hitting a solid .270 with a few homers, and he looked headed for a 50 RBI season, not too shabby for a very young catcher. Meanwhile he had been charged with only two errors all season, so the glove looked OK, too.

But the Royals, in mid-1988, were doing VERY poorly, and Manager John Wathan, an ex-catcher, decided to blame MacFarlane for calling a bad game and handling the pitchers wrong. There is self-evident foolishness when an ex-catcher manager claims that his team (with seasoned pitchers) has gone bad on account of poor pitch selection, but that was the story. Wathan decided that Mike Macfarlane should pack his bags and return to Omaha, which Macfarlane dutifully did. At Omaha, he hit .237. Do you think he may have been a little demoralized?

With all this background information, you can easily understand why the Royals (who, before 1990 always avoided the free agent market) suddenly jumped into the auction for Bob Boone's services, and emerged as the highest bidder.

Marc Bowman:

Mike MacFarlane was a fine $1 catcher in 1990, but don't go bidding him up to the premium level just because he has a full time job now. His power doesn't reach over the fences, his .255 BA for 1990 could be a high water mark, and he runs like a catcher. Only in the RBI column does he add much to your roster.

Rey Palacios has been released, so the new backup catcher will probably come from the rookie crop. Brent Mayne is more highly regarded than Tim Spehr. Mayne won't hit much even if he plays a lot, and Spehr isn't likely to get much playing time unless there is an injury.

Lary Bump:

Brent Mayne is a 23-year-old whose pro career before 1990 consisted of seven games. After a solid season (.267, 2, 61) at Memphis, he shot to the big leagues in September. With the Royals' general overhaul dropping Bob Boone and Rey Palacios from the roster, there is a place for Mayne. He could be a left-handed complement to Mike Macfarlane, who hasn't received too many votes of confidence from Duke Wathan.

If Mayne isn't ready, an intermediate measure

could be right-handed batter Tim Spehr (pronounced Spear). He didn't hit much (.225, 6, 34) at Omaha, but he is a good defensive catcher with an excellent arm.

MILWAUKEE

B.J. Surhoff gets about as many at bats as any AL catcher, and he steals more bases than any of his peers. Just on the basis of youth, playing time, health, and lack of competition, Surhoff is a great commodity. But Surhoff is also a potentially GREAT hitter, just 26 years old, and he can RUN. To be a winner, you need players with clear upward potential. If you are planning to spend some money on a good catcher, this guy is your best bet. After a somewhat disappointing 1989 and just a fair 1990, B.J. should be cheap, and he is an excellent speculation for 1991.

Back in 1989 The Analyst took a stand on Tim McIntosh, saying that Baseball America had erred by not including him in their list of Brewers Top Ten Prospects. And last year, we predicted that McIntosh would appear with the Brewers some time during 1990. Hitting hasn't carried McIntosh very far very fast, however, and his defense still causes anxiety — although he has improved markedly in the last two years.

McIntosh is an excellent possibility to be that one player who can give you about 10 HR for $1 or $2 in 1991. It isn't likely, but it could happen. Since McIntosh's hitting isn't going to hurt you, he would make an excellent backup if you end up owning Surhoff. I like McIntosh somewhat more than Alan Boodman does (see below), but if Surhoff stays healthy all year, Mac can't accumulate too much value.

Lary Bump:

Speaking of good defensive catchers, the 26-year-old McIntosh isn't one. But he sure can hit. In each of his four full minor league seasons, he has had an average between .283 and .302, 15-20 HR, 74-93 RBI and an OBP between .346 and .375. Like every other Brewer, it seems, he bats right-handed. He will not dislodge B.J. Surhoff, but McIntosh can fill in behind the plate on occasion and DH.

Alan Boodman:

You sure know what you get when you pick up B. J. Surhoff, but the question becomes: Is that what you really want? Surhoff has to be one of the most consistent players around, but it would be nicer if he could sacrifice a little consistency to play at a higher level. B. J.'s 1990 season showed a little improvement from his previous two campaigns, as he tacked on 30 points to his batting average and inched forward in just about all other areas as well. Surhoff's BB/SO ratio returned to where it was in his rookie year, which is also a good sign.

B. J. is a medium-average, low-power, contact hitter who has more speed than any other catcher save Craig Biggio. Even with four full major league seasons under his belt, he will only be 26 in 1991, so further development isn't out of the question, and the next couple of years could be big ones for him.

Surhoff is not a small fellow (6'1'' and 190), and he may be able to generate some additional power as he ages, but that's what they've always said about Mike Scioscia too. Scioscia and Surhoff are quite similar players (so are Surhoff and Biggio), and it looks like B. J. just might go on to have a career similar to Scioscia.

If you're looking to the long-term, only Sandy Alomar (in the AL) seems to be in the same ballpark. Many other AL catchers are either past their prime (Parrish, Fisk, Boone, Pena) or just aren't that good anyway (Heath, Petralli, Valle/Bradley, Geren). A couple of others (Steinbach, Harper, maybe Borders) look like they can play, but who knows when they'll get around to it (Steinbach), or how long they can keep it up (Borders, Harper).

Tim McIntosh is supposed to be the hot rookie who's going to make a major-league impact this season, but don't be surprised if it doesn't turn out that way. First of all, if you've read this far, you know that the Brewers already have a catcher, and that catcher is going to play at least 70 percent of the time. Second, McIntosh (26 in '91) is only a few months younger than the man he's trying to replace, so there won't be any changes made on the basis of age. Third, how likely is he to duplicate (or even come close to) his minor-league numbers, which are fairly good?

Remember that throughout Tim's entire minor league career, he has had the benefit of playing in extremely good hitter's ballparks. You can't simply take his El Paso and Denver stats at face value.

In 1991, McIntosh projects to play maybe 50 games, with a little power, some doubles, and a below-average BA.

Rick Wrona has been signed from the Cubs as insurance, but insurance is something that's generally used only in the event of a disaster. Wrona and McIntosh both bat right-handed, so the Brewers might be inclined to choose one or the other as the regular backup, and relegate the other to obscurity on the bench or in the minors for most of 1991.

MINNESOTA

Brian Harper solidified his standing as one of the top offensive catchers in the league, with a .294 BA and 54 RBI last year. While the AL is gradually coming to treat catcher as a position for defensive specialists, Harper offers the probability of decent output, even at age 31.

Back in 1989, many people got excited about Derek Parks, now age 22. The Yankees mentioned some trade interest in Parks, and the media went overboard, comparing him (favorably) to Alomar Jr. But Parks' abbreviated season at Orlando in 1989 did nothing to budge our original assessment: He is a fine all-around athlete, full of potential, but still has a lot to learn and is not ready for the majors. And he his just .177 for Portland in 1990.

Lenny Webster, although three years older than Parks, is following in Derek's footsteps. Webster succeeded Parks as Midwest League MVP in 1988. Webster produced .288, 11 HR, 87 RBI, and 3 SB's. In comparison, Parks in his MVP year 1987 at Kenosha put up numbers of .247, 24 HR, 94 RBI and 1 SB. Webster is just as far away from the majors as Parks is, as Lary elaborates . . .

Larry Bump:

One of the disadvantages of getting so much more information on the minors these days is that we hear too much too soon about some people. Lenny Webster is a case in point. Even before he batted .288 and drove in 87 runs in the Midwest League in '88, he had been touted as the Twins' catcher of the future, and those stats firmly cast him in that mold. Maybe Webster is the Twins next catcher, but last year he was still down in Double-A, where he had fair success (.262, 8, 71). He also has a .308 career major league average in 26 ABs, but that doesn't mean he'll have a big-league job this year. He'll most likely start at Portland, but if either of the 31-year-old Twins catchers, Brian Harper or Junior Ortiz, falters, Webster could make a pre-September visit to the HumpDome, Webster, like Harper and Ortiz, bats right-handed, and he is 26.

Paul Clements:

The Twins don't have a replacement for Gary Gaetti at 3B. Brian Harper came up as a third baseman originally, and he made a few appearances at that position in 1990. If the Twins can't keep Gaetti, Harper might be tried at third for 1991. That means that Junior Ortiz could emerge with a bigger share of the catching chores. The Twins don't see Ortiz as an everyday catcher, however. He would be used mainly against right-handed pitching, depending on who's pitching for the Twins. Manager Tom Kelly likes to arrange pitcher-catcher partnerships.

Tim Laudner has been working out, hoping for a comeback. Laudner had approached the Twins last year, willing to work his way back through the minor leagues, but the organization didn't want to upset their farm system, so they had him wait until 1991.

NEW YORK YANKEES

One of the Yankee coaches told me last September, "It will be real interesting to see who comes back from spring training [1991] with the catcher job." He had just been talking enthusiastically about Matt Nokes' progress in certain defensive skills, and the implication was clear. Look for Nokes to emerge with more playing time.

Since banging the rabbit ball of 1987 for 32 homers, Nokes hasn't done much. But he is still only 27. His swing can be fine-tuned to take advantage of Yankee Stadium. And despite the fall-off from a great rookie season, he has still averaged 17 homers per year during four seasons in the major leagues, and he hasn't been playing full time. I see plenty of upward potential compared to the Nokes of 1989-1990.

Bob Geren is good enough to be the #1 catcher on most major league teams, but his offense really suffered in 1990. One of his former minor league roommates told me that Geren never could hit a good slider, and that major league scouts became increasingly aware of this little deficiency since mid-1989. Geren himself can't explain the sophomore slump, except that he felt a loss of ability to hit the outside pitch to right field. Let's see: Outside pitch? Can't hit it where he wants? Slider? Hmmm.

Geren's defensive skills are outstanding, but that won't help you unless he gets the BA up to a safer level. His power hitting is still fine. He has 17 career homers in just 492 at bats.

Geren and Nokes are both classic cases for second-half analysis of rookie stats. They both hit well over .300 in the first half of their rookie seasons, and both hit .250 in the second half. Both were overvalued in Rotisserie auctions in their sophomore years, as bidders looked only at full-year numbers (.288 in the case of Geren, .289 for Nokes as a rookie). Nokes has leveled off as a .250 hitter. Geren? Well, he just has to learn how to hit that slider.

Dave Sax, who hit .313 backing up Brian Dorsett at Columbus in 1989, tailed off to .249 with 19 RBI at Columbus last year, and no longer looks like a prospect.

Daniel Stone:

Bob Geren's defensive steadiness should assure him of a significant role. Even if he plays only against lefties, the Yankees see so much lefty pitching that he could get 200 AB's without getting any other playing time. Last year, Yankee catchers got 192 at bats against southpaws, not counting what Jim Leyritz did.

Defensively, Geren showed a great deal of improvement in 1990, and the Yankees kept playing him even after his offense became stagnant. The Yankees waited for him to pull out of his slump, but he never did it. Geren's poor minor league batting averages indicate that his 1989 numbers will never be repeated, so don't look for a comeback in 1991. He is probably incapable of hitting over .240 again, although he could poke 10 home runs.

A platoon role could easily make Geren more valuable in Rotisserie, because his batting average would be safer. He hit .254 against lefties last year, and .284 as a rookie. Those numbers won't hurt you, while a .220 BA from a full timer can put a dent in your standings.

Matt Nokes continued to work on his defense in the instructional league, and should get a nice share of playing time at catcher and DH combined.

Rick Cerone was acquired as a backup, but can do more when he's healthy. He had surgery for a knee injury early last year and missed over half the season. Cerone feels that the surgery was unnecessary and, at age 37, a long stay on the DL doesn't look too good in your medical history. Don't expect much in 1991.

Brian Dorsett was a September experiment. His work was adequate, but the Yankees are hoping that platoon/utility player Jim Leyritz can be the

#3 catcher in addition to his other duties. Leyritz disappointed the team by failing to complete his winter league work as a catcher. Leyritz and Yankee management have somewhat different opinions of just how advanced Leyritz is as a defensive catcher. Jim thinks he is good major league material already. Leyritz was, of course, mainly a catcher at Columbus in 1989.

OAKLAND

Terry Steinbach has always held promise of bigger numbers, but 1990 was his third consecutive disappointing season for those who are waiting for him to break out. Even last year, I said I was beginning to think he is destined to play perpetually below his ability, due to injury or bad luck or whatever. Somebody is likely to overbid on Steinbach in almost every league, because of his All Star background and association with post-season play. My advice is to let someone else pay the price if the bidding in your league goes up to full "fair value." Last year Steinbach sold for an average of $13, and often in the $15 to $20 range. If that happens in your league, take a $1 stiff as a backstop, and use the extra money to chase a real star.

The Ron Hassey of 1985 and 1986 was a rotisserie dream player: an inexpensive backup catcher with reasonable production and a nice, high batting average. Since then, he has been more mediocre at best. Ron will celebrate his 38th birthday in Phoenix this year (assuming that he doesn't sign with a new team and that that A's invite him in one form or another). Age has already been a factor in his career. For two years I have felt pretty safe in predicting that Hassey would slip a little further downward, and he has followed suit very kindly. In 1991, expect even more deterioration, if he hangs on at all.

Lary Bump:

Troy Afenir is a 27-year-old right-handed batter who just keeps showing up. He had a good year, for him, at Tacoma last season (.249, a team-leading 15 HR, 47 RBI). The Athletics were well set at catcher at the end of '90, with Terry Steinbach, Ron Hassey and Jamie Quirk. But Quirk was the only one resigned after the winter meetings, so Afenir should get a major league chance. This is another sign of the lack of depth in the Oakland organization. Afenir toiled at Huntsville in 1989 and produced 13 HR and 45 RBI in only 225 AB's. He is no defensive gem, and has frequently filled the role of DH in the minors.

SEATTLE

Scott Bradley and David Valle were both disappointments in 1990. Bradley has always been a "safe" Rotisserie catcher because of his decent batting average. He had his two most prolific seasons, 342 AB and 335 AB, in 1987 and 1988. The most accurate prediction that I made about Bradley last year, was that he would appear on a number of good Rotisserie rosters, and this prediction looked better in mid-season than it did at year-end.

Valle has always offered the good possibility of HR output from a catcher who tends to be overlooked and inexpensive. They both failed at these Rotisserie specialties last year, and they didn't thrill people in "real" baseball, either.

Valle took a dive in the second half of 1989, and never recovered. It was one of those seasons that could have worked out well, but injuries and other factors worked against him. I had an uneasy feeling about Valle last year at this time, and said so in these pages. He hits left-handed pitchers well, with a career average around .290 against them, while having great difficulty against righties. If the Mariners moved him into a strict platoon role, it could enhance his Rotisserie value.

Farmhand Bill McGuire has never impressed anyone with the bat. In two trials with the big team, he hit just .182, and at Calgary in 1990 he hit just .229. AA Williamsport catcher Chris Howard hit just .237 with 5 HR.

Tony Formo, 1991 Left Field Baseball Extravaganza:

Beltin' Backstop Dave Valle (.328 OBA, .331 SA) had a lowly .214 BA and lot of time on the DL, which has been his pattern throughout his career. He is a good defensive catcher, however and likely to play if healthy. Scott Bradley (.264 OBA, .275 SA) had a lousy year offensively. Mariner management would have been a lot more intelligent to seek a catcher who can stay healthy and hit, rather than signing Pete O'Brien.

TEXAS

UPDATE — The Rangers acquired Mark Parent, who will play against left-handed pitching and will pop a few homers.

The Rangers haven't been the best place to look for catching talent in recent years, and 1991 will be more of the same.

Bob Hazlewood:

The Rangers will have Mark Parent, Geno Petralli, Mike Stanley, and Chad Kreuter (not again?) on opening day, with Parent and Petralli the leaders for playing time. At age 30 last year, Petralli ended three consecutive years of .280 to .300 hitting, dropping back to his 1986 BA of .255. Don't expect anything outstanding from Petralli in 1991, and don't expect much from Stanley or Kreuter under any circumstances.

For the long term, the Rangers really like the kid Ivan Rodriguez, who hit .281 with decent RBI output at A-League Charlotte last year. Tom Grieve says he has "all the tools." He is not a prospect for 1991, however.

Lary Bump:

Of several 1991 catching prospects with pretty good bats, the 24-year-old Bill Haselman may be the best. He batted .319 with 18 HR and 80 RBI at Tulsa last season. The Rangers already have let John Russell go, so that leaves Mike Stanley and Chad Kreuter as right-handed competition to Haselman. Geno Petralli is the only Texas catcher who bats from the left side. Haselman is likely to start the season at Oklahoma City, but it isn't far from there to Texas if this shaky catching corps needs help.

TORONTO

The main question about catchers in Toronto is whether lefty-hitting Greg Myers will take any playing time away from right-handed hitter Pat Borders. Borders was everything that a Rotisserie owner could want from a backstop in 1990 (.286 and 15 homers). He cost an average of only $4 to $5 in 1990. People were still focused on Borders' 1989 stats, and hadn't yet thought through the implication of Ernie Whitt leaving. I think Borders will keep his at bats in 1991. He hit over .280 against both righties and lefties in 1990. Myers hit just .174 against lefties and .242 against righties. There is no platoon advantage in using a .242 LHH when you can use a .288 RHH against right-handed pitching. Granted, Myers is only 25 and will improve some, but Pat Borders is age 28 and should be able to hang right in there around the level that he attained in 1990.

J. L. Feinstein:

When "Stand" Pat Gillick overhauled the Blue Jays at the Winter Meetings, he left only two positions manned by the same players who ended the season there. At 3B he had Kelly Gruber, and at catcher he held onto his two-man platoon of Pat Borders and Greg Myers and with good reason.

While everyone knows about Gruber . . . not a lot has been written about the Blue Jays catcher corps. When you think of top offensive catchers in the AL, the names that come readily to mind are Carlton Fisk, Sandy Alomar, Lance Parrish, Mickey Tettleton,& Terry Steinbach.

Yet, when you go to the numbers, Border/Myers rank with those present and former All-Stars in terms of offensive production. The Blue Jay catchers combined to hit a solid .265, with 20 HR and 71 RBI. Of the catchers mentioned above, only

Parrish hit more HRs (24) and none drove in more runs.

For 1991, not a lot is expected to change. They should start the season platooning and end up with Borders getting perhaps 55-60% of the plate appearances.

If Myers can stay healthy, I'd expect him to show a bit more pop than the 22 RBIs he had last season. He was swinging the bat well when he went on the DL last year and never seemed to recover his stroke once he returned.

Borders seized the opportunity created by Myers absence and responded with 15 dings. . . two-thirds of which came before the All-Star break. The Blue Jays would be quite satisfied if he was able to post those numbers again.

Lary Bump:

Carlos Diaz is a 26-year-old right-handed hitting catcher who has plodded his way through the Toronto farm system. His high-water mark was a .250 average at Knoxville in '89. Last season he batted .203 in 77 games at Syracuse, with one of his nine career homers. He went up to the big club in September strictly as a defensive catcher. His most realistic goal might be to grow up to be Orlando Mercado.

NATIONAL LEAGUE CATCHERS

ATLANTA

Bad franchises like the Braves provide excellent case studies for Rotisserie management. Rule 701: Do not pursue power-hitting catchers who are past their prime. Rule 728: Do not trade Stolen Bases for Homers if there is a Low Batting Average involved. Rule 749: Do not trade large quantities of Saves for ANYTHING! The Braves violated all these rules simultaneously when they gave up Steve Bedrosian and Milt Thompson for Ozzie Virgil. Ozzie is gone now, of course, but the lesson remains cogent.

In 1989, the Braves chased Jody Davis down the drain. Then last year they landed one of the great washouts of 1990, Ernie Whitt. While waiting for Whitt to recover from a broken thumb, the Braves launched a youth movement built around 29-year-old rookie Greg Olson

Readers of Winning Rotisserie Baseball were advised to drop Greg Olson when he reached peak value just before the All Star break. Olson had been a .235 hitter at AAA Portland in 1989, with a long minor league history of weak hitting. When he had a .290 BA in mid 1990 with Atlanta, it was obviously a fluke.

Kelly Mann keeps appearing on lists of top rookies for 1991. His only virtue is defense. If you put him on your Rotisserie roster, you will suffer.

Marc Bowman:

Whitt's contract was not renewed by the Braves for 1991. They feel that Greg Olson, Jimmy Kremers, Kelly Mann and others can carry the load into the future. This group certainly can't do any worse than Whitt did in 1990. After the All Star break last year, Olson showed why he has been a career minor leaguer. His excellent play in the first half was an aberration. Expect him to pick up where he left off with his second half 1990 stats (.227-1-11).

Jimmy Kremers had trouble against all kinds of major league pitching. Even the mediocre pitchers made him look bad. Kremers is still developing. There is plenty of room for improvement with a .110 career major league batting average. Kremers hit .232 at AAA Richmond last year, and .235 at AA Greenville. Don't expect much of anything.

The one good-hitting prospect, Francisco Cabrera, has been used primarily at first base, but he will likely be playing more at catcher (only three games last year) now that Sid Bream has knocked everybody down a notch at 1B. In 1989, Cabrera was the fifth best hitter (.300, 9 HR, 72 RBI) in the International League, where pitchers dominate. He is only 24, and headed upward.

Lary Bump:

Braves catchers' love affair with the Mendoza line continued in 1990. Ernie was at his Whitt's end after batting .172. The catching platoon of the future batted .143 from the right side (Kelly Mann) and .110 from the left (Jimmy Kremers). Mann, 23, may win the job with his throwing arm alone; he threw out about two-thirds of those who attempted to steal on him. But his '90 offensive statistics (.316 in 50 games at Greenville, .202 in 63 at Richmond) suggest he should spend most of this season in Triple-A. Kremers, 25, also played

63 games at Richmond, batting .232. He'll probably start the season in Atlanta as the backup to 30-year-old Greg Olson, but it may not be too long before Mann overtakes both of them. There isn't a good Rotisserie pick in the bunch.

CHICAGO CUBS

The Cubs spent the winter trying to trade Damon Berryhill. For example, they wanted to give Berryhill and Dwight Smith to the Rangers for Pete Incaviglia, but had to settle for George Bell instead.

The following advice is still current, so I repeat it verbatim from the 1989 book:

"If you are going to have a backup catcher on your NL Rotisserie roster, you may as well have one from Chicago. Look what would have happened last year [1988] if you had just used Wrigley Field as the criterion to select a backup catcher: you would have got Damon Berryhill for $1. Lloyd McClendon is no Berryhill, but he has a little pop in his bat (led the American Association in homers in 1986). For $1 you should be able to get Wrigley Field, a minor league home run leader, and the ever-present possibility that a front-line catcher can get hurt and create Rotisserie value for his replacement." McClendon, by the way, would have given you 12 HR and 40 RBI for your $1 in 1989.

Adam Stein:

The Cubs catching position is up for grabs. They wanted to trade Damon Berryhill or Joe Girardi, but ended up letting Rick Wrona go the Twins. Berryhill is likely to start (just needs to be able to throw) with Girardi on the bench. Hector Villanueva will have one foot in the minor leagues, and one foot on the 24th roster spot, on opening day.

Lary Bump:

Hector Villanueva was born to hit. Actually, he was born to eat, and hitting came next. The 26-year-old right-handed batter spent 52 games each with Iowa and Chicago, with similar success — .266, 8, 34 for Iowa; .272, 7, 18 with the Cubbies. There is a question whether his arm is good enough for a National League catcher. He also can fill in at first base for Mark Grace when a tough left-hander pitches. But Villanueva's best position in the minors was DH. His bat should keep him in the majors as a pinch hitter and fill-in player.

CINCINNATI

Greg Gajus:

Joe Oliver (.231-8-52-1) was a disappointment for his BA in 1990, but nearly every other facet of his game was satisfactory. Oliver's first full season did reveal a problem with right handed pitching (.179 BA .282 SLG) but his defensive skills are good enough to keep him in the lineup even if he continues to hit .230. Oliver threw out almost 50% of the runners attempting to steal. Look for more of the same in 1991.

Jeff Reed (.251-3-16-0) probably saved his career with a strong second half, hitting .287 after the break. His .360 average against LHP in 1990 was a fluke, as the rest of his career he has been helpless against lefties. Expect another 40 to 50 games starting against RHP and resting Oliver.

Oliver went from catcher of the future to catcher of the present in 1989 when Bo Diaz went down for the year and Reed failed to hit (again). Oliver's minor league stats indicate a Damon Berryhill or Nelson Santovenia type of hitter (10-12 HR, 50 RBI's and .260 to .270 BA) which is not too shabby for an NL catcher. Joe appeared to be solid defensively, and at age 25, he still has room to improve. He had some problems against RHP in 1989, too (hitting .186 in 73 AB) so some time off against righties is a good idea. Barring injury, Oliver should get at least 120 games behind the plate in 1991.

A typical $1 catcher, Reed teased everyone in 1989 by hitting .333 in April and .190 the rest of the year. He is a left-handed hitter and solid defensively, but the emergence of Oliver cut his playing time considerably in 1990. Barring a trade or injury, I'd be surprised to see Jeff get more than 200 AB in 1991. Reed is not suddenly going to become a good hitter at age 28, and he would have to hit more in order to play more. Expect no more than the usual defensive replacement P.T.

Sean Lahman:

Joe Oliver's first full season solidified his position as the everyday catcher. Despite the unspectacular offense, Oliver showed the confidence and durability necessary to be a big league catcher. The righthander has never displayed an abundance of power but has been a good hitter, as his .272 average in his rookie season (1989) demonstrated. That Oliver did manage 8 home runs and 52 RBI is encouraging; the numbers would go up with increased playing time.

Oliver spent most of the season platooning with Jeff Reed, a journeyman lefthanded hitting catcher. Reed got much less playing time but did produce a .251 average. Oliver is better defensively, has a better throwing arm (opponents were 54% successful in steals against Oliver, 81% vs. Reed), and Oliver can handle pitchers very well. It seems likely that the platoon will not continue and that Oliver will be able to take over the job full-time in 1991. As a backup catcher, Reed is more than adequate, but should Oliver miss significant time due to injury, the Reds would probably acquire someone else.

Long time AAA catcher Terry McGriff was sent to Houston in the Bill Doran trade, leaving the Reds without any immediate prospects at catcher.

Lary Bump:

Among those making a cameo appearance (one AB; strike three, you're out) in the majors in 1990 was Glenn Sutko, a 23-year-old right-handed batter. He batted .300 — but in just four games at Cedar Rapids — before being promoted to Chattanooga, where he struggled to a .167 average in 53 games. He struck out 66 times in 174 ABs, walked 8 times.

Want to bet he's a good defensive catcher? Want to bet he'll be in Nashville, or maybe down in Chattanooga again, in '91?

Alex Trevino was in the Reds minor league system during the winter.

HOUSTON

Welford McCaffrey:

1990 will be engraved in Craig Biggio's memory book as a very strange year. The year ended as it had started with Biggio firmly rooted as the Astros catcher, but in between management did its best to confuse the man. The end result was a disappointing year. Biggio took part in the Astros Great Experiment of 1990. When the team was blown out of the division race early in the season, management decided to try players at different positions to see what they could do, Biggio was one of those players.

First it was decided to try Biggio in the outfield. This was done to protect his legs, so that he wouldn't lose any speed, and because of his inability to throw out base stealers. Rich Gedman was obtained in a trade with the Boston Red Sox and out trotted Biggio to the outfield. In the middle of this experiment, Astros GM Bill Wood proclaimed Craig the Astros second baseman of the future, meaning next year. Management even considered playing Biggio at second before the end of the season instead of waiting for Biggio to go to the fall instructional camp to learn the position. In all, Biggio played 50 games in the outfield, most of which was in center.

The Great Experiment failed. Biggio looked like a catcher playing center, especially those times when he did not bend down far enough to field ground ball singles, hit right to him, that ended up going for doubles or triples. Gedman turned out to be another of many failed attempts by Wood to resurrect a flagging veteran's career; Gedman ended up batting a disappointing .202. Most importantly, the experiment failed because Biggio let it be known that he wanted to catch, not play some other position no matter how much it might save on the wear and tear of his legs. The dive in Biggio's offensive numbers made an impression on management that backed up Biggio's words; he plays best when he's a catcher.

It is well known that Biggio has problems throwing out base stealers. Part of the problem is that Astros pitchers do not hold runners on base very well, with their slow deliveries after committing themselves to the plate. But part of the problem was Biggio's. Craig spent the off-season of 1989-90 trying to improve his throwing abilities. He worked on shifting his feet better, timing, and releasing the ball quicker. Early in the 1990 season, Biggio was throwing out more runners than in 1989, but more work was necessary. Biggio has never backed off from extra effort, and he was happy to work on his catching before games. The Great Experiment disrupted Biggio's catching development by making him work on other positions. He had to spend time learning the outfield and he began taking infield practice at second base.

It could be argued that the Great Experiment set Biggio's catching development back one whole year. The lessons that Biggio had learned over the winter and early in the season had to be slowly relearned when Craig put the catching mask back on for good after the failed Experiment. At the least, valuable work time had been wasted so that Craig could learn positions he did not want to learn and may never play.

There are really no catchers in the Astros farm system that can replace Biggio at catcher. Biggio, despite his throwing problems, is a fine defensive catcher who calls a good game. Offensively, he has shown he can hit for average and if he can regain his 1989 form he can drive in runs as well.

Biggio had the second best batting average among National League catchers in 1990, fifth best on-base percentage, but the worst slugging percentage. I expect Biggio to be the catcher for the Astros in 1991. He will come into spring training determined to show that he can make improvements behind the plate and in driving in runs. Establishing Biggio at the catcher position will make him a happier person, a more productive player. Biggio will bat .270, drive in 70 runs and hit 15 homers. And don't forget that speed!

Lary Bump:

At 28, Carl Nichols is no longer a rookie. He's a five-year veteran, or at least he has played in the majors in each of the last five seasons, gathering 135 ABs in 76 games. He has a good arm, good enough to put him in right field at times when he isn't catching. He has a little bit of pop in his right-handed bat, which accounted for a .253 average, 4 HR and 33 RBI last season at Tucson. He also drove in 11 runs in 49 AB with the Astros. With Craig Biggio moving all over the field and Rich Gedman a free agent, there might be an opening. But where Nichols can do a little bit of everything — except play first base, as he showed last season — he may not do anything well enough to hold down a major league job.

LOS ANGELES

Mike Scioscia has become a fixture, and at age 32 is not ready to step aside. Another key factor is that there is no one pushing him. The Dodgers acquired Mets castoff Barry Lyons, but he is a defensive asset only. Scioscia is the one that you want for Rotisserie.

Rick Dempsey was not offered a contract for 1991.

One possibility to make an impression in 1991 is Carlos Hernandez. Hernandez hit .300 at AA San Antonio in 1989, then .315 as a part-time backup to Darrin Fletcher at Albuquerque last year. He has no power, but is still improving at age 23. See Philadelphia for particulars on Fletcher. Farther down in the minors, Brian Barr will probably play at San Antonio this year; he bears watching for 1992-1993.

MONTREAL

Michael Cassin:

Mike Fitzgerald is one of the best backup catchers in the majors. The Expos are fortunate to have such a good backup, because he inevitably becomes their regular catcher when Nelson Santovenia gets hurt every year. Santovenia was injured during most of 1990, and he didn't hit well when he was healthy. In 1991 it appears that Santovenia is in danger of losing his job to prospect Greg Colbrunn. The scene is set: suppose Montreal gives up on Santovenia; Colbrunn becomes the regular catcher, but two months into the season Colbrunn appears overmatched and unready; now starting at catcher for the Expos . . . Mike Fitzgerald, again!

Colbrunn hit .301-13-76 for AA Jacksonville last year. He's expected to start the season at Triple-A Indianapolis, but he goes into spring training with exactly the same chance that Delino Deshields had last year; if he shows enough, he can win a major league job. The biggest question about Colbrunn in 1991 could be the Expos willingness to turn over their pitching staff to a 21-year-old. Montreal may be faced with the question of keeping three catchers on their roster, if Colbrunn is good enough to stick.

The safest approach for Rotisserie is to buy Fitzgerald at $2 or $3 again; he costs the same every year, and always ends up being worth at least that much.

Lary Bump:

Greg Colbrunn is a 21-year-old right-handed batter who is a threat to Nelson Santovenia and Mike Fitzgerald — maybe not this year, but certainly next. He has made the transition from 3B well, but his strong suit is his hitting. At Jacksonville, he batted .301 with 13 HR and 76 RBI.

Jerry Goff found a job in Montreal as the LHH catcher after coming over from the Seattle organization. A .287 start at Indianapolis earned him his first major league opportunity. He has shown some power in the minors, most notably with 20 HR in '88. Batting left-handed should be enough to keep him with the Expos in a sometimes-platoon role.

If you paid $2 for Mike Fitzgerald in 1989, you were delighted with his career-high 42 RBI. Last year, you got .243-9-41-8 for about the same price. More pleasure.They gave Mike 290 at bats, facing both lefty and righty pitchers. Mike had his best season since 1986, when he checked out for the year after trying to stop a fastball with one finger.

NEW YORK METS

Mackey Sasser was a big beneficiary of Davey Johnson's departure. Johnson had been outspoken in giving Sasser a "bad defense" rap. Today there may be one pitcher (Dwight Gooden) who prefers pitching to Charlie O'Brien, but Sasser has proved that Johnson's prejudice was ill-founded. Sasser isn't a young Bill Dickey, but he is competent.

Mets management spent the winter causing confusion about the catcher job. GM Frank Cashen said the number one catcher was Charlie O'Brien. Manager Bud Harrelson said the top guy was Mackey Sasser. Considering that Sasser had the job and continued playing with three injuries (hand, ankle, and elbow) until O'Brien was acquired to give him a rest, I tend to believe Harrelson. The funny aspect of the confusion is that Sasser is going to have value for Rotisserie purposes, anyway, and O'Brien is going to be worthless no matter how much he plays. Obviously, you should tell people that O'Brien has the job, and you should buy Sasser.

Todd Hundley will play all year at Triple-A unless the Mets have a real emergency during the season. The Mets catchers are Mackey Sasser and Charlie O'Brien, in that order, with the Mets looking for a third catcher after the winter meetings. They were unsure whether they wanted a defensive specialist, or a hitter-off-the-bench who could also catch, for their 3 backstop. If it turns out to be a defensive type, Hundley's continued residence at Tidewater in 1991 is even more certain.

Alan Boodman:

Mackey Sasser is the incumbent. He has posted .300-plus batting averages in each of the past two seasons, and now that his playing time has increased, his overall numbers reflect the expectations raised by his minor league record. His recent accomplishments were not a fluke.

I'm not trying to convince anyone that Mackey the Hacker should be on anyone's All-Star team, or that we should get too excited about a guy who managed just 83 base hits in 1990. But he has now established himself as a solid all around catcher who would be an asset to any Rotisserie team, with catching talent as scarce now as it has been since the mid-80's.

Batting average is Sasser's number one talent, although it is unusual for a player with Mackey's notorious lack of patience at the plate to post consistently good numbers in the BA department. Sasser also has fair-to-middling power (he would hit 35 doubles and 10-12 homers in 500 AB). Mackey should be among the top offensive NL catchers in 1991, behind only Santiago, Biggio, Scioscia, and maybe Daulton.

The question that must always be asked about Sasser is "Will he be able to play on a regular basis for a full season?" Contributing factors include his health (or lack thereof), his defense, and his inability to hit left-handed pitching. He's also as slow as a three-legged cat, but show me five catchers who aren't. I don't know if Mackey has fully recovered from his ailments of last season, but I do know that Mackey's health was never a concern before 1990. I'm not sure if that means he was rarely hurt before last year, or if it was just that nobody cared.

Sasser's defense was a bit improved in 1990. Defense isn't a subject which many Rotisserians need to deal with, but it can have a big impact on a player's time in the field. Some players have to hit a lot to overcome defensive weaknesses, and Mackey has generally been thought to be one of them. Defense won't keep Mackey out of the lineup this year. Especially when you consider the alternatives.

Defense (throwing) is the main reason — if not the only reason—that the Mets acquired Charlie O'Brien last August. The fact that he contributes almost nothing else to a major league club is why the Brewers were willing to part with him. If the genius who thought up this trade (Machado and Kevin Brown for O'Brien) keeps pulling rocks like these, the Mets will wind up down in Davy Jones' locker with the Cardinals in a few years. The best that O'Brien's fans can hope for is that he'll get a couple of starts against left-handers early in '91, and that he'll hit better than .105 against them. If he doesn't, and maybe even if he does, Todd Hundley may be in for more action this year. Keep in mind, however, that Hundley has played all of about 2 weeks of AAA ball.

And remember these names: Brook Fordyce and Alan Zinter. Actually, you can forget them until about 1993, but by 1995 all three (including Hundley) will be established in the majors, not all with the Mets and probably not all as catchers. I'd say Hundley's the weakest prospect of the three, and will have to make a living mostly with his glove. Zinter is the one most likely to make the majors as something other than a receiver.

Lary Bump:

Todd Hundley, a 22-year-old switch hitter, and Dave Liddell, a 25-year-old righty hitter, found themselves in the majors under emergency circumstances last season. The son of ex-Cubs catcher Randy Hundley batted .265 at Jackson between trips to New York, where he batted .209 in 36 games. His reputed strength is his defense, but he didn't seem ready to handle a major league pitching staff last season. He most likely will be at Tidewater this season, with Liddell, who batted .212 with the Tides, backing him up.

Alan Zinter, the Mets' No. 1 draft pick in '89, is

a switch hitter who had a good year at Port St. Lucie (.291, 7, 63). Like Hundley, he has a good arm. Fordyce is a 20-year-old right-handed batter whose bat is his greatest asset. He turned in numbers of .315, 10, 54 at Columbia. Look for Zinter at Jackson and Fordyce at St. Lucie this season. The Mets still need catching help, but they will have some options in the next few years.

PHILADELPHIA

Pete DeCoursey:

Darren Daulton's career was resuscitated and given wings when Nick Leyva batted him 2nd, re-introducing him to the fastball, and making his walks valuable, with Von Hayes and Dale Murphy coming up after him. This made Daulton the Phils hottest hitter after July 7, when he first batted in the number two spot. Daulton should be able to hit at least .250 with 8 to 12 HRs, and could easily score 70 to 80 runs if he bats 2nd for most of the season, or drive in 60 if he bats 5th or 6th. He is fast enough to move around the bases if Hayes, Murphy and Chamberlain bang the ball, though he will not steal many bases.

Historically a good April hitter, Daulton struggled through the first half of 1990, and then had the first good hot month hot streak of his career. His new closed, crowd-the-plate stance may cause pitchers to challenge him inside this year, and if he starts to be plagued by hand or knee injuries, watch out — catchers who like to play will never wait long enough to recover from those kinds of injuries, and usually their batting numbers suffer most noticeably. Dutch will continue to be a workhorse, taking a game off each week, and that's it.

The Phils will likely supply Daulton with a new backup next year, in the person of Darrin Fletcher, whom they acquired from the Dodgers for Dennis Cook in a late-season trade. Fletcher has shown a good bat at Albuquerque, hitting .273 in '89 and .291 in '90. He is good at drawing a walk, and he has alley power, with 13 HRs in '90. Since a few clubs have shown interest in Steve Lake, Fletcher could turn out to be a nice $1 catcher, particularly given the reality that nothing breaks down a catcher like a 135 game workload. He should hit for average from the start, and might show the first year power which many players evince at the Vet. Steve Lake, wherever he goes, will play seldom and hit around .240 with no power. If for some reason you want that, he's your man.

PITTSBURGH

And they say funny things happen in Rotisserie baseball. In "real" baseball, Don Slaught is making more than Barry Bonds. Now tell me, who are the people playing with fantasy dollars? You and I, or Larry Doughty and Don Slaught?

Mike Lavalliere will get most of the at bats. He hurt his hand in spring training last year, and never quite got on track. But Lavalliere bats left, and he is better than Slaught for defense. Mike is a .281 hitter over the past four years. Slaught has a .264 BA over the same period.

Adam Stein:

Don Slaught was hitting .405 on June 18 last year, just a flukey little welcome to the National League. From that point to the end of the season, he hit just .202. Wherever he plays in 1991, he won't get much playing time. He will hit closer to .202 than .405, and he will be worth no more than $1 to $3.

ST. LOUIS

Absent a free agent signing, the Cardinals appeared determined to convert Todd Zeile to 3B and install Tom Pagnozzi as the full time catcher. Pags is a decent defensive catcher, with a .252 lifetime average. Last year he responded well to the experiment with Zeile at third base; Pagnozzi hit .293 in the second half.

Zeile is still only 25, and still improving. He should increase his HR output to around 20 this year, and he should get his BA up to about .270. Zeile is also reasonably assured of playing time, if he just stays healthy. Pagnozzi, on the other hand, carries numerous downside risks. If the Cardinals grab a good third baseman by trade or free agency, Pagnozzi sits down. If Zeile can't handle 3B defensively and the Cards install a fielding specialist (Tim Jones or Rex Hudler?) Pagnozzi is the one who pays the price.

Lary Bump:

You can call him Ray; you can call him Carl; you can call him Stephens. But can you call Carl Ray Stephens a major league regular? Probably not, even though the Cards are intent on moving Todd Zeile to 3B. Stephens, a 28-yearold right-handed batter, has spent four of the last five seasons at Louisville, taking time out in '89 to get sent back down to Arkansas. His .221 average last season marked the first time he cracked the American Association Mendoza line. A good defensive catcher, so he may get some time spelling the somewhat shaky Tom Pagnozzi.

SAN DIEGO

After the departure of Mark Parent, the Padres are looking for a catcher to back up their star, Benito Santiago. The vacancy is not as big as it would be on most other teams, because Santiago likes to play every day except Sunday. From Dave Smith, we have an analysis showing that Parent has played 35% of his games on Sundays over the past two years.

The backup job will probably go to Tom Lampkin, a good-field, no-hit veteran who surfaced briefly with Cleveland.

In the minors last year, the alternatives to Lampkin were Ronn Reynolds (.2559-41 at Las Vegas); and Dan Walters and lefty-hitting Kevin Higgins, who both put in time at Las Vegas and Wichita with decent offensive stats. Bob Lutticken also toiled at Wichita, producing just .250-4-20. If I was Joe McIlvaine, I'd be looking real hard for a number two catcher right now. And this is the same team that had Alomar Jr., and couldn't use him.

Brigg Hewitt:

What can you say about Benito Santiago? He lets his bat and his throwing arm do his talking for him. During 1990 Santiago had some minor injuries and minor lapses of concentration, both punctuated with excessive talk and wild throws. Santiago should have a better season in every category in 1991.

Lary Bump:

Benito Santiago's injury last year gave Tom Lampkin, a 27-year-old, an emergency shot at the majors. And all it cost the Padres was Alex Cole. Lampkin hit almost as well in the National League as in the PCL, but only because he batted .224 in the Coast League his .222 was close.

SAN FRANCISCO

When Steve Decker arrived in the major leagues, Roger Craig was talking about what a good year Decker would have at Phoenix in 1991, and Gary Carter was talking about playing one more year. After Decker spent the month of September bashing major league pitching, Craig was talking about Decker in San Francisco in 1991, and Carter was talking about a career in broadcasting.

Terry Kennedy will provide experience, scouting reports, pitcher-handling, and a lefty bat. Kennedy may end up with a good share of playing time.

Rob Wood:

Steve Decker is very likely to win the catcher job. He is a big, strong kid, out of the Joe Oliver mold but with more power than Oliver. Decker's defense is already above-average, so if he sticks he will get loads of playing time. I think he is a great prospect, but Roger Craig has a history of "overhandling" his catchers and thereby stunting their development (cf. Kirt Manwaring).

AMERICAN LEAGUE
FIRST BASE

BALTIMORE

> UPDATE — Glenn Davis gets 1B; Milligan hopes for DH duty, with Evans in RF. Makes you wonder about Milligan's shoulder.

Last year we had all kinds of good things to say about the emergence of Randy Milligan, and he emerged just fine. Only a late-season shoulder injury and ultra-careful treatment during September prevented Milligan from having a very big year. Even with several weeks missed, he delivered much more value than the $9 average price that people paid for him in April 1990.

David Segui is the variable in 1991 that might affect Milligan's role as the regular first baseman. Recognize that Milligan will not be easily pushed aside. He is a former International League MVP. Although he arrived in the majors a little late, and has been banged around some, there is no assurance that Milligan has already had his career year. He was on a definite upward trend when injury interfered with his 1990 performance.

If you picture a platoon, think of something highly unusual. Segui is a switch hitter whose right/left differentials at the major league level have not yet been established. Milligan's differentials are also questionable; before 1990 he had trouble against lefties, but hit righties just fine (.307). In 1990 Milligan exploded against the lefties for a .330 BA and tailed off in his performance against righties. If I were Frank Robinson, I would want to see more evidence before making a decision.

We have a couple of different opinions on the fate of Segui for 1991. I think the critical issue is the ability of Dwight Evans to handle the DH duty, and who else the Orioles might obtain as a tenth bat for their offense.

George Hall:

Randy Milligan has the first base job on opening day, but look for David Segui to push his way into the lineup as the season progresses. Behind them, Sam Horn will provide some left-handed pop off the bench.

Segui's time is now. He is a high-average, low-power switch hitter. Just age 24 in 1991, Segui moved rapidly through the Orioles farm system, and his stats tell why. 1989: .319, 11 homers, 77 RBI at A Frederick and AA Hagerstown; 1990: .336 for AAA Rochester, with 4 HR and 66 RBI for Rochester and Baltimore combined.

The scouts say nice things about Segui, such as "a good swing from both sides of the plate," and "almost never strikes out." In 890 at bats in 1989-1990, David whiffed only 41 times. The scouts also have some concerns, however. They say less enthusiastic things like, "cannot see him as an everyday first baseman considering his lack of power," and "seems content to spray the ball." Any major league team wants long ball delivery from their 1B. The question is: can Segui learn to hit for power? He was age 23 during 1990, and at 6'1" and 170 pounds there is room to bulk out. Segui also has excellent work habits and is a good learner. My conclusion is that he can produce up to 10 or 15 homers per year (maybe not in 1991, but eventually) fitting the mold of a Keith Hernandez or Mark Grace type of hitter. One concern of the scouts will never be fixed; Segui is slow.

Ideally, the O's will eventually use Milligan more as a DH, with Segui at first base. Segui is already ahead of Milligan on defense, but two factors will delay that shift well into 1991 or 1992. Segui will have to prove (to Frank Robinson's satisfaction) that he can hit consistently well at the major league level, and DH Dwight Evans will have to pass into obscurity. There is no clock running on either process; they could happen suddenly and early in 1991, or they could not happen at all during 1991. That's the fun of Rotisserie. But at least you know what to look for. If Evans slumps badly or goes on the DL, Segui's value goes up. If Segui does well with his limited playing time (and he will get some PT no matter what), then Robinson will give him more time, either at 1B or DH, and his value will go up. If both happen early in 1991, Segui's value will soar.

Lary Bump:

Diego Segui's son David is a smooth-fielding, switch-hitting, line-drive hitting 24-year-old. His .336 average at Rochester would have led the International League, but his AAA season was cut short by injury and a couple of trips to Baltimore, where he batted .244. He totaled only 4 HR in 126 games, and his minor-league high was 11 in 1989. But those who argue that he will hit for power can point to the 35 doubles he hit. He also has consistently walked more than he has struck out. Still, he's far from sure of a job with the Orioles. He's not likely to move Randy Milligan off 1B, and the power-starved Birds need a bigger stick at DH. Watch how Segui is used in spring training, and most likely watch him go back to Rochester to start the season.

BOSTON

UPDATE — The Sox signed Jack Clark, as expected. His BA will go up at Fenway. Mo Vaughn will lose a few games, but he still figures prominently.

When the winter meetings ended, the Red Sox were hot on the trail of Jack Clark, who could put up some monstrous numbers in the Boston lineup, IF he could stay healthy. Without Clark, the Sox will displace (or trade) Carlos Quintana anyway, and give first base to Mo Vaughn.

Named Big East "athlete of the decade" for his college play, Vaughn will be in the lineup as DH even if he doesn't have the first base job. Vaughn has made extremely fast progress in two years as a pro, and his 1989 and 1990 seasons were both characterized by weak beginnings and huge second half numbers. If Vaughn starts slowly in 1991, it could be a great sucker punch to grab him from a disappointed owner.

Quintana showed little power in 1990, but he was a pleasant surprise with a .287 batting average. He was good for .319 in the first half and just .261 in the second half, but I don't expect a big fall-off in 1991. Quintana was consistent all year in most of the other offensive categories; he is likely to show improvement at his young age; and he has untapped power potential that should net him double digit homers this year. Quintana may end up in the Bosox outfield, but his best to get 500 at bats again (like he had in 1990) would be a trade to another team.

Fred Percival:

Last year at this time, the Boston first baseman, by default, was Carlos Quintana. He isn't really a first baseman, even though that's where he played at Triple-A Pawtucket in '89. Like many other home-grown Red Sox, Quintana is a left fielder. At 6-3, 210 pounds, the 25-year-old looks like a first sacker, but his defensive play at 1B can be charitably described as indifferent. For 1991, all eyes are on Mo Vaughn.

Lary Bump:

Mo Vaughn's appearance is not deceptive. At 6-1, 225, the 22-year-old Vaughn looks like a power hitter. He started to become just that last season at Pawtucket (.295, 22, 72) and continued in 1990.

CALIFORNIA

Wally Joyner is expected to recover from his 1990 ailments, and could be darn cheap after his disappointing season (.268-8-41-2). He's going to be thrown back into most auctions, and all American League first basemen are pretty good hitters, so he isn't going to stand out among to his peers. Like all injury rehab cases, Joyner should be treated with caution by those who are trying to hang on to a top spot in their league. For those who are looking to make a move in their standings (and should be willing to take a little risk) Joyner offers an excellent opportunity. The Angels are not loaded with people who can play first base. Lee Stevens was the primary fill-in for Joyner while he was on the DL, and they tried Rick Schu during the late-season stretch when they looked like an expansion team (or even a spring training B squad). Stevens was the only serious candidate for 1B on the winter roster, and the Angels like Stevens more as a DH (see DH section).

Lary Bump:

After two good years at Edmonton, 23-year-old Lee Stevens is ready for the show. The question is, with Wally Joyner expected to be healthy again, where? The Angels tried him in LF last year. Stevens' hustle couldn't make up for inexperience, and his arm came up a bit short. He made great progress at Edmonton, raising his average from .247 to .293 and his OBP from .341 to .390, and increasing his HR total from 14 to 16 in 108 fewer ABs. The left-handed batter also improved against left-handed pitching. With Brian Downing opting for free agency, and perhaps finally on the way out anyway, perhaps Stevens will be the Angels' DH in '91, filling in on occasion at 1B and OF positions.

CHICAGO WHITE SOX

Frank Thomas is a potential superstar, improving rapidly at age 23 and already in the class of productive hitters. Thomas is likely to hit for a higher average than most other first basemen, with the full power output that you normally expect from a good 1B. People who have seen Thomas swing have been using the words "Hall of Fame" rather freely; it may be too early to talk about election to the Hall, but it isn't too early to be talking about a highly productive season and an exciting Rotisserie commodity.

Carlos Martinez was once part of the White Sox youth movement, but now he's more of a spectator. He was displaced from the 1B picture during a horrible 1990 season. Last year he forgot to put down his bat before waving at some spectators in winter ball, and spent about half a semester studying the Venezuelan justice system. He got off to a poor start in the regular season, and never recovered. Martinez may fill in at 1B on occasion, and he may get some DH duty against lefties, but he is going to have trouble getting more than the 311 at bats that he has averaged over the past two years, and may get as few as 200 AB.

Steve Lyons was a part-time 1B and utilityman in 1990. He offered little interest for Rotisserie purposes but attracted wide attention in the field of lunar observation. Chicago was apparently fed up with Lyons' antics, and he will probably have to find another team if he wants to play in 1991.

Dan Pasqua may appear at 1B on occasion against righty pitchers.

Jon Dunkle:

Frank Thomas is the starting first baseman for the Chicago White Sox. After punishing minor league pitching, Thomas was called up to the majors. Someone forgot to tell Thomas as he made major league pitching look like Southern League pitching. Expect Thomas to post numbers similar to those of Toronto first baseman Fred McGriff.

Lary Bump:

Thomas is no longer a rookie. Not that he ever looked like one. It's hard to believe some people once thought of him as an Auburn tight end in a baseball uniform. First the 23-year-old toyed with the Southern League, batting .323 with 18 HR, 71 RBI, 112 walks and a .487 OBP in 109 games. Observers were cautious when he was called up to the big leagues, for he didn't show much power at first. When the dust had cleared and they called in the wrecking ball for old Comiskey Park, he had done about as well in the American League — .330,

7 HR, 31 RBI, a .454 OBP in 60 games — as he had in the minors. When this right-handed batter steps to the plate, he should wear a sign saying "Lefties Beware!" He stung them at a .408 rate, with a .538 OBP and .732 slugging percentage. Aha, a weakness! Thomas batted "only" .283 against right-handers, his OBP dropped to .401 against them and they held him to a measly .408 slugging percentage. Time will tell if the new Comiskey becomes The House That Thomas Built.

CLEVELAND

My money is on Brook Jacoby. Jeff Manto has, however, achieved the distinction of making it back into the pages of this book after being dropped. We featured him in 1989 as a genuine prospect, then left him out of the discussion in the 1990 book, because he hit just .277 at Edmonton (where numbers like .330 are not too rare). Now he's back. Jeff's father introduced himself to me at last summer's SABR convention in Cleveland, where the Tribe was helping the visiting Yankees look like a pennant contender. "Does your book have Jeff in it?" he asked. How do you tell a father that his son used to be a prospect but isn't any more? OK, Mr. Manto, Jeff's back. Enjoy it while you can.

The Cleveland 1B slot is the Bermuda Triangle of professional hitters. Prospects and veterans alike get swallowed up. Keith Hernandez, Don Lovell, Willie Upshaw, and Eddie Williams, to name just three, have recently disappeared soon after they were seen holding a first baseman's mitt in Cleveland Municipal Stadium. Keith has to go somewhere when he checks out, I suppose.

Another RHH, young Tim Costo, hit .316-4-42-4 in A-ball at Kinston last year. The Cleveland front office talked up Costo's value during the winter, but all the excitement is way too premature. The Frank Thomas types who soar through the minor leagues with a hop, skip and a jump are not so common that every organization has one. Cut out the BS, Cleveland. Please.

Bill Gray:

Brook Jacoby had an outstanding year in 1990. Actually he played more games at third (99 vs. 78) but Baerga has earned third. Jacoby was one of Cleveland's three All-Stars in 1990. For once he was productive with runners on base (.295 with runners in scoring position). At 31 he (and you) should be content if he comes close to matching last years numbers. His name always comes up in trades. You have to consider this to be a real possibility as his value likely will never be higher.

Keith Hernandez is still on the team thanks to a two year guaranteed contract for $3.5 million. He talked seriously of retiring, then said he may hire a personal trainer to whip him into shape for one last shot. He really hasn't played regularly since 1987. Hank Peters gambled that Hernandez wasn't shot and is determined to have him on the roster in 1991. [Peters should have read the Rob Wood Washed Up List.] If nostalgia overcomes your senses and you want to have him on your team, two bucks would be too much. He is a very old 37. High mileage on the odometer.

Dion James got into 35 games at first. He also qualifies in the OF. James was in MacNamara's doghouse early in the year but worked his way out. If Jacoby leaves, and Hernandez retires, James may get a lot of PT. He didn't play the last three weeks of the season, for what that's worth. Back in the doghouse? He has always hit for a decent average .274 in 87 games, but lacks power (1 HR) and will steal only occasionally (5 of 8).

Mitch Webster played three games at 1st. If your league rules allow for Webster to qualify as a 1B, he would be the most valuable Cleveland first baseman. See Cleveland outfield essay for more on Webster.

Unless Jacoby is traded, he will be the regular at first.

Steve Goldman:

First base remains one of the most uncertain positions for the Tribe as we approach the 1991 season. Keith Hernandez was brought in as a free agent in 1990, but repeated injury problems turned his year into a waste. There have been reports in the press that the Indians will let him go, but GM Hank Peters denies these. This is probably a moot point, however; Hernandez' recent injury problems, combined with his age, dictate that one should not expect much from him.

The most likely scenario is that Brook Jacoby, who did see a lot of action at the position in 1990, will shift over from third on a more permanent basis. Carlos Baerga should continue to develop at third, necessitating that he play every day. But Jacoby did have a good year with the bat, and displayed the ability to play first.

The backup scenario is that 26 year-old Jeff Manto will be given the nod. He is a player who has demonstrated the ability to hit with power in the minors, and he has an outstanding eye for balls and strikes. In a late-season trial with the Indians, he hit only .224 in 76 at-bats, with only two home runs, but he walked 21 times, to yield a .392 on-base percentage. He definitely merits a look in the spring. If he does win the starting first base job, this will very likely result in shifting Jacoby to the designated hitter role.

Lary Bump:

Jeff Manto missed his best chance to make the majors when he couldn't dislodge Jack Howell from 3B with the Angels. Now it appears that Brook Jacoby has moved with him to 1B. Since both bat right-handed, there is no platoon opportunity for Manto. The last three seasons in the minors, he has totaled 65 HR and 250 RBI, including last year's .297, 18, 82 in 96 games at Colorado Springs. In 30 games with the Indians, he checked in at .224, 2, 14. We may never know if this 26-year-old really can hit or whether his success the last three seasons was due to playing in the Texas and Pacific Coast leagues.

DETROIT

Cecil Fielder will play first base for the Tigers in 1991. See the essay, The Biggest Surprises of 1990, for the story on Fielder. Just as an aside, note that the 1989 Analyst cited Fielder for having the third-best home run percentage on the power-packed 1988 Blue Jays.

Lary Bump:

Rico Brogna is one 20-year-old whose 21 HR in 1990 may be legitimate. The left-handed hitter led the Eastern League. He did play in London, one of the league's best hitting parks, which still may not be as easy as, say, Wichita. Brogna hit just 12 HR in his first two pro seasons, but he's young enough that he may still be developing. He was considered the best-fielding 1B in the E.L. as well. He won't have to worry about competing for the 1B job in Detroit this year, though in '92 the Tigers might consider moving Cecil Fielder to DH to accommodate Brogna.

KANSAS CITY

For two consecutive years, George Brett has struggled horribly in the first part of the season, and then come on like a speeding locomotive after the weather gets warm. George's alter ego Graig Nettles did the same thing for years, even in the Senior League. At least Brett is doing it in the majors.

Marc Bowman:

Batting Champion "Boy" George Brett returns. If he stays healthy, he should hit over .300 again, with moderate power, good production, and occasional speed. Brett almost always starts off slowly and then goes on a tear in late May. His birthday is May 15, and he makes an extra effort to feel young whenever reminded of his age. He was hitting only .200 in mid-May last year, but his second half included a two-month stretch of .390 hitting that would boost anybody's stats to high levels.

There is a tactic to highlight here. Try to acquire Brett around May 15. You may be able to steal him for little or nothing.

The Royals looked willing to let go of Gerald Perry during the winter, but if they re-sign him, he will be the most probable backup to Brett. Otherwise, Jeff Conine's readiness is the only question about his arrival. A point worth noting on Perry (wherever he ends up playing) is that he got 11 of his 17 SB in the second half of 1990, evidence that he was learning the AL pitchers. Back in 1987, Perry stole 42 bases to set a Braves record.

Conine made a big impact at AA Memphis and got a September call-up. Big Bob Hamelin is just 23 and has moved up through the minors rapidly, despite a disappointing, injury-shortened season in 1990. He is a definite factor in planning for 1992-1993, with a remote chance of impacting 1991.

Both Conine and Hamelin have attracted attention from people who follow minor leaguers. If there is a sleeper taking shape in the above group, it is probably the low-profile of Gerald Perry.

Lary Bump:

Headline writers in KC are practicing their [Jeff] Conine the Barbarian headline variations. He had nine uneventful games of experience with the Royals last September, and he may not be there again until the leaves start to change this autumn. But few doubt he will be back. Perhaps more impressive than his .320, 15, 95 season, with 21 SB, at Memphis last year were his first two pro years, when he totaled 24 HR in the Florida State League. He could move George Brett to full-time DH duty this season, but '92 is a better bet. Conine is a 24-year-old right-handed batter (and the Royals' lineup already leans too far to the right) who also knows his way around the bag at first.

If you're looking for Luis Delossantos, look in the third base essays.

MILWAUKEE

Alan Boodman:

The Brewers began to phase out Greg Brock after the All-Star break last year, and it looks like Paul Molitor will be playing yet another position (1B) when the 1991 season opens.

Brock only got 130 AB in the second half of '90 as Molitor interned at first base in preparation for full-time play there this season. Milwaukee fans may not believe this, but Greg Brock is, I feel, still capable of helping a major-league ballclub. If Greg hits .255, he is an asset, as he gets his share of extra-base hits, draws a lot of walks, and even steals bases well, if not often. He is also a fine defensive first baseman. Brock doesn't help a club tremendously in any one area, but contributes a little in almost everything, sort of like Sid Bream.

Greg will turn 34 this season, but he seems like the type of player who could play regularly for another 3-4 years in the right circumstances. If Brock remains in Milwaukee, his 1991 playing time looks like it will diminish to almost nothing (at least until Molly gets hurt again). I'd expect less than 250 PA with an average near .250, but close to 10 HR and around 30 walks.

Paul Molitor's new home is first base, which also puts him in a whole new position Rotisserie-wise. That is, he'll be expected to put up numbers comparable to other A.L. first basemen, and that might be a bit much to ask of baseball's ultimate nomad.

Across the board, Paul's stats usually border on the outstanding, and if he could have stayed reasonably healthy in 1980, 1981, 1984 (ouch!), 1986, 1987, or 1990, we'd be talking about Molitor in terms of the Hall of Fame. I guess we still might end up doing just that anyway, but as a first baseman at this point in his career, I don't see too much to get excited about in Rotisserie terms.

As far as homers and RBI, even in Paul's best years he put up numbers that Eddie Murray generally attains by the end of July. Of course, Molitor could well steal 40 bases and hit .325, and even if it's more like 30 bases and .305, he's still got most of them beat. If you're in a league that uses runs scored or emphasizes batting average (by using OBP as a category, for example), Molitor might rank closer to the top among A.L. first sackers.

Assuming Paul appears in 135 games (knock on wood), he'll hit .295 or so, maybe sneak in (barely) to double-digits in homers, steal near 30, and will drive in closer to 50 runs than 80. What do you expect from the only first baseman/leadoff man in the league?

George Canale is a less-than-hot prospect coming off of a season where he hit .254 with 12 homers in 134 games against AAA pitchers while playing his home games in a bandbox. He projects as a very low average, very high strikeout kind of hitter, and if the Brewers' brass is on the ball at all, Canale will do his projecting somewhere other than County Stadium.

Lary Bump:

The lefty-hitting George Canale is in danger of seeing his time as a prospect come and go without fruition. He went back to Denver last season after putting up numbers of .278, 18, 71 in '89. He claims his power production fell off last year (12 HR, 60 RBI) because the Brewers wanted him to cut down on his strikeouts — which he did, from 134 to 103 in 35 fewer ABs — and hit for a better average — which he didn't, dropping to .254. Perhaps they wanted a Greg Brock clone? But shouldn't a 1B be able to hit 30 HR in two years at Denver almost by accident? At any rate, Brock will turn 34 this season, and Canale will turn 26 — more likely in Denver than in Milwaukee.

MINNESOTA

Kent Hrbek is the obvious incumbent. At age 31 he isn't going to reach any new heights, but he's been been remarkably consistent over the past three years. Pencil in about a .280 BA, 20 to 25 homers, and around 80 RBI, and you can't be too far off.

Paul Clements:

The Twins would like to trade Gene Larkin, but the problem is: who wants a slow, low-power first baseman who always hits .266 to .269? Most teams expect much more offense from the 1B position. Larkin simply hasn't developed. If Minnesota can unload him, even as a throw-in, Paul Sorrento would immediately emerge as the backup first baseman and regular lefty-hitting DH. Considering that Herbie Hrbek normally misses 35 games a year, that backup/DH role can add up to a lot of playing time in a good hitter's stadium.

The trade of Larkin is a big variable, but a middle-of-the-road case would give Sorrento about 85 games, 300 AB, .255 and 12 to 15 homers. If Larkin actually leaves, those numbers could all increase.

Lary Bump:

Sorrento, a lefty-hitting 25-year-old, came to the Twins in the Bert Blyleven trade. He put together a solid season at Portland when he wasn't in Minnesota getting major league playing time. His PCL numbers were .302, 19, 72, with a .406 OBP. With the Twins, he did what he is paid to do by hitting 5 HR in 41 games, though his average and on-base ability declined. He played enough so he no longer is a rookie. Depending on how he and Kent Hrbek compare in the field, Sorrento can play 1B or DH against right-handed pitching. He may not be more than a platoon player.

NEW YORK YANKEES

The Yankees had good news and bad news at first base last year. The good news was Kevin Maas; the bad news was Don Mattingly. Maas arrived in the major leagues by hitting 11 homers faster than anyone in history has ever done it. The homers slowed to a trickle, however, after pitchers stopped throwing fastballs whenever they fell behind in the count. Now it's Maas' turn to make adjustments.

Don Mattingly should have been in his prime in

1990, but instead he had his worst year ever, undone by pain in his lower back. He spent seven weeks on the DL and failed to hit a home run in his last 260 at bats. The back pain was nothing new, but the terrible impact on his hitting was unprecedented and unexpected. He went through a streak of 200 at bats with a .208 average before going on the DL. Jack Morris was the last pitcher to face Mattingly in 1990. Don went one for four, and Jack told me that Don didn't look like the old Mattingly. "The old Mattingly would have got four hits off me. You can see that Donnie's making progress, but there's still some stiffness in his back. I can see it. But he still has great hands, and Donnie is a gamer." Don told me that, as long he does his exercises diligently and sticks to the program, he should be just fine.

When he produced a .303 season with 23 homers and 113 RBI in 1989, Mattingly attracted criticism for having a bad year. The same people ("Yankee fans") who said 1989 was a bad year are all silent now. They know they would LOVE to see Don return to the 1989 stats that made them complain so bitterly.

The first base job, or any other position that Mattingly wants, will be his for the asking. Suggestions that Maas should displace him on account of skill or fielding ability are just plain silly. With his excellent positioning based on knowledge of hitters and pitchers and his intense concentration, Mattingly would be an adequate first baseman even if he couldn't move. If Mattingly appears at DH, it will be because he wants to.

Maas will get his at bats just the same. He can always DH, and he was given a course in Outfield 101 while in the minors.

Daniel Stone:

With the emergence of Kevin Maas, many New Yorkers began to wonder who should play first base in 1991, with Mattingly back in the lineup. Some proposed that Mattingly should move to left field, but that is the last thing the Yankees would want to do. It just makes no sense to move the best-fielding first baseman in the league to a foreign position. Maas was erratic at best when he filled in at 1B last year. Seeing Maas at work in the field has educated New York fans about how many runs Mattingly saves with his glove.

Maas is unsuited to the outfield himself. He is still hobbled by a knee injury that caused him to miss half of the 1989 season. The large brace that he wears during games is visible evidence that the knee still bothers him. The natural solution is to put Maas at DH and give him a few spot starts in the field, regardless what Kevin may want for himself.

The problem of fitting both Maas and Mattingly into the same lineup is the kind of problem all managers love. Both are exceptional talents. Maas' power will probably decline. It's very hard to maintain a pace of 1 HR every 12.1 at bats. He should exceed 20 easily, anyway. His average was already dropping in late 1990. Maas may be a great power hitter very soon, but people who expect MVP stats in 1991 are likely to be disappointed.

Mattingly's condition should be visible during spring training. If there is a problem, people will see it and publicize it. Regardless of the facts, however, somebody in every league is like to bid Mattingly up to the value of his 145 RBI, .350 BA seasons. Let someone else be that person.

OAKLAND

Mark McGwire is nice, steady and valuable Rotisserie commodity. For 1991 expect: 35 to 39 HR, 100 to 110 RBI, and a .240 to .250 BA. McGwire's power is not only big, it is also consistent and predictable. He isn't one of those sluggers who gives you 39 HR one year and then 19 the next. The only concern is a batting average that dipped down into the "negative value" category in both of the last two years. McGwire hasn't shown evidence of learning to hit for average, and on a simple linear trend, seems to be getting worse every year. Our prediction is that the BA bottomed out in 1990. He hit .223 in the first half last year, then .247 in the second half.

Doug Jennings can play some 1B, and last year at Tacoma, he hit .346 in 208 at bats, but now has a .195 career major league average at age 26. He isn't the kind of talent who is going to put Mark McGwire on the bench.

A more interesting prospect is lefty-hitting Dan Howitt, who produced 26 HR and 111 RBI with a .281 BA at Huntsville in 1989, and .265-11-69-4 last summer at Tacoma. Howitt is 26 years old, and is likely to make the opening day roster this year.

SEATTLE

Two conflicting forces collided in Seattle last year. Pete O'Brien was on a long and steady downward trend when he arrived in Seattle. The Kingdome, however, has been like an elixir for aging batters, lifting some ruined careers back to respectability. In this case there was no help for O'Brien. He dropped even further than he had fallen before, with a .224, 5 HR performance reflecting the impacts of age and injury. O'Brien will make everyone happy, in Rotisserie and "real" baseball, if he can get back up to 10 HR and a .250 BA. Just a few years ago, O'Brien was second only to Don Mattingly for Rotisserie value and was a marvel of consistency from 1985-1987. Just as we did last year, we will predict a slight up-tick for O'Brien in 1991. That prediction is safer this year, because he is coming off a lower base period. In the larger context of his career, he is fading rapidly, but within the shorter time frame of 1990/1991, there is clearly room for one more lucky bounce upward.

Avin Davis became a DH for Seattle, although he remains a 1B for your purposes. The Mariners are gradually giving up their long-term commitment to Davis, which has always been more than they like to admit. The following anecdote has appeared previously in these pages, but for the benefit of those who haven't seen it, there is a valuable lesson worth repeating.

In the spring of 1987, the Seattle front office were spreading the word that there was great uncertainty about who would play 1B. Yes, Davis is a fine hitter and has a definite edge going into spring training, but Davis is really weak on fielding (so the story continues) and the M's are looking to emphasize more speed and defense in 1987, with people like Harold Reynolds, and it's just not really clear how Alvin Davis is going to fit into their plans if at all.

There is this kid Brick Smith who just hit .344 at Chattanooga with 101 RBI and 23 HR and led the league in doubles, etc., etc., and if Smith has a good spring training (they say) he could be the one who gets the job. So Smith goes down to Tempe and plays quite a bit and really tears up the Cactus league. He hits around .458 with about 11 homers in one month, and he shows tremendous defensive effort and skill. Meanwhile, Alvin Davis is on the bench for some time, watching all of this happen. So what does he do? What would you do? He starts taking a little extra infield practice (compared to the normal Davis when returning home to the town of his undergraduate campus days, that means A LOT of extra infield practice, comparatively speaking) and he hones up his skills a little by fielding bunts, and making nice throws in front of the pitcher covering, and all those other things that good first basemen do so well. Have you guessed the ending yet? Brick Smith (who, by the way, is not really a "kid" but is really a year older than Alvin Davis) goes to Calgary, not to Seattle. And Alvin Davis goes on to have his finest year ever, the most home runs and the highest batting average of his career, and (get this) reduces his errors by 36% from the previous year, while getting 101 more at bats!

There are two little lessons in the above story:

(1) Do not believe ANYTHING stated during spring training about who is going to play what position, especially if it involves a rookie displacing a proven, healthy veteran and especially if it comes from the organization's own PR office. Most of the press releases and "leaks" and manager's comments made during spring training are intended to motivate players, to help managers do their jobs, and to fulfill other organizational purposes such

as building up the value of a player who may be trade bait. Helping Rotisserie people is not high on the list of Principal Accountabilities in a P.R. Director's job description.

(2) Whenever you hear about an up and coming "kid," check his age compared to the other person(s) involved in competition for the job. You might be surprised.

In 1991, the "kid" is Tino Martinez, and he's a serious contender, not another Brick Smith. Martinez is only 23, and there is a road block (or traffic jam) around the 1B/DH positions, but his long term outlook is excellent. If the M's can move O'Brien or Davis, the value of Martinez will soar. Consider that he hit .402 with 20 HR and 70 RBI in just 199 AB for the 1988 U.S. Olympic Team. I think pro-rated numbers are about the last basis that you want for talent evaluation, but I can't resist the temptation to multiply those numbers by 3, and see .402 with 60 HR and 210 RBI in 597 at bats. Scary, even in amateur play. Last year for AAA Calgary, Martinez produced .320-17-93-8 with obvious major league potential. He isn't likely to hit .300 going from the PCL to the AL, but he is within reach of double digit homers as a rookie.

Tony Formo's 1991 Left Field Extravaganza:

Alvin Davis (.387 OBA, .429) had a solid season at DH and first base. The Mariner franchise leader in RBI and HR had only 68 ribbies and 17 taters, and is likely to become full-time DH as Tino Martinez develops.

Signing Pete O'Brien (.308 OBA, .314 SA) as a free agent was a dumb move. He's an anemic hitter in a position where you want a thumper, and his presence in the line-up moved Alvin Davis from first to DH, and Jeffrey Leonard to the outfield. Whatever defensive advantage there might have been in having O'Brien at first instead of Davis was outweighed by having Penface in the outfield instead of someone like Cotto or Briley. O'Brien's offensive stats have been taking a steady nosedive for half a dozen seasons. Moreover, the best prospect in the organization has been another first baseman. At the end of the season when Martinez was called up from Calgary, O'Brien was tried in the outfield, but he doesn't hit well enough to earn a regular spot, and probably won't play much in the future unless the M's can find someone stupid enough to want him in a trade.

Former US Olympic star Tino Martinez has been considered the top prospect in the organization and was hitting .319 with 17 HR and 92 RBI for Calgary on August 20, when he was called up to replace O'Brien, who had injured his thumb (and wasn't hitting).

Lary Bump:

The radio announcer made me sit up and take note: The Mariners had just called up slugging sensation Tino Martinez. Hold on. Martinez may be a lot of good things on the baseball diamond, but a slugger he's not. And after hitting 17 HR at Calgary, an easy mark, he hit 0 in 68 AB with Seattle. The Mariners shouldn't have to depend on him to hit a lot of HRs. But they can expect excellent defense, run production (93 RBI at Calgary), a good average (.320 with the Cannons), on-base ability (.413 OBP), good strike zone judgment (He walked twice as often as he struck out), even a little speed (8 SB). Kind of the best of both worlds, Alvin Davis and Pete O'Brien. This 23-year-old lefty hitter should be in Seattle's '91 lineup often enough to make him valuable in 1991, and his future is all upward.

TEXAS

Rafael Palmeiro really turned his career around in 1990. In late 1989 (he told me) he wasn't enjoying the game of baseball, and just wanted the season to end. He had started 1989 on a very high note. He saw the ball well in April and May, and raised his average to .361 by May 28. The Rangers, meanwhile, made a quick start and attracted attention as a much-improved team. But Palmeiro slumped badly, and so did the Rangers. By season's end, he was playing part time at best, and was clearly in Bobby Valentine's dog house. Being on the outs was especially painful for Palmeiro in 1989, because he had started the year with few friends on the team and relied on a mentor relationship with Valentine to keep his spirits up. When Valentine turned his back, it was a painful rejection.

By the end of 1990, Palmeiro and Valentine were best buddies again. Rafael had more friends on the team, and he was enjoying the game more than ever before. And of course you know that Raffy was in the hunt for the AL batting title right up until the last few days of the season. The most wonderful aspect of Palmeiro is that he is still only age 26. Having achieved major league success at an early age, he has "superstar" written all over him. Just sit back and watch.

There is no "regular" backup to Palmeiro at 1B. Jack Daugherty appeared there in 30 games last year and will pick up any slack in 1991 if he hasn't been traded by opening day. The Rangers have taken a peculiar liking to Daugherty at a late age (31 this year) and will use him in the outfield more extensively than at first base. Despite arriving in the major leagues at a very advanced age, he has handled major league pitching for a .296 career average in 426 at bats.

TORONTO

The Jays are now committed to John Olerud at 1B, with enough confidence in his ability to have let go of Fred McGriff, after letting go of Cecil Fielder to keep McGriff fully active. Olerud must be something special.

J.L. Feinstein:

With Fred McGriff shipped off to San Diego as part of the Winter Meeting blockbuster, 1B was officially handed over to 22-year old John Olerud. The position couldn't be in better hands. In his first full season in the bigs, Olerud got 350 ABs, as a part-time DH and occasional 1B. Olerud had a solid first half, hitting .275 with 10 HRs and 33 RBI, before his bat cooled off a bit and his playing time diminished as Cito Gaston went with the hot hand down the stretch. Over all, Olerud ended up with .265-14-48.

His smooth stroke and quick wrists convinced the Jays they needed his bat in the lineup every day, so he went to Instructional League to learn how to be an OF. He responded so well, that the Jays began to tout him as their Opening Day left-fielder.

Then came the Winter Meetings and the trade of McGriff. In defense of the controversial trade, Gillick indicated that he'd never have traded McGriff if he didn't have Olerud waiting in the wings. The acquisition of Joe Carter puts an end to the Olerud/OF experiment, for the time being, but the point is that Olerud offers extremely versatile athletic ability. He can also pitch.

Indeed, after the trade, Joe McIlvaine when asked to choose between the two, McGriff and Olerud, as first basemen, said that he'd take Olerud. He went on to say that while McGriff would always hit more homers than Olerud, Olerud was a star waiting to blossom. This feeling was seconded by almost all of the "baseball men" present at the winter meetings.

The impression you get from talking to writers, scouts, and front-office personnel from both leagues is that Olerud is very much for real. The thinking is that he's never going to hit 35 HRs a year, but that he has the potential to hit 25 consistently (if you extend his 1990 stats to 600 AB, he'd have 23), drive in 90-100 runs, and hit .300. Plus he plays a slick 1B, and figures to get even better with additional experience. About the only thing he can't do is run. (If your league has a prize for most appearances without a stolen base, he's your man.)

Olerud will get the occasional day off, with either Pat Tabler or Joe Carter getting the call at 1B. Neither are long-term answers, but can do in a pinch. Barring injury, Olerud should get into 150 games.

PS — Don't say we didn't tell you about Olerud last year.

Tony Formo (February 1990):

John Olerud might be the sleeper Rotisserie capitalists dream about. When the Jays selected him in the amateur draft, he was expected to return to Washington State University for his final year, but Toronto made him an offer he didn't refuse. If he had stayed in college another year, he almost certainly would have been a first round pick. He has a picture swing, and in his cameo appearances in September, it worked just fine with major league pitching.

Lary Bump (February 1990):

John Olerud: The next Babe Ruth. Or at least the next Mel Queen or Willie Smith. Until now, John Olerud hasn't played in the minor leagues. His career to date has been the stuff of legends. An All-America pitcher and DH. Recovered from a brain aneurysm to play last spring at Washington State and to tear up the summer Alaska League. Even though he said he would go back to college for his senior year, Toronto drafted him in the third round, paid him a first-round bonus and put him in a major league uniform. Olerud, of course, got a hit in his first at bat.

NATIONAL LEAGUE FIRST BASEMEN

ATLANTA

The biggest question about the Atlanta roster is the possible return of Nick Esasky. People call me every day, wanting to know. These people have Esasky at a $15 salary (for example), and they want to know if they should retain him. My question is: for what reason would you expect Esasky to be better in 1991 than he was in 1990? Did Esasky say he can play? No. Did the Braves say he can play? No. Did the doctors say he can play? No. Did the Braves just go out and sign a new first baseman? Yes. Esasky has nothing going for him but the wishful thinking and occasional prayers of Rotisserians around the world.

Marc Bowman:

If Nick Esasky gets 550 at bats, then Tommy Gregg, Fran Cabrera, Jeff Blauser, Mark Lemke, and Jim Presley (or whoever replaces him) will all lose some playing time.

Esasky's mysterious dizziness in 1990 resulted in a number of fill-ins at 1B and other shifts. The most notable beneficiary was Dave Justice. Justice worked out so well that the Braves finally traded Dale Murphy, about three years too late. When Justice moved from 1B to RF, Tommy Gregg and Francisco Cabrera became a natural left/right platoon, with Jim "Hound Dog" Presley filling in on occasion. Cabrera is the most exciting player in the bunch. He's only 24; he can really hit, and just needs a place to play.

The arrival of Sid Bream puts a damper on the Gregg/Cabrera platoon. Pencil in Bream/Cabrera, and you will be more accurate. Just plain Bream is also under consideration.

Pete DeCoursey:

Sid Bream will become a 20 HR man for the first time in his career, but Tommy Gregg and Francisco Cabrera, whom he will block, would have put up better offensive numbers. Cabrera hit .294 with a .514 SA against the lefties; Bream has hit .230 against southpaws in 627 ABs since 1984 . Cabrera should retain some value this year, but Tommy Gregg, stuck behind Justice, Gant, Smith, McDowell, and the two 1Bs, may find himself without a place to play.

The best reason for the Bream move has to do with something which we don't talk much about in Rotisserie: defense. He and Pendleton will take away 50-75 hits that went through the Braves infield last year. Their dives and grabs won't help you in Rotisserie, but I thought you might want to know why the Braves did it.

Lary Bump:

Is Mike Bell in some kind of trouble in Virginia? Twice the Braves called him up from the minors, but in between they sent him back to Double-A Greenville, not to Richmond. The 22-year-old left-hander played well enough, displaying a good glove and improving his average from .244 to .291 in his second full season in the South Carolina city, to merit a promotion to Triple-A. It's my guess the Braves have this slight (6-1, 175) first baseman working with weights to improve his HR production (6 each season at Greenville). They'll probably send Bell back to the minors. If it's not with Richmond, we may have to call for an investigation.

CHICAGO CUBS

Mark Grace is developing nicely in all aspects of the game. He hasn't had a BA lower than .296 (his rookie year, 1988). At age 27 in 1991, Grace will show you the best he is capable of doing. In a highly-charged, powerful lineup he should have a career year. The only question is: who plays when Grace doesn't?

Adam Stein:

Mark Grace will sit against some tough lefties, and he will take an occasional day off. Someone has to fill in for him. Hector Villanueva performed this role last year, but he may not make the roster in 1991. The Cubs didn't have a first baseman on their bench during the winter; they will probably teach someone how to play first, if they decide to drop Villanueva. Whoever gets the job will be worth $2 to $3 or more. Remember, almost half the starting pitchers in the NL East are lefties, and some of them are truly tough. Check the boxes during the last two weeks of spring training. His name will be there.

CINCINNATI

Another happy ending if you followed out recommendation last year: "Champ Summers taught International League batting champion Hal Morris how to swing for power, without losing contact. Champ nominated him as Yankees' most improved minor leaguer of 1989; he's on my list, too."

Greg Gajus:

If not for the spring training lockout, Hal Morris (.340-7-36-9) may have been the Reds starting 1B for the entire year. Benzinger was hot, until mid-June, keeping Morris on the bench (and eventually a trip to Nashville). Morris won the Player of the Week award and the full time job in early July and held it the rest of the season, hitting .350 after his recall from Nashville. His addition to the lineup was one of the keys in the Reds improvement in 1990.

The only question about Morris is his ability to hit left-handers. Against LHP Morris hit only .224 in 76 AB, with no extra base hits. If he improves some against LHP, a full season for Hal projects to a Mark Grace clone (.300 10-15 HR 60-70 RBI 15 SB). Lou Piniella reads and uses the stats — if Morris struggles early in 1991 against LHP he will be platooned immediately.

Like almost every Red, Todd Benzinger (.253-5-46-3) got off to a hot start in 1990. However, by mid-June he was being platooned with Hal Morris, and a few weeks later was completely out of the picture in Cincinnati. As anyone who owned him knows, Todd was a complete disaster the second half, hitting .190 with 1 HR and 7 RBI after the break. With the emergence of Morris, Benzinger is highly unlikely to have any role with the Reds in 1991 and will probably be traded. Of the Reds 15 players with 100 or more AB, Benzinger had the worst OBA (.291) and next to worst SLG (.340). Avoid him.

World Champions usually don't make many changes, but Terry Lee (.211-0-3-0) has the best chance to make a surprise contribution to the Reds in 1991. Lee is a big (6'5" 215) right-handed 1B who has spent most of the last four years on the DL with severe foot problems. His stats in Cedar Rapids (1983: .262-19-67 in 405 AB), and Vermont (1985: .289-12-62 in 409 AB) are comparable to established Reds like Eric Davis (1982 Cedar Rapids: .276-15-56) and Chris Sabo (1985 Vermont: .278-11-46). Lee hit .304 with 15 HR and 72 RBI in AAA Nashville in 1990 in only 72 games. If you focus on his 1990 season, and his performance in context of his teammates, Lee projects as a solid major league hitter.

As noted, Hal Morris had a huge platoon differential in 1990 and this represents Lee's opportunity in 1991. Given the chance, he would easily outhit Benzinger, and Piniella would not hesitate to platoon at 1B—at the end of 1990 he was platooning everyone except Davis, Larkin, and Sabo.

Sean Lahman:

At the All-star break Todd Benzinger was quietly having a pretty good season (.275, 4 HR, 39 RBI). Just after the break he was injured. Hal Morris took over and never looked back. Before he was even healthy enough to return, Benzinger had lost his job to the rookie. The switch-hitting Benzinger did see some time at first and a little in left field, but was essentially just a bench player in the second half. When he did play, he didn't do very well and was almost non-existent in the final months. The Reds and Astros were reportedly working on a deal to send Todd to Houston for Mike Scott, but Scott nixed the plan.

Hal Morris was the International League MVP in 1989 for the Yankee's Columbus farm team. When they signed GM Bob Quinn and manager Lou Piniella, both formerly of the Yankees, the Reds also got inside information that enabled them to pick up Morris in exchange for Tim Leary (read: they got Morris for nothing). In half a season, Morris hit .344 with 7 HR, 36 RBI, and 9 SB. Morris will provide the Reds with the kind of offensive weapon you need at first base, something Benzinger never was able to do.

Coming up fast are Terry Lee, who got a brief look in September, and Reggie Jefferson, who missed most of the season with a back injury. If either one of these players gets ready, Morris could be moved to the outfield (but in whose place, I don't know). Given the numbers at first base, and the plethora of quality outfielders, it would not be surprising if Benzinger is in another uniform next season.

Lary Bump:

Watch for Adam Casillas, Reggie Jefferson, and Terry Lee. At 29, Lee is older than Benzinger. He had an excellent season (.327 at Chattanooga, .304 at Nashville, with a total of 23 HR and 87 RBI). His reward was his first cup of coffee in the bigs (and his last, if he doesn't play his way into a platoon with Morris).

Jefferson is a 22-year-old switch hitter who a year ago was hailed as the Reds' first baseman of the future. An auto accident reduced last season to 126 AB at Nashville (.270, 5, 23) and seriously clouded that future.

So maybe the real future 1B is Casillas, a left-handed batter who has led the Midwest and Southern leagues in batting the last two seasons. He also joined Nashville for the American Association playoffs, and was the Sounds' hottest hitter. Casillas' problem is that he doesn't have traditional 1B batting skills. Case in point: he hit just 3 HR and drove in 64 runs at Chattanooga. Another case in point: he has walked nearly three times as often as he has struck out the last two seasons. Watch what he does at Nashville this season. If he shows some power, he's a legitimate 1B threat. If he doesn't, expect the Reds to try to find another position for him.

HOUSTON

Welford McCaffrey:

How valuable is Glenn Davis to the Houston Astros? 1990 was the first season Davis did not lead the team in home runs since he joined the club full time in 1985. 1990 was the first season Davis did not lead the team in runs batted in since the 1986 season. In 1990, Davis already had 19 home runs, leading the league, and had 48 RBI, when his season was effectively ended with a back injury, initially mis-diagnosed as a rib cage muscle pull, in late June.

1991 should be a monster season for Davis, especially if the Astros still have him on opening day. Davis made it clear that he wanted a long-term contract before the season, or he would take the free agent route after 1991. He will want to establish his market value. While he will be 30 years old, he has shown no signs of diminishing abilities. In fact, early in the 1990 season he looked better than he had ever looked before, with some incredible home run streaks. Places where he had not done well in hitting homers before, like Wrigley Field, Jack Murphy Stadium and

Candlestick Park, became his favorite haunts in 1990. He even started hitting better in day games which had always given him trouble before; he talked about sitting out some day games in 1990, until he had a great day hitting homers early in the season.

Davis has been described as overvalued, meaning that he hits meaningless home runs in one-sided games. I decided to take a look at Davis and try to measure just what his value was to the team. [For details, write.] This study suggested that, in 1990, Davis did not play as significant a role as for the team as his stats would suggest. The Astros won almost as many games without Davis as they did when he was in the lineup. In fact, they went on a winning streak pulling themselves out of last place about the time Davis was first injured. But remember, further research along the lines of Davis' 1990 season is needed for his career to come up with a definite conclusion on this hypothesis.

Lary Bump:

Luis Gonzalez and Mike Simms are the prospects who might benefit from a Davis departure. An embarrassment of riches in power-hitting first baseman — in the Astrodome: behind Glenn Davis are Simms, who has hit 95 HRs in the minors, one every 20 ABs in his pro career despite having just 13 last year at Tucson, and Gonzalez, who slammed 24 at Double-A Columbus.

Simms, like Davis, bats right-handed. The Astros have seen this 24-year-old coming since '87, when he powered 39 dingers at Asheville. Last year he matched his career high with a .273 average, drove in 72 runs and had a .386 OBP. Watch how the Astros use him in spring training. They may showcase him to make a deal to fill a hole — pitching, catching, outfield.

Gonzalez, 23, has an advantage batting left-handed, and he can also play 3B. He batted .265 with 89 RBI and 27 SB. The Astros don't need any help at 3B, but if they feel need a lefty-hitting 1B this season, they can't call on Franklin Stubbs. So there is a glimmer of hope that Gonzalez may not be back at Tucson.

LOS ANGELES

The answer is: Eddie Murray in 1991. The trivia question is: Who had the highest major league batting average but didn't win their league batting crown? (Willie McGee's overall average was dragged down by his AL at bats, but he still won the NL title.) Murray pounded the geritol in late summer, and hit .361 with 54 RBI after the All Star break.

It seems inconceivable that the recent changes in the Dodger lineup could possibly harm Eddie Murray's production. Brett Butler is the second best leadoff hitter in baseball, and the best in the NL; and Darryl Strawberry's speed/power presence in the middle of a lineup will help those around him. Murray could have another "career year" in 1991. Spend with confidence.

The Dodgers are very high on Eric Karros. When I called in September, simply to verify Luis Lopez' age, all they wanted to talk about was Karros. I agree with Lary that Lopez is a better bet for 1991, anyway.

Lary Bump:

Brian Traxler, a 23-year-old left-handed hitter with a Jim Traber physique, hit so well in '89 and last spring training that he made the big club. Eleven ABs later, no doubt exhausted from running out his only major league hit, a double, he was back at Albuquerque. He did not distinguish himself there, batting just .277 with 7 HR and 53 RBI, not exactly hot numbers in the PCL. Meanwhile, coming up behind him were Lopez and Karros.

Luis Lopez, a 26-year-old right-handed hitter, had pounded PCL pitching in a brief visit in '89, going 37-for-75 for a .493 average and .524 OBP. Surely that was a fluke and he couldn't do it again. No, he couldn't, but he did lead the PCL with a .353 average that included 11 HR, 81 RBI, a .417 OBP and a .487 slugging percentage. He isn't going to beat out Eddie Murray, but he has the best chance of these three rookies to see some time in LA before September. Lopez had been among the top prospects in the California League four years ago, but hadn't been mentioned in '88 or '89. It pays to save your old Baseball America issues.

If Murray ever winds down, Eric Karros, a 22-year-old right-handed batter, is his likely replacement. You know that warehouse in "Raiders of the Lost Ark"? Aside from the ark, that warehouse is filled with batting trophies won by Dodgers minor leaguers, including Karros, who batted .352 at San Antonio last season. Batting behind 109-RBI man Henry Rodriguez, Karros hit 18 HR with 78 RBI.

MONTREAL

Michael Cassin:

Andres Galarraga went into last season with career averages of .263 vs. RHP and .322 vs. LHP (the best mark against lefties among active NL players). So last year he went out and hit .273 vs. RHP and .226 vs. LHP. Maybe Hal McRae helped Andres' swing vs. righties, but he didn't cut down Andres' Ks any, and there were still plenty of times when Galarraga looked totally helpless swinging against the right-handed breaking ball. A .256 BA, 20 HR, 87 RBI, and gold glove defense are more than acceptable, but his 169 strike-outs stand out like a a beacon in the darkness. All the Ks and a fall-off in his offensive numbers have soured a lot of people on Galarraga, but 20 HR and 80 RBI are a given, so you can do worse.

One thing in Galarraga's favor, especially as far as RBIs, is whether he hits 5th or 6th next year, he'll be hitting in back of players like Wallach, Calderon, Grissom, and Walker, all of whom either hit a lot of doubles or steal a lot of bases (or both), putting plenty of men in scoring position for him. That the Expos are always among the league leaders in doubles and stolen bases makes Galarraga's frequent failures to move runners over with outs less costly to Montreal than it might be to another team.

The Expos experimented some last season with Mike Aldrete getting playing time at first, but little came of it. If Calderon, Walker, Grissom, Martinez, and Alou all look solid, Montreal may think of moving one of them in and dealing Galarraga, but for the time being Andres looks locked in as a full time player.

NEW YORK METS

Alan Boodman:

1991 will likely be the most expensive year in Dave Magadan's Rotisserie career. In his first season as a regular, 1990 saw Dave perform at almost exactly the levels predicted for him here last year, but buyers must wonder if he's reached his peak, or if he may refine his skills further this season.

Anyone who bats .328 will be overbid at many auctions, and Mags is the type of hitter who is far more valuable to a major league team than to a Rotisserie League team. His assets are his batting average, his walks, and his doubles. He also has developed into a fairly slick first-sacker. That plus 75 cents will get you a bottle of soda pop.

Bidding high for guys like Magadan to play first base for you is a defeatist strategy; it's possible you would be better off with a Greg Brock-type who could get some HR and RBI, sacrificing some BA to do so. If your team is to have any power at all, first base is one of the positions you have to look to.

Dave's 1990 season is really not at all out of context with his career up to this point. His lifetime batting average is now over .300, and there's every reason to believe that it's going to stay there for some time. Magadan's doubles would be more valuable if they happened to count for something in RLB. Also they would be more valuable if they happened to be home runs. Bill James posited that players who hit doubles but not homers as youngsters might tend to develop home run power as they age, but Dave is absolutely NOT the type of hitter that this is going to happen to.

Magadan is an extremely disciplined hitter who is

not going to be caught in any long batting slumps, and it is conceivable that .328 will not be his best season. As far as the other primary RL categories are concerned:

1. He has no speed and probably never will. I don't remember anybody talking about players developing speed as they age.

2. It's unlikely that he will EVER hit more than 12 homers in a season, and it's REALLY unlikely that he'll ever hit more than 20. You may have noticed that Dave is about as slow as Mark McGwire, and they draw walks at about the same rate, but they don't have similar power stats. The question is: if you have an extra 30 HR and 30 RBI, do you trade them for 70 more points in batting average? And if you do, will you please trade them to me? I'll take them.

3. For the first time, Mags will be in the starting lineup from opening day. If Buddy shuttles him around in the order as in '90, it will help Davey's RBI count as opposed to hitting him second all year, but would cost him a few runs scored. His totals in the main categories should end up close to what they were last year.

If you look around the National League, it's not too difficult to find several first basemen who might be able to help you more in 1991. Magadan's about even with Hal Morris of Cincinnati. Morris has the advantage of being younger (and therefore more potential to develop), and while .340 is a bit much to ask, he was a very good hitter in the minors too. And if Magadan is even with Hal Morris, how does he compare to Clark (either one, but mostly Will), Davis, Galarraga, Murray, Guerrero, Grace, or Justice? I'd say he compares to Mark Grace, but that's about it. Bid mid-range money on Davey, but let someone else win him. You'll probably both end up happy.

Kelvin Torve might end up as the backup here, and Tim Teufel will still be around if he doesn't kill himself first. Torve is a veteran minor-leaguer with Magadan-type skills, but he's older than Kent Hrbek or Ivan Lendl, both of whom have as much chance as Torve at getting significant playing time at Shea Stadium this year. Look at Teufel's minor league numbers, and at his first few seasons in the majors. He could have turned in a fine career somewhere, but circumstances reduced him to a bit player in his mid-to-late-20's. He's a competent backup infielder if you can't get anyone better.

PHILADELPHIA

Pete DeCoursey:

Ricky Jordan is the presumptive starter against LHP and John Kruk the foe of RHP. With a set outfield, it will be hard for Jordan to win the full-time job, since Kruk is a .300 hitter against righties and Ricky isn't. In fact, if Jordan engages in his traditional spring strugglefest, replete with finger and wrist injuries or rumors of them, Dave Hollins may get a chance to displace Ricky at 1B. The Phils were impressed by Hollins' PH power, with 3 pinch-homers, and once Hollins adjusts to major league pitching, his excellent batting eye will make him an on-base threat as well. The Phils think highly of Hollin's defense at 1B.

If Jordan is pushed into the the outer darkness but surfaces someplace with a chance to play in August, he would be a great pick-up. An inordinately large proportion of his HRs and RBIs and hits have come in August and Sept., even in his minor league career. The Phils patience with him may evaporate by midsummer, and he probably isn't as good as say, Pat Tabler, but he turns 26 this year and has always hit in Aug. and Sept. In leagues which count BA rather than OBA, he's a good pickup.

John Kruk will hit for a good average(.280-.300), but his 15-20 HR power and 30 double days are over. If you are looking for more than a high average, 5-10 HRs, 60-70 RBI and large bunches of walks, look elsewhere. Be careful of relying on Kruk for SBs: although he stole 10 last year, he stole 2 of his first 6 and was then given the stop sign for a month. After the break, he picked on Rich Gedman for 3 in one game, humiliating Alex

Trevino and his ilk for 8 SBs in his last 9 attempts. As a base-pilferer, he could be curtailed by Leyva from attempting in 1991.

PITTSBURGH

Orlando Merced and Carmelo Martinez were both elevated by the free agencies of Sid Bream. Merced is a switch hitter but has done better against righty pitchers in his brief major league trials. Martinez bats right and offers the possibility of an old/young, left/right platoon. I think I like Martinez better than the Pirates do; he hit 20 homers in the one year that he got 500 at bats. Redus is the 4th OF and part of the 1B platoon (with Carmelo), if nothing changes.

Pete DeCoursey:

Someone might want to point out to the Pirates that Gary Redus and Carmelo Martinez are both right-handed. Here's how they hit against both kinds of pitching:

Versus lefties in '90

Player	AB	BA	OBA	SA	2B	3B	HR	RBI
Martinez	90	.233	.343	.456	5	0	5	16
Redus	202	.262	.345	.455	15	3	6	23

Versus righties in '90

Player	AB	BA	OBA	SA	2B	3B	HR	RBI
Martinez	127	.244	.324	.394	4	0	5	19
Redus	25	.120	.313	.120	0	0	0	0

From 1984-9, Redus hit .246 with a .395 SA against righties, while hitting .263 and slugging .427 against lefties; Martinez hit .239 and slugged .391 against righties, while batting .261 and .438 against lefties. Gary's faster and a better fielder; Carmelo's better at fielding throws and hitting homers, but on what basis would you platoon these two? By the phases of the moon? As Jeff King also hit a sterling .214 against righties last year, the corners will be weak for the Buccos against two-thirds of the NL's pitchers.

Lary Bump:

Lost and Found? My name is Orlando Merced, and I'm looking for my batting stroke. Where? Somewhere on the Pirates' bench at Three Rivers Stadium. A 24-year-old switch hitter, Merced had batted .341 in 35 games at Buffalo at the end of 1989, and he was off to a similar start last season when the Bucs called him up. He wasn't the same hitter in Pittsburgh (.208) or in Buffalo when he returned (finishing at .262 with a career-high 9 HR and a team-high 55 RBI). Aside: This team tied for the division title. Tell me Pilot Field isn't a pitchers' park. As a major league prospect, Merced seems to come up just a little short. That's in more than his height, which is generously listed at 6-0. He probably doesn't have enough power to be an everyday 1B, and he probably isn't a good enough OF to win a job. If he finds that hitting stroke in spring training, though, pay attention.

ST. LOUIS

For two years, I have been warning people away from Pedro Guerrero, because of his injury history. Well, Pedro didn't break an arm or a leg last year or the year before, but the warnings have been going on long enough, that he has now succumbed to old age. Guerrero slumped to .275-4-29-0 in the second half of 1990. He might bounce up a little from that bottom, but his best days are long gone.

Most people are likely to overvalue Guerrero in 1991; the perception is above the reality of his performance. Even my executive editor Pete DeCoursey leaned toward Guerrero as someone who should compare favorably with Rafael Palmeiro. I was trying to make the point that Palmeiro is a comer for 1991, and I was disparaging a trade in which a novice Rotisserian had given away Raffy for garbage. Guerrero's name came up, and I quickly posed one of my patented, "I'll bet you $$ per category, one on one" challenges, matching Palmeiro against Guerrero head-to-head in the four offensive categories. Pete was mildly surprised to look and see that Palmeiro won every category last year, even HR and RBI. [He then won his money back by substituting Fred McGriff for Guerrero, but that is getting away from the point . . .] Guerrero's power output has slipped below some noted non-HR type of hitters.

Gerald Perry's arrival in St. Louis, combined with the apparent difficulties that might arise with Todd Zeile spending a full year at 3B, fueled rumors that Perry might take over at 1B with Guerrero going back to third, which he played up until 1985 and sporadically thereafter. The Cardinals deny all this conjecture. The company line portrays Perry in a Denny Walling type of role. Perry is surely more valuable than Walling has been. Gerald is younger, has more speed, and more hair.

Lary Bump:

Should the Cardinals decide to trade Pedro Guerrero, the 25-year-old Rod Brewer might be able to step right into the lineup. At least, into a Whitey Herzog-type lineup; it's not clear whether Joe Torre will keep the same kind of set-up. Last season, the lefty-hitting Brewer hit a career-high 12 HR, and he has averaged 10 in his four minor league seasons, so he's not the traditional big bopper 1B. Despite batting just .251, he drove in 83 runs. He has maintained about a 1/1 W/K ratio throughout his career, and he's not a bad fielder. The worst that could happen to him would be another year at Louisville, most likely a productive year. The best would be a Guerrero trade.

SAN DIEGO

Jack Clark is out; Fred McGriff is in. McGriff will not suffer a big power loss coming to San Diego. The park effects might even help him in the HR department. McGriff's batting average is very likely to drop, however. At least he still has Tony Fernandez on base when he comes up.

McGriff's presence diminishes the importance of all the backups at 1B, who figured so prominently when the injury-prone Clark patrolled the cold corner in San Diego. Phil Stephenson and Triple-A standby Rob Nelson both bat left, like McGriff; Fred doesn't like to take days off, anyway. Stephenson and/or Jerald Clark (a righty hitter) are most likely to pick up the slack, if there is any.

The Padres roster in late December looked rather incomplete. No one is going to displace McGriff, but someone might come along who will immediately step ahead of the above-named understudies.

SAN FRANCISCO

Will Clark is due for a big year. At age 27 he should be in his prime, and he is far too talented to stay down around the levels that he produced in 1990.

Mike Laga finally wised up to the fact that waiting in line behind Will Clark will get you nowhere. Laga went to Japan for 1991. The next backup for 1B in the farm system last year was Rich Aldrete, who hit .228 at AA Shreveport. If something happens to Clark, the Giants will shift somebody from another position.

Thom Rogers:

Look for Will Clark to regain his 1989 form after offseason foot surgery. Last year's .295-19-95-8 would be a fine year for most hitters, but Clark is surely capable of doing much better. My personal prediction is .310-25-105-8, in 600 AB.

AMERICAN LEAGUE SECOND BASEMEN

BALTIMORE

Simply stated, Baltimore is a lousy place to look for your Rotisserie second baseman. For some reason, the Orioles have been determined that Billy Ripken should be their 2B. They repeatedly promoted him up the farm system when his numbers didn't support such action. Great fielder? He led the Southern League in errors. Then they continued playing him while better players watched. So, playing against pitchers selected because he should be able to hit them, Ripken kept his lifetime average at precisely .239 in the 1989 campaign, with a career high in homers (2) and fell just 8 RBI short of his career best, driving in 26. Then in 1990 he soared to .291 with 3 HR and 38 RBI, no longer harmful, but not much help either.

The competition offers slim pickin's. Rene Gonzales kept his lifetime BA at exactly .218 in 1989 and then dropping to .217 in 1990. Gonzales is in the game for his defense and, as described by Pete DeCoursey elsewhere, he will continue getting into games despite the fact that no one in Rotisserie baseball wants him to play. The few people who get stuck with Gonzales (because they can't think of another infielder) don't want him to play, and the people who own Billy Ripken and Worthington/Gomez etc. don't want Gonzales in the game, either.

Gonzales reminds me of a question that needs to be addressed somewhere. The "Mendoza Line" means a floating index around .215, not precisely .200. The beauty of the term is that it takes into consideration all the normal variation in baseball statistics: fast starts and slow starts, pitcher-dominated years and hitter-dominated years, etc. The Mendoza line floated up and down with the tides and seasons, always offering a Buoy marker. If you were below Mendoza in the Sunday paper, you were in trouble. Because the origin of this term (George Brett's usage) came to the public via the book Rotisserie League Baseball, we should all protect its definition. The mass media have been misusing this term for over eight years, and with increasing frequency. I am beginning to see why William Safire bemoans the deterioration of the English language. People THINK they know the meaning of a term when they don't; they use it in incorrectly in conversation or writing and thereby misinform those to whom they are speaking. And so the misuse spreads. Maybe if people started calling it the "Rene Gonzales" line, George Brett's original meaning would be restored. At least people would learn that Gonzales (in this case) is spelled with one z and one s, not two z's.

Speaking of the Rene Gonzales line, Tim Hulett looked like an offensive force last year at this time, by default. In 1989, Hulett returned from exile in Rochester (after several marginal years with the White Sox) to do wonderful things like hit .303 against RHP in his late-season appearances with Baltimore. In 1990, Hulett hit a harmless .255, but his production wasn't worth the $1 that he went for in most auctions last spring.

Just before the winter meetings, the Orioles made some remark about Juan Bell being an everyday player in 1991. Where would he play? I adopted the theory that the "Bell in the lineup" story was nothing but a screwy attempt to attract brother George to Baltimore to play with Juan. It didn't work. The value of the rumor is that it made me consider Bell as a 2B, meaning that the notion must have occurred to Baltimore management as well. It isn't a great idea, but the O's have fielded some pretty horrible second basemen in the past few years, and Bell would at least offer variety.

Lary Bump:

A year ago I wrote that the Orioles should let Bell mature and improve his concentration. Now I question whether the 23-year-old ever will mature. On the night Rochester clinched its division championship, Bell precipitated a dugout fight by — I won't put this delicately — farting in teammate Donell Nixon's face. Not a really mature thing to do. Bell is an immensely talented switchhitting shortstop, but it's a quicker road to a big league job in Baltimore going against Bill Ripken than against his brother Cal, who apparently will play shortstop every day until he drops. Bell also swung a pretty good bat — .285 with 6 HR, 35 RBI and 16 SB in another injury-plagued year.

McKnight, 28, is a great guy to have on a Triple-A team. He switch-hits, he gets on base, he hustles, he can play a lot of positions (most notably last season filling in at SS when Bell was injured). Unfortunately, his skills don't quite add up to making him a major leaguer, especially against right-handed pitching. His .280 average last season was the highest of his seven years in the minors. His other superlatives in the minors — 9 HR, 55 RBI, 9 SB. Not quite enough.

BOSTON

The Red Sox have a number of possibilities swirling around the 2B/SS situation. Jody Reed is the obvious choice for 2B and is a nice .280 BA, 50 RBI commodity for Rotisserie (when in doubt, take someone from Boston). After the winter meetings, the Sox were pursuing Japan repatriate Vance Law. Before you get all excited about Fenway effects, consider that Law's most recent NL stats (.235-7-42-2) were accumulated in over 400 at bats with the Cubs. Wrigley field is OK for hitters, too, and Law is now two years older (34).

Marty Barrett had an injury-plagued 1989, and appeared at only 60 games at 2B in 1990. Reports are that Barrett thinks too much (and obviously says too much) to stay on the good side of Boston management. Another trouble is, Barrett is unspectacular even when he is healthy, performing functions that just don't add up to much compared to other (cheaper) players, just like Rotisserie.

CALIFORNIA

UPDATE — Johnny Ray went to Japan, boosting the future of Luis Sojo.

For the third consecutive year, the Rotisserie-magnificent Johnny Ray is due to be traded or benched. He almost went to Cleveland after the 1989 season, and has been shopped widely elsewhere. Ray had an off year in 1990, but he remains a lifetime .290 hitter and wasn't all that bad in his off year. Ray is solid in all areas, but age is becoming a factor. He's 34 now. Frank White is 41, though, and the two have many similarities.

There is a great deal of nonsense about Luis Sojo following the Devon White deal. True, Sojo may be installed as the regular 2B, and true, Johnny Ray is again expendable. But false, Sojo is not a major talent who has pushed Ray out of the picture. Sojo is no more talented than Mark McLemore, and McLemore wasn't good enough to push Ray out of the picture. (The Angels tried, with a ridiculous left field experiment in 1988, but they soon wanted a real outfield bat in the lineup and McLemore back on the bench. Hello, Cleveland.)

Lary Bump:

Luis Sojo, a 25-year-old right-handed batter, jumped straight from Class A to Triple-A, and for most of two seasons was the steadiest SS in the International League. That's still a long stretch from being Tony Fernandez, so Sojo moved to 2B with the Jays, and Nelson Liriano moved to Minnesota. In 75 games with Syracuse, Sojo batted .296 with 6 HR, 25 RBI and 10 SB. More impressive than the SB total was the fact that he improved his SB success from 39% to 83%. At 25, he's nice and youthful compared to his competition.

CHICAGO WHITE SOX

Scott Fletcher reached his peak in 1987 with 63 RBI, 13 steals, and a .287 BA, all good numbers for a middle infielder. Fletcher is still hanging on at age 32 in 1991. He will hit well enough to stay in the lineup, and if he can produce 50 RBI again like he did in 1990, he will have true Rotisserie value. His average should be around .250, which will neither help nor hurt you. His SB speed is really gone now, but the aggressive style of Jeff Torborg will send him running half a dozen times in 1991, anyway.

Jon Dunkle:

Second base for the White Sox is bleak offensively. The duo of Scott Fletcher and Craig Grebeck combined for a .227 batting average. Adding Steve Lyons to the equation makes the situation worse. Avoid the White Sox at this position.

Timothy R. McAvoy:

Fletcher's 1989 arrival ended the Fred Manrique and Donnie Hill Show, which was getting bad ratings and really needed to be canceled. The Sox like Fletcher for his glove work; any offense is a bonus from their point of view, but you of course will be focused mainly on the hitting aspect.

Fletcher's production fell off at Texas (.239 BA) but revived nicely after he returned to Chicago. With Sosa and/or Lance Johnson hitting in front of him, Scott's RBI output should hold up nicely in 1991.

CLEVELAND

Jerry Browne is on my list of best picks for 1991, because of his prime age with 2 years of full time major league experience.

Bill Gray:

Jerry Browne. Again, the job is his. There are no other players in the Cleveland organization who will move him aside. Jerry will be only 25 in February. He has shown signs in the past three years of becoming a premier second baseman. In 1987 at Texas, Browne stole 27 bases at age 22. In 1989, he hit .299. Last year he improved his RBI and runs scored despite hitting "only" .267. However, in the last 57 games, he batted .281 (58 for 206).

Browne was hampered in the first half of 1990 by nagging injuries and was in a terrible slump at the plate. Then he caught fire after the All-Star game. At 25, with 4 major league seasons behind him, the stage is set for Jerry Browne to take a giant step upward. The only negative with Browne is that he will probably not steal as often as you might like. After Browne spent the 1989 season leading off, he was moved to the second spot behind mid season phenom, Alex Cole. Cole will get the majority of the steals on this team. This will continue to allow Browne to have a lot of RBI chances and will keep his average nice and high. Even though he stole just 12 times last year, barring injury he could have a shot a 20. MacNamara wants to use speed to create more offense. Still makes too many baserunning blunders but these should diminish as Browne matures.

With Browne, you don't have to worry about another player taking his place. He will be the Cleveland 2B for years to come. He will get you plenty of AB and is still improving.

Steve Goldman:

There is no question who will play second base for the Tribe in 1991; Jerry Browne is the only candidate.

Jerry struggled at the plate through most of 1990, but came on strong to post decent figures at the plate, a .267 batting average and a .353 on-base percentage. These numbers aren't as good as they were in 1989, but they're still good enough to suggest that he could have a long and prosperous career in Cleveland, especially when you consider that he has the range to play a fine second base. In fact, I think it's way too early to write off the trade in which they acquired him with Pete O'Brien and Oddibe McDowell (both since departed) for Julio Franco. Browne is still only 25, and there's no telling how good he can eventually be.

The ascension of Alex Cole into the leadoff spot should take some pressure off Jerry, who was the leadoff hitter before that. Browne should be more at home in the second spot, to which he is well-suited. His abilities to get on base and to make contact with the bat should give the team a fine 2 hitter who can combine with Cole to set up the offense.

DETROIT

The Tigers acquisition of Tony Bernazard may have tipped their hand. The original question was: what happens with Tony Phillips (a natural second baseman being chased off 3B by Travis Fryman) and Lou Whitaker both eminently qualified to play second? Bernazard's arrival is a sign that the Tigers plan to unload either Phillips or Whitaker, probably the latter. If they both stay, Phillips would get a utility role, but what would Bernazard be? A backup utilityman?

Expect Whitaker to get about 450 to 500 at bats (wherever he plays), with 10 to 15 homers, and about a .250 BA. His RBI count will depend on where he bats in the order, somewhere in the 55 to 75 range.

Rick Burkhardt ("speaking only as a fan"):

It appears at present that Sparky's plans are to keep Lou Whitaker at second base against right-handed pitching, with Phillips there against southpaws. If Fryman has a productive spring, I expect him to be the starter there next year; right now I'd say he has to play himself out of the position. Phillips will also play some short when Trammell needs a rest; third if Fryman needs a day off or goes into a slump, and undoubtedly will get some time in the outfield as well. Sparky's attitude seems to be that as long as he hits and gets on base, Phillips will get almost as many at bats as a regular would get; he just won't have a set position. If his offense stays consistent with this past season, look for him to have 450 at bats. Keep in mind that a trade of Whitaker (a possibility if they could get some good pitching) could make Phillips a regular at second, and if Trammell were to get hurt, Fryman would move to short and Phillips would take over at third.

Michael Lesher:

When the Tigers got Bernazard, I wondered what they wanted with him. Two possibilities:

(1) Cecil Fielder may have created a strong market for players from Japan.

(2) The Tigers may soon make a move to trade Whitaker, one of the few Tigers with trade value, and one of the few regulars that Detroit can (now) afford to deal away. They are reportedly offering Whitaker for a starting pitcher or a left-handed DH with power. At the end of last year, Sparky said that Phillips could expect 500 at bats in 1991, but with all those infielders that doesn't seem mathematically possible. If they trade Whitaker, Phillips takes over at 2B and Bernazard fills in as UI.

KANSAS CITY

One year ago, Terry Shumpert was an unproven minor leaguer coming off a .248 year at Omaha. Today, he has the Royals 2B job locked up.

Marc Bowman:

Frank White was not offered a contract for 1991, so the job officially belongs to Terry Shumpert. It's likely that Shumpert would have won the job anyway. Terry can steal a lot of bases, but he struck out a lot in his brief stint during 1990, a sign that he may not yet have adjusted to major league pitching. In 1991 he will probably struggle early, whiff excessively, and possibly ride the bench a while and think about major league pitching.

After the All Star break, Shumpert could be terrific. Even if he doesn't perform up to expectation, he will get playing time as long as the Royals have no alternative. Better than grabbing Shumpert on draft day (unless he's available for next to nothing) the best strategy is to let someone else have him and keep him during the early-season struggle that seems likely to occur. When he's hitting under .200 in June, and striking out once every four at bats, do the other owner a favor: "I'll take Shumpert off your hands, if you give me a good player to go with him." You will end up with a pile of stolen bases, cheap.

Bill Pecota and Kevin Seitzer are the backups. In fact, the Royals were making noises about putting Seitzer at 2B, but they have apparently abandoned the idea. Pecota will play all over the field during the 1991 season, and qualifies at 2B and SS already, using the 20 game rule. Beware: 1990 was the first year that Pecota ever had any Rotisserie value. He is over age 30 and hit just .206 in 1988-1989. Seitzer may appear at 2B just long enough to let you shift him over there, making room for a good hitter at 3B on your roster.

Lary Bump:

The Royals gave 24-year-old RHH Terry Shumpert, their 2B job last season, and he started to run with it until he was injured. He batted .255 in 39 games at Omaha, then .275 in 32 with the big club. His most impressive offensive stat was his 18-for-18 base stealing at Omaha. He showed signs of coming out of the fielding slump that plagued him in '89. Shumpert didn't especially enjoy being the announced heir apparent to Frank White. Now White's gone, and unless the Royals give the 2B job to Kevin Seitzer [see above] it's Shumpert's to keep.

MILWAUKEE

Jim Gantner must be good in the field, because the Brewers perpetually move aside better hitters to put him at 2B.

Alan Boodman:

Jim Gantner, like a house guest who won't leave, returns to the middle of the diamond for yet another season. Gantner, once the premier (although unrecognized) defensive second baseman in the AL, is apparently still good enough with the glove to justify inclusion in the lineup, but it's got to be embarrassing to management that the Brewer farm system can't come up with anyone better.

But you know, they did come up with someone better—in 1978. If it were my team, Paul Molitor would play second base. He is still physically capable of playing there, and as far as the risk of injury is concerned, don't think that hiding Molitor at first base is going to change anything. If he puts his mind to it, Paul Molitor can get hurt anywhere. Wait and see.

Offensively, would you rather have a combo of Gantner/Molitor or Molitor/Brock? Gantner cannot be SO good defensively that he makes up for the difference between a .265 hitter with no power or RBI (Gantner) and a .250 hitter who could draw 75 walks, hit 20 homers and drive in 80 runs (Brock). [Even Pete DeCoursey says that while defense matters, it doesn't matter that much; he would know.]

However, since the AAA second baseman has the same skills as Jimbo, at a lower level of competition, there won't be any pressure from behind, and Gantner will be expected to play a full season. Actually, a full season means 120 games of about .260 with no homers, 30 RBI, and 10-15 steals.

Edgar Diaz or maybe Gus Polidor (is he still here?) are the main backups, and the fact that neither of them seem to be able to beat out Gantner has to say something. What it says is "Don't pick up Diaz or Polidor."

MINNESOTA

Among all major league teams, the Twins have the highest turnover ratio among second basemen.

Remember Wally Backman? Tommy Herr? Steve Lombardozzi? Now we have Nelson Liriano, Al Newman, Chip Hale, and Chuck Knoblauch. Who's next?

Chip Hale had the 2B job going into spring training 1990. Tom Kelly announced that he didn't want to use Al Newman as an everyday player. He said it had been a mistake to use Newman that way in 1989, and that he didn't intend to do it again in 1990. Hale had a poor spring, however, got shipped out to Portland, and Kelly installed Newman at 2B until Liriano relieved him later in the season.

Paul Clements:

The Twins like Liriano, and I agree with them. He has the potential to be a really good hitter, and is at the right age to improve. An external factor is the probable hole at third base, meaning that Al Newman will be frequently occupied there, making more playing time for Liriano at second. There was no talk of Hale during the autumn, so unless he has a tremendous spring, I would expect him to be back in the minors again in 1991.

Lary Bump:

Hale is a former heir apparent, but his hopes may be evaporating into thin air. With the Twins' 2B slot essentially vacant for two years, they gave Hale, a 26-year-old lefty hitter, all of two major league ABs last year. He hit all right, .280-3-40 with a .366 OBP, at Portland. There must be something that cost him his one-time rightful inheritance.

The newly anointed heir is Chuck Knoblauch, a 22-year-old right-handed batter who was the Twins' No. 1 draft pick in '89. At Orlando, he batted .290 with 2 HR, 53 RBI and 23 SB, and fielded as well as you would expect a former SS to field at the less-demanding 2B position. There is still a Help Wanted sign near the second sack in the Metrodome, and Knoblauch may be hired over Nelson Liriano without the benefit of Triple-A experience.

NEW YORK YANKEES

Bad year? Steve Sax was just 12 hits short of a .280 batting average in 1990. If you ask Steve, he will tell you that he had more than his fair share of hard-hit line drives that went right into fielders' gloves last year, and his teammates and opponents will all agree. Even when Steve's average dropped down around .240, there were no signs of a slumping player: no lunging at bad pitches, no fuming at umpires for call strikes, no dogging while running out ground balls. "It was just one of those years," Steve said in September.

Speed came to the ballyard every day in 1990 for Sax. He was second only to Rickey Henderson in the AL for both total steals and SB success rate. Patience also came to the park every day. Steve drew more walks than he had strikeouts.

Daniel Stone:

A recovery for Sax in 1991 is likely. He has hit .275 or better in eight of his ten major league seasons, and should be able to hit .300 again without making any changes. One of his biggest problems in 1990 was the weakness of the whole Yankee offense.

Sax is the third-best baserunner in the American League, after Rickey Henderson and Alex Cole. He scores a lot of runs, hits for high average, doesn't strike out much. Critics point to Steve's "low" RBI output as evidence that he slumped in 1990 and didn't get hits with men on base. The fact is, the Yankees never had anyone on base. The career high of 63 RBI in 1989 came while he was batting behind Rickey Henderson for most of the season. Think that made any difference?

Sax really turned up the pace at the end of the 1990 season. It was an accomplishment to finish with a .260 average. He had to hit .400 over his last ten games. The outlook for 1991 is excellent. Sax is due to hit a few balls "where they ain't," and the Yankee lineup can't possibly be any worse than it was in 1990. Expect a big year.

Lary Bump:

If you scout enough players, occasionally you get one right. I liked Pat Kelly at Oneonta in 1988, and I liked him last year at Albany. I expect to like him with Columbus this season, but as a Yankee-hater, I draw the line at liking him in Yankee Stadium in '91. He'll be there, but I won't have to like him. Kelly has more ways to beat you than a con man at the county fair. He hit well (.270-8-44) especially good for a 2B in a pitchers' league. And he ran well in 1990, with 31 SB. He also has a good glove and covers a lot of ground. He's a right-handed batter, just 22.

Trivia question:

Who was the last Yankee second baseman to steal more bases than Steve Sax's 43 in 1990? Answer: Snuffy Stirnweiss. You could look it up.

OAKLAND

Willie Randolph played the most games at 2B for the A's in 1990, but he looked unlikely to return after the winter meetings. Oakland acquired veteran utilityman Ernest Riles, backing up Mike Gallego and Lance Blankenship. Gallego will probably be the starter on opening day.

Gallego and Blankenship are both right-handed batters who can't hit either righty or lefty pitchers. Riles bats left, and has been used almost exclusively against right-handed pitching over the past two years. He hit .293 against righties in 1989, but slumped last year.

Neither Gallego nor Blankenship can do much for your Rotisserie roster. They sold for about $2 each in most 1990 auctions, and didn't earn even that much for their owners. Riles is an interesting case, however. He had .340 batting averages in three different minor leagues, and was on his way to a decent career when sidetracked by injuries in 1987. Despite the horrible 1990 season, he is still a .264 career hitter, and should be safer than the alternatives in Oakland. For $1 or $2 my choice would be Riles.

TEXAS

Julio Franco, the man who once disappeared for two days while he was "looking for Jerusalem" in the neighborhoods of New York City, has the 2B job with the Rangers for 1991. Franco is perpetually among the top Rotisserie middle infielders, helping in all four categories. Everybody knows about Julio, however. He cost an average of almost $30 in 1990. He's still only 29 years old.

Switch-hitter Brian House produced a .277 BA and 30 SB for Oklahoma City in 1990. The former Cubs farmhand is 27 years old now, too old to be a top prospect, but he has stolen 30 to 60 bases every year as a pro and has often been chosen as a minor league all star.

TORONTO

Things change. Manny Lee fought for the Toronto 2B job for years. Then as soon as he won it, he got shifted to shortstop. Roberto Alomar has arrived in the American League. Likely to be backing up Alomar is rookie utility player Eddie Zosky, who spent 1990 at AA Knoxville. Don't expect any offense from Zosky.

Brigg Hewitt:

Just before he left San Diego, Roberto Alomar was complaining about a possible shift to shortstop (to replace Garry Templeton). Well, he didn't want to play SS in San Diego, and he isn't going to play SS in San Diego.

Watch for Alomar to start slowly in 1991. His offense and defense may both look bad in the early going. He will be playing without his father's coaching for the first time in years, unless the Jays find a way to put Alomar Sr. on their payroll. Once he begins to concentrate, however, Roberto will produce some outstanding baseball. His numbers should be at least as good in 1991 as they were in 1990, and at age 23 he is still improving, with big stardom in his future.

When it was a toss-up between Lee and Liriano in 1990:

Like many either/or situations involving two players both likely to get playing time (one as a regular and one as a backup and utilityman), there is a clever method to get the one you like best, at a low price. Bring up one of the names (the one you DON'T like) early in the auction. The price will probably be very high, just due to early-auction supply and demand functions. As soon as player A is taken at a high price, congratulate the bozo who bought him: "That was a good price for Manny Lee; I guess you know that Liriano isn't going to play much this year. Nice move!" Don't shout, but say it loud enough for everyone to hear. When Liriano comes up much later, no one will want to bid too high. You could flip-flop Liriano and Lee in this sequence, with the same desired result. Just take your pick, and dig in.

J.L. Feinstein:

Answer: Lloyd Moseby, Tony Fernandez, Nelson Liriano, and Mookie Wilson.

Question: Why did the Blue Jays trade for Roberto Alomar?

For several years, the Blue Jays have had a powerful offense, one that all too often lived (and died) by the 3-run homer. The one thing they lacked was the ability to manufacture runs. Much of the problem could be tied to a lack of productivity from the leadoff hitter. Some of the guys they tried had a decent BA (Fernandez/Mookie Wilson); most had good speed; but they all had sub-par base percentages.

Enter Roberto Alomar. In his 2 years in the bigs, he's reached base over 600 times, scored at least 80 runs every year, and stolen a couple dozen bases each year. He's not another Rickey Henderson, but he figures to be far and away the most productive leadoff hitter, the Blue Jays have had in recent memory.

Defensively, Alomar has outstanding range and the ability to make the spectacular play. His 19 errors are a function of his getting to a lot more balls than the average 2nd baseman, as well as occasional lapses of concentration.

His game is made for the Skydome, both offensively and defensively. His range makes the Blue Jays very solid up the middle, and his ability to get on-base and swipe a bag or two will set up Olerud, Gruber, Carter, etc. very nicely.

As of the winter meetings, the Blue Jays didn't have a legitimate back-up second sacker on the roster. They could always move Gruber to 2B and put Mulliniks in at 3B in a pinch, but the expectation is that they'll look to pick up a utility type between now and spring training, possibly a guy like Luis Quinones. (The Reds were interested in John Cerutti).

The best Toronto 2B prospect, Williams Suero, has both speed and pop. But he is almost certainly going to spend the year in Syracuse.

NATIONAL LEAGUE SECOND BASEMEN

ATLANTA

As you can see below, there isn't unanimity about the Treadway/Lemke rivalry, even though Treadway just had his career year with highs in BA, homers, and RBI. But then the Braves were giving Lemke a good share of playing time last September, and September is a good preview of spring training. My personal opinion is that Treadway should be safe for 1991; Lemke will have to wait or work into the lineup at 3B.

Lemke is the perpetual odd man out in the Braves' game of musical chairs around the infield. At least he made it to the Triple A All Star game in 1989. Lemke has been solid throughout his minor league career. At Durham in 1987 he hit .292 with 20 HR, 68 RBI and 10 SB's with only 11 errors; he led the league in assists and fielding percentage. Then in 1988 he had a fine year at Greenville, hitting .270 with 16 HR, 80 RBI, and 18 stolen bases. In 1989 he produced a .276 average and 61 RBI.

Marc Bowman:

Jeff Treadway is a fine second baseman. He does all things well enough, but doesn't do anything exceptionally well. His range is above average, and he turns the DP well, but you wouldn't say "Treadway" when asked to name the five slickest middle infielders. He hits for a higher average than most 2B's, and he has above-average power, but he doesn't come immediately to mind when you think of good-hitting second basemen. He gets a few SB's but isn't regarded as fast. Briefly stated, Treadway is a nice, underappreciated little Rotisserie package. He cost an average of only $5 last year and was worth more like $10. His position at 2B is more established now than it was a year ago, but his price should remain reasonable.

Mark Lemke is the backup, and a good one. Lemke is still young (25) but appears to be headed down the same road that Paul Runge traveled. Lemke really needs a chance to play regularly before his offensive potential can develop fully, but that chance doesn't seem likely. Unless something breaks in the Atlanta infield, and Lemke starts to play every day, I recommend that you don't waste a roster spot on him.

Adam Stein:

Jeff Treadway faded in the second half. If the Braves knew how to make deals, they would package Treadway and a pitcher for one top-quality infielder. Don't hold your breath. Treadway (28) is now going downhill. Mark Lemke is likely to push him out of a job, this year or next. Lemke's value is enhanced by his ability to play 3B. With Presley out of the picture, Lemke is a serious candidate for the starting job at third.

Watch the use of Treadway in spring training. If he isn't playing every day during the final two weeks, I wouldn't spend more than a few dollars for him.

CHICAGO CUBS

Considering that Ryne Sandberg hit .321 with 19 HR in the second half of 1989, he has now been a 40-homer, .310-BA hitter for a full year and a half. If you don't think he's going to keep it up, the question is: why would Sandberg's performance slip now? One safe prediction, though: he isn't going to improve any in 1991. The only problem with Ryno, even if you feel convinced that he will continue at the high level, is that someone in your league is going to pay every penny that his stats are worth, probably even more. You need bargains to win, and Sandberg isn't going to be a bargain. He could, however, be a $40 player who delivers only $25 worth of production. My advice: get yourself some nice young, Fast, Power-hitting Outfielders (two FPO's for the price of one Sandberg).

Timothy R. McAvoy:

The Cubs were confident enough in Sandberg that they let minor league standout Greg Smith go to San Francisco [see]. Speaking of letting young talent go to other teams, how could the Phillies give up Sandberg (and more) for Ivan DeJesus?

Lary Bump:

Replacing Greg Smith as the prospect buried behind Ryne Sandberg is Jose Vizcaino, from the Dodgers. It has been written for — lo! — these two years or so that Vizcaino would be the Dodgers' 2B. The 23-year-old switch hitter could have been in '91. After batting .279 at Albuquerque, he batted .275 in 61 ABs with the Dodgers, outshining his more heralded DP partner, Jose Offerman. In fact, Vizcaino played a fair amount of SS, his original position, with LA. He may help the Cubs at SS, or even 3B, during 1991.

Don't get all wide-eyed, even if you see Vizcaino winning a job (say at 3B) during spring training. He might get you a dozen SB, but Vizcaino is in the game for defense. He never hit for high average or power, even in the low minors.

CINCINNATI

No discussion of the Reds 33-12 start is complete without noting Mariano Duncan's remarkable start. Playing a new position (39 games at 2B before 1990) with a new team Duncan did a great Joe Morgan impression for the first 6 weeks of the season, hitting over .380 with power and walks until an injury in mid May. He finished with .306-10-55-13, a career year by any definition.

As noted last year, Duncan has always been able to hit LHP. But his platoon split in 1990 bordered on unbelievable. Duncan hit .410 and slugged .606 against lefties, hitting only .227 against RHP. The .410 average against LHP is the second highest since Elias began tracking platoon stats. Duncan's weakness against RHP and some defensive problems contributed to the Doran trade in August.

Duncan's 1991 outlook is somewhat cloudy. With Bill Doran re-signed, Duncan was asking for a trade. The two will undoubtedly platoon at 2B, with Doran also getting some time at 3B resting Sabo. There has been some talk of Duncan playing some OF, although the Cincinnati outfield is already full of part time players. Duncan will not hit .410 off LHP in 1991, but he could improve against righties.

Like every new Red, Bill Doran (.300-7-37-23) made a huge impact immediately on arriving in Cincinnati in late August (see Glenn Braggs, Billy Hatcher, and Hal Morris). Doran hit .373 for the Reds in 17 games before succumbing to back problems (again!) and missing the post season. According to press reports, the back problems were caused by an infection, not by damaged discs, so there is hope that Doran will bounce back in 1991.

Doran was a free agent, and he knew he would not be a full time player due to the presence of Mariano Duncan. Doran offers the Reds two things that Duncan does not: (1) a legitimate lead off hitter (.411 OBA in 1990) which allows Barry Larkin to bat 3rd (Larkin takes too few walks to be an effective leadoff hitter) and (2) much better defensive play at 2B. Duncan has the physical tools to play 2B, but his skills need to be refined. Doran will be 33 in 1991, and given his recent injury history is something of a gamble.

Ron Oester (.299-0-13-1) put together a decent part time season in 1990, and contributed a couple of key hits in the post season. For Rotisserie purposes he should be avoided, in the twilight of a mediocre career.

Sean Lahman:

There was a lot of publicity over the Athletics' late August acquisitions but not much was made of the Reds acquiring Bill Doran from the Astros. At first glance, the move didn't seem to make much sense. Mariano Duncan and Ron Oester were platooning and both hitting around .300, so why acquire another second baseman? Lou Piniella cited Doran's ability to play some other infield positions and also his leadership ability, but anytime you can acquire an infielder who delivers a .300 BA with 20 steals, you have to do it. The cost was minimal (two AA pitchers and a AAA veteran) and the timing was great. Whatever Doran's contributions were, the Reds did end up winning the pennant and the World Series.

At first glance, it seems like the Reds have three solid candidates to start at second; A nice problem to have, right? Think again. First there is Duncan who hit .309 with 10 HR and 55 RBI from the 2 spot. Although Duncan had career bests in nearly every category, his lifetime average before 1990 was .235 and he is 28 years old. Can a player be expected to make such a radical improvement at that age? Was it the chance to play full-time? Was it playing on artificial turf? Maybe it was the fact that he stopped being a switch hitter and batted only right-handed. Who knows. Time will tell if 1990 was a fluke for Duncan, but I wouldn't recommend chasing him in any auction. He is a risky commodity, and someone in every league is going to pay the full value of his 1990 stats, and be disappointed.

Doran, who can put up some impressive numbers, missed the postseason with a back injury. Will he be healthy enough to produce some all-star statistics once again? The Astros weren't sure. The Reds think he will. Even injured, he did put up some impressive numbers to show that his .219 average in 1989 was just a bad year and not an indication of his true ability.

Ron Oester hit .299, but he will be 35 and has had reconstructive knee surgery. Oester said after the World Series that he is considering retirement.

At AAA, the Reds have Billy Bates, acquired from Milwaukee during the season, and Keith Lockhart, who spent time at third base and in left field during the 1990 Nashville season. A good spring and a couple of breaks could land either one of these guys a starting role. Bates got a look in September and made the post-season roster when Doran was injured. Bates will probably compete with Luis Quinones for the utility infielder's job. Lockhart has no experience at the major league level but has had two solid seasons at AAA Nashville.

Note: Does anyone know if any major league second baseman may have gone to the University of Michigan? If so, the Reds would like to know. The current infield of Hal Morris, Barry Larkin, and Chris Sabo all played baseball for the Wolverines. They might as well make it 4 out of 4.

Lary Bump:

It wasn't a great year for Bates, but it certainly was eventful. For the fourth consecutive year, the 27-year-old left-handed batter started the season at Denver. Before it was over he would be brought up to Milwaukee, traded to Cincinnati and sent down to Nashville. There he scored the winning run as the Sounds made the playoffs by winning a one-game division playoff in the 18th inning. Then it was back to Cincinnati, where he completed the major league portion of his year 0-for-29 against right-handers and 0-for-5 in the NL. Then, when Bill Doran underwent surgery, Bates was added to the Reds' Championship Series and World Series rosters. Thus, he found himself in a position to score the winning run in the 10th inning of WS Game 2 by beating out the first of three one-out hits against Dennis Eckersley. Bates is a good ballplayer (.293-0-34-15 in the American Association last year). But he spent his youth behind Jim Gantner in Denver. The departure of Ron Oester gives Bates a chance, but he's still No. 3 on the depth chart behind Doran and Mariano Duncan.

And forever he will be the answer to a Cincinnati trivia question.

HOUSTON

Believers in Andy Mota will be spared much suffering in 1991 if the Astros simply leave him off the roster and make him ineligible for Rotisserie teams. If he makes the roster, you should talk about his great hitting in A-Ball two and three years ago. Don't mention that he didn't make the Baseball America top ten prospect list for the AA Southern League. Don't mention that he is OLDER than all of the ten players who did make the list. Don't mention that Knoxville 2B Williams Suero is infinitely faster, more powerful, and a better fielder than Mota (and nobody has yet heard of Suero). Don't mention any of these things, and don't bid on Mota. If he somehow starts 1991 in the majors, it will be a sorry comment on the hopeless outlook for the Houston franchise.

Welford McCaffrey:

The trade of Bill Doran to the Cincinnati Reds late in the 1990 season left a gaping hole at second base. The 2B job is up for grabs during spring training. Candidates for the position include Casey Candaele, a four-year major league veteran, Dave Rhode, a utility player last year after spending four-years in the Astros minor league system, and Andy Mota, the second base man of the future who played AA ball last year.

The Astros 1991 spring training decision comes down to this: Do they bring up their future now and develop that talent in the majors, or do they go with a veteran for one year and let the future at second spend one year at the AAA level?

My bet is that the Astros will decide to go with Candaele at second for 1991 and let Andy Mota spend a year at AAA. Why? Because of what happened to Eric Anthony in 1990. Some folks in the Astros organization felt bringing Anthony to the majors in 1990 was rushing things, he should have spent another year in the minors. The majority of management wanted to bring him right in and learn whatever he needed to learn right here in the majors; the best way to learn to hit a major league curve ball was to face major league pitchers throwing major league curve balls. When the Astros sent Anthony down to the minors in 1990 the Astros were more or less admitting they had rushed Anthony to the majors. This will prevent the Astros from rushing future players to the majors.

Who is Casey Candaele you may be asking? In 1987, after batting .272 for the Montreal Expos, Casey came in fourth for the National League Rookie of the Year honor. He is also, in case you have forgotten, the son of Helen St. Aubin, a former professional women's baseball player. He was traded to the Astros in 1988 by the Expos for minor league catcher Mark Bailey.

Whatever happened to Candaele, you may further inquire? While playing in 1989 for the Astros AAA farm team, the Tucson Toros, Casey's retina started leaking. The leaking retina caused his vision to blur. His average plummeted from .290 to .218. When the condition was diagnosed it was decided that he would take the remainder of the summer off to rest the eye and hope his vision would come back on its own. Candaele was an early surprise for the Astros, one of the few bright spots in an otherwise dismal season. Some clutch homers led to his being dubbed the "Little Bopper" by his teammates and the "Mighty Mite" by the broadcast crew.

Casey Candaele is no Ryne Sandberg. Candaele is no Bill Doran, Roberto Alomar or Gregg Jefferies for that matter. But Casey can stand shoulder-to-shoulder with the rest of the second basemen in the NL. Casey was fifth among second basemen in batting and slugging average and third in on-base-average. Even though he didn't play a full season last year, his minor league stats are consistent with his 1990 season. In four full seasons of minor league play he averaged between .259 and .305. The Astros could do worse than playing Candaele at second in 1991.

Down on the farm is Andy Mota. Andy will be

25 in 1991, Candaele will be 30 years old. Mota, son of Manny, has led two different leagues in batting on his rise through the minors. In 1988 he led the New York-Penn league with a .351 average. In 1989, Andy led the Florida State League with a .319 average. Andy was batting .286 this year before he broke his thumb in August while playing with the Astros AA Columbus farm team. Andy Mota is definitely someone to watch in 1991 spring training. A strong spring training could land him the Astros second base job.

David Rohde, who will be 27 in 1991, has an outside shot at second. Rohde was in the middle of his best minor league season, his fifth, batting .353 for Tucson when he was called up by the Astros. In limited action he batted .184 for the big club this year. During his minor league career he has batted as low as .261 and as high as .291. Other remote possibilities for the second base job are Eric Yelding, Craig Biggio, and Andujar Cedeno. Yelding is a possibility only if Gerald Young returns to his rookie season form and wins back the centerfield position and then Candaele, Mota and Rohde have serious problems during spring training.

Management considered having Biggio spend the fall instructional league learning second base. It was even announced by management that Biggio was the second base man of the future. As you can imagine, it was much discussed in the press and talk shows. But two things happened to change management's mind. First, Biggio played 50 games in the outfield and looked really bad fielding ground balls; a number of singles went through his legs for doubles and triples. Secondly, Biggio told management he wanted to be a catcher, not an outfielder or infielder.

The Houston 2B picture was summarized long ago by those astute Rotisserie analysts, Bud Abbott and Lou Costello:

"Costello: What's the guy's name on first base?

Abbott: No, no. What is on second base.

Costello: What's the guy's name on second base?

Abbott: That's right!"

Lary Bump:

David Rohde is a 26-year-old switch hitter and former SS who probably has as much right as anybody to claim 2B in Houston. After a .353 start, with a .479 OBP, at Tucson, he went up to the Astros. In 59 games, he had just 98 ABs, and his average tumbled to .184 and his 2/1 W/K ratio in Tucson became 1/2 in the bigs. Eric Yelding, Casey Candaele and Craig Biggio probably have a better chance to be the Astros' regular 2B.

LOS ANGELES

Adam Stein:

Juan Samuel played 2B after the Dodgers sent Willie Randolph to the A's. Samuel has never lived up to his potential. The Dodgers pursued Samuel and offered him arbitration. If the Dodgers bring him back, Samuel will continue to decline and is a good bet to be traded.

Last year's third base platoon of Sharperson and Lenny Harris could move to second for 1991. Wherever they wind up, they're each good for $10 seasons each and can be had for less than that. Play it safe and grab both. The Dodgers second baseman is likely to be their leadoff hitter and should steal plenty of bases.

Bob Whitemore:

Juan Samuel is coming to spring training camp, with the apparent goal of winning the 2B job. From the group of Samuel, Sharperson, and Harris, you probably have second base and third base pretty well covered.

Triple-A second baseman Dan Henly hit .300 at Albuquerque last year, with no speed and no power. Everybody hits .300 at Albuquerque. Eddie Pye at AA San Antonio hit .248 with 2 HR. The only interesting minor league performance by a minor league 2B was at Bakersfield, where Matt Howard stole 47 bases.

Pete DeCoursey:

When they moved Juan Samuel back to 2B, his bat magically returned, and for all of the protestations, 13 HRs and 52 RBIs and 38 SBs from your second baseman is awfully good. Juan will lift his BA over .250 for the first time in 3 years, now that he has adjusted to the pitcher's heaven known as Dodger Stadium. In 1991 Samuel should also produce a few homers and 8-12 more RBIs than he had last year.

MONTREAL

The Montreal 2B situation has gone from utterly confusing to fully settled, very quickly. Just one year ago, there were five candidates. Now there is only Delino Deshields.

Michael Cassin:

Delino DeShields spent the last few weeks of the season moving between the lead-off, 2nd, and 3rd spot in the batting order, and where he hits next season is one of the questions the Expos have to resolve before opening day. The Departure of Tim Raines means that DeShields will probably bat leadoff.

Delino stole 42 bases last year, but was thrown out 22 times, the second highest CS total in the league. As DeShields matures, and learns to read pitchers, this ratio will improve greatly, making him a 70 to 80 SB threat in the near future. He should settle in the .280 to .290 BA range, maybe .300 with the benefit of leg hits. RBI will depend on the batting order, but he doesn't have the home run power to be a big RBI man, even in the third spot. He does have enough power to be among the league leaders in doubles.

DeShields developed quickly (he's 21), making the team a year earlier and at a different position (SS in the minors) than Montreal expected. Coming off a year like this there could be a let down this season, especially early on, so if you have DeShields you may have to show some patience, and if you don't you may have a chance to steal him if he gets off to a bad start. Do it.

Junior Noboa hit enough to become the main infield utility man, surpassing Tom Foley. Noboa will get first shot if there's an injury to a starter, but he doesn't hit righties well enough to keep a full time job. Foley's lefty bat may keep him around as a sixth infielder. Both will be marginal investments at $1 this season, unless something happens.

Pete DeCoursey:

If, like me, you already have Delino Deshields, heavens bless you. If not, then either get him, or prepare to regret your lapse. You will certainly regret what he will do against for you the next 15 years. I would rather have Delino than either Alomar. The only player as young and as good in the majors is Ken Griffey, Jr. DeShields can hit, walk, score runs and he'll turn 22 a few months before the start of the season. Get him, or as I said before, regret him.

NEW YORK METS

The Mets didn't acquire Tommy Herr to play a utility role. He will get plenty of playing time, but his peak value years are long gone. Batting second behind Lenny Dykstra for most of 1990, Herr should have been able to hit better than .260. Actually, he has hit above .263 only once, since his spectacular .302 BA, 110 RBI season in 1985.

Herr's hitting style depends on a good eye and quick hands. Over the course of his career, he has been among the best hitters when it comes to placing a ball in play in a selected location. The hands are not as quick as they used to be, however. Many times in Philadelphia, with .400 hitter Dykstra on first base, and a gaping hole between the two right side infielders, Herr couldn't knock the ball through. The loss of bat speed is now a matter of record. Herr will steal a few bases, using a crafty approach to situations. His leg speed has gone the way of his bat speed.

Although I'm not quite as pessimistic about Herr as Alan Boodman is (below), the facts are still pretty harsh. In most leagues, Tommy is going to be valued based on assumptions that he has a full time role and that he will perform at about his career averages. There is downside risk on both points, and nothing on the upside.

Tim Teufel (age 32) will provide backup help at 2B for Herr and at 1B for Dave Magadan. Teufel hits lefty pitchers 40 points higher than he hits righties, and his slugging percentage is almost 100 points higher. These accomplishments have been recorded mainly against the toughest southpaws in the National League. If your league is based far enough from New York, he might give you 10 homers for $1.

Alan Boodman:

Herr was originally acquired from Philadelphia as a rent-a-player for the 1990 pennant race, but it turned out that Tommy knew his contract status better than the Mets' front office did. He is actually signed through the end of 1991, and I suppose he may contribute something positive to New York this year. Last year for the Mets, he was an offensive zero. This is a trait that doesn't generally sit well with Mets management, but it still might be a good plan to keep Herr around because if they don't, the Mets run the risk of not recording any ground ball outs this year.

Herr has never had any power, his speed has vanished, and Tommy's ability to get on base is not aided by the fact that he now plays in Shea Stadium. It's also not aided by the fact that he can't hit. Go on the assumption that if Herr's healthy, he's better than someone who isn't, and if he's in the lineup, he'll contribute more than the players who aren't. But that's about it. Herr should be among the lower-priced second basemen in 1991, but if there is a Cardinal fan in your league, or anyone who remembers 1985, he will be overpriced.

PHILADELPHIA

Mickey Morandini got a laugh out of the fact that last year's "Top 150 Minor Leaguers" book gave him a peak projection of 17 homers in a major league season. He had 5 homers in 188 Double-A at bats in 1989, but Mickey claims four of them were flukes. Speed yes; power no.

Pete DeCoursey:

Morandini will be sheltered against tough lefties in 30 to 35 games by Randy Ready, and will probably be pinch-hit for in the late innings of close games in April and May. After hitting .223 with 7 doubles and 5 SBs in the first half of '90 at AAA Scranton, Morandini came on to hit .296 with 17 doubles and 11 SBs in the latter half of the season, and showed more improvement during his September call-up after the Herr trade. Mickey is likely to struggle initially, and then come on strong eventually. He underwent strength training in the offseason, rather than play winter ball. While he will not hit more than 3-5 HRs, he should start to hit .280 or higher after June, and finish the season at .250-.260, with up to 20 SBs and again, he should walk a bunch, say 50-60 times.

Ready could be a nice pick; he will play only against lefties and as a pinchhitter. With the Phils crowded outfield, he may be undervalued in some drafts, but he will once again find himself in his usual 100 games and 200 ABs. Expect 7 or 8 HR. If the Phils bring in a veteran back-up with any vestige of ability, be careful on Morandini. Leyva's principal managing skill is to get the most out of weaving veterans into the lineup with spot-starts and midgame substitutions; he tends to be impatient with rookies, and may get tired of watching Mickey learn, and turn to Backman, the kind of veteran he loves.

Lary Bump:

Last year I wrote, "If you make only one future pick, make it Philadelphia's Mickey Morandini; pencil in the left-handed batter for 500-plus ABs in '91." This year I actually feel better about the first part of that assessment than the latter. Even with Triple-A Scranton, and especially with the Phillies, he showed a vulnerability to left-handers that may land him in a platoon with Randy Ready. The 24-year-old batted just .261 at Scranton. But if you've read anything by John Benson, you know what he thinks about second-half figures as an indicator of the next year's performance. And once Mickey found his bearings in the International League, he batted nearly .300 in the second half. He had only 1 HR, but he also had 24 2B and 10 3B. In '89, he had 44 extra-base hits. He also stole 16 bases for Scranton and got three in three attempts for the Phils.

PITTSBURGH

Jose Lind fit two models perfectly last year. He celebrated his 26th birthday (May 1) by soaring to new heights of offensive output, delighting Rotisserians who fill their rosters with 26-year-olds who have 2 years of regular major league experience. The smartest of these owners then traded Lind for some nice Fast, Power-hitting Outfielder (FPO) around the All Star break, when Lind was hitting .300 with 30 RBI. In the second half, he hit just .220 with 18 RBI. Why? Winter league burnout. The July issue of Winning Rotisserie Baseball (page 12) fingered Lind and a number of other players who were likely to be tired in late summer 1990, after playing baseball year round.

Lind is one case where you should not use second half stats to forecast next year performance. He is much better than a .220 hitter. You have to think "context" and take all factors into consideration.

Adam Stein:

Jose Lind lived down to his good-field, no-hit reputation in the second half of 1990. The Pirates would be wise to give Jeff King more at bats, and Lind fewer, by shifting King's 3B platoon partner (Wally Backman?) to 2B against some righties.

ST. LOUIS

At age 27, Jose Oquendo graduated from prospect to veteran rather suddenly. The Cardinals team around him just became much younger. Oquendo had an off year in 1990, like most of the St. Louis hitters. He averaged .280 from 1987 through 1989, and can return to that level without making any big changes. He just needs the youngsters around him to get on base and put up some numbers. Oquendo will make an excellent acquisition if you play in a league where everyone sits around with 1990 $ values and no sense of perspective.

Tim Jones is (surprise) older than Oquendo. Don't expect any big upward movement at age 28. Even if Jones should land a bigger role because of injury or some other change, he won't help a Rotisserie roster.

Lary Bump:

Luis Alicea, a 25-year-old switch hitter and former No. 1 draft pick, began a comeback from a career-threatening injury by batting .348 in 92 ABs at Louisville. He isn't a rookie, for he was the Cards' 2B for 91 games in '88 before going back to the minors.

Geronimo Pena, a 24-year-old switch hitter (these are the Cards, after all), began a comeback from a disastrous trial at 3B, during which he hit like Mario Mendoza's kid brother. The thinking was "Pendleton's gone after this season. Who else can we use at third, a catcher?" Anyway, Pena finished at .249 with 24 SB, but also with 116 Ks. Here's another creative managing suggestion: Jose Oquendo hit poorly last year against lefties, and Pena was no great shakes against righties. Platoon the two switch hitters. That would be creative, but if it was my team, I'd keep Oquendo's glove at 2B virtually every day, unless Ozzie moves on and the Cards need Oquendo at SS.

SAN DIEGO

The departure of Roberto Alomar opened up the 2B job for new candidates. If Bip Roberts wants it, the competition will scatter quickly. Roberts has quickly become one of the top leadoff hitters in the game. At age 27 Roberts is poised for a career year. He hasn't hit under .300 since 1986. He just produced major league highs in hits, doubles, homers and RBI, and he more than doubled his SB output to 46 bases, with 79% success. The "Age 26" factor was definitely at work for Roberts in 1990.

Roberts can play so many positions that opportunities may still emerge at 2B. Joey Cora just turned 25 last year; if you think his major league chances are diminishing, you could miss an opportunity. I think Cora is more attractive than the more recently-touted Paul Faries.

Brigg Hewitt:

The Padres will keep the 2B competition open through spring training. Joey Cora has earned a chance to play, by waiting behind Roberto Alomar. Cora is recognized as a defensive gem, but he hasn't played enough in the major leagues to prove his offensive abilities. In spring training, Cora will have to differentiate himself from the sentimental favorite, Paul Faries, to clinch the starter role.

Lary Bump:

Oh, to be young and a second baseman in San Diego! Oh, to be a second baseman in San Diego and nearly three years older than Roberto Alomar. Faries has had three good seasons in four years in the Padres' farm system, including last year's .312, 5, 64, 48 SB, .399 OBP log at Las Vegas. With Alomar in the way, Faries seemed destined for the old Cora-Roberts utility shuttle. Now, he becomes a viable candidate in a battle with the other utilitymen.

Pete DeCoursey:

For the purposes of Rotisserie, Bip Roberts was better than Roberto Alomar last year, and will continue to be so until at least 1993. Justly rescued after being buried alive, Roberts had a marvelous season which is eminently repeatable, you'll see its re-run next year when the Padres come to town. Young Alomar will have a longer career, and a higher peak (about five years from now), but that doesn't mean he will be better than Roberts in 1991. Bip is the gem for the coming year.

SAN FRANCISCO

Thom Rogers:

Going into last year I thought Robby Thompson's 13 HR in 1989 were a fluke. After hitting 15 more last year, I'm ready to predict 12-15 for 1991. He's too important to the defense to trade; with Uribe potentially moving to the bench or to another team, away the Giants will need Thompson around to break in the new shortstop. For '91 I say: 500 AB, 13 HR, 50 RBI, 12 SB. Keep in mind though, that he has a cranky back that usually flares up in the last third of the season. If anything serious develops, the above numbers must be adjusted downward. Don't overworry about the back however: the last time Thompson didn't amass 500 PAs was 1987, when he had 460. He's a gamer.

Lary Bump:

Three years ago, at age 21 in Triple-A, Tony Perezchica hit .306 with 64 RBI. He has been on the fringe of the major leagues ever since. Now Perezchica has put in three good seasons at Phoenix, and all he has to show for them is 11 major league ABs. In the meantime, he has seen the likes of Greg Litton and Rick Parker elevated to the show. Perhaps the .268-9-49 season he had last year is the best it can get for Perezchica, a right-handed batter. Is Rob Thompson an immovable object? Don't give up on Tony yet.

Don't expect new arrival Greg Smith, a 23-year-old switch hitter, to become a big factor at 2B this year, or in the near future. But do expect him to be a useful utilityman and fill in. His greatest value is offense: .291-5-44-26 at Iowa last year.

AMERICAN LEAGUE THIRD BASEMEN

BALTIMORE

George Hall:

Just like muffing an easy grounder, Craig Worthington mis-handled the Orioles 3B job in 1990, and may be in danger of losing it. He is now up to his neck in competition with Leo Gomez, the hottest prospect in the Baltimore organization. The excess of talent at third base also diminishes the value of reserves Tim Hulett and Rene Gonzales, who weren't all that valuable before.

The rise of Gomez certainly complicates the picture for Worthington, and for manager Frank Robinson. Coming off a promising rookie season in 1989 (.247-15-70 in 497 AB) Worthington collapsed in 1990 (.226-8-44 in 425 AB). After a long period of patience, the O's finally benched Worthington for the last month of the season, to get a look at Gomez and other folks like Marty Brown. Worthington's weak performance may have been a sophomore slump, or it may have been something more serious. The problem for Baltimore is that they don't have a lot time to figure out what happened in 1990. Gomez is clearly ready to produce at the major league level, so it doesn't make a lot of sense to put Worthington on the field for another whole season just to see if he can straighten himself out.

Gomez, age 23, brings slugging potential beyond the best possibilities that Worthington can offer. At Hagerstown in 1989, Gomez hit .281 with 18 HR and 78 RBI. At Rochester in 1990, he hit .277-26-97. For comparison to his peers, check out the highly-touted Yankee slugger, Hensley Meulens, who was .285-20-96 in the same league last year.

Strikeouts and poor fielding have been the negatives in scouting reports about Gomez. He cut down his K's in 1990 (from 102 to 89) and made improvements in his fielding to the point where he can be considered mediocre now. When the Orioles front office compares Gomez and Worthington, they now see isolated power as the key feature that differentiates Gomez. Neither of these two 3B candidates can be considered speedy.

Trading Worthington would be a risk for Baltimore. Gomez has proven that he deserves a lengthy trial in the majors, but he hasn't proven that he can be a major league success. Worthington, at least, has had one good year in the majors, and he is still only 25. Nonetheless, Worthington's name was coming up repeatedly in trade rumors during the winter.

Hulett, Gonzales, Brown, and Jeff McKnight are all age 27 to 30. The first two are career utility players, and the last two are career minor leaguers, all for good reasons.

Lary Bump:

Leo Gomez, 24, can hit. His 97 RBI led the International League last season. He can get on base. In each of his five minor league seasons, excepting an injury-riddled 24 games at Charlotte in '88, he has had OBPs better than .400, and he scored 97 runs last year. He walks about as often as he strikes out — in fact, 89 times each in '90. If he takes over at 3B for Baltimore this year, it will be because of his offense, and not his defense. It's not that he doesn't try; he works as hard as anyone on fielding, but it just doesn't come easy to him. In my mind, Craig Worthington is more valuable as an everyday 3B. Both bat right-handed. But the

Orioles need punch. How about LF for Gomez? He is ready to play in the majors. Watch to see if he gets a chance.

BOSTON

Wade Boggs, a .352 lifetime hitter at the beginning of 1990, had never hit lower than .325 until last year, when he sank to .302. Anyone who hits 50 points below his career average must be scrutinized with concern. How would you feel about Ryne Sandberg if he suddenly produced a .237 season? Actually, Boggs didn't just suddenly drop to .302. He hit .363 and .366 in 1987-1988, then slipped to .330 in 1989, and then down to .302. At this rate of decline, he'll be down in the .270's in 1991.

One theory is that the American League is learning much better defensive positioning to use against Boggs, combined with the right pitches in the right locations. This notion has merit and is supported by some people who see a lot of Red Sox games. There is another idea, though. One analyst (who didn't want to be cited) tells me that Boggs' deterioration can be traced directly to his road performance, and theorizes that Wade simply misses Margo Adams. The statistical base necessary to test that theory will grow in size by 50% in 1991 (the third year after the change in road habits) for those who want to keep track. For Rotisserie purposes, it would be prudent to stop thinking of Boggs as a solid .350 hitter until he proves that he can do it again.

One more knock on Boggs, before we change the subject. He already had a reputation for hiding in the dugout during the last few days of any season when he was trying not to risk a BA title. In 1990 he was fighting for his eighth consecutive season with 200 hits, which would have given some kind of individual distinction. Ask Wade if you want to know what Hall of Famer he would have passed or tied; I'm sure Boggs knows very well who it was. Anyway, Boggs started swinging at anything rather than take a walk in the second half of 1990, when he saw that his 200 hit streak was jeopardized. After four consecutive years with 107 to 125 walks, Boggs got only 87 last year. A real team player, and a big disappointment to Rotisserie people who use esoteric categories like runs scored and OBP.

Lary Bump:

One of the most improved players in the International League last year was 3B prospect Scott Cooper. His final figures (.266-12-44) don't do justice to the line-drive bat he was swinging at the end of last season. His development made Eastern League batting champ Jeff Bagwell expendable [to Houston; see NL3BS]. In Cooper's five-year career, the 23-year-old lefty hitter has done better in even-numbered years. So maybe we shouldn't expect much from him in '91. But in '92, we may be talking about the man who made Wade Boggs expendable.

CALIFORNIA

UPDATE — The Angels expected to sign Gary Gaetti, who will displace Jack Howell. Howell could hang on to some ABs as a DH.

The Angels keep using Jack Howell at 3B. Howell isn't that good, despite the promise implied by an exceptional minor league career. Howell's longevity in the lineup is caused by California's complete inability to come up with anybody better. Last year, Rick Schu, Donnie Hill, Kent Anderson, Pete Coachman, and Bobby Rose (in that order of frequency) all gave third base a try. Those are not exactly household names, are they?

I really liked the chances for Bobby Rose to take time away from Howell last year, and I still like that scenario as likely (unless the Angels trade for somebody much better). Rose hit .359 at Midland with 11 HR and 73 RBI in 1989 but was unjustly snubbed from BBA's Texas League Top Ten list. Then he hit .283 with 63 RBI for Edmonton last year. Rose is only 24 on opening day. He bats right, Howell left. What a coincidence. Give Rose 250 at bats in the Bigs in 1991 — maybe not enough to be worth even $2, but this young man can only go up in value.

Lary Bump:

Pete Coachman, a 29-year-old right-handed batter, had the best of his four seasons at Edmonton in '90, when he batted .291 with 5 HR, 51 RBI, 27 SB and a .401 OBP. His reward was 16 games, and a .311 average, with the Angels. He also can play 2B, and fill in at SS. He makes contact against any kind of pitching. He can't be considered a top prospect, but 3B is wide open in California. He could surprise, but his value is mainly as a utility player.

The better long-range prospect is the 24-year-old Rose, also a right-handed batter. After his .359 season at Midland in '89, it's surprising he didn't get more of a shot with the Angels than his seven last-season games last year. His '90 stats at Edmonton were OK, but nothing like the year before. Rose also can play 2B. It would seem the Angels need more run production at 3B than either Rose or Coachman can provide.

CHICAGO WHITE SOX

Robin Ventura is the currently active case study to see when Olympian hitters develop into good major league hitters. My prediction last year was that Ventura would reach a satisfactory level in the middle of the season. Sure enough, he struggled early, then turned up the accelerator to hit .270 in the second half. Not exactly stardom, but acceptable.

Worth recalling (January 1990):

Ventura may be destined for greatness, but I have serious doubts about him for 1990. The White Sox' stated intention to make Robin their everyday third baseman doesn't jibe with Ventura's absence from the Baseball America list of Ten Best Southern League Prospects. I might put Ventura somewhere on the top ten list, but I wouldn't say he looks any better than Eric Anthony, Marquis Grissom, or Delino Deshields for 1990.

There is a remarkably consistent track record established by the 1984 U.S. Olympians, indicating that a year and a half of minor league ball is the normal prerequisite for major league success after you play as an amateur for the U.S. Olympic Committee. If you think back to the fine players from the 1984 Olympic team who made it as big league hitters, they all needed some seasoning. Will Clark put in a year at Fresno in 1985, started well but then faltered due to injury with the Giants in 1986, and finally hit his stride in 1987. Mark McGwire spent 1985 in Modesto, 1986 at Huntsville and Tacoma, and likewise blossomed in 1987. Cory Snyder spent 1985 in Waterbury, spent part of 1986 with Maine although his Cleveland numbers were pretty decent in 1986, too, and Snyder also had his first full major league season in 1987. Barry Larkin played against Snyder in the 1985 Eastern League, with Vermont, spent most of 1986 in Denver, and makes this group four for four with 1987 as their first full year in the Bigs. Conclusion: 1984 Olympians make the Show for good in 1987. Inference: 1988 Olympians become good major leaguers in 1991.

Back to 1991 White Sox third base:

Using the second half theory applied to rookies, you can expect Ventura to hit .270 in 1991. In two years as a pro, he has been nothing more than a slowrunning singles hitter.

Craig Grebeck was the #2 third basemen in 1990 and will make increased appearances there in 1991. He will improve his .168 career major league batting average, but not enough to have any real value. Grebeck was a consistent .280 hitter in the minors. You want guys who hit .300 somewhere during their lifetime. Grebeck is nice for defense; that's all.

In 1991, Cory Snyder will probably appear at 3B some time during the year. He doesn't qualify on opening day, however.

Jon Dunkle:

Former Olympian Robin Ventura is good enough to be a solid regular third baseman for the Chicago

White Sox, but not yet good enough to be sought after as your starting third baseman. Ventura was second on the White Sox in sacrifice hits, and he had an on base percentage that was higher than his slugging percentage. These stats are fine if you are a speedy outfielder who can effectively utilize the skill of getting on base, but in Ventura's game these skills are essentially wasted. For a third baseman they are way too thin. Check back on Mr. Ventura in a couple of years. Maybe he will develop some power. Until then, let someone else pay the price for him.

Timothy R. McAvoy:

Ventura has apparently adjusted to the wooden bat, and now swings with more confidence. He isn't going to hit for power, but he has a well-composed presence at the plate, and should be good for plenty of RBI if the White Sox can get runners on base for him.

CLEVELAND

Carlos Baerga has marvelous long-term prospects. I think he is still a little on the young side to put up any big numbers in 1991, but if he gets off to a slow start again, like he did last year, he could make a nice, cheap midseason acquisition.

Tom Brookens was reduced to a platooner vs. left-handed pitching back in 1989 with the Yankees, and filled that role only when he was healthy. He had a miserable 1989 with only 169 at bats and a .226 BA, and continued on the path to obscurity in 1990. He should feel fortunate to have a job on the playing field at age 37, and is probably regarded as a quasi-coach by the Indians. That may be nice for a major league franchise, but it's not what you need.

The other Indians who toiled around the hot corner in 1990 were Jeff Manto, Mark McLemore, and Steve Springer. There is no one in that group who would be of any interest.

Bill Gray:

Carlos Baerga will start at third in 1991. Only 22, Baerga looks like he will be a star. Acquired as part of the Alomar for Joe Carter trade, the Padres were very hesitant about giving up Baerga. Last year he had a rough start and was sent down to the minors. When he returned he was a different player. Baerga took over at third in order to have Jacoby fill in at first when Hernandez went down. He looks to be at this position for many years. He will be cheap and is an excellent long range pick.

In his first 60 games Baerga hit only .215 (34-158). Over the last 40 games Baerga hit .305 (47-154), and finished the year with a very respectable .260 average. His 7 HR should grow to 10-12 this year. As he matures, Baerga has the looks of a .300 hitter who can pop 18-20 homers. This is still a couple years away, but you might want to pick him up on a cheap, long term contract, then sit back and enjoy this future star.

The job is Baerga's to lose. At 22 he might still have periods of poor production. The Indians are quick to shuttle the young players down to Canton or AAA Colorado Springs to retool. Stick with this kid. He will pay off long term.

Steve Goldman:

It's time for a change here; Carlos Baerga is ready to assume the position on a full-time basis.

Carlos was acquired with Alomar and Chris James in the deal for Joe Carter, and many people considered him a throw-in, although that was not the case. The Padres did not want to part with Baerga, and with good reason. He was one of their blue-chip prospects, and only age 21 at the time of the trade. However, the Indians were able to pry him away from San Diego, and he is one of the reasons that the trade should be considered a steal for the Tribe when enough time has passed to fairly evaluate it.

At his tender age, Baerga, a switch-hitter, displayed the ability to hit Major League pitching. He displayed some power, and was also the team's best pinchhitter. His performance and age demand that he get the full-time nod over Brook Jacoby, who has held onto that spot for seven years (an eternity for an Indian). This should work out OK for the Tribe, however, as Jacoby can then move to first base on a permanent basis, and settle the line-up a bit.

Another player who may figure somewhat into the third base picture is Tom Brookens, although he has declared himself to be a free agent, and would have to be re-signed. I wish the Tribe would let him go. Ever hear of the saying, "Jack of all trades and master of none?" That's Tom. But I'm afraid that John McNamara has joined a club (chaired by Sparky Anderson) of people who are somehow convinced that Brookens is valuable despite his continued inability to hit or field at a major league level.

Adam Stein:

Carlos Baerga should find a slot in the starting line-up in 1991, at third or at shortstop. He'll hit in the .280's this year with 10 homers. He's only 22 years old and will show more power as he matures.

DETROIT

In 1989, Sparky named comeback project Chris Brown as his regular third baseman. In 1990, the winter nominee was the marvelous prospect Doug Strange. That tells you how desperate Detroit was to get their hands on a true major leaguer who could do the job. Now they have two, Travis Fryman and Tony Phillips.

Adam Stein:

Travis Fryman will be a superstar down the road. He'll fall off in his sophomore season, but will be a good player to have for 1992.

Lary Bump:

What do you do when you're the heir apparent to a guy who just won't abdicate his position? Some players pout and shout. The 22-year-old Fryman, a right-handed batter, did his job as Toledo's SS, batting .257 with 10 HR and 53 RBI in 87 games. Then he answered a call from Detroit and moved over to 3B alongside Alan Trammell. Fryman was even better batting with Tiger Stadium as his home: .297-9-27 in 66 games. Trammell was a year younger when he arrived in the majors to stay, and that was 13 years ago. Don't bet against seeing Fryman as a productive major leaguer in 2003. [Sound like nice, safe five-year contract material.]

KANSAS CITY

In one of the many card shops in Cooperstown, there is a huge assortment of rookie material from the late 1980's, stuff like cards laminated on wood with gaudy trophy-type figures of players bolted to them. No offense to anyone who enjoys collecting this kind of doo-dad, but I think it's silly to take a card that is available wholesale for five cents, and make it the centerpiece of a paperweight monstrosity that sells for $20. And a child should know better. My nine year old son Jim went into this Cooperstown shop, crowded with SABR conventioneers in June 1989, and took a quick look around. He picked up an item like the one described above, waved it under my nose, and squealed (much to my embarrassment): "Look, Dad, they're selling Kevin Seitzer cards for $20. Isn't that stupid? Kevin Seitzer's no good!" We left quickly.

Kevin Seitzer is not a future Hall of Famer, and everyone knows it now, even if they didn't all know it back in early 1989, when Seitzer had two years of .300 hitting under his belt. The pitchers caught up with Seitzer in 1989, just as Jim knew they would. Also, this book predicted his demise. Last year:

It is a negative sign that Kevin's average against lefties dropped 100 points from 1988 to 1989 (.353 to .257) and he showed no improvement versus southpaws in the second half of '89: .252-3-10 in the first half; .263-0-2 in the second half. My money says that lefties learned some little edge against Seitzer in late 1988 or early 1989, word spread quickly, and Kevin either remained ignorant of events or found there was nothing he could do about them. No .300 this year.

Seitzer must have though about hitting lefties during the winter of 1989-90. He came out smokin' and hit .320 against lefties in the first half of 1990. In the second half they cut him down again, however, to a .152 BA. Ah, the ebb and flow of pitcher/hitter struggles (and the natural variation in small stat samples) are the stuff that keeps us guessing.

Luis Delossantos is (amazingly) still only 24. He has been stuck at Ohama for four years. It is easily possible to envision some changes in Kansas City that would create a major league role for Delossantos, a solid .290 hitter in the minors. The Royals are obviously not in love with him, however, or they would have given him a chance by now.

Marc Bowman:

Kevin Seitzer will lead the Royals in plate appearances again in 1991 while starting virtually every game at third base. His gradual decline in all offensive categories is a concern to the Royals, however. If his output continues to decay, the team would want to drop him down to the bottom third of the order. But the Royals don't have much leadoff type talent. With the aging and departure of Willie Wilson, and the failure to come up with anyone better than Brian McRae to bat near the top of the order, Seitzer should stay in the 2 spot unless he really slumps.

Seitzer doesn't have much power. His 15 homers in 1987 were a fluke, partly due to the lively ball and partly due to the friendly "here it comes" pitching style that greets so many rookies in the American League. Seitzer also has little speed. His main Rotisserie value has been his batting average, and when that slipped to .275 in 1990, he lost much of that value. Although he is still a fan favorite, Seitzer could worth as little as $3 to $5 for Rotisserie purposes, if he keeps going downhill. If there are any Royals followers at your auction, bring up Seitzer early, and watch the fish feed.

Royals management has publicized their notion that Seitzer might be moved to second base in 1991. Seitzer would give a bit more offense than Terry Shumpert, and 3B could be opened up for someone like Sean Berry, but the move isn't really likely.

Lary Bump:

You may be hearing that Sean Berry will be the Royals' 3B this season. Let's examine this idea. True, many of the best prospects skip Triple-A ball altogether. True, Berry came of age with the bat (.292-14-77) last season at Memphis. But let's talk about age — the right-handed hitting Berry is 25. Why did it take him three years to get out of the Florida State League? And why, despite reaching first base 22 more times, did his SB total drop from 37 to 18 and his SB percentage from 77 to 67? There are several question marks here, so don't sell your Kevin Seitzer 3B stock yet.

MILWAUKEE

The only mystery about Gary Sheffield is whether he can play. If he plays, the position will be 3B in Milwaukee, and he will do well if he plays.

The Brewers farm system is essentially bankrupt of young talent around 3B. Last year's Triple-A third sacker, Joe Redfield of Denver, is talented, but he isn't young. Redfield was .279-17-71 with 34 SB (!) in 1990, but he's now 29 years old. It is normally a good sign when your experience and knowledge of pitchers can give you an edge in basestealing, but when that happens in the minors, you have a problem.

Alan Boodman:

More and more, Gary Sheffield is showing tendencies like Chris Brown. Five years ago, Brown finished fourth in the Rookie-of-the-Year balloting. Now he is out of baseball, probably forever. Both Sheffield and Brown are high-average type of hitters with questionable fielding skills. Gary has more speed than Chris Brown ever had, and the biggest difference between them is their ages: Brown played his first full season in the majors at

23, Sheffield played his at 20. There is still hope for Sheffield, but the specter is looming.

One of the most notable similarities between Sheffield and Brown is that their teammates couldn't stand them. Brown developed a probably undeserved reputation for faking injuries early in his career, a reputation that followed him throughout his baseball life. It is true that Brown never managed to play 135 games in a season, and it got to the point where his reputation preceded him. Every time he was out of the lineup, Chris faced the additional scrutiny of his teammates, the press, and the fans. Was he faking it, or was he really hurt? Either way, the people around him apparently never forgave him, and Brown is now one of the most talented players not playing anywhere.

The problem with Gary seems to be his attitude. When Dave Parker was signed away from the Athletics, it was envisioned that Parker would play the role that he had seen Willie Stargell play with the Pirates in the '70's. He would take the young, excitable Sheffield under his wing and mold him into a championship-caliber ballplayer, not too large of a task, as Sheffield already posessed great ability. The honeymoon lasted almost until June, and Brewers fans are back to hoping that Gary will mature as he ages.

Of course, Milwaukee fans might have to follow Sheffield's progress from a distance. Sheffield was on the trading block during and after the winter meetings. The Brewers were already facing potential losses (Rob Deer, e.g.) in the free-agent market, and generally do not pursue other team's free agents. The farm system, particularly at AAA, is bone-dry, and the front office is now attempting to deal away two of the best remaining players (Sheffield and Dan Plesac). This is not the way a top-flight organization is run.

A 22-year-old third baseman of Gary's ability is a precious commodity. If he can put in a full season (say 140-150 games), he'll hit above .275, with up to 15 homers and possibly 75 RBI, with 25-35 steals. If Sheffield continues to take steps forward, it won't be too far down the road before we see him putting up Paul Molitor-type stats each season.

MINNESOTA

The Twins spent the winter of 1990-91 worrying about the loss of Gary Gaetti. They talked about Brian Harper as a possible third baseman. They talked about Dan Gladden as a possible third baseman. If they can't re-sign Gaetti and can't get a real third baseman, however, people like Al Newman will pick up most of playing time.

Whenever you see a team talking about moving this player or that player into an obvious vacancy, there is a 90% probability that they are simply jockeying for a better bargaining position. You don't announce to the world, "We need a third baseman very desperately," because the price goes up. It's just like Rotisserie trading. Remember John Olerud the left fielder? Sure, John did just wonderful in the instructional league, and the Jays lost all interest in acquiring another outfielder. Right. Remember Derrick May annointed as the Cubs regular LF for 1991? People who read my newsletter know what I thought about that whopper. So it is with all these Twins who are suddenly able to play 3B.

Gaetti, by the way, hit just .208 in the second half of 1990, and just .202 against righties in the second half. During the first half, it was the lefties who got him out (.197 BA).

At age 32 it's a little early for Gaetti to be washed up, and he stayed out of the worst categories on the Rob Wood lists (he's "in transition") but it really doesn't look good for Gaetti to regain his old form, ever. And consider that there are many ballparks more unfriendly than the Homerdome [and yes, I use that word advisedly; see Fred Percival's tables].

Paul Clements:

If the Twins are going to move somebody to 3B, Brian Harper is the most realistic case. He came up as a 3B originally, and there is NO ONE ELSE who would get serious consideration for such a move.

NEW YORK YANKEES

Jim Leyritz' future may depend on his catching abilities. The Yankees and Leyritz are not exactly on the same wavelength when it comes to asssessing him as a defensive catcher. The front office doesn't think he's lousy or anything like that, but they think he needs improvement. Leyritz himself feels very confident about his defensive ability behind the plate. The issue came to a head when Leyritz declined to complete a winter ball assignment as a catcher.

Leyritz is a self-acknowledged singles and gap type of hitter, with limited power. He can pop a homer, though. He had ten dingers at Albany in 1989. Leyritz can hit a mediocre fastball as well as anyone. In his first 96 major league at-bats, he hit .313 while enjoying the usual "welcome to the American League" as pitchers liked to challenge him with heaters until he proved he could hit them. Then Leyritz hit just .232 in 207 AB.

Getting back to the disagreement about catching skill, Leyritz points to his 45% success ratio throwing runners as a catcher at Albany in 1989. The concern is more about pitcher-handling, game-calling, and ability to stay at top form over a full nine innings, however, according to one Yankee coach. Your "day off" catcher isn't going to do the job if he gets tired after seven innings and you have bring the regular off the bench to work two innings (or more if the game goes longer). Watch Leyritz to see if the Yankees are leaving him in spring training games for a full nine innings; if they do, that's not a vote of confidence; it's a sign of concern. You don't care where he plays, of course, but (like I said) catching may be the key to increased playing time for Jimmy in 1991.

Randy Velarde's .340 BA in 1989 is now widely recognized as a fluke. He never hit much over .270 even in the minors, so you were really sucked in if you formed your 1990 valuation based on 100 major league at bats from 1989. Just like Leyritz hitting around .300 in his first 100 AB, it just doesn't mean anything in the American League when a rookie starts off by smashing a lot of fastballs for base hits. Considering the number of AL pitchers, catchers and coaches who agree with the notion that rookies get a steady diet of cheese in their first trip around the league, you would think that the scouting would improve and somebody would see the wisdom of making a change. Some organizations (like the A's) don't follow the simple approach, and some pitchers and catchers don't accept the notion when I ask them about it, but most organizations do it, and most battery men will confess it.

So the A.L. simply made adjustments with Velarde in 1990, and he went downhill in all offensive categories. The change-up, in particular, is a pitch that now impairs Velarde's performance. Don't expect a return to .300 in 1991, or ever.

Mike Blowers will have one more chance to blossom in 1991, but he'll have to earn his way into the lineup this year. He has tons of talent, but seems easily distracted. In my opinion, he has been too quick to make excuses and too slow to accept responsibility for his own fate, and that is why the Yankees took his fate out of his hands early in 1990.

Daniel Stone:

The Yankee third base situation is just as unclear in the spring of 1991 as it was last year at this time. Jim Leyritz, Mike Blowers and Randy Velarde were all serious candidates during the winter. Even Matt Nokes and Hensley Meulens were being considered. Meulens, at least, has a background as a 3B. He never played any other position before the move to outfield in 1990.

The Yankees pursued Terry Pendleton actively, but lost him to Atlanta. The New York front office moves at a painfully slow pace. Neither the original G.M. tandem of George Bradley and Pete Peterson, nor the late-1990 appointee Gene Michael, made any trades after the All Star break last season. For a last place team loaded with capable but disgruntled veterans, the front office needs to be quick and agile when it comes to trading [again, just like Rotisserie]. It would really be a shame if

George Steinbrenner is somehow preventing all meaningful action, in an unconscious effort to prove that he is vitally needed.

Jim Leyritz got the bulk of action in 1990. [Randy Velarde appeared in more games at third, but often as a late-inning sub; the breakdown in appearances was Velarde 74 games, Leyritz 69, Blowers 45, Tolleson 3, Walewander 2; what a cast!] Leyritz performed adequately both at bat and in the field, but he was nothing to write home about. The Yankees want to use him as a utility player; thus they have an interest in his catching.

If the Yankees fail to get a free agent or make a trade, Leyritz will get most of the 1991 action at 3B. Even though he bats right, none of the other candidates is a lefty hitter, either (except the catcher, Nokes). The worst case for Leyritz, if the Yanks acquire a third baseman, would still be 250 at bats and a safe .260 average.

Leyrtz and Velarde are age 27 and 30, respectively, so don't hold your breath waiting for them to develop. What you see is what you get.

Mike Blowers is an enigma. He could have, or should have been the Yankees regular 3B in 1990, but the team lost patience with him early. He had the job to lose, and he lost it quickly. Blowers tore up the pitching-dominated International League (.339 BA and 50 RBI in 230 at bats) after the Yankees sent him down, but that wasn't good enough for a recall. Blowers also averaged 15 homers per season during three years in the minors before coming up, but that fact doesn't carry any weight in the spring of 1991, either.

Lary Bump:

Mike Blowers no longer qualifies as a rookie, though he may continue to play like one. Last season with the Yankees, when he batted .137 against right-handers, and was essentially a right-handed version of Mike Pagliarulo, only he didn't field as well as Pags. Normally a guy who bats .339 and drives in 50 runs in 62 games in the International League will raise quite a few eyebrows. But knowing what Blowers has done in the majors. Jim Leyritz needn't look over his shoulder at 3B. Blowers might be a right-handed DG-LF candidate, but he's probably not as qualified for that job as Hensley Meulens, and the Yankees are loaded with RHH's while they need lefty hitters. Something will have to change in a big way to give Blowers a long career.

OAKLAND

> UPDATE — Carney Lansford's snowmobile accident threatened his whole 1991 season. The A's signed Vance Law; our tables had value added to Riles, Bordick and Hemond, in that order.

The backups behind Carney Lansford last year were Lance Blankenship, Mike Gallego, Mike Bordick, Jamie Quirk, Scott Hemond, and Dann Howitt, in that order of frequency. Bordick and Hemond are the only third basemen in the group, and the only "prospects." Both are strictly defensive types. Bordick never hit over .270 in the minors, and Hemond is likewise weak with the bat. It's not as if Lansford is being pushed by anyone in the Oakland organization.

Lansford is lucky that no one is breathing down his back, because his career path is going through some rough sledding. At age 34, you don't expect him to improve. Lansford might improve from the .268 BA that he had in 1990, but he isn't likely to raise his .292 career average. Lansford is still capable of putting up some nice valuable numbers, but there is more downside risk every year.

The best auction opportunities will exist in those leagues where everyone is focused on "last year." If there are two or more owners who think that Lansford can return to his pre-1990 form, he isn't going to be cheap. Lansford was one of the most valuable Rotisserie packages just two years ago when he hit .336 and too many people are likely to remember.

Lansford has come back from adversity and bad stats before. He overcame a terrible slump in the second half of 1988 (.216 with no production) to make a neck-and-neck run at the A.L. batting title in 1989. We correctly predicted this comeback, proving that we don't worship second half stats blindly. I like the text so much, I'll reprint it: "The chances of his improving are about 99.999%. Don't act too interested, and don't overdo the bad-mouthing, either, or it will arouse suspicion when you later express an interest. Just spread the word that Carney appears washed up, let it sink in for a while, and casually mention him as a throw-in in later trade talks. If he starts off the year hitting .180, so much the better." Approach 1991 with the same advice in mind.

For 1991: a .280 average with 8 HR, 58 RBI, and 20 SB.

Lary Bump:

Scott Hemond is typical of most of the players at the top of the Oakland farm system; he's not much of a prospect. A former catcher, he's 25, and like just about everybody on the Oakland roster, he bats righthanded. He fell way off his 1989 figures in Double-A last year by batting .243 with 35 RBI. His increase in HR from 5 to 8 reflects a move to the PCL from the Southern League. His SB total plummeted from 45 to 10. Carney Lansford should be at 3B in Oakland well into his dotage.

SEATTLE

Edgar Martinez was one of our best picks last year. We even liked him in 1989, when he would have done better than Jim Presley, if just given a chance. Martinez fit the "age model," and his .424 BA in winter ball was another tipoff. Martinez slipped some in the second half of 1990, just like we said winter players are likely to do after August 1. But on the whole, Edgar was one of the best players available cheap in last year's auctions. He sold for an average of only $4, not bad for a regular player who hits .300 with double digit homers.

Martinez is no longer obscure, but he has given his name to the Martinez Gambit. The idea is to make a list of all the players you can find with the same surname as a prospect you want to buy, and talk about all of them excessively before and during your action. Someone may get confused, and bid on the wrong one. You might be able to use it this year in connection with a guy named Gonzalez. (See Leaguesmanship essay under Namesmanship.)

January 1990:

My pick for Mariners 3B in 1990 is 27 year old Edgar Martinez, who is ready to step in and do the job. Martinez has several good sleeper qualities including:

(1) He is unknown — most people have not heard about him, and those who did hear about him have deliberately forgotten what they heard, because it confuses their thinking about Chicago's young 1B/3B Carlos Martinez who does not have such an established third baseman in front of him, and they are reminded of that NL center fielder named Martinez who keeps changing teams and sometimes plays every day and sometimes plays on just rare occasions, and because Carmelo Martinez is Edgar's cousin, not his brother, and because there used to be two pitchers named Martinez on the same team, and . . . you can see why Edgar is forgettable; and

(2) He plays in a great ball park for Rotisserie hitting; and

(3) He is age 27, which is the age when most hitters show their most rapid improvement and/or reach their peak in major league hitting stats.

(4) Edgar is tearing up Winter Ball at the time of this writing.

(5) I forget — see, Martinez makes you do that a lot.

Tony Formo's 1991 Left Field Extravaganza:

Pee Wee Briley (.319 OBA, .356 SA) was nothing special offensively, just a good dose of speed: 16 SB, 5 HR, and 29 RBI in 337 AB. Briley hustles and can play infield, so he's likely to be around as a role player, but not a star.

TEXAS

The trade of Scott Coolbaugh to San Diego clears the way for Dean Palmer to stand with one foot at the top of the Rangers farm system, and the other foot on the field at Arlington. Notwithstanding the Rangers protestations that Palmer must spend another year in the minors, I see him arriving in the majors and making an impact in 1991, in midseason if not on opening day.

Palmer put on a spectacular display against "major league" pitching in 1989 spring training, becoming a hero at Port Charlotte stadium. He just turned 22 in December 1990, and the fact that he is even mentioned as a major league possibility at this age, is a statement of what kind of talent the young man possesses. He reached top form in 1989 with 25 homers and 90 RBI in Double-A.

1990 was an off year for Palmer. He hit only .218 with 12 HR; thus you can understand the Rangers saying that he needs more seasoning. But if spring training 1991 is anything close to what we saw in 1989, I can't see Palmer going back to the minors. It may have been good for your Rotisserie sleepers list that Palmer had a bad year. If he starts getting attention during spring training, make sure everybody in your league knows that he hit only .218 last year.

Steve Buechele is not going to dry up and blow away. He is still only 29. Given 300 at bats, he could hit 10 homers. The batting average is a problem for Rotisserie purposes, however, and batting low in the order he isn't going to get many RBI.

Lary Bump:

The conventional wisdom last spring was that if Coolbaugh didn't take over 3B for the Rangers, it would be because Palmer rocketed past him. Coolbaugh started the season with Texas in 1990 and played himself out of a job; now he's gone to San Diego. Teams lose interest when you bat .200 with a .264 OBP and a .267 slugging average. Even at SS those numbers can end your playing time. Coolbaugh worsened his case by hitting only .225 in the minors.

Palmer, still just 22, is also a RHH. A 25 homer season at Tulsa in 1989 earned him a late-season trip to the big club. In 1990, he didn't even get a sniff of Texas, and had just 12 HR, 39 RBI, a .218 average and 106 Ks in 316 AB.

TORONTO

One year ago, we said that Kelly Gruber would be great if he could only stay healthy for a full season. He got a career high 592 at bats in 1990, stayed in good shape, and had personal bests in almost every offensive category.

J.L. Feinstein:

For years, the Blue Jays wondered when Kelly Gruber was going to blossom into the hitter they knew he was capable of becoming. He'd shown flashes of stardom, but had never put it all together. Until last year, that is.

He started the season with a bang, and kept it up all year long. During the first half of the season, he almost single-handedly kept the team in contention, with 20 HRs and 66 RBIs at the All-Star break. He ended up with personal bests in all power stats, and hit a respectable .274 with a dozen plus stolen bases.

When injuries hit the Jays, he filled in wherever needed, both in the outfield and at 2B. About the only thing he didn't do was take tickets.

The back-up for Gruber will [once-again] be old reliable, Rance Mulliniks. Following a sub-par 1989, Mulliniks rebounded to be one of the most productive pinch-hitters in the league in 1990. Overall, he batted .289, with 16 RBIs in less than 100 ABs...mostly off the bench. Free agent signee Pat Tabler can also take a turn at 3B, if needed.

NATIONAL LEAGUE THIRD BASEMEN

ATLANTA

For the first time in three years the Braves knew in December who would be playing third base in April. Free agent Terry Pendleton will enjoy the big change from spacious Busch Stadium to the Launching Pad in Atlanta. Pendleton will provide one of the more dramatic case studies in park effects. My expectation is that we will get a lesson about the importance of individual hitter characteristics when considering the impact on hitters of changing ballparks.

Pendleton had 6 homers in 1990. In six and a half years of major league play, he has amassed a total of 44 homers, an average of less than 7 homers per year. In his career year (at age 28) in 1989, Pendleton had 13 dingers, 8 of them in St. Louis. Terry has never had more than 7 road homers in any season, and he had zero (0) homers on the road in 1990. Against this personal history, consider the average HR park effect multipliers, 1.082 for Atlanta and 0.862 for St. Louis [see Fred Percival essay in this edition]. If you divide 1.082 by 0.862, you get 25.5% as the St. Louis to Atlanta HR inflation rate.

So what should you expect from Pendleton in 1991? If you bump up his 1990 output by 25.5%, you get 7 or 8 homers as the 1991 projection. If you bump up his career average, you get 8 or 9 homers.

I think Pendleton will hit more than 8 or 9 homers in Atlanta, even though he is aging. Pendleton has excellent power to straightaway center field, from both sides of the plate. And he has good power to right center batting righthanded, and a nice home run stroke down the right field line batting left. I think Atlanta's dimensions will help him more than 25.5%. And consider that he has a stronger lineup around him now.

Marc Bowman:

The best alternative to Pendleton in Atlanta is Jeff Blauser. He isn't the fielder that Pendleton is, but he is improving. And Blauser might be a better hitter at this stage of his career. Significantly, Blauser hit .284 with 8 HR and 27 RBI in the second half of 1989. I think we have a true case here, where a half season of stats give an accurate indication of what to expect in a full year. Blauser is still only 25, and improving rapidly. Given a full time job, he should produce 15 HR and 50 RBI with a .270 average or better. The size of Pendleton's contract tells you that the Braves intend to play Terry every day, however. If you want Blauser to get more playing time, the shortstop position or a trade would offer the best hope.

Bruce Crabbe (AAA Richmond) and Tom Redington (AA Greenville) were the best minor leaguers in 1990. Redington is likely to reach the majors first, but with San Diego, not Atlanta.

CHICAGO CUBS

The Cubs really need a third baseman. Last year they used Luis Salazar, Domingo Ramos, and Curtis Wilkerson, in that order. The ageless Salazar hit .325 with Chicago in 80 at bats after coming over from San Diego in 1989, and provides stability with the possibility of a full time back-up. In 1990 he remained a satisfactory "sometimes" player for the Cubs, and he was available for $2 to $4 in many 1990 auctions. Cheap players who give you 10 HR are nice, scarce commodities. Salazar has provided that benefit for three consecutive years, but don't bet that he can do it again in 1991. It's time for the price to go up a little, and the output to go down.

Domingo Ramos is not much of interest for Rotisserie.

Lary Bump:

Ty Griffin, Gary Scott, Third Basemen, Chicago Cubs

In the case of the 23-year-old Griffin, the mighty have fallen — hard. There were those who wanted to put the switch-hitting former Olympian in the lineup at Wrigley Field, perhaps even shoving Ryne Sandberg over to 3B, almost from the moment Griffin signed with the Cubs. So I was surprised driving through Charlotte in April to hear on a radio broadcast Griffin's name in the Charlotte lineup again. I'm surprised right now to discover that the reason he batted only 249 times (.209 average) with the Knights was that he finished the season in the Winston-Salem outfield, where in 120 AB he raised his average to just .217. Griffin has had injury problems, and he still has a good batting eye, but he won't be seeing any pitches in the majors for a couple of years, if ever.

As Griffin's star was falling, Scott's was rising fast. He was the Carolina League's MVP, even though he wasn't there after July. His .295 average, 12 HR, 70 RBI and 16 SB had earned him a promotion to Charlotte, where he replaced Griffin and batted .308 in 143 AB. One question about the 22-year-old RHH is his fielding, for he made 29 errors in his brief stay at Winston-Salem. It's not impossible to picture him in Chicago before September, especially given the state of the Cubs' 3B position. But it may be asking too much to expect him to improve his fielding and handle big-league pitching all in the same year.

Pedro Castellano and Jose Viera will not get near the majors in 1991, but they both look good for 1993-1994.

CINCINNATI

Chris Sabo climbed out of the Rotisserie doghouse in 1990. A nice 25/25 season will do that for you. His average price dropped to $15 last April; he ended up earning a lot more than that for the faithful. The sophomore jinx struck Sabo in 1989, but everyone saw it coming. What else would you expect from a 27 year old rookie who had a terrible second half in 1988? A serious knee injury ended Sabo's 1989, and his future as an effective ballplayer was in question just one year ago. No more.

Greg Gajus:

Lou Piniella's biggest tangible contribution to the 1990 Reds was turning around the career of Chris Sabo (.270-25-71-25). To summarize, the pre-1990 Sabo was a fair power, good speed, no brain third baseman who took walks like he was from San Pedro de Macoris and ran the bases "until he was out." He was a fan favorite and an analyst's nightmare, and coming off a serious knee injury, his future looked bleak. I don't know if it was a brain transplant, or Lou Piniella's batting tips, but this new Sabo was an entirely different player.

A key was his improved strike zone judgement. Sabo had taken 54 walks in his career before 1990, in 1990 he drew 61 walks. Hitting better pitches resulted in more home runs, and his overly aggressive base running was reigned in to some extent. It was as if Ron Oester had suddenly hit 15 Home Runs. He topped of the year with a great World Series and SI cover.

Sabo will probably bat 6th the entire year in 1991, which should help his RBI total—He led off 70 games in 1990. Chris tends to have a strong first half, a symptom of all-out play that wears a player down, and 1990 was no exception. Second half stats were .238-9-29-4 SB. I still think he is something of a gamble due to his injury history, but the "new" Sabo is one of the top 3B in the league. The "old" Sabo wasn't one of the top 10.

Luis Quinones started the 1989 season in Nashville

(Pete wanted to keep Manny Trillo) and was brought up after Trillo was released in late May. His major league stats before 1989 showed little evidence that he was anymore than another no-hit middle infielder but he shocked the Reds with 12 HR in 340 AB. The crowded infield in 1990 sent Quinones back to reality.

Sean Lahman:

As in his rookie season, Chris Sabo was on fire for the first three months and burning out for the last three months. Elected to start the All Star game, Sabo hit 50 points higher, and got two-third of his homers, in the first half last year. His average season over the next few years should look like this: .275-15-80-30. If he doesn't win the gold glove there should be a Congressional inquiry. His 12 errors in 1990 represent about half of what you would expect from a full-time 3B playing on an artificial surface.

Lary Bump:

It wasn't a good year for Brian Lane. At Chattanooga, he batted only .239-6-51 and that was better than his performance with Nashville (.193-6-20). A solid '91 season at Nashville though, would put him in a position to back up Chris Sabo in 1992.

HOUSTON

Welford McCaffrey:

Rainbow cladded dome-plated astroturf team: Ken Caminiti, the Astros third base man in 1989 and '90, is the symbol of the Astros in his era. He is a hard working, well intentioned, good conditioned, nice looking marginally talented guy. He won't win the team any championships, but he will win some friends and it won't cost the team an arm and a leg.

The Astros, from the general manager on down, are hard working, well intentioned, well-conditioned (except for Mike Scott), nice looking (at least for the most part) and marginally talented (some more talented than others). GM Bill Wood seems to be a real nice guy who has to deal in a world of cutthroat GM's. So the players he gets in trades seem to be other's castoffs (not that some of them haven't turned out pretty nicely for the Astros) and not stars of the future. [There is a Bill Wood or two in every Rotisserie league. Nice guys. Finish last.]

Manager Art Howe seems real nice and easy going. He has to beg the umpires to throw him out of the game. It's hard to picture Art whipping his squad up for sustained battle. All the players seem laid back. You don't hear about them refusing to talk to the press, bad mouthing a fellow player or threatening an umpire. When its game time the Astros collectively put down their afternoon tea cups and say "Jolly well, it's time we all be sporting about it and play some baseball tonight with these good fellows."

In 1989, Caminiti batted .255, hit 10 homers and drove in 72 runs. Only Howard Johnson, Tim Wallach and Terry Pendleton had better years among NL third sackers. Kenny established himself as the Astros third baseman. It was the best production the team had gotten from third base since the 1986 Western division year.

In 1990, the team hoped for even better production from Caminiti. They got less. Only Terry Pendleton (.230) hit worse than Caminiti (.242) among third basemen in 1990. Worse yet, Caminiti had the worst slugging percentage of the third basemen, including Pendleton. The biggest concern for the Astros is that even though Caminiti hit only 4 home runs, he still struck out 97 times. Not a good combination.

Last year he made 22 errors, in 1990 he made 21. While possessing a cannon for an arm, his aim is not always accurate. Part of the problem is that he is not sure handed, so when he does bobble the ball he'll rush his throw to make up for it.

Third base has always been a problem area for this franchise. Even though Aspromonte, Rader and

Cabell played third for the team's first 18 years they were all average at best.

Don't bet your number one draft pick that Caminiti won't be back at third with the Astros in '91. Kenny has faced the hot seat of a do or die situation before and came out on top. Caminiti faced possible extinction from dome land after a miserable 1988, but his 1989 season saved him.

Caminiti's competition isn't strong, but a late trade or free agent signing could change that quickly. Chief among his competitors is Jeff Bagwell, a minor league third base man picked up by the Astros from the Red Sox in the Larry Andersen trade. He has batted .300 in both years of his pro career, but he has little power. There has been talk of converting Luis Gonzalez, a 1B/DH type, to third base. Gonzalez has been in the Astros minors for three years. His lifetime average in the minors is .286, but he also has shown little power.

Jon Dunkle:

Caminiti hit over .300 at all stages of his minor league career. He has the power to hit 15 home runs a year. His fielding is exceptional and he has an outstanding arm. If the Astros stick with Caminiti, I think he will prosper and become a star.

Lary Bump:

There are several interesting possibilities here. One is that the Astros may think Ken Caminiti isn't all they've cracked him up to be. Another is that they would consider moving Bagwell, perhaps to the OF. A third is that the Red Sox gave up the Eastern League batting champ (.333) for an aging RP because Bagwell doesn't have the power they need. Consider that Bagwell's 4 HR almost led the team in New Britain. A fourth possibility is that the Red Sox may have missed the boat, for Bagwell's EL-leading 34 doubles portend a Jody Reed type right-handed hitter who could bang doubles off the Green Monster at a Boggsian rate. Bagwell is just 22, so there's no rush. Perhaps he can answer some of these questions this season at Tucson, then make his move on Houston.

LOS ANGELES

USA Today summed up the 3B situation pretty clearly on December 11: "Harris/Sharperson or Dave Hansen or Jeff Hamilton or Brooks." The situation got a little clearer when Hubie Brooks dropped out of the picture. And if you like tea-leaf reading, infer that the offer of arbitration to Juan Samuel means that LA does not want to move the Harrperson platoon from third base to second. Hamilton is coming back from rotator cuff surgery, so I would put him on the longshot list. The bottom line, then, is that 22-year-old Dave Hansen will have a chance to win the job in spring training; but failing that, it's another year of Harrperson, with Hansen possibly emerging in mid season.

Bob Whitemore:

Dave Hansen will need a really big spring to displace Harris and Sharperson in 1991. The platoon pair in 1990 produced a .301 BA with 65 RBI and 30 steals. Even allowing for the 700 AB factor, one must ask: is Hansen really likely to do any better?

Barry Wolven:

The Dodgers have played forever without a third sacker (when did Cey leave?) so why should this year be different?

Pete DeCoursey:

If the Dodgers are smart, they won't use Dave Hansen at 3B. He is the kind of doubles power, high walk hitter that the Dodgers already have in the Sharperson-Harris platoon. If they turn the job over to Hansen (or to Hamilton, their young returning veteran) that position will drop both in defense and in production.

MONTREAL

Michael Cassin:

Last season Tim Wallach came up with one of the

great years that have been sprinkled through his good career. Wallach will turn 33 during the '91 season, so expecting anything more this year would be risky. Clear?

The biggest surprise about Wallach's season was that he was able to do what he did without any protection from Galarraga. If Wallach is to remain an effective clean-up hitter, someone (Galarraga or Larry Walker most likely) will have to hit consistently in the 5 spot.

Wallach's .298 average was the best of his career, I can't see him doing it again in 1991, and he has probably hit the 20 homer mark for the last time. The one category where Wallach might improve is RBI; and that depends on the batting order.

Numerous small, nagging injuries have slowed Wallach, and while he's never done a long stretch on the DL, his health can be a problem. One point in his favor is, while everyone else in Montreal was going free agent, Wallach was demanding a no-trade clause. There should be at least a small fall-off from last season, but you can still do much worse than Wallach, and if you own him there's no reason to feel pressure to deal.

Junior Noboa did what little back-up work there was last year (8 games), and there shouldn't be much more this year.

NEW YORK METS

Ever since 1989, we have been telling you that Gregg Jefferies was the Mets third baseman, not a second baseman. The Mets were dragged (kicking and screaming) into accepting their own original plan for a set infield (they always wanted Jefferies at 3B) after Kevin Elster's injury cleared a spot for Howard Johnson at shortstop. The Mets have an expectation that playing one position will help settle Jefferies mentally, and will hasten his development as a hitter. I see no reason to question this theory, and expect that Jefferies should have a giant year in 1991 and/or 1992.

After a massive build-up, Gregg Jefferies flopped in the first two months of his rookie season, 1989. He had been the only player in history named Baseball America minor league player of the year twice, and his September call-up in 1988 heralded the coming of the next Babe Ruth and every other expectation-raising cliche.

After a bad April-May in 1989, Jefferies got on track. He has been a solid .280 hitter ever since, and at age 23 he has lots of upward potential. Within a year or two he will become a perennial 20/20 man. In Rotisserie circles he is already highly regarded as a speed/power combination, rare for an infielder; the rest of the world will appreciate him soon.

Thus far in a short career, the world has seen two different hitters named Jefferies: the one in a slump, and the one who's doing OK. The slumping Jefferies is moody and unproductive; he takes a long time getting back on track when things are going wrong. The OK Jefferies is good but unspectacular. The world hasn't yet seen Jefferies in a groove. That will be something to behold. There was just a glimpse when September 1988 is prorated to a full year: a .321 BA and 33 HR, 93 RBI, and 28 SB per 550 at bats. We may not see that Jefferies over the course of a full season for another year or two, but we will see him for a month here and a month there during 1991.

If for some reason Jefferies can't play 3B, the Mets will slide Howard Johnson from short to third, and insert Kevin Elster at SS. No one else is likely to gain any playing time. Tom O'Malley, who played more 3B than Jefferies last year, is gone to Japan. Prospect Chris Donnels (.272-12-63-11 for Jackson) isn't ready yet.

Alan Boodman:

The Mets are serious about de-emphasizing Kevin Elster's role with the club in 1991. Gregg Jefferies will stay at third base, where he ended 1990. Howard Johnson keeps the shortstop job, and Tommy Herr occupies second, just as they ended 1990.

If you can, acquire Gregg Jefferies and sign him to a long-term contract. Still a couple of years away from turning 25, Jefferies could soon become the top NL infielder of the 90's, assuming Ryne Sandberg will begin to decline before 1995.

Lary Bump:

Chris Jelic, a 27-year-old right-handed batter, started as a catcher and finally made it to the Mets playing LF. He played 3B semi-regularly (92 games) at Tidewater, and turned in respectable batting stats — .306-4-49 with a .406 OBP. He hadn't batted better than .257 since 1987, when he had a .330 average in 224 AB at Lynchburg. Jelic's immediate future probably depends on Mark Carreon's rehab program. If Carreon returns, Jelic becomes a superfluous right-handed bat and utilityman. It's doubtful he could fill the role as well as Tim Teufel.

PHILADELPHIA

Pete DeCoursey:

Third Base: The Phillies think Charlie Hayes, who seldom walks, can drive in 80 runs in '91 by banging his base hits after they've crammed the bases with Dykstra, Daulton, Von Hayes, Murphy, and Kruk, all of whom will reach base more than 200 times next year. Hayes showed some ability to work pitchers to favorable counts last year, but did almost nothing once he got the favorable counts. The problem was most visible in the second half of the season. Similar to his previous error problem, Hayes lack of concentration is a big factor here. While his noticeable defensive improvements show he can learn, he has a much longer way to go with the bat. His full output may be .260 with 10 HRs and 60 RBI; and he has a problem staying focused at the end of the season. Early improvements may fade by Labor Day.

In the his first 76 games last year, Charlie hit .280, but over his last 76, he fell to .237 because of a growing difficulty with RHP. He hit just .207 against righties in the second half. His bat will not bench him, because Charlie is rapidly becoming the best fielding 3rd baseman in the NL.

Dave Hollins will play 3B to rest Charlie, and will probably see around 20 starts at 1st and another 20 at third. If Hayes is hurt, then Hollins will get the job. Don't be surprised if the Phils spend this year letting other clubs be impressed by Charlie's glove, and then deal him late in the year or early next year to play Hollins, a far better and more versatile offensive player, who is average or slightly better defensively at third, but would show the Rose virtues at the plate: hustling speed, walks, doubles power, and high average.

PITTSBURGH

In December the Pirates acquired Milwaukee farmhand Joe Redfield. He is age 29, really too old to be considered a prospect, but the change of organization raises hopes. Jack Daugherty reached the majors at age 29 and found a role at age 30, so it's not impossible. Redfield hit .274-17-71-34 at Denver last year. The speed is the most impressive aspect.

Wally Backman was still unsigned in the final hours of 1990. Jeff King would love to play every day, but he's just learning to hit lefty pitchers; against righties he was only .214 last year. King is a revealing case study in left/right comparisons by first half and second half. The bottom line is that all his improvement during 1990 came against left-handed pitchers. He didn't show any progress against the righties, and actually deteriorated. In the first half, King hit .214 overall, .204 against lefties and .243 against righties. In the second half, King improved to .264 overall. Against lefties he soared to .304, but against RHP he slumped to .204.

Many hitters have made good careers out of bashing righty pitchers, without ever being able to touch the southpaws. It is rare, however, for anyone who has trouble against righties to get much playing time, if they could stay on a roster. There is no doubt that Jeff King will stay on the roster and get plenty of PT, but this writer wants to see

King hit some righties before putting him on a Rotisserie roster. Hitting .204 against RHP just won't make the grade in the major leagues, no matter how well you hit lefties.

Adam Stein:

In the second half of 1990, Jeff King finally showed some signs of becoming the player that the Pirates wanted him to be when they made him a number 1 pick. Even if he gets platooned, he could hit 20 HR with 80 RBI. His value will be enhanced if he can bat directly behind Bonds and Bonilla.

ST. LOUIS

Terry Pendleton is out, and Todd Zeile (?!?) is in. Zeile is discussed in the Cardinals catcher section; catcher is where you want him on your team.

Tim Jones, Craig Wilson and Rex Hudler are the other possibilities. Jones is a light-hitting utility player who won't be of much value even if he plays frequently. He might have some small value as a mid-season pickup if someone on your roster gets hurt, but it wouldn't make any sense to buy him on draft day. Wilson is a 26-year-old rookie who spent three and a half years in A ball. Since 1987, he as been hanging around Louisville. Wilson's 33 RBI in 125 major league at bats would pro-rate to 132 in 500 AB; that's a lesson in the silliness of pro-rating part time numbers. Craig is a singles hitter, and a light one at that. His lifetime OBP is under .300, and his lifetime slugging percentage is only .264. If St. Louis thought he could hit better than Tom Pagnozzi, Zeile would go back behind home plate. Rex Hudler is discussed in the OF essays.

SAN DIEGO

After losing Carlos Baerga and Dave Hollins from their farm system a year ago, and unloading players like Randy Ready, Chris James, Luis Salazar, Chris Brown and Eddie Williams, the Padres have beefed up their 3B depth chart with the additions of Scott Coolbaugh and Tom Redington. Prospect Paul Faries is also a candidate at 3B, if he doesn't get the 2B job. Among this group, Faries is the only player who appeared at third base for the Padres in 1990, and he played just one game there.

Coolbaugh is a high power, low average hitter, just the type whose stats would be exaggerated by playing in Jack Murphy Stadium. He hit .315 against lefties last year, but only .151 against righties. He didn't have enough at bats to prove these tendencies, but the Padres will have to think about them anyway. Redington is also a righty hitter. He attracted wide attention by winning Baseball America player of the year honors for the Midwest League in 1989, but he had an off year in 1990 and fell out of favor with the Braves front office. Promotion to the major league 40-man roster during the winter of 1989-90 proved unhelpful, as Redington reportedly spent the lockout period doing some serious vacationing.

Either Redington or Coolbaugh might make a nice $1 acquisition, but I wouldn't use up a roster spot for either, when San Diego is obviously open to the idea of finding an established major league third baseman. Also, don't forget that Joey Cora (see 2B) and Garry Templeton will be kicking around, looking for a spot to get into games; and Faries is in favor for hitting .312 with 48 SB at Las Vegas in 1990. If you have to pick one in January, it's Faries. The best approach is wait and see. You won't miss much.

Considering all the righties in the talent pool, it's hard to understand why the Padres have been so cool toward Mike Pagliarulo.

Lary Bump:

The chances of 30-year-old Steve Springer resurfacing in the majors are slim, even with the Padres. But Springer, a right-handed batter, deserves a mention for persevering through six consistent Triple-A seasons. His batting averages ranged between .261 and .281, HR 4 to 8, RBI (with one exception) 46 to 56, SB 4 to 10, walks 24 to 41, Ks 67 to 83. His only reward so far has been four games with the Indians. He also can play 2B.

SAN FRANCISCO

We liked Matt Williams way back in 1989, liked him more in 1990, and said so both years. 1989: "dramatic ability to hit major league home runs: 16 of them in 401 ML at bats, and they tend to come in bunches. Overall, Williams is a fine hitter for age 22 to 23, when most people are in Double A ball at best." 1990: "This year, I like Matt Williams even more. The batting average will improve. Williams is a solid .260 hitter against lefties, already. The problem is righty pitching. Williams improved from .078 vs. RHP in the first half last year, to .198 in the second half. If he keeps improving at this rate, he will hit .378 vs. righties in 1990 — not likely, but encouraging!"

Williams hit .274 against RHP in 1990, certainly as high as anyone could expect. He is obviously one of the game's great sluggers for the 1990's.

John Koller:

Williams had trouble hitting curveballs in previous seasons, but he worked on this problem during the winter of 1989-90 and came out of the gate looking for curves and hitting them. Matt's 122 RBI set a Giants record for third basemen.

Thom Rogers:

Future Hall of Famer Matt Williams will continue to improve. His .277 average this year surprised even him. His HRs were consistent all year although his RBI dropped in the second half. He won the RBI title anyway. As he continues to gain confidence, he'll put up increasingly impressive numbers. For '91 I'd expect a .275 BA, 35 HR, 105-110 RBI, and 10 SB.

AMERICAN LEAGUE SHORTSTOPS

BALTIMORE

Two years ago, there was serious consideration of Juan Bell displacing Cal Ripken, who would have moved to first or third. There is no such talk in the spring of 1991. After nine full seasons in the major leagues, Ripken seems like he should be older than his 30 years. He is on a pace to set career records in many offensive categories for AL shortstops. It makes you wonder how people could have seriously considered him "too old" to play shortstop when he was only 28.

There is no reason why Ripken shouldn't hit better than his 1990 batting average of .250. He is a lifetime .274 hitter who is (as just noted) not yet in the twilight of his career. Ripken has been remarkably consistent with 21 to 28 homers in every one of his nine seasons. The only problem with Ripken as a Rotisserie commodity is that everyone knows about him, and he never goes cheap. His average price was $28 in 1990, and he sold for less than $25 in only about 10% of all auctions.

Juan Bell is discussed under the Baltimore 2B section, because that is where he is most likely to appear in the major leagues in 1991. In this section we will make just two comments about why Bell wouldn't get the shortstop job, even if Ripken vanished.

1. At Rochester Bell produced a .285 BA and 16 SB in 1990, and in 1989 he had a .262 average, no power, and 17 SB taken with raw speed. Bell was better in every offensive category back in 1988 when he split time between AA San Antonio and AAA Albuquerque, and hit .300 in 257 Triple A at bats. He isn't showing any rapid development; he is still only 23. His offense would be just marginal against major league competition.

2. Bell is a personality problem, and, although he has made improvements, I believe that Frank Robinson simply doesn't like him. Young Juan, in case you didn't know, is reportedly ruder than his older brother George, who has his own reputation. The best that can be said about Juan, comparatively, is that he has time to change, while George is "grown up."

Long ago, Frank Robinson said that Juan Bell will bat ninth, if and when he makes it to the major leagues.

BOSTON

Tim Naehring is a good bet for 1991, if you can observe during spring training that his back works OK.

Isaac Kaufman:

The 1991 season offers three possibilities for the Red Sox at shortstop.

(1) Tim Naehring may be given the job on opening day; that would be the best move the Red Sox could make, and the most likely. Naehring has an outstanding attitude, and clear potential. Given the job, he could hit .270 with 15 homers.

(2) The Sox could go with Luis Rivera. In my opinion that would be the worst choice. Rivera is a crowd favorite, but his play isn't up to par. Last summer it seemed every time I tuned in channel 38, Rivera was always in the process of making

one of his crazy Looie Looie throws, sending Carlos Quintana into some painful-looking contortions to grab the wild throw. Considering that his offense provides a below-average BA with mediocre power, Rivera just isn't worth using up a place in the lineup.

(3) Boston may trade for a new second baseman, and move Jody Reed to shortstop. Reed is the best natural shortstop on the team, especially when it comes to throwing skill. After the winter meetings it seemed less likely the Red Sox would actually get anyone, but possibilities like Mariano Duncan were still being discussed.

Lary Bump:

I thought Tim Naehring's injury last season would doom Boston's playoff chances. Naehring's absence may have been felt more in the Championship Series. Luis Rivera hit as well as any Red Sox player, but Naehring could have provided another long-ball threat in a lineup that desperately needed one. The 24-year-old right-handed hitter batted .269 with 15 HR and 47 RBI in 82 games at Pawtucket, and had a .271 average in 24 games with the Bosox, often batting third in the lineup. He fields his position pretty well, can also play 3B and is an excellent hit-and-run man. Typical of the Red Sox, he has five stolen bases in three pro seasons. Pencil him in at SS this season, in an important lineup position.

Fred Percival:

Looking at the following numbers:

	Outs made	Runs Created	Ratio
Barrett	250	35	.140
Rivera	240	34	.142
Reed	373	76	.204

It was obvious that the Red Sox had to play Jody Reed somewhere. He has low range as a shortstop, but adequate range as a second baseman. He will hit, and could always return to shortstop, but the Sox will be better off playing him at second.

CALIFORNIA

After three disappointing seasons, it is beginning to look as if Dick Schofield reached his offensive peak in 1986 at age 23, when he hit .249 with 13 HR. In 1989 his BA slipped to .228 and in 1990 he had only 18 RBI. Schofield lost a lot of playing time to "the kid," Kent Anderson. (Perception is often different from reality when a rookie is pressing a veteran. Schofield is only 8 months older than his rival.)

Anderson hit .308 last year, but got only 143 at bats. His 5 RBI in 1990 tell you more about his offensive contributions. In 1989 Anderson hit just .229, but he improved to .244 in the second half. The bottom line is that there is no premier SS in California in 1990. While Schofield has obvious potential and should be doing better than he did in 1989 and 1990, he has suffered enough physical problems to raise doubts. Somebody in your league will be optimistic and expect Schofield to make a complete return to form. Our advice is to let someone else have him.

Gary Disarcina is the Angels shortstop of the future. He hit .305 in Single A in 1988, then .286 with 54 RBI and 11 SB last year at AA Midland. Last year he slumped to .212 with only 25 walks and 46 strikeouts, but there is no serious competition at AAA Edmonton. Time is the only thing that stands between Disarcina and the Angels; he was on the 40-man roster way back in December 1989. With a big spring training and favorable treatment from the front office, he has a chance to reach the majors in early 1991, mainly because the other candidates are weak.

Lary Bump:

You could look at the Angels as being prudent for not rushing the 23-year-old Disarcina into their lineup with Dick Schofield out much of the year. Or you could look at Disarcina's puny .212 average in the PCL, which definitely would be south of Mendoza in any league. With Schofield only 28, there shouldn't be any rush this year to move Disarcina to Anaheim. He should get another year in the Coast League to try to develop his hitting.

CHICAGO WHITE SOX

Ozzie Guillen got off to a marvelous start in 1990, raising expectations and Rotisserie trade values to career high levels. Guillen is not a .350 hitter, however, and he settled back to earth as the season wore on. His .279 full year average is about what you should expect in 1991. If he gets off to a fast start again, trade him.

Guillen is a terrible baserunner. He is blessed with good speed but doesn't know how to use it. At age 27 there is hope that Ozzie is still improving, but he's been in the league six years now, and must be a slow learner if that is the issue. Still, when you look at someone who gets only 13 SB in 30 attempts, you have to see that many runners would get 20 SB given the same opportunities. Manager Jeff Torborg is not suddenly going to lose his interest in the running game, certainly not after the success he had in 1990, so there is upward potential for Guillen in this one category. Guillen stole 36 bases as recently as 1989.

Jon Dunkle:

The American League Wizard of Oz put together a career season in 1991. Ozzie Guillen hit .300 for a good portion of the year, then fell apart in the second half. Even though he won't put up numbers like he did during the first half, Guillen still ranks among the top Rotisserie shortstops. His BA will never hurt you. He scores runs, steals bases, and hits a rare homer that will come in handy in a tight pennant race.

Guillen has some unusual, negative statistics. He is perpetually on the A.L. leader board for times caught stealing. And because he doesn't walk much and gets a "CS" in the box score more often than "SB," he has one of the worst ratios of runs scored per base hit. Ozzie finds all kinds of ways to avoid scoring. Fortunately, most Rotisserie leagues still don't count runs or CS.

Timothy R. McAvoy:

Did you really expect Guillen to hit over .320? I didn't. And the White Sox were delighted with his .279 average and stolen base total (although they would have hoped for a higher SB%). Most of all, Chicago loves his defense. No one plays harder.

CLEVELAND

Bill Gray:

The 1991 SS is Felix Fermin. Not a potent offensive player, but very few shortstops are. Fermin's defense is the reason the Indians like him. He really won't hurt you offensively, and if your league counts errors, note that he improved from 27 in 1989 to 16 last year. He also drove in 25 of his 40 RBI in the second half. Because of Fermin's play, the Indians aren't desperate for their 1988 number one pick, Mark Lewis, to arrive. Lewis will benefit from Fermin's steady play and have a chance to develop in AA Canton. He will not be rushed as Jay Bell was. Cleveland gave up on Bell prematurely and traded him to the Pirates for Fermin.

If Lewis makes some major strides in Colorado, Fermin will be traded or relegated to backup. Felix is a short-term fix, both for you and for Cleveland. Don't overspend for him if your expectation is for 1991. Word on Lewis is that defensively he is not ready. Baseball America rated Lewis the 1 player in the Eastern League in '90. The long-term outlook is very good.

Steve Goldman:

Felix Fermin goes into spring training as the 1 man, but watch out! The Tribe acquired Felix in 1989 as a stopgap, someone who could play the position on a major league level until Mark Lewis is ready to come out of the minors.

Well, Fermin does play shortstop at a major league level, but he's not one of the better ones around. He does field well, but not spectacularly, and he has a weak bat, and doesn't compensate for it by walking. Lewis, on the other hand, has the potential to be a major star. He is still very young, but if Fermin goes bad, the Tribe will want to push Lewis along. It is conceivable (though unlikely) that events in spring training could unfold in a way that makes Lewis the opening day shortstop.

Lewis will not make a big impact in the majors in 1991, even he gets some playing time. Cleveland is not the place to be looking for a Rotisserie shortstop this year.

Lary Bump:

It seems as if we started hearing about Lewis as the Indians' SS of the future back about the time Lou Boudreau left Cleveland. But the Tribe's No. 1 draft pick in '88 is still just 21. In the Eastern League last year, he hit .272-10-60 in 390 AB, and the .306-1-21 in 124 AB in the PCL. His bat really came to life last season, but he still struggled at times in the field, with 31 errors for Canton. He has been promoted in mid-season each of the last two years, and a similar promotion — to Cleveland — isn't out of the realm of possibility this year. A bold move would be for the Indians to say coming out of spring training, "We're in a lousy division that even we can win. We probably can't do it with Felix Fermin in the lineup. Let's give this Lewis a shot." Well, it could happen.

DETROIT

In September 1989, Andy Hawkins told me, "Trammell and I work out together during the off season. I know him real well, and I can tell you he is OK and he's going to have a good year in 1990. He's got the back trouble under control with exercises. Don't pay any attention to 1989. He's going to be real good next year."

Real good? He hit .304 with 14 homers, 89 RBI and 12 steals. Not bad for age 32, and just plain outstanding among major league shortstops. yes, I would say he did "real good."

If anything takes Trammell out of the lineup, Travis Fryman or Tony Phillips can slide over and fill in for him. (See 2B and 3B essays.)

KANSAS CITY

Is it possible that Kurt Stillwell is only 25? Yes. Kurt has had ongoing injury problems, and failed to improve in 1990. But he is far too young to be headed downhill within the context of his career. Look for a return to form in 1990. You need players with upward potential to win, and Stillwell should be on your list.

Marc Bowman:

Kurt Stillwell should achieve his career averages or better in 1990. He is still quite young (25) and is likely to focus his attention on hitting, now that his defense is reasonably solid. At his best, Stillwell can help you in all four categories. For this year, I predict .261-10-54-9. Last year, Stillwell didn't get even one SB, but that was due largely to a shortage of opportunities. He only attempted twice. During the first half of the season, Stillwell did his best hitting when the Royals were behind by two runs or more. When the Royals played better later in 1990, Stillwell was in a slump.

Stillwell has yet to produce even one full season without slumps or injuries. His first two "full seasons" with the Royals ended prematurely when he got hurt. Last year he showed that he is prone to extended slumps. If you get Stillwell on your roster and he gets off to a fast start, trade him. Talk up the value of his youth and upward potential, but recognize that something is likely to go wrong. It always does.

Bill Pecota is the backup SS, but he will see more time at 2B than at short in 1991. Steve Jeltz also filled at SS on occasion during 1990, if you can call his mediocre fielding and a .155 BA "filling in." If the Royals have any sense, Jeltz won't be among them on opening day. Finally, Paul Zuvella was still kicking around the minors, at the top of the KC farm system, in 1990. None of the reserve shortstops can possibly be of any interest in Rotisserie plans.

MILWAUKEE

George Hall:

The Brewers shortstop job belongs to Bill Spiers, until he does something to lose it. Spiers was Milwaukee's first draft choice in 1987, out of Clemson. He moved through the Brewers farm system in a quick hop scotch, reaching Milwaukee as a replacement for the injured Dale Sveum in 1989. He suffered nettlesome injuries in both 1989 and 1990. At age 24, he is still improving, and the injury bug is the only obstacle that he has yet to overcome.

For Spiers 1991 stats, I predict .242-2-36-11 with 363 at bats, based on his track record. If he could get 500 at bats, 50 RBI and 15 steals are easily within reach. Spiers left-handed bat is an asset for a shortstop.

If something goes wrong with Spiers, the Brewers have a problem. He is Edgar Diaz, the 27-year-old career minor leaguer. His .271 BA doesn't look too frightening, but don't expect it again in 1991. He went into an offensive free fall last year, after a good start at the plate. He distinguished himself in the field by making 17 errors without much playing time.

Alan Boodman:

The shortstop job is Bill Spiers' to lose. This is yet another Brewer whose primary contribution is defensive, as there aren't many things he does to help a team offensively. Spiers, as an offensive player, is similar to Jim Gantner, which really isn't a very nice thing to say about somebody, but it's true nonetheless. At best, Bill looks like a .265-range hitter with little power and moderate speed. I can't say what they see in him, except that he's still young and might develop.

Even though there doesn't seem to be much of an alternative (Dale Sveum?), the Brewers may be tempted to try someone else during the season, if they need to shake up the batting order and score some runs. Spiers should bat ninth (so should Gantner), and doesn't stand to produce much even for a number nine hitter. Bill will get into about 100 games, hitting .240 to .250 and staying below 5 homers and 45 RBI. He might steal 20 bases, but his OBP won't be much higher than .300, which tends to cut down on opportunities to steal. If Dale Sveum got the same playing time, he'd be on base more often than Spiers and would add 17-20 homers. Sveum may be unable to play SS any longer, but the Brewers have enough multiple position players that they can consider sliding someone over to 3B and trying Gary Sheffield at short.

MINNESOTA

Greg Gagne still has the shortstop job locked up, but he has dropped from the ranks of good-offense shortstops. A .235 BA was acceptable in 1988, when he produced 14 homers and 15 steals, but in 1990 the .235 BA was just a drag on everybody's roster. Gagne hit just .226 with 14 RBI in the second half last year. At age 29, you can't expect any improvement. Gagne is not in danger of hitting .190 like some shortstops, however, and he plays in a stadium that is kind to hitters. When in doubt, get your middle infielders from Minnesota or Boston.

Lary Bump:

Here's the choice: (A) known commodity Greg Gagne, 29, or (B) the untried Scott Leius, 25. Both bat right. Both tailed off significantly at the plate last season, Leius from a Southern League-leading .303 to a miserable .229 in the Coast League. His true value is somewhere in between there, perhaps at the .240 he posted in 25 September at bats with the Twins. In his other three minor league seasons he finished at .278, .239 and .237. In 103 games at Portland last year, he posted career lows with 2 HR, 23 RBI, a .299 OBP and a .312 slugging percentage. He needs to start this season back at Portland. If he starts well, then perhaps the Twins should consider moving Gagne aside. Much depends, of course, on what Gagne does.

NEW YORK YANKEES

The Yankees got one marvelous year out of Alvaro Espinoza after signing him as a six-year minor league free agent on November 17, 1987. At that point, he was a .266 career hitter in the minors, with no power and little speed. His defense, however, had managed to keep him in professional baseball. When Rafael Santana was injured in early 1989, the Yankees were left with a gaping hole in their infield. Espinoza was the only healthy and experienced SS in the Yankee system. He won the major league starting job in spring training 1989, by default. This sudden elevation had a profound and positive effect on Espinoza, who blossomed at age 27, both offensively and defensively.

Unfortunately, Espinoza couldn't repeat the performance in 1990. The league's pitchers and defenses made adjustments that really undid his hitting. Espi is a free-swinging, good-contact type of hitter. He doesn't strike out excessively, but he almost never draws a walk. When he sees a ball he can put in play, his reflex is to hit it. In 1990, opposition pitchers started throwing him outside fastballs, with the defense shifted toward right. Alvaro didn't strike out as much in 1990 as he did in 1989, but his BA plummeted from .282 to .224. Espinoza drove the ball right at the second baseman or right fielder so many times in 1990, that he started trying to pull the ball late in the year. It didn't work.

The only hope for Espinoza to put up a .280 average like he did in 1989, or even to hit .250 again, would be a change in approach. He has to be more patient, and stop swinging at those pitches that the pitcher wants him to swing at. If he was eight years younger, that would be a reasonable objective for spring training. At this stage in his career, it is doubtful that Espinoza will ever be able to un-learn all his years of experience.

Fortunately for Espinoza, there isn't going to be much competition for the SS position, unless the Yankees trade for somebody. That won't help you in Rotisserie, however, because 500 worthless at bats count the same as 200 worthless at bats. Spend your money elsewhere.

Daniel Stone:

Espinoza is improving his defense, which will help him keep his job. He led AL shortstops in range factor last year. He positions himself wisely, moves well in all directions, and has a good arm.

His minor league career stats say that Espinoza is not going to hit for high average, or high anything. He may hit a little higher than .220 in 1990, but not much higher.

Wayne Tolleson and Randy Velarde are the most likely substitutes when Espinoza doesn't play.

OAKLAND

At age 27, Walt Weiss will begin his fifth year as a fixture at shortstop for the "dynasty" A's. Weiss posted a career high .265 BA last year. There is no reason why he shouldn't hit .260 again this year and next year. Weiss is never going to join the ranks of truly valuable Rotisserie shortstops, however. If anything, his price will move up as becomes better-known as a member of a championship team, but his value will stay right about where is was in 1990.

The only subs at shortstop in 1990 were Mike Bordick and Mike Gallego. Neither of them is going to do anything with the bat that would make you sit up and pay attention, if they receive a big increase in playing time.

Lary Bump:

It was all set up to be the stuff of legends. Mike Bordick steps from the back of the bus into the World Series and becomes a hero. It sort of happened, but to Billy Bates. Instead, Bordick is another guy — and I'm tiring of writing this — who seems to point out the weakness of the Athletics' farm system. The 25-year-old is still another right-handed batter, who has had two totally undistinguished offensive years in the PCL — .240 and .227, with a total of 3 HR and 73 RBI, OBPs in the .320s and sub-.300 slugging percentages. That's poor even for a shortstop, and Oakland gave him some time at 3B. He does have a good glove. And the highlight of his '90 season was improving his SB percentage from 31% to 100%. So what if he only attempted three steals? Bordick is more proof that Tony LaRussa may be trying to surround himself with utility infielders. He may be valuable to LaRussa, but Bordick has no Rotisserie value.

SEATTLE

Omar Vizquel, Mike Brumley, Brian Giles, Jeff Schaefer, and Dave Cochrane were seen playing shortstop for the Mariners in 1990. Vizquel got the biggest share of playing time, and he was the giant among this group of offensive midgets with a .247 BA and 18 RBI. Wow.

Tony Formo's 1991 Left Field Extravaganza:

Switch-hitting Omar Vizquel (.295 OBA, .298 SA) was hurt much of the season. While the Little O's offensive stats seem somewhat anemic, they are an improvement on his woeful 1989 season (when he was rushed to the majors because of the Quinones trade), and seem likely to improve. Vizquel's reliable play at shortstop is a novelty in Seattle, and likely to keep him in the lineup unless his bat completely fizzles and someone better comes along, neither of which seems as likely as his increasing offensive production.

Brian Giles (.336 OBA, .421 SA) had a career day against the Blue Jays, but is not likely to play much if Vizquel remains healthy and continues to improve.

Lary Bump:

Jeff Schaefer's second major league shot came about as a result of an injury to Omar Vizquel. Think maybe it's time for Schaefer, a 31-year-old righthanded batter to hang them up? He posted a typical .241 with 0 HR in 49 games at Calgary, then soared to .206 in 55 games with the Mariners. He has a very slim chance to remain as a utility infielder this season. Actually, in bygone days, he would have been gone in '89, when he was one of the leaders of the Vancouver Canadians' one-day strike when they didn't receive their paychecks. Baseball's less lenient labor policies never would have stood for that 20 years ago.

TEXAS

Jeff Kunkel's .170 batting average in 1990 delivered the shortstop job to Jeff Huson, who will keep the lead role in 1991. Huson is not an offensive force, but he once hit .300 in the minors, and he can steal 10 to 20 bases per year. If he can hit .240 again like he did last year, Huson's speed will create some value for you.

Monty Fariss hit .302 for Oklahoma City, without any speed or power. Watch those spring training box scores.

Bob Hazlewood:

Jeff Huson will get most of the playing time at shortstop this year, while Jeff Kunkel will fill in occasionally. After hitting .085 against righty pitchers last year, Kunkel won't see many of them in 1991. Huson bats left and doesn't have any particular difficulty against righties or lefties.

Lary Bump:

The Padres grew tired of waiting for Gary Green to grow into the prospect they had projected out of UNLV. So last year they moved him over to Texas for the longest major league stint (88 AB) of his career. He had earned the promotion with a .234 start at Oklahoma City. Come to think of it, the presence of two other disappointments, Jeff Kunkel and Jeff Huson, at SS may have played a role as well. Anyway, the right-handed hitting Green, now 29, didn't make much of his chance, batting .216 with 0 HR and 1 SB. He is still considered a good glove man, but probably not good enough to carry his anemic bat to any more major league games, especially if the Rangers find a real SS.

Dic Humphrey:

The Rangers looked at 1984 Olympian Gary Green as a possible back-up. Minor league heir apparent Monty Fariss (1988 number one pick) produced reasonable offensive stats at AA Tulsa in 1989 (.272, 52 RBI, 12 SB) and hit .302 at AAA Oklahoma City last year, but the Rangers were not thrilled with his defense. He may be due for a change in position.

TORONTO

One fixture is gone, and another is implanted. Just in case anyone's curious, I think the Jays got the best of The Trade. Roberto Alomar hasn't nearly reached his peak, while both Tony Fernandez and Fred McGriff are at (or past) their peaks. Manny Lee is on our "age 26 with two or more years of major league experience" list, and Joe Feinstein thinks he is due for a surge. In the above essays, we have warned you away from most of the league's shortstops. Manny Lee isn't in the Fernandez/Guillen category, and he sure isn't a Ripken/Trammell type of value, but he is the shortstop you want for 1991. He is the most likely of all to be a bargain.

J.L. Feinstein:

Good-bye Tony Fernandez . . . helllooooooo, Manny Lee.

I can just imagine the talk in Toronto's pubs in December 1990: "How could Gillick do this? I know we called him 'Stand Pat,' but geez, how could he trade Fernandez? Who's gonna play SS? Manny Lee! He wasn't even a good 2B. At shortstop? You gotta be kiddin."

Well, let me tell ya gang. Not to worry. Shortstop is not going to be a major problem. You heard it here first. To start with, the job goes to Manny Lee. I know, I know. When they handed him the 2B job last season, he played a mediocre 2B and hit a pedestrian .243. How could he be the answer?

Well, Manny's from the Dominican Republic. San Pedro de Macoris, to be precise. A place known for their shortstops. Like Tony Fernandez, for example. Manny came into the Jays organization as a SS. That's all he ever wanted to be. I mean, if you came from Pedro, you WERE a SS. Of course, when he made it to the Jays, he had perennial Gold-Glove SS Tony Fernandez in front of him. So, Manny became the backup SS and did quite a decent job. Then, a couple years back, the Jays converted him to a 2B, to fill a need. Well, it beat going back to the Dominican, so Manny 'agreed,' but he was never really happy there. After all, he was a SS. To turn him into a 2B was a slap in the face. Telling him he wasn't good enough to be a SS. Somewhat predictably, Manny responded by going thru the motions at 2B.

For a while the Jays platooned him with Nelson Liriano, then wondered if that was what was making him so unhappy. So, they traded Liriano . . . and handed Manny the 2B slot. To say he was a disappointment would be an understatement. The Jays had seen enough and were ready to give up on him, when along came Joe McIlvaine to take the moody Tony Fernandez off their hands.

Now, Manny has his shot. To be what he always wanted to be . . . an every day shortstop, like Fernandez before him and Alfredo Griffin before him. Look for a reborn Manny Lee. One who's out early taking grounders and extra BP. One who can't wait to get to the park. After all, he's made it. He's now a SS . . . and he's gonna prove he's up to the task.

Look for him to play a VERY solid SS. With Alomar at 2B and Devon White in center, the team is gonna be very strong up the middle. Look for Manny to be more than an automatic out, too. With his "new" attitude, he'll work at his offense, and a .270 BA is clearly within reach. He hit .291 back in 1988.

If Lee does falter, and we don't think it likely, the

Jays have a real slick glove man named Eddie Zosky in the minors. A first round draft pick in '89, he spent the season in Knoxville [AA] where he made a nice adjustment to being weaned from aluminum bats. After struggling at the plate in 1989, he improved to hit .271 at Knoxville. A year at Syracuse would do him some good, but there's little doubt he can play a major league SS right now. He's got an arm that compares [some say favorably] to Shawon Dunston, and the range to make the spectacular play look easy.

As of the Winter Meetings, Gillick expects to use Zosky as Lee's back-up, but we look for the Jays to pick up a utility infielder [can you say Curtis Wilkerson, three times, fast?] to back up both Lee and Alomar, and let Zosky spend a year at the AAA level.

NATIONAL LEAGUE SHORTSTOPS

ATLANTA

Marc Bowman:

The Braves tried to get rid of Andres Thomas in 1990; he was constantly rumored to be on his way to Houston or Philadelphia or the Yankees. The trade never got done, and the challengers to Thomas in Atlanta were all inconsistent and failed to impress. Thomas actually improved a little during 1990, but the Braves aren't going to be enthusiastic about him until he shows more patience at the plate. He walked only 11 times last year, 12 in 1989. Andres swings at far too many bad pitches, including many in the dirt. He will get less playing time in 1991 as Bobby Cox tries to mix in a variety of platoons and substitutes in the infield.

In a great year, Thomas could produce 10 HR and 50 RBI, but he is likely to stay down around 6 HR and 35 RBI in 1991. His batting average will never be anything helpful; he hasn't hit over .220 since 1988. If he would just lay off those bad breaking balls . . .

Jeff Blauser came close to winning the shortstop job in 1990. He actually ended up with more SS games and more AB than Thomas last year, but Blauser never got Thomas out of the starting lineup for any lengthy period. There has been talk of a Blauser/Thomas platoon — but how? Both bat right. Blauser has a slight preference for lefty pitching; Thomas doesn't care (a .215/.225 split doesn't exactly cry out for someone to be platooned). Blauser hits better against all types of pitching. And Blauser and Thomas both faced about the same mix of righties and lefties in 1990.

Victor Rosario got a late-season look-see but was unimpressive. Mark Lemke can fill in at SS, so don't expect the club to carry Rosario out of spring training; he is marginal prospect anyway.

Lary Bump:

The Braves obtained Rosario, a veteran of seven minor league seasons at the ripe old age of 24, from Philadelphia after he had put together a good second half with the bat to finish at .251 for Scranton. In his second season with the Red Barons, he also surprised with 5 HR and 42 RBI, but he will have to do something about his godawful 12/91 W/K ratio. He has carried a reputation as a good defensive SS, and he is talented. But that talent hasn't kept him from making errors in bunches. He needs some work on his throwing and concentration. Andres Thomas and Jeff Blauser aren't exactly Ripken and Trammell, so it's possible to project Rosario as Atlanta's SS at some time. Not likely for now, though.

CHICAGO CUBS

One caution on Dunston: the new Cubs lineup is so powerful that Chicago was rumored to be viewing Dunston as expendable for a top starting pitcher and a defensive specialist shortstop. I won't argue the merits of moving Dunston (the idea doesn't sound to me like the thinking of a pennant-winner's front office), but I will point out the obvious downside if Dunston leaves Wrigley Field, and the obvious disaster if he gets traded to the AL.

Timothy R. McAvoy:

Shawon Dunston might be a great all-around hitter if he could just learn that baseball rules allow you to let a pitch go by without swinging. He is so eager, sometimes he seems to start swinging before the pitch is thrown. Nonetheless, Shawon will give you a couple dozen stolen bases and 60 RBI every year, and he now seems strong enough to hit 15 HR every year. He is at the age where the pitchers have done all they can to stop him from hitting, and Dunston should now be showing that he can learn from experience. What you see in 1991 will be about as good as Shawon is capable of producing.

CINCINNATI

Greg Gajus:

Barry Larkin (.301-7-67-30) had a good, but not great year in 1990. Larkin had only 38 extra base hits and does not draw that many walks, so his batting average represents most of his offensive value. However, thanks to an injury-free season (158 games played) Larkin created more runs on the Reds than anyone but Sabo.

With the decline of Ozzie, there is no doubt that Barry is the best SS in the league. Larkin will be 27 in 1991, an age when most players peak, so improvement over his 1990 stats is a possibility. The only question is where he will bat in the order. Larkin led off 24 games, hit second 57 times, and batted third 71 times. Despite his lack of power, he seems more comfortable hitting third, but he led off in post season play. Bill Doran's presence is likely to put Larkin in the number 3 spot. A full year batting third will allow Larkin to put up 80 RBI, sensational for a shortstop.

Sean Lahman:

What more needs to be said about Barry Larkin? He is without a doubt the best shortstop in the league. He is a franchise player, more valuable to the Reds than Eric Davis. If there is one downside to Larkin's 1990 season, it was his power shortage. Larkin would normally hit 15 HR in a year but had only 7 last year. Batting leadoff most of the season, Larkin was obviously more concerned with getting on base and scoring runs. If he hits third, the home run numbers will be up there again; otherwise, 7 seems a reasonable number. Larkin did drive in 67 runs, very high number from the leadoff spot.

Luis Quinones will be the utility infielder, backing up 2B, SS, & 3B. Quinones will be 29 years old and is not likely to become a full-time player. His main value is his versatility; he can play three infield positions and is a switch-hitter, hitting left-handed pitchers about as well as right-handed pitchers.

HOUSTON

Welford McCaffrey:

Something strange is going on around here. Rafael Ramirez used to lead the league in errors every year. But now, all of a sudden, he has become an average shortstop. Ramirez committed 25 errors in 1990, the same as Dickie Thon. Garry Templeton and Alfredo Griffin committed more at 26. That's a third of the NL shortstops right there. But most of the others are not too far away. Jay Bell had 22, Shawn-O-Meter Dunston and Jose Uribe had 20 each. Kevin Elster made 17 errors and Jeff Blauser 16 in far fewer games than any of the above. Even the all-time great Ozzie Smith had 12 errors after committing 17 in '89 and 22 in '88. To round it out, Barry Larkin was barely a cut above average with 17 errors in almost a full season of play.

Shortstops continue to be good-field no-hit types. The only shortstop with a high average in the NL last year was Larkin at .301. I went back to look at the good field, no hit shortstops of yore for comparison purposes. When you mention good field, no hit shortstops I think of Mark Belanger, Bud Harrelson, Larry Bowa and their contemporaries. The golden age of the good field, no hit shortstop, I would say, was 1967-1977.

Where have all the fielders gone? We can only hope that it is only a passing trend that the NL shortstops are catching up to Rafael Ramirez.

Eric Yelding is slated to be the Astros shortstop for 1991, according to GM Bill Wood. Yelding is an outfielder converted to the shortstop position. His first year as a shortstop in the minors he committed 58 errors, his second year he did worse committing 59 all together. Eric has great range and gets a good jump on the ball, but he commits a lot of errors still on the balls hit right at him. Overall, he will make as many errors as Ramirez but will get to many more balls because of his superior range.

Yelding is more of an offensive threat than Ramirez. While Yelding has even less power than Ramirez, he can get on base more via the walk. Yelding has much greater speed, so what he lacks in power he can make up for through the stolen base (if he learns not to get picked off as much in 1991) and taking the extra base.

The Astros shortstop of the future (most likely 1992, but possibly 1991) is Andujar Cedeno, age 21. Cedeno is a great offensive force having batted .285 in the rookie Gulf Coast League in 1988 his first minor league season, .300 at Asheville in 1989, but slumping to .245 in 1990 in Columbus of the Southern League. He had gotten off to a great start in the Southern League but slumped badly at mid-season. The big thing against Cedeno right now is that he strikes out an awful lot and makes a lot of errors. Cedeno made over 40 errors at Columbus. These are not good signs for the future. Expect Cedeno to start in Tucson with a possible shot at the majors at mid season if Yelding doesn't work out in the field at short.

Rusty Harris is another name to look out for in 1991. Harris batted .308 in limited action at Tucson in 1990 after batting .265 with 84 walks in 97 games at Osceola in the Florida State League in 1989.

Another shortstop that Astros management likes is Orlando Miller. He batted .319 for Asheville in the South Atlantic League in 1990. Miller was picked up by the Astros in a trade with the Yankees, for 1988 Olympic shortstop Dave Silvestri. Miller had batted .291 for the Yankees New-York Penn League Oneonta in 1989. He should be ready for the majors by 1992-1993.

One major problem all the Astros shortstop prospects have in the minors is that they all make a lot of errors, including the Astros number 1 draft choice in 1990, Tom Nevers.

Yelding is a gem for Rotisserie, because of his stolen bases. He gets on base a lot. One problem Yelding may have had in 1990 is that he never knew where he was playing, appearing at second, short, center and left. If Yelding is stabilized at one position in 1991 he may be able to concentrate on his offense a bit more and have a better year.

Lary Bump:

Andujar Cedeno — What a great baseball name! A great baseball player, though? It's too early to tell. He had an exceptional season at Asheville in '89 — .300-14-93-23. At Double-A Columbus last year, he powered 19 HR, but his other figures dropped, to a .240 BA and just 6-for-16 in SB. He also struck out 135 times. The biggest factor in the right-handed batter's favor is that he's just 21 years old. Given the power he has shown to date, it isn't difficult to project him at another position, perhaps 3B or OF, in the majors. Check out how the Astros use him this year, at Tucson or another try at Columbus.

LOS ANGELES

Jose Offerman was brought up to the major leagues in 1990 (reportedly) for his personal safety. It seems he made so many poor throws that the Albuquerque first baseman wasn't speaking to him any longer, and management feared mayhem. I don't think the Dodgers will send him back to the minors, and I don't think they'll bury him in the dugout.

The problem for Rotisserians is that Offerman is now a career .155 hitter in the majors (just 58 AB). He hit for high average in the minors, but everyone knows that a .300 BA in the Dodger farm system is only normal, and means absolutely nothing when you get to Dodger Stadium. I don't think Offerman is going to hit well at age 22, and I wouldn't want him on my roster for 1991. Somebody in your league is going to pay an outrageous price for him anyway, saving you any tough decisions.

Adam Stein:

The Dodgers want Jose Offerman to win the job from Alfredo Griffin. Still, they aren't going to rush him if he's not ready. Offerman offers superstar talent, with a weakness in his glove (and that doesn't count in Rotisserie baseball; it just affects playing time). Offerman is capable of stealing 60 bases, though it depends on how much the Dodgers use him, and where they bat him. Even if Griffin starts on opening day, Offerman should take over permanently during the season. Griffin is a terrible offensive player (and a bad defensive one too). Don't even waste a $1 on him. Offerman looks like a $10 player now, more if he wins the job in spring training.

Lary Bump:

Although he tailed off from an incredible start at Albuquerque, Jose Offerman, a 22-year-old switch hitter still batted .326 with 0 HR, 56 RBI, 60 SB and a .416 OBP in 117 games. It seemed as if Alfredo Griffin's bags already were packed when the Dodgers called up Offerman. But his .155 average in 29 games gave Alfredo a reprieve. Offerman has a strong arm, but he committed 36 errors at Albuquerque. He may become a player who puts to rest the cliche, "You can't walk off the island. In three pro seasons, he has 190 walks and 224 Ks. Unless something unforeseen happens, he will be the Dodgers' SS this season.

MONTREAL

Spike Owen has been a $3 player in 1989 and 1990 auctions. In '89 he was completely ignored in 10% of Heath Research and Roti-Stats auctions. Expectations are obviously low, so put Owen on your $1 list for late rounds, and you might get lucky. Don't expect him to hit over .240.

Michael Cassin:

Delino DeShields' move to 2B means at least two more years of Spike Owen at shortstop for the Expos. And if Will Cordero doesn't hit better than he did in AA last year, it could be a few more than that. Owens will do what he always does at bat: .240-5-40.

Cordero hit .238 at AA Jacksonville, with 110 strike-outs in 383 ABs. Montreal hasn't been shy about moving players from AA to the the major league starting lineup, but Cordero is only 19 and still needs work. He played an entire year of A ball at 16 years old, which means there is plenty of time to bring him along slow, but which could also mean a burned-out 21-year-old. This is the season to watch if Cordero can bring up the average and bring down the Ks. The Expos can afford to give him another season at AA, making his progress easier to chart. In any case, '93 is now the target year.

Junior Noboa and Tom Foley's infield utility jobs seem secure. Both can look for about 150 ABs, but Noboa has a better shot at playing time if someone goes down with an injury. Johnny Paredes is still around, but doesn't look to be a factor.

NEW YORK METS

The Mets (Frank Cashen) became clear that they want Howard Johnson at shortstop, "until further notice." There was no confidence that Kevin Elster would recover fully, and no expectation that he should displace Johnson even if he did return to form. Johnson helped management articulate about this thinking, by fielding adequately in 73 shortstop games last year, and by saying that he wanted the SS job. Howard thanks Bud Harrelson for helping him with his fielding.

Howard Johnson at shortstop is a Rotisserie cornerstone. Johnson emerged as a tremendous speed/power threat when he started to look curveball and react to the fastball. Strikeouts turned into homers. Hope for 30/30 but expect "only" 20/20.

Alan Boodman:

It is a sign of real offensive weakness from Kevin Elster (and a testimony to Howard Johnson's hitting) when you can remove a glove like Kevin Elster and come out ahead on the deal. Kevin has had nearly three seasons to prove he can handle major league pitching, and all he's done in that time is make people wonder how he ever handled minor league pitching.

There's no doubt that Elster's defensive skills are above average, but players who field well without hitting usually have trouble holding regular positions. The saving grace for Elster was that the Mets were a good enough offensive team (they led the NL in runs scored last season by a wide margin) that they could afford to carry a bat like Kevin's, just to get his glove in the lineup.

Elster has always had some pop in his bat, and usually produces some doubles and homers, so I guess the problem is he doesn't hit enough singles. He's good for 10 homers in a full season, and would drive in 65 runs a year if he plays in an offense like the Mets, even batting eighth. Unfortunately, Kevin's career batting average is now below .220, and he may not get a chance to raise it much if he remains a Met. The hope that he can approach his minor league numbers is still there, but it fades with each passing .207 year.

There are no phenoms coming through the system right now at shortstop, so HoJo is the man for 1991. Kevin Baez (recalled from AA last September) has a major league arm, and when the rest of his body catches up in a few years, he might get a longer look.

Apparently Buddy has decided that he can live with HoJo at short, so Elster's role looks to be that of late-inning defensive replacement. They're not going to take Johnson out too often either, so Kevin's role may be even more limited than that. He's never played an inning at a position other than shortstop, which means a utility infielder job is improbable. Elster's best shot might be to get traded to someplace where they can use him, someplace where they put more value on a glove and less on a bat.

If Kevin remains with the Mets, his playing time will be severely cut in 1991. He was nearly exiled to the Chicago Cubs before the 1990 season in a deal for Shawon Dunston, and I'm sure the Mets wouldn't mind including Mr. Elster in a trade for an everyday outfielder. Until something like that occurs, don't spend too much on a Mets shortstop unless it's Howard Johnson.

For Johnson, the good news is that 1991 is an odd-numbered year. Johnson seems to save his monster years for the odd ones. In 1990, Howard's batting average (.244) was somewhat of a disappointment, but the guy's only hit above .250 twice since becoming a regular 7 years ago. If you want a higher BA pick somebody like Lenny Harris or Wally Backman; if you want production, take HoJo.

Even in an "off-year" for HoJo, he's still more productive than Dunston or Larkin, and both of them were having career years, particularly Dunston, and both of them tailed off big-time towards the end of 1990. Some "off-year" stats for HoJo: .244 BA, 23 HR, 90 RBI, 34 SB, 89 runs scored, and 63 extrabase hits. Don't you wish your shortstop could put up numbers like those even in a good year?

Lary Bump:

The Mets gave Baez a taste of the big leagues after he finished his season at Jackson at .232-2-29. He's a 24-year-old right-handed batter ticketed for Tidewater or perhaps back to Jackson this season. His graduation to the majors will depend on glovework.

Fred Percival:

Kevin Elster never approached his offensive expectations. He was a good hitter in the minors, but has not come close to the major league BA his AAA numbers would predict. Elster has been standing too far from the plate last season, and has been easily handled with outside pitching. Kevin never has seemed to formulate a hitting strategy. There was hope that he might have been helped by new coach Mike Cubbage, but nothing changed much in 1990. Elster hasn't been a hot hitter since the first two weeks of 1989.

PHILADELPHIA

Pete DeCoursey:

Dickie Thon has decided to return to pulling the ball, which should bolster his HR total back to 10-12, but could drop his average below .240. If your league counts errors, Dickie will continue to make more each year, as he is slowing. He is a solid bet to at least repeat and possibly even better all of his offensive numbers, but they are no better than replacement level now. One of the Phils top priorities is to improve their middle infield back-up. If they get someone capable, Thon's playing time will be threatened.

If Rod Booker remains Thon's principal back-up, Thon will play 140-150 games again. Booker will not hit much in any case, and will not play enough to be worth drafting.

PITTSBURGH

Jay Bell is an up-and-comer at age 25. He should deliver about 10 HR and double digit SB, and his BA won't hurt you in 1991. Bell never hit over .300 in the minors, but he started his career at age 18 and has always been young relative to the competition. As he matures in the major leagues, his bat will come along nicely. Also, for the following reason, his RBI should jump to 60 or 70 (not 52).

Pete DeCoursey:

Bell had almost 40 sacrifice hits last year. If you let him swing away in all these situations with men on base, with the pitchers throwing a steady stream of fastballs, Bell would hit more homers and drive in many more runs. Bell is just age 25. The Pirates should see that he is now a solid major league hitter, and let him take those RBI opportunities in 1991.

Lary Bump:

Have the Pirates really persuaded themselves that Jay Bell is the answer to their shortstop prayers? Or have they merely built a case for him to boost his trade value so they can eventually go with Carlos Garcia at SS? The 23-year-old with a live right-handed bat has been promoted during each of the last two seasons, with little dropoff in production. Last year he followed up a .277 start at Harrisburg with a .264 mark in 197 AB at Buffalo. He totaled 10 HR, 43 RBI and 19 SB. He also was considered the best-fielding SS in the Eastern League. His greatest hidden talent is his leaping ability, almost on a par with his future double-play mate, Jose Lind. I expect to hear sometime that Garcia has leaped high to cut off a throw from RF and tagged out a runner rounding second base. The Pirates could do worse than stick him in their lineup on opening day, but he probably will start the season at Buffalo. Keep your eyes on this guy.

ST. LOUIS

Ozzie Smith is fading at age 36. He might steal 30 bases for you again, and his BA won't hurt you, and he will produce above-average RBI, but the .300 average, 40 SB and 75 RBI that we saw as recently as 1987 will never be seen again. Nonetheless, someone in every league builds a roster studded with fading stars, and that person will pay too much for Smith in 1991. Don't stay in the bidding. Last year, Smith went for $20 or more in half of all auctions.

Lary Bump:

Throughout his career, Bien Figueroa has been in the shadow of his old Florida State teammate, Luis Alicea. Figueroa's contributions go far beyond his .240-0-39 figures at Louisville last season. He makes every play at SS, bunts, hit-and-runs and travels the bases intelligently, if not particularly fast (5 SB). In the Cardinals' organization, he's stuck behind Ozzie Smith, Tim Jones and Jose Oquendo, but he's a better SS than many playing in the big leagues today. He has a chance to play in the majors immediately if he's traded.

SAN DIEGO

Tony Fernandez has already had his career years. Jack Murphy stadium and the new look of NL pitching will shave some points more off Tony's batting average. He might get a little boost in HR output; Fernandez has been showing more fly balls and fewer line drives in the past two years, and could now be described as having warning track power. Tony has averaged only 2 HR per year in Toronto's stadiums during his career.

Shortstop is about the only infield position where Paul Faries is not rumored to be the sure starter. After coughing up Robby Alomar, the Padres are likely to want Fernandez in the lineup as an every-day player, but Joey Cora is still young and improving, and Garry Templeton hasn't yet evaporated.

Templeton is now age 35, and he is destined for the bench, a new team, Japan, or someplace other than "6" in the starting lineup. He has weak legs and can't run the bases or field with the old range.

SAN FRANCISCO

It looks like a spring training battle will decide who gets the SS job on opening day. Neither candidate is going to give you much offense, so you shouldn't spend much time agonizing over your prediction. For 1992 and beyond, there are a couple of good possibilities.

Rob Wood:

Mike Benjamin is a decent hitter with a good arm, the same description as Jose Uribe, the man he is trying to beat out. Benjamin is a trifle weaker defensively, so the Giants will not likely give Benjamin much of a chance for a regular position.

Andres Santana is the Giants proclaimed SS of the future. Andres is a good slap hitter with tremendous speed (after an ugly broken ankle in 1989), and dazzling defense.

Royce Clayton is my choice for Giants SS of the future. A real hitter (none of this slap and dash crap) he also has decent defense. Unfortunately, Clayton is far from the majors, and will have Santana to contend with for the foreseeable future.

Thom Rogers:

After Uribe's decent first half (.289-1-18-3) he showed his true colors once again in the second semester (.174-0-6-2). Manager Craig sat him down for most of September as he looked at Mike Benjamin and Andres Santana. They want to trade Uribe as they can no longer afford his miserable average with no power and little speed. He's still a good SS, but in my opinion after watching him last season even this part of his game is slipping. Although his error count hasn't increased, his playing time has gone down, meaning he makes more errors per at bat, and his range looks diminished.

I give the starter's job to Benjamin based upon various things Rosen and Craig have said about him as far back as late fall 1989. The Giants are wealthy at SS with Benjamin, Andres Santana and Royce Clayton in the pipeline. Benjamin is the most advanced of the three, hitting about .255 and averaging 4 HR 35-40 RBI, and about 12 SB the last 2 years at Phoenix. He hit only .214 in 56 AB at SF this year, but management likes his defense and figures he'll eventually hit Uribe's .250 and be able to steal 10-15 bases per year. He's really only keeping the position warm for Santana, who I think will start at Phoenix. Santana hit .291 and stole over 30 bases at Shreveport last year, after suffering a broken leg the year before. He's the future at SS. If he's off to a good start at Phoenix and Benjamin can't hit above .240 by the middle of June, I wouldn't be surprised to see the Giants call Santana up and work him into the starter's job. This position bears some watching over the winter and through April-May, especially if/when the emergence of Santana becomes a clear possibility.

Lary Bump:

Jose Uribe's job has been rumored to be in jeopardy for a couple of years. Mike Benjamin, at age 25, is in a position to take the job. He followed up a .259 average with .251 in his second full season at Phoenix, and improved his power and speed slightly to 5 HR, 39 RBI, 13 SB. He has a pretty good glove. Everything about him is just pretty good. Not as good as Uribe in his prime, but with Jose now 31, Benjamin may be able to move into the lineup for a couple of years.

In a couple of years, the Giants hope that switch-hitter Andres Santana (now 23) will be ready. He stole 91 bases in 1988, then suffered a career-threatening leg injury. He came back last year to bat .292 with 0 HR and 24 RBI in 92 games at Shreveport. His SB mark, though, fell to 31 in 49 attempts. Look for Santana in Phoenix this season, even if Benjamin doesn't make the big club.

AMERICAN LEAGUE OUTFIELDERS

BALTIMORE

UPDATE — The O's hope Evans can replace Finley, who went to Houston. Orsulak will also play RF.

The Baltimore outfield is crowded and unsettled in 1991, just like it is every year. For Rotisserie purposes, you must approach all the O's outfielders as part-time and platoon players as of opening day; if you get 500 at bats from anyone, that would be a surprise. Last year Steve Finley led the group with 464 AB (we told you that Baltimore liked him best). The point is that you should get your 600 AB outfielders from some other city, and use Baltimore to fill in with bargains and gambles.

Frank Robinson likes to have more than three "regular" outfielders, using the DH position as necessary to help him rotate people in and out of the line-up. Take a look at last year's OF at bats: Finley 464, Joe Orsulak 413, Devereaux 367, Anderson 234, Gallagher 126, Komminsk 46, and Nixon 20. Phil Bradley had 422 AB with Baltimore and Chicago. Evans had 445 AB with Boston. For 1991 there are at least five people (Evans, Finley, Devereaux, Anderson, Orsulak) to share outfield time. Frank likes all that switching around.

The new wild card in the deck is Dwight Evans, who isn't accustomed to getting only 400 AB and isn't going to be happy as "just a DH." We think the Orioles will attempt to satisfy Evans with playing time in right field, but they aren't going to make him an everyday outfielder when they wouldn't do it for Phil Bradley.

Last year Evans got 10 of his 13 homers against righties, so there is a big squeeze on lefty-hitting Steve Finley and Joe Orsulak. Their main position is/was right field. There just isn't any big incentive to platoon them in 1991. Orsulak can slide over to left field, and Finley can play all three outfield positions. It is good for both of them that they are flexible. Among those two, Orsulak is the one most likely to lose playing time. The O's love Finley, as we keep telling you, and Orsulak was already losing PT in late 1990 (just 156 AB with a .224 average in the second half). During September the team had Orsulak on the bench for some long stretches. If any other team shows interest, he is obvious trade bait.

Mike Devereaux is the closest thing to a "regular" center fielder. He has no big right/left differentials, and should be safe for 367 at bats again, like he had in 1990.

Brady Anderson was the morning-line favorite for left field after the winter meetings. He won't play much against lefties, but will appear in LF against RHP and will back up Devereaux in center, often on the same days that Finley plays LF.

In summary, Dwight Evans will play RF or DH as long as he's healthy. Devereaux and Anderson are assured of significant playing time in CF and LF respectively. Steve Finley will appear all over the outfield. He will get a large number of at bats for a fourth outfielder, and will take over RF if Evans has trouble with his back again. Joe Orsulak has been relegated to fifth outfielder role. If they are still on the roster, Donnell Nixon, Brad Komminsk, and Darrell Miller will gets looks during spring training but will all have trouble making the team unless something changes.

Concerning performance, Evans is obviously on the wane. If he gets a dozen homers in 1991, he will be doing about as well as you can expect. Finley and Anderson are the best bets to improve (age 26 and 27) while Devereaux and Orsulak (28 and 29) have already shown the best they can do.

Lary Bump:

Luis Mercedes is a 22-year-old right-handed batter who has led the Carolina and Eastern leagues in batting the last two seasons. That's the good part. The negatives are his defense and his attitude. He wasn't successful as a second baseman in '89 or as a center fielder in '90. He will have to shake the reputation, deserved or not, of being a bad guy to have on a team. If he keeps hitting .334 and stealing 38 bases, somebody will take a chance on him within a couple of years.

BOSTON

UPDATE — Tom Brunansky re-signed with Boston. Combined with the Jack Clark signing, that really cuts into Mike Marshall's ABs.

Mike Greenwell is on our "great second half" list, and Ellis Burks made the "age 26 with two or more years experience" list for 1991. If Mike Marshall can just hang on, the Red Sox outfield will be much improved this year.

Mike Greenwell started badly in 1990, but came on strong to hit .328-12-47-6 in the second half. He is a fixture in left field, as the ancient rumors of a trade to Atlanta have become dormant. I expect Greenwell to have a big year in 1991.

Kevin Romine was never anything more than a a late inning defensive replacement for Greenwell. Romine will be 30 this spring. Except for a .358 average in just 148 AB at Pawtucket three years ago, he never had a good year even in the minors. He will give you a decent average, but little or nothing in runs, HR, RBI or SB, even if he gets regular PT.

Randy Kutcher hit only .225 and .230 in the last two years, with no production. He is 31 years old, and has been a weak hitter at all levels of play. You don't want him, even if it looks like he has been given a job.

At the end of the winter meetings, Carlos Quintana was expected to join the outfield (from which he came) if he played in Boston at all in 1991. Away from Fenway, expect his batting average to drop. Although he is still improving at age 25, he never produced any truly big minor league numbers, and his offense at Fenway has been a lesson in park effects.

Adam Stein:

Mike Greenwell was the topic of trade talks during the winter after the 1989 season and in the beginning of the 1990 season. It affected his play. After the Red Sox made it apparent that Greenwell was staying, he settled down and had a typical Greenwell performance. Look for 1989 all over again in 1991. If Boggs can get on base, Greenwell will drive him in a lot.

Fred Percival:

Ellis Burks is a terrific ballplayer, but is the one the Red Sox should trade for pitching. Burks' trade value is as high as his great potential, and Lou Gorman should unload him on someone who has not paid much attention to his injury history. Although he played a lot of games in '87 & '88, he was hobbled in many of them. Things got worse in '89, when he missed 65 games. In 1990 he played 152 games with 588 at bats; there is a good chance that both will stand as career highs. Some guys just get hurt a lot, and it looks like Mr. Burks is one of the Blue Cross group.

How would Ellis perform away from Fenway? He gets on base a lot more in Boston, but his extra base hits are divided very evenly between home and road. So look for his BA to plummet, but his HR and slugging to stay about the same, if he gets traded to a city with an "average" stadium. But bear in mind that he is not a player you can expect 160 games from.

Isaac Kaufman:

Burks might have even more potential than Greenwell (they are different types of players, difficult to compare). Look for Burks to take another step up the ladder toward superstardom: a .300 average, more home runs, more stolen bases. Also, remember that the man is a gifted fielder, who plays with inspiration. He will earn more notice for the glove in 1990, as he learns more about the intricacies of the Fenway Triangle.

Lary Bump:

Mickey Pina, a right-handed hitter who can play right field, had a great half-season (14 homers) at Pawtucket in '89 and a miserable full season (.223, 9 HR, 47 RBI, 118 K) with the PawSox last year. He'll need to start this year there, too, but if he turns himself around, he'll be in Boston before it's over.

Phil Plantier, a lefty hitter, was the leader of what must have been the striking-outest team in baseball. The 22-year-old, just a year out of A-ball, fanned 148 times for Pawtucket. He might have challenged the International League record of 199 had he not been called up to Boston. You see, he also led the minor leagues with 33 homers. His winter assignment: Learn the strike zone. Plantier is a LF/DH candidate who probably will be up at least part of the season to give the Bosox some power.

CALIFORNIA

Junior Felix is just 23 years old, and likely to improve dramatically over the next three years. Normally you wouldn't expect a big jump at this young age, but playing for a team that really seems to want him could be a powerful boost. I certainly wouldn't consider any serious risk that Felix would go down from his 1990 numbers. Why shouldn't he be a 20/20 man in 1991?

Dave Winfield frankly surprised me with his 1990 comeback performance. He may be a physical marvel, but you shouldn't pursue older players unless they are big bargains and/or you have to take chances to move up in the standings. For conservative teams building on a strong 1990 roster, I wouldn't value Winfield on the basis of any more than 12 to 14 homers and a .260 BA.

Chili Davis became a second-look free agent in late 1990. If he ends up leaving the Angels, it will improve the chances for Dante Bichette to get playing time. Bichette had become the fifth outfielder for California, behind Davis, Luis Polonia, Dave Winfield, and Devon White; but in 1991 he could emerge again.

Bichette was a bargain in 1990, due to the "burn me twice" mentality. Too many people overpaid him for him in 1989 auctions. If you want to see another bargain in 1991, make sure everybody in your league knows that Bichette got only 109 at bats in the second half of 1990. You can start the process by seeing that he doesn't get retained for 1991 by the lucky person who bought him last year.

Michael J. Fraser:

The Angels outfield will have a new look in 1991. They always wanted to get rid of Devon White. He has really deteriorated as a player in all aspects, and his defense slipped a long way down in 1990. He had become a defensive nonentity. He even lost his uniform number (30) while vacationing in the minors. The most probable outfield is Junior Felix in center (a lock), Dave Winfield in right, and Dante Bichette in left. Luis Polonia played great in 1990, but looked like the fourth outfielder going into spring training 1991. Polonia should still get 400 at bats, playing left field and right field against LHP.

Chili Davis became a free agent, and the Angels had decided that Davis or Brian Downing (or both of them) would be gone in 1991. Downing is more popular with the fans and front office.

Winfield has been especially impressive since coming to California. He played in 132 games after missing all of 1989. In the second half of 1990, Winnie got into a groove. All the old willpower is still there. You can see it. He doesn't move as quick as used to, but he works hard physically and stays in good shape.

Max Venable appeared to be on the verge of re-signing with the Angels when the winter meetings ended. He isn't going to get any better at age 34, but as he proved in 1990, he can be a valuable

Rotisserie fill-in when he is playing for an injured Angel and you have an injured player yourself.

The Angels farm system is very light on talent. Ruben Amaro at AAA Edmonton was the closest thing to a standout last year (.289-3-32-32).

We told you last year that Lee Stevens was the one to watch at Edmonton. Stevens was in the majors at age 23 in 1990, but not in the outfield. He subbed for the injured Wally Joyner at 1B, and did well enough that he can expect to return as a DH/1B/OF in 1991. Before you start looking into the minor leagues for the sixth, seventh or eighth best outfielder in the organization, don't forget to look at Stevens. Wherever he plays, he is due for bigger and better numbers this year.

CHICAGO WHITE SOX

UPDATE — Ivan Calderon and Tim Raines will trade LF jobs. Raines will pile up SB under the aggressive Jeff Torborg. There was more talk of platooning Sosa/Johnson in CF.

After years of confusion and uncertainty, the White Sox outfield finally took a clear shape in 1990, and a nice shape it is. Sammy Sosa established himself in right field at a very young age. His future looks bright indeed. Lance Johnson finally succeeded against major league pitching, and he became a premier base stealer. He might be platooned some in 1991, as he is still having trouble against some righty pitchers. Ivan Calderon lost weight during the 1989-1990 off season. He began stealing bases last year, to the delight of his Rotisserie owners. There has been talk of Calderon playing CF, but you shouldn't take it too seriously. Dan Pasqua is the fourth outfielder for 1991, as Phil Bradley was still floating around as a free agent after the winter meetings. Cory Snyder has no clear place in the outfield, but will get some at bats anyway.

Adam Stein:

Cory Snyder will be a "tenth man" [actually, an "eleventh man" in the nomenclature of the Designated Hitter Era]. He'll play some DH, some RF, possibly some 3B and CF, etc. He will play mainly against lefties and pitchers who don't have good fastballs. This writer thinks the Indians got a steal.

As noted in the Cleveland essay by Bill Gray, Snyder got in trouble with the Indians, because he sought off-season help from White Sox hitting instructor Walter Hriniak. Cory now has the coach he wants, full time. Make a note to review Snyder in October 1991 as a case study in the value of hitting coaches.

Jon Dunkle:

The 1991 White Sox outfield will be comprised of Lance Johnson, Ivan Calderon, and Sammy Sosa. Calderon was the heart of the White Sox run-producing machinery, as he led the team in combined RBI runs scored. He hits for power with a .270 average and quite a few stolen bases. Lance Johnson is the White Sox equivalent of Willie McGee, without the price tag. He could be quite a steal (no pun intended) in 1991 auctions. Sammy Sosa needs to cut down on his strikeouts, hit right-handers, and draw a few more walks. He was the 2 RBI producer in the lineup last year. He led the team in triples, was third in home runs, and stole several bases but to the tune of a .233 batting average. At his young age (22) you can expect rapid improvement. A batting average of .250 to .260 should be no problem in 1991.

Timothy R. McAvoy:

Sammy Sosa is gifted with an Andre Dawson arm. Not many people will forget that Harold Baines preceded Sosa in RF, but Sosa could be there longer than Baines was. With increased patience and confidence in the hitters who follow him in the lineup, Sosa will cut down his strikeouts and hit for higher average. He just needs to make the pitchers throw strikes to him. Sosa is a fine long-term investment for any Rotisserie franchise.

Phil Bradley just didn't work out. He will be much sought-after as a leadoff hitter for some other team, but he failed to impress the White Sox.

Lance Johnson finished strongly (.298 BA, 23 steals in the second half), solidifying his place in CF. He is now too old to be the "center fielder of the future," a tag he wore in the St. Louis organization. In Chicago, finally, he is the "CF today." Johnson's emergence was one factor in the Sox willingness to let go of Daryl Boston and Dave Gallagher.

Ivan Calderon has found a home. Physically imposing, he really punishes the ball, and now he has speed, too. Look for Calderon to stay at the high levels of offense that he showed in 1990.

Dan Pasqua offers left-handed bench strength. The new stadium, with wind and sunlight reversed from the orientation in the Old Comiskey, may turn out to be kind to left-handed hitters. Pasqua could be overlooked in many auctions this year, because he doesn't have a clear starting role but will get plenty of AB with plenty of homers.

Lary Bump:

Rodney McCray is a scooter, the '90s version of Herb Washington or Allan Lewis. He has played center field in the minors, but his real position is pinch runner, as evidenced by his White Sox line from last season; six steals in six at bats with no hits, and he appeared in 32 games! In seven minor league seasons, he never batted higher than .257, but he has stolen 344 bases. At 27, he may be slowing down; his stolen base percentage has dropped from the 80's into the high 60's. Not worth an investment.

CLEVELAND

It's all very clear. Three outfielders will emerge from a list including Joey Belle, Beau Allred, Chris James, Candy Maldonado, Alex Cole, Mitch Webster, Turner Ward, Alan Cockrell, Luis Medina, and Stanley Jefferson. Last year, we thought it was bad with six "probable" outfielders. The Indians had a genuine glut in December 1990.

The USA Today on December 11 predicted Belle in left and Ward in right. Belle is so tightly wound that I don't think HE knows where he will be in July 1991, but the skill is all there. Turner Ward hit .299-6-65-22 for Colorado Springs, nice enough stats, but the Indians have produced a horde of nice-enough-stats outfielders at Colorado over the past few years, and the vast majority have gone absolutely nowhere. The Tribe's best rookie (Alex Cole) came up through the Cardinals and Padres organizations. Finally, don't be seduced by Ward's .348 BA with Cleveland in September. Forty-six at bats prove absolutely nothing, and Ward never hit above .301 in any league before. He will be 26 in April 1991, not exactly wunderkind material.

Bill Gray:

While there were several standout performances in the Cleveland outfield in 1990, one must still consider all positions up for grabs. At first glance you would have to say that Alex Cole will start in center field, Candy Maldonado and Mitch Webster in left and right, respectively. But all have competition, and Maldonado talked like he wouldn't be back.

The Indians late season surge generated a new closeness and high team spirit with which to carry over into 1991. After the last game, all the players, coaches and John MacNamara ran onto the field and shook hands and had a "wait-till-next-year" celebration. One player; Cory Snyder, skipped the celebration because he knew he would be finding a new team for 1991. Keep your eye on Snyder. His last two seasons were disasters, but the talent is still there. A fresh start on a new team could lead to a repeat of 1988. Snyder got off on the wrong foot with the team in the off-season last year, when he sought hitting instruction from the Chicago White Sox hitting instructor, Walt Hriniak. Do you think Cory might want to play in Chicago? Nah.

Maldonado, after a career year, went the free agent route and asked for big bucks on a long term contract. His agent used the media to negotiate, dropping lines like the Indians aren't going to offer the kind of package it will take, and Candy will go elsewhere. At the same time, Mr. and Mrs. Maldonado were househunting in the Cleveland suburbs. So, Candy will be in Cleveland for a while. Don't expect him to produce similar numbers, however. As I said, he had a career year in 1990 (even better than his '87 rabbit-ball year).

He obviously likes AL pitching and the smaller parks. If he stays close to his 1990 output, he'll remain with the tribe. If he really takes a hard line with his new contract, he'll be let go; and if he falters during the season, he'll be traded or even benched. There are many talented and inexpensive youngsters ready to play.

Alex Cole is already established as a starter after his tremendous success in just 67 games. Cole made headlines almost immediately when he stole FIVE bases in one game shortly after being called up from the minors. If he continues to produce an on base percentage of .379 over an entire season, you're looking at a legitimate 80-100 SB potential. Even if his BA falls way off, he'll play a lot because of his speed.

Beau Allred was one of the few kids who was not shuttled up and down by the Indians. He played in only four games as an expanded roster "lock out" player, then was sent down. When rosters expanded again in September, he was not recalled. People wondered what was going on. Doghouse, injury illness? Nothing of the sort. The team is very high on this kid and so confident that he will be on the team in 1991, they just wanted to look at other kids. At Colorado Springs, Allred, a left handed batter, hit .278 with 13 homers, 74 RBI and 6 SB in 378 AB. If he shows anything in the spring, Webster will become a backup.

Albert (Joey) Belle seems to be winning his battle with alcoholism. If his personal problems are behind him, Belle has the talent to be a superstar. Last year, Belle slowly fell apart in Cleveland and continued his slide at Colorado. Despite his troubles he still managed to get 96 AB in Colorado and batted .344 with 5 HR, 16 RBI and 4 SB. When he hits one out of the park, it is a mammoth shot, similar to Bo Jackson. Until he can prove to the Indians and the world that he is ready to play, he is a risk. However if he pans out, and I believe he will, he can be one of the best baseball (and Rotisserie) players of the nineties.

Mitch Webster has to hope the kids aren't ready yet. Those of you who owned Webster last year had to enjoy his 12 homers and 22 SB and even the 55 RBI. Too bad the Indians looked at his on base percentage of .285 and decided to give Cole a shot. Still, Snyder's exit will give Mitch a chance to play every day. He won't bat leadoff so the OBP won't be that much of an issue. How long can he hold on to a starting job? At the All Star break, Webster had played in 78 games and batted 291 times with 15 SB. After the break he played in just 50 games, batting only 146 times. His greatest asset to a Rotisserie owner is his stolen base potential. The second half saw him swipe only 7 bases. So, why do I think Webster will start? First, MacNamara is the George Allen of baseball, tending to stick with the veterans. Second, Cleveland has improved enough to be a legitimate contender in the weak AL East. Contenders usually don't play too many youngsters. Third, while conceding that Cole is a lock to stay in center, Belle and Allred, while superb prospects, are still unproven.

One other variable that could kill Webster as a starter is Chris James. James was mainly a DH last year but he has played the outfield before. James fell just one hit short of batting .300 for the year despite an abysmal beginning to his season. In mid may, James was hitting only about .100, then he caught fire batting well over .300 the rest of the way. His 12 homers and 70 (career high) RBI were perfect for the DH role to which James finally adjusted. MacNamara also loves the intensity with which James plays. Many knowledgeable folks have said that James' fiery play and attitude really pulled the team up a notch and contributed to their late season success. James has been a potential star for the last several years. He seems to have finally found a good fit with Cleveland and should continue to rack up a lot of AB as a DH and possible platoon with Maldonado in the outfield, and at DH.

As if the Indians didn't have enough OF/DH prospects with Cole, Belle, and Allred, add to your list the names of Alan Cockrell, Turner Ward and Luis Medina. All three spent most of the year in Colorado where the balls tend to carry, however, Cockrell has been added to the 1991 40 man roster going into spring training because he hit .323 with 17 HR, 71 RBI and 6 SB in 378 plate appearances.

Turner Ward, unlike Allred, was called up in September. He batted 46 times with a .348 average, 1 HR and 3 SB. At Colorado, Ward hit .299 with 6 HR and 22 SB. Luis Medina was supposed to have made the club in 1989 after he hit six homers as a September '88 call up. He faltered at the plate in 1989 and was sent down. His season ended with an injury. Medina came back last year to bat .272 with 18 homers. (he hit .310 with 28 homers at Colorado in 1988). Not an adept fielder, Medina was Colorado's DH. With increasing competition, Medina, at 28, must produce now.

Summary: Maldonado may take his big free agent contract elsewhere. Webster will start but will be a platoon player by year end, again. Cole emerges as the surest bet among the OF starters. James is a lock for DH. If you can find equal value in another team's outfield (Milwaukee? Oakland?) take it. Too many unanswered questions in Cleveland.

Fred Matos:

The Orioles defensed Alex Cole with an unusual alignment late last year. The three outfielders all shifted toward left and moved in. The third baseman played on the grass. The pitches were all outside fastballs (Cole bats left). Alex was 0 for 4 that day and looked terrible. He didn't hit a single ball to the right side, not even a foul ball.

DETROIT

Rich Burkhardt ("speaking only as a fan"):

The biggest question the Tigers need answered right now is: can Milt Cuyler hit major league pitching well enough to win the center field job and move Moseby to left? If Cuyler can cut it at the major league level, he'll be a good defensive outfielder with potential to steal 40.

Lary Bump:

It's a testimony to the weakness of the AL East that the Tigers could finish third with Lloyd Moseby trying to cover CF at Tiger Stadium. Another cause for optimism in Detroit is that a real center fielder will be showing up in '91. The big center field in Detroit needs one of the best CF's, and it will get one in Milt Cuyler. Don't expect the 22-year-old switch hitter to hit, especially against right-handers. He was a .258 with Toledo, and .255 in 19 games as a Tiger. But expect him to run (52 SB at Toledo) and run and run. He's a younger Gary Pettis, with only about two-thirds as many strikeouts. Sparky already has Cuyler penciled in to bat ninth. I think he's one of the best players, for baseball if not for Rotisserie, coming up this year.

KANSAS CITY

The Royals outfield was unsettled after the winter meetings. Kirk Gibson was implanted at DH if not in the outfield, and past regulars Bo Jackson and Danny Tartabull were still on the trading block. There was consensus on some items, however. Jim Eisenreich will get playing time but not exceed what he has done in previous seasons, and Brian McRae has the center field job. One local scrutinizer believes that McRae will be overlooked and undervalued; a more distant observer believes that McRae is OK but apparently confirms the belief that he is under-appreciated outside of the KC area. I think the most likely future is somewhere in between. McRae is young, healthy, fast, and has a job, but he is not going to be a great star, not in 1991 anyway.

Marc Bowman:

Much as the Royals would love to trade him, Bo Jackson looked like he would return to LF in 1991. His center field experiment ended when Brian McRae showed that he was already ahead of Jackson in the field. Bo knows how to hit a ball to "East Hell," but he doesn't know how to stay healthy for a full season. Expect more of the same in 1991, wherever Bo plays. If he could stay healthy, he would hit 40 homers with over 100 RBI and 30 stolen bases. He would also strike out 200 times. But don't gamble on Bo's health. If you have him in mid-season and he's doing well, TRADE HIM! So what if he stays healthy and hits 20 homers in the second half? You will get full value in trade, and you won't be pressing your luck. The safest course is not to acquire him at all. Let somebody else drool, get all glassy-eyed, and overbid when his name comes up.

Switch-hitting rookie Brian McRae will win the center field job, if he doesn't have it locked already. If he shows that he can get on base well, he might also be awarded the leadoff slot, in which case he would get many more SB, maybe 30 to 40. McRae stole at least 21 bases in every year in the minors. The other option is that he might bat ninth, ala Roberto Kelly in NY. The ninth spot would help his batting average a little, but he would have fewer chances to steal over the course of a season. No matter what happens, McRae will be offered plenty of playing time, and he should be on your sleeper list for 1991. If your league has other people who see his full value, you have some respectable competition. Most people outside of KC were still unsure of McRae's value in December 1990. Willie Wilson's departure may help focus attention on McRae; hope it doesn't in your league.

Danny Tartabull is displayed on the trading block alongside Jackson, but he will get the nod in right field if he's still with the Royals. Tartabull has had two consecutive bad seasons, both caused by injuries in one way or another. He has changed his hitting style from line-drive to pure power, with a definite uppercut. In a full, healthy season, the new Tartabull should hit 30 homers with 100 RBI, but a lower BA than the old Tartabull. In the KC lineup, Danny would bat fifth, behind Brett and Jackson. He has no speed. After two bad years, Tartabull could be comeback sleeper. You just want to make sure he is going to stay in the AL.

Jim Eisenreich is an extra outfielder and backup DH. He will play whenever Kirk Gibson or one of the three above-named outfielders takes a day off. If Tartabull and/or Jackson is traded, Eisenreich would be the clear candidate for increased outfield PT. The Royals have used him "full time" in the past and still have confidence in him. With the long history of injuries in the KC outfield, Eisenreich has gotten more playing time than many "regular" outfielders in the AL. He will get plenty of AB's in 1991 regardless what other personnel moves may be made. Upward potential for Eisenreich is very little. He's now 32, and he's gotten all the possible breaks to increase his playing time in recent years.

Kirk Gibson has alleviated the Royals shortage of left-handed hitting. He is eager to play in the field (like most DH's) but isn't likely to push anyone aside on account of defense. Gibson is probably better off resting his many damaged parts, and sitting in the dugout when his team is in the field.

Gary Thurman may be the person most helped by Willie Wilson's departure. Thurman really has trouble with right-handed pitching in the majors; that's been the main obstacle to promotion. He is still only 26, however, and will get plenty of SB's even if he plays only against lefties. Speed is his only value, however.

The best minor leaguers are Chito Martinez, Harvey Pulliam, and Bobby Moore. Martinez got 17 HR in just 275 at bats at Omaha, preceded by two good years at Memphis. He is still only 25. Pulliam has strong numbers across the board, and Moore was rated the next in line behind Brian McRae in last year's pecking order. He has 55 stolen bases over the past two years.

Lary Bump:

The Royals have five young outfielders worth watchng: Jacob Brumfield, Brian McRae, Harvey Pulliam, and Gary Thurman.

Until last season, we thought McRae was around only for name-recognition value. But the 23-year-old switch-hitting son of Hal showed a pretty good bat (.286-2-23) in 46 games as KC's CF. He will be part of an overhaul of the Royals' OF, with both Danny Tartabull and Bo Jackson on the trading block. Don't go overboard on McRae; he never has played minor league ball above the Double-A level, he never hit better than .268 for a full season in the minors, and he hits lefties better than righties. He has some speed (21-33 SB each season) and developed some power (10 HR at Memphis) last season, and his age is in his favor.

Part of the Royals' problem, and all of Thurman's, is vulnerability to right-handed pitching. They need another big year out of George Brett and Jim Eisenreich and probably a new LH hitter they acquire [Kirk Gibson, obviously] to get Thurman some platoon playing time in RF or LF. He had an excellent year (.331, 39 SB) at Omaha. At age 26, it is now or never for him.

One of the most solid players on an Omaha club well balanced with veterans and youngsters was the 23-year-old Pulliam. He batted .268 and provided 16 HR, 72 RBI and better defense and throwing ability than most left fielders. One drawback in trying to crack this lineup: He bats right-handed. He may start the season in Omaha, but I expect him to be playing a significant role in KC before September.

On the horizon after starting 1990 'way off in the distance is Brumfield. He led the Florida State League with a .336 average, stole 47 bases and walked more than he struck out. When promoted to Omaha, only his W/K ratio suffered. In 77 AB, he batted .325, stole two bases and even hit two homers. He also has an excellent RF arm. He is — you guessed it — a right-handed batter. Perhaps the Royals need Whitey Herzog back, to turn all these speedy OF's into slaphitting switch hitters. Regardless, put Brumfield on your futures list for 1992.

MILWAUKEE

The Brewers have three regular outfielders, Robin Yount, Greg Vaughn, and Franklin Stubbs. If there is any platooning to be done, lefty-hitting Darryl Hamilton could alternate with RHH Vaughn, and switch-hitter Mike Felder could sub for either Vaughn or LHH Stubbs.

Alan Boodman:

What with sluggers like Spiers and Gantner in the infield, the Milwaukee outfield is counted on to supply a good deal of the offense for the Brew Crew. The cast of players will be the same as in 1990, with the exception that Rob Deer has been exiled to Detroit. You wouldn't think that losing a .200 hitter should adversely affect anything, but Deer has an average OBP (no mean feat for a .205 hitter) and has tremendous power.

There's always been a discrimination in baseball against power hitters who draw walks, but have a low (or very low) batting average, a prejudice emphasized in standard Rotisserie scorekeeping. Deer, a career .225 hitter, is actually a WELL above average offensive player. His career offensive winning percentage is almost exactly the same as Robin Yount's, which is to say it's a heck of a lot better than Vaughn's, Felder's, or Hamilton's. Think about that.

Robin Yount, probably grossly overvalued at most auctions last year, should be thrown back into almost every auction, and should be undervalued going into 1991. Just as there were good reasons for letting someone else take Mr. Yount in 1990, there are several good reasons why YOU should consider adding him to your outfield this year:

1. His previous track record is excellent, as everybody knows.

2. He's got a guaranteed job, and will play literally every day.

3. I can't believe that Yount's sub-par 1990 season means his career is over. Not even an Edsel without brakes goes downhill as fast as Robin did last year.

4. He improved in the second half of 1990.

5. His 1990 season wasn't all that bad anyway.

6. Yes it was.

7. No, it wasn't.

I know that the .247 batting average was the lowest

of his career, but how many negative things can you say about 17 homers, 77 RBI, 98 runs scored, 78 walks, and 15 steals? You can say that those aren't exactly MVP numbers, or that it wasn't a typical Robin Yount season, but so what? There are 25 to 30 starting AL outfielders who won't do as much. In 1991, Robin will bat within 10 points of .285, hit near 15 homers, drive in 85-90 runs, and steal over 10 bases. He'll also score 80 runs and draw 70 walks, if not more.

There's no reason to refer to Greg Vaughn's 1990 season as a disappointment. His numbers are almost all within the ranges expected of him based on the major league equivalencies of his stats at Denver. People who hit .276 at Denver do not hit .276 in Milwaukee. They hit closer to .235.

This season should be one where Greg takes some steps forward. At age 25, Vaughn is entering his prime years, and his minor league record indicates a player capable of dynamite offensive numbers, although he won't be hitting .300 (or close to it) anytime soon. Greg will open the season as the starting right fielder, and the Brewers ought to give him every chance to develop. Playing 140 games, look for a batting average around .250, 20 to 25 homers, 75 RBI, and up to 15 steals. Vaughn should also draw more walks this year, as he was a fairly patient hitter in the minors.

Franklin Stubbs has recently been signed away from the Astros, and, having been liberated from the Astrodome, may be ready to post some power numbers in the high-rent district. In 1990, Stubbs hit the admirable total of 23 home runs (including 9 in the Dome). In addition, Stubbs' other offensive numbers are impressive when you take into account the poor hitting ballpark and the poor hitting ballclub around him. You couldn't really expect Frankie's runs and RBI counts to be much higher than they were, considering the Astros' lineup. In 1990, Stubbs will turn 30, so his developing years are over, yet Franklin's numbers should improve quite a bit. He'll be a fixture in left field unless his problems with left-handed pitching return, so look for as many as 140 games, hitting around .265 with 25 homers, 75 to 90 RBI, and perhaps even 20 steals.

Backups: Mike Felder and Darryl Hamilton. Felder has been loitering at the major-league level for the past several seasons based on the fact that he has outstanding speed. In a full season, he would easily swipe 50 bases at a minimum. That's about all that Felder would add to a team. If you hit him high enough in the order, he'd score some runs. I'd look for Mike to get no more than 200 plate appearances, bat .250 to .265 with fewer than 3 homers, 20 to 30 RBI, and 15 to 25 steals.

Darryl Hamilton is a similar player to Felder: a couple of years younger, but with approximately the same skills. Darryl has less speed than Mike, but would steal 30 bases in a full season, and has absolutely no power with correspondingly limited run-production potential. His career minor-league batting average is well over .300, so Darryl might hit near .300 in the majors within the next couple of years. For 1991, Hamilton should get around 150 PA, hit around .270 with no homers, less than 25 RBI, and 10 to 20 steals.

George Hall:

There is little coming out of the Brewers farm system for the outfield. One creative solution could involve Tim McIntosh, a very good hitter whose progress has been somewhat impaired by lack of defensive excellence. Elsewhere, Matias Carrillo, 27, is unspectacular but reliable if a seasoned sub is needed. Ruben Escalera and Shon Ashley are coming off good seasons at El Paso but are both scheduled for Denver in 1991. Dee Dixon came out of nowhere to hit .286 with 19 homers at El Paso, and he stole 53 bases. Dixon could zoom right past Carillo, Escalera, and Ashley. Still bouncing around is the former "next Willie Mays," the Seattle emigre Mickey Brantley.

[It's interesting how little has changed at the lower levels. The following is from the 1990 book: "Other candidates include Matias Carillo (10 HR and 22 SB at Denver), Mike Felder (26 SB with the Brewers), Daryl Hamilton (.286, 20 SB for Denver), and Shon Ashley (.315, 14 HR, 65 RBI for El Paso). Felder seems likely to get his usual part time role, and ring up some SB while doing little else. Carillo is no kid; he's 26, and if he can only hit .260 at Denver, what does he hope to do in the majors? Hit .209? Ashley is a legitimate prospect, probably still a year too early. Hamilton offers about the same things as Felder. Why would the Brewers want two such people making major league wages, when they only need one?" If only the regular lineup could be so stable.]

MINNESOTA

The Twins are delighted with 27 year-old Shane Mack, picked up from San Diego in the December 1989 draft. Mack missed almost all of the 1989 season with an injury, after two unsuccessful attempts to stick in the major leagues in 1987 and '88. He put up some huge numbers at Las Vegas (.336, .347) these two years, but couldn't come close when he played for San Diego. In Minnesota he rose to the top immediately.

Mack has the CF job, with Kirby Puckett in right. Puckett hit only .270 after the All Star break. He is a better player than that. The whole Twins lineup was flat in 1990. But Puckett is definitely aging. Pedro Munoz could emerge as the regular left fielder, even if Dan Gladden doesn't get traded.

Randy Bush re-signed on December 18. He will complicate the RF picture, competing for time with Munoz and Mack, with Puckett shifting from RF to CF to accommodate him.

Paul Clements:

The Twins are very dissatisfied with Gladden as a leadoff hitter. He simply refuses to take a walk, so the .270 BA really isn't good enough. Who might lead off? Munoz looked very impressive when he first came up; then the pitchers seemed to get a book on him, throwing high, higher and highest, and watching Pedro swing at all of them. The season wasn't long enough to make it clear if Munoz was beating the pitchers, or vice versa. He hit three rockets in the final game of the season, so it looks like a coin-flip. I would want to see a good spring from Munoz, before spending much.

As long as Mack does well in CF, the Twins will keep him there; Puckett's legs will last longer if he can play in RF instead of CF.

Lary Bump:

Get started on a subject, and for some reason you can't get off it. Pedro Munoz is a right-handed batter who absolutely destroys left-handed pitching. He's probably best suited to LF, but can play RF. Apparently it doesn't matter to the Twins that they already have Shane Mack to play LF or RF and absolutely destroy left-handed pitching. Here's an opportunity for Tom Kelly to show some creative managing, perhaps in a DH platoon with Gene Larkin or Kent Hrbek or Paul Sorrento going against right-handed pitching. Or playing Dan Gladden in LF against right-handers, even though he's a right-handed batter. Munoz would have won the International League batting title (.319), but he didn't have enough AB's before being traded by the Blue Jays for John Candelaria. He then batted .318 at Portland and .271 in September with the Twins. He showed fair power (12 HR, 82 RBI total), and Syracuse is a tough home run park. Munoz had 19 HR at Knoxville in '89 and he is only 22. Munoz has tremendous potential. How much playing time he'll get this season is the only question.

NEW YORK YANKEES

The Yankees 1991 outfield will feature Hensley Meulens in left, Roberto Kelly in center, and Jesse Barfield in right. Jim Leyritz can play left field, and he will on occasion during 1991. Mel Hall is fading rapidly, but will hang on as a reserve OF and occasional DH against righties; he's worthless against lefties. Kevin Maas and/or Don Mattingly could appear in the outfield, the former to alleviate a crowded DH/1B situation, and the latter if he thinks his back would be less strained in the outfield. Bernie Williams waits in the wings.

Jesse Barfield is now fully recovered from a 1988 wrist injury. He points to the fact that 16 of his 18 HR in 1988 were hit after he had surgery on the wrist. Barfield's recovery has been traced not only in his revitalized HR output (23 and 25 in the last two years) but also in his walk/strikeout ratio, which has been better in 1989 and 1990 than in any previous year. His BB/K ratio had been slipping from 1984 to 1988 (.43, .46, .40, .41 and .38 respectively). Then in 1989, the number shot up to a career high of .58, and stayed up at .55 in 1990. I discussed the significance of this development with Jesse, and also with Rob Wood, the world's foremost BB/K researcher. There is good evidence that a sudden drop in the ratio is a sign of impending doom in a player's career [see Rob's essay in this edition], but there is no compiled evidence (yet) that a sudden upward movement is a leading indicator of good things to come. Personally, I expected Barfield to recover further in 1990, and he did.

Lary Bump:

You're probably heard so much about Meulens — that he seems old to you. He's 23 and blossomed (.285-26-96 at Columbus) last year. He can hit, especially against lefties, so he can DH if LF doesn't work out. He should be one of the more productive rookies this year.

OAKLAND

Rickey Henderson plays left field for the Oakland A's. If you need an essay on Henderson's value, you should put this book back where you got it. He showed no signs of slowing down during 1990, unless you want to call his second half stats weak; Rickey was .313-11-26-16 after the All Star break.

Way back in the spring of 1987, I thought Dave Henderson was one of the great sleepers in the game of rotisserie, and about to emerge as a star performer. He had hit .290 in the second half of 1986 despite missing some time; he was a ripe age (28) to produce a big season; he played in a great hitter's park; and he was generally overlooked and undervalued by everyone I knew. For 1987, I was obviously wrong. I admitted my mistake; Dave Henderson was worthless, washed up . . . my reading of the numbers had been way off the mark.

1988, not 1987, was Dave Henderson's year to emerge. Not everybody blossoms at exactly age 26. Over the past three years, Henderson has been one of the most consistently valuable outfielders for Rotisserie. Injuries and the sudden arrival of Willie McGee were negative factors for Dave in 1990, but McGee is gone now, and rookie challenger Darren Lewis is also out of the picture (a local boy, playing across the bay in San Francisco now). The competition (translate: backup) in center field in 1991 will be Willie Wilson, no spring chick himself. Henderson is 32 this year, and Wilson is 35.

You can pencil in J. Canseco in RF. He's good, too. For a stat forecast and $ value, see the tables. If you want to read several pages about how and why and in what ways he's good, and who he's as good as or better than, pick up a fan magazine. The only Rotisserie issues for Canseco are health and price. He has had back trouble and missed playing time, and is obviously carrying a great deal of bulked-up muscle, the kind that often leads to a strained rib, a separated rib muscle, a pulled hamstring, etc., etc. Price is the bigger problem. Somebody in your league (a new owner or someone who finished low in the standings last year) will play for a 40/40 year out of Canseco, or even a 50/50 year. Let them have him. Canseco hasn't been on too many first place rosters during the last couple of years, for the reasons noted.

Doug Jennings is a lefty-hitting 26 year-old. He had numbers similar to Felix Jose at Tacoma in 1989, then hit .346 while in AAA in 1990. The departure of Mr. Jose gives a boost to Jennings' career. His nice low batting average (.192) with Oakland in 1990 will keep most bidders away this spring. Playing with an outfield that has an injury history like Oakland's, he could be a valuable mid-season pickup if he doesn't go on draft day.

Susan Nelson:

Dann Howitt attracted attention in 1989 with 26 homers at Huntsville. He spent 1990 at Tacoma without distinguishing himself (.265 BA, 11 HR). At age 27 he is probably not a factor for 1991.

Doug Jennings has an admirable, aggressive attitude. He made a move toward the mound when Nolan Ryan pitched him up and in, one time too many. Not many players would have reacted that way in that situation.

Tony LaRussa likes to use infielders as outfielders and really move people around. You can expect to see the likes of Blankenship, Ernest Riles, and even Terry Steinbach roaming the outfield at times during 1991. There is no outstanding rookie prospect coming along this year.

Lary Bump:

Ozzie Canseco was in the major leagues in '90 for one reason, and he wears No. 33. Unless Jose has a clause in his contract, don't expect to see this guy who batted .225 with 103 Ks in 325 ABs at Huntsville back in the bigs. Ever.

If Ozzie was in the show out of filial loyalty, then Howard was there because of his loyalty to the organization. The 27-year-old right-handed batter has spent seven years in the A's farm system. If you put all of his best years together into one, you'd come up with a .270 average (last year), 17 HR, 78 RBI and 29 SB. His greatest offensive skill is drawing walks, so he has had good to excellent OBPs. Howard probably won't be back in the majors, unless there are injuries in the A's OF. But in this pencil-thin organization, he may have a chance to see some time.

Howitt, a 27-year-old left-handed hitter, had a big year (.281-26-111) at Huntsville in '89 and a medium-sized year (.265-11-69) at Tacoma last season. In case you happened to watch the World Series, you may know the A's need lefty hitters. So Howitt may have a job coming off the bench if he can beat out Doug Jennings.

The A's only real OF prospect was 23-year-old CF Darren Lewis, gone to San Francisco. His '90 half-seasons at Huntsville (.296-3-23-21) and Tacoma (.291-2-26-16) were remarkably similar, and consistent with his record in the lower minors. Lewis has earned mid-season promotions each of the last two years. Look for a third, to the majors, sometime in '91.

SEATTLE

After the winter meetings, the outfield looked like Ken Griffey Junior in center and Jay Buhner in right. The M's were unhappy with Jeffrey Leonard, and trying like heck to trade him, but he could be the left fielder in 1991. Greg Briley will compete, or platoon, with Leonard in left, while Tracy Jones and Ken Griffey Senior provide righty and lefty bats (respectively) and serve as backups in the outfield.

A team with a long losing record should have a strong farm system from all their early draft picks, but the M's don't when it comes to outfielders. The best at Calgary in 1990 were LHH Dave Brundage (.304-3-48-8), Casey Close (.270-12-69-15), LHH Jim Weaver (.257-7-42-20), and switch hitter Ted Williams (.266-6-20-9). In a league with a dozen regulars hitting over .320, Calgary;s outfield didn't stack up against the competition. AA Williamsport farmhands Tom Alfredson, Isaiah Clark, Jeff Hooper, Dru Kosco, Pat Lennon, Mike McDonald, and Mark Merchant were all even less impressive. Lennon was the only one whose year could be remotely linked to the word "progress," and former #1 pick Merchant was going absolutely nowhere.

Tony Formo's 1991 Left Field Extravaganza:

Pee Wee Briley (.319 OBA, .356 SA) was nothing special offensively in 1990, with 16 SB, 5 HR, and 29 RBI in 337 AB. Briley hustles and can play infield, so he's likely to be around as a role player, but not a star.

Jay Buhner (.357 OBA, .479 SA) showed flashes of offensive potential when he was healthy and made contact with the ball, but tied a ML record for consecutive strikeouts. He also hit 7 HR in 163 AB and has the potential to be a star slugger if healthy.

Henry Cotto (.307 OBA, .349 SA) had an unspectacular season at the plate, but played well defensively. Cotto is the sort of player who is valuable coming off the bench when there are injuries, but not a starter for a contending team.

Ken Griffey Junior (.366 OBA, .481 SA) is one of the most exciting young ballplayers ever. He makes miraculous catches and throws, hits clutch home runs, and was among AL leaders in BA (hitting an even .300). He's only 21 years old, and going to get even better, already having had a candy bar named after him, been selected for the All Star team, and been on the covers of Sports Illustrated and Baseball America. The hype is justified.

Junior was scheduled to start the 1989 season in the minors, but played so well (setting a franchise record for total bases) in spring training, that they kept him. The then 19-year-old phenom pointed out that he wasn't nervous, because it was his 12th Major League Spring camp, ten with his father and two with the M's. Although he had only 17 games of Double-A and no Triple-A experience, he had been hitting major league pitches in batting practice since he was a kid in Cincinnati.

The Kid is a delight to watch. He moves like a ballplayer, and is a wonderful product of heredity and environment that caused this gifted athlete to grow up getting a lot of role modeling from the Big Red Machine. After a shaky first week, Junior became an instant superstar, winning AL Player of the Week honors before his first month in the majors was over, having tied the franchise record for consecutive base hits (8) along the way. Not only did Griffey run up good stats, he developed a flair for making big plays in crucial situations. Eight of Griffey's first 10 HR either gave the M's a lead or tied a game, and 5 of them were game winners.

Ken Griffey Senior is an excellent ballplayer who is probably more highly motivated than at any time in his distinguished career. Although he had been selected as an All Star 5 times in his 18-year career, he had never been selected Player of the Week until he was picked up by the M's to play with his magical offspring. With Senior staying on for another season with Seattle, expect him to play better D (as a role player) than did Penitentiary Face. Senior will also DH effectively, and act as a role model, keeping his head in the game and showing Junior the way that major leaguers run out pop flies and routine ground balls.

Tracy Jones (.307 OBA, .397 SA) hit .302 with 15 RBI in 25 games before having surgery for the cartilage in his right knee, which locked up on him while driving home from the Kingdome after a game. Jones is a good hitter, and could surprise with a comeback if healthy.

TEXAS

At the end of 1990, the Rangers outfield for 1991 was penciled as Incaviglia in left, rookie Juan Gonzalez in center, and still-young Ruben Sierra in right. Jack Daugherty was someone that management liked well enough to want in the lineup, especially against righties, but there was no place to play him regularly. Kevin Belcher is emerging rapidly and could become a full time Texas outfielder any time during 1991, and Gary Pettis is likely to become one of the most expensive defensive replacements in baseball. Kevin Reimer is another minor leaguer topping a farm system loaded with good outfielders.

Ruben Sierra had an off year in 1990, creating the possibility of a good buy. Most people don't realize that Sierra is still only 25, and still improving. When you have an MVP type of season at age 23, people credit you with being fully developed, but we have not yet seen the best of Ruben Sierra.

On Ruben Sierra: In the 1987 Baseball Abstract, Bill James picked Sierra as THE great player in the 1986 rookie crop:

"If I could choose any of the fine rookies from the 1986 season to start a ballclub with, I would not hesitate for a second. I would choose Ruben Sierra. I would not trade him for Jose Canseco, although I think Canseco is going to be a tremendous power hitter. I would not trade him for Cory Snyder. I am not sure if I would trade him for both of them.

"The basis of my overwhelming attachment is simply this: that there are very, very few players who can hit major league pitching with authority at the age of 20 — and those few who can, have a tremendously disproportionate history of developing into superstars. When you compound that with his obvious defensive skills (he can run like the wind and throw with the best of them), well, you've got a package there.

"The only comparable rookie, in history, that Sierra isn't far ahead of in some respect is Henry Aaron.

"So I say this is THE man from the 1986 rookie crop. There were probably seven rookies in 1986 who have a CHANCE to develop into Hall of Famers, but Sierra has the best chance."

I repeat this insightful outlook every year, because it is a lesson in the rarity of young players who reach the majors, and performing well, at an age when when most of the top professionals are no higher than Double-A.

Many people ask about Juan Gonzalez, and the answers are yes, he really is that good, and no, he isn't going to ride the bench in Arlington. Unfortunately, like all rookies, he is likely to get over-hyped during spring training and over-priced during your auction. Rookies don't ALWAYS have great years just because they are great talents. Take another look at Ken Griffey Junior's 1989 season (compared to 1990) to see the possible gap between obvious talent and actual performance. Someone in your league is going to pay for a big season out of Gonzalez in 1991. If they are lucky, they will get exactly what they pay for, but no, more. Expect 20 homers and a BA around .250.

The Rangers spent the last few months of 1990 trying their darnedest to trade left fielder Pete Incaviglia. These efforts are likely to continue in 1991 until they are consummated. "What's the big hurry?" you may ask. There isn't so much an urgency to get rid of Incaviglia, as there is to make room for emerging young talent, and soon. Indeed, Inky is appreciated in Texas.

Bob Hazlewood:

One quality that Inky brings to the ball park every day, that doesn't show up in the box scores every day, is that he plays every game at 100%. No one will ever accuse Inky of dogging it. He played in more games last year than everyone except Sierra, Franco, and Palmeiro. He needs a little work on social graces, but so did Babe Ruth.

The five outfielders, Incaviglia, Gonzalez, Sierra, Daugherty, and Pettis (with Belcher possibly replacing Inky later), will get a big share of the DH duty. Most likely that will be Inky or Daugherty. Pettis will provide depth off the bench, and ranks fourth among the outfielders although he may not finish fourth in at bats.

Lary Bump:

It finally may be time to stop the assault on our sensibilities and get Pete Incaviglia out of the Rangers' OF. Gary Pettis, we've been told, was merely holding a place in CF for Gonzalez, but it's conceivable Texas may keep Pettis' glove and legs in center and put Gonzalez in LF. The Rangers are laden with talent that is ready for major league play earlier than the normal age for graduation from the minors. The 21-year-old RHH Gonzalez is a year behind Ruben Sierra's timetable for reaching the majors, but way ahead of all other 21-year-olds. Gonzalez followed up a .258-29-101 season at Oklahoma City with a .289-4-12 month with the Rangers. He looked much more comfortable in the majors than he had in his '89 trial.

Belcher, though two years older than Gonzalez, is in a similar position to where Juan was a year ago. In '89, Gonzalez batted .293 at Tulsa; in '90, Belcher batted .293 at Tulsa, but with less power. Both struggled in their first September call-ups. Belcher, also a right-handed batter, has better strike-zone judgment, so he gets on base more often. He also is faster and can steal bases (29 at Tulsa), though he needs to improve his SB percentage, which hasn't been higher than 67% in his four minor league seasons. Look for Belcher in Oklahoma City this year, unless something changes. In '92, look for a Texas OF of Gonzalez, Belcher and Sierra.

At 27, Reimer isn't a hot prospect, but he and Jack Daugherty provide something that has been in short supply in Texas — bench strength.

TORONTO

J.L. Feinstein:

Christmas came about three weeks early for the Blue Jay pitching staff. In the course of a week, Pat Gillick rebuilt the Blue Jay outfield from a defensive liability to one that figures to lower the team ERA substantially.

Gone is George Bell, who played [badly] the deepest left field in the majors. Gone is Junior Felix, who could often be seen waving off the defensive adjustments from the dugout. Gone from CF is Mookie Wilson . . . a lovely fellow who plays hard, but with the kind of arm that would whip in a two-hopper throwing out the first pitch.

In his place, you now have Devon White in center. Say what you will about White's lack of offensive production, there's no question about his defense. He can run and throw with the best of them and is perfect for the expanses of the outfield in the Sky Dome. His recent offense has been a major disappointment, particularly in light of the promise he showed in his rookie season, when he had 24/87 and 32 SBs.

One of the other two outfield spots belongs to Joe Carter. At the press conference announcing the trade, Cito Gaston indicated he'd open the season with Carter in RF and Mookie Wilson in LF.

They may start that way, but the smart money doesn't see that as the Blue Jay OF for long. Rather, expect one of two other variations on the theme. The most likely scenario has Carter in LF and top Blue Jay prospect Mark Whiten in RF. Whiten comes off a year in AAA [Syracuse] where he was named the #1 I.L. prospect by Baseball America, ahead of guys like Travis Fryman, Leo Gomez, and Mo Vaughn.

International League managers rave about Whiten and with good reason. When he was promoted to the Jays, he was among the leaders in both batting average and HRs. One manager compared him to Bo Jackson, adding "he's got a good arm and great speed . . . . . he's got everything going for him."

Regardless of which option Cito chooses, the key is Joe Carter. The acquisition of Carter helps the team on many levels, not the least of which is leadership. He's a proven run-producer, having driven in over 100 runs in four of the last five years. Given the Blue Jay lineup, Carter's a lock to make it five of six. Someplace between 110-125 seems about right. While it seems unlikely he'll get his average back to the .300 he hit a few years back, .260-.270 doesn't seem like much of a stretch.

That leaves the question of what will happen to Mookie? The answer, I suspect, is the Jays will try to find him a home in the off-season/spring. Everything he does, someone else can do it better. Whiten's got a better arm and more speed. Hill has more power.

Fred Matos:

So far, Glenallen Hill's age and history with Toronto have closely paralleled Cecil Fielder's experience. The Blue Jays gave Fielder, at a young age, the rap of not being able to hit RHP, and they used him only against lefties. So far, the Jays have done the same thing with Hill. Last year, Hill's platoon differential was only 15 points in batting average, similar to Fielder's small differential, despite the bad reputation. Fielder eventually left Toronto and achieved recognition (and playing time against righties and lefties) with some other team. Could the Glenallen Hill story be similar?

NATIONAL LEAGUE OUTFIELDERS

ATLANTA

Last year, our recommendation of Ron Gant was one of our better predictions:

"Gant is on my list of best picks for 1990, because of his prime age (25) and likelihood of being extremely undervalued. He could have a big year and should be dirt cheap after his .177 major league BA last year." So you all went out and bought Gant at the $4 average price that he commanded in 1990 auctions. Right?

If you are looking for reasons why Dave Justice should have a sophomore slump, don't bother looking in his second half 1990 stats. He was .295-23-58 after the All Star break. Pro-rate them apples! Unfortunately, he isn't going to be thrown back by the people who drafted him last year.

Atlanta has obviously not found the "right" way to handle McDowell. Critics must wonder if there is a right way. McDowell was the first of the 1984 Olympians to achieve major league success, beating out the likes of Will Clark, Barry Larkin and Cory Snyder, chronologically. Oddibe had a marvelous rookie season, but since 1985, he has had all kinds of problems including a visit to Oklahoma City (for "motivation") in 1988. Quite surprisingly, Oddibe told people that he liked playing at Triple-A just fine; he didn't have to worry about whether he was going to be in the line-up, and didn't have to feel the discomfort of competing every day to put somebody else out of a job. He expressed a very big-minded view of life, for sure, but not the kind of killer instinct that one normally expects in the professional competitive arena.

Marc Bowman:

After suffering for years with an unsettled outfield with only one known starter in Dale Murphy, the Braves now have two solid regulars and good backups. Ron Gant won the center field job, for a long time to come, with his first 30/30 season in 1990. It was the Braves' first 30/30 performance since Hank Aaron in 1963. Dave Justice, one of the best rookies in years, hit nine homers during a two-week stretch immediately after the Murphy trade. Justice has the RF job locked up for 1991. Left field will be shared by Lonnie Smith and Oddibe McDowell.

Smith will get the lion's share of starts in left field, and he will usually bat leadoff. Lonnie recovered from a tough start to hit .305 in 1990, but he isn't likely to hit .300 ever again. Smith is on a long down-trend from his marvelous 1989 season, and he comes with an assortment of negatives. For a leadoff hitter, he won't steal many bases, because he's too old, and he won't score many runs, because the Braves have an anemic offense behind him.

After a monstrous 1990 season, Ron Gant will be due for a let down in 1991. He isn't going to sneak up on anybody: not in Rotisserie, and not on the playing field. In almost every league, he will be retained by the person who bought him last year; in the few cases where he comes up for bids, somebody will pay a superstar price. Around the National League, pitchers are going to be careful with Gant in 1991; they won't stop him, but they will give him a harder time than he had in 1990. Gant has always been a free swinger, and he will be seeing fewer strikes this year. His average could easily dip to .270. Gant is a natural "bad ball" hitter. He should still be good for 20 homers, 75 RBI, and 25 or more steals. SB is the one category where he might actually improve in 1991, as he learns the pitchers and situations better. Gant is a young and improving, but he is also one of the more inconsistent players over the past three years. Don't expect him to become suddenly steady and reliable.

Dave Justice had two weeks in August that were better than some players 1990 season: .410 BA, 9 homers, 23 RBI. Consider that Justice is still only 24. One year ago, most scouts agreed that young David would be ready for the majors around 1992. If he makes the big improvement that everyone expected in 1991, the world will have something to behold. The short Fulton County Stadium fences will continue to help Justice. He had only 438 at bats in 1990, meaning that his annual HR output could actually increase.

The only question about Justice is how much the pitchers will be able to gain on him in 1991. He will see much more cautious pitching, and will draw more walks, but the power stats are likely to fall off a little.

Oddibe McDowell is one of the most talented fourth outfielders in the NL. He is a better defensive player than either Gant or Lonnie Smith, so he will often get into games that he doesn't start. McDowell's bunting and baserunning abilities will get him into many games as a pinch hitter or pinch runner. Oddibe was used sparingly in September 1990, but he should get about 300 at bats in 1991. He should be good for a dozen steals, and his power production should improve a little, but he isn't likely to hit for good average unless he gets into an everyday role.

Before the acquisition of Sid Bream, Geronimo Berroa and Jim Vatcher looked like the best candidates in a large field of competitors for the fifth outfielder job. Now that Tommy Gregg has been squeezed out of the first base picture, he goes to the head of the OF waiting line. Other possibilities behind Gregg, Vatcher and Berroa include Andy Tomberlin and Dwight Taylor.

Lary Bump:

At times, the Braves' 1990 lineup looked like The Attack of the Munchkins, with Mark Lemke and Oddibe McDowell and Jeff Treadway and the 5'9" Jim Vatcher coming to the plate. The 24-year-old Vatcher may be short in statute, but don't sell his talent short. In '89 he hit better than .300 in two pitchers' leagues, the Florida State and Eastern. He batted only .254 last season in another tough league, the International, before the Phillies called him up and traded him to the Braves. He doesn't have a lot of power, but his walks outnumbered his strikeouts in the minors, and he has a right field arm. It would be a disservice to him if the Braves typecast him as an off-the-bench bat without giving him a chance. What do they have to lose?

CHICAGO CUBS

One of the fun things about writing this book in late December is that I don't have to agonize over questions like Derrick May as the Cubs left fielder. Most of the books and annuals that went to press already have Derrick penciled in. Not me. They will sell more books than I do, because they get to the stores first. But my book will do you more good on draft day.

For the record, I never accepted the "Derrick May is our left fielder" story out of Chicago, and said so in the WINNING ROTISSERIE BASEBALL monthly at the end of the 1990 season. When a team needs a left fielder, they don't say, "We are in desperate need of a left fielder." That would weaken their bargaining position. They say, instead, "We have a marvelous young left fielder named Derrick May." Yeah, right.

The world of Rotisserie is waiting with baited breath to see what George Bell will do in Wrigley Field. Bell should improve his HR output by more than the 25% implied in the park differential between Toronto and Cubland. Bell has outstanding power to left field, especially against southpaw pitchers. He should be parking a large number of shots on Waveland Avenue this summer.

Center field belongs to Jerome Walton. I predict that Walton will have a tremendous comeback year in 1991. He is still only 26. Many people in 1989 didn't think Walton was ready for the major leagues, and didn't think he would do well when the Cubs kept him after spring training. Suppose Walton had gone back to Iowa in 1989, and had a tremendous year in Triple-A. And then suppose he was injured in 1990 and had a horrible season. And then suppose he was coming to spring training in 1991, with the CF job wide open for him to claim. In that case, everyone would think that Walton was the greatest thing since corn flakes. So why should he be downvalued, just because he spent the last two years on a major league roster? You want sleepers, and I say Walton will be undervalued in most auctions, especially those where people are looking at 1990 stats as their basis for valuation.

Walton broke his hand in 1990, on a Ken Howell pitch. After the hand was healed, Walton was reluctant to run, for fear of re-injury. In 1991 he should be more courageous on the basepaths and pile up the SB again like he did in 1989.

Right field is Andre Dawson, as usual. Dawson tailed off a little in the second half of 1990, but I wouldn't be especially worried about him. The only problem with Dawson in that too many people will remember 1987 and value him with that peak performance in mind.

If you gave the Chicago outfield to most managers, they would make Dwight Smith the fourth outfielder and consider playing him against all right-handed pitching. He hit .331 vs. RHP in 1989, and has a 70 point lifetime L/R differential. Don Zimmer isn't your average manager, however. He doesn't like moody people, and Smith is moody. Worse for Smith, once you get in Zimmer's doghouse you don't get out. Ever. And Smith is in Zimmer's doghouse. So the best chance for this marvelous, fast, .295 lifetime hitter is that he should get traded to another team if he wants to have a productive year at age 27. The Cubs were trying to oblige him with a trade, when 1990 drew to a close.

Dave Clark is a high-power, fair-average type of hitter. Given 500 at bats, he could hit 15 to 20 HR in Wrigley Field, but he won't ever get 500 AB. Clark is, at best, a leading contender for the fifth outfield spot. If/when somebody in the Cubs OF gets hurt and Clark gets a couple weeks of regular play, he can be a nice mid-season fill-in, for you and for the Cubs.

Adam Stein:

Derrick May, Dave Clark, Dwight Smith, Doug Dascenzo and Luis Salazar are the candidates for outfield backup time, in that order of likelihood. Salazar will be valuable for the time he spends at 3B, but the best of the others will be worth only $2 to $4.

Lary Bump:

Derrick May is a 22-year-old LH batter and the son of ex-journeyman OF Dave May. Derrick doesn't fit the description of either journeyman or outfielder, for he can hit but can't field. In five minor league seasons, his averages have ranged between .295 and .320. His '90 numbers at Iowa — .296, 8, 69 — no doubt would be inflated in a full season at Wrigley Field. He'll probably be competing for playing time with Dwight Smith, who had similar statistics at Iowa in '88 and batted .324 for the '89 Cubs division-winners. May's advantages are that he is five years younger and he hits lefties pretty well. It would be an interesting exercise to see both of them in a fly ball-chasing contest at Wrigley Field. There might not be a winner. May has a future as a hitter; it may be in the American League. Expect him to get a good shot with the Cubs in '91.

CINCINNATI

Greg Gajus:

Eric Davis (.260-24-86-21)—"Eric Davis had a great year despite playing through some serious injuries and should explode in 1991." (Same comment as 1990). Eric started slow, went on the DL with a knee that never fully healed, seriously bruised his shoulder making a sensational catch at the end of the year, and topped his injury history with the lacerated kidney in Game 4 of the World Series. Hitting .224 as late as August 19th, Eric hit .357 with 9 HR and 29 RBI the rest of the year.

Davis was scheduled for knee surgery after his kidney heals, and should be 100% for spring training. My only advice is to not count on Davis for steals - he now runs only when it is crucial and usually does not run with a left handed batter up (Morris or O'Neill usually follow him in the lineup). His biggest plus in 1991 may be the intangibles—the Cincinnati fans will finally get off his back due to his dramatic injury in the Series, and his maturing led to recognition as THE team leader, a status that had eluded him under Pete Rose. A fully healthy Davis will be 1991's Barry Bonds. With the usual Davis injuries, expect 25-30 HR with 85-110 RBI's.

Paul O'Neill (.270-16-78-13) xeroxed his 1989 stats but took 80 more at bats to do it. In 1990, O'Neill improved against LHP (.259 with .406 SLG) but declined against RHP (.275 with .428 SLG). Despite the improvement against LHP, the arrival of Glenn Braggs may put O'Neill's full time status in jeopardy.

As 1990 drew to a close, the Reds had a serious numbers problem in the outfield, with Billy Hatcher, O'Neill, Glenn Braggs, Herm Winningham, and possibly Todd Benzinger competing for 2 outfield spots. If a trade does not occur to clear out some of the players, you can expect Piniella again to work everyone into the lineup, which would greatly limit O'Neill's chance to greatly exceed his current production. Of those outfielders, O'Neill is the only one that has a chance to develop into a full time performer.

Billy Hatcher (.276-5-25-30) concentrated his contributions into the first month of the season and in the last 4 games (2nd half: .235-3-12-8). From a Rotisserie point of view, the speed is the only aspect with any value. His brilliant World Series will probably make him very overvalued. I wouldn't be a bit surprised if he only got about 300 AB next year due to the crowded nature of the Cincinnati outfield.

The key to Hatcher's playing time will be whether Davis returns to center field next year. Healthy, Davis is the best CF in baseball, but Piniella used him in LF most of the year to ease the strain on his knees. Hatcher's offense is tolerable in CF, but not acceptable in LF. Treat Billy as a major gamble for 1991.

Glenn Braggs (.299-6-28-3) turned in a fine 200 AB in 1990, primarily filling in for Eric Davis's frequent injuries and as a platoon partner with Paul O'Neill. Braggs was very effective against LHP, hitting .339 and slugging .513, making him a good platoon partner for O'Neill. But given the crowd in the Cincinnati outfield, it is hard to see Braggs significantly increasing his playing time unless the team is struck by mass injuries.

Herm Winningham (.256-3-17-6) As Eric Davis's caddy, Herm is usually in line for a decent amount of playing time. If Davis stays in LF this year, Herm could be in line for more playing time in a CF platoon with Hatcher. If Davis stays in CF, ignore Winningham unless Eric goes on the DL.

Adam Stein:

Billy Hatcher epitomizes the Reds' 1990 season. He had a great first half, then coasted on a nice-looking set of stats, while his play became totally mediocre. Finally, he turned on a great display of talent in the LCS and World Series.

Hatcher's stats go up and down with management decisions that affect his playing time and stature on the team. He may have a delicate psyche, or he may just lose his edge when he doesn't play every day. The reason doesn't matter. What you need to know is that Hatcher is likely to have a big year if all the pre-season personnel moves set him up in a full-time role. If he becomes part of an outfield supporting cast, along with Braggs, Benzinger, etc., his play will suffer and he should be avoided.

Sean Lahman:

The biggest change for the Reds outfield in 1990 was the acquisition of Billy Hatcher in early April. When the Pirates decided to move Bobby Bonilla to the outfield, that left Billy Hatcher the odd man out, and he was making too much money to be a bench player. The Reds picked him up for two AAA players and Hatcher was a major part of the Reds success. A lot of scouting reports say Hatcher can't bunt, but he's had a lot of bunt singles when I've been watching. His speed is an important weapon (30 SB in 40 attempts) and he is an excellent baserunner. In the past, he has had problems with right-handed pitchers but last year hit them well enough to stay in the lineup every day. Hatcher's post-season experience and his leadership ability were a main reason he was acquired and an indication that the Reds plan to keep him around.

Nobody plays harder than Eric Davis. People who don't see him play every day (or at all) say he doesn't hustle, that he's not a team player. If he's not running full speed, it's because he's physically unable. If Davis is not in the lineup, he probably should be in the hospital. If he can stay healthy for 162 games (he's never played more than 135) he'll put up better numbers than anyone in history.

Paul O'Neill began to show that he could hit left-handed pitching last year, a new development he attributes to Lou Piniella's hitting instruction. O'Neill still seems hesitant at the plate, something he will have to overcome to fulfill his superstar potential. If he never takes this quantum leap, O'Neill is still a solid everyday outfielder whose numbers last year are a good indication of what he will do in the future.

Glenn Braggs' offensive skills have been refined since he arrived in Cincinnati. He's a more consistent hitter and reduced his strikeouts, a major problem when he first came up. Braggs is a lot like Paul O'Neill; he can hit, he can hit for power, and he can run the bases. Defense has been Braggs shortcoming, but it is something he has worked hard on. Braggs can play left or right field and does a lot of pinch-hitting. He should get about 300 ABs off the bench and hit about .270 with 10-12 HR and 12-15 SB.

There are not any notable outfield prospects at AAA. It's just as well; the outfield is crowded enough already.

HOUSTON

UPDATE — Steve Finley gets a full-time job in RF, with Anthony in LF. Rhodes and Ortiz lose time.

What happens when you bring up all your kids too early? First, the kids go bad. They lose confidence. You send them back to the minors. They suffer more. Second, you finish last, and look stupid doing it.

The Houston outfield of 1991 will include a power-hitting 23-year-old comeback candidate (Eric Anthony), a speedy 26-year-old comeback candidate (Gerald Young), and various rookies. If Young stays with the Astros, and if they put him in center field and leave him alone, he will be one of the great bargains of 1991. Most leagues won't have any bidders who expect Young to return to his 65 SB form of 1988. Most people think Gerald Young is about 39 years old now. He will surprise most people.

Eric Anthony will most likely end up with RF job; the Astros started playing him there when their roster overflowed with left fielders last year. Once again this year, I will tell you that Anthony is a low-average, high-power hitter in the mold of Dave Kingman and Gorman Thomas. He will end up on the rosters of people who don't understand the delicate sensitivity of batting average rankings in Rotisserie baseball, and on rosters that already have Tony Gwynn and a half dozen other .300 hitters. If you take Eric Anthony and win your league in 1991, please send me a copy of the final standings. I will be fascinated to see how you did it.

Going into spring training, it looked like a platoon of Karl Rhodes and Javier Ortiz in left field. Rhodes is the true prospect, just age 22. Last year he was used exclusively against righty pitching. He has good speed, but his minimal power will be lost in the Astrodome. Ortiz was used against righty and lefty pitchers both in 1991. It isn't his weakness that would lead to a platoon; it is the desire to get Rhodes into the lineup.

Just for the record, we claim a victory for second half stats for tipping off Gerald Young's horrible 1990 season. From last year's book: "Gerald lost his base-stealing ability in the second half of 1989; he was cut down in 9 of 12 attempts, netting just three steals." If you acquired Young with the image of 40 to 60 SB in mind, you suffered.

Welford McCaffrey:

The Houston Astros held auditions, during the 1990 championship season, for anyone who would like to play a role in left field. It was hoped that the winner of the audition would play for a long run. 12 players answered the audition call. At the end of the year, no winners were announced. The auditions will continue in spring training.

The first player to audition for the role of left-fielder was Eric Anthony. Anthony has been touted over the last two years as the "Great Hope of the Future." Management decided 1990 was the season, installed Anthony in leftfield and said the position was his. The fans and the press, who had clamored for the home-run hitting Anthony for two years, were delighted.

Anthony was 22 years old in 1990. He did not play high school or college ball. He went from a tryout camp to minor league ball. Baseball is not a game he has grown up playing, the fundamentals are not there. The one thing Eric has is a great home run swing. IF he can learn to hit a curve ball or change-up he'll be an exciting player. Unless he learns to hit over the winter watch for Eric to be down in Tucson come April.

Javier Ortiz' star shone briefly in his left-field audition. He hit .273, hit a few doubles, drew a good share of walks and could drive in a run or two when needed. He's now 28 years old come 1991. It could happen, but not likely.

Karl Rhodes is a long shot to win the left-field role in 1991. He'll be only 22 years old he has had five years of minor league experience. He was impressive at times in his off-Broadway performance towards the end of the season, when the Astros were playing all their games with the intensity that you normally expect during a spring training exhibition schedule.

The Rhodes scholar can take a walk, he actually walked more than he struck out in a number of minor league seasons. "Tuffy" has a real good compact left-handed swing and hangs in there against lefties. This may be the sleeper for the 1991 season.

The Astros have let it be known that they are looking for an entirely new outfield for 1991. The only one of the current crop they would like to keep if they had their druthers is Eric Anthony, and that is only if he can hit for a decent average while clouting mammoth home runs. Look for the Astros to make some deals or even to sign a free agent or two over the winter to round out their outfield for 1991.

Centerfield? Read these extracts from my diary:

April 9, 1990 — In their home opener, the Astros lost 8-4 in 11 innings. Gerald Young, the Astros leadoff hitter and centerfielder, went 1-6. Young got a double to drive in a run in the Astros four run sixth. I hope Gerald does well this year. The man can cover centerfield great and he can sure run around the bases. He just can't get on; he doesn't walk much and he can't bunt worth a damn. The Astros even had Young work with Rod Carew on bunting, and Young couldn't bunt a ball fair unless he bunted right back to the pitcher. Young has a tendency to uppercut the ball resulting in easy fly outs. He really doesn't have any line drive power.

April 11, 1990 — Great news: my friend Rick got some great box seats for the game with the Reds tonight. Two games live in one week! The Astros lost 5-0. Rick is optimistic about the team. For example, he believes that Young should have a full season like the half season he had when he came up in '87. Rick reminded me that Young wasn't too shabby in '88 when he stole 65 bases for a single season club record. I don't share Rick's confidence in the Astros and I told him so. What I haven't told Rick yet is that sometimes I get this creepy feeling all over me when I think about the Astros. It's like there is something hanging over the team, but I just can't put my finger on it.

April 15, 1990: I just don't understand it. The Astros just won their first game of the season, yet some fans are unhappy. It gave me that creepy feeling again. On the radio, I hear, "How can the caller ask such a stupid question? Of course we are concerned about the early difficulties experienced by Gerald Young, but sending him to the minors is rather drastic considering we've only played five games so far. I wish the fans and media people would leave the players alone. Then maybe someone like Gerald could relax. Gerald is a fine young player and we feel he still has a lot of potential. Sending this young man down now could just shatter his self-confidence." You could almost picture the radio guys' mouth begin to foam, "Gerald Young is going to start hitting again and he is going to help this team generate some offense. I only hope when he does you naysayers will call back so we can laugh at you. I've been in baseball my whole life and I know Gerald is going to hit again." Diary, I've decided that I'm not going to any games for a while. I've been seeing BILL at the ballpark and on television, besides hearing him on the radio. I don't want any more nightmares so I'll just think pure Astro fans thoughts. Rick could be right. The Astros could win the division if everything falls into place right. It could.

May 21, 1990: The Astros won today, which makes them 14-24, only 13 and a half games out of first. Gerald Young was optioned to Tucson tonight. Shortly after I fell asleep, I woke up in a cold sweat. I was having the worst nightmare. BILL came. BILL is a short-haired dark grey-suited white longsleeved shirted power red tie black wing-tipped wire-rimmed glassed fanatic.

May 22, 1990: Eric Yelding became the Astros centerfielder today. He seems to be a better hitter than Young, at least he can bunt the ball for a hit. Yelding has better speed on the basepaths though he has a tendency to get picked off. His range is not as good as Young in center. Yelding has been mostly a second baseman and shortstop in his professional career starting with the Blue Jays organization in 1984. He may end up as the shortstop for the Astros in a year or two if nobody else comes up from the minors to take it or if Young or somebody else claims center from Yelding. But for today Yelding is the Astros centerfielder.

June 28, 1990: Craig Biggio, the Astros catcher, playing in center. Poor Craig. A guy hits the ball for a single to center, Craig reaches down to catch the hop, the ball goes through his legs. I'll get back to you later, one of the fantasy league owners wants to make a deal.

Later, June 28, 1990: Somehow, one moment I'm on the phone and the next I'm at the start of a tropical storm. It was BILL. First, bats and balls rained down from the sky. I had to get cover. Then a terrific wind came up from the South and silhouetted against the dark sky was BILL. He laughed and laughed and laughed. "You call that a centerfielder. Ha, ha, ha, ha, ha. Ha, ha, ha, ha, ha."

July 20, 1990: Rafael Ramirez is recovered from his injury so Yelding can go back out to center and Biggio can get back to catching. Yelding hit .309 in 1984, his first year in professional ball in the Pioneer League, and .305 in 1987 in the South Atlantic League, but he has also batted as low as .250 in the International League in 1988. He has never hit much more than a dozen doubles in a season. Walks are not a real specialty of his either.

October 4, 1990: The season's over. Yelding did not end on a very good note. His .254 average made him 11th in average to other centerfielders, only Carter of San Diego did worse at .232, but he drove in 115 runs. Yelding was 11th in centerfielders in on-base-average and last in slugging. Eric is slated to be the starting short stop next year, not the center fielder. Yelding is expected to get together with a nutritionist, who helped Vince Coleman out during the off-season in 1989, to add some more weight and muscles on his small frame. Gerald Young was a persona non grata at the end of the season. I wouldn't be surprised if he was traded during the winter. And I would not be surprised if the Astros traded for a centerfielder since they look totally inadequate to fill their needs. But, if the Astros are unable to get another center fielder for next year then expect to see Yelding out there. Yelding is a hard worker, seems to take to instruction well and showed flashes of brilliance during the course of the season.

"Ha, ha, ha, ha, ha. Ha, ha, ha, ha, ha."

Lary Bump:

Consider Willie Ansley, Jeff Baldwin, Javier Ortiz, and Karl Rhodes

Anybody know who plays the outfield for the Astros? Clearly, there are positions for the taking. At the end of 1990, Javier Ortiz, a right-handed batter, seemed the most likely to take one. After a .352 start at Tucson, he looked impressive (.273) in 30 games as Houston's LF before going down with an injury. At age 28, though, he doesn't project to have a long and productive career.

Next in line: Karl Rhodes, a 22-year-old lefthanded batter nicknamed Tuffy. He batted .275 and stole 24 bases at Tucson, and his .350 OBP was the worst in his five minor league seasons. He provides speed and on-base ability rather than power and run production.

Jeff Baldwin is a 25-year-old LHH who also could have a shot at left field. After five minor league seasons, he finally made it to Triple-A last year, but just for 19 games, in which he batted .135. He returned to Double-A Columbus to bat .316 and reach base nearly 40 per cent of the time. But he stole 0 bases. Not a realistic candidate for the Astros this season. Maybe next year, if — a big if — he can produce in Triple-A.

The Willie Ansley story continues to unfold. Instead of the success story — Texas high school championship, a 596-foot HR in a high school game in Amarillo, playing in an all-star game in the Astrodome, Astros' No. 1 pick in '88 — 1990 was a story of frustration. Ansley, a 21-year-old righthanded hitter, batted just .255 at Columbus, with 9 HR, 37 RBI and 33 SB. Look for him to come back, and to be back in CF at the Astrodome within two years.

LOS ANGELES

Kal Daniels just gave us another lesson in why players are NEVER washed up at age 26. He should continue at a high level in 1991, but the bargain of 1990 is gone now.

Brett Butler is arguably the best leadoff hitter in the National League. His presence will add to the RBI count of all who bat behind him, especially Murray and Strawberry.

Darryl Strawberry's arrival in Los Angeles was founded in some high anxiety about his contract status during the pre-season of 1990. The Mets refused to negotiate during the season to Darryl's satisfaction, and Darryl responded by carrying the Mets during the league's longest winning streak of 1990, 11 games in June. Considering that he hit just .225 in 1989, Straw must regard the 1990 season as very happy adventure. It looks good in the record books, and it helped him find a new home.

I like Stan Javier as a cheapie outfielder, because he stands alone as the fourth OF for playing time, because he's a switch hitter, and because he is age 26. See Pete DeCoursey's notes below. Then make sure everybody in your league knows that the Dodger OF is now 100% locked up, because you don't want people looking at Javier's 1990 value. Just ask, "Where is he going to play?" when his names comes before the auction. Javier is one of the rare cases where it could be a good idea to bring up the name yourself in conversation. "Hey, Sam, where is Javier going to play this year? Where, where, where?" Then bid on him.

Alan Boodman:

Darryl may never get into the 40-40 club, but it looks like he intends to get 30 homers and right around 100 RBI every year. His steals have diminished, but Strawberry scores runs, draws walks, and is capable of hitting in the .270-.285 range. Also his strikeouts have dropped. I think he's finally arrived at the point where he'll turn in a few solid and consistent years, if not flashy ones.

Adam Stein:

Kirk Gibson has left for Kansas City, and the Dodgers signed Darryl Strawberry as as a free agent from New York. Then, facing the same problem they've had for the past year and a half (no true centerfielder) they simply added Brett Butler. Voila! The games best outfield, built on the ashes of 1990.

Darryl Strawberry will spend a lot of time in Disneyland and not enough fine tuning his game. It would have been a great laugh for New Yorkers to see Darryl in center field. Bill James' defensive spectrum (SS, CF, 2B, 3B, RF, LF, 1B) theory noted that as players get older and their skills deteriorate, they should move to the right on the spectrum. The Dodgers have this annoying habit of trying to move players to the left on the spectrum (Guerrero, Gibson, Stubbs, Samuel) and ruining their team defense. With Butler safely buffering Darryl from his worst self, look for a huge (MVP) year from Strawman.

Before they traded Hubie Brooks, Kal Daniels was the one rumored to be on the trading block. Daniels looks like he has finally recovered from knee surgery. If he can stay healthy, and he doesn't lose playing time in the Dodgers crowded outfield, he's one of the top 10 offensive players in the league.

He no longer can steal bases, but he's good for a .300 average and 30 home runs.

Without Butler, the Dodgers might have used Javier five days a week. Now he must share a smaller number of at bats with a larger number of competitors. Javier is a decent player, but is a high risk to get stuck on the bench. Chris Gwynn is not a bad fifth outfielder for your team, but he has no way to break into the Dodger line up at present and thus, little upward mobility. No other Dodger outfielder will get enough playing time to be worth having.

Pete DeCoursey:

Stan Javier, who can run and hit for average, is a good $1-$5 OF. He will play when Daniels and Strawberry are hurt, and when Butler gets 10-12 games off. That will add up to 50-70 starts, and lots of pinch-hitting, pinchrunning, and late inning duty. He should be able to keep his average up and steal 10-15 bases.

Bob Whitemore:

Braulio Castillo was rated the 34th best minor league prospect by Baseball America. He was in rehab for some trouble with his nostrils and isn't a prospect for 1991. He hit just .228 at San Antonio last year.

Henry Rodriguez was the number two prospect in the Texas League according to BBA. He hit .291-28-109-5 at San Antonio.

Tom Goodwin, a lefty hitter like Rodriguez, stole 60 bases for San Antonio. If pennants were decided by Double-A outfields, the Dodgers would have won the NL last year.

MONTREAL

UPDATE — Ivan Calderon is projected to bat third or fifth; he should pile up the RBI.

Michael Cassin:

Ivan Calderon [see Chicago/AL] is in; Tim Raines is out.

Montreal didn't want to commit to moving Tim Raines out of the lead-off spot to the third or fifth spot, despite finding in Delino DeShields a potential lead-off batter who can hit better than Otis Nixon.

Dave Martinez' strong hitting vs RHP may keep Marquis Grissom a platoon player a year longer than expected. Grissom hit 37 points higher vs. righties, but showed more power vs. LHP, and the Expos want some power from Grissom, even if he gets his SB total up near 40 this year. Only if the Expos are sure they can get 25-30 HR from Larry Walker will they let Grissom play strictly as a speed player.

Write in Martinez, Walker, and Grissom each for 2/3 of the CF/RF time as a starting point. I still think Montreal wants Walker's power in the line-up every day. I can't see a significant improvement over Walker's HR/RBI totals of last season (19/51), but I can see a slow and steady improvement heading into 1992.

The arrival of Calderon means that Grissom doesn't have a definitive spot yet. Without Calderon, Grissom would have played every day. Grissom will improve his BA and SB this season, but with the Expos likely to get all they can out of Calderon, I'd put a hold on any giant leaps forward, for at least one more year.

Playing against all RHP, Martinez did as good as he'll ever do. He did what he had to do as a second place hitter, and his 11 HR were more power than he's ever shown, but there's no chance of him getting any more ABs this season than he did last, so it's more likely that his numbers will decrease than increase.

Moises Alou is 24, and ready to play, but finding him playing time won't be easy. It's possible Montreal may decide that Alou is better than either Grissom or Walker and put him into one of their spots, but if it does happen it won't be early in the season. Alou should make the team, but I think all the news of Pittsburgh's throwing its minor league players around will make Alou over-priced at this point. Sooner or later some other major league GM will make a horrible waiver blunder, and you can make your move for Alou while he's being overshadowed by some other phenom who's on the move.

If the Expos had traded Raines without getting a good outfielder in return, you could have concluded that Moises Alou must be ready. The acquisition of Calderon isn't a guarantee that Alou is unready, but there was a possible vote of confidence there, and Montreal didn't pull the lever.

Otis Nixon continues to steal enough bases to give him value to Montreal, and much more for Rotisserie. If the final outfield spot comes down to a choice between him and Aldrete, Rodgers will go with Nixon. You can decide how much 40-50 SB, and nothing else, are worth to you. At this point it seems the best Montreal can hope of Aldrete is that he'll go the Huson/Hudler route and turn into a useful middle relief pitcher. Rolando Roomes was cut early in the winter.

Lary Bump:

Oh, the wailing and gnashing of teeth in Pittsburgh! Larry Doughty traded away Alou! What exactly did he trade? The son of Felipe Alou, and the nephew of the two other big-league Alous. A 24-year-old righthanded batter who's probably better suited to LF than CF. A player with some speed (20 SBs each of the last two seasons) and some power (a total of 25 HRs the last two years. A player who batted .264 in his first partial season in Triple-A. A player who probably doesn't fit into the Expos' OF in '91. Let's look at what he does at Indianapolis this season, and then decide whether we have another Felipe Alou on our hands, or another Jesus Alou.

Pete DeCoursey:

Larry Walker and Marquis Grissom are both base stealers. Grissom is a nascent Willie McGee, while Walker is will be a 24 year old version of HoJo at the plate. He hit 19 HRs and stole 21 bases and drew 49 BBs in 468 PAs. Given Rodger's general confusion and the crowding that new addition Moises Alou may bring, it may not be this year, but Larry Walker will be the next 30/30 clubber on the Spo's. Tell everyone he struck out more than 1/4 of his plate appearances, and pretend that you didn't really want him, you were just trying to get the other fellow to waste his money. But smile inwardly; this guy is a stone winner. Grissom is another 24-year old who stole 22 of 24 bases (see Categories essay) last year, and will follow DeShields in '91, or '92 as the next Expo to hit .300 and steal 50 bases. Grissom has better speed and strike zone judgement than young Mr. Alou has shown so far, and I think he will end up with the playing time, as his learning process distinguishes him even more than Moises' name helps that young man.

NEW YORK METS

Vince Coleman, the prototypical carpet-cruiser, is not exactly built for Shea Stadium. His numbers on grass aren't that bad, but during the course of his career, his longest hot streaks have occurred on the rugs of the NL. If you take away a player's hot streaks, the impact can be remarkably damaging.

The main issue with Coleman is OBP. The .292 batting average in 1990 helped lift the OBP top .340, a good year for Coleman, but not too hot for a leadoff hitter. Compare the 1990 OBP's of Brett Butler (.397), Lenny Dykstra (.418), and Jerome Walton (.350 — just to show the disappointing end of the spectrum) and you can see why Coleman isn't all that highly regarded.

The Mets have used a "wait for the three run homer" style of offense since the early days of Davey Johnson. Coleman is supposed to change that. More likely, the Mets will change Coleman more than Coleman changes the Mets. Consider also that Vince was obsessed with stealing 100 bases in 1990 (to prove his worth to the Cardinals). He would have failed even if the Cards hadn't benched him for September. There is no much number to shoot for in 1991. I foresee a flat year for Coleman, with the New York media hounding him.

Darren Reed might be the $1 player who gives you 10 HR this year. When I asked him to name one factor that led to his August 15 call-up, he said simply, The fly balls were going farther." He decided to swing for power in 1990, noting that his various stances and swings had never carried him beyond spring training before. The result was 17 homers at Tidewater and a ticket to the majors. Reed is a good defensive outfielder with a great arm. He is only 25. You could do worse for a buck.

Alan Boodman:

Kevin McReynolds started the 1990 season slowly (as usual), but finished strong (as usual) to post above-average stats, but not particularly impressive ones by Kevin's standards. 24 homers, 82 RBI, and .269 are decent numbers for most leftfielders, but we all know that Mac is capable of better.

You may have noticed that most of the Mets' big sticks (Strawberry, Johnson) are "consistent" to the point where we can reliably say they're likely to hit anywhere between 15 and 40 homers in '91, drive in from 65 to 120 runs, and bat between .210 and .300. Give or take a little. McReynolds is the one player who can be pinpointed with any degree of accuracy. He's never injured, his Rotisserie stats lie within a predictable range from year-to-year, and he even follows the same in-season patterns, making you wonder what possessed you to get him during April, and by July he's hitting over .300 (for the month), and with a couple of longballs a week. But Kevin's so quiet that nobody bothers to notice. He's pretty consistent about that too.

It's possible that Kevin is going to be shuttled back and forth across the outfield this year, and that the Mets could be facing fewer lefties than ever, and these are factors that aren't exactly in Mac's favor, but he'll get his usual 575 plate appearances, and he'll bat .276 with 27 homers and 93 RBI. He'll steal 16 bases, and remember you read it all here first. You don't really need a very big crystal ball for this guy.

Darryl Boston, cast off by the (then) lowly-regarded White Sox, had to be the biggest Mets' surprise in '90, but he also stands a good chance to be the biggest '91 letdown for a few reasons. First of all, he isn't really that good. While he deserved the chance that he got last season — the Mets had nobody better, and Boston was never as bad as the White Sox made him out to be, he's still a low-average, medium-power hitter with a little speed and a fairly weak glove and arm. I know .273 wasn't bad, but it's as high as Darryl will ever hit, and 12 dingers (in nearly 400 PA) is my idea of medium-range power for a second baseman, but not for an outfielder. Combine this with the fact that 1990 is very likely to be Boston's BEST season, and you see why you probably shouldn't risk much on this particular Mets' outfielder.

Boston has the kind of skills that appeal to a ballclub that has no alternatives, but the 1991 Mets do have alternatives in the outfield. What if Pat Tabler hangs around? What if Darren Reed develops? What about Mark Carreon? What if Keith Miller finally has the season management has been waiting for? Personally, I've been waiting for him to get on base more than 30 percent of the time, but I get the feeling the Mets expect even more. Good luck. I didn't say they were great alternatives, just numerous.

To finish up Boston, I'd look for substantially less playing time this year, as the Mets decide that he is not the centerfielder of the future. If, for some reason, the Mets decide that he is the centerfielder of the future, look for substantially fewer victories in the future. Darryl should get maybe 200-250 PA (that's an upper limit, I hope), and will hit in the .230-.240 range with 5-10 homers.

The rest of the cast:

Mark Carreon, if he has recovered from his surgery of last summer, might be due for more playing time, but I doubt it (I doubt the playing time more than the recovery). I'm not unhappy that the Mets have him, but I don't particularly want him on my Rotisserie team. His role is pinch-hitting, which he has always done very well.

Darren Reed is as close to a "prospect" that the Mets system has as far as outfielders go. He hasn't shown it recently, but Darren has the ability to hit a ton of homers, and he has other power-hitter's skills such as striking out a good many times, being slow for an outfielder (but fast for a DH), and having no real defensive position. He's obviously not a centerfielder, but since nobody else around here is either, he doesn't look quite as bad out there as he really is.

Keith Miller has had enough written about him already. I'd a lot rather have Darryl Boston. If Miller plays more than about 20 games for the Mets, you'll know that whatever good baseball sense and decision-making capability the Mets ever had went right out the window with Davey Johnson and Joe McIlvaine.

Adam Stein:

Hubie Brooks appeared to get better in the second half. Actually with Murray and Gibson hot, he had more runners to drive in, he saw more fastballs which helped his average. He should fall off some in 1991 at age 34, and might get reduced playing time. Note that he wasn't happy about the trade to New York, and is sure to suffer abuse from fans who miss Strawberry.

Welford McCaffrey:

Terry Puhl can play left, center and right. Terry missed most of the 1990 season due to a shoulder problem requiring an operation. He became a free agent at the end of the season. Terry has been making $900,000 thanks to a contract signed when he was an essential starter on the team. For the past few years Terry has been relegated to being the Astros fourth outfielder, someone that Houston did not want to sign for $900,000 again.

Lary Bump:

In 1990, the Mets promoted Chuck Carr (I was going to say "brought up Chuck Carr" but it didn't sound right) from Double-A after Mark Carreon was hurt. Carr did what he does best — steal a base — then he too was injured and out for the season.

After a .259 start at Tidewater, he went down to Jackson and batted .258. Those averages are consistent with his five-year minor league career, and so are the 54 stolen bases he totaled in '90. The question is whether the leg injury took away too much of the 22-year-old switch hitter's speed so he won't be as effective in CF or on the bases. Monitor his progress at Tidewater.

PHILADELPHIA

Pete DeCoursey:

Barring a trade or injuries, pencil in Von Hayes and Lenny Dykstra for 150 games each, and Dale Murphy for 140. If either LF Hayes or RF Murphy is injured, expect Wes Chamberlain, a fast, powerful product of the Pittsburgh organization, to reap most of the playing time. Hayes is the easiest of the three to predict with certainty. He will hit at least 15 HRs, steal at least 15 bases, and score and drive in at least 70 runs. From June 4 to Aug. 4, the day Dale Murphy arrived in Philly, Hayes hit 1 HR in 111 ABs. Hitting in front of a genuine offensive threat, he bashed 4 HRs in a week and 3 more within the same month. Batting ahead of the powerful righty Murphy all season, look for Hayes' walks and homers to be up next season.

One easy way to predict Von's season is to watch the papers to see if he is fined for fighting with umpires. During seasons when he throws gauntlets of harsh words at them, they tend to strike back as they did last season, robbing the selective Hayes of one of his greatest attributes: his ability to force a pitcher to throw a strike. If Hayes is quiet, at least to the men in blue, he will be productive. Unless Murphy, Chamberlain, and Jones are all incapacitated, expect Hayes to deliver 25 HRs and 80 runs and RBIs.

If Hayes is traded, a Jones-Chamberlain platoon might be used until Jones is adequately showcased for a trade to the AL. After that, Chamberlain would be the man (see below).

Lenny Dykstra's season was no fluke. Like anyone who hit .330, a certain number of ground balls found holes due to luck, but by the end of the season, he slumped to a September BA of only .269. When your worst month of the season, tops your six-year career batting, slugging and on base averages, you're doing well.

Dykstra changed fundamentally as a hitter last year, and could easily become a Brett Butler clone, hitting .280-.310 every year, with a lot of runs scored. Do not expect his RBI column to stay at last year's lofty height, however: he hit .435 with runners in scoring position last year, a level which is not sustainable. None of his occasional injuries should affect his stealing another 30 bases at a very high success rate as in '90. His bulking up last year helped him stay strong; if you read in the spring that he has jettisoned his mini-hulk look, prepare for a drop in performance in August and Sept, as was true in '88 and '89. If your league counts either OBA or runs, he becomes invaluable. For his BA and SBs, he is only going to be very good next year.

Dale Murphy was acquired to hit 20-25 HRs and drive in 80 runs. If, like the Phillies, you are willing to endure a batting average between .235 and .255 to get that production, he's your man. Look for him to rest 20-25 times per year, mainly against righties with good curveballs. Murphy hit lefties at a .311 clip and slugged .617, while lefties held him to .214 BA and .324 SA. With Dykstra, Von Hayes, Daulton, and Kruk bracketing him, he will see more lefties next year, and be buoyed somewhat by that advantage.

Ron Jones can still hit, but so far has been unable to play more than 20 games in RF without blowing out one of his knees. Since he doesn't have three knees, the genetic defect that has felled him twice now, may have run its course. Look for him to get a spot start or two in LF and lots of PH activity early, and then to be sent to the AL for pitching, as the Phillies believe, with two consecutive season-ending knee injuries to back them up, that DH is his best chance to have a career.

Wes Chamberlain hit .270 with 2 HRs and 4 SBs in 46 ABs, including two thefts of third base last year, and will provide 20 HRs and 20 SBs as soon as he is given 400 ABs to acquire them. Chamberlain is more experienced in RF than in LF, and if you count errors in your league, be aware that he will make 10 or more before he masters LF.

Don't overestimate his opportunity to play. Wes will probably not get more than 40 games of playing time caddying for Von and Dale, and he will probably start the season in the minors. While September rosters allow 40 players, April goes back down to 25. Chamberlain is not thrilled about the idea of the minors. He hit better in Philadelphia than he did in AAA Buffalo. Don't let a poor start in Scranton fool you. If Chamberlain is brought up, grab him.

Sil Campusano will caddy for Dykstra, pinch-bunt, and play when a defensive replacement is needed in the late innings. Given Leyva's confidence in the defensive abilities of his trio, that will be seldom. If Dykstra misses a game or two, Campusano will replace him; if Nails were knocked out for a long period, the Phils would attempt to play Hayes there or acquire someone else, not go with Campusano full time. Sil will not get many more than 100 ABs, and there is no reason to expect much production from him.

John Kruk is a good left fielder and competent RF, and would be another backup if disaster struck one of the starters. If Jordan became the everyday 1B, then Kruk will spell Murphy occasionally against those tough RHP, but currently Jordan is much more likely to get that kind of treatment than Murphy. Randy Ready will only see OF action if lots of other people get hurt, because his defense is awful out there in the pasture.

Lary Bump:

Another one that Doughty let get away! Actually, Doughty's crime in letting Wes Chamberlain get away was not getting enough in return (unless you go by weight with Marshmelo Martinez, that is). It was not a happy year for Chamberlain in Buffalo. Coming off an Eastern League MVP year, a lot was expected from him, and when he started miserably, he and his teammates got down on him. One of the few failures in Terry Collins' masterful managing of the Bisons was an inability to get more out of Chamberlain and keep him and his teammates from each other's throats. Actually, Wes had a pretty good second half, to finish at .250, 6, 52. The 25-year-old righthanded batter needs to get more out of his talent. He can run, but was caught stealing 19 times in 33 attempts. He has a good arm, but he sometimes can't find a fly ball with a compass. Moving from RF to LF with the Phillies might ease the defensive pressure, and keep him in the lineup every day.

For Ron Jones, a lefthanded batter now 26, every year it's the same thing. Hit .290 with the Phillies, get hurt and miss the rest of the season. Actually, last year was a little different. He batted .276 for Philly, after rehabbing at Scranton (.264, 3, 26 in 148 ABs) before another season ended with a knee injury. He no longer qualifies as a rookie, but in the equivalent of less than half a major league season, he has a .286 average, 13 HR and 37 RBI. The question is whether his rickety knees will allow him to finish that or any season. Still worth a gamble.

PITTSBURGH

Andy Van Slyke will stay in center. His good 1990 season was lost between two giant bookends, Bonds and Bonilla. He is 30 years old now, but could still improve slightly over the .284-17-77-14 that he posted in 1990. Van Slyke is still coming back from a seriously pulled rib cage muscle that felled him in early 1989, when he slumped to a .237 BA. Someone is likely to bid Van Slyke up to the full value of his marvelous 1988 (.288-25-100-30) if his name comes up early. If he comes up late in your auction, you might get lucky.

Let's replay some of the comments from 1990 (this is really fun):

"Barry Bonds has been one of the best players for Rotisserie for three years."

"You have to expect Van Slyke to rebound [from .237-9-53] to 15-20 HR and 70-80 RBI."

"If I had to pick the one player most likely to increase output with a Kevin Mitchell style season in 1990, I would pick Bobby Bonilla." [P.D.]

And Bonds was age 26. How could you miss the Pittsburgh outfield with all that advice? You couldn't.

Pete DeCoursey:

Barry Bonds taught me an important lesson last year. It's a very good idea to expend months, blood, and sweat trading for one of your three favorite players in the majors, when he is in the process of winning an MVP. Just perks up the whole damn season. Going to try to do it again, this year. Come on, Von Hayes! Barry should repeat in every category except runs scored, where the ancillary weakening of the lineup (all those guys who took the money and scooted) may affect his total. This could, however, make him even more aggressive on the bases, a good thing for his stolen base total. If you ever want an example of a smart ballplayer with natural tools, watch Barry Bonds. Watch him steal at a high rate of success, watch him work counts for walks and extra-base hits, watch him rundown a deep fly. He is marvelous, and will stay so.

Rich Burkhardt:

Barry Bonds is like Bobby Bonilla plus great speed. The turf may already be starting to take it's toll on Bonds' knees; he was complaining an awful lot about them at the end of last season. If they start giving him too many problems and take away his speed, it reduces the talent gap between him and Bonilla.

Lary Bump:

Steve Carter is the only OF prospect remaining in Pittsburgh. He is a 6-4, 200-pound left-handed batter, and has been a singles hitter. At age 26, he has developed some power. His .303 average, 8 HR and 45 RBI don't look like much until you consider he played his home games at Buffalo's Pilot Field. Moving from old War Memorial Stadium into the new ballpark was roughly the equivalent of moving from Switzerland to the Sahara. Carter can play CF or LF, and should be able to contribute off the bench in Pittsburgh.

ST. LOUIS

The Cardinals may not have the best outfield in baseball, but they certainly have the newest. All three outfielders in 1991 will be newcomers to the National League.

Left field will be Bernard Gilkey, or a platoon with Gilkey and Milt Thompson. Thompson bats left, and he had terrible problems with lefties last year. Gilkey played against both righty and lefty pitchers (and did just fine against both) during his September call-up, so Thompson would have to earn his way into a platoon role. Gilkey hit .314 against righties in his brief callup, so there hasn't yet been any reason to sit him down against northpaws. Gilkey was .295-3-46-45 at Louisville last year.

Milt Thompson is clearly relegated to the fourth outfielder role. But he has been a fourth outfielder most of his career, and a highly productive one at that. Considering that Thompson was a consistent .290 hitter for six years before 1990, you must expect him to rebound from the horrible 1990 season. Consider also that Thompson is backing up three players who have never played even one full ML season among them, and you will see why I think a .265 BA with 15 steals make a conservative case for 1991.

Most people don't realize that Ray Lankford had an off year in 1990. He hit only .260 at Louisville, and had only 13 HR, 84 RBI, and 37 SB in AAA and NL combined. Back in 1989, Lankford was Texas League MVP, with a .317 BA and 98 RBI.

I like Lankford just as much as Juan Gonzalez for 1991 stats.

Felix Jose has been on my list of breakthrough candidates for three years now. Last year: "Felix Jose is the true prospect for the A's outfield. He has done just about everything you could ask at Tacoma: hit for average, hit for power, drive in runs, steal bases. The A's should find a place for him in 1990." The A's did find a place for him, in St. Louis. For the price of renting Willie McGee for one month, I think the A's got robbed. Watch Jose in 1991.

Rex Hudler is the best candidate for fifth outfielder and infield utility rolled into one. Now age 30, Hudler's career got squished in 1984-1985 when he couldn't make a role out of backing up Willie Randolph for the Yankees. Now Hudler has the equivalent of one big major league season (650 at bats) under his belt, and has produced 17 homers. Thanks to pinch-running chores, he has produced 63 SB in this distorted sample, but you get the idea. He can fly, and it's no illusion. For a $2 to $3 sub he is a fine investment. Hudler hit .327 in the second half last year. And don't forget all those rookies who need backing up.

And one more "I told you so," Alex Cole appeared in this section last year, right alongside Lankford and Gilkey. In fact, he was listed first, and made it to the majors first.

Pete DeCoursey:

The Cards pasture crew will be the best source of bargains and sleepers in any NL draft. Lankford will be overpriced, but Gilkey, Thompson and Jose will all steal bases and hit for a decent average. Thompson fell back to his old inability to hit lefties, but even playing only part-time as the 4th OF could easily steal 20 bases and hit 5 HRs. Jose may also be undervalued in some drafts, and he will hit 12-20 HRs next year. Gilkey and Lankford will carry on the Cards tradition of hitting for average and stealing bases, Lankford will show line drive power and hit 6-10 HRs; Gilkey will have to pay a public utility for any power he wants to display.

Adam Stein:

With 600 at bats apiece, based on 1990 pro-rata major league performance, Ray Lankford would hit .286 with 15 HR, 60 RBI and 40 SB; Bernard Gilkey would be .297-9-28-54; and Felix Jose would be .271-21-91-28. They may fall short of these projections, but they will still be worth $15 each.

Lary Bump:

At last summer's SABR convention, John Benson asked me what minor leaguers I liked. The names Bernard Gilkey and Ray Lankford jumped into the front of my mind. John asked if either one could replace Milt Thompson in '91, and I replied that both could replace him right then. Actually, it's more likely that Gilkey will replace Vince Coleman in LF (if he's traded) and Lankford will — in fact, already has — take over CF from Willie McGee. Gilkey, a 24-year-old righthanded batter, appeared to have the better season in '90 — .295 and 45 SB at Louisville to .260 and 29 steals. But add in 10 HR, 72 RBI, an 81 per cent SB success rate and superior defense, and Lankford, a 24-year-old lefty batter, moves closer. It also was the poorest-hitting season he has had. Gilkey's season was his best of six as a pro. He needs to improve his SB percentage (He was thrown out 32 times last year) and his indifferent fielding. After last season, the last thing the Cardinals need is another poor-fielding OF. Gilkey has consistently walked more than he has struck out. Last year's OBPs at Louisville — .388 for Gilkey, .362 for Lankford — were typical of their careers. Joe Torre can put them at the top of his lineup and watch them go.

SAN DIEGO

The Padres outfield in December 1990 was "Tony Gwynn and four question marks." It sounds like a pop music group. Question Mark and the Mysterions, resurfaced in San Diego as gray-haired rockers. Seriously, any analyst would have to believe that the Padres were looking for an established outfielder or two in January 1991.

Tony Gwynn you know already. The four-time NL batting champ. The .329 lifetime hitter. The guy who was hitting .237 in mid June with a damaged thumb and still won a batting title. Chris Gwynn's older brother.

Gwynn is highly likely to rebound from his "poor" .309 season in 1990. He should also add a few SB to the total of 17 that was so disappointing to Rotisserie people. We won't see .370 with 56 SB again, but we will see another BA title from Tony Gwynn, in 1992 if not in 1991.

And the question marks:

Thomas Howard is a high-speed switch-hitter coming off a .328 season at Las Vegas. You have to be cautious with PCL batting averages, but Thomas is a genuine talent, likely to give you 20 SB if he gets about 450 AB (which seems likely). Howard was used against both righty and lefty pitching in his 1990 call-up, and could play LF full time. He also might platoon with rightyhitting Jerald Clark. Howard did you a favor by hitting only .188 in the majors, keeping his talent a secret from people who don't look beyond the October USA Today stats.

Clark has been around the majors, off and on, for four years counting 1991. He has more power than Howard, and the same high-average background at Las Vegas. Clark won't produce much if he faces only lefty pitching. Based on 100 at bats in 1990, he likes facing righties better, anyway: .354 vs. RHP and .189 vs. LHP.

Shawn Abner is the best talent in the bunch. He's still only 25, younger than either Clark or Howard. Abner has been promoted faster, and accordingly hasn't accumulated the same minor league credentials. At age 21 he had one good year (.300-11-85) in 1987 at Las Vegas, and has devoted his efforts to helping the Padres ever since. They sent him down twice for half-seasons in the minors, and he failed to hit even .270. As a .219 lifetime hitter he isn't going to attract many high bids.

Darrin Jackson was my favorite in this group a year ago, but he was such a flop in 1990 (even as a midseason pickup) that I have to force myself to be objective in 1991. Maintaining a sense of perspective, Jackson now has the equivalent of one season in the majors, 487 at bats, with stats of .248-13-49-8, not too bad if you could squeeze them all into one year. Jackson bats right and plays CF just like Abner; he hits lefties better while Abner doesn't have any overwhelming preference. Absent other names coming along, I foresee Abner getting more PT while sharing with Jackson.

Oscar Azocar became one of numerous contenders to share the San Diego outfield. With New York his job was to keep Deion Sanders interested in baseball. When Deion went to the Atlanta Falcons, Oscar lost his outfield job. He's a heck of a nice guy, but a horribly free swinger unlikely to go anywhere. I asked Oscar about his second (and final) walk of the 1990 season. Was he learning patience? "No, no," he said, "They give me the take sign." And this was on a 3-2 pitch. Wow.

Lary Bump:

A 26-year-old switch hitter, Thomas Howard has been touted for several years as strong defensive OF candidate. He also has batted .300 three of the last four seasons. Last year at Las Vegas, he averaged .328 with 5 HR and 51 RBI in 89 games. He probably doesn't have the arm to play RF in the majors, but he can fill in at LF and CF.

This book is full of suggestions to study spring training box scores. In some cases, we may be agonizing over the 5th outfielder or the 24th man on a roster. In the case of San Diego's outfield, we are probably talking about a new regular. If you can use another 400 at bats and the numbers that go with them, pay attention to this situation! If you can't get Florida/Arizona stats, get the WINNING ROTISSERIE BASEBALL newsletter, and we'll summarize them for you.

SAN FRANCISCO

Batting champ Willie McGee has never shown the ability to put together two consecutive seasons of star performance. He was a marvelous bargain in 1990 auctions, but will likely be overpriced this year. The silliest thing about following Last Year values is that you are always a year behind. When a player is soaring to new heights, you're looking back at his jumpoff point, and passing. When he crashes back to earth, you're staring at the apogee of the smoke trail, and bidding your ass off. If you can't stand forecasts, go with two-year averages.

Thom Rogers:

Kevin Mitchell had bone spurs removed from his wrist in the off-season. Even with them he had a great season(.290-35-93) His second half numbers were weaker than the first half, but still decent. The dropoff can be attributed to the wrist problem. I'm looking for a big year from Mitchell: 550 AB, and .290-40-100-4.

After sitting out most of last year with a leg injury (and a new free agent contract), Kevin Bass will have enough pride and talent to show he was worth the price. Candlestick is good (hmmmm . . . better) to LH hitters, so he should do well against righties.

Rob Wood:

Kevin Bass (RF) is fully recovered from knee surgery, and looks to be an integral part of the Giants offense in 1991. Don't shy away from Bass.

Rick Parker (RF): This was the guy who was hitting .237 at Double-A when the Giants acquired him in the Bedrosian deal in August 1989. Pass.

Lary Bump:

Mark Leonard, a 26-year-old lefthanded hitter, has been a solid run-producer in the minors. Last season he batted .333 with 19 HR and 82 RBI in 109 games at Phoenix before joining the right field derby in San Francisco. An injury cut short his season. There's no reason why he can't challenge for a job this year. He doesn't run much (6-for-9 at Phoenix), but he has a good arm.

The Giants have a penchant for taking infielders from Phoenix and making them outfielders (possibly because they have such a gaping hole in RF). Rick Parker, late of the Phillies' organization, played 3B at Phoenix, and earned his first major league shot by batting .335. He has little power (19 HRs in 6 pro seasons), but runs on occasion (24 steals with the Giants and their top farm last year). The righthanded hitter is 28, so his future is limited. Leonard would be a better choice.

AMERICAN LEAGUE DESIGNATED HITTERS

As Susan Nelson reminded me last year, "You do not build your team around the DH." True in baseball, true in Rotisserie. We are not going to make a major effort of scrutinizing likely DH candidates.

Most of the people who will appear at DH have already been discussed, especially in the 1B/OF essays. Few of the AL teams use a roster spot for a player who is just a DH. Every day, when the field manager gives the ump a line-up card, the team must say, "Here is the name of our DH." But at the end of spring training, no team is required to say, "This guy is our DH." Most teams choose not to give the DH role permanently to one individual, or even to a pair of platooners.

Many changes revolve around the DH spot. Fading veterans stop at DH on the way out. Some linger for years; others vanish rapidly. Emerging rookies often pause at DH during their arrival in the majors. They show what they can do with a bat, then take a position in the field. Players in the process of losing their jobs take the DH role while watching the new guy in the field. Players nursing injuries use the DH role for short term rehab purposes.

Anybody can be a DH. That means that the selection of the DH can impact more positions than any other decision. If the manager says, "Joe Bimbleman is my shortstop," or "Bimbleman is my catcher," such statements affect only a couple of MI's or a couple of catchers. But if the manager says, "Joe Bimbleman is my DH," that decision could change the total at bats available to seven other players: four outfielders, two infielders, and perhaps a catcher or two.

Because the DH is used as an entry level position for emerging talent, and a counseling-out position for aging stars, it pays to study the DH assignments in the box scores. You can often see the future in DH selections. At a minimum, you can see who is in the manager's doghouse, who has favored status, and who will most benefit from (or be hurt by) changes in other players' roles.

Finally, remember there are very, very few minor league "DH prospects." Any youngster who can hit has been discussed in the essay covering the position that he plays best.

BALTIMORE

The acquisition of Dwight Evans does not imply that the Orioles like his outfield play. They had too many outfielders already. Don't listen to the protests and denials. Evans may want to play RF, and the O's may have a sincere hope that Evans is healthy enough to play some in the field, but "Evans, 9" in their lineup is not a plan for the future; it's "Evans, DH."

Mickey Tettleton and Sam Horn appeared in a combined total of 103 games at DH last year. You must expect that they will lose some at bats with Evans in the lineup. Dwight hit 26 of his 33 HR against righties in 1989 and 1990, so you can't expect Horn's left-handed bat or Tettleton's switch hitting to help them compete against Evans.

The RHH backup to Evans, aside from the numerous outfielders and cornermen who will appear as DH, is catcher Chris Hoiles.

BOSTON

Jack Clark is likely to emerge as the regular DH with Boston, appearing occasionally at 1B or even OF. Somebody who has the time can study the historical success of teams that have an everyday DH. In 1989, the five teams that played Dave Parker, Harold Baines, Brian Downing, Dwight Evans, and Jeffrey Leonard, were a combined 429-381, a .530 winning percentage. In 1990, the four teams that had a 100-game DH on their Roster (Evans, Baines, Chris James, Dave Parker) were .528.

If there is a change in Boston, it will be a switch within the lineup. Clark may play 1B with Mo Vaughn at DH. Carlos Quintana (if he stays with the team) will make an occasional DH appearance, as will Mike Marshall, Phil Plantier, and almost every one of the Red Sox hitters.

CALIFORNIA

The DH slot could provide a safety gap for young Lee Stevens, if the return of Wally Joyner displaces him from 1B. In December the Angels were considering free agents Chili Davis and Brian Downing as possible "full time" DH's. If either signs, Stevens will feel just a little more pressure.

CHICAGO WHITE SOX

The arrival of Cory Snyder puts a squeeze on Carlos Martinez, who might have expected to DH against lefty pitching. Now it looks like Snyder against the southpaws, and Dan Pasqua vs. RHP. Going into the winter meetings, Dan Pasqua was the favorite to get the most DH duty. If Snyder gets off to a good start, the White Sox will be less inclined to make him sit down for Pasqua. Snyder had 10 HR against RHP last year, and just 4 against lefties.

Matt Stark is a credible candidate to play his way into some DH time if he has a good spring training, or to get in as a mid-season call-up if he starts the year at Triple-A and puts up good numbers.

Adam Stein:

One of the popular questions related to Rotisserie is "Who is the WORST player in baseball?" Every year, baseball fans and baseball magazines have opinions and/or statistics as to who is the best player — Rickey Henderson, Ryne Sandberg, Barry Bonds, Jose Canseco, Eric Davis — but little is ever said or studied on who the worst player is.

The "worst" player shouldn't be a part-time player, or someone who just barely gets a spot on a roster. I don't think it means a lot to say that Dann Bilardello is the worst player in the majors, and I don't want to talk about THAT player. If the best player is the one who helps his team (or an arbitrary team) most, then the worst player should be the one who hurts his team most. Players can hurt their team in two ways — bad defense and using up offensive outs without getting as much production as a player who would replace him.

Cory Snyder is probably not the worst player in the major leagues, but he comes close.

CLEVELAND

Chris James was the regular DH in 1990, handling lefty and righty pitching both just fine. The biggest threat to James' playing time was probably Joey/Albert Belle, but Belle had winter ball problems.

Bill Gray:

Joey Belle was canned by his winter ball employer, Ponce, on November 20, because of (you guessed it) behavior problems. He has severely jeopardized his future with the Indians; they are simply not counting on him for 1991. Although Cleveland didn't offer arbitration to Candy Maldonado, his return looked probable because no other team wanted him enough to make a big offer.

Steve Goldman:

Among those most likely to fill the DH spot or see action there are Chris James, Albert Belle, Beau Allred, Jeff Manto and Brook Jacoby. Should Candy Maldonado re-sign with the team, he could see action here also. However, the picture is so unclear, it's impossible to speculate with any kind of certainty as to what will happen.

DETROIT

The Tigers will parade a horde of outfielders, first basemen and utility infielders through the DH slot. Last year, Sparky Anderson used 18 different people at DH (everyone except the pitchers), with Dave Bergman leading the long list.

Tony Bernazard may end up getting more time at DH than in the field. The switch hitter, who peaked with Cleveland in 1986 (.301-17-73-17) played for the Fukuoka team in Japan last year. Please don't ask me how to pronounce Fukuoka.

KANSAS CITY

The arrival of Kirk Gibson led to the abandonment of Gerald Perry. KC will award Gibson the lion's share of at bats, with the remainder going to Danny Tartabull (if he stays with the Royals), George Brett (if and when he doesn't well enough to play 1B), and an assortment of backup outfielders and utilitymen. Jeff Conine's first major league impact may be delivered through the DH role. Watch Conine very carefully, before shelling out big bucks. He fractured his wrist in winter ball, and may need surgery. If you want to know how badly a wrist injury can affect a hitter, ask Jesse Barfield. Ouch.

MILWAUKEE

Dave Parker continues to amaze people. At age 39 he led the Brewers in hits and RBI. He isn't going to improve in 1991, but his half life seems to be about 15 years, making him worth a gamble if the price is right.

MINNESOTA

The Twins have long been dissatisfied with Gene Larkin as their "regular" DH. They tried to trade Larkin, but discovered that slow singles hitters are the least marketable commodity in the hitting department. Minnesota eventually tested 16 different people in the nonfielder slot last year. For 1991, look for Larkin to spend more time on the bench, with Dan Gladden (if he's still around) and Paul Sorrento leading another large field of DH candidates.

NEW YORK YANKEES

With Don Mattingly back at 1B, Kevin Maas will move to DH, and (hopefully) he will like it. Steve Balboni and Matt Nokes will provide a right/left combo that leads an assortment of alternatives. Credit the Yankees with rediscovering the value of left-handed hitting. Seeing Balboni at DH on a regular basis over the past two years made me want to raise the question: of the many championship teams that ever played in Yankee Stadium, which one didn't have an arsenal of left-handed power hitters? (Answer: none.)

OAKLAND

Harold Baines restores the regularity of DH duty, that was lost when Dave Parker went to Milwaukee. Baines is just age 32 this year. A full year in the Oakland lineup will enhance his stats, more than a year of aging detracts from them. Expect a slight but definite increase in value.

SEATTLE

The purpose of obtaining Pete O'Brien was (supposedly) to give Alvin Davis the DH job, but 11 others helped Davis do that job in 1990. Assuming that A.D. stays in Seattle, he will be the premier full time DH in baseball. It is unusual to see the job handed to someone only 29 (30 this year). The man with no position, Tino Martinez, will appear extensively at DH if Davis leaves or gets into the doghouse, or if Davis or O'Brien gets injured.

TEXAS

The Rangers follow the Sparky Anderson approach to designated hitting, i.e. giving the job to the largest possible number of co-workers. Jack Daugherty is likely to be the number one beneficiary in a large field. Steve Buechele could keep his AB count up with DH duty, if someone like Dean Palmer pushes him aside.

TORONTO

J.L. Feinstein:

The Blue Jays DH scenario appears half-settled. Rance Mulliniks figures to get the call against all righties, but the DH against southpaws will depend on the resolution of the outfield battle.

If Gaston elects to go with Mark Whiten in RF, Carter moves to left. In that scenario, look for Glen Hill to be the right-handed DH. He'll get spelled occasionally by Mookie Wilson and/or Pat Tabler. If the Jays go with Hill in LF and Carter in right, look for Tabler to split the righty ABs at DH with Mookie. And, if Gaston really decides to play Mookie in left every day, Hill should get the lion's share of the ABs.

AMERICAN LEAGUE STARTING PITCHERS

BALTIMORE

Jeff Ballard and Bob Milacki in 1990 sunk back into the obscurity from which they had come. They were a combined 7-19 with a 4.70 ERA. Milacki was the workhorse of the staff in 1989, compiling 243 IP (a club record for rookies). A big guy (6' 4", 220 lbs.), he also threw 239 innings over three leagues in 1988. Milacki is one more living example of the lesson: don't project next year stats on the basis of performance during a September call-up. He impressed tremendously during his short stint with the O's in '88, giving up just 9 hits in 25 IP and posting a 0.72 era in his 3 starts, then produced a worthless ERA and ratio in his rookie year of 1989.

Credit Barry Wolven with projecting Jeff Ballard's downfall in last year's book: "Jeff Ballard is not as good as his 1989 W/L record. The high-flying baby birds might come down to earth and drag Ballard down with them." There were storm clouds on the horizon for Ballard during the winter of 1989-1990, arising from arthroscopic surgery to remove bone chips from his elbow. During this procedure a bone spur was found, so a follow-up operation was necessary. The fact that Ballard was once described as a potential staff ace is another lesson. You shouldn't fool around with the low-strikeout type of pitchers, certainly not with high expectations. Stick to the hard throwers, and concentrate on those who are healthy.

Take Ben McDonald, for example. He is the only Baltimore starter who throws hard enough to be half-way reliable, and McDonald is more than half way to being a sure thing in Rotisserie. There are few exceptions to the rule, "Don't waste money on starting pitchers." McDonald is one of those exceptions.

Pete Harnisch, the 1988 Baseball America number 1 prospect in the Southern League, managed a .500 record last year, and is a serious candidate for a full time starting role again in 1991. Curt Schilling had a chance to take the 5th starter's job in 1990, and has the same chance in 1991. He might also go to the pen. Schilling was a starter at Rochester in 1990, but was used exclusively in relief by the Orioles. His 2.54 ERA in 1990 is encouraging.

David Raglin:

The Orioles weren't making any announcements about starters during the winter. Ben McDonald is the only pitcher who obviously has a starting role for 1991. Pete Harnisch, Bob Milacki, Jeff Ballard and Dave Johnson are all good possibilities for the rotation. Jose Mesa pitched well in September (3-2, 3.86 in 7 starts), and he will get a chance to make the rotation. Curt Schilling is up in the air, but still can't be ruled out.

John Mitchell is out of the SP picture. Youngsters Francisco Delarosa, Jose Bautista, and Anthony Telford are nothing better than longshots. Telford is talented, and he made some good appearances last year, but he really came up too early. I was surprised that Baltimore promoted him. Keep in mind: there are plenty of minor league hurlers with great stats, especially in the "pitcher leagues" like the IL and EL. Most of the minor league stars never achieve success in the majors.

BOSTON

The Red Sox started the winter of 1990-91 with a decimated pitching staff. Roger Clemens took a long, forced rest in September. Greg Harris was also near collapse at the end of the year. After the season ended, Mike Boddicker quickly left for greener pastures in Kansas City.

Boston started climbing out of this hole by acquiring Matt Young and Danny Darwin. Young is of questionable value, with a long history of bad pitching. He is coming off a 1990 season that was a career peak, however, as he posted a 3.51 ERA in a hitters park, and deserved better than the 8-18 record. Darwin (from Houston) will give us one of the most severe tests of park effects in recent history. Both Darwin and Young are likely to ascend immediately to the number two and three spots in the rotation, behind Clemens. The fourth and fifth spots will likely go to two from the group including Tom Bolton, John Dopson, and Dana Kiecker. Dopson's physical condition is less than assured, and there is widespread curiosity about whether Kiecker and Bolton can repeat their unexpected effectiveness in 1990.

Tony Formo:

Matt Young (3.51 ERA, 8-18) was a solid starter for the Mariners in 1990, and would have had a better record with adequate offensive support. Despite a career history of injuries, Matt threw 225.1 innings, and seems likely to remain effective. Young broke in with the M's in 1983, and before he was traded to Los Angeles (and then Oakland) after the 1986 season, placed himself among Mariner career leaders in strikeouts, walks, and shutouts.

Isaac Kaufman:

Raising the Red Sox starting rotation in 1991 will be an act worthy of Lazarus. After leading the league in ERA by starting pitchers in 1990, they now need help.

Greg Harris was abysmal over the last six weeks of the season (after he beat the Blue Jays in Toronto with a masterpiece on August 26). When the injury to Clemens put the pressure on him, he struggled. With the new acquisitions, Harris is very likely headed back to the pen.

Dana Kiecker is the biggest question mark. Kiecker threw some great games last year, but in the end he had a losing record with a good team. Manager Morgan likes him, but there isn't room for a sixth starter. Kiecker, too, could end up as a reliever in 1991. If he keeps his spot in the rotation, I think he will mature, and I would predict 15 wins and a 3.65 ERA.

Tom Bolton has got me stumped. He was so bad for so long, and he IS a southpaw in Fenway. Despite the great half season, I still say: beware of the jinx.

Bill Gilbert:

From the moment Danny Darwin became a starter on July 1, 1990, he was one of the top 2 or 3 pitchers in the National League. His 2.21 ERA and 1.03 ratio were the lowest for pitchers with 162 or more innings. At age 35, Darwin's arm is sound. He would have been the ace of the Astros' staff in 1991. In Fenway he will very probably fall short of his brilliant 1990 figures, but fifteen wins with an ERA down around 3.00 and a ratio near 1.20 should be achievable. [10-12 wins with an ERA of 3.50-4.00 or worse is more likely. (PD)]

Fred Percival:

While the importance of strikeouts in the overall scheme of pitching varies from pitcher to pitcher, strikeouts are very important indeed to Roger Clemens. Over the past four seasons he has averaged more than seven strikeouts per start, every year. Clemens gets his high K totals the old-fashioned way: he pitches to a LOT of people. Actually, too many people in the opinion of Project Scoresheet's Boston staff.

	IP	K/Start	IP/Start	CG	ERA	BB/Start
1987	282	7.1	7.8	18	2.97	2.31
1988	264	8.3	7.5	14	2.93	1.77
1989	253	6.6	7.2	8	3.13	2.66
1990	228	6.7	7.4	7	1.93	1.74

No, Billy Martin wasn't Roger's manager in 1987-88. But John McNamara did ride his best horse awfully hard, and by the time Joe Morgan took over in mid-'88, the Rocket's arm was definitely out of warranty. A ribcage injury that ruined the last two months of his 1988 season masked some disturbing inconsistency; then 1989 and 1990 raised the likelihood that Clemens will never be the in-your-face, complete game dominator of yore.

Boston's ace has obviously lost much of his strength, and Tom Seaver observed that his was a very tired looking arm back in 1989. And although Roger's IP total declined once again in 1990, only Jack Morris and Chuck Finley pitched more 1990 AL innings. As those innings have piled up, it has become increasingly important for Clemens' curve to find the strike zone; when it doesn't, the fastball can look a bit larger to the hitters.

The key question is whether this pitcher can make the classic transition from power to finesse and still be effective (a la Seaver). The indications during 1990 were mixed. The ERA was great, but the failing arm was disturbing. So far, it looks like Roger is still relying on what worked in the past to win. A connection between Clemens' strikeouts and success can be made by breaking individual starts into two groups based on the number of strikeouts/outing. Look at 1988. Roger had 18 starts in which he struck out 9 or more batters. In these games his record was 12-3 with a 1.57 ERA. He had 17 starts with fewer than 9 K's, going 6-9 and 4.51. For 1989, the K divider is lower, but the dichotomy still exists.

	Starts	IP	ER	ERA	IP/Start
7 or more Ks:	16	124	34	2.47	7.75
6 or fewer Ks:	20	129	54	3.76	6.47

On average, Roger pitched well into the seventh inning in his low-K games, so early showers don't account for the difference in per-game strikeout totals. In fact, the opposite is true. When Roger is on his game he strikes hitters out. When he isn't, the hitters strike back. And Roger's game is still raring back and getting the ball to the plate just as fast as he can make it go. Unfortunately, his arm is not the same rocket launcher that he brought into the league in 1985.

One big variable in 1990 was the catching. Tony Pena was a great help, after working with the worst catchers in the league in 1989. Hopefully, in 1991, Pena can help with that transition which Seaver accomplished so well.

Lary Bump:

Rookie possibilities include Tom Fischer, John Leister, Derek Livernois, and Kevin Morton. Leister was one of the few who failed the open tryouts for starters with the Bosox last year. I was surprised one day when I heard manager Joe Morgan on a pre-game radio show, and he said Leister was one guy he saw at Pawtucket who could help the Boston club. The ex-Michigan State QB had a 1.61 ratio and 5.78 ERA with the PawSox, so his 1.94 and 4.76 in two games with the big club shouldn't have come as a surprise. At 30, he's probably out of chances.

That means the Sox may have to dip down to Double-A New Britain if they need to come up with a starter. They had three promising young lefties there — Fischer (1.41, 4.19), Livernois (1.15, 1.98) and Morton (1.22, 3.81). One or more may see some time in Boston this summer.

CALIFORNIA

When Bud Black signed his huge contract with San Francisco, his supporters justified the price by saying that Black had been better than Mark Langston over the last two years. This isn't so much an elevation of Black as it is a condemnation of Langston.

Langston suffered a bad case of BCS (big contract syndrome) in 1990. His performance slipped a little in every observable category, adding up to results that were totally unsatisfactory. From 1989 to 1990, on a per-inning basis, Langston gave up 22% more hits, 4% more walks, and he got 7% fewer strikeouts. The net result is that he became mediocre. Nonetheless, the fastball is still there. Langston is good bet for a comeback season. He will be cut loose by almost everyone who bought him last year, and there is one owner who won't be bidding against you. People who lost Langston to the NL during 1989 (and those who lost him from the NL to the AL last winter) also harbor bitter feelings toward him. I expect bargain prices on Langston in many auctions this year.

Chuck Finley rises to the ace role while Langston is down in the dumps. Finley has been consistently excellent for two years. His ratio was up a trifle in the second half of 1990, but don't worry. If you need an ace pitcher and you are willing to pay, Finley is your man. Last year he cost an average of only $13, and often went for less than $10. Don't expect widespread bargain prices in 1991. In fact, Finley will be retained and unavailable in most auctions. Love that splitter! By the way, we claim another "I told you so" on Finley last year: "a good quality southpaw just coming into his own ... don't let his minor second half injury cause you undue worry (although it would be great to tell your opponents what a big deal it is). He gives up much less than a hit per inning, and has an average Game Score of 59 — tops among all A.L. lefties." How could he have been so inexpensive after that recommendation? Doesn't everybody read this book?

More from 1990 [I love picking these quotes]: "Bert Blyleven had no business producing the kind of numbers he had in 1989. Expect him to take a big tumble." Send money, please, no cards or flowers. For 1991: Bert Blyleven? How many 40-year-old pitchers can one league support? Blyleven had shoulder problems last year, and he produced only half the innings that he was pitching three, four, and five years ago. He may get a spot in the rotation, but I still say 1989 was a fluke. Steer clear.

Kirk McCaskill couldn't seem to make up his mind last year, if he wanted to be a bum or a savior. He pitched like both at different times, ending up with a season that was clearly inferior to his 1989 campaign. Elbow bone chips (no, that's not a new organic snack) may have been cleared up by surgery, but McCaskill must be treated with suspicion. He has gone from "diamond in the rough" to "talent impaired by wear and tear," without stopping in between to deliver even one great season.

Jim Abbott was plagued by inconsistency during 1990. He may have helped the Angels, but he sure didn't help you. At age 23 he should be improving, so the question is: why was his second half ratio last year 1.50?

Finley, Langston, McCaskill, Abbott and Blyleven were the five starters (in that order) are the most likely rotation. Floyd Bannister, a Yakult Swallow during 1989, will challenge for a spot. Mike Fetters had a 0.99 ERA after five starts for Edmonton last year; he was used as a reliever by the Angels.

Lary Bump:

The good prospects are Joe Grahe and Scott Lewis.

Grahe, a 23-year-old U. of Miami right-hander, drew mixed reviews last season. After starting with a 1.50 ratio and 5.14 ERA at Midland, he moved up to Triple-A Edmonton. His numbers of 1.15 and 1.35 there earned him a trip to California, where his 1.71 ratio and 4.98 ERA indicated he may not be ready for prime time. Or perhaps he'll have to make it in a spot relief role. Major-league left-handed batters clipped for a .370 average.

The unheralded Lewis, also a right-hander, was the ace of the Edmonton staff at 1.32 and 3.90. He pitched extremely well (0.73, 2.20) in two starts with the big club. Lewis, 25, is the kind of pitcher who could plug along and be a solid contributor as a fourth or fifth starter, especially if Bert Blyleven can't cut it anymore. Grahe has better potential to be a star, but probably not this year.

Kirk McCaskill and Willie Fraser improved markedly in the second half last year. McCaskill has been mentioned in many trade talks. Fraser might be able to regain the starter spot that he earned as a rookie, then lost.

CHICAGO WHITE SOX

Charlie Hough signed with Chicago on December 20. By order of the Commissioner, all reports of this transaction must include mention that White Sox manager Jeff Torborg was the catcher for Hough's first major league game. Hough threw 252 innings when he was 40 (in 1988) and continues to average 200 IP per year since then. He still works as hard as any pitcher, practicing infield play and anything else that can give him an edge. For Rotisserie, of course, he is basically worthless.

Greg Hibbard is a very consistent, intelligent, finesse-type pitcher, assured of a spot in the rotation on opening day. Melido Perez keeps missing the strike zone with his split-finger pitch. If he improved his accuracy by just a couple of inches, he could be highly effective, but he hasn't shown any progress in two years. Wayne Edwards is a good candidate for the fifth starter role.

Jack McDowell had a fine second half (9-5, 3.62 ERA, and 1.24 Ratio) and begins 1990 as the staff ace, now that Eric King is gone. The next emerging talent is Alex Fernandez. If he doesn't succeed in 1990, it won't be on account of too little practice. Last year Alex worked 280 innings in total. The White Sox are frankly not careful about abusing young arms. Who was the last Chisox pitcher who had several consecutive good seasons? Tommy John? Billy Pierce?

Jon Dunkle:

McDowell is now approaching the level of greatness that was once expected of him. Rotisserie veterans remember McDowell well from the campaign of 1988. He had produced a 3-0 record and 1.97 ERA in his September 1987 call-up, and he attracted sky-high prices in 1988 auctions. Jack won only 5 games 1988, and spent all of 1989 in the minors. His name always comes up now as an example of misleading September stats. Last year McDowell led the team in strikeouts and tied for the lead in wins as he and Greg Hibbard went 14-9. McDowell still has problems with the home run ball. In the new Comiskey Park I expect the number of homers to escalate. If he can avoid a surge in HR, he has the potential to win twenty games in a season.

When talking about the Chicago White Sox, the image of youth comes to mind. Before Hough, the White Sox rotation of Greg Hibbard, Melido Perez, Jack McDowell, and Alex Fernandez had an average age of only 23 at the start of the season.

Hibbard, the best left-hander and potentially the staff ace, posted a 14-9 record with a 3.16 ERA. however, he allowed 202 hits in 211 innings pitched. A typical Hibbard line looks something like this:

	IP	H	R	ER	W	K
Hibbard	6	10	2	2	2	3

Well, his ratio wasn't really 2.00 (it was 1.26), but you get the idea. He isn't going to hurt you in 1991 if he puts up numbers like he had in 1990, but his 1990 stats were helped by 25 double plays that often got him out of big jams. There is a clear possibility that he could do much worse in 1991, if his luck changes. For a premier Rotisserie selection, you want someone more overpowering. As a fourth or fifth Rotisserie starter, he should be adequate.

The supposed staff ace at the beginning of 1990, Melido Perez, did not resolve his old problem of giving up runs early. Perez is often unable to get through the early innings without getting in trouble. His average appearance lasts only 5 innings, giving him a losing record and a 4.61 ERA. For the second year in a row, he led the team in walks, while striking out an average of over seven batters per nine innings. While they have not given up hope on him yet, the Sox will consider moving Perez (either out of the rotation or out of Chicago in a trade), especially if/when Alvarez and Hall make it to the majors.

After refusing to become a Brewer so he could go to college, Alex Fernandez was drafted by the White Sox and took the Ben McDonald route to the majors. Although he started only thirteen games and allowed a .265 batting average by opponents, Fernandez should be an immediate success in the majors. He tied for second in most complete games for a White Sox pitcher as his average start lasted 6.74 innings. He is a good, power pitcher, highly recommended for Rotisserie. Unless he has a flashy spring training, he could be a steal in many auctions.

Last year I predicted greatness for Grady Hall and I am doing it again this year. There is one negative point about Grady Hall, that he is older than any current White Sox starter. The positive aspects of Hall are plentiful. He tied for third in AAA for games started and was second in innings pitched. His starts averaged over six and a half innings. Hall was third in complete games in the Pacific Coast League, second in wins, and was named the top left-handed pitcher in the PCL. If Hall makes the roster, look for him as a decent $1 buy, late in the auction.

Dic Humphrey:

For your long-term farm system, don't forget 21 year-old Wilson Alvarez. Proceeds of the trade that sent Harold Baines to Texas, young Alvarez produced a 2.06 ERA and 1.17 ratio for Tulsa in 1989, then struggled at Vancouver last year (7-7, 6.00). He will probably start the year back in the minors, but could emerge in midsummer. Alvarez has the potential to succeed quickly.

Lary Bump:

The young guns in Chicago are backed up by more young guns coming out of the minors. The best for 1991: Wilson Alvarez, Tom Drees, Alex Fernandez, and Jerry Kutzler.

Fernandez, 21, isn't officially a rookie any more. But I had to say what a great prospect he is. The righty didn't pitch like a rookie last year anyway (1.40 ratio, 3.80 ERA with the Chisox) after picking on batters in the Gulf Coast (0.79, 1.84) and Southern (1.04, 1.08) leagues.

Kutzler, a 26-year-old right-hander has been on the fringes of the big leagues for a couple of years. He followed up his 1.40, 4.20 performance at Vancouver with brutal statistics of 1.66, 6.03 in seven starts for Chicago.

As for Drees, a 26-year-old lefty, if the White Sox didn't call him up after he pitched three no-hitters in Triple-A in '89, do you think they'll ever bring him to the majors? His numbers in his second season at Vancouver weren't bad for the PCL — 1.49 ratio, 3.98 ERA. Having an ERA almost identical to your team's (4.03) is not the way to get promoted, though.

After becoming the first major leaguer born in the '70s and a focal point in a trade from Texas, southpaw Alvarez, 21, slid backward last season — 1.50 ratio, 4.27 ERA at Birmingham, 1.89, 6.00 with Vancouver. If Alvarez starts better, look for him in Chicago before the season's out. Don't hold your breath on Drees or Kutzler.

CLEVELAND

Bill Gray:

Look for Cleveland to supply Rotisserie leagues with only two known quantities in Greg Swindell and Tom Candiotti. Eric King is a clever and accomplished pitcher, but his physical condition is questionable, and you don't want to gamble on Cleveland's group of youngsters at the beginning of the year. Swindell, while less than a sure thing now, can regain his dominance at age 26. Candiotti, 34, may fade away rapidly. With a more productive offense, strengthened middle relief, and a bulletproof closer, the starting pitchers can win often.

In 1990, Greg Swindell reversed his old trend of "Good first half, bad second half." He was out of shape when the season began and did not want to injure his arm by throwing his bread and butter pitch, the slider. Consequently, he was ineffective in his first seventeen starts going 4-5 with 8 no-decisions. His ERA in mid-July was 4.45 after 115 innings. His ratio was 1.37. In the second half, Swindell went 8-4 although the ERA and ratio remained high. I think there is reason to be concerned about Swindell. He was lucky to have made it to the All-Star break at 4-5. He could easily have been 4-10. The second half wins were due largely to great work out of the bullpen by Steve Olin and Doug Jones.

Compared to 1989, Swindell gave up 2 more hits per nine IP in 1990. Don't be misled into thinking he was anything close to what he was in previous seasons. Anytime pitchers give up more than a hit per inning, be concerned. You could make a case that Swindell has a lot going for him. He is still young, and has produced great Rotisserie numbers before. There is always a chance that he will finally have that 20 win season that has eluded him. Swindell always generates a lot of interest. My advice, however, is to let someone else pay the optimistic price in 1991. If he continues to get hit, he'll get killed, and he'll kill you, too.

Tom Candiotti pitched over 200 innings for the fifth consecutive year. That's good. He also spent time on the disabled list for the third straight year. That's bad. The arm trouble may be taking a toll on Candiotti. His ERA rose to 3.65 last year after an excellent 3.10 in 1989. Like Swindell, the hits per inning were also up from 1989 to 1990: 0.91 to 1.02. His 15-11 record led the team. Keep one thing in mind when Candiotti's name comes up at your auction. He is now throwing his knuckleball about 85% of the time. It is less strain on his arm than the curves and sliders. A pitcher in this mode is risky.

The knuckleball specialists of our time can never say just what that pitch is going to do. In the windy stadium Cleveland calls home, Candiotti presents the risk of a high ratio and ERA. Coming off 1989 with an excellent 1.17 ratio, Candiotti's 1.29 last year might be viewed as an anomaly. I view it as a knuckleball. I don't blame Tom for wanting to protect his arm and extend his fine career. I just don't think that his roti-owners will be getting the type of numbers that they have come to expect from him. He could be good trade bait if you have him. If you can move him early in the season for some value, then you can sit back and watch his ratio kill somebody else. Remember, you read it here first.

Who will fill the number three, four and five spots in the rotation? John Farrell won't. He had elbow surgery on October 4, with no definite schedule for a return to the rotation, or even to begin throwing again. Late 1991 is the earliest estimate that anyone would mention during the winter. He had torn ligaments, bone chips and needed a relocation of the ulnar nerve. Bring up Farrell's name in conversation during March, to see who's paying attention. He's a good litmus test to find out who read the papers during the winter, and who didn't.

Speaking of news, the Tribe pursued and obtained Eric King and Shawn Hillegas from the White Sox. King is a question mark; his future will depend on the condition of his back and arm. "He is damaged goods," according to one source in Cleveland. As a child, King suffered from Sherman's disease, a degeneration of the spine with decaying vertabrae. Last year, King was on the DL from June 12 to July 16, and again from August 1 to September 2. When he pitched, the White Sox like to give him 6 or 8 days rest for his back to recover. King won't get much rest from Cleveland; they intend to work him hard. He will be installed as the number three starter on opening day. If healthy (one of the larger ifs of 1991), Eric is capable of a fine season. He was the White Sox most complete pitcher, in terms of repertoire.

In exchange for Bud Black last year, the Indians got three legitimate prospects in Mauro (Goose) Gozzo, Alex Sanchez and Steve Cummings. All have the potential to be solid major league pitchers, especially Sanchez. Hank Peters would be a dangerous Rotisserie manager.

Jeff Shaw (1.53, 4.29) pitched better for the Sky Sox than Mike Walker (1.67, 5.58), but Jeff was little better than a batting-practice pitcher (1.91, 6.66) with the Tribe. He is an equal-opportunity batting-practice pitcher; both lefties and righties stung him for a .356 average. Walker was less-than-sterling 1.64, 4.88 with the big club. Both are 24.

DETROIT

The morning-line rotation was Jack Morris, Frank Tanana, Walt Terrell, Bill Gullickson, and a pitcher to be named later.

When you look to Detroit for Rotisserie pitchers, consider that Sparky Anderson will often leave his more experienced starters in, to pitch out of trouble. It isn't so much that Sparky has changed his quick-hook approach to managing, as it is a recognition that he doesn't have a great bullpen with today's Tigers, while he trusts his veterans. The implication is that Frank Tanana, Walt Terrell and (especially) Jack Morris will often be on the mound in the 7th-8th-9th innings, risking damage to the ERA, when other pitchers would be safely in the clubhouse.

David Raglin:

Jack Morris is not a definite to return, but he is likely. Morris is a gutsy veteran, growing more vulnerable to the home run as years go by. He is a better pitcher than the 1990 numbers would indicate. Morris just needs to complete his adjustment to the loss of raw power. He is still only 35, and less-accomplished pitchers have been able to hang on with fewer tools than Morris now possesses.

In retrospect, 1990 may turn out to be the year when Morris began his new career as an ex-power pitcher. Late in the season, with some horrible 1990 stats already in the record books, he seemed to get on track and pitch within himself. Jack finished with four consecutive victories in September. He was only 7-9 in the second half, but kept his ERA under 4.00 and, perhaps the most encouraging sign, had a ratio of only 1.25 after the All Star break.

Tanana and Terrell are reasonably assured of spots in the rotation. They will continue to produce about the same as what you saw in 1990. Bill Gullickson will give plenty of innings, too. Jeff Robinson is someone the Tigers would like to get rid of. Kevin Ritz is simply not ready. Scott Aldred is a big talent, but for Rotisserie purposes he gives up too many walks. In a couple of years, Aldred should be very good.

Lary Bump:

Going into the winter meetings, Detroit was loaded with possibilities for promotion to the starting rotation: Scott Aldred, John DeSilva, David Haas, Randy Marshall, Rusty Meacham, Randy Nosek, and Steve Searcy. Here come the Tigers' young pitchers! Maybe not this year, but soon. Maybe Toledo finally will have a good team. Or perhaps the Tigers will be the White Sox of 1991.

Lefties Aldred, 22, and Searcy and righty Nosek, 24, have been tried somewhat and found somewhat lacking. All three pitched last season for Toledo — Aldred 1.75, 4.90; Searcy 1.18, 2.92; Nosek 1.63, 5.19 — and for Detroit — Aldred 1.60, 3.77; Searcy 1.69, 4.66; Nosek 2.29, 7.71. Searcy no longer is a rookie, but he is only 26.

The real hope for the Tigers lies in the youngsters coming up. Meacham, 23, led the Eastern League with 15 wins and compiled a 1.10 ratio and 3.13 ERA in one of the league's better parks for hitters. Haas, 25, came a long way in '90 — from 7 wins to 13 — with a 1.27 ratio and 2.99 ERA for London. After starting 0.87, 1.48 at Class A Lakeland, DeSilva joined them at London, where he had a 1.28 ratio and 3.74 ERA. He is a power pitcher (189 Ks in 180 IP.) Meacham has the best chance to hit Motown this year. Those three are right-handers, but the best of the lot last season was southpaw Randy Marshall, who followed up a 13-0 start at Fayetteville (0.72, 1.33, 9 walks in 101 innings) with a 7-2 log for Lakeland (1.18, 3.00). If he continues to show any sign of progress, he'll be in Detroit in '92.

Gary Gillette (1990):

Randy Nosek, Detroit's number 1 draft pick in 1985, is a power pitcher who can't get the ball over the plate.

Jeff Robinson's problems date back to the lack of blood circulation in the fingertips of his pitching hand, which terminated his awesome '88 season in August. Since then, although he professes to be completely recovered from that injury, he's had a series of nagging injuries which have sometimes kept him out of the rotation and sometimes kept him pitching poorly. Jeff's best out pitch is an excellent split-finger; his injury was caused by him jamming the ball deep between his index and middle fingers. Without his splitter, he's just another big young pitcher with a good, but not great, fastball.

Morris's problems are well-known — he's an aging power pitcher who has yet to convert his style effectively. Late last year, he seemed completely recovered from his elbow injury, turning in his best month of the season in September. Still, even his best was a 4.41 ERA. Jack's glory days are probably gone forever, but he should be good for 200 or so IP with an ERA around the league average next year.

Detroit management is really taken with Kevin Ritz, even though he has been mediocre when given a chance to pitch.

DuBois is a lefty control artist with a fastball in the low 80s, although he walks too many for a finesse pitcher.

Aldred is a sleeper. He's a young LHP whom the Tigers have their eyes on, but he may not be ready for the big time. Scott had an impressive year in AA in '89 (only 98 hits in 122 IP). Given the unsettled nature of the Detroit mound corps, Aldred could be called up during the season.

KANSAS CITY

Mike Boddicker pitching in Kansas City is "fantasy baseball" for real. He had a 1.40 ratio in the second half of 1990, but that was at Fenway. Unless the physicians give you a reason to be skeptical, you have to love Boddicker for your roster this year. Kevin Appier was 8-5 with a 2.66 ERA and a 1.19 ratio in the second half last year. Put his name on your "wanted" list. He might even improve. Saberhagen is always capable of a great season, but I expect he will be priced beyond anything reasonable. The other Royals starters don't excite me as individuals, but you should scout all of them. When in doubt, taking any KC pitcher is usually better than the alternative.

Marc Bowman:

Kansas City is a great place to look for pitching. The Royals staff is young and throws hard, and they play in a great pitcher's park. In most Rotisserie leagues, eight to ten Royals pitchers will be taken. John Wathan doesn't like to pull his starters early, so they get ample opportunity to accumulate wins. The relief corps was a disaster last year, but should be helpful to the starters in 1991, especially if Mark Davis can produce a "normal" season. Pat Dobson will help all of them, especially Davis. I am really optimistic about the Royals pitchers helping their team (and yours) this year.

Bret Saberhagen is an odd pitcher, odd years that is. After two or three years, the odd/even theory sounded silly, but it's been going on for seven years now. In 1985, 1987, and 1989 Saberhagen was a combined 61-22 with two Cy Young awards. In 1984, 1986, 1988, and 1990 he was 36-48, and his ERA has been a run and a half higher in the even-numbered years. Superstitions have given way to serious consideration of this phenomenon. The current theory is that Saberhagen works himself harder when he is succeeding, finishing every successful year totally burned out (but with great stats in the books). In the even-numbered years, according to this theory, Sabes is tired and below par when the season starts, never gets on track, and never bears down like he does when he's riding a good year. 1991 is an odd year, in case you hadn't noticed. Saberhagen had elbow surgery in July last year, but he looked fine in September.

Mike Boddicker is the number 2 starter. He has one of the great curve balls in the game today, and excellent control. In Fenway he won 39 games in 2½ years — 15 games per year — with a 3.49 ERA. IN KC he should be even better.

Mark Gubicza was hurt during the last few days of 1989. People who knew that fact (or found it here in these pages) did very well by staying away from him in last year's drafts. When he's right, Gubicza is marvelous. But after rotator cuff surgery, what can you expect? If you end up obtaining Gubicza and he does OK, remember that he has a history of fading after August 1, and trade him. Safer still, don't touch.

Two starters (or three, ex Gubicza) will come from the group of Kevin Appier, Tom Gordon, and Storm Davis. Appier was the best last year (2.76 ERA was fourth best in AL), but the Royals may look to Davis because of his experience. Forget Davis; his ratio will sink you. Also, Davis needs six supporting runs per game, like the A's gave him, to be a winner. The Royals are improved in 1991, but they aren't going to give him six runs per game. He pitches many good games; don't be fooled. When Storm Davis explodes on the mound, the shockwaves reach both coasts. Gordon was the only KC starter who stayed in the rotation all year in 1990 (leading the team by far with 32 starts), but he may get shifted to long relief, anyway. The Royals will use a four man rotation until May.

Appier didn't make the Royals in spring training, but he turned out to be their best starter. (Major league GM's don't know any more than you do about selecting pitchers.) Beware of the sophomore slump for Appier.

MILWAUKEE

The Milwaukee starting rotation looked like Ted Higuera, Ron Robinson, Chris Bosio, Jamie Navarro, and one Mr. X, going into spring training. In January, Bosio was still recovering from knee surgery.

The Brewers released three pitchers who have been hanging around their starting rotation for the past few years: Mike Birkbeck, Tom Filer, and Juan Nieves. They also removed Don August from the major league roster. If you can't pitch for the Brewers, you can't pitch.

Teddy Higuera has been one of the great second-half pitchers of the late 1980's (46-17 after the All Star break before last year) but had a genuinely lousy second half in 1990.

Kevin D. Brown will be a sleeper in some leagues, but he spent the whole winter freeze-dried with a 2.57 ERA in the October 9 USA Today. Anyone who has been staring at those numbers is probably fascinated with Brown by now.

Alan Boodman:

Milwaukee Brewers' starting pitchers probably won't be too much in demand. You'll be able to get most of them cheap, for obvious reasons. The rotation "anchor" Teddy Higuera is a 32-year-old returning free agent lefty coming off the worst two seasons of his life. Also, he's been injured, but has been a top notch pitcher when healthy. But that was at least 3 years ago. Higuera attracted considerable interest in the free-agent market; when people are writing blank checks for Dave LaPoint and worse, Higuera must be considered valuable. Save your own money, though. Teddy is no longer a premier pitcher.

Higuera has averaged 200 innings a year since he was 21, and you'd have to say the strain is beginning to show. His health being a major question mark, Teddy is definitely a high-risk prospect right now. I'd wait until I see him pitch before I'd want him.

The number two man is Ron Robinson, who is coming off the best season of his career. Ronnie was bounced around a lot in his Cincinnati days, going from exclusive bullpen work, to spot starting, to the disabled list. His 27 starts in 1990 were by far a career high, and his stats look marvelous, but Robinson wasn't really dominant. He gave up more than a hit per inning, and the 14 wins were very much a function of Ron's getting over 5.5 runs/game to work with. That won't happen again.

NEW YORK

UPDATE — The Yankees expanded their collection of number three starters with Scott Sanderson. He won 17 for Oakland; will likely lose 17 for New York.

The Yankees have one of the largest collections of mediocre pitchers in the history of major league baseball. The two pitchers who anchored the staff, by virtue of early announcements that they had starting roles, were Dave Eiland and Chuck Cary. Not exactly Koufax and Drysdale, are they?

After a rough outing against the Angels on September 6, I asked Cary how much he was using the screwball that made him so effective in 1989. "Not enough," he replied, "I should remember to mix it in more." In his five remaining starts in 1990, Cary never gave up more than three runs. "If you put on a uniform, John, you could be a pitching coach," he told me. Unlike Star Trek, there is no prime directive in Rotisserie.

Daniel Stone:

As always, the Yankees have a huge number of average pitchers competing for spots in the starting rotation. Tim Leary, Andy Hawkins, Dave LaPoint, Pascual Perez, Dave Eiland, Mike Witt, Chuck Cary, Steve Adkins, Greg Cadaret, Eric Plunk, Kevin Mmahat, and new acquisition Steve Farr were all possibilities.

Tim Leary was one of the better Yankee starters last year. That's a condemnation of the staff, not a compliment to Leary. Even that year, however, Leary went sour after August 1. At age 32, you can forget about further improvement. Leary would have lost 20 games last year if the Yankees hadn't benched him to avoid the embarrassment.

The enigmatic Pascual Perez is, or was, capable of star quality pitching, but he missed almost all of 1990 with a bad shoulder. He repeatedly rejected the team's requests that he get surgery, but finally gave in. Perez has been a spectacular comeback player once in his career already. Strong comebacks are usually limited to one per career. Perez is only slightly more interesting than the average rehab project. One attraction is that the Yankees have so many alternatives, that they will DL Perez quickly if it's clear that he can't pitch effectively, saving you some risk.

Andy Hawkins had a bizarre season in 1990. He was off to horrible start, and rumored to be on the verge of release. The Yankees reportedly postponed his departure, only because of ongoing injuries to other pitchers. Given a life, Hawkins worked well in relief, got back into the rotation, and threw his famous 0-4 no hitter loss on July 1. Then he came back and threw another 11 shutout innings on July 6, only to lose that game, too, in the 12th inning. After a two-year ERA of 5.04 with the Yankees, he is likely to get a diminished role in 1991.

Dave LaPoint is also likely to get pushed aside by younger talent this year. He has done just about what the Yankees should have expected, but getting a high salary for a journeyman has made him the subject of much unfair criticism, and the front office is looking for alternatives.

Not too long ago, Mike Witt was an all star and a Cy Young candidate. No more. Since winning 18 games in 1986, he has gone downhill. He experienced a minor revival with the Yankees in 1990, however. The Angels had exiled him to the pen; now that episode is over. He held righties to a .207 average last year, and showed other signs of life. Among the veterans, he is as likely as

OAKLAND

The A's have re-signed both Bob Welch and Scott Sanderson, and acquired Eric Show during the winter, giving them their usual six starters going into spring training. Dave Stewart, Welch, Sanderson, and Mike Moore will take the first four spots in the rotation.

Stewart and Welch are premier pitchers. The only problem is that they won't go cheap. Sanderson, Moore, Young and Show (if applicable) will be protected by the quick hook and the readiness of a superb bullpen. All A's pitchers are helped by the best scouting and the best field positioning in the league. Pitching in a great pitcher's ballpark, and having a winning team to score for them, are two more benefits enjoyed by Oakland pitchers.

Susan Nelson:

The A's have a history of turning washed-up veterans into productive major league starters. Don't assume that Eric Show is finished, just because he couldn't produce for San Diego in the last two years.

The guy to watch is Reggie Harris, the 22-year-old righty drafted from Boston just two and a half years after the Red Sox made him a first round pick. Harris has been a successful starter in the minors, but was used mainly as a reliever by the A's last year. He has a great fastball, and Oakland made him look good by using him carefully in spots during 1990. Tony LaRussa and Dave Duncan understand very well that success build on itself, and they are intent on making a success out of Harris.

Mike Moore had a bad year. First the excuse was that he had missed spring training and just wasn't ready. But when spring turned to summer, Moore continued pitching poorly. What's the excuse now?

Curt Young thinks too much. The problem, though, is his elbow. No one will tell you this, but Young has an elbow problem that flares up from time to time. When he's in pain, he can't throw his slider. Hitters see what is happening and sit on the fastball, which is not an outstanding pitch. When Curt's elbow is OK, however, and he can throw his slider, he is a great pitcher.

Todd Burns is one of the more likely alternatives to become a starter if and when one is needed. He has good stuff, but lacks the proper frame of mind to fill in for Eckersley if that should become necessary.

Lary Bump:

Todd Van Poppel? Not yet. Northern California may not be far from Southern Oregon, but it's still a long way from Coos Bay or North Bend — no, Medford, knew that — to the majors. Still, the 19-year-old righty didn't spend long at Southern Oregon (24 innings, 32 Ks, 0.79 ratio, 1.13 ERA) before the A's No. 1 pick moved up to Madison (1.38, 3.95), where he had some control problems. No doubt you'll hear more from him.

Prospect Ray Young went to Japan in late 1990.

SEATTLE

Seattle is not the same stadium that it used to be. The fences are now farther from home plate, turning old-time homers into track outs.

Pete DeCoursey:

The big change in Seattle is the quality of fielding. Now, when you get a Seattle pitcher, you also get Mike Brumley, Omar Vizquel, Edgar Martinez, Harold Reynolds, and Ken Griffey Jr., one of the best defensive units in the game today. It's like pitching for the '65 Dodgers or '70 Orioles. Brian Holman I like a lot. Also, Billy Swift and Rich Delucia are growing in value.

Randy Johnson suffers from Nolan Ryan syndrome; he tries to strike out every hitter and gets tired and gets in trouble as a result. With that defensive excellence behind him, he should wise up.

Mike Jackson is going down in value. He has poor control (the first pitcher to yield a major league walk to Oscar Azocar, the most impatient hitter in baseball). Despite the poor control, Jackson tries to hit the corners. He falls behind, tries to blow the fastball by, and fails.

Erik Hanson was 9-3 with a 2.59 ERA and a 1.10 ratio after the All Star break. Yes, he is that good.

Tony Formo's Left Field Extravaganza:

Erik Hanson (3.24 ERA, 18-9) took Scott Bankhead's place as the Seattle staff ace, setting a franchise record for strikeouts by a RHP, with 211 in 236 IP.

Bankhead (11.08 ERA, 0-2) pitched only 13 innings in 1990 before going on the DL for the rest of the season. In 1989 Bankhead was the ace of the rotation (3.34 ERA, 14-6) and might be undervalued and overlooked going into the 1991 season. Seattle pitchers should be a good deal, partly because of the increasing depth of quality young arms, and partly because the fences in the Kingdome have been moved back, transforming it from pitchers' nightmare into a good pitchers' park. In 1990, Oakland and Chicago were the only teams with staff ERA's lower than the M's. Take note!

Brian Holman (4.03 ERA, 11-11) was much more effective than his record would indicate. In April he came one out away from becoming the first Mariner to throw a no-hitter. Bone chips in his right elbow ended his season in September. Assuming recovery from minor surgery, look for Holman to be an effective starter for seasons to come.

Randy Johnson (6'10'', 3.65 ERA, 14-11) is the tallest head case in baseball history, with a talented left arm and capacity for self-destruction reminiscent of Dave Stieb. Like Sir David, Johnson has temper tantrums and is easily upset by bench jockeying that more professional pitchers ignore. A clue to Johnson's psychodynamics came when he threw the first no-hitter in Mariner franchise history; when he phoned home after the game, his mother was pleased, but his father wanted to know why he walked six batters. Too bad the Mariners didn't trade him right after the no-hitter, when he was selected for the All Star game and before his lousy second half of the season. Although talented left-handers are desirable, I believe that Johnson is programmed for a career of self-inflicted underachievement.

Rookie left-hander Russ Swan (3.64 ERA, 2-3) had moments of brilliance in his 47 IP. In his first start after being acquired from San Francisco for Gary Eave, Knackert went 7 innings against Detroit without allowing a hit, and had another 7-inning hitless performance against the Royals in September. Given Seattle's recent wealth of quality young pitchers, it is uncertain how much Swan will be used or in what roles (in 1990, 8 of his 11 appearances were starts).

Lary Bump:

Rich DeLucia, Mike Gardiner, Russ Swan are the up-and-coming SP's. At season's end, righties DeLucia and Gardiner and lefty Swan were starting for the Mariners. Unless free agent Matt Young signs elsewhere, there may not be room for any of them this year. DeLucia, 26, started last season as Gardiner's teammate at Williamsport. After a 1.06, 2.11 start, he went to Calgary, where his numbers — 1.31, 3.62 — were equally impressive in a hitters' ballpark. With the Mariners, he had a 1.08 ratio and 2.00 ERA, and is clearly the frontrunner to land a spot in the rotation.

Gardiner, a 25-year-old Canadian, may not be far behind. He was the best of the best in the Eastern League, as its most valuable pitcher and ERA champion (1.90). He also had an 0.92 ratio and a 5/1 K/W ratio. He was clearly over his head in the majors (2.13 ratio, 10.66 ERA in five games). Keep in mind, too, that the last pitcher to lead the EL in ERA and go on to be a major league star was Juan Marichal.

Swan, 27, came over from San Francisco. In the PCL, he had a 1.71 ratio and 4.45 ERA. His totals with the two major league teams were 1.42, 3.65. He is no longer classified as a rookie, but he might have to push aside Keith Comstock to get a job in the bullpen.

TEXAS

With Charlie Hough out of the picture, Bobby Witt can be gracefully handed the number two spot behind Nolan Ryan. Witt just completed his best year ever, highlighted by a 12-2 record with a 2.64 ERA after the All Star break. Note that Witt has had a good second half before (1988 — not as good as 1990, but a standout half-season within the context of Witt's career), and then Witt collapsed the following spring. Nonetheless, for 1990 Bobby looks like his great talent is genuinely emerging.

Nolan Ryan has been a big risk every year for ten years, and he has been Grade A Rotisserie material almost every one of those years. He is obviously the kind of player who should be drafted by a team that wants to take chances and shake things up. For hanging on to first place, you want somebody younger.

The number three starter is Kevin Brown, who was dominant when he first won a starting role, and then faded. Brown's second half last year produced a 2-4 record with a 4.06 ERA and 1.46 ratio. Someone is going to overpay for him because of his once-bright outlook. Stay out of the bidding to be safe.

The Rangers are going to field two starting pitchers who are either very bad or very surprising. The prime candidate is young Scott Chiamparino, proceeds of the Harold Baines deal from Oakland. I like him. After Chiamparino, someone from the group of Gerald Alexander, Brian Bohanon, Robb Nen and Roger Pavlik is likely to emerge; or Kenny Rogers could come out of the pen.

Lary Bump:

The best three young arms are Gerald Alexander, Brian Bohanon, and Scott Chiamparino. Righty Alexander made people show interest with his 6-1, 0.90, 0.63 start at Port Charlotte. But they really stood up and took notice when he jumped all the way to Triple-A and recorded a 13-2 record for an Oklahoma City team that was 45-85 when anyone else got a decision. That's a percentage of .867 compared to .346. With OK City, his ratio was 1.45 and his ERA 4.10. He was unsuccessful (2.71, 7.71) in three games as a Ranger, but his first three starts at OK City were worse than that.

TORONTO

Three aces and two discards . . .

J.L. Feinstein:

The starting rotation shapes up as Dave Stieb, David Wells, Jimmy Key, and Todd Stottlemyre, with Frank Wills battling Al Leiter and possibly Denis Boucher for the number five slot. Wills seems better suited for long relief, so give a slight edge to Leiter, at least going in to spring training. If Boucher happens to make it, the Jays'll have as many Canadians as Dominicans.

Stieb has become one of the most consistent pitchers in the AL. Since 1987 he hasn't had an ERA above 3.35 or a ratio above 1.17, and he hasn't won fewer than 16 games. Clemens and Stewart can't match that consistency.

David Wells has adopted magnificently to the starting role. Over the past two years his ratio is only 1.10. Given a full season as a starter on a team that fields a strong lineup in a weak division, Wells could win 18 to 20 games.

Jimmy Key gives all evidence of recovery from his arm miseries. In the second half he was 8-3, 3.10, 1.08.

Stottlemyre in the second half was 4-9 with a 4.22 ERA and 1.34 ratio. At least he has the potential to improve.

Al Leiter has been a huge disappointment in the major leagues. Yankee fans screamed when he was traded for Jesse Barfield, but Rotisserie people know that a good hitter is always better than a pitching prospect, especially for the next year or two. So it has been with the Leiter trade. He was 3-8, 4.62 at AAA Syracuse last year. He'll need a good spring just to stay on the roster. The competition in the minors, both at Syracuse and Knoxville, is very thin.

NATIONAL LEAGUE STARTING PITCHERS

ATLANTA

Marc Bowman:

As a rule, Atlanta pitchers give up more hits and runs than their counterparts on other teams; Fulton County Stadium is cosy. The Braves are also a weak offensive team, cutting into the wins for their starters. Atlanta might win 75 games in 1991. It is obvious that the starters cannot average more than about 11 wins apiece, and probably less. Check recent history if you want to see how much less. In 1988, the top three starters won 9, 8, and 7 games respectively. Last year, the five man rotation was 14, 10, 9, 5 and 3. If your league counts losses or W/L record, you should really be careful here. Obviously, you don't go for a Braves pitcher unless he is very good. Fortunately for Atlanta, there are a few worth taking a look.

John Smoltz has emerged as the ace of the staff. The rest of the rotation in 1991 will be Charlie Leibrandt, Pete Smith, Tom Glavine and Steve Avery. Several prospects have a chance to break into the rotation, notably International League ERA leader Paul Marak. Leibrandt appears to be fully recovered from a shoulder injury. Smith missed four months of last season with arm troubles, but he should be ready for spring training. Smoltz, Glavine and Avery are all very young.

Smoltz had a few streaks in 1990 when he was nearly unhittable, and a few spells when he was very hittable. The good streak were enough to give him the only winning record on the staff. He still gives up too many walks and homers (indicated ERA a full run higher than actual), but with two and a half years under his belt, he is moving toward consistency and reliability.

Leibrandt's 1990 season is reminiscent of his 1984-1988 numbers, making 1989 look like an unpleasant anomaly. Expect more of the same low-ERA performance for about two more years. Compared to 1990 actual value, he is one of the likely bargains in 1991 auctions.

Pete Smith is better than his career 18-37 record would indicate. He has been the Braves hard luck pitcher in three seasons. Still just 25, he is certified healthy and could be a decent $1 pick.

Tom Glavine gets all the good luck for Atlanta. He wins games when he shouldn't. It is a mystery that he's achieved double digit wins for two consecutive years. He gave up the most runs, hits, and ER of all Braves pitchers, and was just behind Smoltz in HR and walks allowed. Although he is only 25, it isn't likely that Glavine will get any better.

Young Steve Avery was roundly clobbered in his four month welcome to the National League. Based on minor league stats, he should have done better than 3-10 with a 5.47 ERA, but minor league stats don't always give a good indication. Avery needs to improve his control before he can expect kinder treatment around the league.

Marty Clary was wretched last year and is probably washed up as far as Atlanta is concerned. Paul Marak looked good in six September starts. Rusty Richards and Andy Nezelek are the next best prospects — but if you're digging that deep into the Atlanta system for SP's, you have a problem.

Lary Bump:

A late-blooming discovery or the Marty Clary of

1990? Righthander Paul Marak, 25, started last season as a middle reliever at Richmond, and finished it with an International League ERA title (2.39, with a 1.22 ratio) and seven major league starts (1.49, 3.69) under his belt. Marak may be better suited to a relief role; he held major-league righthanded batters to a .118 average, but lefties belted him to the tune of .347. Clary, of course, followed up a surprisingly good 1989 as a superannuated rookie with an ugly 1-10 season in 1990. Isn't it something how the Braves have all these great-looking young pitchers who keep getting upstaged by these journeyman types? Is anybody up there in the Atlanta front office noticing? Is there anyone up there?

CHICAGO CUBS

Our general advice, year in and year out, is to treat Cubs pitchers with the same disdain that you have for Braves pitchers. All pitchers are accidents waiting to happen. Wrigley Field and Atlanta Stadium are conducive to accidents, like leaving spilled grease on the floor, wearing loose clothing around speeding conveyors and pulleys, smoking while pumping gas, etc. Chances are you may get through unscathed, but why chance it? If you can get what you want, without exposing yourself to danger, it's better to avoid it altogether. Buy a hitter, and stop looking in Wrigley Field for your star pitcher.

There are exceptions to every rule. Greg Maddux is exceptional. He's one of only ten major league pitchers to have 20 or more quality starts in both of the last two years (see essay). He is, simply, an excellent pitcher.

Considering that the Cubs look like a winning team for 1991, you may want to take a flyer on Danny Jackson. He is a groundball, curve/slider type of pitcher who won't be hurt too badly by the close walls, and the grass will help him. The problem with Jackson isn't Wrigley Field, it's his health. He has had a lot of arm problems.

Jose Nunez has a good arm; the Cubs always seem to need pitchers and will probably make use of him during 1991. Nunez led the International League in ERA in 1989. He's a dark horse to do something really good in 1991.

Rick Sutcliffe has abused his arm for years. He will keep pitching with a sore arm and not tell anyone. Steve Wilson didn't do very well in 1990, but he has a pretty good arm. He will most likely end up in the bullpen.

Mike Bielecki had a terrible year, but Zimmer seems to like him. That makes him one of the most dangerous cancers on a Rotisserie roster: the high-ERA, high-ratio pitcher who is favored by his team to get many innings.

Mike Harkey has a history of arm problems. I regard him as very iffy for 1991. He had more problems late last year, that many people didn't notice. He is a great talent but must be labeled physically unsound. Lance Dickson was just drafted last year. He has a good curveball. He got injured and was rested.

Shawn Boskie is a possible starter but hasn't shown much in the major leagues.

Adam Stein:

The Cubs rotation will include Greg Maddux, Rick Sutcliffe, and Mike Harkey. All three should have good years, especially Harkey. Sutcliffe always walks a lot of men, but pitches out of trouble.

Shawn Boskie is the prime candidate for fifth starter (if Jackson is the fourth). And if something should go wrong with one of the regulars, the backups include Steve Wilson, Jeff Pico, Mike Bielecki, Kevin Blankenship, Jose Nunez, Joe Kramer, Kevin Coffman, Lance Dickson, Les Lancaster, and the peanut vendor at Ho Ho Kam park. The only one of these worth a long look is Dickson, and he's probably a year away from being effective.

Greg Gajus:

Danny Jackson (6-6 3.61 ERA 1.36 Ratio) is one of the best Rotisserie sleepers for 1991. His numbers were off due to injuries for the second year in a row but when he was healthy he displayed his 1988 form. At one point he allowed 2 runs or less in 10 of 11 starts, but received only 4 wins during that stretch due to poor run support. Jackson is a conditioning fanatic and is an excellent bet to bounce back. Jackson was a free agent, and the Reds never seemed likely to sign both Browning and Jackson (Marge wouldn't let a little thing like keeping a World Championship staff together to stand in the way of a few hundred thousand dollars additional profit). Unlike Browning, Jackson is an extreme groundball pitcher who will benefit from natural grass.

Lary Bump:

It's hard to figure out Kevin Blankenship, a 28-year-old who started as a prospect in the — hmmm — Atlanta farm system. You can explain his 10-9 record at Iowa two ways. Either he wasn't the same pitcher after coming back from a mid-season promotion to Chicago, or he was darn lucky. His 1.55 ratio and 3.42 ERA at Iowa, coupled with figures of 1.54 and 5.84 in three big league games, tend to support the lucky theory.

Lefthander Lance Dickson, 21, the Cubs' No. 1 draft pick, had a whirlwind tour of the Chicago system — twin ratio and ERA of 0.53 at Geneva; 0.94, 1.51 at Peoria; 0.70, 0.38 at Charlotte; a reality-checking 1.76, 7.24 in three reality-checking, losing starts for the big club. Expect the Cubs to be more rational with him this season, starting him at Charlotte or possibly Iowa and keeping him out of the majors until September.

CINCINNATI

Jose Rijo is getting divorced from Juan Marichal's daughter. If you placed any value on Marichal tutelage, you may now subtract it.

Greg Gajus:

All the publicity given the "Nasty Boys" has taken away from the performance of the Reds starters. At no time during the year did the Reds have fewer than three very effective starting pitchers going at any one time. Injuries and changing roles prevented any starter from running up big numbers, but they were all very effective and the key to the Reds World Championship (the Reds were only 5th in runs scored, but first in fewest runs allowed). With all due respect to the Nasties, there would have been nothing to save had the starters been hammered. The principals:

Jose Rijo (14-8 2.70 ERA 1.16 Ratio): After his World Series performance, Rijo is not likely to be undervalued. However, Rijo has always been about this effective since coming to the Reds. The only changes that Rijo made this year were (1) to junk his forkball in favor of his great slider and (2) to throw between starts which has helped Rijo's endurance. Before 1990, Jose was a brilliant 6 inning pitcher, by the end of 1990 he was finishing his starts (6 career CG before 1990, 7 CG in 1990). Although it seems like he has been around forever, Rijo will be only 26 in 1991. All the signs point to another great year.

Tom Browning (15-9 3.80 ERA 1.26 Ratio) was on his way to a typical Browning season when he injured his ankle swinging at a pitch in mid-August. In his next 5 starts, he allowed 23 runs in 22 innings and inflated his ERA from 3.12 to 3.80. 1990 was the 4th year of the last 5 that Browning has pitched over 220 innings. Browning was a free agent with big contract demands. The Reds know better than anyone else knows, what to expect from him, and they resigned him. Browning is 31, has thrown a lot of innings the past few years, and his hits per inning rate is steadily increasing while his strikeouts per inning rate is dropping. If Browning loses his control, he could become Rick Mahler in a hurry.

Norm Charlton (12-9 2.74 ERA 1.30 Ratio): Lou Piniella's promotion of Norm Charlton was one of the keys of the 1990 season. In his first 14 starts,

Norm was 6-3 with a 1.94 ERA. Charlton's only weakness is somewhat shaky control (4 walks per 9 innings). An excellent draft pick for 1991.

Jack Armstrong (12-9 3.42 ERA 1.26 Ratio) was brilliant the first half and disappeared the 2nd half. Armstrong tried to pitch with a bad elbow, which destroyed his stats until he finally went on the DL in August. When he returned, he pitched sparingly in middle relief. There is no reason to believe that Armstrong cannot return to his first half form in 1991. He was healthy at the end of the year and should return to the rotation, unless the Reds sign all of their free agent pitchers. A reasonably safe pick, but behind the other Reds starters.

Rick Mahler (7-6 4.28 ERA 1.24 Ratio); Scott Scudder (5-5 4.90 ERA 1.45 Ratio); and Chris Hammond (0-2 6.35 ERA 2.20 Ratio) are the remaining candidates for the rotation. Mahler is another free agent who has a spot on the team if he will accept the role of middle relief/spot starter. Scudder shows flashes of brilliance and would benefit from a full year at AAA. Hammond was brilliant at Nashville and a disaster with the big club. He will get a shot with free agent Mahler not likely to return. Scudder is the most likely to get the first shot at the rotation if a spot opens up.

Sean Lahman:

Jack Armstrong started the all-star game and disappeared. He had a record of 11-4 at the break but lost his next 5 decisions and went on the DL. He didn't start a game after mid-August. Armstrong had two previous tastes of the big leagues under Pete Rose, both times as an emergency starter. Then Lou Piniella made him the third starter. Armstrong is a big pitcher with a good fastball, and a good assortment of finesse pitches. American League fans who haven't seen him pitch, think of Ben McDonald; these two are very similar. Because of his poor second half, Armstrong may be cheap in 1991 drafts. He should be number one on your "must get" list. This guy is the real thing.

Tom Browning had another typical season. Fifteen wins and a 3.80 ERA. Part of Tom's success comes from being a control pitcher in a rotation of power pitchers. Browning throws two fastballs with different types of movement. After facing Rijo, Jackson, Dibble and the like, how can anyone be expected to hit Browning? He spent time on the DL for the first time in his career, but it was not a pitching injury; he pulled a hamstring trying to beat out a groundball. Otherwise, he has been the most durable pitcher over the past four years.

Norm Charlton finally got his wish and was moved from the bullpen back to the starting rotation, where he did fairly well. With the abundance of starters, it seems likely the Reds would want to keep Charlton in their bullpen. In the rotation, Charlton is a number two or number three starter. Should the Reds put him there, he'll win 12-15 games and strikeout 180-220 (see comments on Charlton under relief pitchers).

Scott Scudder was shuffled between Cincinnati and Nashville last year, but not because he didn't pitch well in the majors. Scudder is one of the players on the bubble with the Reds rotation. He has been highly sought by other teams and it seems likely that the Reds would trade him if they can't find a spot for him by mid-May. Scudder is a finesse pitcher who needs to spend a big stretch of time in the majors to develop confidence in his pitches.

Rick Mahler is a fair pitcher who won't be back with the Reds. He may hook on with an American League team, were I think he could have some success. Mahler has an excellent curve, but sometimes has problems getting it over and has problems setting it up with other pitches. It looks like his playing days are pretty much over.

Chris Hammond got a taste of the big leagues while dominating the American Association's hitters. He's probably half a year away and the Reds don't want or need to rush him. Hammond is a big left-handed power pitcher who is definitely in the Reds blueprint for the future.

Lary Bump:

Nobody was talking dynasty about the Reds, not

with potential starters Tom Browning, Danny Jackson and Rick Mahler testing free agency. And are there replacements in sight?

Chris Hammond, a 25-year-old lefty, tore up the American Association as its most valuable pitcher and ERA leader (2.17). He also posted a 1.21 ratio and 15-1 record. It was a different story in the majors, where he was shelled in three starts, allowing more than one hit and one walk per inning. Other heralded Reds' farmhands, such as Jack Armstrong and Scott Scudder, have struggled before him, so Hammond may make it. But he's not a sure thing.

Neither are 24-year-old righthanders Rodney Imes and Luis Vasquez, who spent all of last season at Nashville. Imes had a 1.45 ratio and 3.75 ERA with the Sounds, and Vasquez was 1.45 and 3.28. In Imes' favor is that he comes from the Yankees' organization favored by Lou Piniella and Bob Quinn. Vasquez hasn't yet shown the results his talent, particularly a devastating curveball, would seem to dictate.

Gino Minutelli. The name rolls right off the tongue. But this 26-year-old lefty isn't ready yet, if he ever will be, for the majors. He finally worked his way out of Double-A with a 1.41, 3.99 start at Chattanooga. At Nashville, his numbers were 1.23 and 3.23. Keep an eye on him. He may be a late bloomer, in which case he may move into the Reds' rotation during the season.

HOUSTON

Bill Gilbert:

Mike Scott is not as bad as he appeared in 1990 (9-13, 3.81) and not as good as he looked in 1989 (20-10, 3.10). After the abbreviated spring training, he was not ready to pitch and had a terrible start. He began turning his season around with a strong outing at Chicago on May 26, and from that point he pitched well in 18 of his 23 starts.

At age 36, Scott is unlikely to regain the form that made him the leagues' dominant pitcher in 1986 when he struck out 1.11 batters per inning. Since that year, his ratio of strikeouts to innings pitched has declined each year to 0.59 in 1990, below the league average of 0.64. Scott ended the year with a tender arm, missing his last start and a chance to win 10 or more games for the sixth straight year. He had arthroscopic surgery on his shoulder in December but was expected to be ready on schedule for 1991. Assuming his arm is sound in 1991, he should win between 10 and 15 games with an ERA and ratio slightly better than the league average.

For the first time in Jim Deshaies' five-year career with the Astros, he failed to hit double figures in wins. He led the team in starts with 34 for the second straight year, but his numbers dropped off in every category: wins from 15 to 7, ERA from 2.91 to 3.78 and ratio from 1.15 to 1.29. However, Deshaies pitched well enough to win in 21 of his 34 starts and finished with six strong outings in his last seven starts. His biggest problem was control. Walks were up and strikeouts down as batters began laying off his enticing, high fastball. Based on his strong finish, Deshaies should turn in better numbers in 1991. About twelve wins with an ERA and ratio around the league average would be reasonable.

Despite his usual bad start, Mark Portugal was the second best starter for the Astros in 1990. On June 17, he was 1-7 but rallied to finish 11-10, repeating his strong second half performance in 1989. He would be a great acquisition in a mid-season trade. Portugal has a strong arm with good enough stuff to be a consistent winner. He pitched well enough to win in 22 of his 32 starts including 10 of his last 11. With a better start he could win 15 with an ERA and ratio better than the league average.

The Astros are in need of a fifth starter. Bill Gullickson (10-14, 3.82) was released and Jim Clancy was even worse in 1990 (2-8, 6.51) than he was in 1989, and will be tried in middle relief.

Candidates within the system are all considered long shots. Xavier Hernandez spent the entire season with the Astros after being drafted from Toronto. He only pitched 63 innings and his one start was in the next-to-last game of the season. He could benefit from a full year in AAA to improve his repertoire which now consists primarily of a sinker ball. Randy Hennis was 10-8, 4.41 at Tucson and was impressive in a late season trial with the Astros, allowing only one hit in nine innings. However, he did not demonstrate that he could throw a breaking ball for strikes. The other pitching prospects in the high minors, Darryl Kile, Ryan Bowen, Jose Cano, William Brennan and Blaise Ilsley all faltered badly at Tucson.

Lary Bump:

It's possible the Astros' youth movement will take in righthander Randy Hennis, 25, but not lefty Butch Henry. At Tucson, Hennis had a 1.54 ratio and a 4.41 ERA. He then recorded 0.41 and 0.00 in the Astrodome.

The 22-year-old Henry is included here as one whose progress you should monitor. After a big '88 season at Cedar Rapids, arm trouble has slowed him down. He put in 143 innings (1.46, 4.22) last season at Chattanooga. He's important to the Astros because he represents part of the payment for Bill Doran.

LOS ANGELES

Los Angeles is a great place to look for pitching, any kind of pitching. The Dodgers deserve credit for excellent scouting and player development. Dodger stadium also deserves some credit. Almost any time during the season, you can look at the LA stats in USA Today (sorted in order by ERA) and right in the middle of the pack will be people with an ERA like 2.91. Sometimes, I have seen median numbers like 2.64, meaning you could just take any Dodger pitcher, and get a high probability of getting some excellent numbers. Look at Mike Morgan in 1989: leading the league in ERA, and the Dodgers take him out the rotation because he is pitching poorly. Ramon Martinez came up from the minor leagues, pitched a 3-hit shutout, and got sent back down. You figure it out.

The Dodgers have both quality and quantity in their starters for 1991. They weren't all that bad in 1990. Since then, they added Kevin Gross and Bob Ojeda; they are hoping for the return of Orel Hershiser, and they retained Fernando Valenzuela. Jim Neidlinger and Mike Hartley were good starters last year. Mike Morgan and John Wetteland achieved high points in 1989. Ramon Martinez was the ace last year. That makes nine credible starters, and we haven't even mentioned the bullpen or the prospects that come up like wildflowers every spring. The Yankees would (or should) trade their whole pitching staff for just three of the Dodgers top nine SP's.

My personal opinions:

Hershiser is washed up. Don't touch him. There are too many nice, young, healthy, hard-throwing CHEAP pitchers. Don't mess with a blown out shoulder. It's Tommy Lasorda's fault, by the way. He can't count pitches.

Kevin Gross is a skilled cheater, and the Dodgers will add to his bag of tricks. Remember how Mike Morgan went from being a bum, to leading the NL in ERA, the moment he arrived in LA, and the team had the nerve to announce that he had tried a new grip that gave his pitches a downward motion? Did you believe that a guy would pitch in the major leagues for five years, and never think of turning the seams 90 degrees just to see what happened? Anyway, Gross could turn out to be a gem. If he isn't, he'll stop pitching real fast; that's one of the many nice qualities of Dodger starters.

Ramon Martinez worried me a little by returning from the Japan series early. The Dodgers claim he is OK, but they have a history of causing arm problems. I believe that Ramon is probably healthy, and if he's healthy he will be dominant again.

Tim Belcher was once great, but Lasorda wrecked him, too. It isn't as serious as Hershiser, but I have to ask: why take a sore arm when you can have a healthy arm?

Bob Ojeda will be fine with the Dodgers. He wasn't

that bad with the Mets, even though they kicked him out of the rotation. The bullpen in LA will be better than what he had in New York, and the stadium is just as friendly. I like Ojeda's chances.

Take ANY Dodger pitcher. They're all just fine for Rotiserrie.

Adam Stein:

Even before Fernando Valenzuela returned from free agency, the Dodgers were blessed with several quality starting pitchers.

If Orel Hershiser has recovered fully by the start of the year, he's the team ace and will dominate again. Hershiser will go cheap, as much because of his unimpressive numbers before he got hurt, as because of his injury. When he's on, he's still the best pitcher in the league. His career ERA is 2.70.

Tim Belcher has great stuff but didn't show it because of injuries that plagued him for most of the season. In 1989, he won 15 games with an ERA of 2.82. The Dodger offensive has become significantly better since, then which should mean more wins. His ERA of 4.00 last year was the first time he finished a season with an ERA greater than THREE. Look for a return to 1989 form.

When Orel Hershiser was injured last year, Ramon Martinez became the Dodgers' ace and one of the top five pitchers in the league.

Kevin Gross was signed as a free agent during the winter meetings in Chicago. Perhaps the Dodgers were unaccustomed to the cold weather and got frost bite of the brain. Gross has a career ERA over four, and in his best year was 15-13 with a 3.41 ERA. If I managed the Dodgers, Gross would be my seventh or eighth starter. At $2 million a year, he'll hold down either the fourth or fifth spot in the rotation. Either way, you don't want him on your team, unless your league allows you to bid negative dollars. Long term thought question: if Kevin Gross is worth $2 million, what's Orel Hershiser worth?

Jim Neidlinger was the Dodgers' number two starter at the end of 1990. He may have to battle for a spot in the rotation this spring. He pitched well last year but many sophomore pitchers have trouble, since most of the hitters have seen them once or twice before. Pitching half his games in Dodger stadium, and on a team that has plenty of replacements if he struggles, he's a safe guy to fill out your staff.

Mike Hartley, Dennis Cook, Mike Morgan, and John Wetteland will battle for Neidlinger for the final slot in the rotation and three roster spots. One or two of these pitchers are likely to be traded (in a package for a third baseman or centerfielder). Hartley posted impressive numbers last season after the Dodgers took him out of the bullpen. Worth a look if he starts, otherwise don't bother with him. None of the others are anything special. Still, the Dodgers are going to win a lot of games in 1991, so ANYONE who starts for them is going to be worth a buck or two.

Pete DeCoursey:

Kevin Gross could very easily be the Tim Belcher Annual Hot Dodger Pitcher next year. Pitching in the league's best pitcher's park, and with the kind of offensive support Butler, Murray, Daniels and Strawberry can produce, Kevin could be a big winner if they give him 33 starts. Dennis Cook, if he recovers from shoulder surgery, could also be well worth $1. He's camouflaged by all the pitchers around him, but he is a solid pitcher and could do well for the Dodgers, although his tenuous roster position and uncertain health make him a medium-sized gamble.

MONTREAL

I nominate Chris Nabholz as the NL pitcher most likely to be overvalued in 1991 auctions. He was 0-6 with a 4.83 ERA at Indianapolis, where he gave up more than a hit per inning and walked 4 per nine IP. His performance in the majors was a silly fluke. When he beat the Mets, effectively ending the pennant race, he was pitching from behind in the count, getting timely bounces, and (for a rookie) was treated kindly by the umpires. The Mets choked and beat themselves. Larry Bearnarth could have been pitching.

Michael Cassin:

The Expos have shifted the focus of their annual search for pitching, away from reclamation projects and toward young arms in 1991. And they have some good ones.

Dennis Martinez is still the ace, despite his 10-11 record. He was among the league leaders in ERA and innings pitched, a nice combination for Rotisserie. Opposing batters hit only .228 against him. At age 35 he isn't likely to forget the skills that brought him this far. Mark him down for another year of the same.

Oil Can Boyd was the pleasant surprise of 1990, with a 10-6 record and 2.93 ERA. He was pampered to the extreme, rarely throwing more than 100 pitches. His health is still a concern. It is unlikely that the Expos will ever let Boyd be a hard worker, so he isn't like to win more than a dozen games in a season, even if he keeps pitching well for many years. For 1991 you just need one more year, and Can should deliver it for you.

Mark Gardner was having his ups and downs before getting hurt in 1990. If the arm problems are cleared up, he will be back in the middle of the rotation. Gardner produced 135 K in 152 IP, and the Expos are very skilled at turning throwers into pitchers. If Gardner is throwing well in spring training, I think he will make an excellent investment, likely to be undervalued.

Chris Nabholz will start camp as the number 4 starter, but he'll need to hold off Howard Farmer and Scott Anderson to keep the job. Nabholz was very sharp in his late season audition, going 6-0 with a 2.83 ERA; opponents hit .176 off him (.116 by LHH). His rotation spot looks reasonably solid and I have to like what I've seen so far. I think he's one of the best bets among rookie pitchers this year. Nabholz pitched two high profile games against the Mets, so his name will be known, so watch the price.

Howard Farmer didn't show much in a September call-up, but he's progressed nicely through the minors, and with Kevin Gross gone, he has the best shot at the number 5 slot in the rotation. Farmer has a good collection of pitches, and the organization is very high on him, and I have a feeling they'll let him spot start in the majors rather than lead the AAA staff. I don't see any big numbers, but he could be a decent pick at a low price, who'll pay off later down the line.

Scott Anderson helped out at years' end, but isn't in the team's plans. Montreal and Kevin Gross have seem to have lost all interest in each other, and if Gross is somehow still on the roster come spring, he'll be fighting for his life amid all the young arms. Whatever part of his future that isn't behind him will be somewhere else.

Brian Barnes looked good in 4 late starts after a very solid season at AA and is a definite candidate for the 5th spot. At this point I think Farmer is a little further on in his development to win the job over Barnes if they have comparable springs, but if Barnes outpitches him by any kind of margin he'll go north. If Barnes does turn out to be a factor this season I think it will be later down the line, and if faced with a choice, I'd recommend Barnes.

Lary Bump:

Even stranger than the Dodgers' remaining in the race was the Expos' charge at the Pirates and Mets. Never mind that all those free agents left after the '89 season; the replacements that had kept their fingers in the dike all of 1990 also started to go down. So here were the Expos with a Triple-A pitcher and two Double-A hurlers forming three-fifths of their contending rotation.

The bubble finally burst with a seven-game losing

streak right after Nabholz, 24, pitched a two-hit shutout against the Mets. A great feat, until you realize that Nabholz is a lefthander and all those Darryl Strawberry-vs.-lefty jokes are true. Actually, in '90, he was Mr. Nabholz and Mr. Hyde and Dr. Jekyll and then Mr. Hyde again. At Jacksonville, the 24-year-old was 7-2 with 1.20 ratio and 3.03. Then he stunk up Indianapolis, going 0-6, 1.49, 4.83. In the majors, he won his first six decisions, including the shutout of the Mets, before losing his last two. In all, he had a 1.07 ratio and 2.83 ERA for Montreal and is a force to be considered in '91.

Howard Farmer, a 25-year-old righthander, was expected to help last season. He did help Indianapolis (1.34 ratio, 3.89 ERA). But he was next to useless (1.56, 7.04) to the Expos. With Kevin Gross a free-agency defector, Farmer will be given another chance. And probably another.

Down the road, if not in '91, it isn't hard to see Brian Barnes, a 24-year-old lefty, as a staff ace. He was voted the Southern League's outstanding pitcher for his 1.15 ratio, 2.77 ERA and 213 Ks in 201 IP. He throws hard, but also mixes speeds well. Especially if your league counts strikeouts, this is a man to consider. His cup of coffee yielded a 1.14 ratio and 2.89 ERA.

NEW YORK METS

Gooden's 3.83 ERA in 1990 was the worst he ever produced, as was the .256 batting average that he allowed. Dwight amassed 19 wins nonetheless, with a .731 W/L percentage. It is obvious that Gooden is going through a transition in his career. He can't punch out hitters like before, but he can battle and use more pitching savvy. If Gooden completes this transition, as the greats like Tom Seaver did so successfully, he will return to dominance. If he doesn't make the adjustment fully (e.g., work on holding baserunners) to be a well-rounded pitcher, he will soon be just another hard thrower who needs his curve on any given day to be effective.

Sid Fernandez remains one of the toughest pitchers to hit. He held the opposition to a measly .201 BA in 1990 and .198 in 1989. Sid was very much better than his 9-14 record in 1990. In his 14 losses, the Mets scored a total of only 14 runs for him. For years, Davey Johnson denigrated Fernandez to the New York media, especially with references to Sid's portly profile. "We have a little food storage area in the clubhouse and you can really tell when Sid has been in there, because he puts such a dent in the supply." If you sow the seeds of thinking that your team should lose whenever Pitcher X takes the mound, you impact your players' performance. Opposing managers generally rate Fernandez the toughest pitcher on the Mets staff, ahead of his Cy Young candidate colleagues. And Sid is a great money pitcher, winner of many of the biggest games in Mets franchise history. His World Series record boasts a 1.35 ERA and 10 strikeouts with 1 walk in 6 IP.

The net result is that Fernandez is a perennial bargain in Rotisserie auctions, especially around New York. The losing record of 1990 will help that trend continue in 1991.

David Cone is becoming another Rotisserie gem. You simply pick him up in late May when his ERA is around six, and accrue his numbers from June through October, when his ERA is under three. Cone has just about the nastiest assortment of pitchers in baseball; the frustration of his opponents can be measured in his league-leading strikeout total. He know how to use his fielders, too, and doesn't try to overpower everybody.

Frank Viola is emerging as the ace of the Mets staff. He is getting adjusted to the National League faster that the NL is getting adjusted to Viola. He has excellent stuff and pitches for a winning team in a pitchers' ballpark. Don't be too worried about Viola's big IP totals. The Mets count his pitches carefully, keeping him under 130. Viola gets the most outs per pitch of any Mets starter; he is very efficient, and thus able to throw a complete game (he had 7 in 1990) without overdoing it. You have to consider him as valuable as any pitcher in your draft.

Julio Valera displaced Ron Darling in the Mets rotation, in the heat of last year's pennant race. It was a controversial move at the time, and didn't work out. Valera remains a strong candidate for a starter role for 1991. He has been pitching against major league hitters in Puerto Rico winter ball since was only 15, and is now mature beyond his 21 years. He has a fine assortment of pitches (88 MPH fastball which sinks, slider, change, and forkball) and amazing poise on the mound. He really knows how to set up a hitter. I think the Mets will stick with him, over Darling, in 1991, and he is one of the rarest Rotisserie commodities, a rookie pitcher worthy of a bid.

Ron Darling is not washed up. He got off to a bad start in 1990 and never recovered enough to make his full year stats look good, but he pitched well in some big games. His main problem was irregular use. If he stays with the Mets, the benefits of a good team and a good ballpark will probably be outweighed by the disadvantage of a management that doesn't seem to appreciate him.

Alan Boodman:

The New York Mets' starting rotation consists of 4 easy picks and one tough call. Frank Viola, Dwight Gooden, David Cone, and Sid Fernandez are locks, and you might look for Julio Valera to emerge as the number five starter. Ron Darling (if he returns) could serve as a spot starter or longer reliever.

Frank Viola must be considered to be the rotation anchor, coming off of a solid, if unspectacular 20-win season. Frank almost singlehandedly kept the Mets from sinking to the bottom in April and May, winning nearly every time out, while Cone and Gooden struggled to keep their ERA's below 7.00. The pace that Frank set was too tough for even him to maintain throughout the campaign, and Viola's 7-9 record after the break could be taken to mean a couple of things:

(1) Nothing at all.

(2) He may have worked a few too many innings.

Frank led the NL in innings worked, which may not mean anything, but just ask Orel Hershiser or Fernando Valenzuela what can happen if you make a habit out of that.

Viola is anything but injury-prone, and he'll most likely be around to get 32-35 starts in a good pitcher's park for a team that stands to score a few runs. And twenty wins isn't always a sign of tremendous offensive support; Frank received only 4.3 runs per start in 1990, compared to a team average of 4.8 runs/game. Being deprived of half a run each appearance is enough to cost quite a few pitchers any shot at fifteen wins, much less twenty. When you get the support Frank Viola got, you usually end up with the record Sid Fernández had. By comparison, Ramon Martinez had nearly 5 runs per game to work with and Doug Drabek had almost 5.4! Even a mediocre pitcher will win half his starts with that kind of punch behind him.

Dwight Gooden, on the other hand, was at the top of the NL with 5.88 runs per game to use, and he needed just about every one of them, particularly early in the season. Late in the season, one or two was all the Doc needed. It's easy to think that the most prolonged slump in Doctor K's career (April through early June) was a result of his less-than-rapid recovery from the arm miseries of 1989, and that's exactly what I do think. He probably won't benefit from that kind of offensive production again this year, but there's no reason why he'll need it. Gooden's fastball and curve were noticeably healthier late last summer, and a return to previous form (like 19 wins is a bad season, huh?) could be expected. Dwight may start slow — not like 1990, I hope — but the Doc will get 30 starts and nearly a K an inning along with his 16 wins. He'll also allow nearly a hit an inning, as has been his pattern in recent years.

David Cone was an enigma through most of the 1990 season. He pitched lousy in April and May, but won some games thanks to the hitters, and pitched in a more Cone-like fashion down the stretch, but had to scrape for victories. The strong second half bodes well for a solid 1991. Cone combines strikeouts with the second best control in the rotation (I know it doesn't always seem like it), and the opponents don't come close to averaging a hit an inning off of him. David, like Sid Fernandez, has the ability to come out and throw a complete-game 2 hitter with 13 strikeouts, and then last 4 innings next time out. It might be irritating, but Cone comes out ahead on balance. Check out his second-half stats.

Sid Fernandez though, is just plain irritating. Sid averaged over a strikeout an inning last year, and the opponents' batting average against him was the lowest in the league, a category which Sid almost always has a shot at leading, if not dominating. Fernandez is capable of being one of the most unhittable pitchers in either league, but he shows up with that kind of stuff maybe only half the time. Other times, Sid's control deserts him suddenly, and the hitters, who would much prefer not to swing anyway, are more than happy to walk around the bases. Fernandez is not the type to report to spring training in any kind of condition to play, and consequently is not the type of pitcher to win consistently in April and May. He seems to fare much better in the hot weather of July and August.

Sid generally misses a few turns over the course of the year, so he'll wind up with around 30 starts (maybe a little less), and will guarantee you well-above-average numbers in ERA, ratio, and strikeouts. His career high in wins is 16, but you've got to figure that he's got a shot to put it all together one of these years. . .

The fifth starter will be chosen from among Julio Valera, Ron Darling, or maybe a long-shot like Wally Whitehurst. My money (but not much of it) would be on Valera, for several reasons: First: Why the hell not? You can take Darling if you want, but even if he makes the rotation, he won't help you much, and if he doesn't make it, he won't help anyone at all. I can't really picture Whitehurst as more than a very occasional starter. The Mets don't seem to have a whole lot of use for the Ed Lynch/John Mitchell/Terry Leach type of pitcher, and I can't say that I blame them. Valera might not make the grade as a starter, and may even wind up back in AAA, but he's got the potential.

Some Stats:

	W-L	ERA	RATIO	RUN SUPPORT
Frank Viola				
1st half:	13-3	2.20	1.106	NA
2nd half:	7-9	3.13	1.192	NA
overall :	20-12	2.67	1.150	4.31 runs/start
Dwight Gooden				
1st half:	8-5	4.21	1.283	NA
2nd half:	11-2	3.45	1.287	NA
overall :	19-7	3.83	1.285	5.88 runs/start
David Cone				
1st half:	5-4	4.40	1.267	NA
2nd half:	9-6	2.44	1.058	NA
overall :	14-10	3.23	1.143	4.93 runs/start
Sid Fernandez				
1st half:	5-5	3.53	1.163	NA
2nd half:	4-9	3.41	1.044	NA
overall :	9-14	3.46	1.099	4.20 runs/start

Adam Stein:

David Cone has become a chronic slow starter who's great in the second half. Let someone else draft him; then take him away from a disgruntled owner. Or, if you play Ultra, put Cone on your reserve list for April and May; when he starts throwing shutouts, dust him off and place him on your active roster for the remainder of the season.

Lary Bump:

Bud Harrelson's decision to start Julio Valera against Pittsburgh in September didn't cost the Mets the pennant, but didn't help them win it. The 22-year-old righthander started very well at Tidewater, and even after cooling off, he finished with a 1.17 ratio and a 3.02 ERA. With the Mets he had an ugly 2.08 ratio and 6.92 ERA. Unless they ditch Ron Darling, the Mets should be able to give Valera another year in the minors. That could set up an interesting battle a year from now if Anthony Young, a 24-year-old righthander, continues the progress that made him the Texas League pitcher of the year, top winner (15) and ERA champ (1.65). His ratio at Jackson was 1.06. He's a fastball-slider pitcher.

PHILADELPHIA

Pete DeCoursey:

Terry Mulholland, Ken Howell, Pat Combs, Jose DeJesus are the set starters, with Steve Ontiveros, Jason Grimsley, and Tommy Greene as the competitors for the 5th slot. These are all risks, gambles, potential nuclear incidents, capable of mushrooming your ratio and ERA.

Mulholland finished the season strongest, turning his season around after hurling a no-hitter at the Giants, his former mates. He is probably the NL pitcher most likely to be 1991's Neal Heaton: fireballing like a nova for a few months, and then burning away in a grey semblance of mediocrity. In his last 10 starts of the year, Mulholland pitched 78 innings, allowing 50 hits and 16 BBs for a 1.85 ERA, and may be the Phil most likely to benefit from a Johnny Podres change-up. If you need a last starter, and you can get him for under $5, take him, but be aware of two things: (1) Last year was the first full major league season he had not finished with an ERA perilously close to 5.00; and (2) Leyva loves him, and sent him regularly to the mound until August with an ERA well over 5.00. If Terry pitches ineffectively, Nicky will not protect you.

Pat Combs is the only Phillies pitcher whom you may be able to judge in spring training. If you can see him throw his breaking ball smoothly, without telegraphing and hanging it up as his arm drags after his body, draft him. If his motion continues to be erratic, expect another season of awful and awesome alternating from turn to turn. If he resolves his mechanical flaws and uses his fastball aggressively, he has the potential to win 15 games, even with the Phils; if not, 10-15, 4.00, is probably his downside.

Ken Howell is one the very few pitchers who was ever disabled for a long period of time because of a sore armpit. He still has great stuff, and in '89, he pitched better and better as the season wore on. If you get him, do not give up on him early. His downside performance in ratio and ERA are likely to be the least disastrous of any Phillie. He also wins a few ugly games each April and May, despite unsightly box score lines, so if he's healthy, and drops several pounds from the start, he could be a good bargain.

DeJesus is a neat pitcher, but he strikes out very few men for a premium fastballer, and will compile another poor ratio. He has never recorded a winning season, and given the support he got last year and is likely to get this season, will likely continue this record. If however, you have a minor league option, and can pick up DeJesus cheap, do so. He and Combs are the two pitchers on the staff likeliest to win 20 one of these years.

The 5th slot should go to Steve Ontiveros or Tommy Greene. Ontiveros will pitch well until his shoulder breaks down again, and he claims that the reconstructive surgery he underwent makes him a new pitcher. He is probably the best bet for a sleeper on the staff, but he may not pitch at all after a few starts, given his history. If you can get him for $1-$3, okay, but any more than that may only buy you a few good starts.

If Ontiveros breaks down, Tommy Greene, who finally began to adjust to the Vet in Sept., may well benefit, and help the team. Greene is another example of how early publicity can hurt a career. At 23, Greene has good stuff, is a fine athlete and good hitter. He could easily become a steady double figures winner, a la Kevin Gross.

The one guy you should not invest in is Jason Grimsley, who has an awful ratio, and whose good ERA is a function of several extremely quick hooks by Leyva. Grimsley will be good this decade, but not next year. His control is nowhere near ready for the majors.

Danny Cox is the comeback longshot who will toil in Clearwater this March. If he's healthy, who knows?

Adam Stein:

Bruce Ruffin and Don Carman have done about much harm as any two teammates over the years. If some weird turn of events causes you to consider either of these names, stop thinking and leave the room. Even if they surface somehow in 1991, don't be fooled when they have three or four excellent outings. They're just trying to set you up for the kill, when they will give up six runs in one inning. Stay away from them!

Thom Rogers:

If you review second half stats for pitchers, the name Terry Mulholland jumps out at you. On opening day, he'll be 28, prime age for a lefty. In the second half, he had a 2.86 ERA and a 1.05 ratio. In the fourth quarter (his last 77 IP) Mulholland boasted a 1.99 ratio and a 0.86 ERA.

Lary Bump:

Tommy Greene and Jason Grimsley are both 23-year-old righthanders. Greene is another one of those disappointments out of the Atlanta organization. In the International League, he had a 1.38 ratio and 3.49 ERA. In the National, the numbers were 1.48 and 5.08. Grimsley's numbers at Scranton were similar (1.48, 3.43), but in 11 starts for the Phillies he had a 3.30 ERA despite a 1.57 ratio. Wildness (43 walks in 57.1 IP) plagued him in the bigs.

PITTSBURGH

Readers of this book and the WINNING ROTISSERIE newsletter are well aware that I spend long winter nights perusing second half numbers, searching for clues. NEAL HEATON is my favorite example from 1990, showing why baseball forecasters must pay careful attention to second half stats.

Media people were crawling all over Heaton in April, May and June last year, dutifully asking questions: Who is this guy? Why is he winning every game? How is he getting people out? How did a mediocre thrower (with a firmly established lifetime ERA of 4.45) suddenly become unhittable? What kind of pitches does he throw?

"Did anything CHANGE?" they asked Heaton. They asked Mike Lavalliere. They asked Jim Leyland. They even asked Don Slaught, who wasn't around in 1989 to see the old Heaton. "What is Heaton doing different this year?"

Well, sure enough, something did CHANGE. Early in July 1989, Heaton developed a simple yet effective off-speed pitch, delivered with motion identical to his fastball, and with good control. The pitch has decent movement, and baffling low velocity. Every time Heaton pitched in May and June 1990, the TV news gave another "flash report" telling the amazing story of Heaton's "new" screwknuckle-change. (It is really, just a split-finger pitch, but Mike LaValliere had his fun with the media by giving it a weird name.)

I have just one question for all the analysts and commentators: why didn't somebody ask the same, simple question in 1989, in July, August or September: Did something change? What is it about April 1990 (4-0, 2.59 ERA) that is so much more captivating than September 1989 (3-0, 1.51 ERA) or August 1989 (0.61 ERA) or even July 1989 (2.45 ERA)?

We all know the answer, of course. Nobody bothered to write down Heaton's numbers for the second half of 1989, and all of his great performances got mixed-in and buried among his first half 1989 record of 1-6, 4.56 (the typical Neal Heaton we had all come to know).

Our 1990 RBA book isolated Neal Heaton's outstanding record for the second half of 1989: 5-1 with a 1.66 ERA and a 1.03 ratio. Based on this strong evidence that SOMETHING CHANGED during 1989, we forecasted Heaton to produce an unprecedented ERA of 2.89 and a 1.20 ratio for 1990, and we measured his "quality" rating as 9 on a scale of 10.

Some pitcher is going to experience a change in 1991, and hopefully before October, some media people will be asking him questions like, "Hey, Neal, what changed?"

As we said in June last year, "Heaton may go down the tubes any time. Things change, and pitching is a fragile skill." And Heaton had a rough second half. But his total 1990 performance, including 12 wins and a 3.45 ERA, must have been pleasing to the people who paid an average of only $3 for Heaton in 1990 auctions, Heck, he wasn't even taken in about one third of all drafts. Can't you use 12 wins and a 3.45 ERA?

Bill Gray:

Same comment as last year: "Doug Drabek is a gem starter. He is of the few consistent pitchers over the last year and a half. The only problem is a shortage of wins. Drabek produced several splendid games last year, including some CG's, that ended up in the loss column. Drabek's average price was only $12 last year, and he is certainly worth more than that. The basic problem in pitching is to get quality innings with minimal risk. Drabek gives you both."

If you acted on that advice, you got Drabek for an average price of only $15 in 1990; sometimes this game is surprisingly easy. Last year we valued Drabek higher than Dwight Gooden (who cost $26), Mike Scott ($25), and Bruce Hurst ($22), for example.

John Smiley: my prediction is that the next no-hitter by a Pirates pitcher will be tossed by Smiley. When he is good, he is great. He has all the talent in the world, and the brains to make it work for him. He could easily become the Steve Carlton of the 1990's. Grab him now, while he's dirt cheap after last year's problems.

Zane Smith cost only $4 (average) last year and was left untaken in many auctions. In the second half he was 7-3 with a 2.19 ERA and a 0.92 ratio. Sometimes talent emerges. It isn't possible that everyone who ever pitched in the Braves system is destined to be a bum, is it?

Adam Stein:

Randy Tomlin will be the next pitcher to suffer from Bruce Ruffin disease. Symptoms: (1) Come out of nowhere and soar to heights among best starting pitchers in the National League. (2) Sell for $15 or more in most Rotisserie auctions after delivering one streak. (3) Turn out to be utterly worthless, even destructive, for Rotisserie roster purposes.

Neal Heaton and John Smiley both suffered physical problems in the second half of 1990. Both should be quality starters again in 1991, meaning that Randy Tomlin could return to the minors.

Lary Bump:

We can project Randy Tomlin, a 25-year-old lefty, as a rotation starter for the Pirates, because he was last year. He pitched well in virtually every one of his 12 starts. In fact, he found hitters in the National League, where he had an 0.95 ratio and 2.55 ERA, about as easy as the weaklings in the Eastern League, where he went 1.07, 2.28.

Mike York, a 26-year-old righty, has been around the block — in fact, around several blocks. He started in the White Sox organization, and has spent seven years in the minors and some time in alcohol rehab. He pitched well enough at Buffalo (1.54 ratio, 4.20 ERA in a pitchers' park) to earn a four-game look in Pittsburgh (1.42, 2.84). If he has a future, it may be in the bullpen, for lefty hitters give him trouble.

ST. LOUIS

Busch Stadium is a great place to look for pitching. The stadium itself is great, and the one-run strategy installed by Whitey Herzog and continued by Joe Torre is great for pitchers. The Cardinals' philosophy is simple. The method is to take away the one-run strategy from the other team, with a huge stadium, high velocity carpet-cruisers in the outfield and guys like Ozzie Smith playing infield, and pitchers who can runners close. The other team may hope to wait for the big inning, which never comes. When is the last time you saw two homers in one inning in Busch Stadium? Name last year's HR leader for the Cardinals. Guerrero? Almost. He had 13. It was Zeile, with 15.

So the opposition sees there is no point in waiting for the three-run inning. They try to steal, or bunt, or hit-and-run, and they find their runners picked off, their stealers caught, and their bunts being fielded by people like Zeile and handled by people like Smith for the DP.

What happens when the Cardinals come to bat? Guess what carpet-cruisers do at the plate and on the basepaths. They hit for high average. They steal bases, thousands of them. They score runs. Back to Rotisserie:

The relevance of the above is that, before you even start, you have a team and a manager that are planning a lot of low-scoring games. That is how you get people like Joe Magrane to lead the league in ERA and with only five wins.

Big stadiums, left-handed pitchers, managers who use one-run strategies and impose them on the other team, are all good things to have involved in your rotisserie staff. Now, down to specifics.

We recommend Joe Magrane every year. He has been good to people who follow our advice. In January 1989, for example: "Prime value can be had for a bargain price, because of the low "W" count. Spend on Magrane. Trust us."

Bryn Smith didn't work out in 1990, but he has been a decent pitcher for years. He is probably the best comeback candidate among all the aged pitchers in the NL. The track record of pitchers acquired by the Cardinals is one of consistent (and sometimes dramatic) improvement.

Jose DeLeon is one of the acquisitions who became a star with the Cardinals. After learning to throw the ball over the plate (I don't know what Whitey told him, but it must have been an offer he couldn't refuse) DeLeon became a whole new pitcher. But he had his problems in 1990 (1-12, 5.16 ERA in the second half). It isn't a good idea to take pitchers coming off dreadful performances.

After Magrane, Smith and DeLeon, the picture gets cloudy. John Tudor is unlikely to return. (If he does, grab him; if he can't pitch well, he will stop pitching, and put you out of your misery.)

Bob Tewksbury pitched very well in the second half of 1990 (1.14 ratio) and is the best candidate for fourth starter. He dominated the American Association in 1989 (13-5, 2.43, 1.08) and looked just fine in a stint with the Cards.

Ken Hill sucked in a few myopic people in 1989 when he started the year with a low ERA. Every year, the Cardinals have two or three rookies who get off to great starts (most recently Hill, Cris Carpenter, Greg Mathews, Scott Terry, etc.) and then fade. You have to look at their minor league numbers, or look at SOMETHING other than the June 7 USA Today, to see what to expect from these kids over the course of a year. Before 1989, Ken Hill had never had an ERA under 4.50 in any league above the "A" level. All you have to do is look at the last five lines in the Baseball Register, and read: 5.14, 4.50, 5.20, 5.14, 4.92. This isn't multi-variate regression analysis; this is doing your homework. When Hill produced a 4.65 ERA in the second half, with a sickening ratio, and proceeded to lose 15 games, anyone who was genuinely surprised should stop playing Rotisserie baseball. If you know anyone who traded FOR Ken Hill and his superb ERA in June 1989, please have them call me; I would like to babysit their teenage girls while they go to look at this piece of real estate . . .

Adam Stein:

Joe Magrane had a 2.90 ERA in the second half, and has had extended periods of quality pitching in previous years, without attracting much attention, and certainly not attracting any high prices. Within the treacherous world of starting pitchers, he offers a nice combination of safety and economy.

Omar Olivares is a young pitcher to keep your eye on. He has an excellent chance to take John Tudor's place in the starting rotation. If he's bad, he will go back to Louisville, cutting your losses. If he's good, he will be a nice bargain.

Lary Bump:

Cris Carpenter is an ex-Olympian, ex-can't miss prospect, and a current 25-year-old righthanded suspect. He pitched well (1.17 ratio, 3.70 ERA) as a starter at Louisville, then the Cardinals dumped him back in their bullpen (0.88, 4.50) when he came back up in September. They haven't seemed to know how to use him. He isn't a rookie anymore. Last season, he wouldn't talk to reporters; he told one of them, "I'm giving it the Steve Carlton treatment." Maybe after another 294 or so career wins, Cris.

In contrast, Omar Olivares, a 23-year-old righty acquired from the Padres before last season, is a shining hope for St. Louis. His numbers at Louisville were 1.17 and 2.82. He went 1.26 and 2.92 with the Cardinals. There is talk of putting him into the crowd in the bullpen, but he seems too valuable an addition to the oft-crippled rotation. Olivares has a very real shot in '91; Carpenter's chance may be slipping away.

[To keep Olivares differentiated from Francisco Oliveras, exaggerate the pronunciation. Oli-vay-reez is the Cardinal; Oli-vee-rahs is the Giant.]

SAN DIEGO

Bruce Hurst was mysteriously horrible in the first half of 1990, but I like him for 1991, anyway. When an established star, a lefty on a good team in a good stadium, produces a second half record of 6-2 with a 1.94 ERA and a 1.01 ratio, I get all excited. If you traded for Hurst in mid 1990, congratulations.

Everybody wants to know about Andy Benes. He has had some shoulder problems that took a few MPH off his fastball. Is there really any such thing as a minor injury in a pitcher's working parts? Benes has been most popular with bidders who are determined to prove that a little knowledge is a dangerous thing. They all know that Benes was the first player drafted in 1989, taken before Gregg Olson, Jim Abbott, and Robin Ventura. Possibly, they also know that Tim Belcher was the most recent pitcher taken as the very first selection. Benes might turn out to be very good. But there are 75 other pitchers who might turn out to be very good, and they will all be cheaper.

Greg W Harris will be joining the starting rotation in 1991. If you wanted him for saves, forget it. If you wanted a quality pitcher, he is still OK.

Wes Gardner, over from the Red Sox, can't possibly be any worse than he was in the AL. He is still a power pitcher, featuring a fastball and slider. He might just be better suited to the NL, and could surprise some people. The Padres might use him as a starter or reliever.

Suspects for the rotation include Derek Lilliquist, Mike Dunne, Calvin Schiraldi, free agent Dennis Rasmussen, and a horde of minor leaguers. I wouldn't get real excited about any of them.

Brigg Hewitt:

Ed Whitson surprised the Padres, the fans, and the Rotisserie world with his two tremendous seasons in 1989-1990. I think Whitson, like Mark Davis, benefitted very much from the coaching of Pat Dobson. Remember, Whitson's problems with the New York Yankees were not exactly physical. With Dobson now practicing psychiatry in Kansas City, you should be worried about Whitson for 1991.

Andy Benes has become the sentimental favorite of the Padres organization. He is a home-grown talent. In my opinion, he was rushed to the majors too early, and is still learning how to pitch. He probably won't do much in 1990 either, but on the optimistic side, you don't have to shave much off a 3.60 ERA to make a real good pitcher.

Lary Bump:

Rafael Valdez was a 15-game winner in '89. The 22-year-old righty struggled last season at Las Vegas (1.71, 4.92). It's surprising that the Padres used him only in relief in a September trial, where he was ineffective (2.29, 11.12). He could surprise and move into the rotation sometime this season, but he probably needs a solid Triple-A season. In 1989, Valdez was 5-0 with a 1.94 ERA in 6 starts at Wichita.

SAN FRANCISCO

Supporters of Bud Black like to point out that he has better stats than Mark Langston over the last two years. Black wouldn't be the first pitcher who excelled after arriving in San Francisco. I like his chances.

Scott Garrelts was 7-4 with a 3.18 ERA in the second half of 1990; his 1.33 ratio tells you he still isn't the old Garrelts, but he has come a long way back from the disaster of early 1990, when he had a pain in the neck and shared it with all his Rotisserie followers. He is going to get plenty of work from Roger Craig. Hopefully, he won't start the year with any posterior inflammations.

John Koller:

Giants pitchers gave up 710 runs in 1990; that's 110 more than the year before. Injuries were the central problem. Rick Reuschel and Mike LaCoss both had knee surgery and missed three months each. Don Robinson had hip and knee injuries, and Scott Garrelts a problem with his neck. Kelly Downs had rotator cuff surgery and didn't pitch until August.

Thom Rogers:

The Giants were still in the hunt for another starter (LH hopefully) but in December 1990, it looked like a rotation of Scott Garrelts, John Burkett, Bud Black, Don Robinson, and Kelly Downs, with Rick Reuschel, Mike LaCoss, and Trevor Wilson in the pen.

Rob Wood:

Al Rosen likes his young pitchers to dominate in the minors, so he normally keeps them down long after they could help the Giants. Contrary to this rule though, Trevor Wilson was brought up to San Francisco in 1989 before he was ready. But June 13, 1990 marked the turning-point in Wilson's career, the night he took a no-hitter into the ninth inning versus the Padres. Trevor has a very good arm, and once he learned an effective delivery he became a winner in the majors. Looking at his poor second half, the Giants are threatening to make a reliever out of Wilson. I think he may be worth a flyer for 1991.

Rafael Novoa went from Single-A to the majors in a little over half a season. Not overpowering, but may be a strikeout pitcher. I would wager that Novoa will be in the Giants 1991 plans.

John Burkett was a career minor leaguer before making it big in 1990. Has four average pitches, but has "pitching smarts". More than anything else, as we Rotisserie hounds know, Burkett's success shows how difficult it is to evaluate pitchers. Everyone in the Giants organization thought Gunderson was the future star and that Burkett was simply a warm body filling out a TripleA uniform. Now it looks reversed.

Eric Gunderson's pitching style is reminiscent of Dave Dravecky. His 1990 season was one disappointment after another: demoted from the Giants to Phoenix in late April. Then, after pitching poorly in Triple-A, demoted to Double A. The Giants may try Gunderson in the bullpen in 1991. He is no longer a viable prospect.

Mike Remlinger has gone significantly backward the past two seasons. Pass.

Lary Bump:

As a pitcher on the way up, Novoa has promise, at least for the future despite his 1.82, 6.75 record in SF. Gunderson's future is dim.

AMERICAN LEAGUE RELIEF PITCHERS

BALTIMORE

Is Gregg Olson losing his touch? Lefty hitters had only a .138 BA and .152 SA against him in 1989; then in 1990 they hit .200 and slugged .238. I wouldn't worry about it. The curve ball is still devastating. Olson is a phenomenon.

Gregg Olson could have been either a starter or a reliever for Baltimore in 1989. The Orioles apparently made the right decision by giving him the stopper's role. Rookies who step right in and become the bull pen ace are rare. Almost all of them become established stars. If there was any uncertainty about Olson as a one-year phenom, that doubt is entirely gone in 1991.

We have a nice track record recommending Olson in both of the past two years. Back in 1989, we recommended Olson as a sleeper and possible bull pen ace. Then in 1990, we expressed confidence that Olson's 1989 success would continue.

Olson offers a rare opportunity to compare college numbers to major league performance, without an intervening minor league career. At Auburn, he struck out 113 batters in 72 innings, with a Ratio under 1.00 and an ERA of exactly 2.00. Another lesson in Olson's quick rise to prominence: he gave up ten hits and ten walks in 11 IP with Baltimore in 1988, a classic case of why you should ignore any stats involving less than 30 innings, and ignore September call-up stats in general.

The setup man is 31-year-old Mark Williamson, a residual from the trade of Storm Davis for Terry Kennedy. Williamson got his first good measure of success in 1989, especially in the first half, when he got 7 saves with a 2.81 ERA and 1.02 ratio.

Another candidate for the rare saves that don't go into Olson's record could be Curt Shilling. A starter by profession, Schilling looked impressive in relief when he filled in for Williamson late in 1990.

Like most bullpens, the Orioles relief corps could use another lefty. On the winter roster and worth a quick look are Brian Dubois (a starter from the Detroit organization), Kevin Hickey (a 34-year-old journeyman), and two starters from Hagerstown, Mike Linskey and Chris Myers.

Hickey staged a minor comeback in 1989, after a five year absence from the major leagues (last with the White Sox). Hickey earned another shot at the majors with a 1.46 ERA at Rochester in 1988. He is a relatively weakthrowing, control type pitcher. Like many lefty relievers, he offers the good possibility that you can buy saves for less than $1 apiece.

Lary Bump:

Now that Mississippi Mike Smith is out of baseball (released by Columbus), Texas Mike Smith might be able to make a name for himself — if he can stay in baseball. Last season, he was an inconsistent 1.55, 4.96 at Rochester and 1.67, 12.00 in a Baltimore cameo. He might not even get a cameo this season, for it's left-handers the Orioles need.

BOSTON

Jeff Reardon has an excellent history and a lot of heart. In late August 1990, I heard the Red Sox trainer say that Reardon couldn't possibly pitch again before the end of the year, and you know what happened. He was back by playoff time. The back problems must be a cause for concern, however. Reardon missed enough games last year, that he had his lowest save total since pitching for Montreal in 1984.

Lefty Rob Murphy could have soared in value when Reardon went on the DL. He didn't. he flopped. One must conclude that he just isn't built for Fenway Park, physically or mentally.

The one who produced unexpected saves in 1990 was Jeff Gray. The former Phillies and Reds farmhand had attracted the Red Sox attention as far back as 1986, when he was 14-2 with a 2.35 ERA in the Eastern League.

Gray illustrates the value of subscribing to Winning Rotisserie Baseball (see page 111). We saw his potential value in May, and alerted our readers to pick him up. Reardon and Murphy both cooperated in helping Gray emerge with nine very cheap saves.

Greg Harris will back in the bullpen in 1991, we expect. A former save artist (yes, he is the same Harris who pitched for the Rangers in 1986), Greg could be a splendid relief sleeper for 1991, because of the uncertainties swirling around Reardon and his setup men. Larry Andersen, of course, is gone to San Diego to set up for Craig Lefferts.

Dennis Lamp has 150,000 miles on his odometer, but just keeps on rolling. He is strictly a middle relief type, not a closer, but is capable of quality innings. Joe ("Death in Rotisserie") Hesketh clung to the 40-man roster during the winter meetings; don't touch him.

Dan O'Neill and Jeff Plympton, the closing combo at AA New Britain last year, were both on the winter roster and will have a chance to help the ailing Boston pen in 1991. Lefty O'Neill was 7-0 with a 0.72 ERA and a 0.75 ratio in 1990. When you have trouble telling which is the ERA and which is the ratio, you have a darn good pitcher; he sure couldn't be any worse than Rob Murphy was last year.

Lary Bump:

You may have heard that Daryl Irvine is a prospect. But the right-hander is 26 already, and if he's so great, why didn't he get more than an 11-game trial last year, when the Bosox were desperate. He was 1.32, 3.24 with 12 saves at Pawtucket, then 1.44, 4.67 (no saves) with Boston. Given Jeff Reardon's physical condition, Irvine has a chance to stick, but not likely to be more than a a set-up man.

CALIFORNIA

After two years of skepticism about Bryan Harvey, I am starting to like him. He has lowered his ratio nicely, after posting a 1.40 that didn't deserve to earn 25 saves in 1989. In the second half of 1990, he got 14 saves despite missing some turns. In September, I was impressed with Harvey's fastball and hard splitter, and I was more impressed with Doug Rader's confidence in Harvey. We all know that saves are 60% management discretion and 40% skill. Harvey has that 60% in his pocket going into 1991.

Mark Eichhorn, the wunderkind of 1986, surfaced again in 1990 and delighted his Rotisserie enthusiasts with 13 saves. Don't expect anything remotely similar in 1991. Bring up Eichhorn's name early (don't bring it up late; you might get stuck with him) and you can find out quickly who, in your league, is looking at 1990 full year stats. In the second half, Eichhorn had zero saves, a 4.56 ERA, and a 1.86 ratio. Anyone who thinks that a winning Rotisserie roster can be assembled without careful consideration of the second half, should be sentenced to spend the summer of 1991 with nine Mark Eichhorns. He calls his pitching style "doo-doo." Nuff said.

Mike Fetters is an exciting commodity. Someone has got to pick up the slack left by the departed Willie Fraser and the failed Eichhorn. He's no puppy at age 26, but he has good stuff.

Lary Bump:

The RP prospects include Jeff Richardson and Cliff Young. After middling success as a starter in the Mets' organization, right-hander Richardson started a new career as a closer in the Angels system. He's 27, so it may be now or never for him. His 1.86 ERA in the thin air of Edmonton may be one of those "You don't judge a reliever by ERA" statistics, for he had a 1.52 ratio. He made it to California for one game last season. Don't count him out for a minor bullpen role this year. Last year, left-hander Young, 26, had his career year (1.06 ratio, 2.42 ERA at Edmonton; 1.53, 3.52 with the Angels). The Blue Jays once liked him so much they drafted him out of the Braves' organization. But after three years in which he yielded more hits than innings pitched, they gave up on him. Last year was also the first Young pitched exclusively in relief.

Greg Minton was still a free agent after the winter meetings.

Willie Fraser is an emerging talent. See Toronto.

CHICAGO WHITE SOX

The Chisox have obvious confidence in Bobby Thigpen and Scott Radinsky, having let go of two setup men. It will be fascinating to see Thigpen's 1990 $ value, as calculated by those analysts who spend their time crunching last year's numbers with excruciating detail. It should be astronomical, to the point that other relievers will be diminished. No one, of course, will ever go to an auction and bid with the expectation that a pitcher is going to get 50 saves, or even 40. Make sure you don't.

Radinsky got limited use (18 IP) in the second half, while his ERA and ratio went berserk as Radinsky walked a hitter per inning. He is still only 23. He throws from the left side. He jumped from A-ball to the majors (although he spent a lifetime at the "A" level). I like him.

The Sox have two more lefties in the pen, Wayne Edwards and Ken Patterson. Patterson will be promoted toward the game-ending situations in 1991, and will surely get more than the two saves that he had last year. He just needs to cut down the walks to be a nice little Rotisserie gem. At age 26 he is young enough (for a lefty) to be making improvements. Wayne Edwards shared the control problem in 1990. Edwards will pick up any slack in the lefty setup role if Patterson slips.

And one lefty from Vancouver: Steve Rosenberg is still kicking. He seems older than 26, but isn't. One White Sox insider tells me he is rated ahead of Radinsky for 1991 planning purposes.

Donn Pall is well-positioned to get the righty setup job in 1991. He has been excellent at times during the past three years, and was a candidate to emerge with the closer role back when the Chisox were open-minded to trading Thigpen.

Adam Peterson, a four year veteran of Triple-A, is notably unaccomplished in the major leagues. He will be a swing man.

Jon Dunkle:

The bullpen is what held the White Sox together all season. Led by recordbreaker Bobby Thigpen, the Sox posted the most saves by any major league team ever. Thigpen, of course, is the primary reliever and the closer. Before you go spending bundles of dollars on him, though, remember Mark Davis.

The main setup man, Barry Jones, is gone to Montreal, and Shawn Hillegas is gone to Cleveland. Scott Radinsky, arguably the hardest throwing pitcher in the American League, will give you plenty of strikeouts and will surely cut down his 1.59 ratio to a more reasonable number when he learns that the pitcher's Prime Directive is to throw the ball over the plate.

CLEVELAND

The key change to notice is the addition of Shawn Hillegas, who was 5-3 with a 1.74 ERA, 0.96 ratio, and 9 saves for AAA Vancouver.

Bill Gray:

Doug Jones, with 43 saves in 1990, continues to improve. After Thigpen broke the 50 save barrier, the Cleveland press wondered in print if Jones could get 50 saves. Sure he could, but it is unlikely that 50 will happen again soon. Jones has 112 saves over the last three years and if you have him, keep him. It is unlikely he'll be available in any established league. If you're starting a league, Jones should go fast and be expensive. Jones has been so reliable he is almost boring. The only excitement Doug seems to generate is guessing precisely when in August will Jones have his yearly collapse. The collapse lasts a few games and everyone thinks the hitters are figuring out his delivery and waiting for the changeup. Last year the crash came during the last week of August. Jones pitched 5 innings in 4 games and lost three while giving up 13 runs. He gave up 7 runs to Boston in one game. Then, in his next twelve outings, he got eight saves and a win. He blew only eight saves last year.

Steve Olin attracted some attention last year. If ever there was a pitching utility man, it was Olin in 1990. He worked in long and middle relief (primarily setting up Jones) as well as closer (1 save). Late in the year he started a game and won. Olin will be the closer when Jones is finished, but that won't be soon. He still gives up too many hits at this point, but his submarine delivery is rapidly making him a dominant pitcher in the Quisenberry-Tekulve mold. Look for his ERA and Ratio to improve dramatically in 1991. He is a future closer.

Jesse Orosco had his last hurrah in 1989. He's rapidly losing it. Once considered Jones' backup closer, the role now belongs to Olin. Jesse will get an inning or two in the middle innings. His Ratio and ERA will not help you and he will not suddenly improve as he did upon arriving in the AL in 1989. [I thought he was cooked when the Dodgers had him — J.B.]

Rudy Seanez will be 22 in 1991. He has a fastball in the mid 90's and has no idea where it is going. If and when he gets control of his fastball and develops another "out" pitch, grab him. It will probably be a couple more years. Reminds me of Rijo when he came up and Rijo has just now learned to pitch after six years in the majors.

Efraim Valdez was 1-1 with a 3.04 ERA in 23 innings. Has a good screwball but is inexperienced and has some control problems. A Juan Agosto type of pitcher who could last in the majors (he's a lefty) for years without anybody ever noticing. Not a Rotisserie candidate in 1991.

Steve Goldman:

Mauro Gozzo, was acquired in the trade for Bud Black in September, will certainly be given a chance, and has the potential to be a good one. And fireballing Rudy Seanez, if he ever can find control, also has star potential. And, although I expect them to get consideration as starters, it is possible that the other two pitchers acquired in the Black deal, Alex Sanchez and Steve Cummings, could see action as either set-up men or long relievers.

Lary Bump:

Watch Mauro Gozzo, Efrain Valdez, Rudy Seanez, and Colby Ward. A side effect of writing these player previews is happening on information in older publications. Thus, in Marty Noble's rookie preview in Street & Smith's Baseball, 1990, we find Gozzo sandwiched between Mark Gardner and Mike Harkey, as one of seven rookie pitchers mentioned. That was after a season in which he totaled a 16-2 record at the three highest levels in the Toronto system. Last year Goose found himself back at Syracuse (1.34, 3.58) and finally with Cleveland for four innings after the Bud Black trade. Let's look at this logically. He isn't going to displace Doug Jones. So it's middle relief, a possible starting role or — most likely — a summer in Colorado Springs.

A left-handed bullpen hope is the 24-year-old Valdez, not to be confused with the Tribe's sometimes starter, Sergio Valdez. At Colorado Springs, Efrain went 1.36, 3.81 with 6 saves. With Cleveland, he was at 1.44, 3.04. Should Jesse Orosco falter, this Valdez could move in as a left-handed complement to Jones. In any event, look for EValdez in Indians box scores this year.

Seanez is a smoke-throwing 22-year-old righty who has shown enough talent to spend parts of the last two seasons in Cleveland. But he has to go back to the minors to learn to throw strikes. In 56 innings at three stops last year, he struck out 58 — but walked 47. His numbers — Canton, 1.26 ratio, 2.16 ERA; Colorado Springs, 2.08, 6.75; Cleveland, 1.72, 5.29.

Ward is a 27-year-old who has started one game in his pro career. Last season a 1.19, 2.00 start at Colorado Springs earned him a major league shot in Cleveland, where his record was 1.44, 4.25. Not bad for an Indian, but not good enough to keep him on the 40-man roster.

DETROIT

Sparky Anderson's roster plans read like a child's Christmas list: "I want Torey Lovullo to play 160 games at first base, and I want Tony Phillips and Lou Whitaker to play second every day, and I want my eight regulars and six utilitymen to get 600 at bats apiece, and I want a solid five man rotation, and I want a six-man bullpen with three lefties and three righties, and I want . . ." OK, OK, Sparky. Here's a piece of candy, now get lost.

If you follow Sparky's stated intentions (THIS is fantasy baseball), then you must foresee a bullpen with Jerry Don Gleaton, Paul Gibson, and Mike Munoz (?) coming at you from the left side. Munoz was on the Albuquerque-L.A. shuttle during 1990. At age 25 he has a bright future. Gibson you know already, and Gleaton just came out of nowhere to blossom as a closer at age 33. Alternatives to Munoz could be Dave Richards or Jose Ramos, or even would-be starter Steve Searcy in a relief role.

The righty half of this fantasy starts with Mike Henneman, who got only five saves in the second half of 1990. After that, look at Yankee castoff Clay Parker, and Eric Stone (2-4, 4 saves at Toledo). Roster actions like dumping Lance McCullers would indicate that Detroit is expecting to get more pitchers, soon.

KANSAS CITY

Mark Davis brought Rotisserie people and real baseball together in 1990. Everyone agreed that Davis was the biggest bust, money-wise, in both games last year.

In these pages last year, we went on (at great length) about the impact of Pat Dobson's coaching on Mark Davis' pitching. Some readers (in January-February) thought we overdid the topic. Kansas City management, who hired Dobson away from San Diego to straighten Davis out, obviously think the topic is worthy of attention. In any event, it is amusing to see all the national media now reporting what we told you a full year ago: Dobson knows how to talk to Davis.

Mark has marvelous natural stuff, as the world now knows. He made Bo Jackson look like an overbulked Little Leaguer in the 1989 All Star game: three pitches, three strikes, you're out (after Jackson had homered in his first at bat). Before the San Diego days, Rotisserie people generally dismissed him. Some noticed that he was among the league leaders with a 1.13 ratio in 1985, and many noticed that had an ERA under three in 1986, but the bids for Davis tended to be pessimistic. Only a few die-hard followers kept buying Davis year after year, waiting for his talent to surface. Major league franchises also devalued the man, who looked just as good on the mound as he did on paper.

I thought the turning point came on Tuesday March 15, 1988, in a spring training game against the Mariners. Get last year's book if you want the anecdote. Anyway, in the two years after that, Davis had a 1.93 ERA and 72 saves; and you saw those numbers here first.

Pat Dobson does not have a reputation for straightening out Ebby LaLoosh types, but maybe he should have. There are quite a number of talented hurlers who have become less enigmatic and more successful while pitching for San Diego.

Jeff Montgomery was helped immensely by the failure of Davis. Montgomery also has great stuff, featuring a high-BTU heater. Montgomery stepped back into the closer role, from which Davis had evicted him, and simply did it all.

Kansas City re-signed Andy McGaffigan and Steve Crawford, and picked up Dan Schatzeder. Lefty Shatzeder is the most likely to get a save or two; all three are potential contributors.

Marc Bowman:

Davis suffered from two severe problems. He couldn't throw strikes consistently, and when he did throw strikes, they were hit over the fence. Otherwise, he was perfectly fine! There has been much discussion about Davis' collapse from the Cy Young form of 1989. Part of the story is that he suffered a hairline fracture of a finger bone during spring training. It wasn't serious enough to disable him, but it affected his control. Control has always been critical, and the minor problem caused a major loss of confidence. Davis finally went on the DL late in the year.

The good news is that Davis pitched very well in September, after coming off the DL. He threw strikes, and he got saves. The bad news is that these games didn't mean anything, either for the Royals, or for Davis' hopeless 1990 stats.

Reuniting Davis with coach Pat Dobson could make Davis a dominant closer again. He could be a bargain in 1991, certainly for people who want to take a chance. You already know one factor that will keep his price down: in every league, there will be one person who simply will not bid on Davis. That's the person who bought him last year!

Jeff Montgomery did all he could to rescue the Royals failing bullpen in 1990. He was good, but he wasn't the unhittable closer that the team needed. He had a 1.43 ratio in the second half, giving up almost a hit per inning. His attitude is similar to Rob Dibble's. He has the stopper's mentality and loves to bear down, producing high strikeout ratios.

Steve Crawford re-signed and now figures in a picture that includes Luis Aquino and Mel Stottlemyre Jr. Deeper in the pen, you find Carlos Maldonado (2.91 ERA, 20 saves at Memphis), Victor Cole, and Hector Wagner. Failed prospect Jay Baller (last up with the Cubs in 1987) got the saves at AAA Omaha in 1990. Maldonado is the only minor leaguer with a chance of Rotisserie value in 1991.

Lary Bump:

Stottlemyre Junior, at 27 a year older than his brother Todd, was probably the best closer in the minors when the Royals called him up from Omaha, where he went 0.90, 1.51 with 13 saves. Even though the KC short men struggled, for some reason Duke Wathan used righty Stottlemyre as a starter and middle reliever. He had a 1.50 ratio and 4.88 ERA with the big club. He was a starter before knee surgery curtailed his 1988 season at Memphis, but he has come back strong as a reliever the last two seasons. How about it, Duke? Will you let Jeff Montgomery blow another 10 saves this year, or give Mel a chance?

Long before "Wild Thing" became a ballpark organist's cliche, Luis Encarnacion had his own theme music, "Louie, Louie," at Waterbury in 1986. Despite 44 saves in three Double-A seasons, he found himself back at Memphis to start '89. He finally made it to Triple-A later that year. And after a successful 1.32, 2.96 season with 7 saves as Jay Baller's set-up man at Omaha, Louie made it to the majors (1.74, 7.84). The 27-year-old righty could be a successful set-up in th majors, if there's anyone to set up in KC. Don't spend a lot, but think about him at the end of the draft.

The name "CsMaldonado" found its way into box scores as the Royals played out the string last year. Turns out to be a 24-year-old right-hander up from

Memphis, where he led the team in saves. He was out of his league with KC (2.17, 9.00). Look for him at Omaha this season, and if KC can't find a closer, you may see old Cs back in the boxes.

MILWAUKEE

Alan Boodman:

The Milwaukee bullpen will be much improved in 1991. And Lord knows there's plenty of room for improvement. Dan Plesac is coming off of his worst year since AA ball. Chuck Crim pitched poorly until after the All-Star break last year; a full year of prime time Crim will give a big lift to the pen. And Julio Machado is now around to help out for a full season.

Plesac can normally be counted on for about 30 saves and a sub-2.50 ERA. That didn't happen in 1990; Dan supplied 24 saves, but his ERA ballooned to nearly 4.50, and his control was way off. The Brewers have apparently decided that now would be a good time to unload Danny (I thought you were supposed to buy low and sell high), and by the time you read this, he may be gone. Plesac did much better in the second half, dropping his ratio from over 1.50 to below 1.30. He should be undervalued at lots of auctions this year, so this would be a good time to add one of the best relievers in the league to your staff, without spending a lot of cash. A return to form can be expected, if Plesac is given a chance. Are you listening, Harry Dalton?

Chuck Crim has averaged 10 saves and 6 wins per year since joining the Brewers in 1987. Crim had a difficult first half in 1990, with symptoms like a 4.29 ERA and a 1.45 ratio. But he came on strong after the All Star break; his ERA was 2.29 and his ratio 1.08. Every year, Crim offers high quality, a proven track record, and good upward potential in the save count. All these nice attributes are not lost on the people who buy Crim. They paid an average of more than $10 last year, and will probably go higher this year because of the doubts about Plesac.

If Plesac gets traded or benched, Julio Machado could emerge as the righthanded half of a closing combo (with Crim). Machado had a 1.12 ratio and a 2.53 ERA when the Mets sent him down to the minors in early 1990. (That tells you how good the Mets THOUGHT their bullpen was). Machado really is that good. He is a very hard thrower, stolen by the Mets from a sleepy Phillies system. Machado definitely has nothing left to prove at AAA, and, if Dan Plesac falters again, Julio may establish himself as the right-handed closer. Machado's fortunes will be the inverse of Plesac's 1991 experience in Milwaukee. A strong performance by Plesac will mean no saves for Machado. Absent Plesac, Julio could get 15 or 20 saves.

Other suspects and pretenders in the Brewers' bullpen include names like Randy Veres, Mark Lee, Tony Fossas, Dennis Powell, and Bob Sebra. They're just waiting for the next flight to Denver. Starters Mark Knudson, Bill Wegman, and Don August (who was taken off the major league roster) may surface in the Milwaukee pen during 1990.

Lary Bump:

In 1990, the Brewers' bullpen consisted primarily of cannon fodder, pitchers called up from the minors to soak up a few middle innings in each game after the starters failed and before it was time for the short relievers. Righthander Randy Veres, 25, was the most successful of those shoved into the breech His 1.74 ratio and 5.19 ERA at Denver, even a mile high, hardly qualified him for a major league job, but these were desperate times. His numbers (1.30, 3.78) were much better with the Brewers. He now has exactly 50 IP in the majors, so he's still a rookie. If he gets one man out this season, he won't be a rookie next year. And he pitched well enough to merit a middle relief, spot-starting role for '91.

Narciso Elvira is a 23-year-old lefty whose height (5-10) and nationality (Mexican) have caused him to be compared to Ted Higuera. His performance, slowed by injuries, hasn't caught up. He moved up last year from Beloit (1.20, 2.35) to El Paso

(1.28, 4.50) and Milwaukee (2.10, 5.40), totaling just 61.1 IP. He may return to the big leagues, but not before September of '91. Look for him at Denver, or maybe for a third season at El Paso.

Machado, a hard-throwing 25-year-old, wasn't the right-handed closer the Mets thought he would be, but in 10 games with the Brewers, he saved 3. Another acquisition in the Charlie O'Brien trade, he had a 1.14 ratio and 1.69 ERA with 8 saves at Tidewater. His performance with the Mets (1.43, 3.15) wasn't bad, but he was very good (1.31, 0.69) with Milwaukee. He's no longer a rookie, but he could be a complement to lefty Dan Plesac, or could even supplant him as the bullpen ace. In either event, Chuck Crim would go back to more middle-relief and set-up work.

The only thing wrong with Machado is that he gave up just one run in 13 IP with the Brewers last year. If he had given up three or four runs, fewer people would have noticed him. The 0.69 ERA that placed him at the top of the USA Today Brewers pitcher stats last October, undoubtedly attracted attention during the winter. You want your sleepers to be low profile people, not guys walking around with placards that say, "Hey, look at me!"

MINNESOTA

Also at the top of his team's ERA listing in 1990 was Rich Garces of the Twins. I wish I had a dollar for every bozo who believes that Garces is going to be a big impact closer in 1991. Yes, he's very young, but youth is not a Rotisserie category. Garces had an excellent summer at class A Visalia, piling up 28 saves. Then he got promoted to AA, and finished the season notching two saves in the major leagues. Against Double-A hitters, Garces' ratio exploded to 1.78, and he allowed eight baserunners in five innings for the Twins. If you can induce people in your league to pay big bucks for Garces, do it. Pray that he makes the roster and keeps the possibility alive. In general, the people who expect Garces to emerge are the same people who believed in the phenom Park Pittman last year at this time.

The arrival of Steve Bedrosian will put a damper on the daydreams involving Garces. The belief that a 20-year-old rookie might push aside Rick Aguilera could be characterized as optimism; the belief that he could push aside a multi-million dollar free agent like Bedrosian, AND Aguilera needs a stronger word, something along the lines of "delusion."

Bedrosian is no more deserving than Aguilera, but money talks. Bedrock will be given every chance to prove that 1990 was a fluke. My personal opinion is that Bedrosian is washed up, and that the Twins better keep Aguilera, and keep him ready. Bedrosian got ten saves in the second half of 1990, but he had a 3.93 ERA and a 1.53 ratio. He could become a genuine incendiary in the Hump Dome.

Rick Aguilera had tendinitis problems last year, but he has recovered from the same problem before. If the Twins are simply concerned about using Aggie without hurting him, there is no evidence that a starting role will be easier on his arm. He has to throw hard to be effective, anyway.

Three thoughts on Aggie's uncertain future: (1) My hunch for 1991 is that, if he stays with the Twins, Aguilera will reclaim the stopper role, after Bedrosian fails. (2) The Twins' posturing after they acquired Bedrosian, when they asserted that Aguilera was not automatically out of the bullpen, could be a prelude to a trade of Aguilera to one of the may teams that needs a stopper (Yankees, Astros, e.g.); you don't tell the world, "This guy is no good for the closer role," and then try to trade him. (3) You should know Aggie's role by draft day. He asked the Twins to tell him, starter or stopper, before spring training begins. If you can't be bothered reading every newspaper during February and March, subscribe to Winning Rotisserie Baseball (203-834-0812).

The Rich Garces bandwagon makes me want to want to ask the question: "What happened to Park Pittman?" Last year he was the Twins Great Young Closer. BS, I say. Pittman stunk up the joint at Portland last year (6.99 ERA and a ratio way over 2) while leading the Beavers in saves with 6. Big deal. And now Garces? He had a Ratio around 2 after promotion to Double-A last year.

Aging in the wings is lefty Gary Wayne, whose role will increase significantly if Juan Berenguer isn't re-signed. Terry Leach is a groundball pitcher who might revive his career in Minnesota, but will never again have Rotisserie value.

Finally, two more "I told you so" predictions from last year: "Aguilera given the closer role," and "Park Pittman a high ERA with control problems."

Lary Bump:

In little over half a season at Visalia, Rich Garces, a 19-year-old righty, saved 28 games with an 0.91 ratio and a 1.81 ERA. At Orlando, his numbers were 1.82, 2.08 [the 1.82 is the BPI Ratio, in case you're unsure] with 8 more saves. When Rick Aguilera had some arm trouble, the Twins looked around for a closer and spotted Garces. In five games with the big club, he saved two of them and had a 1.41 ratio and 1.59 ERA. His performance was so encouraging you may have heard rumors about returning Aguilera to the rotation. It's a big jump for a youngster who wasn't overpowering in Double-A. Portland or a return trip to Orlando seem more likely than a '91 big-league job. But keep watching.

NEW YORK YANKEES

The Yankees ended the winter meetings without Dave Righetti, and with a long list of potential closers. It was obvious that the Yankees had plans for more personnel changes. New acquisition Steve Farr hadn't been assigned to the bull pen or the starting rotation at the end of December; there was only widespread discussion of his flexibility. That makes 17 flexible pitchers on the staff, now. Farr is a logical candidate to get closer duty, if the Yankees can't come up with anyone else in trade. He failed in the closer role with Kansas City, and the Yankees would be wiser to let him keep the starter job that made him such a marvelous comeback in 1990, but there was no one ahead of him as 1991 dawned.

Lee Guetterman is the biggest beneficiary of Righetti's departure. He is capable of 15 to 20 saves per year as half of a left/right tandem. Guetterman is nice for Rotisserie rosters, because his ERA and ratio won't hurt you.

My favorite sleeper in the Yankee pen is Eric Plunk. During the summer of 1990, he added a variety of breaking balls and off speed pitches to his repertoire, making his 90 MPH fastball much more effective. He now possesses a slider, a straight change, a cut fastball, and a forkball, and he has confidence in all of them. Plunk was a special project of Mark Connor, who earned a promotion from bullpen coach to head pitching coach for 1991. One of the little-noticed happy stories in the Yankee pitching department was Eric's finish last year. He had a 1.52 ERA and 35 K his last 18 appearances covering 29 innings.

The Yankees had no sense of urgency about keeping Jeff D. Robinson, but they should have. The once-great setup man for San Francisco and Pittsburgh, who failed when given the Pirates closer role, looked like he regained his dominance in the final weeks of 1990. Robinson gave up no runs in 17 of his last 18 appearances, with a 1.69 ERA.

Greg Cadaret was the first Yankee other than Dave Righetti to record a save during 1990, getting two in a July 29 double-header against Cleveland. During the month of July, he had a 1-0 record, with 2 saves and a 1.93 ERA. The Yankees have moved Cadaret from the pen to the rotation, and back to the pen, in both 1989 and 1990. He is clearly better as a reliever than a starter, and clearly a better reliever when he is left undisturbed in that role. In his six starts last year, Greg had a 1-3 record with a 6.11 ERA. In 1989 he had a 2.70 ERA in relief during the first half, and then came unglued after the Yankees made him a starter in mid-season. If the Yankees do something miraculous, like clarifying Cadaret's role as a reliever before the season starts, you will find him a nice, safe middle reliever who will get you saves for less than $1 apiece.

Alan Mills jumped from A-Ball to Triple-A, then to the majors during 1990. He had become dominant in the low minors in late 1989. My only question is: if Mills is such a great talent, why did he spend four years at the A level without even a brief trial at Double-A?

Willie Smith is the reason why people are saying that the Yankees got a good deal for Don Slaught. Willie reminds everyone of Lee Smith, in terms of appearance and pitching style. He could turn out to be a gem. After promotion to AA Harrisburg in 1989, he produced a 2.45 ratio, a 1.16 ratio, and more than a strikeout per inning. He struggled at Columbus in 1990, and is unlikely to reach the majors before 1992.

Lary Bump:

Coming along faster than Willie Smith is Mike Gardella, a 22-year-old lefty. In the Carolina League with Prince William last year, he tied the league record with 30 saves, and posted a 1.30 ratio and 2.01 ERA with 86 Ks in 71 IP. In just a year and a half as a pro, the former Oklahoma State pitcher has 49 saves in 53 opportunities. Color him reliable. Also color him with a good fastball and curve. In a couple of years, color him in pinstripes. Hey! The Yankees didn't seem to want Righetti for 1992-1993.

OAKLAND

Dennis Eckersley suffered a 33% increase in walks last year. That's a joke to the cognoscenti; he gave up three walks in 1989 and four in 1990. Seriously, Eck had his best year ever at age 35, breaking Dave Righetti's record of 46 saves in one year. Eckersley had 48, but Bobby Thigpen made it a forgettable achievement by notching 57. Eckersley had a 0.61 ERA and a 0.61 ratio, both better than Thigpen. And Eck didn't want to pitch from the bullpen.

In 1989 there was widespread suspicion that Eckersley had arm problems even more serious than indicated by his visit to the 21 Day DL.

Nobody said much about the subject last year. It is pointless to raise doubts about pitchers when no one can get a hit off them, and they haven't walked anybody in three years. Eckersley is an extremely valuable commodity, but the fact is: he can't possibly go up in value at this point of his career. He could, however, go down. From the heights of $40, it's a long fall.

After trading away Eric Plunk and Greg Cadaret, Oakland quickly re-stocked their middle relief and setup corps with outstanding performers. Gene Nelson has a become a nice little Rotisserie gem. He cost an average of only $3 to $4 last year. When you get saves for less that $1 apiece, you have a good buy, and Nelson offers the wonderful benefit of 70 innings per year, with a ratio under 1.00 and an ERA under 2.00.

Rick Honeycutt will continue to get the left-handed setup work and an occasional save. If the A's need a closer on opening day 1991, and Eckersley isn't available for some reason, they would probably go with the veteran Honeycutt. The backup in the lefty role is Joe Klink. Klink is no puppy (age 29), and isn't going to challenge for closer duties, but he is thriving in the Oakland system after frustration and failure with other teams. He got most of the saves at Huntsville in 1989.

Todd Burns has been an effective reliever; he is likely to function as a swing man during 1991.

Susan Moore:

The next Eckersley is likely to be Steve Chitren. The A's are easing him into the role. They like to use their pitchers carefully, in spots, to build confidence. Success then builds on itself. Last year, Chitren pitched for AA Huntsville, AAA Tacoma, and Oakland, producing combined stats of 27 saves with a 1.50 ERA. Expect to see more of Chitren in 1991.

Lary Bump:

There are teams in the majors that would kill for a closer like Steve Chitren, the 24-year-old righty.

His 1.02 ratio and 1.68 ERA at Huntsville weren't as good as his 0.62, 1.02 September in Oakland, but he did have 27 saves with the Double-A club. He has just one slight obstacle in Dennis Eckersley.

SEATTLE

Everyone wants to know about Mike Schooler. He has already broken most of Bill Caudill's records in Seattle, and playing for an obscure team has made it possible for numerous Rotisserians to get him on a cheap, long-term contract. The whole story sounds too good to be true; now people are worried about Schooler's condition. He was 0-4 with only 8 saves over the second half of 1990, and his ratio soared to 1.53.

People keep asking me for "medical information." That's a humorous oxymoron like "military intelligence." Most players with physical problems are not on a schedule. Their doctors and trainers don't know if/when they will be back to normal. The players themselves don't know. How should I know? I can tell you some observations to put a situation into perspective, however. Ace relievers are almost all subject to minor arm trouble, requiring them to take time off. Dennis Eckersley took off three weeks in the middle of 1989, and he was just fine afterward. Dave Smith has taken time off to rest his arm. Tom Henke has just about stopped trying to be a closer during the month of April. The disturbing fact about Schooler is that he didn't take time off to rest. He kept on pitching during 1990, and got knocked around. The pre-season of 1991 is a good time to consider trading Schooler. His value is never going to be higher. Most people don't know that he had any difficulty in late 1990. He is good enough to attract an ace closer in return. If Schooler starts the season with a 5.00 ERA and just a couple of blown saves, he won't be tradeable again until July, and won't ever be worth what he's worth today.

Pete DeCoursey:

Billy Swift and Rich Delucia will both go up in value. Swift had a 2.47 ERA in the second half of 1990, and he gave up so few walks and homers that his Indicated ERA was only 0.56. Delucia is another low walk, low homer pitcher.

Tony Formo's Left Field Extravaganza:

Last season's prediction that Billy Swift could make impressive improvements deserves congratulations to my Seattle scouts, Uncle Coach and Gary Waddington. Swift went from 4.43 ERA (4.78 lifetime) to 2.39, 6-4, 6 SV in 1990, being used both as a starter and reliever and had a 22-inning scoreless streak. The pitching heroics of the former U.S. Olympic performer were overshadowed by the play in which Swift was hit on the forehead by a line drive by Gary Gaetti, which ricocheted into the stands for a rare infield ground rule double (which must have caused fits for Project Scoresheet scorers).

Bryan Clark (3.27 ERA, 2-0, 0 SV) was considered a reasonably hot prospect when the Mariners traded him to Toronto for Barry Bonnell before the 1984. Since then he has kicked around with the Indians, White Sox, and other teams and hasn't distinguished himself in any way other than by throwing left-handed. His performance over 11 IP in 1990 is probably insufficient to convince anyone that he's a competent major leaguer rather than Calgary Cannon-fodder.

At times lefty reliever Keith Comstock (2.89 ERA, 7-4, 2 SV) would look terrific, despite occasions when he would get shelled. After a checkered career up and down from the minors, Comstock is likely to continue to be used as a left-handed set-up man, whose screwball makes him tough on right-handed batters.

Gene Harris (4.74 ERA, 1-2, 0 SV) is reported to have an excellent arm, but has yet to pitch well consistently since coming to Seattle in the Langston deal.

Brent Knackert (6.51 ERA, 1-1, 0 SV) is a talented teenager taken from the Mets organization in the draft where the player must remain on the major league roster or be returned for half the drafting price. Knackert was not ready for prime time in 1990, and was used in mop-up roles rather than key situations.

Lary Bump:

Dave Burba, Vance Lovelace, Scott Medvin, Jose Melendez, Relief Pitchers, Seattle

Formerly a starter, 24-year-old Dave Burba moved to the bullpen last season at Calgary (1.50 ratio, 4.67 ERA). In six games with Seattle, he went 1.25, 4.50. To make it in a set-up role, the righty would have to muscle past Mike Jackson and Gene Harris.

At 29, right-hander Scott Medvin is running out of time. He was acquired from the Pirates' Buffalo club, where he was 1.00, 1.46. At Calgary, his numbers were 1.42, 4.97, with 11 saves. His 2.08, 6.23 performance in five games for Seattle doesn't promise a quick return trip. And if the Pirates can't use him in their bullpen, can anyone else?

Jose Melendez, a 25-year-old righty, earned a trip to Seattle with a 1.26, 3.90 performance in a tough pitchers' park at Calgary. His Mariners ledger read 2.06, 3.90. He has an outside chance to spend some of '91 in Seattle, probably behind Burba.

Vance Lovelace, a 27-year-old lefty, has been a prospect for most of the '80s. Yet his 2.1 IP in 5 games with the Mariners late last season marked his high-water mark in the majors. Perhaps the six walks he gave up had something to do with his lack of big-league time. Despite a 1.54 ratio at Calgary, he posted a 3.47 ERA and 6 saves. If the 6-5 flamethrower hasn't learned control yet, will he ever?

TEXAS

UPDATE — The Dodger ace reliever at San Antonio, Jim Poole, has a shot at the Rangers pen for 1991.

Last September, Bobby Valentine was not much interested in considering the possibility that Jeff Russell might not make a strong comeback in 1991. When he was in a talkative mood, I asked him who figured in his plans for a closer. He said, "Jeff Russell." And he emphasized the "." That makes Russell valuable, because saves are 60% management discretion. Also on the plus side, Russell has had elbow surgery before (1987) and obviously came back strong. He has learned to come directly at the hitters, without nibbling; that knowledge isn't something that needs to be rehabilitated.

If you want skepticism, consider that Russell has had only one successful major league season in eight years. His September 1990 comeback wasn't all that impressive, either. I hate drawing conclusions based on tiny samples of stats, but Russell didn't give us much to look at. In 4.1 IP, he gave up only one run, but he walked three with only one K. If he had struck out three or four batters, I would be just a little more sanguine.

Other names in the pen include righty Brad Arnsberg, who just achieved his first major league success at age 26, and lefty Mike Jeffcoat, a 31-year-old swing man. Both of them had five saves last year, thanks mainly to the absence of Russell. Brian Bohanon is just 22 and still developing; he will be given a chance to impress the Rangers in spring training and might emerge with a middle-inning lefty role.

Jose Guzman has been on the comeback trail since 1988. He wasn't that impressive when he was healthy. Although Guzman is a hard thrower who was highly touted within the Texas organization, he never achieved any big success. Check Guzman's winter ball stats for an early indicator; at least he's throwing again.

Kenny Rogers is probably back in the starting rotation for 1991. Free agent Craig McMurtry was drifting away from the team in December. Lefty John Barfield is still maturing at age 26; he will have to improve further to be of value in 1991.

Lary Bump:

With Oakland, Joe Bitker, a 27-year-old righty, was clearly the odd man out, with Eckersley ahead of him and Chitren on his heels. His 1.27 ratio, 3.20 ERA and 26 saves at Tacoma were good enough to earn him a place in the Harold Baines deal. With the Rangers, he stands an excellent chance, especially if Jeff Russell isn't 100 per cent. After five seasons in Triple-A, the last two as a reliever, Bitker should be ready.

TORONTO

The Blue Jays have become systematic about working Tom Henke into the closer role gradually in April and May. It is now a standard sucker ploy to trade for Henke around May 10, when his ERA is over 5.00, and when Duane Ward (or Ken Dayley this year) has most of the saves. The other half of this ploy, obviously, is to unload Ward (or Dayley) when he looks like a premier closer. Last year was the third consecutive season for this cycle.

Ward and Dayley will be valuable on draft day for the above-stated reason. Jim Acker is coming off a bad year in 1990. In the second half, he had a 5.02 ERA and a 1.59 ratio. You can turn off the oven; he's done.

Willie Fraser looked great when he first came up in 1987; then he collapsed in the second half. In the last three years, his ERA has been 5.41, 3.24, and 3.08 respectively. In the second half last year, he had a 2.11 ERA and a 1.03 ratio. I say that Fraser has found his niche. If the Jays keep him out of the starting rotation and use him like California did late last year, he will be a magnificent $1 middle relief sleeper. Last year he wasn't even taken in most auctions, and his lifetime ERA is still way up there at 4.26. Ssshh.

J.L. Feinstein:

The pen features Dayley, Ward, and Acker setting up the Terminator, Tom Henke. Ward and Dayley will get the occasional save, but shouldn't prevent Henke from getting his 25 or 30.

Tony Formo:

At the end of May 1989, Terminator Tom was 3-3 with 2 Saves, and a 5.40 ERA. People were calling him "The Perpetrator". Cito showed the confidence to use him a lot, and Henke regained his status as one of the top closers in the bigs.

Lary Bump:

The Blue Jays can use a lefty in their bullpen, with David Wells in the rotation and John Candelaria a free agent. The question is whether the 25-year old Bob MacDonald is that lefty. His numbers at Knoxville were good — 1.16 ratio, 1.89 ERA, 15 saves. At Syracuse, he didn't do as well — 1.56, 5.40, 2 saves in 9 games. In four games with the Jays, he got seven men out without giving up a hit. So perhaps his role should be pitching in spots, at least until he proves he can be a big-league closer. If Toronto proceeds cautiously, so should you.

NATIONAL LEAGUE RELIEF PITCHERS

ATLANTA

If Mike Stanton is healthy, Kent Mercker will share the stopper role. If Stanton can't hack it, the job is all Mercker's. Like a typical Braves closer, Mercker (and/or Stanton) will have plenty of saves with an ERA and ratio higher than what you expect from a relief ace. Also, it is just about mathematically impossible that a Braves closer can get more than 30 saves. They just don't create that many save situations.

Mike Stanton was supposed to be the closer last year, but succumbed to arm trouble early. The prognosis is not good. At the end of 1990, Stanton simply couldn't pitch. The Braves would like their 24-year-old phenom to take the closer job and run with it. He still has more than a strikeout per inning in his brief major league career.

Jeff Parrett, acquired in the Dale Murphy trade, will get a handful of saves as the righty setup man. His ERA and ratio won't be bad for a Brave, either.

Mark Grant, proceeds of the Derek Lilliquist swap, actually pitched quite well for the Braves. If he stays in the long relief role for Atlanta, he is worthless for Rotisserie, however.

Depending on Stanton's condition, one or two other spots will be open in the pen. Tony Castillo, Dwayne Henry, Marvin Freeman, and Marty Clary are the suspects that you will generally want to avoid. Castillo is the one remote possibility to be an exception. The best minor league relief candidates are John Kilner and Matt Turner, both at AA Greenville in 1990. They are not likely to reach the majors this year.

Lary Bump:

Kent Mercker, 23, came up from Richmond (1.50 ratio, 3.55 ERA) last season to become the Braves' lefthanded bullpen ace. And he picked up 7 saves with a 3.17 ERA and a 1.39 ratio. Wait a minute. Up from Richmond, lefthanded bullpen ace, seven saves. Sound familiar? Yes, about like Mike Stanton, 1989 version. Last year, in seven games, Stanton had a 2.86 ratio and an 18.00 ERA before he and Nick Esasky went on the DL and took Atlanta's season with them. Now Stanton's still a rookie, and Mercker's not. But Mercker is the Braves' lefty closer. Look for Stanton to be Richmond's closer until he can prove himself. If he returns to Atlanta, perhaps Mercker would return to the rotation.

CHICAGO CUBS

Dave Smith will benefit from pitching for a winning team; he might soar to 35 or even 40 saves. But his ratio and ERA will be subject to one of the severest tests of park effects ever. If you put Wrigley Field and its surrounding neighborhood inside the Astrodome, Waveland Avenue would be somewhere around the left field warning track. And then there's the wind to consider. Anyway, you get the idea.

Les Lancaster was a superb setup man in 1989. Then in 1990 he was then used in every conceivable role, including RP at Iowa. He showed his talent in all of these different trials, including two consecutive outstanding starts, but on the whole, his 1990 season was a nightmare. I think Lancaster will return to form with Dave Smith anchoring the pen. Now, if Zimmer just doesn't ask him to start any games . . .

By the way, we made two key predictions about the Cubs pen last year. The first was Mitch Williams "pitching himself out of the closer role, could happen any day." We noted that an ace reliever cannot have a ratio of 1.50, and valued Williams down below Greg Harris and and Bill Landrum. That much was good. The other prediction, that Lancaster would emerge with the closer role, looked good, right up to the point of Lancaster getting into the save situations, with the ball in his hand. From that point, the forecast really went off the tracks.

Mark Giannini has been saying since October, 1986, "Dave Smith's arm is dead." Some day, he'll be right. But I think not in 1991.

Lary Bump:

Joe Kraemer, Dave Pavlas, Dean Wilkins? Think what the Cubs' bullpen would have been like the last two seasons if Mitch Williams hadn't pitched out of his mind. Or think what it might have been if they had turned Dennis Eckersley loose in the pen. Such thoughts, and thinking about having such nonentities as Kraemer, Pavlas and Wilkins coming along to try to rectify the situation, must have given Don Zimmer and Jim Frey nightmares about the unemployment line. The answer: Dave Smith.

At Iowa, lefty Kraemer, 26, was a starter with a 1.25 ratio and 3.76 ERA. With the big Cubs, he was a reliever with numbers of 1.80 and 7.20. Righthander Pavlas, 28, found himself back in the Cubs' organization, in the Iowa bullpen. He had his first good year since '86 — 1.33, 3.26, 8 saves, and 1.36, 2.11 with the big club. Wilkins, a 24-year-old righty, was Iowa's bullpen ace with 1.55, 3.70, 11 saves. With the Cubs, except for one game in which he had a save, he couldn't find home plate, and compiled a 2.45 ratio and 9.82 ERA.

Thom Rogers:

Paul Assenmacher had a 1.96 ERA and 1.04 ratio in the second half. In the fourth quarter of 1990, he has 1.16 and 1.00.

CINCINNATI

Sean Lahman:

A substantial portion of the Reds success in 1990 was based on their bullpen, the self proclaimed "Nasty Boys". Randy Myers, Rob Dibble, and Norm Charlton would all probably rank among the top five closers in the league, and at least one of them was always rested. The Reds had no MVP candidates and no starter won more than 15 games. Without the bullpen, they not only wouldn't have swept the World Series, they might not have won the division.

Start with the save guy, Randy Myers. He throws a mid-90s fastball and has some good breaking stuff. His intensity gives him the temperament necessary to be a closer. When he was a Met, he kept saying that he could save 30 games if given a chance, and he did (31 saves in 66 games). Myers effectiveness is enhanced by having Dibble and Charlton behind him. Not only does he not have to pitch as often, but I don't think you'll see him pitch more than one inning ever. This means that when he comes in, Myers knows he'll only have to throw fifteen pitches and he won't have to save anything for later. He should save closer to forty games next year.

The right-handed stopper is Rob Dibble. If you don't know him by now, you've missed a lot. Dibble is so intense, he makes Dave Stewart look like Pee Wee Herman. His fastball comes in at 100 mph or more and he has a wicked slider. He struck out only 136 in 98 innings (as compared to 141 K in 99 IP in 1989). Don't think for a minute that because he has such awesome speed that he has no control; he walked only 36 batters (96 in 257 IP for his career). I don't know with 100% certainty but I'd wager that never before has a team had two relief pitchers in an All Star game (both Myers and Dibble in 1990). Dibble's selection was overdue. He could close for any other team in the majors except Oakland and the White Sox (both of whom would love to have him anyway, I'm sure). Dibble knows this and wants to be treated accordingly. The Reds would be foolish to trade him so they're going to have to pay him closer money to keep him happy.

Norm Charlton is a "stopper" too; he stops the opposition. But he's the third guy, so you may see him as early as the sixth inning. If you do, say goodnight. The Nasty boys lost only 15 games in 174 combined relief appearances. Charlton is intense, has a high 90s fastball, and has good breaking stuff like the other two closers. The difference is Charlton has more stamina. Originally a starter, he can pitch two or three innings at full speed. If the starter gets into trouble in the fifth, Charlton could pitch 6 & 7 with Dibble in the 8th and Myers in the 9th. This would be a tough trio to score on and they could all pitch the next day! Because of the uncertainty of where he'll be pitching, Rotisserie prices for Charlton should be pretty low.

The middle/long man in 1989 was right-hander Tim Layana. The Reds drafted him from the Yankees AA affiliate before the start of the season. Part of the reason he was on the roster all year was that the Reds would have had to send him back to New York if they demoted him. He did pitch well, winning Tim Birtsas's bullpen job (partially due to Birtsas being a lefty). It seems likely he'll be back even though he was left off the post-season roster (the Reds went with only nine pitchers, Tim was the odd man out).

The fifth starter/long reliever role figures to go to Scott Scudder if he doesn't win a rotation spot. Tim Birtsas seems to have seen his last days with the Reds. Rick Mahler (see comments on Mahler under starting pitchers) may get the job or possibly Chris Hammond.

Greg Gajus:

Not to knock Randy Myers, who had a great season, but if one examines the stats, it is clear that Rob Dibble was the better pitcher:

	ERA	K/9	W/9	Hits/9	HR/9	Ratio
Dibble	1.74	12.5	3.1	5.7	0.3	0.97
Myers	2.08	10.2	3.9	6.1	0.6	1.12

Dibble had a better ERA, struck out more batters, had better control, and allowed fewer hits and home runs than Myers. (Dibble is also better when you compare career stats). Dibble and Myers both have the mental makeup to be a closer (slightly brain damaged) so it is hard to see why Piniella favored Myers over Dibble most of the year.

For Rotisserie purposes, Myers is still the first choice for the saves, but Dibble could easily move up to the 20 save category at Myers' expense. Piniella has expressed interest in keeping Dibble happy, and the easiest way to do it in 1991 will be to give Dibble more saves. While pitchers are notoriously unreliable, power pitchers like Myers and Dibble are much less likely to suddenly lose effectiveness.

Norm Charlton is very likely to remain in the rotation in 1991. His setup role will probably be taken over by Tim Layana (5-3 3.49 ERA, 1.44 ratio, 2 saves) who was effective in the role most of the year, and/or Ted Power (3.66 ERA, 1.30 ratio, 7 saves with Pittsburgh). Other bullpen candidates will include Scott Scudder and Chris Hammond.

Lary Bump:

Keith Brown, Kip Gross, Rosario Rodriguez, Scott Scudder. You ever get the feeling there are too many pitchers named KBrown cluttering up boxscores? I first typed in "Kevin Brown" as this guy's name. Keith, a 27-year-old righthander, was an important part of Nashville's division-winning club, with a 1.12 ratio, 2.45 ERA and team-high 9 saves. In his second September with the Reds, he was 1.32, 4.76. He doesn't really have much chance to break into this bullpen, unless Tim Layana is sent out for more seasoning.

And how about the invasion of the R. Rodriguezes in the NL West. This one — a 21-year-old lefty we'll call Rosey — started 1990 poorly at Nashville and went down to Chattanooga, where he saved 7 games despite a 1.89 ratio and 4.36 ERA. He was no great cog (1.65, 6.10) in the Reds' September pennant express. He needs at least a year at Triple-A.

Righthander Gross, 26, had a 1.26 ratio and 3.33 ERA at Nashville and figures of 1.26 and 4.26 with the Reds. One of the legion of ex-Mets minor league pitchers, like Brown he's a converted starter — and probably a minor leaguer again in '91.

The 23-year-old Scudder, on the other hand, solidified a job as a righthanded middle reliever and possible spot starter with some good post-season work for the world champs. His '90 regular-season numbers — 1.05, 2.34 at Nashville; 1.45, 4.90 with the Reds. He is no longer a rookie, nor a hot prospect. He has too much trouble with lefthanded hitters to be a consistent major league starter.

HOUSTON UPDATE — Curt Schilling from Baltimore is a candidate for closer duty.

The Astros really cleaned house in 1990. Dave Smith, Larry Andersen, Danny Darwin, Dan Schatzeder, and Juan Agosto are all gone. What's left? I've been saying, "Watch Brian Meyer," for three years, now. Last spring, Art Howe told me that Meyer would become a credible major leaguer as soon as he proved his consistency in the major leagues, or words to that effect. Pitching in the minor leagues, he couldn't prove major league consistency. Lacking major league consistency, he couldn't be promoted to the major leagues. Are there any government people in Houston management?

Having jettisoned every other possibility, the Astros will finally give Kid Meyer his chance in 1991. The kid turned 28 in January 1991.

Lary Bump:

Brian Meyer has been the darling of some would-be baseball cognoscenti. "Live arm; great prospect" are some of the things you've heard about this righthander. Bunk! He's 28. And one of the Astros' avowed priorities was resigning Dave Smith. Meyer did have a pretty good year in '90 — 1.29, 2.97, 15 saves at Tucson; 1.08, 2.21, a save, but an 0-4 record with Houston. He may stick this year, but most likely as a set-up man, and not as a closer.

Lefthander Osuna, 25, never has started in 179 professional games. He was a strong 1.30, 3.38 with 6 saves for Double-A Columbus before moving up to the big club for a 1.41, 4.76 finish. With Juan Agosto heading for free agency, Osuna could be an important Astro in the bullpen.

Bill Gilbert:

Jim Clancy will be given a try at middle relief, and rookie lefthander Al Osuna 7-5, 3.38, 6 saves at AA is the likely replacement for Schatzeder. Brian Meyer, 5-7, 2.97 and 15 saves at Tucson has been groomed as Smith's eventual successor and will probably stick as a set up man. Without an overpowering fastball, he needs to develop another pitch if he is to make it as a major league closer.

LOS ANGELES

Bob Whitemore:

The pitching-rich Dodgers have Jay Howell at the head of their relief corps. Howell's injury in 1990 was a leg, not an arm, which minimizes the risk. And he is fully healed after surgery on the knee, anyway. In the second half, Howell had 12 of his 16 saves, a 1.45 ERA, and a 0.96 ratio. Case closed.

Tim Crews is the likely number two man, but there are many candidates. Howell is the only one with a clear role going into spring training. Jim Gott and Mike Hartley were credible candidates for setup work at the end of 1990. Lefty Dave Walsh has a good chance to get late work in close games in 1991. Dennis Cook, Jim Neidlinger, John Wetteland, Mike Morgan, and any rookies who make the roster, will be in the pen.

Adam Stein:

Jay Howell recovered from an injury to be an effective stopper in the second half. He should have a $25-$30 season as he did in the past. With the additions of Strawberry and Butler, and the pending return of Hershiser and Belcher (who missed most of last year), save opportunities should be abundant.

Tim Crews was effective as a right-handed set up man last year after two good seasons in middle relief. His numbers should be similar to last year's.

Ray Searage is the only returning left hander in the Dodger pen. Despite a 2.78 ERA, the Dodgers' young pitchers could force him off the roster. Dennis Cook is unlikely to make the rotation and will compete for a pen role in the spring.

Whoever among Cook, Mike Hartley, John Wetteland, Mike Morgan, and Jim Neidlinger don't make the rotation will battle for the middle relief jobs. A cast of pitchers who appeared briefly for the Dodgers in 1990 also may factor into the equation. Dave Walsh is the best talent in the group, but there will be a problem with any of these men getting enough work to be worth considering.

Lary Bump:

Darren Holmes, a 24-year-old righthander, moved back to the bullpen last season with outstanding results — 1.27, 3.11, 13 saves — at Albuquerque. His 14 games with the Dodgers were not as good — 1.50, 5.19. David Walsh, a 30-year-old lefty, may have finally come of age last season. He went 1.31, 2.61 with 12 saves at Albuquerque, and 1.29, 3.86 with a save for LA. It's apparent the Dodgers need help in their pen. Walsh could make Ray Searage history. And Holmes should get a shot as a righthanded closer.

MONTREAL

Michael Cassin:

Montreal's strong stable of middle relievers, boosted by the addition of Barry Jones, means Tim Burke can't afford a slump of any length without jeopardizing his closer role. Burke should still reach the 20 mark in saves, but not much more, ERA-wise he's a better bet.

Dave Schmidt had a good season, and before Jones arrived, he looked like he was first in line behind Burke. Free agency then raised doubts about Schmidt even staying. Steve Frey, Scott Ruskin, Bill Sampen, and Drew Hall all had good stretches, especially Frey, but I wouldn't recommend any of them for a big breakthrough year. Frey was 8-2 2.10, with 9 saves, and was especially tough on righties, but he got those 19 decisions in only 55 IP in 51 games, and it's hard to see how he can do that again. Frey should become the lefty set-up man in the absence of Schmidt, and should keep a good ERA and the occasional save, without the wins.

Adam Stein:

Tim Burke recovered from a minor injury and finished 1990 in top form (1.73 ERA, 1.06 ratio in the second half). If the Expos can win a few games in 1991, Burke could be worth $35.

Lary Bump:

Scott Anderson, 29, abandoned the sidearm motion he had as a Ranger in '87 and earned another trip to the majors by starting at Indianapolis (1.25, 3.31). With the Expos, he was 0.94, 3.00. It's hard to project the righthander into the rotation, but he could make it as a middle reliever and spot starter.

Mel Rojas, a 24-year-old righty, was 1.35, 3.13 as a starter at Indy, but pitched exclusively out of the pen for Montreal (1.45, 3.60, 1 save). He, too, could become a starter, but he has shown some success as a set-up man. Expect him to spend the entire season in Canada. Some wild optimists place him ahead of Tim Burke in the bullpen. What a whopper that one is.

Kevin Bearse, a 25-year-old lefty, was penciled into the Cleveland rotation last April, but a 2.74 ratio and 12.91 ERA in three starts earned him a ticket to Colorado Springs. He wasn't a lot better (1.51, 5.00) there. But the Expos under Buck Rodgers have had a lot of success with cattle-call pitching tryouts the last few years. If they try enough pitchers, they're likely to find 9 or 10 to fill a staff. Since I have to think Rodgers has a good idea what he's doing expect him to give Bearse a shot in his bullpen, where he had success before becoming a starter in '89.

NEW YORK METS

John Franco leads the major leagues in saves over the past five years.

A lesson in second half stats: some people, who don't know what a forecast is, got the idea that my prediction for John Franco's 1990 season would have to be gloom and doom, because Franco had a bad second half in 1989. There was an implicit statement that a forecast is a mechanical projection, which it isn't. When you are forecasting the weather, and you see gray clouds, and observe a northeast wind at 15 mph, and someone five miles northeast tells you it is raining there, you forecast rain. You don't study yesterday's maps, and you don't fiddle with computerized histories.

For the record, I discussed the second half of '89 with Franco. He hates talking about the Pete Rose days, for understandable reasons, but kindly accommodated me anyway. It was just one of those difficult periods, easily forgotten. My forecast for Franco for 1990 was a 2.99 ERA with 27 saves, up nicely from 10 saves and 4.48 ERA in second half '89. Nothing mechanical about it. The fact that the Mets coughed up Randy Myers to get John Franco is another piece of information that can't be mechanically projected. Think context. Big picture.

While setting the record straight: Franco doesn't throw a screwball. I don't know what that has to do with Rotisserie, but it renders obsolete a great deal of printed matter. Whatever kind of pitch it is (would I tell?) it induced a great many ground balls and helped Franco lead the NL in saves in 1990.

Al Pena didn't help much in April through July, but after August 12 he gave up only one run in 17 IP, finishing with a 0.53 ERA over the last seven weeks. He walked only one batter during the month of September. I say he's back.

Alan Boodman:

The 1991 Mets' bullpen will be led once again, obviously, by John Franco. Although John cooled after the All-Star break, there's no particular cause for concern. And even if there was, these days a closer's numbers are mostly a product of circumstances and the team behind him, unless you believe that Bobby Thigpen is far and away the greatest reliever God ever created.

Of course, it doesn't hurt to be able to pitch. Franco, not a strikeout pitcher, hardly fits in with the image of Mets' pitchers of recent years. Randy Myers, traded to Cincy for Franco just before Christmas 1989, fits in a lot better, but Randy's 1989 season was a bit of a roller-coaster ride, and the top brass must have figured they'd be better off with the consistency of Franco.

John's 1990 stats aside from saves weren't awesome, but remember that a reliever's main task is to acquire saves, and a 2.53 ERA won't hurt you any. Franco's ratio was a little on the high side of average, and he won 5 games while losing three. Be wary of any so-called bullpen ace who winds up with a record of something like 8-12, or even 12-8 for that matter. Closers generally don't get decisions (losses OR wins) unless they're doing something wrong. Since these guys are the only ones on a Rotisserie team capable of getting saves, I would suggest they do so. We have a whole rotation of starters to get us wins.

As to what may be in store for Franco and the Mets this season, I would just like to point out that John stands a good chance of saving more games than Bobby Thigpen in 1991. John may save about 35 or so. Franco has been a remarkably steady closer since 1986, and I see no evidence that he won't continue to be one. He'll earn a save in more than one-third of the Mets' victories this year, and the Mets always win at least 90 games, so you figure it out.

The rest of the actors in the bullpen could use a little help. Alejandro Pena returns as the top right-handed reliever (shudder) after an excellent second half, following a brutal first half. Unless something awful happens to Franco, Pena probably won't make it to 10 saves, but he might post a low ERA and a good ratio, with some K's.

Wally Whitehurst may be a promising young-to-middle-aged pitcher, but nobody running the Mets is promising him a shot at anything. His best prospects are for Julio Valera to flop, for the Mets to trade Darling in addition to Ojeda, and maybe Wally gets a shot at the rotation. Probably won't happen this year. At worst, he'll be a middle-innings guy with just about the best control in the National League, but with nothing to offer to a Rotisserie team.

Jeff Innis is still here. So is Jeff Musselman. Anybody care? If I ran the team, Musselman would have to pay his way into the ballpark, and I'd make sure he got a bad seat. This guy's got a degree from Harvard, and I'd like to see the Mets make him put it to use.

PHILADELPHIA

Pete DeCoursey:

The Phils saves will be divided between Roger McDowell and Joe Boever, with both likely to finish the season in double figures. McDowell will begin the year as the stopper, with the rubber-armed Boever as his set-up man. Boever will pile up saves by staying in some games through the 9th, since Leyva has lost some confidence in Roger, and the former Brave will be the man Leyva can turn to when McDowell hits his annual slump. If McDowell is traded, look for Boever to assume the stopper's role unless they acquire a fireballer. If both pitch for the Phils, McDowell should finish near 25 saves and Boever with around 10.

One reason McDowell will slump is that the Phils infield is not good enough defensively to sustain a ground ball stopper: with Morandini's education slowing the DP, Thon's eroding range, and Jordan's merely average glove, Charlie Hayes will be the only above average defender. You need more than one hot glove to catch the ground balls Roger will give up. McDowell was most successful with guys like Keith Hernandez standing behind him.

Darrel Akerfelds will record another 80 innings, another ERA in the mid to high 3's, but will have under 5 saves. He wore out last season due to overly frequent use, but Joe "Can I Pitch Today" Boever will get the use which overtaxed Akerfelds. Darrel's ratio is in danger of rising however, past last year's 1.28, as he was hit harder in the second half last year. Don't be fooled by Akerfelds high walk totals: he is an unusual pitcher who allows hits rarely and walks frequently.

After these three comes a left-hander who isn't ready, Chuck McElroy, or a lefty who has proven his lack of ability, Don Carman. "Goggles" McElroy, a short slender man who is a dead ringer for Spike Lee, will be a decent middle reliever, but at age 23, he isn't ready yet. Carman was unable to establish himself as someone who could get lefties out. While he held them to a .175 BA in 103 ABs, that .175 included 7 HRs and 3 doubles. The one class of hitters Carman was supposed to retire tatered off him as often as Mike Schmidt homered during his career.

That leaves Brad Moore and Tommy Greene. Greene is out of options, so he will probably stick as a righty long man if not in the rotation, particularly because Moore is another ground ball pitcher, a commodity not prized by a team whose middle infield consists of one man starting to climb the hill and another tumbling down it.

Lary Bump:

There is talk of moving Chuck Malone, a hulking 6-7, 250-pound 25-year-old, back to a starter. It doesn't really matter when he comes in to pitch if he can't throw strikes any better than he has the last two seasons. The righty walked 106 in 106 IP at Reading in '89, then 89 in 83.1 IP with Scranton and Philly last year. With the Red Barons, he had a 1.64 ratio and 6.39 ERA; with the Phils he was 1.91, 3.68.

Chuck McElroy, a 23-year-old lefty, checked in at 1.26, 2.72, 7 saves for Scranton. He was pounded for 24 hits (2.43 ratio, 7.71 ERA) in 14 IP for the Phillies. But this is a team in need of lefthanded bullpen help, so he will get a chance.

PITTSBURGH

The Pirates have been conditioning Stan Belinda to become their closer, ever since he finished 20 of 22 games and got 7 saves for Bradenton back in 1986. Belinda has never started a game and now has 74 saves in the Pirates organization. He is still only 24, so you needn't be too concerned that he hasn't yet been a dominating closer. With only 8 saves in 1990 and an unclear plan, he should be cheap, too. Recommended for good value, good probability.

And if Lary Bump says watch Vicente Palacios, watch Vicente Palacios.

Adam Stein:

Bill Landrum lost the closer role and had only one save in the second half of 1990. Stan Belinda and Ted Power got the saves. Power is gone, of course, to Cincinnati, and Belinda wasn't especially good at getting batters out. Watch spring training box scores. Forget the save count. Just see who comes in and pitches one inning at the end of a game, four times a week. That's your closer.

Lary Bump:

After a 1.18, 1.90 start with 6 saves at Buffalo, Stan Belinda, a 24-year-old sidearming righty, lost his rookie status with 58.1 IP (1.32, 3.55, 8 saves) in 1990. He apparently also found an ability to get out lefthanders, for they batted just .176 against him. He was a junior member of the Bucs' bullpen by committee, and apparently won't gain much stature this season.

The winter-book favorite to be their righthanded closer is Vicente Palacios. The 27-year-old also lost his rookie status, with a spectacular 0.40 ratio, 0.00 ERA and his first 3 major league saves. He was exclusively a starter at Buffalo, going 1.23, 3.43, and become Pittsburgh's bullpen ace seemingly by accident. He has been overpowering at times in an oft-injured minor league career. Allow yourself to speculate: What might have happened to the Pirates if he had been eligible for the NLCS? And go after him for your own team.

Mike Roesler, a 27-year-old righty, was half of the payment the Pirates received in the Billy Hatcher fleecing — uh, trade. Roesler's career went backwards — from a 1.60, 4.29 start at Buffalo to a 1.17, 3.00 stop in Pittsburgh to a 1.52, 4.18 finish at Harrisburg. Not a good choice for '91.

ST. LOUIS

Lee Smith. What else do you need to know? Oh, the setup guys, etc. Well . . . Scott Terry was supposed to be the closer last year. All he did was add a sense of urgency to getting hold of Smith.

Juan Agosto will get first chance at the setup role, but this isn't the same Juan Agosto whom we have known and loved in previous seasons. In 1988 he got 10 wins and 4 saves with a 1.13 ratio. In 1989 his ratio ballooned to 1.36, but he still had a 2.93 ERA. Last year the ratio was a damaging 1.41, and his ERA soared to 4.29; and he was much worse in the second half. Agosto has appeared in more games than any other pitcher over the past three years; now he's age 33. I say he's got too many miles on the odometer, and the move to St. Louis won't help. Busch Stadium is very friendly to pitchers, but so is the Astrodome.

Considering the gaping holes in the setup corps, you have to like the chances for Mike Perez, the Louisville stopper. Omar Olivares (see starting pitchers) is also a serious candidate for pen work. Finally, Todd Worrell just had elbow surgery; they didn't amputate anything. He's not out of the question.

Adam Stein:

Scott Terry was a flop as a closer. However, once he shook off that failure, straightened out some physical problems, and got into another role, he became a good reliever. In the second half of 1990, he had a 2.50 ERA and a 0.91 ratio. He should be a steal for a buck or two. This is the same Scott Terry who had a 2.92 ERA and 1.18 ratio in 1988. He's still only 31.

The nicest thing about Omar Olivares, whether he starts or relieves, is that he will go back to Louisville if he pitches badly. There aren't too many pitchers who come with a built-in insurance policy.

Lary Bump:

Righthander Mike Perez, 26, has had phenomenal success as a closer the last four seasons — 123 saves, including 31 at Louisville and one with the Cards in 1990. This despite a 1.45 ratio and 2.82 ERA in Triple-A and a 3.95 ERA (1.10 ratio) in the majors. He doesn't seem likely for more than a set-up role in St Louis, except that no matter where he is, there always seems to be talk of trading Lee Smith. If Smith is traded, jump on Perez.

The 27-year-old Howard Hilton has made a minor league career as a set-up man. Last season he had a 1.34 ratio and 3.60 ERA, but no saves, in 55 relief appearances at Louisville. His two games with the Cardinals (1.67 ratio, 0.00 ERA) may have been more a tribute to an organization workhorse than a real major league shot. If he returns to the bigs this year, it would be in middle relief.

SAN DIEGO

Craig Lefferts was supposed to replace Mark Davis, and everybody talked about Lefferts coming up short. Now the Padres wouldn't trade the 1990 stats of Lefferts for the 1990 stats of Davis, would they? No one else would, either. Lefferts may get more saves now that Greg Harris is slated to be starter; he shouldn't get any less.

Larry Andersen, over from Houston via Boston, will get the setup work that Harris vacates. After Andersen, the relief roles are unclear. Anyone who doesn't make the starting rotation will be considered for long and short relief: Atlee Hammaker and Derek Lilliquist are possibilities to get plenty of work and produce very little Rotisserie value.

San Diego acquired John Costello from Montreal during the winter. He may be a candidate for a few trickle-down saves after Greg Harris is moved from the bullpen to the starting rotation. When he was with St. Louis, Costello had some minor success in situational relief but attracted little attention.

Lary Bump:

Darned if I didn't type "Rick Rodriguez" for this one; it's Rich Rodriguez, a 28-year-old lefty late of the — what else? — Mets organization. He had an exceptional Triple-A debut at Las Vegas (1.22, 3.51, 8 saves) and kept up the good work with the Padres (1.43, 2.83, a save). He's a very likely middle reliever or setup man for Craig Lefferts.

SAN FRANCISCO

Dave Righetti will provide the left-handed half of a closing tandem with Jeff Brantley.

The Yankees indirectly helped Righetti by sending him to instructional camp after 1989 to work on his third and fourth pitches in preparation for a return to the starting rotation. The starter's role never happened, but Righetti's pitching improved with the bigger repertoire. Righetti was dominant when he first went to the pen back in 1984. But starting in 1987, he was losing it. His career took a turn upwards in 1990 when he began to mix in curves and changes with the fastball and slider.

Another note for the Giants: Righetti responded very well to careful usage in 1990. The Yankees attempted to use him only one inning, only in save situations, and in all save situations. After working 1.43 IP per outing from 1987 through 1989, Rags worked exactly 1.00 IP per game in 1990. He was 92% (36 for 39) converting save opportunities, far better than the three previous seasons. Roger Craig, are you reading this?

We'll finish with the opposite of an "I told you so." Here's one "You told us so." Last year Michael Duca put in a well-reasoned case for Jeff Brantley's emergence as a closer in San Francisco:

"Jeff Brantley could be the next stopper in this bullpen; I expect Roger to let him close out a lot more games than last year. Brantley came into 5 games with bases loaded in 1989. He got 4 DP's. A great middle reliever, his time will come. If he's still cheap in your draft, go for it."

The message was lost on me. I didn't get Brantley. But lots of other people around the country did get Brantley, and they all called to thank me. After just a few calls, I stopped saying, "Jeff Who?" and took the credit. Thanks to Mike Duca.

Rob Wood:

A person cannot overestimate how much Roger Craig likes Jeff Brantley, and will do everything possible to get him his share of saves.

Lary Bump:

Mark Dewey, a 26-year-old righty, was extremely effective last season — 1.24, 1.88, 13 saves at Shreveport; 1.20, 2.67, 8 saves with Phoenix; 1.14, 2.78 with the Giants. There's no reason why he can't throw his hat into the derby for short relief work. Dewey is likely to stick in some bullpen capacity. Even if he doesn't, injuries to the Giants' staff almost certainly will land him in San Francisco sometime in '91.

Lefty Ed Vosberg, 29, is a Pacific Coast League fixture (1.53, 2.65 last year at Phoenix) who made it to the Giants (1.36, 5.55) to fill a hole when still another pitcher went on the disabled list. Don't look for him in the majors this year unless there's another injury epidemic.

Despite what the Giants say, it would take an injury plague to get Paul McClellan, a 25-year-old righty, back in the majors. It was one of those last-week-of-the-season games, and I was the only person north of Georgia and east of California watching TBS late at night. The Braves already had a couple of touchdowns and a field goal, and McClellan was in the game just to get the last outs. But the Braves kept burning him deep. That must be how he got his 2.61 ratio and 11.74 ERA with San Fran. But what did they expect from a guy who was 7-16 with a 1.57 ratio and 5.17 ERA at Phoenix?

III
THE NUMBERS

HITTERS 1991 FORECAST STATS

NAME	TEAM	LG	B	POS	AB	AVG	HR	RB	SB
ABNER	SD	N	R	8	196	.229	3	19	2
AFENIR	OAK	A	R	2	104	.217	5	22	1
ALDRETE	MON	N	L	7	101	.231	1	11	1
ALLRED	CLE	A	L	7	320	.269	6	42	1
ALOMAR,R	TOR	A	S	4	589	.285	6	56	30
ALOMAR,S	CLE	A	R	2	441	.287	10	67	4
ALOU	MON	N	R	7	50	.200	0	4	0
ANDERSON,B	BAL	A	L	7	347	.238	5	35	23
ANDERSON,D	SF	N	R	6	50	.293	0	4	0
ANDERSON,K	CAL	A	R	6	175	.268	1	10	0
ANTHONY	HOU	N	L	9	389	.212	17	50	8
AZOCAR	SD	N	L	7	226	.248	4	24	6
BACKMAN	PITF	N	S	4	298	.268	1	25	4
BAERGA	CLE	A	S	5	560	.275	12	89	0
BAEZ	NYM	N	R	6	50	.193	0	4	0
BAGWELL	HOU	N	R	5	280	.278	1	29	1
BAILEY	SFX	N	S	2	50	.192	2	7	0
BAINES	OAK	A	L	10	486	.293	17	74	0
BAKER	MINX	A	S	4	32	.281	0	4	0
BALBONI	NYY	A	R	10	178	.208	12	28	0
BALDWIN	HOUX	N	L	7	50	.172	0	4	0
BARFIELD	NYY	A	R	9	488	.237	24	73	4
BARRETT	BOSX	A	R	4	230	.243	0	19	4
BASS	SF	N	S	9	434	.275	10	63	7
BATES	CIN	N	L	4	79	.164	0	7	4
BATHE	SFX	N	R	2	50	.214	3	9	0
BELCHER	TEX	A	R	8	50	.184	0	4	5
BELL,G	CHC	N	R	7	525	.277	27	96	3
BELL,JN	BAL	A	S	4	265	.237	2	23	6
BELL,JY	PIT	N	R	6	508	.254	10	63	12
BELL,M	ATL	N	L	3	55	.221	1	6	0
BELLE,J	CLE	A	R	7	101	.217	3	17	1
BELLIARD	ATL	N	R	6	50	.212	0	4	1
BENJAMIN	SF	N	R	6	306	.217	12	33	4
BENZINGER	CIN	N	S	3	220	.241	4	26	1
BERGMAN	DET	A	L	10	277	.270	4	30	3
BERNAZARD	DET	A	S	4	250	.242	5	25	6
BERROA	ATL	N	R	7	50	.245	1	4	0
BERRY	KC	A	R	5	140	.270	3	18	4
BERRYHILL	CHC	N	S	2	165	.242	3	22	0
BICHETTE	CAL	A	R	7	288	.252	12	41	5
BIGGIO	HOU	N	R	2	500	.270	7	48	21

HITTERS 1991 FORECAST STATS

NAME	TEAM	LG	B	POS	AB	AVG	HR	RB	SB
BILARDELLO	PITX	N	R	2	87	.137	0	8	0
BLANKENSHIP	OAK	A	R	5	132	.204	0	8	4
BLAUSER	ATL	N	R	6	354	.266	8	36	4
BLOWERS	NYY	A	R	5	329	.245	13	51	3
BOGGS	BOS	A	L	5	590	.312	4	57	1
BONDS	PIT	N	L	7	543	.278	27	92	47
BONILLA	PIT	N	S	9	600	.280	27	103	5
BOOKER	PHI	N	L	4	101	.215	0	8	2
BOONE	KCF	A	R	2	50	.262	0	5	0
BORDERS	TOR	A	R	2	300	.276	9	40	1
BORDICK	OAK	A	R	5	104	.171	0	8	0
BOSLEY	TEXX	A	L	7	50	.177	1	5	1
BOSTON	NYM	N	L	8	202	.263	6	23	10
BRADLEY,P	J	J	R	7	0	.0			
BRADLEY,S	SEA	A	L	2	248	.245	2	32	0
BRAGGS	CIN	N	R	9	374	.263	10	48	9
BREAM	ATL	N	L	3	516	.265	20	88	11
BRETT	KC	A	L	3	482	.292	14	85	9
BREWER	STLX	N	L	3	50	.213	0	5	0
BRILEY	SEA	A	L	7	432	.252	11	52	18
BROCK	MIL	A	L	3	188	.252	5	25	3
BROOKENS	CLEF	A	R	5	50	.250	1	6	0
BROOKS	NYM	N	R	9	506	.269	16	78	3
BROWN	BALX	A	R	4	50	.200	0	4	0
BROWNE	CLE	A	S	4	533	.283	6	59	14
BRUMLEY	SEAX	A	S	6	173	.213	0	9	4
BRUNANSKY	BOS	A	R	9	485	.246	16	71	5
BUCKNER	BOSX	A	L	10	96	.208	1	8	0
BUECHELE	TEX	A	R	5	356	.227	11	44	1
BUHNER	SEA	A	R	9	379	.273	17	70	4
BULLOCK	MONX	N	L	10	50	.211	0	5	0
BURKS	BOS	A	R	8	511	.297	22	90	14
BUSH	MIN	A	L	9	235	.256	8	28	1
BUTLER	LA	N	L	8	606	.303	3	40	44
CABRERA	ATL	N	R	3	269	.275	12	42	2
CALDERON	MON	N	R	7	594	.275	13	74	19
CAMINITI	HOU	N	S	5	280	.244	3	30	4
CAMPUSANO	PHI	N	R	8	105	.207	3	11	1
CANALE	MIL	A	L	3	50	.174	0	4	0
CANDAELE	HOU	N	S	4	238	.273	1	19	7
CANGELOSI	PITF	N	S	7	151	.218	1	8	7
CANSECO,J	OAK	A	R	9	413	.268	30	88	14

HITTERS 1991 FORECAST STATS

NAME	TEAM	LG	B	POS	AB	AVG	HR	RB	SB
CANSECO,O	OAK	A	R	10	50	.170	2	10	0
CARR	NYM	N	S	7	50	.192	0	5	1
CARREON	NYM	N	R	7	86	.271	4	11	1
CARTER,G	SFF	N	R	2	50	.230	1	5	0
CARTER,J	TOR	A	R	7	590	.249	26	101	19
CARTER,S	PIT	N	L	8	150	.200	0	14	0
CASTILLO	MIN	A	R	9	169	.236	3	20	0
CEDENO	HOU	N	R	6	110	.202	0	15	7
CERONE	NYYF	A	R	2	50	.267	1	6	0
CHAMBERLAIN	PHI	N	R	7	101	.260	3	11	3
CLARK,D	CHC	N	L	7	110	.254	3	13	3
CLARK,JA	BOS	A	R	10	389	.262	26	77	5
CLARK,JE	SD	N	R	3	193	.251	8	25	1
CLARK,W	SF	N	L	3	573	.313	29	94	7
COACHMAN	CAL	A	R	5	135	.252	0	14	0
COCHRANE	SEA	A	S	5	103	.207	2	6	0
COLBRUNN	MONM	N	R	2	50	.245	0	5	0
COLE	CLE	A	L	8	540	.270	2	35	62
COLEMAN	NYM	N	S	8	507	.273	4	35	68
COLES	DETF	A	R	9	150	.236	3	16	0
COLLINS	CINX	N	S	7	0	.0	0	0	
CONINE	KC	A	R	3	189	.270	2	24	2
COOLBAUGH	SD	N	R	5	353	.202	6	35	2
COOPER	BOS	A	L	5	51	.196	0	5	0
CORA	SD	N	S	4	334	.253	2	22	20
COTTO	SEA	A	R	9	320	.250	6	32	14
CUYLER	DET	A	S	8	300	.227	0	39	13
DANIELS	LA	N	L	7	488	.286	27	97	9
DASCENZO	CHC	N	S	8	75	.230	0	8	5
DAUGHERTY	TEX	A	S	7	315	.295	5	47	1
DAULTON	PHI	N	L	2	431	.252	12	57	8
DAVIDSON	HOU	N	R	9	182	.265	3	21	1
DAVIS,A	SEA	A	L	10	497	.291	20	84	0
DAVIS,C	CALF	A	S	7	399	.265	13	60	1
DAVIS,E	CIN	N	R	8	472	.273	28	95	23
DAVIS,G	HOU	N	R	3	390	.260	23	66	6
DAVIS,J	ATLX	N	R	2	0	.155	0	0	0
DAWSON	CHC	N	R	9	477	.287	22	88	13
DECKER	SF	N	R	2	350	.273	11	46	2
DEER	DET	A	R	9	510	.210	29	74	2
DELOSSANTOS	KC	A	R	5	135	.257	0	8	0
DEMPSEY	LAF	N	R	2	50	.189	1	5	0

HITTERS 1991 FORECAST STATS

NAME	TEAM	LG	B	POS	AB	AVG	HR	RB	SB
DESHIELDS	MON	N	L	4	516	.284	4	51	40
DEVEREAUX	BAL	A	R	8	392	.252	12	51	18
DIAZ,C	TOR	A	R	2	53	.207	0	5	0
DIAZ,E	MIL	A	R	6	158	.257	0	11	2
DIAZ,M	NYMX	N	R	6	50	.180	0	4	0
DISARCINA	CAL	A	R	6	107	.168	0	5	1
DORAN	CIN	N	S	4	410	.270	7	42	21
DORSETT	NYYX	A	R	2	50	.176	0	3	0
DOWNING	CALF	A	R	10	299	.280	10	40	0
DUCEY	TOR	A	L	7	50	.252	0	6	0
DUNCAN	CIN	N	R	4	255	.289	5	30	8
DUNSTON	CHC	N	R	6	504	.263	12	59	25
DWYER	MINX	A	L	10	128	.281	2	12	1
DYKSTRA	PHI	N	L	8	541	.285	8	46	31
EISENREICH	KC	A	L	8	295	.286	4	33	9
ELSTER	NYM	N	R	6	132	.216	3	17	1
EPPARD	TORX	A	L	10	55	.200	0	5	0
ESASKY	ATL	N	R	3	50	.267	2	9	0
ESPINOZA	NYY	A	R	6	460	.247	1	29	2
ESPY	TEXX	A	S	8	100	.231	0	6	9
EVANS	BAL	A	R	10	450	.268	14	73	3
FARIES	SD	N	R	4	295	.225	2	30	17
FARRIS	TEX	A	R	6	125	.257	2	16	1
FELDER	MIL	A	S	7	258	.257	3	24	21
FELIX	CAL	A	S	8	417	.254	11	52	12
FERMIN	CLE	A	R	6	505	.252	0	39	5
FERNANDEZ	SD	N	S	6	594	.271	7	63	27
FIELDER	DET	A	R	3	560	.271	39	106	0
FINLEY	BAL	A	L	9	366	.254	4	40	24
FISK	CHW	A	R	2	388	.289	15	62	5
FITZGERALD	MON	N	R	2	250	.240	7	35	3
FLETCHER,D	PHI	N	L	2	90	.233	3	16	0
FLETCHER,S	CHW	A	R	4	524	.248	3	54	2
FOLEY	MON	N	L	6	208	.221	3	19	1
FORD	PHIX	N	L	9	50	.205	0	4	1
FRANCO	TEX	A	R	4	562	.304	12	76	29
FRANCONA	MILX	A	L	3	96	.229	1	9	1
FRYMAN	DET	A	R	5	490	.271	17	60	6
GAETTI	MINF	A	R	5	546	.232	17	79	6
GAGNE	MIN	A	R	6	503	.250	9	50	12
GALARRAGA	MON	N	R	3	575	.255	23	88	11
GALLAGHER	CAL	A	R	8	216	.262	0	16	1

HITTERS 1991 FORECAST STATS

NAME	TEAM	LG	B	POS	AB	AVG	HR	RB	SB
GALLEGO	OAK	A	R	4	382	.222	3	31	7
GANT	ATL	N	R	8	501	.271	22	61	29
GANTNER	MIL	A	L	4	427	.267	0	32	24
GARCIA	PIT	N	R	6	70	.222	0	6	0
GEDMAN	HOUF	N	L	2	50	.210	1	4	0
GEREN	NYY	A	R	2	238	.235	8	29	0
GIBSON	KC	A	L	10	318	.245	9	35	26
GILES	SEAX	A	R	6	145	.220	8	16	2
GILKEY	STL	N	R	7	418	.266	4	31	19
GIRARDI	CHC	N	R	2	309	.258	1	28	5
GLADDEN	MIN	A	R	7	441	.276	5	37	21
GOFF	MON	N	L	2	75	.215	3	8	1
GOMEZ	BAL	A	R	5	271	.251	8	32	0
GONZALES	BAL	A	R	4	98	.218	1	9	2
GONZALEZ,JO	LA	N	R	7	114	.256	1	8	3
GONZALEZ,JU	TEX	A	R	8	492	.262	19	66	0
GONZALEZ,L	HOU	N	L	5	100	.210	3	14	5
GRACE	CHC	N	L	3	554	.319	12	84	14
GREBECK	CHW	A	R	5	169	.177	2	14	0
GREEN	TEX	A	R	6	50	.210	0	5	0
GREENWELL	BOS	A	L	7	597	.308	16	86	11
GREGG	ATL	N	L	3	184	.255	4	20	3
GRIFFEY,JR	SEA	A	L	8	555	.288	20	75	15
GRIFFEY,SR	SEA	A	L	10	228	.280	8	36	4
GRIFFIN	LA	N	S	6	168	.222	0	11	2
GRISSOM	MON	N	R	9	294	.257	5	30	21
GRUBER	TOR	A	R	5	563	.275	24	97	14
GUERRERO	STL	N	R	3	494	.291	14	88	1
GUILLEN	CHW	A	L	6	550	.260	1	58	18
GWYNN,C	LA	N	L	7	94	.263	3	15	0
GWYNN,T	SD	N	L	9	573	.319	4	68	23
HALE	MIN	A	L	4	52	.192	0	7	0
HALL	NYY	A	L	10	204	.257	8	28	0
HAMILTON,D	MIL	A	L	7	231	.269	2	24	12
HAMILTON,J	LA	N	R	5	84	.235	2	8	0
HANSEN	LA	N	L	5	101	.235	1	10	1
HARPER	MIN	A	R	2	439	.300	6	52	4
HARRIS	LA	N	L	5	301	.283	2	22	12
HASELMAN	TEX	A	R	2	195	.279	5	25	1
HASSEY	OAKF	A	L	2	258	.224	5	23	0
HATCHER,B	CIN	N	R	7	381	.249	4	28	18
HATCHER,M	LA	N	R	7	89	.254	1	9	0

HITTERS 1991 FORECAST STATS

NAME	TEAM	LG	B	POS	AB	AVG	HR	RB	SB
HAYES,C	PHI	N	R	5	456	.252	9	51	4
HAYES,V	PHI	N	R	7	486	.258	23	79	20
HEATH	DETF	A	R	2	375	.256	8	40	6
HEEP	BOSF	A	L	9	169	.272	2	24	0
HEMOND	OAK	A	R	5	163	.210	4	17	5
HENDERSON,D	OAK	A	R	8	478	.265	16	66	4
HENDERSON,R	OAK	A	R	7	496	.300	20	58	65
HERNANDEZ,C	LA	N	R	2	70	.200	0	6	0
HERNANDEZ,K	CLE	A	L	3	164	.219	2	12	0
HERR	NYM	N	S	4	508	.273	3	46	7
HILL,D	CALF	A	S	4	100	.273	1	9	1
HILL,G	TOR	A	R	9	302	.226	13	35	10
HOILES	BAL	A	R	2	275	.230	7	32	0
HOLLINS	PHI	N	S	5	214	.259	5	30	0
HORN	BAL	A	L	10	155	.239	8	26	0
HOWARD,S	OAKF	A	R	9	102	.215	0	6	0
HOWARD,T	SD	N	S	7	94	.234	0	5	0
HOWELL	CAL	A	L	5	335	.229	11	36	2
HOWITT	OAK	A	L	9	72	.180	0	6	0
HRBEK	MIN	A	L	3	441	.285	23	80	3
HUDLER	STL	N	R	7	264	.268	9	24	23
HUGHES	NYMX	N	L	7	50	.208	1	6	0
HULETT	BAL	A	R	4	50	.259	1	6	0
HUNDLEY	NYM	N	S	2	50	.229	0	3	0
HUSON	TEX	A	L	6	405	.228	0	31	13
INCAVIGLIA	TEX	A	R	7	492	.231	22	81	4
INFANTE	ATLX	N	R	4	50	.141	0	3	0
JACKSON,B	KC	A	R	7	416	.264	29	85	17
JACKSON,D	SD	N	R	8	136	.247	3	13	3
JACOBY	CLE	A	R	5	538	.280	12	70	1
JAMES,C	CLE	A	R	10	512	.281	13	67	4
JAMES,D	CLEX	A	L	3	250	.279	2	26	3
JAVIER	LA	N	S	8	261	.276	2	22	12
JEFFERIES	NYM	N	S	5	568	.286	13	62	14
JEFFERSON	CLE	A	R	8	176	.238	4	20	13
JELIC	NYMX	N	R	7	50	.180	2	5	0
JELTZ	KCF	A	S	6	50	.209	1	5	1
JENNINGS	OAK	A	L	7	209	.234	4	20	1
JOHNSON,H	NYM	N	S	6	540	.262	26	88	34
JOHNSON,L	CHW	A	L	8	397	.292	1	35	33
JOHNSON,W	MONX	N	S	3	0	.0			
JONES,R	PHI	N	L	7	258	.240	14	39	0

HITTERS 1991 FORECAST STATS

NAME	TEAM	LG	B	POS	AB	AVG	HR	RB	SB
JONES,TI	STL	N	L	6	157	.242	1	15	4
JONES,TR	SEA	A	R	7	186	.258	5	25	1
JORDAN	PHI	N	R	3	300	.284	5	42	2
JOSE	STL	N	S	9	445	.272	12	55	10
JOYNER	CAL	A	L	3	440	.275	12	58	2
JUSTICE	ATL	N	L	9	501	.286	31	95	14
KARKOVICE	CHW	A	R	2	283	.251	8	34	3
KELLY	NYY	A	R	8	563	.291	17	67	46
KENNEDY	SF	N	L	2	218	.257	2	20	1
KING	PIT	N	R	5	321	.236	14	51	5
KINGERY	SF	N	L	7	208	.274	2	25	5
KITTLE	BALF	A	R	10	100	.242	5	15	0
KOMMINSK	BALX	A	R	8	50	.235	2	6	1
KREMERS	ATL	N	L	2	73	.146	1	4	0
KREUTER	TEX	A	R	2	96	.191	3	6	0
KRUK	PHI	N	L	3	374	.297	7	55	7
KUNKEL	TEX	A	R	6	187	.219	4	17	2
KUTCHER	BOS	A	R	9	50	.231	0	5	1
LAGA	J	J	L	0	0	.0			
LAKE	PHI	N	R	2	101	.254	1	8	0
LAMPKIN	SD	N	L	2	103	.212	2	8	0
LANCELLOTTI	BOSX	A	L	3	58	.172	0	6	0
LANKFORD	STL	N	L	8	469	.267	10	58	23
LANSFORD	OAK	A	R	5	100	.288	0	10	4
LARKIN,B	CIN	N	R	6	498	.309	6	53	19
LARKIN,G	MIN	A	S	10	294	.263	4	29	4
LAUDNER	MINX	A	R	2	96	.218	2	11	0
LAVALLIERE	PIT	N	L	2	327	.275	4	38	0
LAW	JF	N	R	4	163	.233	3	17	1
LAWLESS	TORX	A	R	5	62	.177	0	6	0
LEACH	SF	N	L	9	175	.285	2	17	1
LEE,M	TOR	A	S	6	506	.270	6	59	5
LEE,T	CIN	N	R	3	69	.202	0	8	0
LEIUS	MIN	A	R	6	125	.223	3	15	0
LEMKE	ATL	N	S	4	162	.224	1	16	1
LEMON	DET	A	R	9	373	.246	5	37	2
LEONARD,J	SEAX	A	R	7	476	.254	14	75	3
LEONARD,M	SF	N	L	9	50	.194	1	5	0
LEWIS	SF	N	R	8	50	.211	0	4	1
LEYRITZ	NYY	A	R	5	340	.247	5	28	3
LIDDELL	NYMX	N	R	2	50	.215	0	5	0
LIND	PIT	N	R	4	533	.270	2	46	10

HITTERS 1991 FORECAST STATS

NAME	TEAM	LG	B	POS	AB	AVG	HR	RB	SB
LINDEMAN	DETX	A	R	9	50	.207	2	8	0
LIRIANO	MIN	A	S	4	492	.250	5	54	17
LITTON	SF	N	R	6	170	.244	2	20	1
LOMBARDOZZI	HOUX	N	R	4	50	.196	0	5	0
LOPEZ	LAM	N	R	3	50	.178	0	4	0
LUSADER	DET	A	L	9	193	.247	4	27	2
LYNN	SDF	N	L	7	200	.239	6	25	2
LYONS,B	LA	N	R	2	95	.241	2	10	0
LYONS,S	CHW	A	L	3	50	.241	0	5	1
MAAS	NYY	A	L	10	482	.251	27	76	3
MACFARLANE	KC	A	R	2	476	.245	8	69	0
MACK	MIN	A	R	8	449	.295	12	64	22
MAGADAN	NYM	N	L	3	442	.309	5	64	2
MALDONADO	CLEF	A	R	7	440	.259	14	67	4
MANN	ATL	N	R	2	93	.235	2	11	1
MANRIQUE	CAL	A	R	4	135	.267	2	18	1
MANTO	CLE	A	R	3	251	.231	7	35	0
MANWARING	SF	N	R	2	88	.204	0	8	1
MARSHALL	BOS	A	R	9	125	.259	4	16	0
MARTINEZ,CM	PIT	N	R	3	337	.232	11	53	3
MARTINEZ,CS	CHW	A	R	3	190	.264	3	16	1
MARTINEZ,D	MON	N	L	8	362	.274	8	32	15
MARTINEZ,E	SEA	A	R	5	450	.288	9	46	3
MARTINEZ,T	SEA	A	L	3	267	.249	5	26	0
MARZANO	BOS	A	R	2	133	.225	0	11	0
MATTINGLY	NYY	A	L	3	451	.283	11	66	1
MAY	CHC	N	L	7	75	.225	1	11	1
MAYNE	KC	A	L	2	100	.206	0	10	0
MCCLENDON	PIT	N	R	7	170	.235	6	23	2
MCCRAY	CHWX	A	R	8	56	.178	0	5	7
MCDOWELL	ATL	N	L	8	303	.252	9	39	15
MCGEE	SF	N	S	8	503	.312	4	61	22
MCGRIFF,F	SD	N	L	3	525	.279	36	88	7
MCGRIFF,T	HOU	N	R	2	50	.169	0	4	0
MCGWIRE	OAK	A	R	3	510	.235	36	102	2
MCINTOSH	MIL	A	R	2	256	.266	7	34	2
MCKNIGHT	BAL	A	S	3	50	.218	1	4	0
MCLEMORE	CLEX	A	S	4	50	.194	0	5	1
MCRAE	KC	A	S	8	493	.262	7	62	12
MCREYNOLDS	NYM	N	R	7	514	.275	22	79	11
MEADOWS	PHIX	N	L	7	50	.166	0	3	0
MELVIN	BAL	A	R	2	202	.243	3	24	0

HITTERS 1991 FORECAST STATS

NAME	TEAM	LG	B	POS	AB	AVG	HR	RB	SB
MERCADO	MONX	N	R	2	50	.209	2	4	0
MERCED	PIT	N	S	3	50	.202	0	3	0
MEULENS	NYY	A	R	7	446	.250	14	54	2
MILLER	NYM	N	R	8	107	.248	1	5	8
MILLIGAN	BAL	A	R	3	330	.266	15	47	6
MITCHELL	SF	N	R	7	516	.285	37	102	4
MOLITOR	MIL	A	R	3	488	.299	10	48	21
MORANDINI	PHI	N	L	4	417	.258	3	35	12
MORMAN	KC	A	R	7	87	.229	2	8	0
MORRIS,H	CIN	N	L	3	490	.313	9	54	15
MORRIS,J	STLX	N	R	9	50	.206	1	5	0
MOSEBY	DET	A	L	7	454	.235	13	50	18
MOSES	MINF	A	S	9	200	.250	1	21	5
MOTA	HOU	N	R	4	200	.220	4	29	9
MULLINIKS	TOR	A	L	10	267	.257	3	34	3
MUNOZ	MIN	A	R	7	414	.266	8	43	8
MURPHY	PHI	N	R	9	457	.241	18	67	5
MURRAY	LA	N	S	3	580	.303	24	95	8
MYERS	TOR	A	L	2	247	.234	4	22	0
NAEHRING	BOS	A	R	6	400	.267	10	48	0
NELSON	SDX	N	L	3	50	.181	0	5	0
NEWMAN	MIN	A	S	4	412	.247	0	33	16
NICHOLS	HOU	N	R	2	50	.202	0	8	0
NIETO	PHIX	N	R	2	50	.187	0	6	0
NIXON,D	BALX	A	R	7	50	.269	0	4	4
NIXON,O	MON	N	S	8	222	.235	1	18	43
NOBOA	MON	N	R	4	106	.265	1	11	2
NOCE	CINX	N	R	6	51	.215	0	5	0
NOKES	NYY	A	L	2	372	.253	14	53	3
OBERKFELL	HOU	N	L	5	152	.230	1	14	1
OBRIEN,C	NYM	N	R	2	233	.197	2	30	0
OBRIEN,P	SEA	A	L	3	456	.245	8	39	1
OESTER	CINF	N	S	4	100	.271	0	6	0
OFFERMAN	LA	N	S	6	416	.236	4	37	30
OLERUD	TOR	A	L	3	474	.270	17	60	0
OLIVER	CIN	N	R	2	264	.234	6	39	0
OLSON	ATL	N	R	2	237	.250	4	26	2
OMALLEY	J	J	L	5	0	.0			
ONEILL	CIN	N	L	9	469	.268	14	74	14
OQUENDO	STL	N	S	4	483	.271	2	48	3
ORSULAK	BAL	A	L	9	334	.268	7	45	5
ORTIZ,JN	MIN	A	R	2	144	.278	0	15	1

HITTERS 1991 FORECAST STATS

NAME	TEAM	LG	B	POS	AB	AVG	HR	RB	SB
ORTIZ,JV	HOU	N	R	7	268	.255	5	30	2
ORTON	CAL	A	R	2	164	.194	2	13	0
OWEN	MON	N	S	6	435	.229	4	34	6
PAGLIARULO	SDF	N	L	5	200	.232	4	18	1
PAGNOZZI	STL	N	R	2	386	.260	4	39	1
PALACIOS	KCX	A	R	2	50	.216	2	7	1
PALMEIRO	TEX	A	L	3	583	.303	15	95	5
PANKOVITS	BOSX	A	R	4	50	.200	0	5	0
PAREDES	DETX*	A	R	4	50	.203	0	5	0
PARENT	TEX	A	R	2	290	.211	9	31	2
PARKER,D	MIL	A	L	10	538	.264	19	82	2
PARKER,R	SF	N	R	9	104	.245	3	15	5
PARRISH	CAL	A	R	2	454	.253	20	59	2
PASQUA	CHW	A	L	10	302	.258	11	54	1
PECOTA	KC	A	R	4	231	.229	5	21	7
PENA,G	STL	N	S	4	125	.274	2	18	6
PENA,T	BOS	A	R	2	459	.259	6	48	10
PENDLETON	ATL	N	S	5	495	.252	10	67	10
PEREZCHICA	SF	N	R	4	50	.207	0	5	2
PERRY	STL	N	L	3	259	.254	4	27	11
PETRALLI	TEX	A	S	2	298	.272	2	23	0
PETTIS	TEX	A	S	8	309	.247	1	17	27
PHELPS	CLEF	A	L	3	50	.200	1	5	0
PHILLIPS	DET	A	S	5	375	.259	4	37	8
PLANTIER	BOS	A	L	10	215	.209	12	30	0
POLIDOR	MILX	A	R	6	79	.177	0	6	1
POLONIA	CAL	A	L	7	390	.325	2	38	18
PRESLEY	ATLF	N	R	5	472	.233	16	57	1
PRINCE	PIT	N	R	2	50	.183	0	4	0
PUCKETT	MIN	A	R	9	544	.313	9	76	7
PUHL	NYM	N	L	7	66	.277	0	6	1
QUINLAN	TOR	A	R	5	50	.211	0	5	0
QUINONES	CIN	N	S	4	145	.242	4	16	1
QUINTANA	BOS	A	R	3	340	.277	4	43	1
QUIRK	OAK	A	L	2	95	.252	2	20	0
RAINES	CHW	A	S	7	505	.286	10	66	49
RAMIREZ	HOU	N	R	6	268	.252	2	25	3
RAMOS	CHC	N	R	5	127	.265	1	11	0
RANDOLPH	OAKF	A	R	4	336	.272	2	31	7
RAY	J	J	S	4	0	.0			
READY	PHI	N	R	4	222	.254	4	25	3
REDFIELD	PIT	N	R	5	251	.231	5	30	10

HITTERS 1991 FORECAST STATS

NAME	TEAM	LG	B	POS	AB	AVG	HR	RB	SB
REDINGTON	SD	N	R	5	200	.230	8	39	1
REDUS	PIT	N	R	3	268	.262	6	29	16
REED,D	NYM	N	R	8	109	.232	2	9	1
REED,JE	CIN	N	L	2	220	.236	3	19	0
REED,JO	BOS	A	R	4	569	.288	4	45	5
REIMER	TEXX	A	L	7	50	.251	1	8	0
REYNOLDS,H	SEA	A	S	4	595	.272	4	45	27
REYNOLDS,RJ	J	J	S	9	0	.0			
REYNOLDS,RN	SDX	N	R	2	50	.169	0	5	0
RHODES	HOU	N	L	7	241	.241	3	14	5
RILES	OAK	A	L	5	484	.242	8	66	0
RIPKEN,B	BAL	A	R	4	364	.277	3	34	3
RIPKEN,C	BAL	A	R	6	590	.252	21	86	3
RIVERA	BOS	A	R	6	90	.240	2	11	1
ROBERTS	SD	N	S	4	462	.311	6	36	38
ROBIDOUX	BOSX	A	L	3	94	.191	2	9	0
ROHDE	HOU	N	S	4	256	.219	1	17	3
ROMERO	DETX	A	R	5	50	.214	0	3	0
ROMINE	BOS	A	R	9	50	.272	1	5	1
ROOMES	MONX	N	R	7	50	.251	1	5	1
ROSARIO	ATL	N	R	6	50	.192	0	4	0
ROSE	CAL	A	R	5	319	.238	10	35	0
ROWLAND	DET	A	R	2	175	.210	4	17	2
RUSSELL	TEXX	A	R	2	50	.235	1	3	0
RYAL	PIT	N	L	7	50	.177	0	4	0
SABO	CIN	N	R	5	456	.258	16	52	16
SALAS	DET	A	L	2	350	.227	9	49	0
SALAZAR	CHC	N	R	5	338	.260	9	35	2
SAMUEL	LA	N	R	4	432	.243	11	46	30
SANDBERG	CHC	N	R	4	565	.282	26	80	18
SANDERS	NYYX	A	L	8	0	.0			
SANTANA,A	SF	N	S	6	50	.192	0	6	0
SANTANA,R	CLEX	A	R	6	0	.206	0	0	0
SANTIAGO	SD	N	R	2	386	.243	12	54	7
SANTOVENIA	MON	N	R	2	219	.223	6	29	1
SASSER	NYM	N	L	2	282	.293	5	40	0
SAX	NYY	A	R	4	601	.281	5	50	43
SCHAEFER	SEA	A	R	6	157	.203	0	11	4
SCHOFIELD	CAL	A	R	6	370	.251	2	27	7
SCHROEDER	CALX	A	R	2	90	.211	5	11	0
SCHU	CAL	A	R	5	251	.238	7	21	0
SCHULZ	KCX	A	L	9	50	.247	0	5	0

HITTERS 1991 FORECAST STATS

NAME	TEAM	LG	B	POS	AB	AVG	HR	RB	SB
SCIOSCIA	LA	N	L	2	417	.258	10	56	3
SEGUI	BAL	A	S	3	50	.251	1	7	0
SEITZER	KC	A	R	5	589	.272	5	39	11
SHARPERSON	LA	N	R	5	283	.292	3	27	12
SHEETS	DETF	A	L	10	225	.250	6	31	1
SHEFFIELD	MIL	A	R	5	432	.273	8	50	19
SHELBY	DETX	A	S	8	150	.216	2	9	3
SHUMPERT	KC	A	R	4	348	.255	2	28	7
SIERRA	TEX	A	S	9	610	.292	23	115	10
SIMMS	HOU	N	R	3	163	.222	5	18	0
SINATRO	SEAX	A	R	2	100	.250	0	9	1
SKINNER	CLE	A	R	2	155	.238	2	15	0
SLAUGHT	PIT	N	R	2	267	.265	4	32	1
SMITH,D	CHC	N	L	7	290	.289	7	35	10
SMITH,G	LA	N	S	4	50	.202	0	5	1
SMITH,L	ATL	N	R	7	402	.285	12	48	7
SMITH,O	STL	N	S	6	501	.266	2	44	29
SNYDER	CHW	A	R	10	434	.231	14	51	2
SOJO	CAL	A	R	4	440	.248	4	40	7
SORRENTO	MIN	A	L	10	366	.257	17	56	2
SOSA	CHW	A	R	9	388	.253	10	48	25
SPIERS	MIL	A	L	6	368	.252	3	42	14
SPRINGER	CLEX	A	R	5	50	.193	0	5	0
STANLEY	TEXX	A	R	2	50	.246	1	5	0
STARK	CHW	A	R	10	185	.264	4	39	2
STEINBACH	OAK	A	R	2	404	.261	8	53	0
STEPHENS	STL	N	R	2	65	.184	2	6	0
STEPHENSON	SD	N	L	3	239	.212	7	29	4
STEVENS	CAL	A	L	10	375	.212	12	50	2
STILLWELL	KC	A	S	6	482	.244	7	55	5
STONE	BOSX	A	L	10	52	.211	0	6	0
STRAWBERRY	LA	N	L	9	516	.251	33	95	13
STUBBS	MIL	A	L	7	322	.270	15	51	17
SURHOFF	MIL	A	L	2	458	.262	6	65	17
SUTKO	CINX	N	R	2	51	.196	0	5	0
SVEUM	MIL	A	S	5	167	.237	2	17	0
TABLER	TOR	A	R	3	239	.264	2	27	0
TARTABULL	KC	A	R	9	365	.273	16	62	2
TAUBENSEE	OAK	A	L	2	150	.230	5	30	0
TEMPLETON	SD	N	S	6	183	.248	3	18	0
TETTLETON	BAL	A	S	2	421	.232	18	52	2
TEUFEL	NYM	N	R	4	143	.248	5	15	0

HITTERS 1991 FORECAST STATS

NAME	TEAM	LG	B	POS	AB	AVG	HR	RB	SB
THOMAS,A	ATL	N	R	6	332	.214	7	36	2
THOMAS,F	CHW	A	R	3	510	.309	21	81	2
THOMPSON,M	STL	N	L	7	420	.254	5	40	21
THOMPSON,R	SF	N	R	4	503	.244	14	50	13
THON	PHI	N	R	6	487	.262	12	51	11
THORNTON	NYMX	N	L	8	50	.200	0	5	0
THURMAN	KC	A	R	7	159	.245	1	11	9
TINGLEY	CALX	A	R	2	53	.188	0	5	0
TOLLESON	NYYX	A	S	4	50	.160	0	3	1
TORVE	NYMX	N	L	3	50	.238	0	4	0
TRAMMELL	DET	A	R	6	500	.284	11	70	10
TRAXLER	LAM	N	L	3	50	.180	0	4	0
TREADWAY	ATL	N	L	4	427	.275	7	44	3
TREVINO	CIN	N	R	2	84	.259	1	11	0
URIBE	SF	N	S	6	207	.226	1	12	3
VALLE	SEA	A	R	2	316	.221	7	33	0
VANSLYKE	PIT	N	L	8	499	.263	15	70	14
VARSHO	CHC	N	R	7	98	.224	0	6	2
VATCHER	ATL	N	R	9	214	.253	3	21	0
VAUGHN	BOS	A	L	3	350	.270	14	67	1
VAUGHN	MIL	A	R	9	478	.242	22	79	10
VELARDE	NYY	A	R	5	277	.237	6	25	0
VENABLE	CAL	A	R	7	165	.274	2	17	5
VENTURA	CHW	A	L	5	499	.256	5	57	6
VILLANUEVA	CHC	N	R	2	143	.265	7	23	1
VIRGIL	TORX	A	R	2	55	.181	0	5	0
VIZCAINO	CHC	N	S	4	161	.248	1	11	2
VIZQUEL	SEA	A	S	6	355	.233	2	22	4
WALEWANDER	NYYX	A	S	4	0	.0			
WALKER,G	BALX	A	L	3	0	.196	0	0	0
WALKER,L	MON	N	R	9	411	.248	19	51	23
WALLACH	MON	N	R	5	584	.288	16	85	6
WALLING	STLF	N	L	3	50	.240	0	7	0
WALTON	CHC	N	R	8	510	.275	6	42	20
WARD,G	DETF	A	R	7	150	.256	5	21	1
WARD,T	CLE	A	S	9	144	.270	3	19	2
WASHINGTON	NYYX	A	L	7	50	.241	1	5	1
WEBSTER,L	MIN	A	R	2	72	.258	1	5	3
WEBSTER,M	CLE	A	S	8	410	.245	10	49	18
WEISS	OAK	A	S	6	421	.263	1	35	8
WHITAKER	DET	A	L	4	472	.247	21	68	9
WHITE,D	TOR	A	S	8	504	.232	11	49	28

HITTERS 1991 FORECAST STATS

NAME	TEAM	LG	B	POS	AB	AVG	HR	RB	SB
WHITE,F	KCF	A	R	4	100	.237	1	9	1
WHITEN	TOR	A	S	9	325	.259	7	28	5
WHITT	ATLF	N	L	2	50	.225	1	5	0
WILKERSON	CHCF	N	S	5	176	.227	0	14	3
WILKINS	CHC	N	L	2	50	.200	0	5	0
WILLARD	CHWX	A	L	2	50	.221	1	7	0
WILLIAMS,E	J	J	R	5	0	.0			
WILLIAMS,K	TOR	A	R	9	196	.211	2	17	9
WILLIAMS,M	SF	N	R	5	480	.254	27	90	5
WILSON,C	STL	N	R	5	177	.240	1	17	1
WILSON,G	HOUF	N	R	9	200	.256	5	30	0
WILSON,M	TOR	A	S	8	305	.265	2	26	11
WILSON,W	OAK	A	S	8	328	.260	2	40	19
WINFIELD	CAL	A	R	9	410	.275	18	73	0
WINNINGHAM	CIN	N	L	8	146	.255	2	11	6
WORTHINGTON	BAL	A	R	5	436	.236	10	51	1
WRONA	MIL	A	R	2	50	.240	1	6	1
WYNNE	J	J	L	7	0	.0			
YELDING	HOU	N	R	6	452	.250	1	26	61
YOUNG	HOU	N	S	8	486	.245	2	33	24
YOUNT	MIL	A	R	8	595	.277	19	88	17
ZEILE	STL	N	R	2	406	.251	11	46	1

INTRODUCTION TO PITCHERS
1991 FORECAST STATS

The chapter on Forecasting tells you my general approach to the numbers. At this point I have a few detail comments to add.

All of my forecasts are "rationalized" — meaning that I examine them from different angles, looking for internal inconsistencies and/or combinations of implicit statements that cannot all be true. One of the tests for rationality is to sort all pitchers (and hitters) by major league team, and see that the big picture makes sense. Accordingly, if you go through the following tables and sort the players be team, you will find exactly 162 win/loss decisions, a sensible number of innings pitched for each pitching staff, and a realistic total for saves.

When we went to press, there were still 20 pitchers classified as free agents, and numerous others who had been cut, released, demoted, designated for assignment, or otherwise removed from their team's major league roster.

They are noted with a suffix after their team abbreviation:

F = Free agent.

M = Minor league contract.

X = Removed from major league roster.

We did not include these non-roster pitchers in the rationality tests. Many of them will end up on major league rosters and have an impact in 1991, but I think it is much better to avoid assumptions that this player or that player will sign will this team or that team, when building forecasts. [The only exception is that I assumed that Jack Morris will return to Detroit, because I don't want to forecast Kevin Ritz with 220 IP.] The free agent pitchers are not Cy Young types, anyway. The BEST of them are Dave Schmidt, Juan Berenguer, Dave LaPoint, Dan Petry, Dennis Rasmussen . . . you get the idea. If there is a big free-agent signing, you will hear about it in the news, and read about the impact in WINNING ROTISSERIE BASEBALL (203-834-0812). If I had assumed that Dennis Rasmussen was going to sign with the Seattle Mariners, and he didn't, the newspapers wouldn't alert you to my error. Maybe in ten years, USA Today and ESPN will be reporting "flash updates to Benson forecasts," but not in 1991.

The non-roster pitchers all have forecast stats, anyway, representing what they would do if they played in 1991. Many will sign. Obviously, if/when the free agents sign, they will displace someone less deserving. I wouldn't worry about any of them. The forecasts are going to run into bigger problems than blockbusters like Tom Niedenfuer joining the Yankees.

All major league teams have more than 10 or 11 pitchers with forecast stats in the rationality test. These are full year stats, and every team will use more than 10 or 11 pitchers over the course of a season. The dollar values for 1991 are based on the constraints that exist on draft day ($260 and 23 players per team). The full year stats allow a longer outlook.

Finally, someone out there is going to add up all the wins and losses for their favorite team, maybe even for a whole division, to see my implicit predictions for league champions. The forecasts aren't intended for that purpose. My method draws all player performances back toward the norms for their league. Dave Stewart is the only pitcher who wins 20 games in these forecasts, and no major league team wins more than 91 games this year. Obviously, extremes will occur in real baseball, but extreme forecasts aren't what you need on draft day. [If this warning made you curious: Toronto, Oakland, Mets, Dodgers. Don't quote me.]

PITCHERS 1991 FORECAST STATS

NAME	TEAM	LG	T	W	L	ERA	RATIO	SV	IP
AASE	LAF	N	R	1	2	4.72	1.40	0	29
ABBOTT,J	CAL	A	L	9	12	4.28	1.50	0	205
ABBOTT,P	MIN	A	R	5	8	4.78	1.55	0	97
ACKER	TOR	A	R	4	3	3.54	1.38	1	96
ADKINS	NYY	A	L	1	1	4.74	1.57	0	32
AGOSTO	STL	N	L	4	5	4.26	1.42	2	83
AGUILERA	MIN	A	R	3	4	3.11	1.24	19	113
AKERFELDS	PHI	N	R	3	2	4.39	1.39	2	71
ALDRED	DET	A	L	1	1	3.76	1.51	0	27
ALDRICH	BALX	A	R	1	2	4.66	1.56	1	19
ALEXANDER	TEX	A	R	5	8	4.47	1.60	0	97
ALLEN	HOU	N	L	9	10	3.71	1.34	0	130
ALVAREZ,J	SFX	N	R	1	1	2.86	1.35	1	35
ANDERSEN	SD	N	R	3	2	2.75	1.16	9	64
ANDERSON,A	MIN	A	L	10	12	4.02	1.28	0	186
ANDERSON,S	MONX	N	R	0	1	3.52	1.38	0	29
APPIER	KC	A	R	13	10	2.87	1.24	0	184
AQUINO	KC	A	R	3	3	3.25	1.29	0	85
ARD,J	SF	N	R	0	0	4.00	1.40	0	20
ARMSTRONG	CIN	N	R	6	8	4.43	1.41	0	110
ARNSBERG	TEX	A	R	4	4	3.08	1.43	8	63
ASSENMACHER	CHC	N	L	6	2	2.82	1.23	8	92
AUGUST	MILM	A	R	3	6	5.35	1.52	0	42
AVERY	ATL	N	L	7	12	4.88	1.47	0	150
BAILES	CAL	A	L	3	2	5.10	1.55	0	61
BAIR	PITF	N	R	1	1	3.88	1.53	0	63
BALLARD	BAL	A	L	9	10	4.12	1.39	0	155
BALLER	KCX	A	R	0	1	4.39	1.58	0	21
BANKHEAD	SEA	A	R	8	8	4.24	1.49	0	171
BANNISTER,F	CAL	A	L	3	2	4.18	1.30	0	75
BARFIELD	TEX	A	L	1	3	5.08	1.25	5	58
BARNES	MON	N	L	9	11	3.40	1.24	0	134
BAUTISTA	BAL	A	R	1	2	4.72	1.31	0	33
BEARSE	CLEX	A	L	0	1	5.09	1.60	0	24
BEDROSIAN	MIN	A	R	4	5	3.70	1.40	19	77
BELCHER	LA	N	R	10	8	3.45	1.23	0	141
BELINDA	PIT	N	R	2	3	4.41	1.42	13	52
BENES	SD	N	R	9	8	3.65	1.31	0	175
BERENGUER	MINF	A	R	6	5	3.21	1.30	3	96
BIELECKI	CHC	N	R	11	7	3.94	1.38	0	173
BIRTSAS	CINX	N	L	1	2	4.26	1.54	0	45
BITKER	TEXX	A	R	0	0	3.40	1.40	0	26

PITCHERS 1991 FORECAST STATS

NAME	TEAM	LG	T	W	L	ERA	RATIO	SV	IP
BLACK	SF	N	L	15	13	3.70	1.19	0	191
BLAIR	CLE	A	R	4	4	4.53	1.42	0	53
BLANKENSHIP	PIT	N	R	0	2	3.30	1.50	0	21
BLYLEVEN	CAL	A	R	7	6	4.04	1.34	0	139
BODDICKER	KC	A	R	15	11	3.43	1.34	0	214
BOEVER	PHI	N	R	3	6	3.26	1.37	12	86
BOHANON	TEX	A	L	1	2	5.04	1.53	0	57
BOLTON	BOS	A	L	11	8	3.38	1.33	0	151
BOOKER	SF	N	R	0	1	4.29	1.61	0	16
BOONE	BALX	A	L	0	0	3.56	1.50	0	25
BOSIO	MIL	A	R	6	8	3.61	1.26	0	124
BOSKIE	CHC	N	R	5	4	3.94	1.38	0	109
BOYD	MON	N	R	11	8	3.18	1.23	0	184
BRANTLEY	SF	N	R	4	3	2.87	1.44	10	74
BROWN,KD	MIL	A	L	10	11	3.34	1.20	0	174
BROWN,KEITH	CIN	N	R	2	1	3.97	1.33	0	46
BROWN,KEVIN	TEX	A	R	10	10	3.71	1.35	0	163
BROWNING	CIN	N	L	15	12	4.11	1.28	0	217
BURBA	SEA	A	R	0	0	3.88	1.27	0	44
BURKE	MON	N	R	4	3	2.72	1.18	20	82
BURKETT	SF	N	R	13	10	3.91	1.33	0	187
BURNS	OAK	A	R	3	4	2.89	1.29	4	107
CADARET	NYY	A	L	7	6	3.97	1.50	1	128
CAMACHO	STLX	N	R	2	1	3.63	1.52	0	22
CAMPBELL	KC	A	L	1	0	4.65	1.52	0	25
CANDELARIA	TORF	A	L	4	6	4.52	1.40	1	82
CANDIOTTI	CLE	A	R	12	12	3.53	1.26	0	204
CAPEL	MILX	A	R	0	0	4.01	1.63	0	20
CARMAN	PHIF	N	L	6	6	4.76	1.42	1	97
CARPENTER	STL	N	R	2	2	3.18	1.18	0	43
CARY	NYY	A	L	8	12	3.87	1.27	0	175
CASIAN	MIN	A	L	6	6	3.56	1.35	0	91
CASTILLO	ATL	N	L	4	5	4.39	1.50	1	71
CERUTTI	TORX	A	L	9	8	4.50	1.47	0	136
CHARLTON	CIN	N	L	10	8	2.93	1.26	1	155
CHIAMPARINO	TEX	A	R	11	11	3.21	1.28	0	179
CHITREN	OAK	A	R	4	0	2.91	1.15	9	78
CLANCY	HOU	N	R	5	9	5.38	1.49	0	116
CLARK,B	SEAX	A	L	1	0	3.65	1.53	0	26
CLARK,T	HOUX	N	R	0	0	4.64	1.60	0	22
CLARKE	STLX	N	L	0	0	3.67	1.35	0	22
CLARY	ATLX	N	R	1	8	4.74	1.45	0	118

PITCHERS 1991 FORECAST STATS

NAME	TEAM	LG	T	W	L	ERA	RATIO	SV	IP
CLEAR	CALX	A	R	0	0	4.09	1.54	0	24
CLEMENS	BOS	A	R	16	7	2.67	1.17	0	214
CLEMENTS	SDF	N	L	2	1	3.87	1.57	0	32
CODIROLI	KCX	A	R	0	1	4.95	1.61	0	25
COFFMAN	CHCX	N	R	0	1	5.39	1.59	0	29
COMBS	PHI	N	L	13	11	3.70	1.36	0	187
COMSTOCK	SEA	A	L	5	4	3.30	1.28	6	72
CONE	NYM	N	R	15	10	2.92	1.19	0	228
COOK	LA	N	L	3	2	4.25	1.39	0	84
CORBETT	CALX	A	L	0	1	4.18	1.57	0	18
COSTELLO	CAL	A	R	2	2	3.87	1.30	5	41
COX	PHIM	N	R	0	0	4.00	1.40	0	20
CRAWFORD	KCM	A	R	4	4	3.74	1.29	0	93
CREWS	LA	N	R	2	2	3.02	1.17	4	61
CRIM	MIL	A	R	4	4	2.89	1.22	10	90
CUMMINGS	TORX	A	R	1	1	3.61	1.58	0	21
DARLING	NYM	N	R	11	10	3.86	1.34	0	164
DARWIN	BOS	A	R	11	10	3.40	1.27	0	158
DAVIS,J	SDX	N	R	0	1	4.14	1.39	0	25
DAVIS,M	KC	A	L	3	4	3.72	1.41	16	78
DAVIS,S	KC	A	R	11	9	4.23	1.45	0	139
DAYLEY	TOR	A	L	4	4	3.27	1.23	3	74
DEJESUS	PHI	N	R	12	10	3.80	1.31	0	188
DELEON	STL	N	R	9	13	4.13	1.32	0	193
DELUCIA	SEA	A	R	10	12	2.92	1.20	0	138
DESHAIES	HOU	N	L	9	11	3.44	1.22	0	207
DEWEY	SF	N	R	1	1	3.40	1.30	0	31
DIBBLE	CIN	N	R	7	3	2.40	0.98	11	92
DICKSON	CHC	N	L	0	2	4.64	1.54	0	27
DIPINO	STL	N	L	4	2	3.71	1.30	2	81
DOPSON	BOS	A	R	5	6	3.76	1.26	0	92
DOTSON	KCX	A	R	4	7	4.87	1.57	0	30
DOWNS	SF	N	R	9	8	3.65	1.24	0	152
DRABEK	PIT	N	R	19	12	2.84	1.14	0	236
DRUMMOND	MIN	A	R	2	3	3.96	1.50	0	84
DUBOIS	DETX	A	L	2	5	3.52	1.51	5	65
DUNNE	SD	N	R	2	6	4.77	1.51	0	73
EAVE	SF	A	R	1	2	3.09	1.50	0	35
ECKERSLEY	OAK	A	R	4	2	2.40	1.00	36	75
EDENS	MILF	A	R	4	6	4.72	1.38	2	94
EDWARDS	CHW	A	L	5	4	3.33	1.31	1	78
EICHHORN	CAL	A	R	2	3	3.66	1.46	1	77

PITCHERS 1991 FORECAST STATS

NAME	TEAM	LG	T	W	L	ERA	RATIO	SV	IP
EILAND	NYY	A	R	8	10	4.66	1.25	0	143
ELVIRA	MIL	A	L	0	0	3.93	1.57	0	23
ENCARNACION	KCX	A	R	0	0	4.59	1.53	0	25
ERICKSON	MIN	A	R	14	10	2.99	1.38	0	183
FARMER	MON	N	R	7	9	4.87	1.45	0	132
FARR	NYY	A	R	3	2	3.10	1.21	15	109
FARRELL	CLE	A	R	3	3	3.78	1.32	0	58
FERNANDEZ,A	CHW	A	R	11	8	3.73	1.38	0	131
FERNANDEZ,S	NYM	N	L	15	11	3.26	1.14	0	203
FETTERS	CAL	A	R	6	5	3.84	1.47	2	81
FILER	MILX	A	R	5	3	3.95	1.51	0	83
FILSON	KCX	A	L	0	2	4.76	1.51	0	38
FINLEY	CAL	A	L	16	10	2.78	1.28	0	224
FISHER	HOUX	N	R	0	0	4.13	1.53	0	23
FLANAGAN	TORX	A	L	4	4	4.17	1.54	0	85
FOSSAS	MILX	A	L	2	3	4.47	1.55	0	55
FRANCO	NYM	N	L	3	4	2.91	1.38	31	70
FRASER	TOR	A	R	5	5	2.81	1.19	3	90
FREEMAN	ATL	N	R	1	2	4.94	1.28	1	49
FREY	MON	N	L	6	2	3.00	1.33	3	52
FROHWIRTH	PHIX	N	R	1	1	3.84	1.62	2	25
GARCES	MIN	A	R	0	4	3.48	1.41	1	33
GARDINER	SEA	A	R	0	1	5.21	1.58	0	46
GARDNER,M	MON	N	R	4	7	4.20	1.29	0	153
GARDNER,W	SD	N	R	2	5	4.48	1.32	0	78
GARRELTS	SF	N	R	14	9	3.40	1.30	0	185
GIBSON	DET	A	L	5	4	3.78	1.38	2	101
GIDEON	MONX	N	R	0	1	3.18	1.62	0	16
GILLES	TORX	A	R	1	0	3.85	1.45	0	21
GLAVINE	ATL	N	L	10	12	4.33	1.39	0	194
GLEATON	DET	A	L	0	3	3.55	1.20	12	61
GOODEN	NYM	N	R	17	10	3.44	1.25	0	215
GORDON	KC	A	R	14	12	3.77	1.43	0	199
GOTT	LA	N	R	2	3	3.31	1.37	5	61
GOZZO	CLE	A	R	2	1	4.65	1.36	0	33
GRAHE	CAL	A	R	2	2	4.39	1.53	0	42
GRANT	ATL	N	R	3	5	4.28	1.42	3	105
GRAY	BOS	A	R	2	3	4.18	1.38	8	54
GREENE	PHI	N	R	7	8	4.40	1.35	0	105
GRIMSLEY	PHI	N	R	3	5	3.76	1.51	0	75
GROSS,KE	LA	N	R	11	8	4.33	1.38	0	148
GROSS,KI	CIN	N	R	2	1	3.82	1.29	0	43

PITCHERS 1991 FORECAST STATS

NAME	TEAM	LG	T	W	L	ERA	RATIO	SV	IP
GUANTE	CLEX	A	R	4	4	4.30	1.35	1	62
GUBICZA	KC	A	R	10	9	3.71	1.48	0	141
GUETTERMAN	NYY	A	L	3	3	3.46	1.20	10	85
GULLICKSON	DET	A	R	10	13	4.34	1.49	0	170
GUNDERSON	SF	N	L	1	1	4.32	1.54	0	30
GUTHRIE	MIN	A	L	6	8	3.73	1.32	0	176
GUZMAN	TEX	A	R	2	2	4.17	1.34	0	75
HABYAN	NYY	A	R	0	0	3.45	1.39	0	24
HALL	MON	N	L	2	3	5.17	1.44	1	47
HAMMAKER	SD	N	L	4	8	4.25	1.28	1	76
HAMMOND	CIN	N	L	5	3	4.04	1.42	0	100
HANSON	SEA	A	R	16	10	2.92	1.15	0	207
HARKEY	CHC	N	R	11	7	3.14	1.24	0	179
HARNISCH	BAL	A	R	10	11	4.53	1.49	0	183
HARRIS,GA	BOS	A	R	9	8	4.16	1.46	0	158
HARRIS,GENE	SEA	A	R	1	2	5.12	1.51	0	34
HARRIS,GW	SD	N	R	11	9	3.14	1.23	0	174
HARRIS,R	OAK	A	R	9	5	3.61	1.19	0	141
HARTLEY	LA	N	R	3	2	2.85	1.19	0	68
HARVEY	CAL	A	R	4	4	3.31	1.24	27	60
HAWKINS	NYY	A	R	5	8	5.04	1.48	0	110
HEATON	PIT	N	L	7	7	3.25	1.24	0	125
HENKE	TOR	A	R	3	4	2.55	1.12	31	81
HENNEMAN	DET	A	R	9	4	3.25	1.33	17	90
HENNIS	HOU	N	R	8	9	3.43	1.38	0	135
HENRY	ATLX	N	R	1	2	5.02	1.53	0	34
HERNANDEZ	HOU	N	R	9	8	3.74	1.28	0	169
HERSHISER	LA	N	R	6	6	3.01	1.25	0	90
HESKETH	BOS	N	L	1	1	4.56	1.35	1	53
HETZEL	BOS	A	R	1	3	5.32	1.53	0	57
HIBBARD	CHW	A	L	12	9	3.39	1.28	0	203
HICKEY	BAL	A	L	1	3	3.92	1.47	2	38
HIGUERA	MIL	A	L	11	12	3.94	1.29	0	188
HILL	STL	N	R	8	10	4.63	1.39	0	137
HILL,M	CIN	N	R	2	1	4.00	1.40	0	40
HILLEGAS	CLE	A	R	2	3	3.76	1.25	5	44
HILTON	STLX	N	R	0	0	3.49	1.51	0	22
HOLMAN	SEA	A	R	9	10	3.82	1.34	0	197
HOLMES	MILX	A	R	0	1	4.19	1.49	0	29
HOLTON	BALX	A	R	2	2	4.83	1.52	0	52
HONEYCUTT	OAK	A	L	2	2	3.16	1.19	5	58
HOOVER	TEXX	A	R	0	0	4.57	1.58	0	22

PITCHERS 1991 FORECAST STATS

NAME	TEAM	LG	T	W	L	ERA	RATIO	SV	IP
HORTON	STLX	N	L	1	2	4.84	1.54	0	67
HOUGH	CHW	A	R	11	11	3.87	1.41	0	193
HOWELL,J	LA	N	R	3	3	2.67	1.09	28	69
HOWELL,K	PHI	N	R	10	7	3.99	1.33	0	143
HUISMANN	PITX	N	R	1	1	5.39	1.57	0	17
HURST	SD	N	L	15	10	2.94	1.19	0	221
INNIS	NYM	N	R	1	2	3.00	1.20	1	42
IRVINE	BOS	A	R	1	1	4.03	1.44	0	29
JACKSON,D	CHC	N	L	9	8	4.00	1.34	0	125
JACKSON,M	SEA	A	R	4	7	4.58	1.50	1	56
JEFFCOAT	TEX	A	L	6	6	4.03	1.34	6	122
JOHNSON,D	BAL	A	R	10	10	4.07	1.29	0	175
JOHNSON,R	SEA	A	L	13	13	3.89	1.40	0	206
JONES,B	MON	N	R	5	4	2.72	1.25	9	54
JONES,D	CLE	A	R	5	7	3.14	1.20	30	81
JONES,J	NYYX	A	R	1	2	5.11	1.52	0	85
KAISER	CLEX	A	L	0	0	3.70	1.54	0	26
KERFELD	ATLX	N	R	2	2	5.26	1.57	0	30
KEY	TOR	A	L	14	9	3.62	1.22	0	169
KIECKER	BOS	A	R	10	10	3.86	1.32	0	157
KILGUS	BAL	A	L	9	10	4.53	1.51	0	90
KING	CLE	A	R	8	9	3.38	1.22	0	135
KINZER	DETX	A	R	0	0	4.25	1.60	0	21
KIPPER	PIT	N	L	4	2	3.30	1.26	4	58
KLINK	OAK	A	L	0	0	2.90	1.31	1	40
KNACKERT	SEA	A	R	2	2	5.05	1.56	0	49
KNEPPER	SFX	N	L	6	8	4.81	1.53	0	85
KNUDSON	MIL	A	R	9	10	3.85	1.27	0	167
KRAEMER	CHC	N	L	0	1	5.33	1.54	0	28
KRAMER	CHCX	N	R	2	5	4.17	1.47	1	75
KRUEGER	MILF	A	L	4	6	3.93	1.45	1	110
KUTZLER	CHW	A	R	1	2	4.75	1.52	0	36
KYLE	HOU	N	R	3	9	4.30	1.44	0	110
LACOSS	SFF	N	R	8	6	3.89	1.46	1	119
LAMP	BOS	A	R	3	4	4.67	1.33	1	110
LANCASTER	CHC	N	R	6	2	3.32	1.20	5	82
LANDRUM	PIT	N	R	5	3	3.07	1.28	6	71
LANGSTON	CAL	A	L	15	15	4.27	1.42	0	214
LAPOINT	NYYF	A	L	5	8	4.08	1.48	0	150
LAYANA	CIN	N	R	5	5	3.90	1.42	2	77
LEACH	MIN	A	R	3	3	3.62	1.42	1	89
LEARY	NYY	A	R	10	14	4.13	1.35	0	189

PITCHERS 1991 FORECAST STATS

NAME	TEAM	LG	T	W	L	ERA	RATIO	SV	IP
LEE	MIL	A	L	1	0	3.18	1.30	0	31
LEFFERTS	SD	N	L	4	4	2.73	1.16	25	77
LEIBRANDT	ATL	N	L	9	13	3.50	1.30	0	188
LEISTER	BOSX	A	R	0	0	3.88	1.55	0	23
LEITER,A	TOR	A	L	8	7	3.24	1.33	0	153
LEITER,M	NYY	A	L	1	1	5.31	1.51	0	28
LEWIS	CAL	A	R	1	1	3.30	1.30	0	28
LILLIQUIST	SD	N	L	7	8	4.59	1.43	0	132
LONG	CHCX	N	R	5	2	3.88	1.51	3	72
LOVELACE	SEAX	A	L	0	1	3.88	1.61	0	16
LUECKEN	ATLX	N	R	1	3	4.96	1.55	0	48
LUGO	DETX	A	R	1	0	5.00	1.54	0	32
MACDONALD	TOR	A	L	1	1	3.54	1.21	0	71
MACHADO	MIL	A	R	2	1	3.09	1.38	14	35
MADDUX,G	CHC	N	R	18	13	3.07	1.31	0	229
MADDUX,M	LAX	N	R	1	2	4.86	1.36	0	48
MAGRANE	STL	N	L	13	12	3.12	1.25	0	203
MAHLER	CINF	N	R	7	8	4.32	1.31	3	147
MALDONADO	KC	A	R	0	0	4.43	1.57	0	23
MALLOY	MONX	N	R	0	0	3.57	1.30	0	21
MALONE	PHI	N	R	1	0	3.74	1.55	0	44
MANON	TEXX	A	R	0	0	4.21	1.59	0	21
MARAK	ATL	N	R	6	8	3.72	1.48	0	120
MARTINEZ,D	MON	N	R	12	10	3.09	1.13	0	207
MARTINEZ,R	LA	N	R	15	8	2.90	1.18	0	219
MATHEWS	STLX	N	L	2	4	5.05	1.52	0	73
MCCAMENT	SFX	N	R	1	1	4.41	1.58	0	27
MCCASKILL	CAL	A	R	11	10	3.32	1.27	0	187
MCCLELLAN	SFX	N	R	0	1	5.03	1.60	0	24
MCCLURE	CAL	A	L	3	2	3.11	1.39	3	36
MCCULLERS	DETF	A	R	3	2	3.41	1.30	5	61
MCDONALD	BAL	A	R	15	10	2.92	1.14	0	181
MCDOWELL,J	CHW	A	R	14	10	3.80	1.31	0	206
MCDOWELL,R	PHI	N	R	5	8	3.22	1.31	21	88
MCELROY	PHI	N	L	0	1	3.99	1.59	0	42
MCGAFFIGAN	KCM	A	R	5	4	3.28	1.36	1	87
MCMURTRY	TEXF	A	R	0	2	4.04	1.54	0	41
MCWILLIAMS	KCX	A	L	2	7	4.43	1.59	0	30
MEDVIN	SEAX	A	R	0	1	3.99	1.56	0	22
MELENDEZ	SEA	A	R	0	0	4.70	1.56	0	43
MERCKER	ATL	N	L	2	4	3.43	1.39	18	64
MESA	BAL	A	R	2	1	3.81	1.37	0	43

PITCHERS 1991 FORECAST STATS

NAME	TEAM	LG	T	W	L	ERA	RATIO	SV	IP
MEYER	HOU	N	R	3	6	3.39	1.25	15	90
MIELKE	TEXX	A	R	1	2	3.50	1.39	1	52
MILACKI	BAL	A	R	9	10	4.00	1.37	0	155
MILLS	NYY	A	R	1	3	3.93	1.56	0	41
MINTON	CALF	A	R	3	2	2.91	1.25	4	53
MINUTELLI	CIN	N	L	2	1	3.88	1.52	0	41
MIRABELLA	MILF	A	L	3	1	4.25	1.51	0	46
MITCHELL	BAL	A	R	4	5	4.71	1.48	0	104
MOHORCIC	MONX	N	R	1	2	3.85	1.43	1	61
MONTELEONE	NYY	A	R	1	1	3.94	1.37	0	27
MONTGOMERY	KC	A	R	4	5	2.76	1.27	19	84
MOORE,B	PHIX	N	R	0	0	3.73	1.56	0	21
MOORE,M	OAK	A	R	14	14	4.36	1.41	0	199
MORGAN	LA	N	R	6	8	3.77	1.32	0	119
MORRIS	DETF	A	R	13	16	4.23	1.30	0	237
MOYER	TEXX	A	L	3	6	4.79	1.49	0	85
MULHOLLAND	PHI	N	L	10	11	3.56	1.21	0	198
MUNOZ	DET	A	L	0	1	3.68	1.50	0	23
MURPHY	BOS	A	L	1	5	4.67	1.54	7	64
MUSSELMAN	NYMF	N	L	2	3	4.72	1.51	0	46
MYERS	CIN	N	L	4	6	2.80	1.16	26	80
NABHOLZ	MON	N	L	9	13	3.84	1.29	0	187
NAGY	CLE	A	R	9	11	4.90	1.48	0	143
NAVARRO	MIL	A	R	11	10	3.71	1.34	0	172
NEIDLINGER	LA	N	R	3	2	3.49	1.22	0	82
NELSON	OAK	A	R	3	3	2.75	1.14	3	75
NICHOLS	CLE	A	R	2	4	4.76	1.55	0	79
NIEDENFUER	STLF	N	R	0	5	4.24	1.50	1	51
NIPPER	CLEX	A	R	1	2	4.88	1.59	0	32
NOLES	PHIX	N	R	0	1	3.94	1.59	0	20
NORRIS	OAKX	A	R	0	0	3.45	1.35	0	34
NOSEK	DET	A	R	1	1	4.34	1.58	0	24
NOVOA	SF	N	L	0	1	4.70	1.54	1	29
NUNEZ,E	MIL	A	R	2	2	3.33	1.47	6	72
NUNEZ,J	CHC	N	R	4	4	5.40	1.50	0	49
O'NEAL	SFX	N	R	1	1	4.92	1.52	0	49
OJEDA	LA	N	L	13	10	3.42	1.33	0	159
OLIN	CLE	A	R	4	4	3.35	1.32	7	97
OLIVARES	STL	N	R	5	5	3.29	1.26	0	115
OLIVERAS	SF	N	R	2	1	3.05	1.23	1	55
OLSON	BAL	A	R	4	4	2.96	1.30	35	75
ONTIVEROS	PHI	N	R	5	7	3.54	1.25	0	105

PITCHERS 1991 FORECAST STATS

NAME	TEAM	LG	T	W	L	ERA	RATIO	SV	IP
OROSCO	CLE	A	L	5	3	3.45	1.42	2	70
OSUNA	HOU	N	L	3	6	3.97	1.41	9	80
OTTO	OAKF	A	L	0	0	3.34	1.58	0	16
PALACIOS	PIT	N	R	0	0	2.96	1.19	9	28
PALL	CHW	A	R	4	5	3.55	1.22	3	72
PARKER	DET	A	R	3	4	3.64	1.34	0	106
PARRETT	ATL	N	R	6	8	3.98	1.50	6	104
PATTERSON,B	PIT	N	L	6	4	3.18	1.20	5	76
PATTERSON,K	CHW	A	L	3	1	3.17	1.40	1	53
PAVLAS	CHC	N	R	1	1	3.18	1.36	0	31
PENA	NYM	N	R	3	3	2.99	1.19	7	75
PEREZ,ME	CHW	A	R	11	12	4.84	1.43	0	190
PEREZ,MI	STL	N	R	1	3	3.80	1.20	5	47
PEREZ,P	NYY	A	R	3	4	3.49	1.22	0	80
PERRY	LAX	N	L	0	0	4.37	1.57	0	23
PETERSON	CHW	A	R	2	6	4.92	1.42	0	85
PETRY	DETF	A	R	7	6	5.06	1.50	0	102
PICO	CHC	N	R	2	3	4.30	1.52	2	78
PLESAC	MIL	A	L	4	6	3.73	1.31	10	61
PLUNK	NYY	A	R	2	3	3.14	1.34	13	94
POOLE	LA	N	L	0	0	3.85	1.41	0	25
PORTUGAL	HOU	N	R	11	9	3.14	1.25	0	197
POWELL	MILX	A	L	1	3	5.39	1.57	1	36
POWER	CIN	N	R	4	5	4.06	1.33	5	88
PRICE	BALF	A	L	3	4	4.12	1.37	0	63
QUISENBERRY	SFX	N	R	1	1	5.07	1.59	0	18
RADINSKY	CHW	A	L	2	2	5.38	1.55	2	41
RASMUSSEN	SDF	N	L	11	15	4.52	1.46	0	182
REARDON	BOS	A	R	4	2	3.37	1.23	20	48
REED,J	BOSX	A	R	1	2	5.37	1.54	1	36
REED,R	PIT	N	R	1	4	5.13	1.49	0	69
REUSCHEL	SF	N	R	6	5	3.26	1.34	1	84
RICHARDS	ATLX	N	R	0	1	5.27	1.58	0	16
RICHARDSON	CAL	A	R	0	0	3.72	1.53	0	20
RIGHETTI	SF	N	L	3	6	3.59	1.37	25	95
RIJO	CIN	N	R	14	11	3.06	1.24	0	190
RITZ	DET	A	R	5	7	4.08	1.62	0	92
ROBINSON,D	SF	N	R	11	9	4.21	1.32	0	172
ROBINSON,JD	NYYF	A	R	4	4	3.33	1.31	3	114
ROBINSON,JM	DET	A	R	8	7	5.30	1.50	0	112
ROBINSON,R	MIL	A	R	14	7	3.34	1.32	0	193
ROCHFORD	BOSX	A	L	0	1	5.03	1.61	0	22

PITCHERS 1991 FORECAST STATS

NAME	TEAM	LG	T	W	L	ERA	RATIO	SV	IP
RODRIGUEZ,RH	SD	N	L	1	2	3.25	1.43	1	54
RODRIGUEZ,RK	SF	N	R	0	0	4.08	1.56	0	22
RODRIGUEZ,RO	PIT	N	L	1	2	4.65	1.52	0	20
ROESLER	PIT	N	R	1	1	3.86	1.22	0	28
ROGERS	TEX	A	L	12	8	3.07	1.30	0	167
ROJAS	MON	N	R	2	1	3.68	1.45	5	40
ROSENBERG	CHW	A	L	2	5	5.01	1.49	0	69
ROSS	PITX	N	R	1	0	3.70	1.40	0	26
RUFFIN	PHI	N	L	4	9	5.23	1.53	0	138
RUSKIN	MON	N	L	2	2	3.20	1.46	1	85
RUSSELL	TEX	A	R	3	5	3.34	1.50	20	47
RYAN	TEX	A	R	12	10	3.29	1.15	0	201
SABERHAGEN	KC	A	R	11	9	3.20	1.24	0	158
SAMPEN	MON	N	R	9	8	3.65	1.50	1	91
SANCHEZ	KCX	A	L	0	0	4.65	1.56	0	25
SANDERSON	NYY	A	R	9	12	3.95	1.31	0	173
SAVAGE	MINX	A	R	0	1	5.30	1.55	1	33
SCHATZEDER	KC	A	L	1	1	2.71	1.25	0	62
SCHILLING	HOU	A	R	1	2	3.89	1.25	12	43
SCHIRALDI	SD	N	R	4	9	4.11	1.49	1	108
SCHMIDT	MONF	N	R	5	6	4.88	1.48	7	70
SCHOOLER	SEA	A	R	3	6	2.87	1.29	15	53
SCHWABE	DETX	A	R	1	1	5.30	1.42	0	17
SCOTT	HOU	N	R	10	12	3.30	1.23	0	195
SCUDDER	CIN	N	R	11	10	4.44	1.41	0	157
SEANEZ	CLE	A	R	1	1	4.55	1.53	0	29
SEARAGE	LAX	N	L	1	2	3.23	1.24	1	35
SEARCY	DET	A	L	2	7	4.87	1.52	0	89
SEBRA	MILX	A	R	1	2	5.38	1.59	0	27
SHAW	CLE	A	R	2	2	5.14	1.56	0	44
SHERRILL	STL	N	L	2	2	3.99	1.60	0	42
SHOW	OAK	A	R	7	6	4.62	1.45	0	125
SISK	ATLX	N	R	0	0	3.76	1.56	0	21
SMILEY	PIT	N	L	11	10	4.36	1.33	0	164
SMITH,B	STL	N	R	10	8	3.88	1.27	0	142
SMITH,DR	KCX	A	R	0	1	3.79	1.36	0	23
SMITH,DV	CHC	N	R	3	4	3.02	1.30	29	56
SMITH,L	STL	N	R	4	4	2.65	1.19	23	74
SMITH,M	BALX	A	R	1	1	5.42	1.52	0	14
SMITH,P	ATL	N	R	7	9	4.50	1.31	0	117
SMITH,R	MINX	A	R	6	8	4.46	1.49	0	150
SMITH,Z	PIT	N	L	15	11	2.89	1.15	0	176

PITCHERS 1991 FORECAST STATS

NAME	TEAM	LG	T	W	L	ERA	RATIO	SV	IP
SMOLTZ	ATL	N	R	12	14	3.41	1.25	0	210
STANTON	ATL	N	L	1	4	4.25	1.60	8	28
STEWART	OAK	A	R	21	10	2.93	1.20	0	257
STIEB	TOR	A	R	17	10	2.98	1.19	0	208
STOTTLEMYRE,M	KC	A	R	0	1	4.25	1.50	0	36
STOTTLEMYRE,T	TOR	A	R	11	12	4.10	1.36	0	188
SUTCLIFFE	CHC	N	R	7	6	3.97	1.48	0	114
SWAN	SEA	A	L	2	3	3.72	1.30	0	45
SWIFT	SEA	A	R	6	4	2.88	1.20	9	132
SWINDELL	CLE	A	L	12	10	4.19	1.34	0	180
TANANA	DET	A	L	9	8	4.60	1.40	0	168
TAPANI	MIN	A	R	10	8	4.09	1.24	0	158
TAYLOR	BALX	A	R	0	1	3.64	1.51	0	22
TELFORD	BAL	A	R	2	2	4.32	1.53	0	43
TERRELL	DET	A	R	10	12	4.60	1.43	0	166
TERRY	STL	N	R	4	5	3.52	1.20	5	84
TEWKSBURY	STL	N	R	12	12	3.55	1.24	0	182
THIGPEN	CHW	A	R	3	5	2.77	1.14	37	82
THOMPSON	MONX	N	R	0	1	3.11	1.30	0	34
THURMOND	SFF	N	L	2	3	3.78	1.36	4	59
TIBBS	BALX	A	R	2	4	4.62	1.37	0	40
TOMLIN	PIT	N	L	9	7	2.88	1.20	0	128
TUDOR	STLF	N	L	10	3	2.90	1.15	0	130
VALDEZ,E	CLE	A	L	4	2	3.32	1.39	0	58
VALDEZ,R	SD	N	R	1	2	4.66	1.58	0	53
VALDEZ,S	CLE	A	R	3	3	4.47	1.41	0	71
VALENZUELA	LA	N	L	8	8	4.48	1.50	0	106
VALERA	NYM	N	R	8	8	3.78	1.39	0	157
VERES	MIL	A	R	0	2	3.94	1.31	0	36
VIOLA	NYM	N	L	17	13	3.08	1.19	0	243
VOSBERG	CALX	A	L	1	1	4.43	1.36	0	32
WAGNER	KC	A	R	0	1	5.15	1.55	0	32
WALK	PIT	N	R	7	5	3.93	1.30	0	144
WALKER	CLE	A	R	2	3	4.97	1.52	0	98
WALSH	LA	N	L	1	0	3.78	1.29	1	28
WAPNICK	DETM	A	R	0	0	4.15	1.59	0	24
WARD,C	CLEX	A	R	2	5	4.16	1.44	5	62
WARD,D	TOR	A	R	4	6	3.61	1.24	6	119
WAYNE	MIN	A	L	1	4	3.66	1.32	5	67
WEGMAN	MIL	A	R	7	8	4.88	1.45	0	131
WELCH	OAK	A	R	18	11	3.03	1.24	0	224
WELLS,D	TOR	A	L	14	10	3.03	1.20	0	185

PITCHERS 1991 FORECAST STATS

NAME	TEAM	LG	T	W	L	ERA	RATIO	SV	IP
WELLS,T	LAF	N	L	1	1	5.06	1.55	0	30
WEST	MIN	A	L	10	11	4.99	1.46	0	187
WESTON	TORX	A	R	0	1	5.40	1.52	0	26
WETTELAND	LA	N	R	3	3	3.93	1.41	0	87
WHITEHURST	NYM	N	R	0	0	3.75	1.20	1	57
WHITSON	SD	N	R	14	11	3.01	1.23	0	213
WICKANDER	CLE	A	L	0	1	3.46	1.48	0	21
WILKINS	HOU	N	R	1	3	4.90	1.50	3	49
WILLIAMS	CHC	N	L	2	4	4.30	1.53	9	68
WILLIAMSON	BAL	A	R	5	3	2.83	1.21	2	83
WILLS	TOR	A	R	4	3	4.07	1.34	0	91
WILSON,S	CHC	N	L	4	6	4.84	1.32	1	109
WILSON,T	SF	N	L	4	8	4.78	1.32	0	91
WITT,B	TEX	A	R	17	10	3.53	1.35	0	213
WITT,M	NYY	A	R	9	12	4.51	1.32	0	140
WORRELL	STL	N	R	2	2	3.11	1.26	6	43
YETT	MINX	A	R	1	1	4.67	1.51	0	33
YORK	PIT	N	R	1	1	3.53	1.42	0	26
YOUNG,CL	CAL	A	L	1	1	3.65	1.50	0	35
YOUNG,CU	OAK	A	L	4	6	4.71	1.46	0	109
YOUNG,M	BOS	A	L	11	9	3.44	1.37	0	171

AL CATCHERS 1991 $ VALUES

NAME	TEAM	LG	$VAL	OPT%	BID$
FISK	CHW	A	19	75%	15
HARPER	MIN	A	18	75%	14
ALOMAR,S	CLE	A	18	75%	14
SURHOFF	MIL	A	17	75%	13
PARRISH	CAL	A	13	65%	9
PENA,T	BOS	A	12	65%	8
NOKES	NYY	A	11	80%	9
BORDERS	TOR	A	10	75%	7
HEATH	DETF	A	9	65%	6
STEINBACH	OAK	A	9	85%	7
TETTLETON	BAL	A	8	75%	6
MCINTOSH	MIL	A	7	65%	5
MACFARLANE	KC	A	7	65%	4
KARKOVICE	CHW	A	6	80%	5
HASELMAN	TEX	A	6	65%	4
SALAS	DET	A	5	65%	4
PETRALLI	TEX	A	5	75%	4
GEREN	NYY	A	3	70%	2
ORTIZ,JN	MIN	A	2	55%	1
BRADLEY,S	SEA	A	2	75%	1
HOILES	BAL	A	2	55%	1
MELVIN	BAL	A	1	55%	1
AFENIR	OAK	A	1	55%	1
WEBSTER,L	MIN	A	1	55%	1
QUIRK	OAK	A	1	55%	1
PARENT	TEX	A	1	70%	0
MYERS	TOR	A	0	NA	NA
VALLE	SEA	A	0	NA	NA
SKINNER	CLE	A	0	NA	NA
SINATRO	SEAX	A	0	NA	NA
CERONE	NYYF	A	0	NA	NA
SCHROEDER	CALX	A	0	NA	NA
WRONA	MIL	A	0	NA	NA
HASSEY	OAKF	A	0	NA	NA
PALACIOS	KCX	A	0	NA	NA
ROWLAND	DET	A	-	NA	NA
STANLEY	TEXX	A	-	NA	NA
BOONE	KCF	A	-	NA	NA
LAUDNER	MINX	A	-	NA	NA
RUSSELL	TEXX	A	-	NA	NA
WILLARD	CHWX	A	-	NA	NA
TAUBENSEE	OAK	A	-	NA	NA

NOTE: Hitters and Pitchers not listed in this section have no value.

NL CATCHERS 1991 $ VALUES

NAME	TEAM	LG	$VAL	OPT%	BID$
BIGGIO	HOU	N	17	80%	13
DAULTON	PHI	N	11	80%	9
DECKER	SF	N	11	70%	7
SCIOSCIA	LA	N	10	75%	7
SANTIAGO	SD	N	9	75%	7
SASSER	NYM	N	9	75%	6
ZEILE	STL	N	8	75%	6
LAVALLIERE	PIT	N	7	75%	5
PAGNOZZI	STL	N	6	65%	4
SLAUGHT	PIT	N	5	65%	3
FITZGERALD	MON	N	4	65%	3
GIRARDI	CHC	N	4	65%	3
VILLANUEVA	CHC	N	4	65%	3
OLSON	ATL	N	3	55%	2
OLIVER	CIN	N	3	55%	2
KENNEDY	SF	N	2	55%	1
SANTOVENIA	MON	N	2	55%	1
BERRYHILL	CHC	N	1	55%	1
REED,JE	CIN	N	0	NA	NA
FLETCHER,D	PHI	N	0	NA	NA
TREVINO	CIN	N	0	NA	NA
MANN	ATL	N	0	NA	NA
LYONS,B	LA	N	0	NA	NA
LAKE	PHI	N	0	NA	NA
GOFF	MON	N	0	NA	NA
BATHE	SFX	N	0	NA	NA
CARTER,G	SFF	N	-	NA	NA
MERCADO	MONX	N	-	NA	NA
WHITT	ATLF	N	-	NA	NA
COLBRUNN	MONM	N	-	NA	NA
BAILEY	SFX	N	-	NA	NA
LAMPKIN	SD	N	-	NA	NA
GEDMAN	HOUF	N	-	NA	NA
HUNDLEY	NYM	N	-	NA	NA
DAVIS,J	ATLX	N	-	NA	NA
LIDDELL	NYMX	N	-	NA	NA
NICHOLS	HOU	N	-	NA	NA
STEPHENS	STL	N	-	NA	NA
DEMPSEY	LAF	N	-	NA	NA
MANWARING	SF	N	-	NA	NA
WILKINS	CHC	N	-	NA	NA
SUTKO	CINX	N	-	NA	NA

AL FIRST BASEMEN 1991 $ VALUES

NAME	TEAM	LG	$VAL	OPT%	BID$
FIELDER	DET	A	31	85%	26
PALMEIRO	TEX	A	27	85%	23
THOMAS,F	CHW	A	26	80%	21
MOLITOR	MIL	A	24	75%	18
BRETT	KC	A	23	75%	17
HRBEK	MIN	A	20	85%	17
MCGWIRE	OAK	A	16	75%	12
MATTINGLY	NYY	A	14	75%	10
OLERUD	TOR	A	13	65%	8
JOYNER	CAL	A	12	75%	9
MILLIGAN	BAL	A	11	70%	8
VAUGHN	BOS	A	10	65%	7
QUINTANA	BOS	A	6	65%	4
JAMES,D	CLEX	A	4	55%	2
OBRIEN,P	SEA	A	2	75%	2
BROCK	MIL	A	2	70%	1
CONINE	KC	A	2	55%	1
TABLER	TOR	A	1	70%	1
MARTINEZ,CS	CHW	A	0	NA	NA
MARTINEZ,T	SEA	A	0	NA	NA
MANTO	CLE	A	0	NA	NA
SEGUI	BAL	A	-	NA	NA
FRANCONA	MILX	A	-	NA	NA
LYONS,S	CHW	A	-	NA	NA
MCKNIGHT	BAL	A	-	NA	NA
WALKER,G	BALX	A	-	NA	NA
HERNANDEZ,K	CLE	A	-	NA	NA
PHELPS	CLEF	A	-	NA	NA
ROBIDOUX	BOSX	A	-	NA	NA
CANALE	MIL	A	-	NA	NA
LANCELLOTTI	BOSX	A	-	NA	NA

NL FIRST BASEMEN 1991 $ VALUES

NAME	TEAM	LG	$VAL	OPT%	BID$
MURRAY	LA	N	29	80%	23
CLARK,W	SF	N	28	85%	24
GRACE	CHC	N	28	85%	24
MCGRIFF,F	SD	N	26	85%	22
MORRIS,H	CIN	N	22	75%	17
BREAM	ATL	N	19	85%	16
GALARRAGA	MON	N	18	85%	16
GUERRERO	STL	N	18	85%	15
MAGADAN	NYM	N	15	80%	12
DAVIS,G	HOU	N	15	80%	12
KRUK	PHI	N	13	80%	11
REDUS	PIT	N	8	75%	6
CABRERA	ATL	N	8	75%	6
PERRY	STL	N	5	65%	3
JORDAN	PHI	N	5	65%	3
MARTINEZ,CM	PIT	N	5	65%	3
CLARK,JE	SD	N	3	55%	1
GREGG	ATL	N	2	55%	1
BENZINGER	CIN	N	0	NA	NA
STEPHENSON	SD	N	0	NA	NA
SIMMS	HOU	N	-	NA	NA
ESASKY	ATL	N	-	NA	NA
WALLING	STLF	N	-	NA	NA
BELL,M	ATL	N	-	NA	NA
TORVE	NYMX	N	-	NA	NA
JOHNSON,W	MONX	N	-	NA	NA
BREWER	STLX	N	-	NA	NA
LEE,T	CIN	N	-	NA	NA
MERCED	PIT	N	-	NA	NA
NELSON	SDX	N	-	NA	NA
TRAXLER	LAM	N	-	NA	NA
LOPEZ	LAM	N	-	NA	NA

AL SECOND BASEMEN 1991 $ VALUES

NAME	TEAM	LG	$VAL	OPT%	BID$
FRANCO	TEX	A	37	85%	31
SAX	NYY	A	33	85%	28
ALOMAR,R	TOR	A	29	85%	25
REYNOLDS,H	SEA	A	23	85%	19
BROWNE	CLE	A	20	85%	17
REED,JO	BOS	A	16	75%	12
GANTNER	MIL	A	16	75%	12
WHITAKER	DET	A	15	80%	12
LIRIANO	MIN	A	13	65%	8
RANDOLPH	OAKF	A	9	65%	6
RIPKEN,B	BAL	A	8	75%	6
NEWMAN	MIN	A	8	65%	5
SOJO	CAL	A	6	70%	4
SHUMPERT	KC	A	5	55%	3
FLETCHER,S	CHW	A	4	75%	3
BERNAZARD	DET	A	4	55%	2
PECOTA	KC	A	2	55%	1
BELL,JN	BAL	A	2	55%	1
MANRIQUE	CAL	A	1	55%	1
BARRETT	BOSX	A	1	55%	0
HILL,D	CALF	A	0	NA	NA
GALLEGO	OAK	A	0	NA	NA
WHITE,F	KCF	A	-	NA	NA
HULETT	BAL	A	-	NA	NA
BAKER	MINX	A	-	NA	NA
GONZALES	BAL	A	-	NA	NA
WALEWANDER	NYYX	A	-	NA	NA
MCLEMORE	CLEX	A	-	NA	NA
PAREDES	DETX	A	-	NA	NA
PANKOVITS	BOSX	A	-	NA	NA
BROWN	BALX	A	-	NA	NA
HALE	MIN	A	-	NA	NA
TOLLESON	NYYX	A	-	NA	NA

NL SECOND BASEMEN 1991 $ VALUES

NAME	TEAM	LG	$VAL	OPT%	BID$
SANDBERG	CHC	N	27	85%	23
ROBERTS	SD	N	27	85%	23
DESHIELDS	MON	N	24	85%	20
SAMUEL	LA	N	15	80%	12
DORAN	CIN	N	14	80%	11
THOMPSON,R	SF	N	11	80%	9
HERR	NYM	N	10	85%	9
TREADWAY	ATL	N	9	75%	7
DUNCAN	CIN	N	8	75%	6
OQUENDO	STL	N	8	75%	6
CORA	SD	N	8	75%	6
LIND	PIT	N	4	65%	3
CANDAELE	HOU	N	4	65%	3
FARIES	SD	N	4	65%	3
MORANDINI	PHI	N	4	65%	3
BACKMAN	PITF	N	4	55%	2
PENA,G	STL	N	3	55%	2
READY	PHI	N	3	55%	1
MOTA	HOU	N	2	55%	1
TEUFEL	NYM	N	1	55%	0
QUINONES	CIN	N	0	NA	NA
NOBOA	MON	N	0	NA	NA
VIZCAINO	CHC	N	-	NA	NA
LAW	JF	N	-	NA	NA
OESTER	CINF	N	-	NA	NA
LEMKE	ATL	N	-	NA	NA
ROHDE	HOU	N	-	NA	NA
PEREZCHICA	SF	N	-	NA	NA
BOOKER	PHI	N	-	NA	NA
SMITH,G	LA	N	-	NA	NA
BATES	CIN	N	-	NA	NA
LOMBARDOZZI	HOUX	N	-	NA	NA
INFANTE	ATLX	N	-	NA	NA

AL THIRD BASEMEN 1991 $ VALUES

NAME	TEAM	LG	$VAL	OPT%	BID$
GRUBER	TOR	A	27	85%	23
BOGGS	BOS	A	21	85%	18
SHEFFIELD	MIL	A	17	70%	12
FRYMAN	DET	A	16	70%	11
BAERGA	CLE	A	15	75%	11
JACOBY	CLE	A	15	80%	12
SEITZER	KC	A	14	65%	9
MARTINEZ,E	SEA	A	13	70%	9
GAETTI	MINF	A	8	85%	7
VENTURA	CHW	A	8	65%	5
RILES	OAK	A	7	75%	5
PHILLIPS	DET	A	6	65%	4
BLOWERS	NYY	A	6	65%	4
WORTHINGTON	BAL	A	2	75%	2
GOMEZ	BAL	A	2	55%	1
BERRY	KC	A	2	55%	1
LEYRITZ	NYY	A	2	55%	1
ROSE	CAL	A	1	55%	1
HOWELL	CAL	A	1	70%	1
BUECHELE	TEX	A	1	55%	0
LANSFORD	OAK	A	0	NA	NA
SCHU	CAL	A	-	NA	NA
VELARDE	NYY	A	-	NA	NA
HEMOND	OAK	A	-	NA	NA
COACHMAN	CAL	A	-	NA	NA
SVEUM	MIL	A	-	NA	NA
DELOSSANTOS	KC	A	-	NA	NA
BROOKENS	CLEF	A	-	NA	NA
BLANKENSHIP	OAK	A	-	NA	NA
QUINLAN	TOR	A	-	NA	NA
ROMERO	DETX	A	-	NA	NA
COCHRANE	SEA	A	-	NA	NA
COOPER	BOS	A	-	NA	NA
SPRINGER	CLEX	A	-	NA	NA
LAWLESS	TORX	A	-	NA	NA
BORDICK	OAK	A	-	NA	NA
GREBECK	CHW	A	-	NA	NA

NL THIRD BASEMEN 1991 $ VALUES

NAME	TEAM	LG	$VAL	OPT%	BID$
WALLACH	MON	N	22	85%	18
JEFFERIES	NYM	N	21	85%	18
WILLIAMS,M	SF	N	18	85%	15
SABO	CIN	N	15	80%	12
PENDLETON	ATL	N	11	80%	9
SHARPERSON	LA	N	10	75%	7
HARRIS	LA	N	8	75%	6
HAYES,C	PHI	N	8	80%	6
KING	PIT	N	7	75%	5
PRESLEY	ATLF	N	6	80%	5
SALAZAR	CHC	N	6	75%	5
HOLLINS	PHI	N	4	65%	3
BAGWELL	HOU	N	4	65%	3
REDFIELD	PIT	N	4	45%	2
REDINGTON	SD	N	3	45%	1
CAMINITI	HOU	N	2	55%	1
GONZALEZ,L	HOU	N	0	NA	NA
PAGLIARULO	SDF	N	0	NA	NA
RAMOS	CHC	N	0	NA	NA
WILSON,C	STL	N	-	NA	NA
HANSEN	LA	N	-	NA	NA
HAMILTON,J	LA	N	-	NA	NA
OBERKFELL	HOU	N	-	NA	NA
WILKERSON	CHCF	N	-	NA	NA
COOLBAUGH	SD	N	-	NA	NA

AL SHORTSTOPS 1991 $ VALUES

NAME	TEAM	LG	$VAL	OPT%	BID$
TRAMMELL	DET	A	21	85%	18
RIPKEN,C	BAL	A	15	85%	13
GUILLEN	CHW	A	15	75%	11
LEE,M	TOR	A	13	65%	8
GAGNE	MIN	A	11	65%	7
SPIERS	MIL	A	9	65%	6
NAEHRING	BOS	A	9	65%	6
WEISS	OAK	A	8	65%	5
STILLWELL	KC	A	6	80%	5
SCHOFIELD	CAL	A	5	75%	3
FERMIN	CLE	A	4	70%	3
HUSON	TEX	A	3	55%	1
ESPINOZA	NYY	A	1	55%	1
GILES	SEAX	A	1	55%	0
FARRIS	TEX	A	1	55%	0
ANDERSON,K	CAL	A	0	NA	NA
DIAZ,E	MIL	A	0	NA	NA
VIZQUEL	SEA	A	0	NA	NA
RIVERA	BOS	A	-	NA	NA
KUNKEL	TEX	A	-	NA	NA
LEIUS	MIN	A	-	NA	NA
JELTZ	KCF	A	-	NA	NA
BRUMLEY	SEAX	A	-	NA	NA
SANTANA,R	CLEX	A	-	NA	NA
SCHAEFER	SEA	A	-	NA	NA
GREEN	TEX	A	-	NA	NA
POLIDOR	MILX	A	-	NA	NA
DISARCINA	CAL	A	-	NA	NA

NL SHORTSTOPS 1991 $ VALUES

NAME	TEAM	LG	$VAL	OPT%	BID$
JOHNSON,H	NYM	N	29	85%	25
LARKIN,B	CIN	N	23	85%	19
YELDING	HOU	N	22	75%	16
FERNANDEZ	SD	N	21	85%	18
DUNSTON	CHC	N	19	85%	16
SMITH,O	STL	N	16	85%	14
THON	PHI	N	13	80%	11
BELL,JY	PIT	N	13	75%	9
OFFERMAN	LA	N	11	70%	8
BLAUSER	ATL	N	8	80%	6
BENJAMIN	SF	N	3	55%	2
RAMIREZ	HOU	N	2	55%	1
OWEN	MON	N	2	55%	1
TEMPLETON	SD	N	1	55%	0
JONES,TI	STL	N	1	55%	0
LITTON	SF	N	0	NA	NA
THOMAS,A	ATL	N	0	NA	NA
CEDENO	HOU	N	0	NA	NA
ELSTER	NYM	N	-	NA	NA
FOLEY	MON	N	-	NA	NA
ANDERSON,D	SF	N	-	NA	NA
URIBE	SF	N	-	NA	NA
GRIFFIN	LA	N	-	NA	NA
BELLIARD	ATL	N	-	NA	NA
GARCIA	PIT	N	-	NA	NA
NOCE	CINX	N	-	NA	NA
SANTANA,A	SF	N	-	NA	NA
BAEZ	NYM	N	-	NA	NA
ROSARIO	ATL	N	-	NA	NA
DIAZ,M	NYMX	N	-	NA	NA

AL OUTFIELDERS 1991 $ VALUES

NAME	TEAM	LG	$VAL	OPT%	BID$
HENDERSON,R	OAK	A	48	85%	41
KELLY	NYY	A	40	75%	30
RAINES	CHW	A	36	85%	31
COLE	CLE	A	33	75%	25
SIERRA	TEX	A	30	85%	26
GREENWELL	BOS	A	30	85%	26
BURKS	BOS	A	29	85%	25
GRIFFEY,JR	SEA	A	26	85%	22
YOUNT	MIL	A	26	85%	22
MACK	MIN	A	25	70%	17
PUCKETT	MIN	A	25	85%	21
JACKSON,B	KC	A	24	85%	20
CANSECO,J	OAK	A	24	85%	20
CARTER,J	TOR	A	22	85%	19
JOHNSON,L	CHW	A	22	75%	16
POLONIA	CAL	A	21	70%	15
STUBBS	MIL	A	16	75%	12
GLADDEN	MIN	A	16	75%	12
SOSA	CHW	A	15	75%	11
BUHNER	SEA	A	13	70%	9
VAUGHN	MIL	A	13	70%	9
WINFIELD	CAL	A	13	65%	8
DEVEREAUX	BAL	A	13	65%	8
BRILEY	SEA	A	13	65%	8
WHITE,D	TOR	A	13	65%	8
HENDERSON,D	OAK	A	12	65%	8
FINLEY	BAL	A	12	65%	8
MCRAE	KC	A	12	65%	8
TARTABULL	KC	A	11	75%	8
GONZALEZ,JU	TEX	A	11	70%	8
WEBSTER,M	CLE	A	11	65%	7
FELIX	CAL	A	10	75%	8
MALDONADO	CLEF	A	10	75%	7
MOSEBY	DET	A	10	80%	8
WILSON,W	OAK	A	10	65%	6
BARFIELD	NYY	A	9	85%	8
PETTIS	TEX	A	9	65%	6
LEONARD,J	SEAX	A	9	65%	6
FELDER	MIL	A	9	65%	6
MUNOZ	MIN	A	9	65%	6
ANDERSON,B	BAL	A	9	75%	7
BRUNANSKY	BOS	A	9	80%	7

AL OUTFIELDERS 1991 $ VALUES

NAME	TEAM	LG	$VAL	OPT%	BID$
EISENREICH	KC	A	9	65%	6
DAVIS,C	CALF	A	8	65%	6
DAUGHERTY	TEX	A	8	65%	5
INCAVIGLIA	TEX	A	8	85%	7
ORSULAK	BAL	A	7	80%	5
COTTO	SEA	A	7	80%	5
MEULENS	NYY	A	6	70%	4
BICHETTE	CAL	A	6	65%	4
HAMILTON,D	MIL	A	6	55%	3
WILSON,M	TOR	A	5	55%	3
ALLRED	CLE	A	4	55%	2
HILL,G	TOR	A	4	70%	3
WHITEN	TOR	A	4	55%	2
DEER	DET	A	4	75%	3
JEFFERSON	CLE	A	3	55%	2
BUSH	MIN	A	2	55%	1
VENABLE	CAL	A	1	70%	1
LEMON	DET	A	1	55%	0
THURMAN	KC	A	0	NA	NA
JONES,TR	SEA	A	0	NA	NA
WARD,T	CLE	A	0	NA	NA
MOSES	MINF	A	-	NA	NA
HEEP	BOSF	A	-	NA	NA
WARD,G	DETF	A	-	NA	NA
LUSADER	DET	A	-	NA	NA
ESPY	TEXX	A	-	NA	NA
MARSHALL	BOS	A	-	NA	NA
GALLAGHER	CAL	A	-	NA	NA
WILLIAMS,K	TOR	A	-	NA	NA
NIXON,D	BALX	A	-	NA	NA
JENNINGS	OAK	A	-	NA	NA
CASTILLO	MIN	A	-	NA	NA
CUYLER	DET	A	-	NA	NA
MCCRAY	CHWX	A	-	NA	NA
ROMINE	BOS	A	-	NA	NA
COLES	DETF	A	-	NA	NA
BELLE,J	CLE	A	-	NA	NA
KOMMINSK	BALX	A	-	NA	NA
BELCHER	TEX	A	-	NA	NA
WASHINGTON	NYYX	A	-	NA	NA
REIMER	TEXX	A	-	NA	NA
SHELBY	DETX	A	-	NA	NA

NL OUTFIELDERS 1991 $ VALUES

NAME	TEAM	LG	$VAL	OPT%	BID$
BONDS	PIT	N	37	85%	32
BUTLER	LA	N	30	85%	25
COLEMAN	NYM	N	30	85%	25
JUSTICE	ATL	N	29	75%	22
MITCHELL	SF	N	28	85%	24
GWYNN,T	SD	N	28	85%	24
DAVIS,E	CIN	N	28	85%	24
DANIELS	LA	N	26	80%	20
BONILLA	PIT	N	25	85%	21
GANT	ATL	N	25	80%	20
DAWSON	CHC	N	24	85%	21
MCGEE	SF	N	24	85%	20
STRAWBERRY	LA	N	23	85%	19
DYKSTRA	PHI	N	23	85%	19
BELL,G	CHC	N	22	85%	19
MCREYNOLDS	NYM	N	21	85%	18
CALDERON	MON	N	21	85%	18
HAYES,V	PHI	N	21	85%	18
SMITH,L	ATL	N	21	70%	14
LANKFORD	STL	N	17	75%	13
ONEILL	CIN	N	17	80%	14
WALKER,L	MON	N	17	75%	13
VANSLYKE	PIT	N	17	85%	14
WALTON	CHC	N	16	75%	12
BROOKS	NYM	N	15	85%	13
JOSE	STL	N	14	75%	11
BASS	SF	N	13	80%	11
HUDLER	STL	N	13	80%	10
NIXON,O	MON	N	13	80%	10
MARTINEZ,D	MON	N	12	75%	9
GILKEY	STL	N	11	75%	8
THOMPSON,M	STL	N	11	75%	8
SMITH,D	CHC	N	11	75%	8
MURPHY	PHI	N	11	85%	9
BRAGGS	CIN	N	11	75%	8
GRISSOM	MON	N	10	75%	7
MCDOWELL	ATL	N	10	80%	8
YOUNG	HOU	N	9	75%	7
HATCHER,B	CIN	N	8	75%	6
JAVIER	LA	N	7	75%	5
BOSTON	NYM	N	6	65%	4
ANTHONY	HOU	N	6	65%	4

NL OUTFIELDERS 1991 $ VALUES

NAME	TEAM	LG	$VAL	OPT%	BID$
JONES,R	PHI	N	4	65%	3
KINGERY	SF	N	4	65%	3
ORTIZ,JV	HOU	N	3	55%	2
AZOCAR	SD	N	3	50%	2
WILSON,G	HOUF	N	2	55%	1
LEACH	SF	N	2	55%	1
DAVIDSON	HOU	N	2	55%	1
LYNN	SDF	N	2	55%	1
WINNINGHAM	CIN	N	1	55%	1
MCCLENDON	PIT	N	1	55%	1
PARKER,R	SF	N	1	55%	1
RHODES	HOU	N	1	55%	1
MILLER	NYM	N	1	55%	0
CHAMBERLAIN	PHI	N	1	65%	1
VATCHER	ATL	N	1	55%	0
CLARK,D	CHC	N	1	55%	0
CARREON	NYM	N	1	55%	0
JACKSON,D	SD	N	1	65%	0
GWYNN,C	LA	N	0	NA	NA
GONZALEZ,JO	LA	N	0	NA	NA
ABNER	SD	N	-	NA	NA
CANGELOSI	PITF	N	-	NA	NA
DASCENZO	CHC	N	-	NA	NA
PUHL	NYM	N	-	NA	NA
HATCHER,M	LA	N	-	NA	NA
REED,D	NYM	N	-	NA	NA
ROOMES	MONX	N	-	NA	NA
ALDRETE	MON	N	-	NA	NA
MAY	CHC	N	-	NA	NA
CAMPUSANO	PHI	N	-	NA	NA
BERROA	ATL	N	-	NA	NA
VARSHO	CHC	N	-	NA	NA
HUGHES	NYMX	N	-	NA	NA
HOWARD,T	SD	N	-	NA	NA
MORRIS,J	STLX	N	-	NA	NA
LEWIS	SF	N	-	NA	NA
COLLINS	CINX	N	-	NA	NA
JELIC	NYMX	N	-	NA	NA
FORD	PHIX	N	-	NA	NA
LEONARD,M	SF	N	-	NA	NA
BULLOCK	MONX	N	-	NA	NA
CARR	NYM	N	-	NA	NA

AL DESIGNATED HITTERS 1991 $ VALUES

NAME	TEAM	LG	$VAL	OPT%	BID$
DAVIS,A	SEA	A	20	85%	17
BAINES	OAK	A	18	75%	13
CLARK,JA	BOS	A	16	70%	11
JAMES,C	CLE	A	15	75%	12
PARKER,D	MIL	A	14	75%	10
MAAS	NYY	A	14	80%	11
GIBSON	KC	A	13	75%	10
EVANS	BAL	A	12	75%	9
SORRENTO	MIN	A	8	70%	6
DOWNING	CALF	A	7	80%	5
GRIFFEY,SR	SEA	A	6	65%	4
PASQUA	CHW	A	5	75%	4
BERGMAN	DET	A	3	55%	2
LARKIN,G	MIN	A	3	55%	2
SNYDER	CHW	A	2	75%	2
STARK	CHW	A	2	55%	1
MULLINIKS	TOR	A	1	55%	1
HALL	NYY	A	1	55%	1
SHEETS	DETF	A	0	NA	NA
HORN	BAL	A	-	NA	NA
DWYER	MINX	A	-	NA	NA
BALBONI	NYY	A	-	NA	NA
STEVENS	CAL	A	-	NA	NA
PLANTIER	BOS	A	-	NA	NA
KITTLE	BALF	A	-	NA	NA
CANSECO,O	OAK	A	-	NA	NA
STONE	BOSX	A	-	NA	NA
BUCKNER	BOSX	A	-	NA	NA
EPPARD	TORX	A	-	NA	NA

AL PITCHERS 1991 FORECAST VALUES AND OPTIMAL BIDS

NAME	TEAM	LG	T	$VAL	OPT%	BID$
ECKERSLEY	OAK	A	R	38	85%	32
THIGPEN	CHW	A	R	35	85%	30
HENKE	TOR	A	R	32	85%	27
STEWART	OAK	A	R	30	85%	26
OLSON	BAL	A	R	29	85%	25
JONES,D	CLE	A	R	27	85%	23
HANSON	SEA	A	R	26	85%	22
CLEMENS	BOS	A	R	24	75%	18
STIEB	TOR	A	R	24	85%	20
MCDONALD	BAL	A	R	23	85%	20
FINLEY	CAL	A	L	23	85%	19
WELCH	OAK	A	R	22	85%	19
HARVEY	CAL	A	R	22	85%	19
AGUILERA	MIN	A	R	21	80%	17
RYAN	TEX	A	R	20	85%	17
MONTGOMERY	KC	A	R	20	80%	16
WELLS,D	TOR	A	L	19	85%	17
SWIFT	SEA	A	R	19	80%	15
APPIER	KC	A	R	19	75%	14
FARR	NYY	A	R	18	80%	15
HENNEMAN	DET	A	R	17	80%	13
REARDON	BOS	A	R	16	85%	14
SCHOOLER	SEA	A	R	14	75%	11
CHITREN	OAK	A	R	14	75%	11
CRIM	MIL	A	R	14	80%	11
RUSSELL	TEX	A	R	14	85%	12
SABERHAGEN	KC	A	R	13	75%	10
BEDROSIAN	MIN	A	R	13	85%	11
HIBBARD	CHW	A	L	13	75%	10
CHIAMPARINO	TEX	A	R	13	65%	8
DELUCIA	SEA	A	R	13	65%	8
ROGERS	TEX	A	L	13	75%	9
MCCASKILL	CAL	A	R	13	75%	9
CANDIOTTI	CLE	A	R	12	75%	9
PLUNK	NYY	A	R	12	80%	10
BROWN,KD	MIL	A	L	12	75%	9
KEY	TOR	A	L	12	75%	9
ERICKSON	MIN	A	R	12	65%	8
ROBINSON,R	MIL	A	R	11	75%	9
GUETTERMAN	NYY	A	L	11	80%	9
BODDICKER	KC	A	R	11	85%	9

AL PITCHERS 1991 FORECAST VALUES AND OPTIMAL BIDS

NAME	TEAM	LG	T	$VAL	OPT%	BID$
FRASER	TOR	A	R	11	70%	7
DARWIN	BOS	A	R	10	85%	8
DAVIS,M	KC	A	L	10	80%	8
WITT,B	TEX	A	R	10	85%	8
GLEATON	DET	A	L	10	80%	8
HARRIS,R	OAK	A	R	9	75%	7
BURNS	OAK	A	R	9	70%	7
KING	CLE	A	R	9	65%	6
NELSON	OAK	A	R	9	70%	7
MACHADO	MIL	A	R	9	80%	7
WARD,D	TOR	A	R	9	75%	7
WILLIAMSON	BAL	A	R	9	65%	6
OLIN	CLE	A	R	8	75%	6
LEITER,A	TOR	A	L	8	65%	5
MCDOWELL,J	CHW	A	R	8	65%	5
BOLTON	BOS	A	L	7	65%	5
PLESAC	MIL	A	L	7	80%	6
COMSTOCK	SEA	A	L	7	75%	5
BERENGUER	MINF	A	R	7	70%	5
LANGSTON	CAL	A	L	6	75%	5
ROBINSON,JD	NYYF	A	R	6	70%	4
HONEYCUTT	OAK	A	L	6	75%	5
YOUNG,M	BOS	A	L	6	65%	4
ARNSBERG	TEX	A	R	6	75%	5
KNUDSON	MIL	A	R	6	65%	4
DAYLEY	TOR	A	L	6	70%	4
CARY	NYY	A	L	6	65%	4
HIGUERA	MIL	A	L	6	65%	4
MINTON	CALF	A	R	5	55%	3
BOSIO	MIL	A	R	5	55%	3
NAVARRO	MIL	A	R	5	55%	3
TAPANI	MIN	A	R	5	55%	3
PALL	CHW	A	R	5	55%	3
ANDERSON,A	MIN	A	L	5	55%	3
MCCULLERS	DETF	A	R	4	55%	2
JEFFCOAT	TEX	A	L	4	55%	2
GUTHRIE	MIN	A	L	4	55%	2
BROWN,KEVIN	TEX	A	R	4	55%	2
HOLMAN	SEA	A	R	4	55%	2
KIECKER	BOS	A	R	4	55%	2
JOHNSON,D	BAL	A	R	4	55%	2

AL PITCHERS 1991 FORECAST VALUES AND OPTIMAL BIDS

NAME	TEAM	LG	T	$VAL	OPT%	BID$
SANDERSON	NYY	A	R	3	55%	2
FERNANDEZ,A	CHW	A	R	3	55%	2
MORRIS	DETF	A	R	3	55%	2
EDWARDS	CHW	A	L	3	55%	2
SCHATZEDER	KC	A	L	3	55%	2
PEREZ,P	NYY	A	R	3	55%	2
AQUINO	KC	A	R	3	55%	2
MCGAFFIGAN	KCM	A	R	3	55%	2
HILLEGAS	CLE	A	R	3	55%	2
WAYNE	MIN	A	L	3	55%	2
JOHNSON,R	SEA	A	L	3	55%	1
NUNEZ,E	MIL	A	R	3	55%	1
GRAY	BOS	A	R	3	55%	1
DOPSON	BOS	A	R	2	55%	1
COSTELLO	CAL	A	R	2	55%	1
GORDON	KC	A	R	2	55%	1
MACDONALD	TOR	A	L	2	55%	1
CASIAN	MIN	A	L	2	55%	1
CRAWFORD	KCM	A	R	1	55%	1
MCCLURE	CAL	A	L	1	55%	1
OROSCO	CLE	A	L	1	55%	1
ACKER	TOR	A	R	1	55%	1
KLINK	OAK	A	L	1	55%	1
GIBSON	DET	A	L	1	55%	1
SWINDELL	CLE	A	L	1	55%	1
PARKER	DET	A	R	1	55%	0
STOTTLEMYRE,T	TOR	A	R	1	55%	0
HOUGH	CHW	A	R	1	55%	0
DUBOIS	DETX	A	L	1	55%	0
LEARY	NYY	A	R	1	55%	0
PATTERSON,K	CHW	A	L	0	NA	NA
MILACKI	BAL	A	R	0	NA	NA
BLYLEVEN	CAL	A	R	0	NA	NA
SCHILLING	BAL	A	R	0	NA	NA
VALDEZ,E	CLE	A	L	0	NA	NA
WARD,C	CLEX	A	R	0	NA	NA
LEACH	MIN	A	R	-1	NA	NA
FARRELL	CLE	A	R	-1	NA	NA
EILAND	NYY	A	R	-1	NA	NA
BARFIELD	TEX	A	L	-1	NA	NA
FETTERS	CAL	A	R	-1	NA	NA

NL PITCHERS 1991 FORECAST VALUES AND OPTIMAL BIDS

NAME	TEAM	LG	T	$VAL	OPT%	BID$
DRABEK	PIT	N	R	28	85%	24
HOWELL,J	LA	N	R	26	85%	22
MYERS	CIN	N	L	25	85%	21
LEFFERTS	SD	N	L	24	85%	21
FRANCO	NYM	N	L	23	85%	20
CONE	NYM	N	R	23	85%	19
VIOLA	NYM	N	L	23	85%	19
MARTINEZ,R	LA	N	R	22	85%	19
DIBBLE	CIN	N	R	22	85%	19
SMITH,L	STL	N	R	22	85%	19
SMITH,DV	CHC	N	R	22	85%	19
HURST	SD	N	L	22	85%	18
BURKE	MON	N	R	21	85%	18
MARTINEZ,D	MON	N	R	21	80%	17
SMITH,Z	PIT	N	L	20	85%	17
FERNANDEZ,S	NYM	N	L	19	85%	16
WHITSON	SD	N	R	18	80%	14
MCDOWELL,R	PHI	N	R	18	85%	15
RIGHETTI	SF	N	L	17	85%	15
MADDUX,G	CHC	N	R	16	85%	13
RIJO	CIN	N	R	15	80%	12
MAGRANE	STL	N	L	15	80%	12
MEYER	HOU	N	R	13	80%	11
GOODEN	NYM	N	R	13	85%	11
BOYD	MON	N	R	13	75%	10
MERCKER	ATL	N	L	13	80%	10
HARRIS,GW	SD	N	R	13	75%	10
HARKEY	CHC	N	R	13	75%	10
ASSENMACHER	CHC	N	L	13	80%	10
CHARLTON	CIN	N	L	13	85%	11
SCOTT	HOU	N	R	12	75%	9
DESHAIES	HOU	N	L	12	75%	9
BRANTLEY	SF	N	R	11	85%	10
ANDERSEN	SD	N	R	11	80%	9
BLACK	SF	N	L	11	80%	9
MULHOLLAND	PHI	N	L	11	75%	8
PORTUGAL	HOU	N	R	10	65%	7
JONES,B	MON	N	R	10	80%	8
PENA	NYM	N	R	10	75%	7
TEWKSBURY	STL	N	R	9	80%	8
BOEVER	PHI	N	R	9	80%	7

NL PITCHERS 1991 FORECAST VALUES
AND OPTIMAL BIDS

NAME	TEAM	LG	T	$VAL	OPT%	BID$
GARRELTS	SF	N	R	9	80%	7
SMOLTZ	ATL	N	R	8	80%	7
PATTERSON,B	PIT	N	L	8	75%	6
OJEDA	LA	N	L	8	80%	7
LANCASTER	CHC	N	R	8	75%	6
BELCHER	LA	N	R	8	65%	5
BELINDA	PIT	N	R	8	80%	6
LANDRUM	PIT	N	R	7	75%	6
BARNES	MON	N	L	7	55%	4
HEATON	PIT	N	L	7	75%	5
TUDOR	STLF	N	L	7	55%	4
TOMLIN	PIT	N	L	7	65%	5
TERRY	STL	N	R	7	75%	5
DOWNS	SF	N	R	6	75%	5
CREWS	LA	N	R	6	75%	5
PALACIOS	PIT	N	R	6	80%	5
HERSHISER	LA	N	R	6	75%	4
LEIBRANDT	ATL	N	L	5	65%	4
OLIVARES	STL	N	R	5	65%	3
WORRELL	STL	N	R	5	75%	4
HERNANDEZ	HOU	N	R	5	65%	3
HARTLEY	LA	N	R	5	65%	3
KIPPER	PIT	N	L	5	65%	3
BENES	SD	N	R	4	65%	3
DEJESUS	PHI	N	R	4	65%	3
SMITH,B	STL	N	R	4	75%	3
FREY	MON	N	L	4	65%	3
NABHOLZ	MON	N	L	4	55%	2
BROWNING	CIN	N	L	4	85%	3
ONTIVEROS	PHI	N	R	4	65%	2
COMBS	PHI	N	L	3	80%	3
OSUNA	HOU	N	L	3	80%	3
GOTT	LA	N	R	3	75%	2
REUSCHEL	SF	N	R	3	65%	2
PEREZ,MI	STL	N	R	3	75%	2
BURKETT	SF	N	R	3	80%	2
OLIVERAS	SF	N	R	3	55%	1
NEIDLINGER	LA	N	R	3	65%	2
HENNIS	HOU	N	R	3	55%	1
ALLEN	HOU	N	L	2	55%	1
DARLING	NYM	N	R	2	65%	1

NL PITCHERS 1991 FORECAST VALUES AND OPTIMAL BIDS

NAME	TEAM	LG	T	$VAL	OPT%	BID$
POWER	CIN	N	R	2	75%	1
VALERA	NYM	N	R	2	55%	1
DIPINO	STL	N	L	2	55%	1
INNIS	NYM	N	R	2	55%	1
ROJAS	MON	N	R	1	75%	1
WILLIAMS	CHC	N	L	1	80%	1
PARRETT	ATL	N	R	1	65%	1
WALK	PIT	N	R	1	55%	1
CARPENTER	STL	N	R	1	55%	1
STANTON	ATL	N	L	1	75%	1
MORGAN	LA	N	R	1	55%	1
THURMOND	SFF	N	L	1	65%	1
HOWELL,K	PHI	N	R	1	65%	1
WHITEHURST	NYM	N	R	1	55%	0
SEARAGE	LAX	N	L	0	NA	NA
ALVAREZ,J	SFX	N	R	0	NA	NA
SAMPEN	MON	N	R	0	NA	NA
MAHLER	CINF	N	R	0	NA	NA
JACKSON,D	CHC	N	L	0	NA	NA
RUSKIN	MON	N	L	0	NA	NA
BIELECKI	CHC	N	R	0	NA	NA
DELEON	STL	N	R	0	NA	NA
ROBINSON,D	SF	N	R	0	NA	NA
WALSH	LA	N	L	0	NA	NA
HAMMAKER	SD	N	L	-1	NA	NA
RODRIGUEZ,RH	SD	N	L	-1	NA	NA
GROSS,KE	LA	N	R	-1	NA	NA
LAYANA	CIN	N	R	-1	NA	NA
THOMPSON	MONX	N	R	-1	NA	NA
DEWEY	SF	N	R	-1	NA	NA
GROSS,KI	CIN	N	R	-1	NA	NA
PAVLAS	CHC	N	R	-1	NA	NA
GARDNER,M	MON	N	R	-1	NA	NA
LONG	CHCX	N	R	-1	NA	NA
ROESLER	PIT	N	R	-1	NA	NA
SCHMIDT	MONF	N	R	-2	NA	NA
BOSKIE	CHC	N	R	-2	NA	NA
SMILEY	PIT	N	L	-2	NA	NA
BROWN,KEITH	CIN	N	R	-2	NA	NA
LACOSS	SFF	N	R	-2	NA	NA
MALLOY	MONX	N	R	-2	NA	NA

INTRODUCTION TO SECOND HALF STATS

For a full explanation of second half stats and their significance, see the essay on Second Half Signals.

Just a few words before rolling out the numbers from second half 1990:

1. We included only those players who had enough playing time during 1990 to be "significant" for Rotisserie purposes. If a player had only 90 at bats last year, it really isn't worth looking for a change in performance during the year; there just isn't enough data to mean anything.

2. Second half stats include "dollar values" based on second half 1990 performance. These values are mechanical allocations of $2600 (National League) to 230 players, including 140 hitters and 90 pitchers, and $3120 for AL.

If the second half were the whole year, these amounts are what the players would have "earned." I really have no serious interest in backward-looking arithmetic that spreads money to players. Who really cares what Carney Lansford was worth in the second half of 1990? Nonetheless, I enjoy playing with these numbers, and I know other people have fun with them, too. Just PLEASE don't go taking these numbers out of context. They might help you spot unusual performances when you scan the tables; otherwise they are for entertainment purposes only. If you look at them during your auction, I will find out about it, and take them out of the book next year. OK? Thank you.

HITTERS 1990 SECOND HALF STATS

NAME	TEAM	LG	$VAL	BA	AB	H	HR	RBI	SB
ALOMAR	CLE	A	17	.286	217	62	6	35	2
ALOMAR	SD	N	16	.258	264	68	3	23	12
BACKMAN	PIT	N	5	.298	131	39	0	8	2
BAERGA	CLE	A	13	.309	162	50	4	28	0
BAINES	OAK	A	14	.273	194	53	7	32	0
BALBONI	NYA	A	7	.177	130	23	10	16	0
BARFIELD	NYA	A	17	.228	224	51	13	38	1
BELL	PIT	N	9	.236	292	69	4	24	3
BELL	TOR	A	9	.247	235	58	4	26	1
BENZINGER	CIN	N	0	.190	116	22	1	7	0
BICHETTE	CAL	A	13	.284	109	31	7	18	2
BIGGIO	HOU	N	13	.281	253	71	1	17	9
BLAUSER	ATL	N	10	.257	218	56	4	22	3
BOGGS	BOS	A	14	.298	312	93	1	32	0
BONDS	PIT	N	47	.261	257	67	18	52	28
BONILLA	PIT	N	27	.282	308	87	13	59	2
BORDERS	TOR	A	11	.290	162	47	5	21	0
BOSTON	NYN	N	20	.262	221	58	6	25	12
BRADLEY	CHA	A	16	.236	199	47	3	20	10
BREAM	PIT	N	17	.259	197	51	8	34	4
BRETT	KC	A	42	.388	278	108	12	58	4
BRILEY	SEA	A	9	.233	150	35	3	12	5
BROCK	MIL	A	7	.231	130	30	4	14	2
BROOKS	LA	N	23	.285	281	80	10	53	1
BROWNE	CLE	A	15	.281	221	62	2	32	4
BRUNANSKY	BOS	A	17	.245	253	62	9	36	3
BUECHELE	TEX	A	7	.229	153	35	4	20	1
BURKS	BOS	A	24	.290	290	84	11	45	1
BUTLER	SF	N	33	.337	300	101	1	20	25
CALDERON	CHA	A	26	.262	332	87	7	34	11
CAMINITI	HOU	N	7	.225	275	62	2	25	5
CANDAELE	HOU	N	8	.306	173	53	0	16	2
CANSECO	OAK	A	30	.257	249	64	15	47	7
CARTER	SD	N	29	.244	316	77	11	56	14
CLARK	SD	N	24	.301	183	55	14	36	2
CLARK	SF	N	18	.311	270	84	5	34	2
COLEMAN	STL	N	30	.291	182	53	3	18	30
COTTO	SEA	A	7	.208	149	31	1	15	6
DANIELS	LA	N	31	.302	225	68	16	57	3
DAUGHERTY	TEX	A	11	.277	159	44	4	29	0
DAULTON	PHI	N	26	.303	251	76	10	41	7
DAVIS	CAL	A	5	.250	120	30	2	18	0

HITTERS 1990 SECOND HALF STATS

NAME	TEAM	LG	$VAL	BA	AB	H	HR	RBI	SB
DAVIS	CIN	N	33	.280	264	74	13	51	13
DAVIS	HOU	N	8	.247	93	23	3	16	3
DAVIS	SEA	A	22	.280	250	70	12	46	0
DAWSON	CHN	N	24	.294	248	73	8	43	7
DEER	MIL	A	14	.219	233	51	13	30	0
DESHIELDS	MTL	N	24	.276	275	76	2	31	19
DEVEREAUX	BAL	A	23	.252	222	56	9	32	9
DORAN	CIN	N	23	.340	191	65	6	17	11
DOWNING	CAL	A	18	.291	203	59	9	35	0
DUNCAN	CIN	N	18	.310	229	71	4	31	5
DUNSTON	CHN	N	18	.239	243	58	4	22	16
DYKSTRA	PHI	N	27	.292	301	88	5	29	17
EISENREICH	KC	A	14	.282	234	66	3	24	3
ELSTER	NYN	N	1	.158	57	9	2	6	0
ESPINOZA	NYA	A	1	.220	209	46	1	11	1
EVANS	BOS	A	10	.269	160	43	3	19	2
FELIX	TOR	A	7	.226	164	37	4	19	2
FERMIN	CLE	A	10	.281	210	59	0	25	2
FERNANDEZ	TOR	A	30	.296	301	89	2	31	16
FIELDER	DET	A	31	.258	267	69	23	57	0
FINLEY	BAL	A	19	.258	233	60	2	20	12
FISK	CHA	A	24	.289	242	70	11	38	3
FITZGERALD	MTL	N	8	.236	148	35	5	21	1
FLETCHER	CHA	A	10	.251	255	64	2	37	1
FRANCO	TEX	A	33	.299	274	82	5	28	17
GAETTI	MIN	A	11	.208	289	60	7	38	3
GAGNE	MIN	A	8	.226	159	36	2	14	5
GALARRAGA	MTL	N	25	.252	286	72	14	47	6
GALLEGO	OAK	A	5	.206	209	43	2	14	4
GANT	ATL	N	43	.290	317	92	15	44	23
GANTNER	MIL	A	19	.261	261	68	0	16	14
GEREN	NYA	A	2	.188	112	21	3	15	0
GIBSON	LA	N	24	.263	228	60	5	21	20
GIRARDI	CHN	N	5	.249	197	49	0	17	3
GLADDEN	MIN	A	15	.250	232	58	1	16	11
GRACE	CHN	N	30	.351	285	100	7	50	6
GREENWELL	BOS	A	36	.328	305	100	12	47	6
GRIFFEY	SEA	A	23	.263	274	72	10	40	5
GRIFFIN	LA	N	-2	.179	179	32	0	11	1
GRISSOM	MTL	N	13	.250	124	31	3	19	9
GRUBER	TOR	A	28	.247	271	67	11	52	9
GUERRERO	STL	N	11	.275	193	53	4	29	0

HITTERS 1990 SECOND HALF STATS

NAME	TEAM	LG	$VAL	BA	AB	H	HR	RBI	SB
GUILLEN	CHA	A	8	.240	262	63	1	32	2
GWYNN	SD	N	18	.306	255	78	2	37	6
HALL	NYA	A	4	.237	114	27	3	12	0
HARPER	MIN	A	11	.279	233	65	1	19	3
HARRIS	LA	N	15	.316	212	67	1	14	8
HASSEY	OAK	A	4	.238	122	29	3	13	0
HATCHER	CIN	N	9	.235	217	51	3	12	8
HAYESC	PHI	N	10	.236	275	65	5	28	2
HAYESV	PHI	N	21	.256	258	66	8	36	9
HEATH	DET	A	5	.209	172	36	3	20	2
HENDERSOND	OAK	A	15	.307	166	51	6	22	1
HENDERSONR	OAK	A	47	.313	211	66	11	26	26
HERR	NYN	N	10	.268	261	70	1	28	3
HILL	CAL	A	9	.291	175	51	2	18	1
HILL	TOR	A	9	.220	118	26	5	12	4
HOWELL	CAL	A	6	.239	134	32	3	16	1
HRBEK	MIN	A	24	.309	236	73	11	38	1
HUSON	TEX	A	5	.201	174	35	0	15	6
INCAVIGLIA	TEX	A	13	.218	248	54	9	37	2
JACKSON	KC	A	22	.277	119	33	12	29	5
JACOBY	CLE	A	12	.271	273	74	3	37	0
JAMES	CLE	A	20	.310	271	84	7	32	1
JAVIER	LA	N	12	.285	158	45	2	11	8
JEFFERIES	NYN	N	15	.262	309	81	5	32	5
JOHNSON	CHA	A	35	.298	272	81	1	21	23
JOHNSON	NYN	N	29	.248	290	72	10	45	17
JORDAN	PHI	N	3	.233	129	30	1	17	0
JOSE	OAK	A	13	.289	152	44	4	20	3
JOYNER	CAL	A	0	.0	4	0	0	0	0
JUSTICE	ATL	N	41	.295	278	82	23	58	7
KELLY	NYA	A	46	.285	326	93	11	36	24
KENNEDY	SF	N	4	.272	136	37	1	12	0
KING	PIT	N	19	.259	216	56	11	37	3
KITTLE	BAL	A	0	.188	101	19	2	6	0
KRUK	PHI	N	20	.310	210	65	5	36	6
LANSFORD	OAK	A	10	.253	198	50	0	18	6
LARKIN	CIN	N	20	.295	305	90	3	29	9
LARKIN	MIN	A	5	.246	138	34	1	10	2
LAVALLIERE	PIT	N	6	.257	148	38	2	19	0
LEE	TOR	A	2	.222	225	50	0	22	1
LEMON	DET	A	4	.244	197	48	1	14	1
LEONARD	SEA	A	4	.260	146	38	0	20	0

HITTERS 1990 SECOND HALF STATS

NAME	TEAM	LG	$VAL	BA	AB	H	HR	RBI	SB
LEYRITZ	NYA	A	6	.232	207	48	3	17	2
LIND	PIT	N	4	.220	241	53	1	18	4
LIRIANO	MIN	A	8	.250	208	52	0	13	5
MAAS	NYA	A	24	.249	229	57	19	36	1
MACFARLANE	KC	A	10	.244	197	48	5	32	0
MACK	MIN	A	29	.343	210	72	5	31	10
MAGADAN	NYN	N	19	.312	279	87	3	48	2
MALDONADO	CLE	A	23	.278	299	83	9	51	2
MARTINEZ	CHA	A	1	.241	79	19	1	3	0
MARTINEZ	MTL	N	14	.271	203	55	5	18	6
MARTINEZ	SEA	A	14	.301	216	65	4	22	1
MATTINGLY	NYA	A	2	.265	102	27	0	9	0
MCDOWELL	ATL	N	4	.217	106	23	2	2	4
MCGEE	STL	N	18	.365	170	62	2	25	6
MCGRIFF	TOR	A	37	.331	293	97	17	42	4
MCGWIRE	OAK	A	25	.247	263	65	17	52	1
MCREYNOLDS	NYN	N	25	.294	269	79	11	39	5
MELVIN	BAL	A	6	.250	152	38	3	17	0
MILLIGAN	BAL	A	9	.268	97	26	5	13	1
MITCHELL	SF	N	23	.266	248	66	14	43	2
MOLITOR	MIL	A	21	.279	229	64	5	20	9
MORRIS	CIN	N	20	.327	248	81	4	25	6
MOSEBY	DET	A	18	.243	202	49	7	30	7
MURPHY	PHI	N	21	.264	280	74	11	40	3
MURRAY	LA	N	39	.361	299	108	15	54	5
MYERS	TOR	A	2	.231	121	28	1	11	0
NEWMAN	MIN	A	8	.250	196	49	0	15	5
NOKES	NYA	A	5	.217	161	35	3	14	2
O'BRIEN	SEA	A	5	.247	219	54	3	15	0
OLERUD	TOR	A	6	.252	143	36	4	15	0
OLIVER	CIN	N	5	.214	145	31	3	23	0
OLSON	ATL	N	2	.227	132	30	1	11	1
ONEILL	CIN	N	14	.252	242	61	5	32	5
OQUENDO	STL	N	4	.261	207	54	0	12	1
ORSULAK	BAL	A	7	.224	156	35	3	19	3
OWEN	MTL	N	2	.218	197	43	0	10	3
PAGLIARULO	SD	N	8	.254	209	53	4	23	0
PALMEIRO	TEX	A	26	.327	300	98	6	44	2
PARKER	MIL	A	18	.263	308	81	10	36	1
PARRISH	CAL	A	14	.253	233	59	8	28	1
PASQUA	CHA	A	8	.238	185	44	4	29	0
PENA	BOS	A	16	.249	233	58	3	26	8

HITTERS 1990 SECOND HALF STATS

NAME	TEAM	LG	$VAL	BA	AB	H	HR	RBI	SB
PENDLETON	STL	N	4	.198	177	35	1	13	6
PERRY	KC	A	18	.266	192	51	2	19	11
PETRALLI	TEX	A	3	.272	162	44	0	9	0
PETTIS	TEX	A	18	.238	206	49	0	10	16
PHILLIPS	DET	A	16	.273	256	70	3	22	6
POLONIA	CAL	A	26	.354	240	85	1	23	9
PRESLEY	ATL	N	9	.210	248	52	8	30	1
PUCKETT	MIN	A	16	.290	248	72	2	34	3
QUINTANA	BOS	A	10	.261	283	74	2	33	1
RAINES	MTL	N	35	.289	246	71	7	37	25
RAMIREZ	HOU	N	4	.243	189	46	1	18	1
RANDOLPH	OAK	A	8	.276	152	42	0	11	4
RAY	CAL	A	10	.277	220	61	3	26	0
REED	BOS	A	14	.282	301	85	2	22	3
REYNOLDS	SEA	A	25	.258	314	81	4	23	15
RIPKENB	BAL	A	12	.316	187	59	2	21	1
RIPKENC	BAL	A	20	.248	290	72	12	45	2
RIVERA	BOS	A	12	.238	164	39	5	29	3
ROBERTS	SD	N	33	.333	270	90	4	20	24
SABO	CIN	N	15	.238	269	64	9	29	4
SALAZAR	CHN	N	7	.238	235	56	5	18	1
SAMUEL	LA	N	22	.277	206	57	7	30	11
SANDBERG	CHN	N	31	.270	281	76	16	43	9
SANTIAGO	SD	N	5	.215	158	34	2	20	2
SASSER	NYN	N	7	.276	127	35	3	20	0
SAX	NYA	A	32	.250	300	75	3	24	24
SCHOFIELD	CAL	A	10	.283	212	60	0	17	3
SCIOSCIA	LA	N	12	.266	199	53	4	29	3
SEITZER	KC	A	10	.248	303	75	2	15	5
SHARPERSON	LA	N	15	.287	202	58	3	18	8
SHEETS	DET	A	12	.244	176	43	6	32	1
SHEFFIELD	MIL	A	23	.272	224	61	5	26	11
SIERRA	TEX	A	22	.289	304	88	5	51	3
SMITH	ATL	N	20	.335	257	86	4	23	5
SMITH	CHN	N	3	.227	88	20	1	12	1
SMITH	STL	N	19	.278	248	69	1	21	16
SNYDER	CLE	A	3	.215	158	34	3	13	0
SOSA	CHA	A	26	.201	254	51	7	38	18
SPIERS	MIL	A	7	.222	212	47	0	18	6
STEINBACH	OAK	A	9	.257	152	39	4	30	0
STILLWELL	KC	A	1	.208	236	49	2	18	0
STRAWBERRY	NYN	N	28	.247	271	67	16	52	6

HITTERS 1990 SECOND HALF STATS

NAME	TEAM	LG	$VAL	BA	AB	H	HR	RBI	SB
STUBBS	HOU	N	30	.275	255	70	11	42	14
SURHOFF	MIL	A	15	.258	236	61	1	34	7
TARTABULL	KC	A	15	.296	159	47	7	33	0
TEMPLETON	SD	N	5	.236	246	58	2	26	0
TETTLETON	BAL	A	3	.203	197	40	4	13	1
THOMAS	ATL	N	3	.216	148	32	2	19	0
THOMPSON	SF	N	14	.249	213	53	7	19	6
THOMPSON	STL	N	9	.229	188	43	2	11	9
THON	PHI	N	17	.263	281	74	6	25	8
TRAMMELL	DET	A	26	.317	243	77	8	43	4
TREADWAY	ATL	N	8	.262	195	51	2	19	2
URIBE	SF	N	-2	.174	149	26	0	6	2
VALLE	SEA	A	2	.198	167	33	3	15	0
VANSLYKE	PIT	N	19	.272	228	62	8	37	5
VAUGHN	MIL	A	15	.205	200	41	11	32	4
VENTURA	CHA	A	10	.270	256	69	2	32	0
VIZQUEL	SEA	A	7	.244	246	60	1	17	3
WALKER	MTL	N	20	.232	198	46	9	25	12
WALLACH	MTL	N	22	.288	312	90	8	44	4
WALTON	CHN	N	6	.254	177	45	2	8	4
WARD	DET	A	11	.269	130	35	5	24	1
WEBSTER	CLE	A	17	.244	172	42	6	23	8
WEISS	OAK	A	7	.258	186	48	0	18	3
WHITAKER	DET	A	19	.268	198	53	7	25	6
WHITE	CAL	A	15	.222	180	40	4	22	9
WILLIAMS	SF	N	27	.254	291	74	16	53	4
WILSON	HOU	N	7	.250	136	34	3	23	0
WILSON	KC	A	12	.310	129	40	1	16	5
WILSON	TOR	A	20	.287	300	86	2	29	8
WINFIELD	CAL	A	23	.290	255	74	11	52	0
WORTHINGTN	BAL	A	2	.234	167	39	1	14	0
YELDING	HOU	N	27	.244	279	68	1	14	33
YOUNT	MIL	A	25	.255	286	73	10	41	8
ZEILE	STL	N	13	.264	239	63	7	27	1

PITCHERS 1990 SECOND HALF STATS

NAME	TEAM		$VAL	W	L	ERA	RATIO	SV	IP
ABBOTT	CAL	A	-5	5	7	4.28	1.50	0	107.3
ACKER	TOR	A	-2	3	2	5.02	1.59	0	37.7
AGOSTO	HOU	N	-1	5	5	5.73	1.62	3	37.7
AGUILERA	MIN	A	11	3	1	2.88	1.36	11	25.0
AKERFELDS	PHI	N	-9	2	2	5.40	1.49	2	45.0
ANDERSEN	HOU	N	14	1	0	0.34	0.90	4	26.7
ANDERSON	MIN	A	13	5	7	3.83	1.13	0	87.0
APPIER	KC	A	23	8	5	2.66	1.19	0	108.3
AQUINO	KC	A	3	1	1	2.25	1.25	0	20.0
ARMSTRONG	CIN	N	-8	1	6	5.96	1.64	0	51.3
ARNSBERG	TEX	A	5	4	0	2.52	1.53	5	39.3
ASSENMACHER	CHN	N	18	5	0	1.96	1.02	7	46.0
AVERY	ATL	N	-10	2	8	6.18	1.67	0	71.3
BALLARD	BAL	A	-3	1	2	4.64	1.36	0	42.7
BEDROSIAN	SF	N	7	6	4	3.93	1.53	10	36.7
BELCHER	LA	N	3	2	3	4.46	1.25	0	38.3
BELINDA	PIT	N	2	1	2	4.46	1.49	5	34.3
BENES	SD	N	2	4	5	3.80	1.42	0	85.3
BERENGUER	MIN	A	8	2	4	2.72	1.15	0	49.7
BIELECKI	CHN	N	7	5	3	3.76	1.38	1	69.3
BIRTSAS	CIN	N	-5	0	1	5.40	2.40	0	15.0
BLACK	TOR	A	9	6	7	4.26	1.21	0	82.3
BLAIR	TOR	A	2	2	0	4.50	1.30	0	10.0
BLYLEVEN	CAL	A	-5	1	2	5.81	1.63	0	26.3
BODDICKER	BOS	A	7	6	4	3.33	1.40	0	102.7
BOEVER	PHI	N	15	2	3	2.55	1.26	6	49.3
BOLTON	BOS	A	12	9	5	3.21	1.33	0	109.3
BOSIO	MIL	A	-2	0	3	4.24	1.41	0	23.3
BOSKIE	CHN	N	6	2	2	3.43	1.22	0	39.3
BOYD	MTL	N	13	6	3	2.68	1.15	0	94.0
BRANTLEY	SF	N	7	2	2	1.69	1.83	6	21.3
BROWN,K	TEX	A	-1	2	4	4.06	1.46	0	57.7
BROWNING	CIN	N	-3	7	4	5.05	1.39	0	98.0
BURKE	MTL	N	20	3	2	1.73	1.06	9	52.0
BURKETT	SF	N	5	5	5	4.08	1.33	1	106.0
BURNS	OAK	A	3	1	1	3.28	1.39	2	46.7
CADARET	NYA	A	6	3	0	3.88	1.47	3	51.0
CANDELARIA	TOR	A	-3	0	3	5.06	1.80	2	26.7
CANDIOTTI	CLE	A	12	6	7	3.71	1.27	0	104.3
CARMAN	PHI	N	-7	2	2	5.50	1.54	1	37.7
CARY	NYA	A	4	2	8	3.93	1.27	0	94.0
CASTILLO	ATL	N	4	3	0	3.96	1.50	1	38.7
CERUTTI	TOR	A	-29	4	3	6.26	1.74	0	46.0
CHARLTON	CIN	N	11	6	6	2.63	1.25	0	106.0

NAME	TEAM		$VAL	W	L	ERA	RATIO	SV	IP
CLANCY	HOU	N	-6	0	0	10.34	2.04	1	15.7
CLARY	ATL	N	-10	0	5	7.09	1.63	0	39.3
CLEMENS	BOS	A	33	9	2	0.97	1.06	0	92.7
COMBS	PHI	N	7	6	3	4.12	1.38	0	96.0
COMSTOCK	SEA	A	2	3	2	4.10	1.33	2	26.3
CONE	NYN	N	28	9	6	2.44	1.06	0	125.7
COOK	LA	N	-16	4	2	4.95	1.62	0	60.0
CRAWFORD	KC	A	6	3	3	4.31	1.33	1	48.0
CREWS	LA	N	18	3	2	2.44	0.89	2	55.3
CRIM	MIL	A	12	1	1	2.29	1.08	5	35.3
DARLING	NYN	N	1	5	5	4.19	1.41	0	68.7
DARWIN	HOU	N	29	9	3	2.22	1.06	0	105.3
DAVISM	KC	A	-4	1	1	4.54	1.49	1	33.7
DAVISS	KC	A	4	5	4	4.18	1.43	0	56.0
DAYLEY	STL	N	8	3	2	3.32	1.18	1	43.3
DEJESUS	PHI	N	5	7	6	3.83	1.27	0	101.0
DELEON	STL	N	-6	1	12	5.16	1.42	0	83.7
DESHAIES	HOU	N	9	3	5	3.47	1.23	0	106.3
DIBBLE	CIN	N	20	4	1	1.81	0.95	4	49.7
DIPINO	STL	N	7	1	1	3.92	1.21	3	43.7
DOWNS	SF	N	11	3	2	3.43	1.21	0	63.0
DRABEK	PIT	N	40	13	2	2.29	0.91	0	121.7
DRUMMOND	MIN	A	1	2	2	3.50	1.50	0	36.0
ECKERSLEY	OAK	A	35	2	1	0.73	0.54	23	37.0
EDENS	MIL	A	-1	2	4	4.74	1.37	2	57.0
EDWARDS	CHA	A	9	5	1	3.33	1.31	1	54.0
EICHHORN	CAL	A	0	2	1	4.56	1.83	0	25.7
ERICKSON	MIN	A	3	7	3	2.63	1.37	0	95.7
FARR	KC	A	19	7	4	1.80	1.16	1	70.0
FARRELL	CLE	A	3	0	1	3.86	1.07	0	9.3
FERNANDEZ,A	CHA	A	5	5	5	3.80	1.40	0	87.7
FERNANDEZ,S	NYN	N	19	4	9	3.41	1.04	0	97.7
FETTERS	CAL	A	1	0	0	3.15	1.47	1	40.0
FINLEY	CAL	A	17	7	5	2.27	1.30	0	119.0
FRANCO	NYN	N	14	1	3	3.23	1.53	16	30.7
FRASER	CAL	A	13	3	2	2.11	1.03	2	42.7
FREY	MTL	N	13	5	1	0.77	1.23	5	35.0
GARDNER	BOS	A	3	1	2	3.68	1.25	0	36.7
GARDNER	MTL	N	1	2	5	4.89	1.33	0	57.0
GARRELTS	SF	N	8	7	4	3.18	1.33	0	82.0
GIBSON	DET	A	1	3	2	3.69	1.34	1	46.3
GLAVINE	ATL	N	-2	5	7	4.78	1.50	0	107.3
GLEATON	DET	A	12	0	2	3.38	1.21	11	34.7
GOODEN	NYN	N	19	11	2	3.45	1.29	0	117.3
GORDON	KC	A	-5	7	5	3.91	1.50	0	103.7
GOTT	LA	N	10	3	3	2.16	1.34	3	41.7

NAME	TEAM		$VAL	W	L	ERA	RATIO	SV	IP
GRANT	ATL	N	1	1	2	4.64	1.51	3	52.3
GRAY	BOS	A	8	1	2	3.82	1.33	7	35.3
GREENE	PHI	N	-3	2	3	4.15	1.36	0	39.0
GRIMSLEY	PHI	N	4	3	2	3.30	1.57	0	57.3
GROSS	MTL	N	-8	1	7	6.25	1.68	0	59.0
GUETTERMAN	NYA	A	6	5	4	4.29	1.32	2	35.7
GULLICKSON	HOU	N	-17	5	8	4.20	1.44	0	96.3
GUTHRIE	MIN	A	21	5	7	3.27	1.21	0	110.0
HALL	MTL	N	-7	0	0	13.00	2.33	0	9.0
HAMMAKER	SD	N	3	0	5	4.65	1.23	0	31.0
HANSON	SEA	A	34	9	3	2.59	1.00	0	125.0
HARKEY	CHN	N	17	6	3	2.79	1.14	0	87.0
HARNISCH	BAL	A	-10	4	6	4.75	1.50	0	83.3
HARRIS,GA	BOS	A	-9	6	6	4.79	1.56	0	97.7
HARRIS,GW	SD	N	15	4	5	2.30	1.23	4	54.7
HARTLEY	LA	N	16	5	2	2.09	0.87	0	47.3
HARVEY	CAL	A	13	2	2	3.56	1.22	14	30.3
HAWKINS	NYA	A	-15	4	6	5.53	1.49	0	70.0
HEATON	PIT	N	2	2	5	3.42	1.30	0	50.0
HENKE	TOR	A	14	2	3	2.94	1.34	16	33.7
HENNEMAN	DET	A	9	4	1	3.59	1.31	5	42.7
HERNANDEZ	HOU	N	9	2	1	2.30	1.02	0	27.3
HIBBARD	CHA	A	13	8	4	3.69	1.29	0	109.7
HIGUERA	MIL	A	0	5	8	4.75	1.40	0	102.3
HILL	STL	N	2	5	6	4.92	1.35	0	75.0
HOLMAN	SEA	A	1	3	4	4.06	1.31	0	77.7
HOLTON	BAL	A	-7	0	0	10.80	2.52	0	8.3
HONEYCUTT	OAK	A	7	1	1	3.67	1.26	5	27.0
HOUGH	TEX	A	-4	5	6	3.65	1.44	0	106.0
HOWELL	LA	N	20	2	1	1.45	0.96	12	37.3
HOWELL	PHI	N	-4	0	1	9.00	2.25	0	8.0
HURST	SD	N	29	6	2	1.94	1.01	0	111.3
JACKSON	CIN	N	5	3	4	4.19	1.30	0	53.7
JACKSON	SEA	A	-10	2	4	6.82	2.05	1	31.7
JEFFCOAT	TEX	A	4	2	3	4.50	1.42	2	24.0
JOHNSON,D	BAL	A	3	5	5	3.82	1.22	0	75.3
JOHNSON,R	SEA	A	-2	5	8	3.61	1.38	0	109.7
JONES,B	CHA	A	5	1	3	2.64	1.24	0	30.7
JONES,D	CLE	A	20	1	3	3.86	1.08	20	39.7
JONES,J	NYA	A	-16	0	0	6.59	2.05	0	27.3
KEY	TOR	A	22	8	3	3.10	1.08	0	95.7
KIECKER	BOS	A	12	6	6	3.81	1.26	0	85.0
KING	CHA	A	9	4	2	3.83	1.26	0	51.7
KIPPER	PIT	N	6	2	1	2.12	1.15	2	29.7
KNUDSON	MIL	A	9	5	5	4.40	1.27	0	71.7
KRUEGER	MIL	A	-2	2	4	4.09	1.56	0	55.0
LACOSS	SF	N	-10	3	3	4.86	1.66	0	50.0

NAME	TEAM		$VAL	W	L	ERA	RATIO	SV	IP
LAMP	BOS	A	-7	1	3	7.28	1.49	0	47.0
LANCASTER	CHN	N	10	2	0	3.16	1.03	1	37.0
LANDRUM	PIT	N	4	4	2	3.07	1.43	1	29.3
LANGSTON	CAL	A	-3	6	8	5.19	1.51	0	104.0
LAPOINT	NYA	A	2	2	4	3.69	1.49	0	70.7
LAYANA	CIN	N	-2	2	3	4.57	1.45	1	43.3
LEACH	MIN	A	3	0	3	3.94	1.56	2	32.0
LEARY	NYA	A	2	6	7	4.47	1.34	0	88.7
LEFFERTS	SD	N	16	2	1	1.26	1.19	12	28.7
LEIBRANDT	ATL	N	18	6	10	3.04	1.24	0	109.7
LILLIQUIST	SD	N	-1	3	3	4.33	1.39	0	60.3
LONG	CHN	N	-4	3	1	5.09	1.70	3	23.0
LUECKEN	ATL	N	-5	0	2	5.25	2.08	0	24.0
MADDUX	CHN	N	22	11	7	2.63	1.30	0	136.7
MAGRANE	STL	N	13	6	5	2.90	1.21	0	83.7
MAHLER	CIN	N	3	4	3	4.52	1.27	3	75.7
MARTINEZ,D	MTL	N	22	4	4	3.09	1.03	0	96.0
MARTINEZ,R	LA	N	29	11	2	2.66	1.02	0	122.0
MCCASKILL	CAL	A	10	6	6	3.75	1.24	0	93.7
MCDONALD	BAL	A	24	8	5	2.50	1.05	0	115.0
MCDOWELL,J	CHA	A	15	9	5	3.62	1.24	0	117.0
MCDOWELL,R	PHI	N	16	3	5	2.23	1.24	90	44.3
MCGAFFIGAN	KC	A	6	4	3	3.15	1.37	0	65.7
MILACKI	BAL	A	-6	1	3	4.81	1.40	0	33.7
MIRABELLA	MIL	A	-3	2	0	4.03	1.66	0	22.3
MITCHELL	BAL	A	-9	5	4	4.52	1.67	0	75.7
MOHORCIC	MTL	N	0	0	1	3.82	1.49	1	37.7
MONTGOMERY	KC	A	17	2	3	2.18	1.43	16	41.3
MOORE	OAK	A	-9	6	8	5.32	1.62	0	86.3
MORGAN	LA	N	0	4	8	4.10	1.38	0	96.7
MORRIS	DET	A	8	7	9	3.95	1.25	0	123.0
MOYER	TEX	A	2	2	3	4.78	1.48	0	52.7
MULHOLLAND	PHI	N	25	6	7	2.86	1.05	0	119.7
MURPHY	BOS	A	-9	0	1	7.13	2.66	3	17.7
MYERS	CIN	N	18	1	4	1.93	1.17	14	42.0
NABHOLZ	MTL	N	11	6	2	2.77	1.05	0	65.0
NAVARRO	MIL	A	15	6	5	3.61	1.26	1	99.7
NEIDLINGER	LA	N	16	5	3	3.28	1.11	0	74.0
NELSON	OAK	A	12	2	1	1.89	1.08	2	38.0
NIEDENFUER	STL	N	-5	0	3	4.97	1.86	1	25.3
NUNEZ	DET	A	2	0	1	3.33	1.64	4	24.3
NUNEZ	CHN	N	-3	3	2	7.53	1.43	0	28.7
OJEDA	NYN	N	2	3	3	3.63	1.52	0	44.7
OLIN	CLE	A	11	3	2	3.09	1.30	1	64.0
OLIVERAS	SF	N	11	2	0	2.02	1.15	2	40.0
OLSON	BAL	A	14	2	2	4.20	1.53	20	30.0
OROSCO	CLE	A	-4	2	0	3.60	1.60	0	30.0

NAME	TEAM		$VAL	W	L	ERA	RATIO	SV	IP
PALL	CHA	A	2	3	3	3.90	1.24	2	32.3
PARKER	DET	A	-4	2	2	3.18	1.37	0	51.0
PARRETT	ATL	N	-4	2	4	4.22	1.65	1	49.0
PATTERSON,B	PIT	N	11	3	2	2.88	1.20	3	40.7
PATTERSON,K	CHA	A	6	1	0	2.00	1.48	1	27.0
PENA	NYN	N	12	1	1	2.01	1.14	3	40.3
PEREZ,M	CHA	A	-7	6	7	5.40	1.54	0	95.0
PETERSON	CHA	A	-8	2	4	5.17	1.42	0	55.7
PETRY	DET	A	-10	4	3	5.85	1.53	0	52.3
PICO	CHN	N	-1	0	2	4.40	1.71	2	28.7
PLESAC	MIL	A	12	3	4	3.71	1.29	10	34.0
PLUNK	NYA	A	10	4	1	2.40	1.04	0	41.3
PORTUGAL	HOU	N	14	8	2	2.90	1.25	0	96.3
POWER	PIT	N	2	1	1	4.61	1.50	3	27.3
PRICE	BAL	A	1	2	2	4.35	1.35	0	31.0
RADINSKY	CHA	A	-6	1	1	9.82	2.51	1	18.3
RASMUSSEN	SD	N	-17	4	10	4.93	1.54	0	95.0
REARDON	BOS	A	8	2	1	3.00	1.42	7	12.0
REED,J	BOS	A	-5	0	1	9.95	2.53	0	12.7
REED,R	PIT	N	-10	0	3	5.64	2.01	0	22.3
REUSCHEL	SF	N	5	1	0	1.20	1.40	1	15.0
RIGHETTI	NYA	A	15	0	1	3.21	1.21	19	28.0
RIJO	CIN	N	27	9	5	2.03	1.12	0	111.0
ROBINSON	SF	N	1	6	6	4.71	1.39	0	99.3
ROBINSON,JD	NYA	A	8	2	1	2.49	1.21	0	47.0
ROBINSON,JM	DET	A	-14	4	3	7.17	1.57	0	47.7
ROBINSON,R	MIL	A	20	10	4	3.24	1.29	0	116.7
ROGERS	TEX	A	17	7	2	1.94	1.23	8	46.3
RUFFIN	PHI	N	-20	0	5	7.88	1.98	0	48.0
RUSKIN	MTL	N	2	1	1	2.90	1.49	0	40.3
RYAN	TEX	A	24	5	5	3.15	1.00	0	111.3
SABERHAGEN	KC	A	-1	0	2	5.79	1.79	0	14.0
SAMPEN	MTL	N	-2	5	6	4.29	1.74	1	42.0
SANDERSON	OAK	A	4	8	6	3.98	1.29	0	101.7
SCHATZEDER	NYN	N	12	0	0	0.59	0.89	0	30.3
SCHIRALDI	SD	N	-6	1	7	4.60	1.55	0	62.7
SCHOOLER	SEA	A	6	0	4	3.06	1.53	8	17.7
COTT	HOU	N	17	3	5	2.82	1.07	0	99.0
CUDDER	CIN	N	1	4	3	4.13	1.30	0	61.0
SEARCY	DET	A	-15	2	7	4.66	1.68	0	73.3
SHOW	SD	N	-2	5	2	4.80	1.52	1	60.0
SMILEY	PIT	N	-7	5	7	5.24	1.45	0	92.7
SMITH,B	STL	N	3	3	2	4.93	1.47	0	45.7
SMITH,D	HOU	N	11	4	4	2.28	1.16	7	27.7
SMITH,L	STL	N	18	1	2	1.99	1.23	16	31.7
SMITH,R	MIN	A	-13	1	3	5.19	1.69	0	59.0
SMITH,Z	PIT	N	35	7	3	2.19	0.92	0	111.0

NAME	TEAM		$VAL	W	L	ERA	RATIO	SV	IP
SMOLTZ	ATL	N	11	8	5	3.06	1.23	0	123.7
STEWART	OAK	A	29	11	4	2.22	1.17	0	134.0
STIEB	TOR	A	23	7	3	2.73	1.15	0	108.7
STOTTLEMYRE	TOR	A	4	4	9	4.22	1.34	0	91.7
SWIFT	SEA	A	21	4	2	2.47	1.14	5	73.0
SWINDELL	CLE	A	9	8	4	4.21	1.37	0	113.3
TANANA	DET	A	-4	4	2	4.66	1.42	1	77.3
TAPANI	MIN	A	5	3	3	4.37	1.25	0	47.3
TERRELL	DET	A	-2	6	4	4.54	1.46	0	75.3
TERRY	STL	N	9	2	1	2.50	0.91	0	39.7
TEWKSBURY	STL	N	20	6	8	3.69	1.14	0	95.0
THIGPEN	CHA	A	32	0	3	1.71	1.07	30	42.0
THURMOND	SF	N	2	1	1	3.74	1.48	2	21.7
TOMLIN	PIT	N	22	4	4	2.55	0.95	0	77.7
TUDOR	STL	N	23	5	1	1.49	0.75	0	54.3
VALDEZ	CLE	A	5	4	1	3.04	1.37	0	50.3
VALENZUELA	LA	N	-10	7	6	5.50	1.63	0	93.3
VIOLA	NYN	N	20	7	9	3.13	1.19	0	126.7
WALK	PIT	N	6	3	1	4.01	1.20	1	58.3
WALKER	CLE	A	-14	2	6	5.01	1.67	0	73.7
WARD	TOR	A	16	1	5	3.43	0.93		460.3
WELCH	OAK	A	13	14	3	2.99	1.25	0	114.3
WELLS	TOR	A	20	5	4	2.99	1.13	0	108.3
WEST	MIN	A	-13	3	3	5.72	1.54	0	56.7
WHITEHURST	NYN	N	7	0	0	3.86	1.18	0	37.3
WHITSON	SD	N	25	8	3	2.26	1.22	0	107.3
WILLIAMS	CHN	N	0	0	3	5.61	1.87	7	33.7
WILLIAMSON	BAL	A	7	3	1	3.48	1.16	1	31.0
WILLS	TOR	A	0	1	2	4.11	1.33	0	50.3
WILSON,S	CHN	N	5	2	4	5.15	1.27	0	64.7
WILSON,T	SF	N	-9	2	7	5.55	1.41	0	61.7
WITT,B	TEX	A	23	12	2	2.64	1.21	0	116.0
WITT,M	NYA	A	2	5	5	4.72	1.27	0	68.7
YOUNG,C	OAK	A	-11	5	3	5.56	1.62	0	56.7
YOUNG,M	SEA	A	10	5	9	2.90	1.34	0	121.0

IV
GRADUATE STUDIES

LEAGUESMANSHIP

(with apologies to Stephen Potter)

By Pete DeCoursey

Work, work, work. Any book that assigns you to read newspapers by the quarter-ton is not exactly fun city. Nobody questions that becoming a Bensonite will help you win, but it sure does feel like loathsome toil.

So you ask yourself, "Self," you say, "Isn't there some part of winning that is distinguishable from manual labor?"

Continuing to interrogate the best and wisest spirit you know, you inquire, "Self, isn't there some part of the game where my natural attributes will help me? If this is supposed to be a proper pursuit for adults, where are my opportunities to fib? To enrage my friends? To display my erudition, regardless of whether or not I've acquired any? To sow doubt and confusion in the bosoms of my closest pals?"

As you surmised, all of these activities not only have their place in Rotisserie, but can help you achieve a goal greater than mere success, as you glance back and watch your intimate friends suck dust. The fond pursuit of this goal has many names: the CIA call it psychological warfare; the media have termed it a kind of war between classes, ages, sexes, or races; most families call it dinner-table chat.

Following devoutly in the great steps of Stephen Potter's Gamesmanship and Lifemanship, when it concerns our game, we will call these arts Leaguesmanship, an art wherein you demonstrate that the other owners are not only not in your league, they have in fact leagues and leagues to travel before even your aforementioned dust is visible. Like its famous cousin, Leaguesmanship is the art of winning your league without improving your game, committing a felony, or breaking any of the major Commandments on a regular basis. Leaguesmanship gives you the tactics to dominate your league.

In a game only 10 years old, there is understandably little formal literature on Leaguesmanship, although there is already a formidable wealth of oral history on the subject. In fact, viewed in one light, the formal yearly Rotisserie Guide edited by Glen Waggoner is a chronicle of Leaguesmen and their ploys. But there are other games afoot than in New York, and therefore, this essay will review some of the basic areas of research, and reveal some of the fine work currently being done.

The first choice an enterprising Leaguesman faces is whether to choose to play as an Expertman or Rooneyman.

EXPERTMANSHIP:

The key to this gambit is often misunderstood to be the carrying around of more reference materials than anyone else, toting more tomes than anyone else can carry. A true Expertman normally can't use his rear view mirror on the drive to the draft, because the stack of materials in the back seat is crammed from door to door and rises to the roof. In some leagues where rivalling Expertmen duel every year for draft supremacy, there have been distressing stories of fully-loaded North American moving vans pulling up in front of suburban lawns of draft hosts, disgorging volumes by the ton. This deadly stockpiling of competing stores of statistical references has long since reached the point where more volumes arrive at the draft than anyone can read or even crack the spine of. But despite plaintive calls for gradual reduction or strict numerical treaties, it remained to Preslain to end this mad competition.

Playing as he did in a league situated in Manhattan, Preslain soon saw that the leading Expertman was simply the man most willing to pay extravagant sums to a moving company. So he brought one book to the Thanatopsis League '89 draft: a collection of Clapp's treatises on pre-cellular structures. He dropped it in front of him, where it sat lonely next to the sheet on which he recorded his selections. Leaning back in the leather recliner the host had originally reserved for himself, Preslain gave his reference a predraft perusal, and whistled as he read, with an occasional cluck of the tongue. His competitors became frantic as he ignored their every wink, nod, and stat. They even opened some of the books they had brought. But Preslain closed off any lane of escape with his first selection. Signing Kevin Mitchell at $15, he lovingly fondled the black leather spine of his treatises — "If you understand the building blocks of life," he grinned, "that's all you need to know about this guy. Anybody with a pre-DNA modular structure like that is due to explode." After Mitchell went on to hit 47 home runs in '89, rare book dealers all over the island were scouring for Clapp; the other Thanatopsians had, of course, missed the point. Preslain has laid plans to bring the T'ai Ch'i in 1991.

Expertmanship also has post-draft implications, but these mostly concern mastering the minutiae contained in this book, for fact-dropping during trade talks, and spin-control during conversations. John wrote in the introduction that the trick to applying the stores of knowledge in this tome is context. Your challenge as an Expertman is to use your study to get your opponents to constantly misread the terrain, doing the right thing at the wrong time. For instance, if a player had a great 2nd half but is unlikely to get playing time, or is a notorious slackard in the first half, point out his good 2nd half. Or if a player is indentured to a management which fails to see his benefits or trade him, point out his advantages in detail, and trade the misunderstood player for someone whose manager is using them properly.

Expertmanship can also be a good way to denigrate the value of the players you would receive in a trade, and perhaps persuade your interlocutor to add a nugget or two to the talent lode. It is said that facts cannot lie, but they can be presented in such away as to make interpreters misconstrue them. The Expertman makes numbers talk to him straight up, like a dutch uncle, but gives them spin and context like a presidential press secretary when he introduces them to company.

ROONEYMANSHIP

The antithesis of the Expertman is the Rooneyman, the enfant terrible of Leaguesmanship. The heart of Rooneymanship is contained in the following statement: "Well, all of my friends told me about this Rotisserie thing, and my uncle has a barn . . ." A good Rooneyman is differentiable from a moron only after the fact.

A good Rooneyman constantly talks about how he wants to acquire Bimbleman only because when he took his dad to the game last Father's Day, Bimbleman hit 2 HRs to crush the despised Mets, and he just wants to add Bimbleman in memory of his father, who has since died. Frivolous behavior at the draft can also aid the Rooneyman in the later rounds. For instance, when Enguerrand started the bidding for Juan Samuel at $12 In the Poitiers League, beaming "He's my favorite," he not only acquired 13 HRs, 52 RBIs and 38 SBs cheaply, he also set the stage for starting the bidding on Delino DeShields at $8, which also functioned as an opening and closing price.

The most difficult part of Rooney ploy is making the intentional mistake early. This usually involves paying $5-$10 more for Andres Galarraga or Joe Carter than they're worth. The Rooneyman is essentially the tar baby, and the so called "expert" who trades with him is B'rer Rabbit, who enters the skirmish confident, but leaves tangled and tarred. Rooneymanship, however, is actually nothing more than an apple-cheeked snare, in which overconfident Expertmen get caught up every season.

Another exemplary Rooneyman tactic is to make a number of trades for hometown players immediately after joining a league. This is the equivalent of painting the letters "RUBE" across one's forehead, and is frequently successful in bringing in trade offers. As we look at each gambit individually, we will come back to these two persona, which are the Yin and Yan of Leaguesmanship.

DRAFTMANSHIP

A few forms worth noting:

Namesmanship (e.g., The Martinez Gambit): Pick any common name (Gonzalez is good for 1991) and rave incessantly before the auction starts, "How about that game last night? Isn't Martinez a splendid young ballplayer?" If anyone attempts to pierce the veil of Martinezdom, with a question like, "Which Martinez do you mean?" The Namesman deftly parries them. "The Seattle Martinez, of course. The one on ESPN last night." No one will admit that they missed anything on ESPN during the 24 hours before draft day; such a confession would ruin any hope they had of making bluff bids, by exposing the fact that they lead a relatively normal life and couldn't possibly be prepared for a serious draft.

In the sixth round of the auction, Namesman chugs a can of Coke (any finger food, chewed for display, will do) and belches, "Aeschxw Martinez, four dollars!" The only bidder who would have had the nerve to ask, "Which Martinez?" is the same fellow who missed ESPN (because he spent the evening at his daughter's birthday celebration). The dumbfounded league lets the bid go unchallenged, and the Draftman then chooses his Martinez. In round fifteen, a misguided soul makes the mistake of bidding on Ghfarlgrbr Martinez, and acquires the rights to a career .188 hitter.

It is important to be a leader, not a follower, in Namesmanship. Horning in on another man's ploy could be disastrous, as it was for Albemarle of the Windsor League last year, who was distressed to discover at the end of the draft the he had Expo Dave Martinez slotted as a starting pitcher.

For 1991, given the gaggle of Gonzalezes up for bids, the Rotisserie Baseball Analyst will guarantee a Leaguesman Hall of Fame plaque to any Namesman who manages to belch or chew an opponent into paying Juan dollars for Tony or Speedy.

Pizza Breakmanship:

A few hours into the draft or auction, the pizza arrives, and small groups form in the kitchen and toilet to discuss what has happened. Where the Leaguesman distinguishes himself from the novice is in his use of this time. If for instance, the Leaguesman is waiting to grab Delino DeShields or Bip Roberts late, then the break is the perfect time to trill a few well-chosen words on the marvels of Billy Doran, the incredible promise of Mickey Morandini, and the timeless wonder of Tommy Herr. If a Leaguesman is crossing his fingers and praying for Sammy Sosa, then it's time to talk about how marvelous it is that Cory Snyder and Greg Vaughn have slipped so far. Then, after the break expires, return to the table and offer Doran and Snyder's name at the draft at the first opportunities and bid vigorously until you reach 80 percent of their valuations, then drop off, grumbling about everyone snatching your personal favorites, inwardly glowing that you have taken someone's draft dollars and apportioned them to a player you don't want.

Pizza breaks are also good for commiserating with either half of a partnership about how well he'd be doing if he were not saddled with a partner possessing the judgment of a mid 1980s S & L regulator. It is also a fine time to congratulate anyone who has been conducting a nickel and dime draft on having spurned the superstars whom you just couldn't stop yourself from buying.

Other Draftmanship ploys include the Treegoob Statue Gambit, named after Rennie Treegoob, who generally refuses to draft any player until the draft begins its 3rd hour. A large, pleasant man, Treegoob sits still, doing nothing until everyone else has overpaid, and then entering with a long list of good players who cause everyone else to bang their forehead angrily, saying "Dammit, I forgot he was available." If you ever observe a large group of white men emerging from a suburban Philadelphia home in early April with small, hand-pounded depressions in their scalps, you are watching men who have just emerged from being "Goobed." In fact, at one recent draft, during the last three hours, every time Rennie nominated someone, 11 other men consulted their dwindling store of available cash, goddamned a few times, and pounded their heads in unison: the gathering resembled nothing so much as a prayer session of a particularly masochistic group of monks.

Positionmanship: A ploy for the known Expertman, this stratagem is used to mislead neophytes, and decrease competition. Essentially, the Expertman prepares a list of the 10 or 12 most versatile players, who qualify at several positions, but cannot hit or will not receive much playing time. Wayne Tolleson and Ron Washington are good examples from the past, while Tim Jones, Francisco Cabrera, Tommy Gregg, Rod Booker, and Hector Villanueva are some names for 1991. Then put their names on a separate sheet of paper, headline it MOST VERSATILE, then list their names and all of their marvelous position possibilities. Make sure then, that it is seen by the owner with whom you share some roster holes, and then let nature take its course. Once used by Pszyborski in the famed Dougherty League draft of 1970, it allowed the man known as Mr. Consonant to pick up Frank Robinson and Dave Johnson while his opponent greedily grabbed Mickey Stanley and Dalton Jones. But after the draft ends, there's a big world out there, and here is some of the best work being done currently in the field during the regular season.

Drago's Steinbrenner Sneer: Popularized by the owner of the San Drago Chicken, the Steinbrenner sneer requires a prominent beak and an ability to sneer a la Buckley or big George. Winning big, spending often, and ending most of his sentences by snorting, Mike Drago has become the most hated man in a Central PA league mostly notable for being largely comprised of members of the Reading Eagle sports section. The sneer is particularly good for reminding other owners that you destroyed them on trades, so they have to redeem themselves by going to the well once more. If like George and Mike, you have a nose to look down with, and a God-given ability to treat your fellow men as if they spilled your vintage wines on your Persian carpet when they so much as mention baseball players, this may be the gambit for you. It should be noted however, that like Mike and unlike George, it is very important to approach this gambit with clear idea of what works, and a good accountant.

The Bernstein Bunch Principle: Named after Mark Bernstein, a nascent Philadelphia litigator, this gambit involves sending job lots of perfectly nice fellows clumped by the baker's dozen off to some rookie for Roger Clemens or Darryl Strawberry or George Bell. This worked so well for Bernstein that he is planning to defend his first murder case by offering to plead to two misdemeanours, three burglaries and an indecent exposure to be named later.

The Mallin Value Helium Gambit: Ken Mallin sells and rents real estate to large businesses. This of course has made him a frequent and welcome visitor in the land of Hyperbole. So when, for instance, Ken makes Tim Burke available before the midseason trade deadline, Tim Burke becomes an amalgam of Rollie Fingers and Bruce Sutter, a Dennis Eckersley you could acquire for your very own. "He's the best reliever available," Ken will say. "That makes him incredibly valuable in this market. Saves are rare, no, saves are precious. If you want them, you'll have to pay for them." Okay, but when told that Kal Daniels or Eric Davis is the price, then you start to be aware, that like the Atlantic City casinos, a Mallin trade talk is packed with oxygen, and unless you fight it down, you will be seized by an inordinate desire to be much more generous than you should. That is why Ken continually does well, and why I never quite end up trading with Ken, because the diamond in his window always appears to me to have more flaws than he sees. Sells a whole lot of real estate, and keeps getting nifty guys in trades, however. Makes you wonder what Pat Robertson or Jimmy Swaggart would do in Rotisserie.

Benson's Poormouth Rant: Saving the best for last, those of you who haven't been able to savor the experience of playing in a league with our author, editor and Leaguesman about town, should know something about the way he wages psychological war against his competitors. The first thing he does when he takes over an abandoned franchise is to suggest that his best player is Jose Lind. (This is on a team which possessed Tony Gwynn, Jack Clark, Roger McDowell, and Mike Scott). "My best player is Jose Lind. Or maybe Tommy Herr. It's hard to tell." Within a month, you have given him Randy Myers and Eddie Murray for Jose Lind, Tommy Herr, and a warm feeling that you support truth, justice, and the American way. Benson's idea is to make you feel sorry for him, which is about as appropriate as Robert Shaw feeling sorry for the shark.

This concludes our sampler, for now, although an update is planned as an occasional feature for the WINNING ROTISSERIE BASEBALL newsletter. Having armed you with new and dangerous ideas, we recall the words of Stephen Potter, who termed Gamesmanship "the art of winning without actually cheating. "Now, as we send you forth into a dangerous and unsettled league; work like a coolie, but don't forget these words: Anything which helps you which is neither knowledge nor cheating, is Leaguesmanship; and boy, is it fun.

THEIR BATTING STATS WILL DECEIVE YOU

By Pete DeCoursey

Rotisserie stats are deceptive in a number of ways, but one particular problem is that if a player's value is largely defensive, it is easy to underestimate the playing time they may receive. Therefore, using Defensive Average information from 1988-1990, this essay aims to tell you some names of players whose defense should, has, and probably will continue to earn them playing time their batting performance cannot justify.

National League:

Sid Bream is the best fielding 1B in the majors. Tommy Gregg and Francisco Cabrera were two of the worst in 1990. That is why they were replaced. So if Sid does not set the world on fire, don't hold your breath waiting for him. Jeff Treadway and Mark Lemke are also both well above average at turning ground balls into outs, while Blauser and Presley were awful. Bream, Lemke// Treadway, and Pendleton could convert one of '90s worst defensive infields into one of '91s best. Be careful of what it does to your offensive numbers in the process. And keep in mind that if they ditched better bats at the corners to get better D, it's hard to regard Blauser as safe.

Tommy Herr dissolved defensively in '90 and then, fittingly, became a Met, where he has an excellent shot of hitting .250 with no power, few steals, and rotten defense. HoJo, on the other hand, was slightly above average at 3B and slightly below average at SS, although the Mets turn one third fewer DPs than the League average when he is at short.

Domingo Ramos and Curt Wilkerson were two of the worst defenders at third in '90, in addition to what they do with the bat. Defensive Average is not followed as such by teams, but it is a good predictive tool when players are on the bubble. Scott Coolbaugh had a poor defensive year in Texas, but faces weak opposition in San Diego.

American League:

Pete O'Brien was again one of the best fielding 1Bs, so don't be surprised to see him again grab a share of at-bats inexplicable by offense alone. Kent Hrbek's defense was awful, and if his hitting continues to decline, those inviting Metrodome walls may ask someone else to dance soon.

Nelson Liriano, Fred Manrique, and Steve Sax are all well below average defensively, which may give Chip Hale and Donnie Hill an immediate shot, but shouldn't affect Sax until his bat fades, which does not appear to be an imminent event. Billy Ripken's merely average defense may also hurt him. Generally a player of his vintage has risen to whatever level he's going to reach; look for Juan Bell to take that job. Mike Gallego will hold the Oakland job because he will stop 34 more hits than the league average. Gallego plus 34 hits is a tenable player for Tony LaRussa, but not for you.

Tony Phillips is way above average at 2B and 3B and had a very under-recognized year in '90. His ability to spell Whitaker, Fryman, and OFs will get him in the line-up, but his Rotisserie value is much less than his value to the Sparkster. Steve Buechele is another terrific defender who will continue to get more games than you might wish, as will Randy Velarde. Leyritz displayed slow feet and rock hands. Leyritz was the only AL 3B to face 200 ground balls and turn less than half into outs. Velarde, who faced 178 GBs, turned more than 70 percent into outs. Over the course of a season, that's roughly a hundred hit theoretical difference, and I would be shocked if Leyritz kept that position. Carlos Baerga was also overmatched by the defensive demands of 3B.

At SS, Stillwell and Spiers glovework might impair their future, while Gagne, Huson, Vizquel, and Weiss ensured their PT with above average abilities in stopping hits and starting DPs.

BETTER MODELS OF BASEBALL

By Pete DeCoursey

BATTING

Baseball offense is made up of power and efficiency. Anyone reading this book is a student of two games, baseball and Rotisserie. If it isn't already apparent to you that Rotisserie's eight categories don't really measure either power or efficiency accurately, examine the following players.

	BA	HR	RBI	SB
Roberts	.309	9	44	46
Coleman	.292	6	39	77

Given only this data, most teams (Rotisserie or "real" baseball) would obviously choose Vince Coleman of these two: 31 stolen bases more than make up for 3 HRs and 5 RBI, and 17 points of batting average. But that choice doesn't show that Coleman was better; it merely points out the inadequacy of our measuring tools. Let's split the job into its component parts. The first job of a leadoff man is to score runs. Roberts scored 104 and Coleman 73. In order to score runs you have to reach base. Roberts drew 55 walks for a .375 on base average, while Coleman's OBA was .340.

So Roberts would reach base 20 more times in a full season of leading off, which might have been a large factor helping him score 30 more runs. Just as important is Robert's power advantage. He hit 18 more doubles as well as three more HRs. Now let's ask those questions again — in real baseball, would you trade 20 more times on base, 15 more extra base hits and 31 more runs for 31 stolen bases? No, you wouldn't make that trade, because the stolen bases would be outweighed by the other contributions. unless you were playing regular Rotisserie. Let's look at three more players, and look at power and efficiency, and how well they are represented by the traditional categories.

	BA	HR	RBI	SB
Lance Parrish	.268	24	70	2
Darren Daulton	.268	12	57	7
Mike Scioscia	.264	12	66	4

Not hard to see who you would prefer from that trio. Parrish clearly has more power. Right? But are home runs the only power a player has? How about doubles or triples? Here's how the three men compared in extra base hits:

	2Bs	3Bs	HRs	XBs	PP
Parrish	14	0	24	86	.183
Scioscia	25	0	12	61	.141
Daulton	30	1	12	68	.148

XBs are Total Bases minus hits — a 2B is 1 XB, a triple 2 XBs, and a home run is 3 XBs — PP is Power percentage, which is slugging average minus batting average, identical to Bill James' isolated power average. renamed because IP as an offensive category is confusing. Parrish indeed had more power than Scioscia or Daulton, but as this comparison shows, he had nowhere near twice as much power; if he did in your league, that was a fluke in your rules, not a difference in the boom of the player's bats.

Equally important is the way that batting average deceives us as to how often each man reaches base. Despite virtually identical batting averages, Parrish reached base less often than the other two men.

	BBs	OBA
Daulton	72	.367
Scioscia	55	.348
Parrish	46	.338

On Base Average measures how often a player reaches base far better than batting average. A walk puts a man on base as surely as a hit; the main advantage a hit offers is that it can move runners more than one base at a time, and is much more likely to drive them home. But every hit that drives in a run is counted already in the RBI column; the other function we need to measure is how efficiently a player uses his opportunities to reach base, because a hit or a walk puts men on base and conserves outs, both key activities in scoring runs.

And that brings up the question of runs: Daulton scored 62; Parrish, 54; Sciosica 46. So Parrish had a little more power and 12 more home runs; Daulton reached base more often, made up for much of the power difference with doubles, and scored more runs. So why would any traditional categories Rotisserie owner prefer Parrish? BECAUSE WE MEASURE WHAT PARRISH DOES WELL, AND IGNORE WHAT DAULTON DID WELL, THAT'S WHY. That seems to me to be more of a reason to change the rules than a defense of Rotisserie's categories.

There's another category we do a bad job of measuring: stolen bases. Here are the National League leaders for 1990:

Player	SB	CS	Net
Vince Coleman	77	17	60
Eric Yelding	64	25	39
Barry Bonds	52	13	39
Otis Nixon	50	13	37
Bip Roberts	46	12	34
Tim Raines	49	16	33
Brett Butler	51	19	32
Lenny Dykstra	33	5	28
Ozzie Smith	32	6	26
Howard Johnson	34	8	26
Barry Larkin	30	5	25
Kirk Gibson	26	2	24
Marquis Grissom	22	2	20
Milt Thompson	25	5	20
Shawon Dunston	25	5	20
Billy Hatcher	30	10	20
D. DeShields	42	22	20

The NL stolen base leaders list changes noticeably when you measure the benefits of their activity rather than the frequency of the activity. As you can see, the current ways we measure would make Delino DeShield's SB total more valuable than that of 10 men who accrued the same benefit without having to expend 22 outs to gain it. Tim Raines and Brett Butler both stole more bases than Bip Roberts, but also were caught more often, so that Roberts actually did his team more good by amassing more net SBs. By the same measure, Billy Hatcher's 30 SBs and DeShields 42 did no more good for their team's than Marquis Grissom's extremely efficient 22 SBs. We see the same effect in the American League

Player	SB	CS	Dif.
Rickey Henderson	65	10	55
Steve Sax	43	9	34
Alex Cole	40	9	31
Roberto Kelly	42	17	25
Gary Pettis	38	15	23
Julio Franco	31	10	21
Mookie Wilson	23	4	19
Henry Cotto	21	3	18
Willie Wilson	24	6	18
Mitch Webster	22	6	16
Dan Gladden	25	9	16
Sammy Sosa	32	16	16
Ivan Calderon	32	16	16
Paul Molitor	18	3	15
Devon White	21	6	15
Gary Sheffield	25	10	15
Harold Reynolds	31	16	15
Lance Johnson	36	22	14

When you measure how well they steal bases rather than how many, you get a notion of what they did for or to their own team, and what they should have done for your team. And now for your edification: The "Why Even Bother" All Stars:

Player	SB	CS	Net SBs
Tom Brunansky	5	10	-5
Ozzie Guillen	13	17	-4
Jim Eisenreich	12	14	-2
Ellis Burks	9	11	-2
Lonnie Smith	10	10	0
Mike Devereaux	13	12	1
Carney Lansford	16	14	2
Paul O'Neill	13	11	2
Alan Trammell	12	10	2

Last year these players helped you in the stolen base column without helping their teams, because of their inability to steal efficiently. Incidentally, Pete Palmer, one of the best baseball analysts living, estimates that the proper adjustment is not to subtract CS from SB but to double CS and then subtract them from SBs, because making an out is twice as likely to prevent you from scoring a run as stealing a base is likely to aid you in scoring. If in real baseball a caught stealing is twice as harmful as a stolen base is helpful, then we should at least count them once against stolen bases in our game. If you count them twice, you get Brownie points in Stat Heaven.

So what should we measure? First, it's obvious that we should measure runs scored and driven in, because runs win baseball games.

Then we should measure power, either by extra bases (TB-H) or Power Percentage (SA-BA), and stolen bases (using net stolen bases, SB-CS). Finally we will balance these measures of power and speed by adding a measure of efficiency in reaching base, by measuring On Base Average. Someone is no doubt saying by now, "He doesn't count home runs!" Nonsense. A home run under these categories remains the most valuable use of an at-bat. It scores a run, knocks in a run, and gives the player either three extra bases or a power percentage of 3.000 for that at-bat.

Using either method is not de-emphasizing the home runs, it is bringing doubles and triples out of the statistical dungeon where we have left them to languish. Nor are these categories hard to figure out: each week USA Today publishes 2Bs, 3Bs, TBs, hits, BA, OBA, and SA. As far as the stolen base reform I proposed earlier, that is also available from USA Today and most boxscores.

I have given you two choices on power statistics to let your league decide whether you prefer to give the benefit to players who play the most and amass more extra bases, by measuring extra bases (TB-H) or power percentage (PP), which (like Batting Average) can show a gaudy number over limited playing time. Because three of our measures already gauge quantity (Net SBs, RBIs, and Runs) I prefer to use PP, so that two quality measures balance the three volume categories. That would give us five categories, and our first comparisons would look like this:

Player	OBA	PP	R	RBI	Net SBs
Roberts	.375	.124	104	44	34
Coleman	.340	.108	73	39	60
Daulton	.367	.148	62	57	6
Parrish	.338	.183	54	70	0
Scioscia	.348	.141	46	66	3

Coleman and Parrish still have their attractions: the point of this essay is not to convince you of their worthlessness, but to let you make the same choices about offensive performance that you would if you were their manager. If they draw walks or score runs or don't, they should do that on your team, just as they do for Doug Rader or Tommy LaSorda.

PITCHING

Pitching performance has better measurements than Rotisserie's offensive measurements. ERA and Ratio are good measures of efficiency, but just as RBIs, runs, and Net SBs balance OBA and PP, we need measures of quantity in pitching. The first and most obvious of these is innings. ERA and ratio tell us how good the innings were, measuring innings pitched tells us how many of them there were. For instance, Darrel Akerfeld's 93 innings of 1.28 ratio and 3.77 ERA are not as valuable as John Burkett's 204 innings of 1.28 ratio and 3.79 ERA. By counting innings, you recognize that teams value players according to how much they can pitch. This also means that if someone loads up on relief pitching, he will have one category in which he loses.

Most leagues now require that a staff pitch a certain number of innings, but the more innings a pitcher hurls, the more valuable he is to his club. Note that an Inning Pitched is an accomplishment: getting three men out. It is not a simple cumulative process measurement (like pitches thrown, or batters faced). A pitcher must be successful to record an IP. On every club, the pitcher with the most innings is one of the team's most valuable pitchers. The IP is not like the hitters's at-bat, a reward bestowed by management. The worst athlete in the world could get some major league at bats; it takes skill to pitch a major league inning.

Also, while Saves are a good category, IP allows pitchers like Akerfelds, Paul Gibson, Terry Leach, or Lee Guetterman, who don't save games but pitch 80-90 innings in relief, give you the same benefit they gave their team. Adding IP to the traditional categories gives us Wins, IP, ERA, Ratio, and Saves.

If your league would like to add a 6th category, then I recommend home runs allowed. Strikeouts are gaudy, but are not necessarily important; allowing the least home runs while amassing innings, wins, and saves is what pitchers hope to accomplish when they rise in the morning. Also, remember that ratio only tells you how often opponents reach base; not how hard your pitcher is being hit.

Since it is not currently possible to measure the doubles and triples allowed by a pitcher, HRs allowed lets you get a notion of how many homers a pitcher serves up. A number of leagues have added either losses or net wins (W-L) as a category, but this simply amplifies the record of pitchers on good teams, at the expense of pitchers on poor teams. If we're measuring how good a pitcher is, the number of innings he throws, homers, hits and walks he allows are a more direct measure of his performance than any measure of losses, which necessarily measures team performance.

CONCLUSION

In addition to pointing out some improvements that can be made in the categories to make our game a better model of baseball, the purpose of this article is to encourage you to contribute. Change your league rules, and if you come up with a breakthrough, send a note on it to the newsletter. Next year, maybe this article will feature your rule, in its annual attempt to make analyzing and managing your talent as fun and challenging as it is for big league general managers.

EXTRA INNINGS

ASK JOHN BENSON

1-900-PRE-PLAN (1-900-773-7526)

Got a question?

Can't decide who to retain?

Trade offer keeping you awake at night?

Trouble getting your draft list prioritized?

Don't despair. Call for a private, one-on-one chat with the author of this book. When it's your dime, you will get patient listening, and prompt, clear advice. The price is only $1.99 per minute. Get your parents' permission first. Seriously, this rate is rock bottom for live access to a professional of any kind.

Talk as long or as short as you want. Obviously, it will help you to assemble your notes (if any) before calling, and be ready to state your question concisely. If you want to shoot the breeze, that's OK, too, and won't cost you any more than a cheap psychiatrist.

Last year, when Jeff Russell went down, numerous people called and asked who would get the saves in Texas. The Rangers weren't talking. But everyone who called got the story here: Kenny Rogers. Info like that should be worth $1.99.

The hours are 1 p.m. to 11 p.m.

WINNING ROTISSERIE BASEBALL (Monthly!)

When a player gets hurt, traded, demoted or called up during the season, you know all about it from the newspapers and TV. But do the media tell you the other players who will be affected? And how? Who will play while Davis is on the DL, and how long will Davis be out? Why did Chicago trade for Jones, and how will they use their new acquisition? Who will replace Martinez, and what is the new batting order? Why was rookie Smith brought up? Will he play? Who will sit down to make room for him?

These are the types of questions that are answered every month in WINNING ROTISSERIE BASEBALL, the first, best, largest publication for serious readers on this subject. Our mission is to give you an informed vision of the future. The same 50 writers who make this book a success also contribute to WRB, and more join the group every month. Scheduled for January to April 1991:

• Comprehensive post-spring-training Draft Day issue listing every position on every team, and % of playing time that will be given to each player.

• More detailed lists like the "Age 26 with 2 years ML experience" population, with assessments of who will be most undervalued and overvalued in 1991 auctions, and why.

• Final wrap-up of 1991 winter ball: who helped themselves and who didn't.

• Complete list of all players who changed teams during the winter, and the likely effect of the change on the player, his old team, and his new team.

Last year, before draft day, the newsletter (for example) warned NL owners to stay away from Brunansky, because Whitey Herzog wanted to send him to Boston. In May, we said Jeff Gray would get some saves. Imagine 25 pages of tips like that every month, and you get the idea.

If you like this book, you will love the "newsletter" — a modest term considering that the monthly is 20 to 40 pages in length. WRB is published year round. In the winter, we take advantage of the fact that the stats have stopped changing, long enough to do some in-depth analysis. The monthly includes many scholarly, quantitative essays from leading authorities. We have letters to the editor, debates, and state-of-the-art research findings. I once thought of calling it the New England Journal of Rotisserianism; but who wants to be pretentious?

Just like this book is the most current annual publication for your needs, WRB is the most current monthly publication. You get the same type of information, year round, twelve time a year. Most people who read WRB win their leagues. That's partly because people who like to win like to read WRB, and partly because WRB gives you the edge you need to finish first in your league.

The best statement I can make is that WINNING ROTISSERIE BASEBALL is now in its third year (started 1989), has always been sold with a 100% money back guarantee, and NO ONE HAS EVER WANTED THEIR MONEY BACK! Some people have had suggestions to make the newsletter better. It isn't perfect. But when I suspect that someone may be unhappy and I urge them to take their money back and get off my mailing list, they always change their tune. Most people renew months before their subscriptions expire, to make sure they don't miss a single issue. New subscribers call up and want to buy back issues. During the first year, I didn't even bother with renewal notices, because 90% renewed without being reminded. We still don't have any regular system to send reminders; it just hasn't been necessary.

No, it isn't cheap. It's not for cheap people. If you think playing Rotisserie should cost less than going bowling once a month, well, you can't be getting much enjoyment out of the game, and there isn't much that I can do for you. If you don't like the idea of a CPA-MBA-scout-writer-analyst working his tail off for a small group of elitist readers, well, eat cake; you know.

The vital information? A sample issue is $7. A six month subscription is $35. One year is $59. Two years is $99. Most people try six months and then renew for two years, in case you want a profile of the average reader. Yes we take MC/Visa credit cards. Telephone 203-834-0812 or write to Wilton Britannica, PO Box 7302, Wilton, CT 06897.

COMPUSERVE SPORTS FORUM

Finding Sports Forum was one of the highlights of 1990 for me. There is a whole world out there, with hundreds of Rotisserie [they call it FBB] leaguers on line, humming and chattering away all year round. They can be accessed instantly through any computer modem. If you have Compuserve, you can sign on immediately and see what I mean. If you don't know what I'm talking about, or haven't taken the plunge yet, just go to your local computer store and tell them you want to access Compuserve. It's very easy.

Once you have Compuserve, just get the "!" prompt, and type "GO FANS" and you're in. What can you do when you're in? All kinds of neat stuff. Some of my favorites last year:

- Play in a league, or two. At any time, you can look over the rosters and standings of fifty leagues. Before the season starts, you can select one of the rosters abandoned by the bozo who mangled it last year; with a core of gem players and a fistful of fantasy money, you can go to auction and turn your franchise around. If rehab projects aren't your specialty, you can join one of the many new leagues that form every spring.

Last year, Forum boss Harry Conover kindly publicized the fact that I would play in two newly-formed leagues, one AL and one NL. The sharks came swarming to feast on poor, helpless Benson. They were fierce competition. They traded relentlessly. They sat at their screens 24 hours a day waiting to claim Dave Justice. They came after me in every category. They colluded [well, I mean I sort of wonder about some trades; but actually Harry's people watch everything pretty carefully]. Benson did OK, anyway. I was able to win the NL, and took third in the AL (after coasting in second all year and blipping into first for one week around September 1). If you had been a Sports Forum user last summer, you could have followed my agony every step of the way; it's all there for public viewing.

Seriously, the Forum staff provides a highly professional, unique service combining timely stats with league secretarial, commissioner, and social services. The competition is only as serious as you want to make it. It's fun, fun, fun. If you want to see what's going on, look at my rosters in the Spahn NL and Palmer AL. My Spahn team is a dynasty already. Going into 1991, I have Ramon Martinez at 7, Kal Daniels at 10, Willie McGee at 11, Carmelo Martinez at 2, with fair prices on Sandberg, Bonilla, Eric Davis, Sid Fernandez, Gooden, Lefferts, Burke, and Roger McDowell. The Palmer roster was a two-year project in the first place. Watch me in 1991!

And just as serious: any hot shot Rotisserie "expert" who wants to test his skill in a public forum, against two leagues of 20 strangers, with the world watching, just sign on and ask Harry to fix you up. If you are a famous author, the competition will be worthy. If you can add two leagues to your existing workload and finish first and third, I'll read YOUR book.

- Messaging: a few hundred Rotisserie nuts generate a huge volume of chatter and transactions. I found it enlightening to sign on every night, check the major league transactions (which are posted right off the AP wire), and then scan the claims and waivers to see who's hot and who's not. You can, of course, look at other people's trades, kibbitz, etc.

- Conferencing: with hundreds of people around, you quickly make friends. Chances are, someone you know is on line every time you connect. You shoot them a message, "Wanna CO?" and next thing you know, you're in a conference room with one or two, or twenty friends, drinking beer and telling lies. The Forum also schedules formal conferences with famous guests like Alex Patton and John Benson to answer your questions on line, live.

- Libraries: every imaginable baseball stat, player value, league historical archive, etc. is there for your perusal. The Forum had first half and second half stats, average auction prices, etc. on line (everything is downloadable of course) within a day or two after the season ended.

And that's just a few baseball-related items. Tip of the iceberg and all that. There are many other sports, too. Check it out. I know you will like it. And tell Harry I sent you. Telephone 508-443-0142.

THE ROTISSERIE LEAGUE BASEBALL VIDEO: JOHN BENSON ON TAPE

The video business is simpler than the book business, at least when it comes to choosing topics. Book publishers must experiment with all kinds of new and unproven ideas. Sometimes they create books that nobody wants to read. No such problem exists in the video business. Producers simply watch the book market; when a subject generates enough interest to support several successful books, then it must be time to do a video on that subject. That time has come today for Rotisserie baseball.

The Rotisserie League Baseball Video (hosted by Reggie Jackson) is a look inside the world of serious Rotisserians. You will meet Glen Waggoner and Dan Okrent. Hear the insiders at USA Today and The National Sports Daily tell how Rotisserie people have secretly taken over both publications.

On scouting and roster building, you get the previously-unpublished secrets of the first Grandmaster, Harry Stein: The Ten Homers for a Dollar Theory, The Five Outfielders / Four Categories Theory, and more. And you hear from other luminaries including Steve Wulf and Jody McDonald, John Benson, and Pete DeCoursey.

Two more features make this video a treasure:

(1) The game is described clearly for all to understand. If you have family and friends who don't appreciate what you're doing, just give them this video, and say, "Here, look." Then they will comprehend your passion, and be better equipped to help you deal with it.

(2) Speaking of problems, at the end of the filming, with cameras still rolling, Reggie tells the producers what he really thinks of them and their work. It's great.

You can go to any store and buy the regular, general-public version of this video, OR . . .

For my readers, I have negotiated something special: better product, better price. Call 212-595-1995, mention "John Benson" and tell them you want the DELUXE version. The deluxe edition is longer and better. The price is $19.95, but for readers of this book, there is a $5 DISCOUNT. Don't forget: ask for the Deluxe Version — not the regular — and tell them John Benson says you get it for $14.95, not $19.95. You can order by mail: Blue Flame Productions, Dept. JB, 109 West 85th Street, New York, NY 10024. Whether using mail or phone, there is a $3 charge for shipping.

One final point: this video is NOT going to become dated. It contains general advice and information useful all year for many years to come. Buy several and use them for gifts this year and next year. Don't miss it.

FANTASY BASEBALL MAGAZINE

If you like Rotisserie information, you can now get it six times a year in a colorful, clear and attractive presentation. Kit Kiefer and Greg Ambrosius oversee the delivery of timely and useful essays, stats, rankings and analyses. Don't tell them I said this, but their magazine is terribly inexpensive. It's as good as any value in the industry.

It has been fun and personally rewarding to see FBB Magazine evolve since late 1989. Every issue has been better than the ones that went before, and the energy and enthusiasm that go into each issue make it likely that this trend will continue for a long time. I urge you: try it, you'll like it.

THE OFFICIAL ROTISSERIE LEAGUE STATPHONE: SPONSORED BY JOHN BENSON
1-900-990-JOHN (1-900-990-5646)

If you are serious about Rotisserie baseball, you already know about the Official Statphone. For just 95 cents per minute, you get round-the-clock updates.

Personally, I like to check in every day for the injury status reports. Much of this information never gets onto the wire services, and never gets into the news. Statphone has saved me from numerous horrible trades and transactions, and tipped me off with obvious opportunities created by other players' injuries, etc. There is absolutely no substitute for timely information. Don't shoot with your eyes closed. Use Statphone.

The other reason I like Statphone is to cure insomnia. When I've got six points at risk in the ERA and ratio categories, I NEED TO KNOW how my starting pitcher did, before I can go to sleep. Statphone tells me.

In case you haven't figured it out already, the above phone number generates a small amount of revenue for yours truly. Please remember 1-900-990-JOHN when you call Statphone. Write it down. Carry it with you. Accept no substitutes.

"We'll give you the stats before your pitcher hits the showers"

IMAGINE... INSTANT BOXSCORE STATS, BY PHONE!

THE 1990 ROTISSERIE BASEBALL ANALYST — IS YOUR LIBRARY COMPLETE ?

Numerous essays on drafting, bidding, managing your roster, and scouting talent at all levels, have NOT been repeated in the 1991 Rotisserie Baseball Analyst. If you don't have the 1990 book, you need it.

The 1990 Grand Champion of Bill James Fantasy Baseball, Richard Miller, had this book. The 1990 Compuserve Sports Forum Champion of Champions, Bill Boersma, had this book. If anyone finished ahead of you in 1990, they undoubtedly had this book.

If you can afford to let your opponents keep an edge over you, go right ahead. But if you want to make sure that your arsenal is just as full as your opponents' then you need the 1990 book.

The 1990 Analyst is a complete data bank of everyone who was somebody in early 1990. Just like Cecil Fielder and Jeff Manto appeared in the 1989 book but not in 1990, some names from the 1990 book are not in the 1991 edition. If and when they should resurface, you will want scouting reports at your fingertips.

The 1989 edition is already a rare collector's item — completely sold out and unavailable anywhere. Act now before 1990 is gone, too.

Call Devyn Press: 1-800-274-2221. (No longer available in stores.)

TO ORDER THE 1990 OR 1991 ROTISSERIE BASEBALL ANALYST
Call Toll Free (U.S. & Canada)

1-800-274-2221

8 AM TO 8 PM
VISA or MASTERCARD ACCEPTED
or Mail to:
DEVYN PRESS, INC., 3600 Chamberlain Lane, Suite 230, Louisville, KY 40241

Please send me _____ copies of "Rotisserie Baseball Analyst 1990," at $17.95 each and _____ copies of "Rotisserie Baseball Analyst 1991," at $17.95 each. For each copy I enclose the correct amount + $3 for shipping/handling per book.

We accept checks, money orders and charge card orders, send your card number and expiration date.

Rotisserie Baseball Analyst 1990 $17.95 x _____ = $ _____
Rotisserie Baseball Analyst 1991 $17.95 x _____ = $ _____
Subtotal $ _____
Shipping/Handling ($3 per book) $ _____
Amount enclosed $ _____

Name _____
Address _____
City _____ State _____ Zip _____

(WHOLESALE INQUIRIES ARE WELCOME)